The **Rough Guide** to

Soul
and R&B

by

Peter Shapiro

D0893218

Rough Guides online
www.roughguides.com

Rough Guides Credits

The Rough Guide to Soul and R&B

Additional contributions: Bill Lord
Editors: Tracy Hopkins and Greg Ward
Layout: Dan May
Design: Duncan Clark and Dan May
Picture research: Tracy Hopkins
Proofreading: Janet McCann
Production: Aimee Hampson

Rough Guides Reference

Series editor: Mark Ellingham
Editors: Peter Buckley, Duncan Clark,
Tracy Hopkins, Matthew Milton,
Joe Staines, Ruth Tidball
Director: Andrew Lockett

Picture Credits

Richard E. Aaron/Redferns: 7, 128, 297, 317. Paul Bergen/Redferns: 35, 416. Bettmann/Corbis: 376. Grant Davis/Redferns: 203. GEMS/Redferns: 22, 158, 419. Harry Goodwin/Redferns: 151. Herman Leonard/Redferns: 90. Michael Ochs Archives/Redferns: 49, 61, 97, 147, 156, 167, 174, 181, 190, 217, 246, 257, 270, 291, 310, 323, 332, 353, 364. Don Paulsen/Redferns: 389, 396. Martin Philbey/Redferns: 114. Neal Preston/Corbis: 198, 227. Christina Radish/Redferns: 15. RB/Redferns: 428. David Redfern/Redferns: 77, 123. Ebet Roberts/Redferns: 81. Richard Upper/Redferns: 260, 405.

Publishing Information

This first edition published September 2006 by
Rough Guides Ltd, 80 Strand, London WC2R 0RL
345 Hudson St, 4th Floor, New York 10014, USA
Email: mail@roughguides.com

Distributed by the Penguin Group:
Penguin Books Ltd, 80 Strand, London WC2R 0RL
Penguin Putnam, Inc. 375 Hudson Street, NY 10014, USA
Penguin Books Australia Ltd, 250 Camberwell Road, Camberwell, Victoria 3124, Australia
Penguin Books Canada Ltd, 90 Eglinton Avenue East, Suite 700, Toronto, Ontario M4P 2Y3, Canada
Penguin Books (New Zealand) Ltd, 67 Apollo Drive, Mairangi Bay, Auckland 1310, New Zealand

Printed in Italy by LegoPrint S.p.A

448pp; includes index
A catalogue record for this book is available from the British Library

ISBN 10: 1-84353-264-6
ISBN 13: 978-1-84353-264-4

Contents

Feature boxes

Introduction

The *Rough Guide to Soul and R&B* traces the evolution of soul music from a rootsy righteousness born in the Pentecostal churches in cotton country to its present-day incarnation as the dream weaver of ghetto-fabulous fantasies. The church of soul music explored here is a broad one, so there's room for Louis Jordan and The Clovers, Latin Freestyle and New Jack Swing, Chic and Teena Marie, Cameo and The Gap Band. There are undoubtedly those who think that housing both Mahalia Jackson (or, even worse, Sylvester) and Otis Redding under the same musical banner is a heresy but, as this book will hopefully prove, soul has never been about purity. From Nat "King" Cole to Destiny's Child, all of these artists are indisputably part of the same continuum.

While everyone from 11-year-old prodigies to former folk singers from London gets a look-in, this book does not cover certain digressions (e.g. house music) from soul's main conversation between its religious roots and its material longings. Nor does it cover either of the crucially distinct genres that bookend it – the blues and hip-hop (but both of these musical styles have their own *Rough Guides*). However, discussing soul and R&B in the twenty-first century without engaging with hip-hop is impossible, so artists who span the divide like Missy Elliott and Lauryn Hill are included as well.

Unfortunately, there was not enough room to cover gospel adequately either. Soul music, and perhaps the bulk of today's popular music, would not exist without the language of ecstasy and longing created by the great gospel singers. There would be no Temptations without the Swan Silvertones, no James Brown without Archie Brownlee, no Aretha Franklin without Clara Ward, but their music is sadly beyond the ambit of this book.

What *The Rough Guide to Soul and R&B* does cover is just about every key figure in soul and R&B, from Aaliyah to Zapp, from The Chairmen of the Board to The Trammps, from The Average White Band to Hot Chocolate. It encompasses soul music's major arteries, such as Southern soul, Philly soul and Motown, as well as the side roads the genre followed in Africa, Jamaica, Spanish Harlem and the north of England.

This book is not intended to be the most comprehensive, end-all reference book about soul and R&B, but one that will spark debate, recommend some truly great albums, songs and playlists, perhaps help you win a couple of quid at your local pub quiz and hopefully introduce you to music that will make you want to do the Popcorn in your underwear.

Note

Within the artist entries, you will notice groups and individuals in this font, which means they have their own individual entry that can be referred to for more detail. Musicians, producers and other key figures in **this font** can be found in the index.

Recommended albums at the end of each entry are arranged chronologically and the symbol before the title indicates the format: ⊙ for an album on CD, and ◉ for vinyl.

Acknowledgements

Thanks to everyone at Rough Guides who was involved with this project – particularly my editors Tracy Hopkins, Greg Ward and Andrew Lockett who put up with endless delays caused by a herniated disc and law school – and thanks, most of all, to my wife Rachael, who once again tolerated my bouts of insomnia more than any reasonable person should have to.

Aaliyah

Aaliyah hit the headlines just twice in her short life: the first time was when she was 15, for allegedly marrying her then-mentor R. Kelly, and the second was when she was 22, for dying way too young, in an airplane crash in the Bahamas in August 2001. However, the title of her debut album, *Age Ain't Nothing But A Number*, says it all. She deserves to be remembered for her talent, not her age.

Aaliyah Dana Haughton – "Aaliyah" is Arabic, Hebrew and Swahili for "the highest" or "the exalted one" – was born on January 16, 1979, in Brooklyn, but soon moved with her family to Detroit. As a child she appeared, unsuccessfully, on the proto-*Pop Idol* television show *Star Search*, but her career really took off when her uncle, **Barry Hankerson**, signed her to his Blackground

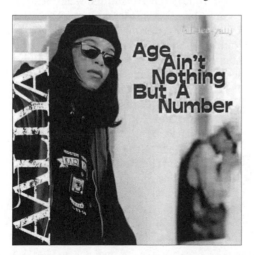

record label and introduced her to R. Kelly. Kelly wrote and produced most of the tracks on her massive-selling debut *Age Ain't Nothing But A Number*. Although the album included two top-ten pop hits – "Back & Forth" and The Isley Brothers cover "At Your Best" – what attracted far more attention was the rumour that Aaliyah and Kelly had married in 1994, although she was under age and he was ten years her senior.

When the media firestorm finally died down, Aaliyah returned sans Kelly in 1996 with *One In A Million*. Of the various producers and songwriters featured, the most fruitful partnership was with **Timbaland** and Missy Elliott. Both the title track and "If Your Girl Only Knew" were huge R&B hits, and established the trio as a potent force. They produced one of the most startling R&B singles of recent years, 1998's landmark "Are You That Someone?", with its bionic human beatboxing and Swiss-cheese rhythm track. Aaliyah sounded like the "baby girl" that Timbaland called her, a point he emphasized with gurgling baby noises in the background.

Aaliyah was still the breathy ingenue on "Try Again", her first pop #1, which came from the soundtrack to *Romeo Must Die*, in which she starred alongside **Jet Li**. On 2001's *Aaliyah*, however, she sounded as though she had grown into her movie-star looks, and took us on an engaging journey through the complexities of relationships. Timbaland wove a snake-charmer beat out of a shehnai-like synth riff and a stop-start drum pattern on "We Need A Resolution", while Aaliyah slithered through the spaces, singing as a woman desperately trying to keep it together as her relationship breaks down. Where most of her contemporaries might have turned histrionic, Aaliyah aimed for composure – something that's all too rare in the current pop climate. It's a damn shame that it's even rarer now.

⊙ **Aaliyah**
2001, Blackground/Virgin

Even if it occasionally tries too hard to please, covering all the bases from the industrial rock of "What If" to the piano ballad "I Refuse", this is turn-of-the-millennium state-of-the-art R&B. The Orientalist "We Need A Resolution" helped to kick-start R&B and hip-hop's love affair with the Far East.

Colonel Abrams

Detroit-born **Colonel Abrams** was one of soul's most distinctive voices during the dark years of the mid-80s. With his heavily masculine, straining voice poised somewhere between Teddy Pendergrass and Keith Sweat, Abrams' closest contemporary was Alexander O'Neal, but what set him apart was his talent with the proto-house rhythms emerging out of New York.

Abrams started out in the mid-70s as a session singer in New York. He was then chosen by producer **Pepé Willie** as the lead vocalist for **94 East**, a Minneapolis group signed to Polydor that just happened to include a young **Prince Rogers Nelson** on guitar. Their single went nowhere, however, and Abrams was soon working with New Jersey group **Surprise Package**.

Colonel Abrams first made a name for himself in 1984, when the ballad "Leave The Message Behind The Door", released on Streetwise, made the lower reaches of the R&B chart. However, the real action was on the flip side, the proto-house "Music Is The Answer", with its clipped rhythms, prominent hand claps and austere synths.

Thanks to the dancefloor success of "Music Is The Answer", Abrams signed to MCA and released the classic single "Trapped" in 1985. A modest R&B hit in the US, "Trapped" was a smash in Europe, reaching #3 in the UK thanks to its prime mid-80s drum machine matrix. It also featured on his 1986 debut album, *Colonel Abrams*, which included production work from **Sam Dees** and arch-Eurodisco conceptualist **Cerrone**.

Abrams' follow-up "I'm Not Gonna Let" also hit the British pop chart, but subsequent singles "How Soon We Forget" and "Nameless" failed to maintain the impetus. Abrams released "Bad Timing" in 1990, produced by Larry Blackmon from Cameo, but unfortunately the title said it all. He then pursued a more soulful direction on 1992's *About Romance*, released on the Acid Jazz label. Uptempo tracks like "Good Things" were popular on European dancefloors, while ballads like "You Don't Know (Somebody Tell Me)" did OK on black radio in the US.

Since the mid-90s Abrams has concentrated on house music, releasing several 12-inches on dance labels Strictly Rhythm, ZYX, Smack, King Street and MicMac, and joining Roger Sanchez, Michael Watford and Jay Williams as **Brotherhood of Soul** for the fine single, "I'll Be Right There".

⊙ **The Best Of Colonel Abrams**
2000, Universal

Although it lacks "Music Is The Answer", this does have Abrams' finest dancefloor movers for MCA: "Trapped", "I'm Not Gonna Let", "The Truth" and "How Soon We Forget". It also proves that with the right production, he can turn in a pretty mean ballad as well.

Johnny Ace

A fine ballad singer who became the first rock'n'roll martyr, **Johnny Ace** was youth culture's first fallen angel. The first pop star to live fast and die young, he was also the first to be turned into an icon far beyond his true talent or stature.

John Marshall Alexander was born the son of a preacher in Memphis in 1929. After being discharged from the Navy in 1947, he joined the Adolph Duncan Band as a pianist, and then **BB King's Beale Street Blues Boys** with fellow bandmate Bobby "Blue" Bland. When King left, Alexander took over, and the group – also including **Roscoe Gordon**, **Earl Forrest** and **Tuff Green** – became **The Beale Streeters**.

In spring 1952, the group – now billed as **Johnny Ace & The Beale Streeters**, to spare Alexander's preacher father – recorded "My Song" for the Duke label. Off-pitch they may have been, but Ace's warm vocals made the girls swoon, and the record was an R&B #1 for nine weeks. The follow-ups "Cross My

Heart" and the echo-filled "Clocks", both from 1953, were also big R&B hits. Now a solo artist, Ace teamed up with the **Johnny Otis Orchestra** and released the moderate hits "Saving My Love For You", "Please Forgive Me" and "Never Let Me Go".

By the autumn of 1954, as one of the biggest draws on the R&B scene, Johnny Ace was headlining a tour with labelmate **Big Mama Thornton**. Clowning backstage with a loaded gun after a Christmas Eve show in Houston, Texas, he shot himself in the head. He died the following day.

Johnny Ace had his biggest hit after his death. The sickly ballad "Pledging My Love" stormed to the top of the R&B charts, where it stayed for ten weeks. It also reached #17 on the pop chart, but was stalled by cover versions by Theresa Brewer, the Four Lads and Tommy Mara. Thanks to the manner of his death, and the sheer mawkishness of "Pledging My Love", Ace became an icon. He was also the subject of several tribute records: "Johnny Ace's Last Letter", by both Johnny Fuller and The Three Blazers, "Johnny Has Gone" by Varetta Dillard, "Salute To Johnny Ace" by The Rovers and "Why Johnny Why" by Linda Hayes.

Johnny Ace Memorial Album
1973, MCA

While Ace possessed a smooth baritone, he was often stiff and had a love-hate relationship with pitch. In other words, his fame was far more radiant than his talent. Collecting just about everything he recorded, this compilation will let you judge for yourself.

Barbara Acklin

Barbara Acklin was one of the main figures of Chicago soul in the late 60s and early 70s. Her voiced ranged from gritty gospelisms to a floaty, Minnie Riperton-style high pitch. Although she was a powerful singer unusually blessed with decent material, her contributions as a songwriter were just as notable.

Born in Oakland, California in 1943, Acklin's career began in the mid-60s as a background singer for Chess/Checker. Her first solo release, as **Barbara Allen**, was a single on her cousin Monk Higgins' Secret Agent label, "I'm Not Mad Anymore" in 1966. That same year she got a job at the Brunswick label as a receptionist, but quickly showed her worth as a songwriter by co-writing Jackie Wilson's "Whispers (Gettin' Louder)".

Acklin soon found her way into the studio where she recorded a couple of solo singles, "Fool, Fool, Fool" and "I've Got You Baby", before teaming up with Gene Chandler for "Show Me The Way To Go" and "From The Teacher To The Preacher" in 1968. It was her third solo single for Brunswick, "Love Makes A Woman", that truly established Acklin. Displaying her full vocal range on top of a definitive Chicago production of singsong melody, gently uplifting horn charts, finger-popping rhythm and sweet chorus, it was a #3 R&B hit.

Acklin's soprano was in equally fine form on the punchy, organ-heavy "Just Ain't No Love", while "Am I The Same Girl" and "A Raggedy Ride" showed that she could ride the day's funkier rhythms with ease. On slower tracks like "After You" from 1969, she indulged in a bit too much Mariah-like melisma, even if her interaction with the falsetto choir was delightful.

Working with **Eugene Record** from The Chi-Lites, whom she eventually married, Acklin continued to release funky-sweet singles with little success. However, her partnership with Eugene Record flourished, and the duo co-wrote "Have You Seen Her", "Stoned Out Of My Mind", "Toby" and many other Chi-Lites hits.

After 1973's bizarre, and pretty terrible, proto-disco trifle "I'll Bake Me A Man", Acklin left Brunswick for Capitol and released "Raindrops", her second biggest R&B hit despite the strained extended metaphor of the lyrics. After a couple more minor R&B hits, "Special Loving" and "Give Me More Of Your Sweet Love", both from 1975, and a new version of "Love Makes A Woman" in 1983, Barbara Acklin died of pneumonia in 1998, while apparently working on material for a new album.

Greatest Hits
1995, Brunswick

It probably could have done without her version of "To Sir With Love", but this is an excellent compilation of Acklin's career at Brunswick. All the hits are here, as well as excellent obscurities "By My Side" and "You've Been In Love Too Long".

Johnny Adams

Although he didn't always use it wisely or to the best of its capabilities, **Johnny Adams** was blessed with one of the most remarkable instruments of any soul vocalist. The so-called "Tan Canary" could pass from a whisper to a piercing scream at the drop of a hat. One moment he might sound like a playboy in a smoking jacket; the next he might be on his knees, testifying like a preacher at a revival meeting.

Born in New Orleans on January 5, 1932, **Lathan John Adams** was a member of several gospel groups as a teenager, including Bessie Griffin's Soul Consolers. He was working as a gardener in 1959 when songwriter Dorothy LaBostrie, who lived in the same building, overheard him singing in the shower. She begged him to record her secular ballad "I Won't Cry" for the Ric label. With its end-of-the-night rock'n'roll arrangement and Adams sounding alternately like Sam Cooke, Charles Brown and Solomon Burke, the recording was the perfect bridge from the proto-soul of the period to the classic soul style that was about to emerge. Although it was a big hit in the Crescent City, Adams had to wait until 1962 for his first national success, the slow ballad, "A Losing Battle", written and produced by a young Mac Rebenack, aka **Dr John**.

Adams moved across town to the Watch label, where he worked with producer **Wardell Quezergue** on such tracks as "I'm Grateful" in 1965. That formulaic Southern

soul ballad was rescued when Adams finally broke down in a preposterous shriek that has to be heard to be believed. He then continued in this histrionic vein on a few singles for Huey Meaux's Pacemaker label.

Adams entered his most fertile period in 1968, at Shelby Singleton's Nashville-based SSS International label. His version of the old chestnut "Release Me" was ridiculously melodramatic, but it did redefine a song that had become mouldy and stale. Thrown in the studio with a bunch of country musicians the next year, Adams recorded the remarkable "Reconsider Me", making like **Little Richard** with his falsetto squeals and yelps on top of a real cowpoke backing.

A spell with Atlantic during the early 70s resulted in the disappointing 1976 standards album *Stand By Me*, but Adams returned to the R&B charts for a final time in 1978 with an excellent reading of Conway Twitty's "After All The Good's Gone". He also became a fixture on the New Orleans nightclub circuit during the 70s, indulging in his penchant for Vaudevillean shtick alongside guitarist **Walter "Wolfman" Washington**.

A long Indian summer in his career was instigated by Adams signing to Rounder in 1984. With Washington and saxophonist **Red Tyler** in tow, he released the startling *From The Heart* that same year, followed by further releases *After Dark, Room With A View Of The Blues, Walking On A Tightrope, Johnny Adams Sings Doc Pomus: The Real Me, Good Morning Heartache, The Verdict, One Foot In The Blues* and *Man Of My Word* throughout the 80s and 90s. Moving with ease and effortless flair between deep soul, harrowing blues and intelligent pop – and even kitschy antics like his "mouth trombone" – on these albums, Adams proved himself to be one of the great interpreters of the African-American vocal tradition.

From The Heart
1984, Rounder

An outstanding album of blues/soul classicism. Adams's Rounder releases functioned in essentially the same way as Ella Fitzgerald's "Songbook" albums: as a redefinition and reaffirmation of tradition in the face of changing times.

Reconsider Me
1996, Collectables

This retrospective of Adams' Ric and SSS International recordings includes all of his great 60s singles, from "A Losing Battle" to "I Can't Be All Bad", and shows him to be one of the most original balladeers of his time.

After 7

A vocal trio from Indianapolis, **After 7** were among the prime predecessors of the overly declamatory, melismatic, whining, pappy ballads that have taken over R&B. **Keith Mitchell** and **Kevon Edmonds**, who met as members of Indiana University's IU Soul Revue, decided to form their own group after graduation, and enlisted Kevon's brother **Melvin Edmonds**. Conveniently, Mitchell happened to be the cousin of **Antonio "LA" Reid**, while the Edmonds brothers had another sibling, Kenny "Babyface" Edmonds. LA and Babyface were then two of the hottest R&B producers around and, when they signed a production deal with Virgin in 1989, they took their relatives with them.

The group's 1989 self-titled debut, *After 7*, was a sensation on the quiet storm circuit. Slow jams like "Heat Of The Moment" and "Ready Or Not" rode LA and Babyface's characteristic watery keyboards and the group's rather wimpy harmonies to the pinnacle of the R&B chart. The slightly more syncopated "Can't Stop", meanwhile, got a pop shine; the remix was a huge club hit in the US and a pop top-ten hit.

In 1991 the vaguely doo-woppy "Nights Like This", taken from the film *The Five Heartbeats*, gave After 7 their fourth R&B top-ten hit. Although LA and Babyface were no longer behind the boards, 1992's *Taking My Time* stuck to the tested formula. The late-night slow jams "Kickin' It" and "Baby I'm For Real" (a cover of The Originals' song of the same name with a 20-second sample of Bloodstone's "Natural High") were huge hits on urban radio.

Reflections in 1995 held another big R&B hit in "'Til You Do Me Right", which seemed to stay on the radio for the entire year. However, as the R&B climate changed, and shiny bouncy tracks became the vogue, the softly spoken love men of After 7 were soon relegated to the sidelines.

The Very Best Of After 7
1997, Virgin

Unsubtle, gritless and whiny, to be sure, but unlike most of their peers After 7 are not adenoidal huffers and puffers. This has all their big hits, as well as a decent cover of Hall & Oates' "Sara Smile" and other previously unreleased tracks. It's also the best introduction to the group.

Arthur Alexander

A lthough his records never made much of an impact on the R&B chart, let alone the pop chart, **Arthur Alexander** is a key figure in the development of not only soul, but rock'n'roll as well. He is, after all, the only artist to have his songs covered by Elvis Presley, The Beatles, The Rolling Stones *and* Bob Dylan – not to mention The Osmonds.

Alexander was born the son of a blues guitarist on May 10, 1940 in Florence, Alabama. While he was in gospel groups as a youngster, he was equally influenced by the country music all around him, and his recordings blended the two traditions. While working as a bellhop, Alexander was introduced to white R&B nuts like **Tom Stafford**, Spooner Oldham, Dan Penn, **Rick Hall** and Billy Sherrill. In 1960, as **June Alexander**, he recorded "Sally Sue Brown", a blues number he had written with Stafford, for the Judd label.

The following summer, Alexander helped Rick Hall build a recording studio across the river in Muscle Shoals. Fame Studio's first release was his "You Better Move On". A ghostly blend of countrypolitan chorales, big hi-hat and a simple guitar figure, it reached #24 on the pop charts. Alexander's strange vocal, somehow weepy and forlorn at the same time, seemed to anticipate **Mick Jagger**'s snarl, and he was whisked away by Dot, the record label, to Nashville.

Although the flip of "You Better Move On" was the uptempo rocker "A Shot Of Rhythm & Blues", Alexander was mostly saddled with saccharine pop and country-styled material in Nashville. "Where Have You Been All My Life" was his 1962 follow-up, but the flip, his own "Soldier Of Love", was far better. That same year, "Anna (Go To Him)" beautifully replicated the atmosphere of his debut "You Better Move On".

In 1965, he moved across town to John Richbourg's Sound Stage 7 label, but after a few so-so singles, illness and (allegedly) substance abuse caused him to drop out of sight. He returned in 1968 with "I Need You Baby" before working as a staff songwriter. He then recorded a self-titled album for Warner Brothers in 1972 that included the definitive

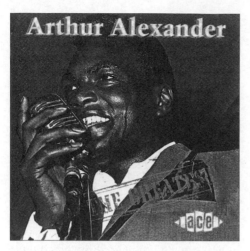

Arthur Alexander

version of "Burning Love", later made famous by **Elvis Presley**.

Alexander signed to Buddah in 1975, and recorded the minor hit "Every Day I Have To Cry" back in Muscle Shoals, Alabama. After a couple more singles, he became disillusioned and quit the music biz, moving to Cleveland and working as a bus driver. Suddenly, years later in 1993, Alexander emerged with *Lonely Just Like Me*, a pretty decent collection of renditions of his classics plus some new originals. However, a few days after signing a new contract, he died of a heart attack.

The Ultimate Arthur Alexander
1993, Razor & Tie

This excellent collection of Alexander's Dot recordings (both singles and obscurities) shows that, had he been given better material, his rich voice would have made him one of the biggest stars of Southern soul. His slow-burning intensity would have made him a perfect interpreter of the Nashville weepies that formed the backbone of country soul.

Ashford & Simpson

Nickolas Ashford (born May 4, 1942) and **Valerie Simpson** (born August 26, 1946) rank among the greatest songwriting teams in the history of soul. As a recording duo, they were a huge presence on disco dancefloors, and their vision of the good life, as spelled out on disco hits like "Bourgie Bourgie", helped to move soul from the chicken shack to the penthouse.

The two first met as members of the choir at White Rock Baptist Church in Harlem, and released a couple of singles together in the early 60s that went nowhere. They then landed songwriting jobs at Scepter/Wand, working with Joshie Jo Armstead on songs for **Maxine Brown**, **Chuck Jackson**, **The Shirelles** and **Ronnie Milsap**. After "Let's Go Get Stoned", which they wrote for **Ray Charles**, became #1 on the R&B chart in 1966, they were recruited by Holland-Dozier-Holland as staff writers at Motown. There Ashford & Simpson were responsible for such classics as "Ain't No Mountain High Enough", "You're All I Need to Get By", and "Your Precious Love" for **Marvin Gaye & Tammi Terrell**, and "Remember Me" and "Reach Out And Touch Somebody's Hand" for **Diana Ross**. When Tammi Terrell became too sick to continue to record with Marvin Gaye, Simpson ghost-recorded her tracks for her.

In 1971 Simpson tried her hand at a solo recording career, but the two were always most effective together, and, in 1973, they signed as a duo to Warner Brothers. Their slickly produced, uptempo records, and in particular Ashford's piercing falsetto – sometimes he's a dead ringer for Sylvester – helped lay the groundwork for disco. Released after the pair were married in 1974, "Main Line", from their second Warners album *I Wanna Be Selfish*, was a huge hit in New York's early discos, with its propulsive bassline and its love-as-addiction metaphor. "Tried, Tested And Found True", the proto-boogie of "Don't Cost You Nothing" and "Over And Over" were their other popular dancefloor records; coincidentally, the latter was covered by Sylvester.

"It Seems To Hang On", six minutes of absolute disco perfection, became their biggest hit to date in 1978, reaching #2 on the R&B chart. The next year, another percolating dancefloor monster, "Found A Cure", also reached #2. Around that time, Ashford & Simpson also wrote the smash hit "I'm Every Woman" for **Chaka Khan**, but finding an R&B #1 for themselves was proving elusive.

After a couple of decent-sized R&B hits, "Nobody Knows" and "Love Don't Make It Right", Ashford & Simpson moved to

Muscle Shoals and Fame Studios

The city of Florence, Alabama on the shores of the Tennessee River was the birthplace of some of the biggest figures in American music: "Father of the Blues" **W.C. Handy**; "Father of rock'n'roll" **Sam Phillips**; and country music titans **Buddy Killen** and **Billy Sherrill**. However, the city's biggest contribution to the sound of American music – the Muscle Shoals sound – came courtesy of Fame (Florence Alabama Music Enterprises). Housed in an old tobacco warehouse on Wilson Dam Highway across the river in Muscle Shoals, Fame Studios was opened by **Rick Hall** in 1961.

Fame was responsible for some of the deepest soul sides. The irony of this is that, with the exception of the singers, the music was entirely crafted by hillbillies. Rick Hall thought that the studio would be his ticket to Nashville, but the musicians and songwriters he drafted in – **Spooner Oldham**, Jimmy Johnson, **Dan Penn**, Roger Hawkins, **Peanut Montgomery**, Junior Lowe, **David Briggs**, **Norbert Putnam**, Donnie Fritts, **Terry Thompson**, Barry Beckett, David Hood, Duane Allman and **Jerry Carrigan** – played R&B on the Southern frat house circuit. The merger of Hall's country roots and his musicians' and songwriters' soul and R&B backgrounds became Muscle Shoals' legacy.

The first record cut at Fame Studios was Arthur Alexander's strangely ghostly "You Better Move On" in 1962. The record reached #24 on the pop charts and Alexander was promptly whisked away by his label, Dot, to record in Nashville. However, the record's success and its special sound prompted acts like The Tams and **Tommy Roe** to record in Muscle Shoals.

After Rick Hall and his crew recorded **Jimmy Hughes**'s "Steal Away" in 1964, they couldn't find anyone to license it, so Hall formed his own Fame label to release the record. With Hughes's anguished performance, "Steal Away" went on to become perhaps the archetypal R&B cheating song and a big hit for Fame. Hughes was at his best on slower songs like "Steal Away" or his cover of Jerry Butler's standard "I Stand Accused" (on which Hughes sounded like he was trapped in an echo chamber), but he also recorded some fine uptempo songs for Fame in the mid-60s: "You Really Know How To Hurt A Guy" and "Neighbor, Neighbor".

It was Percy Sledge's 1966 smash, "When A Man Loves A Woman", which was recorded

in nearby Sheffield, Alabama with backing from Fame musicians, that truly heralded the arrival of the Muscle Shoals sound. Over the next few years, Muscle Shoals was responsible for landmark records by **Wilson Pickett**, **Aretha Franklin** (1967's "I Never Loved A Man (The Way I Love You)"), **Joe Tex**, **Mighty Sam**, **Candi Staton**, **James & Bobby Purify** (1966's "I'm Your Puppet"), **Laura Lee**, **Arthur Conley** (1967's "Sweet Soul Music"), The Staple Singers, Joe Simon and Etta James (1968's "Tell Mama"). Even lesser-known records, such as **Bobby Moore & The Rhythm Aces**' aching "Searching For My Baby" or **Maurice & Mac**'s irresistible "You Left The Water Running", were tinged with the Muscle Shoals magic.

The golden age of the Muscle Shoals sound was the late 60s when Bary Beckett, David Hood, Roger Hawkins and Jimmy Johnson were Fame's house band. However, when they left the studios to found the Muscle Shoals Sound Studio in 1969, Fame's fortunes started to diminish. Their studio recorded soul sessions by Bobby Womack, Millie Jackson, **The Soul Children** and **R.B. Greaves**, but it became more famous when it branched out into other genres and recorded rock sessions with Boz Scaggs, **Joe Cocker**, Rod Stewart, Bob Seger, Leon Russell and **The Rolling Stones**.

Although the Fame label was hurt by the defection of these key musicians, Rick Hall continued to release fine records in the early 70s by **Spencer Wiggins** ("I'd Rather Go Blind") and **Willie Hightower** ("Back Road Into Town") and instrumentals by **The Fame Gang** (Travis Wammack, Clayton Ivey, Jesse Boyce and Freeman Brown). Hall finally closed the Fame label in 1974. The Fame Studios continue to record and produce material for a variety of fine artists to this day, but sadly, Muscle Shoals lost its unique country-soul blend in the mid-70s.

Various Artists: The Muscle Shoals Sound
1993, Rhino

From the classic 6/8 country gospel ballad sound to funkier, more uptempo grooves, the Muscle Shoals sound defined country and deep soul. This excellent 18-track collection includes a healthy proportion of the masterpieces recorded in the Florence-Muscle Shoals-Sheffield area of Alabama and features such soul greats as Arthur Alexander, Jimmy Hughes, Aretha Franklin, Wilson Pickett, Percy Sledge and Clarence Carter.

Capitol in the early 80s, where they immediately had an R&B top-ten hit with "Street Corner". In 1984, "Solid" finally provided

the huge crossover hit they were looking for. Mixed by longtime disco stalwart François Kevorkian, who suggested the

Songwriters Ashford & Simpson give a solid performance of their own

a cappella intro, "Solid" was emblematic of the fractured R&B that was then starting to take hold, and it stayed at #1 for three weeks.

By the late 80s, the duo had moved away from the dancefloor, becoming sappy balladeers on top-five R&B hits like "Count Your Blessings" and "I'll Be There For You". They continued to tour and record throughout the 90s, and in 1996 recorded the horrendously cod-spiritual album *Been Found*, with poet Maya Angelou.

⊚ The Very Best Of Ashford & Simpson
2002, Rhino

While it doesn't have the obscure but great "Main Line", and it begins with a tacky medley of their Motown songs, this is probably the best available collection of Ashford & Simpson's work, ranging from "It Seems To Hang On" to "Solid".

Atlantic Starr

B efore they redefined the R&B power
ballad, **Atlantic Starr** were a fairly run-
of-the-mill funk-disco band. Hailing from
suburban White Plains, New York, the
group revolved around the **Lewis brothers**:
keyboardist Wayne, guitarist David and
trumpeter/trombonist Jonathan. Along with
lead vocalist **Sharon Bryant**, bassist **Cliff
Archer**, trumpeter **William Sudderth**, saxophonist **Damon Rentie**, percussionist
Joseph Phillips and drummer **Porter
Carroll**, the group signed to A&M in 1977.
Veteran Philly session man Bobby Eli produced their first two albums, *Atlantic Starr*
(1978) and *Straight To The Point* (1979),
which provided a fair-sized R&B hit in 1978
with the medium-tempo funker "Stand Up".

For their third album, *Radiance* (1981),
Atlantic Starr brought in James Carmichael,
who had turned **The Commodores** into
superstars, as producer. He lightened the
group's sound and shifted the focus to Sharon
Bryant – a change that paid immediate dividends when "When Love Calls" reached the
R&B Top 10. Then, in 1982, the Chaka Khan-
esque "Circles", typical of the post-disco sound
then ruling the East Coast, became an R&B #2.

Bryant went solo in 1984, and was replaced
by **Barbara Weathers** for the appropriately
named 1985 album *As The Band Turns*, which
featured a pared-down line-up of the Lewises,
Weathers and Phillips. Although the album
featured uptempo groovers like "Freak-A-
Ristic", its signature track was "Secret Lovers".
A classic cheating ballad, its arrangement and
production (now handled by the Lewis brothers) were pure 80s schmaltz. Even more saccharine was "Always", which was, inevitably,
an even bigger hit and reached #1 on the pop
chart in 1987.

Weathers, in turn, left in 1988, but the hit
adult contemporary ballads kept on coming
with new singer **Porscha Martin**. "My First
Love" was yet another R&B chart-topper,
drenched in sickly keyboards and overwrought but wimpy singing. More huge hits
followed in the form of "Love Crazy" and
"Masterpiece" in the early 90s, with new
vocalist **Rachel Oliver**, before the record-
buying public finally wearied of the group's
monotonous style. Atlantic Starr continued
to perform and record with constant line-up
changes into the twenty-first century, but
their commercial peak ended back when big
hair went out of fashion.

Ultimate Collection
2000, Hip-O

By far the best way to listen to Atlantic Starr. This is the
only collection that includes tracks from their first and
best phase, as a faceless disco-funk band, as well as from
their slow jam apotheosis, and it's not in chronological
order, so there are some respites from the relentless
candyfloss.

Patti Austin

P atti Austin has one of the most familiar
voices in popular music. A professional
singer since the age of five, she has been
heard on countless commercial jingles and
back-up gigs. It's a shame that her own
records are rarely as memorable.

Born in New York on August 10, 1948,
Austin's precocious talent first came to light
when **Dinah Washington** invited the five-
year-old on stage at the Apollo to sing
"Teach Me Tonight" – only to have her scold
the band when they played it in the wrong
key. She soon appeared on TV with **Sammy
Davis, Jr.** and on Broadway productions of
Finian's Rainbow and *Lost In The Stars*.

Blessed with one of the purest tones in the
business, Austin's voice wasn't exactly suited
to the strains and emotions of classic soul
singing, but that didn't stop her or numerous producers from trying. Her first singles
were for the Coral label in 1966. Tracks like
"Take Away The Pain Stain" – not as bad as
the title, but a sub-par **Supremes** rip nonetheless – and "Leave A Little Love" –
Bacharach-style arrangements anchoring
Austin's teensy-weensy easy-listening vocals
– became favourites on the Northern Soul
scene, as did the surging "Music To My
Heart", released on ABC in 1968.

"The Family Tree" was Austin's first
record to achieve any kind of commercial
success, reaching the R&B Top 50. Despite
releasing singles in assorted styles for United
Artists, Columbia and CTI, and duetting
with **Michael Jackson, George Benson,
Quincy Jones, Tom Browne** and **Yutaka
Yokokura**, chart placings were few and far

between. However, her three albums for Creed Taylor's progressive jazz CTI label – *End Of A Rainbow* (1976), *Havana Candy* (1977) and *Body Language* (1980) – pointed the way forwards.

The emergence of the quiet storm/smooth jazz radio format provided Austin and her tone with her raison d'être. After singing on Quincy Jones's "Razzamatazz", she scored a pop #1 with James Ingram, "Baby Come To Me". The breezy melody and killer hook – and its role as the theme song for the popular soap *General Hospital* – made it a surefire chart-topper and one of the ballads of the decade.

Austin has continued in a similar vein ever since, with tracks like "How Do You Keep The Music Playing", "It's Gonna Be Special", "The Heat Of Heat" and "On The Way To Love" getting peak drive-time plays on smooth jazz radio stations throughout the 80s, 90s and 00s. While providing the female antidote for all the husky love men, she also recorded a couple of albums of standards – *The Real Me* in 1988 and the well-received tribute to Ella Fitzgerald, *For Ella*, in 2002 – and remains active on the touring circuit.

The Real Me
1988, Qwest

Austin is all about technique, rather than emotion, so her records are all too often uninvolving. *The Real Me* may not have her only big hit, "Baby Come To Me", but this collection of standards, including "Smoke Gets In Your Eyes" and "Cry Me A River", is where her voice really shines.

The Average White Band

Despite their facetious name (the gift of another funky ofay, Bonnie Bramlett), the **Average White Band** are among the very few white artists – along with Elvis Presley, Teena Marie, Hall & Oates, Madonna, Ricky Nelson, Lisa Stansfield, The Bee-Gees, Tower of Power and, umm, Kenny G – to have made a significant impact on the American R&B charts. Not only were all the members of the band Scottish, but their run of 14 R&B hits was originally triggered by an **Eric Clapton** concert.

Singer/bassist **Alan Gorrie**, guitarists **Hamish Stuart** and **Onnie McIntyre**, keyboardist **Roger Ball** and saxophonist

Malcolm Duncan were all members of soul tribute bands, while drummer **Robbie McIntosh** had played with Brian Auger's Oblivion Express. They anonymously backed **Chuck Berry** on his first #1 record, 1972's "My Ding-A-Ling", before getting together as Clapton's opening act in 1973. Although they released their debut album, *Show Your Hand*, later that year, it was their self-titled 1974 album, *The Average White Band*, that first proved their name to be a misnomer.

Produced by **Arif Mardin** – the man who turned the Bee-Gees into a worldwide phenomenon – the album's stand-out track was "Pick Up The Pieces". Released as a single, it topped the US pop chart in February 1975 thanks to its catchy horn line, James Brown-style guitar interplay – check out The J.B.'s' "Gimme Some More" for comparison – and in-your-face hi-hats. However, that initial success was marred by McIntosh's death on September 23, 1974, after ingesting heroin and morphine at a Hollywood party.

McIntosh was replaced by former Bloodstone drummer **Steve Ferrone** for *Cut The Cake* in 1975. Led by the title track, which reached the pop Top 10, and the preposterously funky and oft-sampled "School Boy Crush", this was AWB's most consistent album, and their last before they began to water down their street funk sound in the face of the disco juggernaut.

Their subsequent albums – *Soul Searching* (1976), the live *Person To Person* (1977), *Benny & Us* (1977), a collaboration with Ben E. King, *Warmer Communications* (1978), *Feel No Fret* (1979) and *Shine* (1980) – marked a steady decline. The group split in 1980, only to re-form after a decade of session work for *Aftershock* in 1989. Despite working with the great **John Robie**, and the modest success of the single "The Spirit Of Love", which featured vocals by Chaka Khan and **Ronnie Laws**, the album tanked. AWB nevertheless continued to work the nostalgia circuit, releasing *Soul Tattoo* in 1997 and the live *Face To Face* in 1999.

Pickin' Up The Pieces: The Best Of The Average White Band (1974–1980)
1992, Rhino

Although 1975's *Cut The Cake* is AWB's finest studio album, this has all the hits and their best album tracks. Their secret was a glossier take on the formulae created by Kool & The Gang and The Meters, which owed much to producer Arif Mardin.

Roy Ayers

The godfather of acid jazz and one of the most sampled artists of all time, vibraphonist **Roy Ayers** is among the more controversial musicians in the soul pantheon. That's not for any stance he's taken, but because his legacy tends to leave critics and traditional soul fans cold, while new bucks and hip-hop heads are in ecstasy.

According to legend, Ayers, who was born in LA on September 10, 1940, was a budding five-year-old pianist when his parents took him to see **Lionel Hampton**, who gave him his first pair of mallet sticks. It was not until 1957, however, that he took up the instrument in earnest. By 1961 he was gigging on the local jazz scene with Chico Hamilton, Teddy Edwards and Jack Wilson, and he recorded his first date as a leader in 1963 with *West Coast Vibes* on United Artists.

Between 1966 and 1970, Ayers was a member of flautist **Herbie Mann**'s band. He contributed to the Mann albums *Live At The Whisky A Go Go*, *Memphis Underground* and *Concerto Grosso In D Blues*, as well as recording four of his own: *Virgo Vibes*, *Daddy Bug And Friends*, *Stoned Soul Picnic* and *Daddy's Back*, the last of which featured **Herbie Hancock** and Ron Carter.

After signing to Polydor in 1970, Ayers recorded the heavy jazz fusion set *He's Coming* in 1971, featuring drummer **Billy Cobham** and saxophonist **Sonny Fortune**, and including the classic "We Live In Brooklyn Baby". That same year, influenced no doubt by the crossover success of **Donald Byrd**, Ayers formed **Roy Ayers Ubiquity**, along with mainstays Harry Whitaker, Wayne Garfield and Edwin Birdsong, and released *Ubiquity*. With tracks like "Pretty Brown Skin", the album foreshadowed the airy, light soul-jazz/jazz-funk fusion sound with which he would make his name. *Virgo Red* followed in similar style in 1973, though on that year's *Red, Black & Green*, and particularly the title track, Ayers shifted the emphasis towards the grooves and songs, and dispensed with most of the noodly fusion bits.

With master drummer **Bernard "Pretty" Purdie** on board, 1974's *Change Up The Groove* did exactly what it said on the sleeve, especially on "The Boogie Back", a favourite among serious collectors and crate diggers.

Purdie returned, along with Jon Faddis, Dee Dee Bridgewater, Al Foster and Calvin Brown, for *A Tear To A Smile* in 1975, the album most responsible for establishing Ayers' success and reputation. However, later that year, Ayers largely dumped the formula on the more straightforwardly funky *Mystic Voyage*, with cuts like the clavinet-heavy "Brother Green (The Disco King)", "Funky Motion" and "Spirit Of Doo Do".

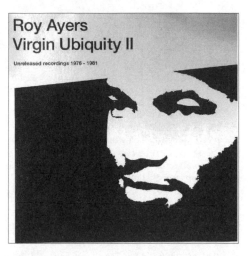

Everybody Loves The Sunshine, in 1976, was filled with sun-drenched grooves, such as "The Golden Rod" and "Keep On Walking", constructed from soft tempos and whining keyboards. There was plenty more Jacuzzi jazz on Ubiquity's *Vibrations* that same year, while Ayers reprised "Everybody Loves The Sunshine" for *Come Into Knowledge* in 1977, his one album with **RAMP** (the Roy Ayers Music Project).

Disco began to rear its ugly head on Ayers' late-70s albums, although it has to be said that his first foray into the genre, "Running Away", from 1977's *Lifeline*, is a stone-cold classic. Ayers abandoned the Ubiquity name soon afterwards and released a series of uninspiring, formulaic albums. He found his way out of the rut, in 1980, by going to Africa and recording the slightly awkward *Music Of Many Colors* with Afrobeat kingpin **Fela Kuti**. The African theme continued the following year with the more consistent *Africa - Centre Of The World*. Meanwhile, Ayers also founded his Uno Melodic label for which he produced cult records by Ethell Beatty, 80's Ladies and **Sylvia Striplin**, whose *Give Me Your Love* in 1980 was the best of the bunch, with its bouncy title track and the rather amazing "You Can't Turn Me Away".

Although Ayers continued to record throughout the 80s, he became overly reliant on new synthesizers, sacrificing his unique tone in favour of technology. After guesting on **Masters At Work**'s Nu Yorican Soul project in 1996, he set up his own AFI label and released several instrumental albums. In 2003 *Mahogany Vibe*, on the BBE label, saw

him remaking some of his old hits with vocalists like Erykah Badu and Betty Wright.

Destination Motherland: The Roy Ayers Anthology
2003, Universal

With two CDs and 33 tracks, this compilation holds just about all the Roy Ayers a casual fan could want. Since it focuses on his grooves, Ayers' tendencies to noodle and overload on smarm are tempered by dancefloor imperatives.

Acid Jazz

Growing out of the jazz-dance and rare groove scenes in both Europe – particularly the UK and Germany – and Japan, **acid jazz** was a retro-fixated movement that began in Britain in the late 80s as a reaction to the explosion of house. Its very name was a play on the acid house craze. The scene's prime mover, pirate radio DJ **Gilles Peterson**, championed unfashionable jazz-funk and soul-jazz by **Roy Ayers**, **Miles Davis**, **Donald Byrd**, **Charles Earland** and **Herbie Hancock**, at a time when Smiley and "Aciiiid" ruled Britain.

In 1987 Peterson and Eddie Piller, who ran the Mod revivalist labels Countdown and Re-Elect the President – which introduced scene stalwarts, organist **James Taylor** and **Chris White** of Mother Earth, in more rocking guises – formed the Acid Jazz label. They released the first in the scene-defining series of *Totally Wired* compilations, and also Galliano's "Frederick Lies Still", an affectionate parody of **Curtis Mayfield**'s "Freddie's Dead". Acid Jazz went on to release dozens of records of boho jazziness by such artists as **Brand New Heavies**, Snowboy, The Apostles, **Jamiroquai**, D-Influence, Corduroy and even proto-rappers The Watts Prophets.

Peterson set up his own Talkin' Loud label in 1989. His first signing was **The Young Disciples**,

a group of British musicians fronted by American singer **Carleen Anderson**, the daughter of Vicki Anderson and Bobby Byrd. The group released perhaps the two finest singles to emerge from the scene, "Get Yourself Together" in 1989 and "Apparently Nothin'" in 1990. Later releases from Incognito, United Future Organization, Urban Species, 4 Hero, Roni Size, Innerzone Orchestra and Nuyorican Soul stuck to Peterson's original aesthetic of smooth but funky cod-jazz, but also pushed it in new directions to embrace hip-hop, house, techno and drum'n'bass.

While acid jazz started and had its biggest impact in the UK, the virus spread across the world, with labels such as Luv 'n' Haight and Ubiquity in the US, Compost in Germany, Japan's Bellissima! and Italy's Right Tempo preaching the boho gospel.

Various Artists: Totally Wired 1/2: The Beginning
1992, Acid Jazz

The cream of the first two volumes of the *Totally Wired* series, which launched acid jazz as a mini-genre of its own. This compilation includes tracks from Brand New Heavies, Galliano, The Night Trains, Jazz Renegades and Ulf Sandberg Quartet.

🔊 PLAYLIST

1 FREDERICK LIES STILL Galliano from **Totally Wired 1**
Galliano reads his poetry over a jazzy cover of Curtis Mayfield's "Freddie's Dead" and a scene is born.

2 GET YOURSELF TOGETHER Young Disciples from **Road To Freedom**
Carleen Anderson proves herself to be the finest singer of this mini-genre.

3 APPARENTLY NOTHING Young Disciples from **Road To Freedom**
Based on an old Marvelettes' record, this is one of the few acid jazz tracks to carry weight beyond its own enclave.

4 NEVER STOP Brand New Heavies from **Heavy Rhyme Experience Vol 1**
Acid jazz at its most upwardly mobile.

5 STARSKY AND HUTCH THEME James Taylor Quartet from **Wait A Minute**
A party-hardy Hammond organ workout.

6 LOUNGIN' Jazzmatazz from **Jazzmatazz Volume 1**
The all-star crew of acid jazzers on this side project by Gang Starr's Guru almost make you forget DJ Premier.

Babyface

For better or for worse, **Kenneth "Babyface" Edmonds** was probably the most important R&B presence in the 90s. Fusing the traditions of suave pop crossover à la Nat "King" Cole and quiet storm love man à la Barry White, Babyface remade R&B as anodyne office music and Hollywood schmaltz. Not only a hugely successful artist in his own right, Babyface wrote and produced monster hits for everyone from Boyz II Men to Céline Dion and, as CEO of LaFace Records, he introduced and shaped the careers of artists like **OutKast**, TLC, Usher and Toni Braxton.

Edmonds was born on April 10, 1959, in Indianapolis, Indiana. As a teenager he joined **Bootsy Collins**'s touring band as a guitarist and earned the nickname "Babyface". In 1977 he joined the funk group **Manchild** with reed player **Reggie Griffin**, who went on to fame as an electro producer in the 80s. Manchild had a minor R&B hit with "Especially For You" and released three unheralded albums before they broke up.

Babyface Edmonds then hooked up with **Antonio "LA" Reid** (born **Mark Rooney** on June 7, 1957, in Cincinnati, Ohio) and the two formed **The Deele** with vocalists Carlos "Satin" Greene, Darnell Bristol, Stanley Burke and Kevin Roberson in 1982. On early records like "Body Talk" and "Material Thangz", The Deele were walking in the very large footsteps of Prince. After Babyface recorded his first solo album, *Lovers*, which produced a top-ten R&B hit in "I Love You Babe", he and Reid

started producing records for other artists – most significantly The Whispers' LinnDrum funk ballad "Rock Steady" that would herald the production duo's signature sound.

For The Deele's 1987 album *Eyes Of A Stranger*, Babyface and Reid shifted the group's sound away from that of Prince wannabes towards the sound that would become their calling card. The single "Two Occasions" was a cringe-worthy ballad with Hallmark card lyrics, keyboards that wallowed in the depths of MOR cliché and puppy-love falsetto vocals. It was a top-five R&B smash and it finally established the producers' reputations. Babyface and Reid rapidly became super-producers – over the next two years they had big hits with Pebbles ("Girlfriend"), the **Mac Band** ("Roses Are Red"), **The Boys** ("Dial My Heart"), **Sheena Easton** ("The Lover In Me"), **Karyn White** ("Superwoman") and **Bobby Brown** ("Every Little Step" and "Don't Be Cruel") – and distanced themselves from The Deele, who finally broke up in 1989.

That same year, Babyface released his second solo album, *Tender Lovers*, which established him as a superstar. The middle-of-the-road ballads "It's No Crime", "Tender Lover", "Whip Appeal" and "My Kinda Girl" were very much in the style he established with "Two Occasions" and were all R&B top-three or pop top-ten hits. Over the next few years, Babyface the singer concentrated on soundtrack work – his songs had all the subtlety and nuance that Hollywood love scenes and date montages demand – but as a producer and songwriter, he achieved stratospheric success: Boyz II Men's "End Of The Road" and "I'll Make Love To You" spent 27 weeks atop the American singles chart, **Madonna**'s "Take A Bow" was at #1 for seven weeks and Whitney Houston's "I Will Always Love You" for fourteen weeks.

By such standards his 1993 album *For The Cool In You*, which only managed triple platinum, was a disappointment. In 1995 he scored the film *Waiting To Exhale*, writing and producing the soundtrack's big hit, Whitney Houston's "Exhale (Shoop Shoop)". That same year he also won the first of three consecutive Grammy Awards as producer of the year.

Featuring more guest appearances than a Robert Altman film (Mariah Carey, Stevie Wonder, **Kenny G**, Shalamar, **LL Cool J**...), 1997's *The Day* spawned the two enormous singles "For The Lover In You" and "Every Time I Close My Eyes". Although he continued working on soundtracks as well as producing and running his record label, *The Day* was Babyface's last significant new release until *Face2Face* in 2001. *Face2Face* featured the uncharacteristic "There She Goes", a **Timbaland**-style production with skidding synths, skittering syncopation and a divebombing bassline that was actually likeable, and the more familiar "What If", an icky ballad made even worse by adenoidal vocals reminiscent of Jodeci's KCi.

A Collection Of His Greatest Hits
2000, Epic

With fourteen somewhat oddly chosen tracks – including a couple of non-single album cuts – this may not be the perfect introduction to Babyface's crass commercial craftsmanship, but it does cut to the chase. If you like your R&B to remind you of a dentist's waiting room, then this is the disc for you.

Erykah Badu

Perhaps the most under-appreciated virtue in soul is restraint. In a climate of cookie-cutter melismatic warblers, **Erykah Badu** stands out on the strength of a voice that doesn't have to shout to be heard, that doesn't have to over-enunciate to emote and that doesn't have to be breathily girly to be sexy. That said, restraint and economy don't necessarily mean simplicity and naturalism, and Badu's mannerisms can sometimes be just as annoying as those of the hyperactive divas to whom she's such a welcome antidote.

Badu was born with the rather more prosaic name **Erica Wright** in Dallas, Texas on February 26, 1971. She was working there as a teacher in 1995 when she landed an opening slot for a local gig by D'Angelo. Her performance caught the ear of D'Angelo's manager **Kedar Massenburg**, who signed her to his Kedar label. Her first single was released the next year: a cover of Marvin Gaye and Tami Terrell's "Your Precious Love", performed as a duet with D'Angelo, which appeared on the *High School High* soundtrack.

In 1997, she released the *Baduizm* album, on which she co-wrote eleven of the twelve songs. Her songwriting ability, superficial vocal resemblance to **Billie Holiday**, and Afro-inspired garb prompted many critics to hail her as the priestess of neo-soul. However, although tracks like "On & On" and "Next Lifetime" indicated great potential, her singing rarely went below the sur-

PLAYLIST
Erykah Badu

1 **ON & ON** from **Baduizm**
The updated spin on the "Top Billin'" drum beat and Badu's Billie Holiday shtick helped make neo-soul a critical sensation.

2 **NEXT LIFETIME** from **Baduizm**
The sleazy synth sounds on this track are the yang to Dr. Dre's yin.

3 **DRAMA** from **Baduizm**
A lush Jacuzzi of Fender Rhodes.

4 **TYRONE** from **Live**
Badu gives her man plenty of shit, to the delight of the ladies in the house.

5 **BAG LADY** from **Mama's Gun**
This is kinda preachy, but Badu sounds like a real person, not just a persona.

6 **DIDN'T CHA KNOW** from **Mama's Gun**
Badu is as mannered as ever here, but her astringency cuts through the smarmy jazz licks.

7 **BACK IN THE DAY (PUFF)** from **Worldwide Underground**
It's got Lenny Kravitz on guitar, but is pleasantly nostalgic nevertheless.

8 **LOVE OF MY LIFE WORLDWIDE** from **Worldwide Underground**
Badu's little-girl voice grates, but the minimal production grounds her.

Erykah Badu covers up another bad hair day

face, and was often just as mannered as her headwrap – the jazz pretensions were nothing but boho shtick. While *Live*, released in the same year, might have seemed like a quick cash-in on the surprising success of her debut, it nonetheless held worthwhile tracks, like the single "Tyrone" and the covers of Heatwave's "Boogie Nights" and Roy Ayers' "Searching".

Live was released on the same day that Seven, Badu's son with **Andre Benjamin** – aka Dre 3000 of **OutKast** – was born. The fallout from her subsequent break-up with Benjamin produced one of the decade's best

singles in OutKast's "Ms. Jackson". Badu told her side of the story on *Mama's Gun* in 2000, in often harrowing and, at times, melodramatic detail, turning her fragile voice to the blues. The blues may be the age-old and eternal verities of life, but here they merely sounded age-old. The album was tinted with the jazzy, Afro-Bohemian patina, so characteristic of producers **Jay Dee** and ?uestlove, that tainted albums by Badu collaborators Common and The Roots. The one time it didn't sound retrogressive was on the magnificent "Bag Lady", which derived its sound from a Dr. Dre sample and found Badu singing lines like, "Bag lady, you gone miss your bus/You can't hurry up 'cause you got too much stuff/When they see you comin', niggas take off runnin'/From you, it's true, oh yes they do."

Badu's 2003 "EP" *Worldwide Underground* clocked in at 50 minutes and consisted mostly of sketches and extended jams. It was little more than a commercial stopgap even if "Danger" and "Love Of My Life Worldwide" – a tribute to old school rappers Sequence – were more fully realized and more street than almost anything Badu had done previously.

Baduizm
1997, Kedar

Badu's voice can be as irritating as Macy Gray's, her Afro metaphysics as received as Common's, and her boho image all but one-dimensional, but when the incense smoke subsides and the jazziness seeps below the surface, this is a fine contemporary retro-soul album.

Anita Baker

One of the biggest R&B success stories of the 80s, **Anita Baker** was the jazzier, female counterpart of Luther Vandross. She sang rich, heavily produced ballads that nodded towards jazz complexity and adult sophistication but retained a firm commercial grounding.

Born in Toledo, Ohio, on December 20, 1957, Baker was raised in Detroit. She joined the group **Chapter 8** in 1976 as lead singer, and they achieved a few modest R&B hits – "Ready For Your Love", "I Just Wanna Be Your Girl" and "Don't You Like It" – before she left to go solo in 1983.

After signing to Otis Smith's Beverly Glen label, Baker released *The Songstress* later that year. Very much a singer's album, it flew in the face of contemporary trends, but Baker's ballad style found an audience on the emerging quiet storm radio shows and the gentle "Angel" became a top-five R&B hit. Despite this success, Baker had to work as a secretary to pay her bills, and spent the next couple of years trying to extricate herself from her contract with Beverly Glen Records.

In 1985, Baker eventually signed with Elektra, who were willing to accede to the demands of the talented singer who was starting to get a reputation as a control freak. She insisted that her album be produced by her old Chapter 8 cohort, **Michael Powell**, and the label eventually gave in – a smart move. Perhaps even more of a singer's album than her debut, *Rapture* was blessed with better material and excellent arrangements from Powell, particularly on the soaring ballad "Sweet Love" and the sensuous, Vandross-like "Caught Up In The Rapture". Released in 1986, the album went multi-platinum and won two Grammy Awards. Baker was suddenly one of the biggest female stars in R&B.

Although 1988's *Giving You The Best That I Got* contained two R&B #1s – the title track and "Just Because" – it was less successful than *Rapture*, both commercially and artistically. Perhaps the album was simply less of a surprise, or perhaps it was because so many imitators had followed in her wake, but Baker sounded more traditional, more run-of-the-mill. On *Compositions* in 1990, she just sounded terrible – and the material didn't help either. Baker then suffered a series of personal problems and didn't record again for several years.

She returned with *Rhythm Of Love* in 1994, which was mostly an album of standards, including "My Funny Valentine", "Body And Soul" and "The Look Of Love", but by now her style sounded contrived. After a decade of raising a family and being involved in protracted contractual disputes, she came back once again in 2004 with *My Everything*. Despite being released on the legendary jazz label Blue Note, the album offered the familiar mix of adult soul, jazzy touches and half an ear to contemporary urban radio.

Rapture
1986, Elektra

The album that confirmed adult-oriented R&B was here to stay. A smooth and sophisticated mix of R&B, gospel and jazz singing made this the Holy Grail of the quiet storm format, and turned Baker into a megastar. "Sweet Love", "Caught Up In The Rapture" and "Same Ole Love" were unquestionably revolutionary, and seemed to herald a new age for women in popular music. Unfortunately, things didn't quite work out that way.

LaVern Baker

Born **Delores Williams** in Chicago on November 11, 1929, **LaVern Baker** ranks alongside **Ruth Brown** as the greatest of the female rock'n'roll singers. While she's most often remembered as a singer of rollicking novelty numbers, in truth, she was one of the finest singers of her generation, and her facility with bluesy ballads is one of the cornerstones of the female soul style.

Baker was discovered by bandleader Fletcher Henderson at age 17, appearing as "Little Miss Sharecropper" at South Side Chicago clubs. She made her vinyl debut under that name for RCA Victor in 1949, but changed her *nom de disque* to Bea Baker in 1951 when she recorded for Okeh with Maurice King's Wolverines. The following year, she fronted Todd Rhodes's band as LaVern Baker on the smoky torch song "Trying". More emotional and straining, and less mannered than most classic torch singers, her style attracted Atlantic enough to sign her in 1953.

That year, Baker belted out her first single for her new label, the bluesy ballad "Soul On Fire", with a power then heard only in Baptist churches. Atlantic, however, preferred her to record novelty numbers, which she did with style and grace. In 1955 the Latin-flavoured "Tweedlee Dee" was a huge hit on both the R&B and pop charts, but it was undone by Georgia Gibbs' whitewashed version. Baker continued in that vein on "Bop-Ting-A-Ling", "Play It Fair" and "Still" before the rockin' tall tale "Jim Dandy" become her biggest R&B hit in 1956. The follow-up was the absurd "Jim Dandy Got Married" a year later.

The mournful, stroll-tempoed "I Cried A Tear" gave Baker her biggest pop hit in 1958, reaching #6, despite being a bit over the top at some points and a bit trad at others. With records like "So High, So Low", based on the spiritual "Oh Rock My Soul", and the Pentecostal pastiche "Saved", written by **Leiber & Stoller**, she flirted explicitly with gospel, growling and testifying like the best of them.

After recording tributes to Ma Rainey and Bessie Smith, Baker left Atlantic to record for Mayhew and Brunswick. Aside from 1966's sassy duet with Jackie Wilson, "Think Twice", her material from this period failed to make the charts. A few of her releases became big favourites with the Northern Soul crowd, however, particularly "I'm The

One To Do It" and "Wrapped, Tied And Tangled", on which the backing is more than a little reminiscent of George Benson's "On Broadway".

As her career went into decline, thanks in part to the soul singers she had helped to inspire, Baker went to Vietnam to entertain the troops. She then moved to the Philippines, where she ran an officers' club for twenty years, before returning to the US in 1988 when Ahmet Ertegun invited her to take part in Atlantic's fortieth anniversary celebrations.

Baker's performance at the anniversary show at New York's Madison Square Garden led to renewed public and critical acclaim. She went on to record new songs for the soundtracks to *Dick Tracy* and *Shag*, and appeared in the Broadway musical *Black & Blue*. Although she had suffered two strokes and had both her legs amputated due to complications arising from diabetes, Baker once again proved her worth when she recorded *Woke Up This Mornin'* in 1992. A decent comeback effort, it featured some of the best session musicians in the business: Cornell Dupree, Bernard Purdie and Chuck Rainey. LaVern Baker died of heart failure on March 10, 1997.

Soul On Fire: The Best Of LaVern Baker
1991, Atlantic

This chronological collection of Baker's singles for Atlantic gives short shrift to her ballad singing in favour of her rock'n'roll records, but it nevertheless highlights the belting, growling talents of one of R&B's most underrated singers.

Hank Ballard & The Midnighters

Billy Ward & The Dominoes may have laid the groundwork, but if there was a group that ensured that R&B and soul would use God's language to describe the devil's deeds it was **Hank Ballard & The Midnighters**. The Midnighters instituted a change in popular music nearly as great as that of **Elvis**, only hardly anyone noticed because mainstream radio wouldn't go anywhere near their records. However, the Midnighters aren't in this book because of their lyrics – they're included because they came up with a style of music that was as salacious and wild as the topics they sang about.

The Midnighters began life as a Detroit gospel group called **The Royals**. The group – Henry Booth, Sonny Woods, Lawson Smith and Charles Sutton – started singing secular material at the turn of the 50s in a style that owed much to **The Orioles**. They were discovered at a talent show by Johnny Otis, who was working as a talent scout for King/Federal Records at the time. They signed to King and released their debut record, "Every Beat Of My Heart", in 1952. Their second record, "Moonrise", is now considered a classic of the pre-rock'n'roll vocal group style, but at the time, it – along with their subsequent records "Starting From Tonight", "Are You Forgetting" and "The Shrine Of St. Cecilia" – failed to sell.

Frustrated, Lawson Smith left the group and was replaced by **Hank Ballard** (born November 18, 1936), who had previously written the flip side to "Moonrise", "Fifth Street Blues". Ballard's voice was much rougher than Smith's, but he was a more distinctive singer. His writing style was also just as coarse. His first single with The Royals was 1953's "Get It", which was about as suggestive as early 50s R&B got, particularly with the yelps and grunts in the background. "Get It" was a top-ten R&B hit, but that was nothing compared to what was about to happen.

Changing their name to the **Midnighters**, the group released their breakthrough record in 1954. Ballard had written a song called "Sock It To Me Mary" as their next single, but producer **Ralph Bass** thought the title was too outrageous and the song was renamed "Work With Me Annie". The title change didn't prevent the record from being denounced as "smut" by several publications or from being banned by several radio stations, though. "Annie, please don't cheat/Gimme all my meat", sang Ballard with an intensity almost unheard of in popular music. The record was an absolute sensation and spent seven weeks at the top of the R&B chart.

The follow-up, "Sexy Ways", was perhaps even more shocking. Ballard sang in whoops and slight melisma about the pleasures of the flesh in the most graphic terms imaginable at that time: "Wiggle, wiggle, wiggle, wiggle/I just love your sexy ways/Upside down, all

around/Any old way, just pound". The electric guitar riff that announced the song was heavily distorted and eventually became one of the cornerstones of rock'n'roll. The aftermath of all this carrying on was detailed in "Annie Had A Baby", another R&B #1, but after "Annie's Aunt Fannie" and about a dozen answer records, the Midnighters left the poor girl alone. They released several fine records in the mid-50s, including "Henry's Got Flat Feet" and "Tore Up Over You", but without much commercial success.

In 1959 the group, now billed as **Hank Ballard & The Midnighters**, hit the R&B Top Five with the lachrymose "Teardrops On Your Letter", but the flip side "The Twist" was where the action was. "The Twist" reached #16 on the R&B chart when it became the plug side, but it failed to really take off nationally. However, the record was huge in the city of Baltimore, Maryland and Buddy Dean, the host of a dance TV show in Baltimore, told **Dick Clark** about it. Clark invited Ballard to perform the song on American Bandstand, but Ballard chose to pursue a woman in Atlanta instead. Clark hastily hired Ernest Evans, who became **Chubby Checker**, to do a note-for-note cover on the show and the rest is dance-craze history.

"The Twist" was absolutely electric. Ballard attempted to replicate its energy on a whole slew of dance-craze discs in the early 60s: "The Coffee Grind", "Finger Poppin' Time", "Let's Go, Let's Go, Let's Go", "The Hoochi Cocchi Coo", "The Continental Walk", "The Switch-A-Roo" and, unfortunately, "Do You Know How To Twist". However, by this point the group had run out of steam and they soon disbanded.

Ballard popped up from time to time at the King studios and cut some funky records, such as 1966's "Get That Hump In Your Back", that were never released. In 1968 he hooked up with James Brown, who wrote the ridiculously funky black-is-beautiful anthem "How You Gonna Get Respect (You Haven't Cut Your Process Yet)" for Ballard. He recorded a few more records under the Godfather's aegis, including "Butter Your Popcorn", "Blackenized" and "From The Love Side", but by 1974 Ballard was on his own again and recorded trash like "Let's Go Streaking". He then re-formed the Midnighters, with an altered line-up, in the mid-80s to perform on the nostalgia circuit. Having been inducted into the Rock & Roll Hall of Fame in 1990, Ballard died of throat cancer on March 2, 2003 in Los Angeles.

(○) **Sexy Ways: The Best Of Hank Ballard & The Midnighters**
1993, Rhino

Containing all of the group's hits from 1953 to 1961 in chronological order, this is the only Midnighters collection to get. This superb compilation makes a stong argument for Hank Ballard to be talked about as one of the all-time soul greats and one of the most influential figures in the history of popular music.

Darrell Banks

Although he only released seven singles and two albums, **Darrell Banks** remains one of the most revered singers on both the Northern and deep soul circuits. Equally adept at the styles of Detroit and Memphis, he was a powerful, soulful singer who was impeccably smooth but had enough grit to lend an air of gravitas to his records.

Born **Darrell Eubanks** in 1938, in Mansfield, Ohio, Banks was raised in Buffalo, New York. His first taste of success came in 1966 when his very first single, "Open The Door To Your Heart", stormed to #27 on the pop chart and #2 on the R&B chart. Released on the Detroit-based Revilot label, it was firmly in the Motown style but without the sweetening – the lack of adornment allowed his voice to sound rich and full.

Later that year, "Somebody (Somewhere) Needs You", a Northern stormer with thoroughly engaging vocals, also hit the R&B

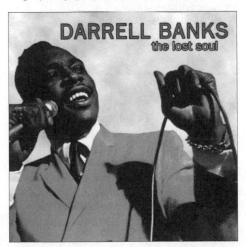

chart. Banks then moved to Atco for 1967's "Here Come The Tears", a slow dragging ballad from his debut album *Darrell Banks Is Here!* that showed off his poignant voice to fine effect. "Angel Baby (Don't You Ever Leave Me)" and "The Love Of My Woman" were more uptempo, but he rode their tricky rhythms passionately, and both became Northern Soul classics.

Banks signed to Stax/Volt in 1969 and released *Here To Stay*, an album of deep soul ballads produced by **Don Davis**. Standouts like "Just Because Your Love Is Gone", "I Could Never Hate Her" and "Forgive Me" marked a rapprochement between the string-heavy arrangements of Detroit and Chicago and the more downhome feel of the South. Sadly, however, Darrell Banks was not here to stay. He was shot dead in Detroit in March 1970, by a policeman who was having an affair with his girlfriend.

(○) **The Lost Soul**
1997, Goldmine

This 27-track compilation of Banks's Revilot, Atco, Cotillion and Volt records holds just about everything he ever recorded. The sound isn't up to the talent of a man who's sometimes called the greatest soul singer of them all, but it's an excellent album nevertheless.

Homer Banks

Despite his legendary status among soul cultists, and his major role in the development of Southern soul, **Homer Banks** remains all but unknown to the vast majority of soul fans.

Born in Memphis on August 2, 1941, Banks was a co-founder of the **Soul Consolidators** gospel group. In the late 50s, he landed a job as a secretary at Satellite Studios, which was to transform into Stax in a couple of years. He never recorded for the label, but Stax songwriters Isaac Hayes and **David Porter** helped him to get his first recording date for Genie in 1965. The first song he recorded was their "Lady Of Stone", which started out as a chugging weepy, before Banks let rip at the end. It was a very solid performance, much like **Aaron Neville** might sound if he ever let loose and testified, but it was let down by raggedy instrumentation.

Moving to the Minit label, Banks released the classic "A Lot Of Love" in 1966. While he

Most Expensive Soul Records

In 1959, as the doo-wop style was dying out, **Irving "Slim" Rose** started buying up all the deleted doo-wop records he could get his hands on and sold them at his legendary Times Square Records shop in the Times Square subway station in New York. Fuelled by both nostalgia and a desire to overcome the ignorance fostered by the enforced segregation of the pop charts, people began buying the old doo-wop records that no one was interested in when they were first released. This was the birth of the first true record collector subculture.

Of all the African-American musical recordings, doo-wop records still command the highest prices. However, thanks to a renewed interest in Northern Soul in recent years and the collectors' mentality of hip-hop fans, soul and funk records are also now commanding serious prices on the collectors' market. If you stumble across any of these records in your uncle's attic, they should keep you in polyester and beer for at least a few months.

1 DO I LOVE YOU (INDEED I DO) Frank Wilson (1965, Soul)
This is the Holy Grail of soul collectors and the world's most expensive 7". Only two copies of this unreleased record are known to exist. It was discovered in 1977 by Motown historian Tom Dieperro, who shared it with legendary record dealer Simon Soussan. Soussan leaked acetates of the disc to the UK's Northern Soul scene, where it became a sensation. Changing hands several times over the next twenty years, the record finally fetched a record-breaking £15,000 from Scottish DJ Kenny Burrell in 1996.

2 STORMY WEATHER Five Sharps (1952, Jubilee)
"Stormy Weather" is to doo-wop collectors what Frank Wilson's "Do I Love You (Indeed I Do)" is to soul collectors. Only three copies of this 78rpm are known to exist, and two of them are cracked. It was recently offered for sale on the Internet auction site eBay for $19,990.

3 ROCKET 88 Ike Turner and His Kings of Rhythm (1951, Memphis Recordings And Sound Service)
Discovered in 1995, this 16" acetate is an alternative take of what is generally considered to be the first rock'n'roll song. It was offered for auction in 1998 for $20,000.

4 I CAN'T BELIEVE The Hornets (1953, States)
This early doo-wop obscurity was sold at auction for $18,000 in 2002.

5 CHEATIN' KIND Don Gardner (1969, Sedgrick)
£8000

6 I REALLY DON'T KNOW The Flamingos (1995, Parrot)
$8000 on red vinyl

7 NO ONE ELSE CAN TAKE YOUR PLACE The Inspirations (1968, Breakthrough)
£5000

8 BECAUSE OF MY HEART The Butlers with Frankie Beverly (1966, Rouser)
£5000

9 NOTHING'S TOO GOOD FOR MY BABY The Springers (1966, Wales)
£4000

10 THIS WON'T CHANGE Lester Tipton (1966, La Beat)
£4000

11 WHERE ARE YOU (NOW THAT I NEED YOU) The Mello-Moods (1952, Robin)
$5000–7000

12 LET ME MAKE YOU HAPPY Billy Woods (1971, Sussex)
£3000

13 LIKE A NIGHTMARE The Andantes (1964, VIP)
£3000

14 TELL THE WORLD The Dells (1955, Vee Jay)
$5000

15 FOR YOUR PRECIOUS LOVE Jerry Butler & The Impressions (1958, Vee-Jay)
$5000

was in full-on church mode, screaming, shouting and pleading, the song became more famous for its arrangement: the riff formed the basis for **The Spencer Davis Group**'s "Gimme Some Lovin'". Although it was ripped off hook, line and sinker, and failed to achieve any chart impact, Banks's record did at least become a Northern Soul anthem. The flip side, "Fighting To Win", showed him to be equally adept at deep soul ballads.

Written with Deanie Parker, "A Lot Of Love" was the only one of his own compositions that Banks ever recorded. Most of his singles, including "60 Minutes Of Your Love" and "Foolish Hearts Break Fast", were Hayes/Porter songs that were very much in the mould they perfected with Sam & Dave.

Fine singer though he was, Banks's records didn't sell, and he started to concentrate on songwriting. With Betty Crutcher and

Raymond Jackson, Jr., he became part of the **We Three** songwriting team, creating hits like "Who's Making Love?" for Johnny Taylor, "If You're Ready (Come Go With Me)" for the Staple Singers, "(If Loving You Is Wrong) I Don't Want To Be Right" for Luther Ingram, "I Can't Stand Up For Falling Down" for Sam & Dave and "I Like What You're Doing (To Me)" for Carla Thomas. Banks later worked with **Carl Hampton**, writing "Woman To Woman" for Shirley Brown, and "Caught In The Act (Of Gettin' It On)" for Facts of Life.

Homer Banks briefly returned to recording in 1977, making the *Passport To Ecstasy* album with Hampton. It was a collection of cheating songs done in the bluesy, slightly funky style that was to characterize the Malaco label over the next few years, and indeed Banks went on to work for Malaco as a producer and songwriter. He wrote **J. Blackfoot**'s surprise hit "Taxi" in 1983, and continued to work with him throughout the 80s and 90s before dying of cancer on April 3, 2003.

(o) **Hooked By Love: The Best Of Homer Banks**
2005, Stateside

The first readily available compilation of Banks's 60s recordings undeniably holds a lot of filler, including previously unreleased material that perhaps should have stayed that way – "Danny Boy". Nevertheless, this 20-track CD provides a fine overview of the career of a very underrated vocalist.

The Bar-Kays

O riginally known as The River Arrows and The Imperials, **The Bar-Kays** were discovered by Otis Redding playing at the barbershop next door to the Stax studios in Memphis. Redding chose them as his backing band, as an alternative to the overworked Booker T & The MG's and **Mar-Keys** line-ups that usually supported the label's singers.

In 1967, before touring with Redding, the group – bassist **James Alexander**, guitarist Jimmy King, keyboardist Ronnie Caldwell, trumpeter **Ben Cauley**, saxophonist Phalon Jones and drummer Carl Cunningham – recorded a couple of singles under their own name. The first was one of the greatest instrumental discs ever, featuring "Soul Finger" – quite simply joy transposed to vinyl – and "Knucklehead", a consummate

slice of greasy early funk. "Give Everybody Some" followed in a similar, if less well executed, style.

On December 10, 1967, all The Bar-Kays except Alexander were on the plane with Otis Redding that crashed into a lake near Madison, Wisconsin. Only Cauley survived. The following year, Alexander and Cauley formed **The Bar-Kays Mark II** with guitarist Michael Toles, keyboardist Ronnie Gordon, saxophonist **Harvey Henderson** and drummers Willie Hall and Roy Cunningham. Key session players at Stax, the group appeared on Isaac Hayes's landmark *Hot Buttered Soul* album, as well as records by Albert King, the Staple Singers and Rufus Thomas. They also released several singles themselves, including the enjoyable "Don't Stop Dancing To The Music" and "Sang And Dance".

Cunningham and Gordon left the group in 1970, while **Winston Stewart** and former Temprees singer **Larry Dodson** were drafted in. After the me-too but damn funky "Son Of Shaft" hit the R&B Top 10 in 1971, Toles and Cauley joined Isaac Hayes's group, to be replaced by Vernon Burch and Charles Allen. That year's *Black Rock* was a heavy funk album that found the group borrowing both sonically and visually from Funkadelic. Their 1972 album *Do You See What I See?* and 1974's *Cold Blooded* followed in a similar vein, but enjoyed little commercial success. However, the Bar-Kays' performance was the clear highlight of the **Wattstax** concert in 1972.

After Stax folded in 1975, The Bar-Kays signed with Mercury. Their first release, "Shake Your Rump To The Funk", was their best fusion of P-Funk and Sly Stone to date and hit the R&B Top 5. It featured on that year's *Too Hot To Stop*, one of the best funk albums of the decade. Neither *Flying High On Your Love* (1977) nor *Light Of Life* (1978) was quite as good, even if the latter boasted the yowsah-licious "Holy Ghost".

The Bar-Kays were now at their commercial apex, but their records became nothing but combinations of novelty synth sounds, bouncy basslines and smarmy ballads. On the dancefloor you didn't really mind, but it's hard to differentiate between hits like "Boogie Body Land", "Hit And Run" and "Freaky Behavior". At least in 1984, with "Freakshow

The Bar-Kays were the highlight of the Wattstax festival (the black Woodstock) in 1972

On The Dancefloor" and "Sexomatic", they got a little angular, but that also meant they were merely aping popular styles.

Now basically a trio of Dodson, Stewart and Henderson, The Bar-Kays continued to record until the late 80s. Various line-ups toured through the 90s, and they even managed to hit the lower reaches of the R&B chart in 1995 with "Old School Mega Mix" and "The Slide".

Soul Finger
1967, Volt

Soul Finger is a prime slice of the classic Stax sound and the only album recorded by the original Bar-Kays line-up that served as Otis Redding's back-up band. The title cut, their first smash hit single, captures the band's dance party sound, while a few slow tunes and lots of boogaloo grooves fill out the rest of the CD.

Too Hot To Stop
1976, Mercury

Their debut on Mercury Records, this was recorded the same year that The Bar-Kays went on tour with George Clinton's P-Funk. Filled with good, tight, contemporary funk, *Too Hot To Stop*'s highlights are "Shake Your Rump" and the title track, but the slower grooves show the versatility of this slick band.

The Best Of The Bar-Kays
1988, Stax

The strange break-up of Stax and the division of its back catalogue goes some way towards explaining the lack of a decent Bar-Kays compilation. This is the best available, but it's by no means perfect – it doesn't have "Soul Finger" and the only track from their commercial heyday is "Holy Ghost". It does, however, hold their other Stax singles, most of which are solid funk efforts, and it avoids the synth fatigue that mars their later work.

J.J. Barnes

A true favourite of the UK's Northern soul circuit, **James Jay Barnes** gained more fame in Europe, and in the UK in particular, than he ever had back home in the US. He was an excellent singer, held short of greatness perhaps only by generally formulaic arrangements and his tendency toward the mannered.

Barnes was born in Detroit on November 30, 1943. He began his career in gospel music, singing with the **Halo Gospel Singers**, before releasing his first solo soul single, "My Love Came Tumbling Down", in 1960. A series of singles followed on small local labels; the most successful, "Just One More Time", was picked up for national release by Scepter in 1963. The finest of all his early records, though, was probably 1964's "She Ain't Ready", a bluesy finger-popper with nice, gospel-tinged vocals.

He moved to Ric-Tic in 1965, and recorded the Northern soul landmark "Please Let Me In". While the record, produced by Don Davis, unquestionably owed a lot to the Motown formula, Barnes' performance was every bit as impassioned as, and much grittier than, anything released by Ric-Tic's crosstown rivals. The harder-driving and equally impressive "Real Humdinger" found its way onto the R&B charts in 1966, and in the same year he recorded a cover of **The Beatles**' "Day Tripper", with **George Clinton** producing. Barnes joined Steve Mancha and Eddie Anderson in **The Holidays**. Their first single, "I'll Love You Forever", featuring an additional overdubbed contribution from Edwin Starr, was a big R&B hit.

Barnes also signed to Motown around this time, where he wrote songs for Martha & The Vandellas and **The Marvelettes**. However, none of the tracks he recorded himself was ever released by Motown, supposedly because Marvin Gaye felt that he sounded too much like him. Whatever the truth, Barnes left Motown and released "Baby Please Come Back Home" for Groovesville in 1967, in a style that owed more than a little to Marvin Gaye. It became his first – and biggest ever – solo hit, reaching #9 on the R&B chart. The similar "Now That I Got You Back", released shortly afterwards, also made the lower reaches of the R&B chart that year.

Although sales dried up Stateside for Barnes, he had a smash on the Northern soul set in 1969 with the hook-laden "Our Love Is In The Pocket". Another George Clinton production, it was popular enough on US dancefloors to land Barnes singles deals with Buddah and Volt, but his subsequent singles "Evidence" and "Snowflakes" went nowhere.

Despite recording his debut album, *Born Again*, for the New York-based Perception label in 1973, Barnes soon turned his attentions towards Europe, recording "How Long" for the UK label Contempo Records that same year. However, none of his later Contempo recordings, including the 1978 album *Sara Smile*, recaptured the Motor City magic that had first won him his European fans. He went on to cover Frank Wilson's Northern soul shibboleth "Do I Love You (Indeed I Do)" in 1985, and released an album for Ian Levine's Motor City project in 1991, *Try It One More Time*.

The Groovesville Masters
1997, Goldmine

Even if 38 tracks and two CDs is slight overkill, Barnes remains one of soul's great unsung heroes. This compilation includes his best records: "Our Love Is In The Pocket", "Please Let Me In" and "Baby Please Come Back Home".

Archie Bell & The Drells

If not exactly blank slates, Houston's **Archie Bell & The Drells** were hardly the most forceful or characterful vocal group around, but they carved out a solid career by riding whatever rhythm was hot and not getting in the way of their producers. **Archie Bell** was born on September 1, 1944, in Henderson, Texas. He started out singing with **Little Pop & The Fireballs** in the early 60s, but, eager to have his own group, he soon hooked up with three high-school friends – James Wise, Huey "Billy" Butler and Joe Cross – and formed Archie Bell & The Drells, naming them after The Dells.

The Drells soon came to the attention of KCOH DJ and Berry Gordy wannabe **Skipper Lee Frasier**, who signed them to his new Ovide label. Their first single, "She's My Woman, She's My Girl", was a regional hit in 1967, but its momentum stalled when Bell was drafted and sent to Vietnam. He was home on leave that December when the group hastily added vocals to a riff-heavy instrumental vamp by local band The TSU Tornados. "Tighten Up" sounded like a more lightweight version of Sly Stone's "Dance To The Music", but it was utterly delightful nevertheless. Licensed by Atlantic, it became a #1 hit in 1968.

With Bell away in the army, much of 1968's *Tighten Up* album was allegedly sung by different singers: "1000 Wonders", a Northern Soul classic, was sung by James Taylor (no, not that one), and "You're Mine" was apparently sung by TSU Tornados' leader Cal Thomas. The album did, however, showcase Bell's talents as a songwriter on "Soldier's Prayer 1967" and "When You Left Heartache Began".

Bell was given leave to tour with the Drells in 1968. In New Jersey, **Kenny Gamble** and **Leon Huff** took them into the studio to record "I Can't Stop Dancing" and "Do The Choo Choo", both more fully realized but similar in style to "Tighten Up". The snappy, sassy "There's Gonna Be A Showdown", later reprised by the New York Dolls and sampled by the Wu-Tang Clan, followed at the end of the year. In 1969 Bell finally received his discharge papers from the army and the group recorded the very fine album *There's Gonna Be A Showdown*. Also that year, Archie's brother Lee and Willie Pernell replaced Cross and Butler.

After 1970's "Wrap It Up", an unsuccessful blend of Sam & Dave with The

Northern Soul

The strange phenomenon that came to be known as **Northern soul** was born in the north of England during the mid- to late 60s. The young men from the industrial wastelands who gathered at the Twisted Wheel club, at 6 Whitfield Street in central Manchester, worshipped American soul records – the rarer and more obscure the better – with a zeal and piety that would shame all but the most devout religious believers.

The UK's soul scene was an outgrowth of London's jazz scene. It started to develop in the very early 60s at clubs like The Flamingo, beneath the Whiskey-à-Go-Go on Wardour Street, which hosted weekend all-nighters that were popular with West Indian immigrants and American GIs stationed in Britain, and The Scene in Soho's Ham Yard, where **DJ Guy Stevens** played urban blues like **BB King**, the lounge blues of **Mose Allison**, and the Hammond organ jazz of **Jimmy Smith**. This strange and explosive combination of fanatic DJs/collectors/curators, immigrants from the African diaspora and American military personnel was to define not only Northern zoul, but also the next 40 years or so of European popular music.

When, thanks to the hit-making prowess of Motown, soul music attracted a more mainstream following, this crowd began to search for more obscure records to set them apart from the pop flock. As early as 1965, the most influential DJ on the scene, **Roger Eagle** of Manchester's Twisted Wheel club, was searching out soul records that were rare even in America: **Chubby Checker**'s "At The Discothèque", **The Sapphires**' "Gotta Have Your Love", Darrell Banks's "Open The Door To Your Heart", **The Flamingos**' "Boogaloo Party" and **Earl Van Dyke**'s "Six By Six".

With the exception of "Open The Door To Your Heart", these records – and most of those that really moved the dancefloor at the Twisted Wheel – all shared the monolithic, stomping, 4/4 **Holland-Dozier-Holland** Motown backbeat and uptempo, uplifting chords (usually masking the pain of the lyrics). High-energy rave-ups, these tracks fit the amphetamine-laced atmosphere of the Twisted Wheel perfectly. This unique subculture now had a signature sound that would remain unchanged for years. In a 1970 article for *Blues & Soul* magazine, journalist and leading light of the British soul scene **Dave Godin** coined the term "Northern zoul" to distinguish it from the funkier, more contemporary soul music that was being played at clubs in London.

Many of the ultra-rare records that fuelled the Northern zoul scene were first "discovered" by **Ian Levine**, who was the son of two well-off Blackpool club owners. His parents' comfortable financial position enabled him to travel to the US at a time when foreign holidays were still a rarity for the vast majority of the British population. On those trips, usually to Miami, Levine found the records that gave birth to the Northern zoul subculture.

Levine at first supplied his records to DJs at the Twisted Wheel and then the Blackpool Mecca, watching with delight as the countless hours he had spent scouring junk shops to uncover records such as J.J. Barnes's "Our Love Is In The Pocket", **Rose Batiste**'s "Hit & Run" and **Pat Lewis**'s "No One To Love" resulted in dancefloor gold. In 1971 Levine finally became a DJ in his own right at the Blackpool Mecca. However, Northern zoul was ultimately an aesthetic cul-de-sac, an ultra-conservative, anachronistic sound doomed to cause its own demise. Determined to keep the spirit alive, Levine branched out into rare contemporary records that had the old Northern soul vocal feel but a more discofied beat, such as

Temptations, the Drells failed to chart for a few years. A brief sojourn with the Glades label produced a hit with the nostalgic "Dancing To Your Music" in 1973, before the group were lured back into the Gamble & Huff fold. *Dance Your Troubles Away* in 1975 saw the group paired with Instant Funk for a set of solid, if slightly over-orchestrated, disco tracks – the best being "I Could Dance All Night" and the O'Jays-style "The Soul City Walk".

The 1976 album *Where Will You Go When the Party's Over*, which included the thumping "Don't Let Love Get You Down" and "Everybody Have A Good Time", was significantly better. However, the Drells seemed to lose their way again on the very mediocre *Hard Not to Like It* (1977) and *Strategy* (1979). After they disbanded, Bell had a short-lived solo career with Becket Records before reuniting the Drells in the 80s. The new line-up played the UK's nostalgia circuit and released "Look Back Over Your Shoulder", a yucky faux Northern soul track, in 1988.

First Choice's "This Is The House (Where Love Died)", **The Carstairs'** "It Really Hurts Me Girl" and **Patti Jo's** "Make Me Believe In You".

When Levine championed these new records in the early 70s, the scene broke in two – the purists who wanted to hear the 60s stuff went to the Wigan Casino, while the faithful stayed with Levine at the Mecca. Although disco and changing economics scarred the Northern soul scene irrevocably in the mid-70s, it was nursed back to health at various all-nighters throughout the UK and monthly parties at London's 100 Club, and Northern soul continues to exert its pull on Britain's soul scene to this day.

 The Golden Torch Story
1995, Goldmine

This compilation of tracks that set the dancefloor alight at the Torch club in Stoke-on-Trent is a perfect introduction to Northern soul. As well as classics such as J.J. Barnes's "Our Love Is In The Pocket", The Just Brothers' "Sliced Tomatoes" and Rose Batiste's "Hit & Run", it holds eccentric tracks such as N.F. Porter's stunning "Keep On Keeping On".

PLAYLIST

1 DO I LOVE YOU (INDEED I DO) Frank Wilson from **Northern Soul Connoisseurs**
The most expensive record in the world, but also one of the best.

2 PLEASE LET ME IN J.J. Barnes from **The Groovesville Masters**
As impassioned as, and grittier than, anything released by Ric-Tic's more famous crosstown rivals.

3 STORM WARNING The Volcanos from **Northern Soul: On The Philadelphia Beat**
Woefully underrated early Philly soul, rescued by British soul fans.

4 HIT & RUN Rose Batiste from **The Golden Age Of Northern Soul**
Certainly more soulful and sassy than The Supremes.

5 EXUS TREK Luther Ingram Orchestra from **Hipshaker**
Big, bold colours and dramatic arrangement make for a three-minute instrumental epic.

6 (COME ON BY) MY SWEET DARLING Jimmy (Soul) Clarke from **The Golden Age Of Northern Soul**
As uplifting and joyful as any record in the Northern soul canon.

7 TAINTED LOVE Gloria Jones from **The Wigan Casino Story: The Final Chapter**
One of the better examples of dancing as exorcism.

8 SLICE TOMATOES Just Brothers from **The Golden Torch Story**
Sounds like it was recorded for a 60s surf flick, but so groovy that it was sampled by Fatboy Slim.

9 KEEP ON KEEPING ON N.F. Porter from **The Golden Torch Story**
The driving, ghostly arrangement keeps this track shrouded in mystery.

10 IT REALLY HURTS ME GIRL The Carstairs from **Dazzle: Disco Delights From New York City**
The record that tore the Northern soul scene asunder, but at least it's worth fighting over.

Tightening It Up: The Best Of Archie Bell & The Drells
1994, Rhino

While you couldn't ask for a much better compilation, this unintentionally makes the case that the Drells were only as good as their backing band and producers. Luckily, they worked with some of the best in the business, and the music is rarely less than scintillating – though the vocals are a little more workmanlike.

I Can't Stop Dancing / There's Gonna Be A Showdown
2005, Collectables

While missing the group's first hit, "Tighten Up", this Collectables CD combines their 1968 and 1969 albums for Atlantic and, coincidentally, their best work with producers Gamble & Huff. Located right at the junction of 60s soul dance music and the slick 70s sound of Philadelphia International, this mostly upbeat collection doesn't quit from start to finish.

William Bell

William Bell was one of the great practitioners of country soul. Sadly, however, for much of his recording career he was saddled with an uptempo R&B style that didn't suit his particular gifts. He was born **William Yarborough** in Memphis on July 16, 1939, and started out singing with the **Del-Rios** as a teenager, along with Louis Williams, Norman West and James Taylor. In 1956, for finishing second in a talent competition, they won the opportunity to release a single on the local Meteor label. Bell wrote both sides, "Lizzie" and "Alone On A Rainy Night", which were recorded with The Bearcats as the back-up band. The Del-Rios broke up in 1960, but Bell had

caught the attention of **Chips Moman** at Stax.

Bell's first Stax release, in 1961, was the poppy and inconsequential "Formula Of Love". However, the flip side, a self-penned composition called "You Don't Miss Your Water (Until Your Well Runs Dry)", became a cornerstone of the emerging country soul style. While the lyrics were pure cornpone country, Bell's brilliantly understated vocal and Moman's echoey, churchy arrangement were pure black gospel in 6/8 time. Perhaps the first record of its kind, it stood – despite its complete lack of chart success – as a genuine milestone. The next year's "Any Other Way", on the other hand, might have been released on Stax, but could just as easily come out of the Brill Building.

When Bell was subsequently drafted into the army, he recorded several sides in a two-week frenzy that trickled out throughout the mid-60s. The best of these, "Somebody Mentioned Your Name", "I'll Show You" and "Share What You Got", featured slower arrangements that beautifully framed Bell's relaxed voice. By contrast, both "Monkeying Around" and "Don't Stop Now" showed how uncomfortable he could be at higher tempos.

Bell's first new record after his discharge from the army in 1967, "Everybody Loves A Winner", featured countrypolitan piano that must have been shipped in from Nashville. "Everyday Will Be Like A Holiday", released later that year, was perhaps his finest hour, a beautiful hopeful ballad with a chorus that melted your heart as much as the sleigh bells in the background. In 1968, after the excellent ballad "Private Number" with Judy Clay, Bell once again redefined Southern soul with "Forgot To Be Your Lover". The song's dangling guitar notes and surging strings would come to characterize the soul ballad over the next few years, as would Bell's softly overstated phrasing and confessional lyrics.

Bell stuck with Stax until the label's demise, but he got lost in the mix and released a succession of character-free singles until 1975. He then re-emerged on Mercury with the biggest hit of his career. "Tryin' To Love Two" followed the Southern-soul formula he had helped to create, with perfect period backing from **Chocolate Milk**. He enjoyed a few more moderate R&B hits in a similar style from the late 70s to the mid-80s, including "Easy Comin' Out (Hard Goin' In)", "Bad Time To Break Up" and "I Don't Want To Wake Up (Feelin' Guilty)", a duet with Janice Bullock. The best of his albums from the period was the well-crafted *Passion* from 1986, which was filled with modern break-up and cheating ballads.

Do Right Man
1984, Charly

As with most Stax artists, Bell's back catalogue has been poorly served by the division of Stax's output between Atlantic and Fantasy. Nonetheless, this compilation highlights his country soul golden age, including "You Don't Miss Your Water", "Everybody Loves A Winner" and "Everyday Will Be Like A Holiday".

Wow… / Bound To Happen
1997, Stax

A nice slice of late-60s Stax produced and co-written by Booker T., 1969's *Bound To Happen* is paired here with 1971's Muscle Shoals release *Wow…*. This includes the hits "I Forgot To Be Your Lover" and "My Whole World Is Falling Down" and is the most coherent introduction to the deep Southern soul of William Bell.

Regina Belle

New Jersey's **Regina Belle** made her mark as one of the biggest names in the crowded field of "adult" vocalists – the singers of those enormous, melodramatic MOR love songs that are the soul equivalent of the power ballad. Half Broadway showbiz, half gospel glitz, Belle's powerful pipes are perfect for belting out overwrought paeans to lost love.

Belle was born on July 17, 1963, in Englewood, New Jersey, and sang gospel and soul as a child, before studying jazz and opera at university. She was discovered by quiet storm DJ **Vaughn Harper** after she sang the national anthem before a Lisa Lisa concert in New York. He hooked her up with The Manhattans, and she sang back-up on their *Too Hot To Stop* and *Back To Basics* albums. In 1987 Belle signed with Columbia and recorded *All By Myself* with veteran dance producer **Nick Martinelli**. He tried to turn her into a disco diva, with mixed results, but two slow tracks – "Show Me The Way" and "So Many Tears" – became big R&B hits and showed where her strength really lay.

Hollywood soundtrack producers immediately cottoned on, and Belle was called in to over-emote that same year with **Peabo Bryson** on "Without You" for the hopeless Bill Cosby flick *Leonard Pt. 6*. The similar "All I Want Is Forever", a duet with Kool & The Gang's James Taylor from the movie *Tap*, followed in 1989, complete with a ludicrous he-man guitar solo.

Belle's 1989 album, *Stay With Me*, was produced by Martinelli and **Narada Michael Walden**. It was followed by "Baby Come To Me", her first R&B #1, which was recorded in Hawaii in a candlelit studio, and sounds just like it – it's that smarmy. In much the same vein, "Make It Like It Was" also went to #1, while "A Whole New World", yet another Hollywood schlock fest for Disney's *Aladdin*, hit #1 on the pop charts in 1992.

Passion, in 1993, was more of the same, with unrestrained gospel-tinged vocals unleashed over paper-thin, tinkly backing on tracks like "If I Could". In 1995, *Reachin' Back* was dominated by Philly soul covers like "Love TKO", "Could It Be I'm Falling In Love", and "Didn't I (Blow Your Mind This Time)". For a woman to cover such definitively male songs was potentially an interesting idea, but Belle only brought her signature style – the production was as weedy and overdone as ever.

Believe In Me, in 1998, marked a radical makeover. No longer was Belle biding time between soundtrack appearances; she sounded like she was actually listening to the radio and lightened up considerably, even sounding sexy on tracks like "Don't Let Go" and "I Got It". However, 2001's *This Is Regina!* marked a step backwards into big-haired

ballad territory; one of the few exceptions was the dire R&B track "La Di Da", which featured a phoned-in rap from MC Lyte.

On Belle's most recent release, 2004's *Lazy Afternoon* – the inevitable jazz standards album – producer/keyboardist **George Duke** managed to keep her showbiz tendencies largely in check, with pretty creditable results.

◉ **Believe In Me**
1998, MCA

Regina Belle's best album by some distance. Sure, it errs on the jazzy side and is still resolutely quiet storm in tone and content, but for once she doesn't sound like she's stranded on a desert island with only David Foster for company. This is about as modern as Adult Contemporary soul is going to get, and in a genre bound by conservatism and convention that's a very good thing.

Eric Benét

Probably better known for being the former Mr **Halle Berry** than for his records, **Eric Benét** is a middle-of-the-road love man in the typical mould whose music is as pretentious as the accent in his name.

He was born **Eric Benét Jordan** on October 5, 1969 in Milwaukee, Wisconsin. As a teenager, he formed a group called Benet (ba-nay) with his sister Lisa Marie and cousin George Nash Jr. They had modest success with "Only Want To Be With You" in 1992 before disbanding soon afterwards. Eric Benét became a solo artist and released his debut album, *True To Myself*, in 1996. The tracks "Let's Stay Together" (not the **Al Green** song), "What If We Was Cool" and "Spiritual Thang" tried to disguise his Adult Contemporary intentions with nouveau-retro stylings, but they just weren't hip enough to pull it off.

His 1999 album *A Day In The Life* was more direct about its ambitions with relentlessly MOR R&B schlock. The biggest singles from the album were a cover of Toto's "Georgy Porgy" with **Faith Evans** and the wretched and mawkish "Spend My Life With You" with **Tamia**, which topped the R&B chart for two weeks. Even worse was a version of Kansas's "Dust In The Wind", which ranks alongside Duran Duran's "911 Is A Joke" and Joan Baez's "The Night They Drove Old Dixie Down" as the most inappropriate covers ever made.

Benét appeared in the fantastically awful film *Glitter* alongside Mariah Carey in 2001, the same year he married Halle Berry. He soon became tabloid fodder when their relationship fell apart amid allegations that Benét cheated on Berry. This manifested itself on his 2005 album *Hurricane*, released after the couple separated, which was another in the long line of terrible, self-serving break-up albums.

◉ **A Day In The Life**
1991, Warner Bros

Eric Benét is a smooth-talker in the standard quiet storm love man fashion with nothing to single him out from the hordes except for his high-profile relationship. Benét really is for quiet storm addicts only, but if you must, this is the album to go for simply because it contains his only significant hits, "Georgy Porgy" and "Spend My Life With You".

George Benson

George Benson languished in anonymity as a session player for much of his career. A well-respected jazz guitarist, even after he started to record albums under his own name he remained known primarily to his fellow musicians. Only when he was finally allowed to sing, in a voice somewhere between Nat King Cole and Stevie Wonder, did Benson become an R&B superstar.

Born March 22, 1943, Benson grew up in the Hill section of Pittsburgh, Pennsylvania, where he was taught guitar by his stepfather, Thomas Collier. In 1953, at the age of 10, he released a single for RCA as Little Georgie Benson, "She Makes Me Mad/It Should Have Been Me". As a teenager, he became lead vocalist for The Altairs, a doo-wop group who recorded for Amy, and subsequently worked with a group led by Neal Hefti, composer of the *Batman* theme. In 1963 he landed a gig with organist Jack McDuff, and stayed in his band for two years, recording the 1964 album *New Boss Guitar Of George Benson With The Brother Jack McDuff* along the way.

After being signed by the legendary **John Hammond** to Columbia, Benson recorded *It's Uptown* in 1965 and *The George Benson Cookbook* in 1966, with a group that included organist **Lonnie Smith**. Verve Records tried, unsuccessfully, to turn him into a lounge star on his next two albums, 1967's

Giblet Gravy and 1968's *Goodies*. The crossover attempts continued at A&M, where Benson worked with **Creed Taylor** on *Shape Of Things To Come* in 1968, and *The Other Side Of Abbey Road* and *Tell It Like It Is*, both from 1969.

When Taylor left to form his own CTI label, he took Benson with him. As well as recording his own albums – *Beyond The Blue Horizon* (1971), *White Rabbit* (1972), *Body Talk* (1973), *Bad Benson* (1974) and *Good King Bad* (1975) – Benson also recorded with Stanley Turrentine and Freddie Hubbard at CTI. However, dissatisfied by the way Taylor drowned him in strings and denied him freedom, Benson started to moonlight for Paul Winley. There he recorded the almighty "Smokin' Cheeba Cheeba" as part of the Harlem Underground Band

and a cover of "Soul Makossa" as part of the Mighty Tomcats, as well as his own *Erotic Moods* album in 1973.

Benson jumped ship again in 1976 to join Warner Bros, where he was teamed with Barbra Streisand's producer **Tommy LiPuma**. That year's *Breezin'* album was entirely instrumental, except for a cover of Leon Russell's "This Masquerade", a scatting, Stevie Wonder-influenced ballad that became a surprise pop hit and launched Benson's singing career. "Everything Must Change" and "The Greatest Love Of All", both from 1977, provided more of the same and cemented Benson's position as jazz's biggest crossover star.

In 1978 a version of The Drifters' "On Broadway" gave Benson another top-ten smash, and led to his being accused of selling out by the jazz community – even though the live album it came from, *Weekend In LA*, was almost entirely instrumental. When **Quincy Jones** produced *Give Me The Night* in 1980, however, and the infectious title track became his biggest hit to date, Benson's fate was sealed.

"Turn Your Love Around" in 1981 – a near-perfect early 80s record with its Linn drums and Toto-style bassline – was almost as big. Now firmly an R&B singer, Benson went on to work with **Kashif** on "Inside Love (So Personal)" in 1983, and with **Narada Michael Walden** on "Kisses In The Moonlight" in 1986. Inevitably, however, his commercial prime passed, and he returned to his ACR jazz roots, working with Earl Klugh, the **Count Basie Orchestra** and Joe Sample.

The George Benson Collection
1981, Warner Bros

The album that marked the peak of Benson's career as a commercial entity. The tracks are all slick, well-crafted, slightly jazzy pop numbers that highlight Benson's creamy vocals perfectly.

The Best Of George Benson
1989, Columbia

If you're a greater fan of George Benson's guitar than his singing, then try this collection of his work at CTI – though, be warned, you'll have to fight through strings to get to it.

PLAYLIST
George Benson

1 SMOKIN' CHEEBA CHEEBA from **Harlem Underground Band**
Before Benson became a sensation he donned his pimp threads for this classic ode to Mary Jane.

2 THIS MASQUERADE from **Breezin'**
Taking a break from the instrumentals, Benson scats his way to the top of the charts.

3 NATURE BOY from **In Flight**
Benson is a dead ringer for Stevie Wonder on this string-filled ballad.

4 ON BROADWAY from **Weekend in LA**
A catchy version of The Drifters' classic that made Benson a superstar.

5 GIVE ME THE NIGHT from **Give Me The Night**
Thoroughly professional craftsmanship courtesy of Quincy Jones.

6 OFF BROADWAY from **Give Me The Night**
Perhaps the perfect George Benson track: plenty of tasty licks for the jazz diehards and a smooth quasi-disco funk groove for the new fans.

7 MOODY'S MOOD from **Give Me The Night**
Benson's no King Pleasure, but this will still get your girl in the mood.

8 TURN YOUR LOVE AROUND from **The George Benson Collection**
It may whiff of British group Shakatak, but this is classic post-disco early 80s R&B.

Brook Benton

Born **Benjamin Franklin Peay**, on September 19, 1931, in Camden, South Carolina, **Brook Benton** was perhaps the biggest R&B star of the very late 50s and early 60s. Thanks to a creamy, easy-going baritone that was one step closer to soul than Nat "King Cole" and **Billy Eckstine**, while remaining buttoned-down enough for the masses, Benton enjoyed sixteen top-ten R&B hits between 1959 and 1963.

Despite his easy-listening appeal, Benton's roots were in the church. Having spent much of his adolescence as part of the Camden Jubilee Singers gospel troupe, he moved to New York in 1948 and linked up with Bill Langford's Langfordaires. After a brief spell in the Golden Gate Quartet, he joined the Jerusalem Stars. He cut his first secular material for Okeh in 1953, under his own name. He then recorded as Brook Benton for Epic and Vik, where he scored a minor hit with "A Million Miles From Nowhere" in 1958.

Benton signed with Mercury the following year, and was teamed with producer **Clyde Otis**, with whom he was to co-write nearly all of his hits. The first, 1959's "It's Just A Matter of Time", was a string-soaked combination of Slim Whitman and Billy Eckstine that stayed atop the R&B charts for nine weeks. "Endlessly", "Thank You Pretty Baby" and "So Many Ways" followed swiftly in the same style, and all reached the R&B Top 3 in 1959. Despite overtly courting a crossover audience, Benton tried to hire black string players for his sessions whenever he could.

"Baby (You've Got What It Takes)", a 1960 duet with **Dinah Washington**, had the same syrupy strings, but it rocked a little bit harder; their interaction was rather delightful, even if it had about as much heat as Rock Hudson and Doris Day in *Pillow Talk*. It spent ten weeks on top of the R&B charts, where it was promptly followed for a further month by their sexier duet "A Rockin' Good Way". Benton quickly reverted to his avuncular style on pop trinkets like "Fools Rush In", "For My Baby", "The Boll Weevil Song", "Hit Record" and the almost bluesy "Hotel Happiness".

By 1964, when records like "A House Is Not A Home" and "Lumberjack" seemed to have more in common with Burt Bacharach and Burl Ives than the rest of the soul scene, Benton was out of fashion even on the Adult Contemporary charts. He signed with Cotillion in 1969, and was paired with producer and rescuer of lost causes **Arif Mardin**. The result was 1970's "Rainy Night In Georgia" – a widescreen record if ever there was one, it was his biggest hit in almost a decade and by far his most soulful record. None of Benton's other Cotillion releases caught fire, however, and he spent several years bouncing around labels like Stax, All Platinum and Brut, before charting modestly with the bizarre disco disc "Makin' Love Is Good For You" in 1978. He died from complications arising from spinal meningitis on May 9, 1988.

40 Greatest Hits
1989, Mercury

This includes all 39 of Benton's Hot 100 chart entries for Mercury, plus his definitive version of Tony Joe White's "Rainy Night In Georgia". Aided by excellent liner notes by pop scholar Colin Escott, it's an essential package for anyone interested in hearing how soul developed out of crooning R&B as well as gospel.

Today / Home Style
2004, DBK Works

This recent CD reissue brings together Brook Benton's two landmark deep soul albums produced by Arif Mardin for Cotillion Records in 1970. Alongside the soul classic "Rainy Night In Georgia" lies a wealth of covers sung in the same smooth, laid-back style that rank him as a great song interpreter on a par with Lou Rawls and Jerry Butler.

The Blackbyrds

After building a prestigious and eclectic career for himself in the late 50s and 60s, jazz trumpeter **Donald Byrd** (born December 9, 1932) became something of a superstar in 1972. That was the year he recorded *Black Byrd* with producers **Larry & Fonce Mizell** and support from a largely unheralded line-up comprised mostly of his music students from Howard University. The album was a breezier version of **Herbie Hancock**'s funk-fusion experiments on *Crossings* (1972) and *Sextant* (1973) and it laid the foundations for *Hancock's Head Hunters* (1974). *Black Byrd* became the best-selling album in Blue Note Records' history.

Following on from the album's success, Byrd created **The Blackbyrds** out of the backing group of Howard students: reed

player **Allan Barnes**, guitarist **Barney Perry**, keyboardist **Kevin Toney**, bassist **Joe Hall**, drummer **Keith Kilgo** and percussionist **Pericles Jacobs**. While maintaining his solo career, Byrd recorded as part of the group throughout the 70s, moving further away from traditional jazz (whatever that is) and more towards straight-ahead funk and R&B. The group's first album, simply entitled *The Blackbyrds* (1973), was their best, featuring funk bombs such as "Do It Fluid", "Gut Level" and "The Runaway".

Their second album, 1974's *Flying Start*, included the group's biggest hit, "Walking In Rhythm", as well as "The Blackbyrds' Theme", a tune which could have been funky had it not succumbed to fusion's most garish tendencies. Instead of becoming too noodly the way most fusion groups did, however, The Blackbyrds simply became boring. The soundtrack for the 1975 blaxploitation film *Cornbread, Earl And Me* was a dull trudge over the same territory as their previous two albums.

City Life offered a brief respite later in 1975 and contained perhaps their finest track, "Rock Creek Park", a gurgling, simmering funk track with a Moog synthesizer line that would give **Dr. Dre** an idea or two, and "Happy Music", a lite jazz-funk hit with a hypnotic keyboard riff. *Unfinished Business* (1976), on the other hand, was thoroughly pedestrian, except for the fact that it contained "Party Land", which was perhaps their most influential track. "Party Land" was the first record to use the high-pitched "whoop whoop" synth sound that soon became emblematic of disco. Around this time guitarist Barney Perry was replaced by

Orville Saunders and saxophonist **Jay Jones** joined the group.

The Blackbyrds continued to hit the R&B chart in the late 70s and very early 80s with the records "Supernatural Feeling" and "What We Have Is Right". However, with Donald Byrd now concentrating his efforts on a new group, 125th Street, The Blackbyrds broke up after the release of the very lacklustre *Better Days* album in 1980.

Greatest Hits
1989, Fantasy

With their very successful, streamlined appropriation of funk rhythms and their put-it-on-the-back-burner approach to improvisation, The Blackbyrds made jazz safe for its mid-70s crossover. Guaranteed to annoy jazz purists, The Blackbyrds had the equal and opposite effect on the funk mob who lapped up tracks like "Do it Fluid", "Rock Creek Park" and "Happy Music".

BLACKstreet

After **Teddy Riley** changed the face of R&B with **Guy**, and the invention of New Jack Swing, he emerged from behind the scenes to become the most in-demand producer on the circuit. When Guy broke up in 1991, Riley worked with everyone from labelmates Heavy D and **Mary J. Blige** to Bobby Brown and Hammer. He was also responsible for the only decent tracks on **Michael Jackson**'s *Dangerous* album, "Remember The Time" and "Jam", and took the credit for Wrecks-N-Effect's sublime "Rump Shaker".

As Guy fans clamoured for a reunion in 1994, Riley took time out from trying to re-launch New Kids On The Block as a bunch of street toughs, and formed a new group. Relocating to Virginia Beach with vocalists **Chauncey "Black" Hannibal**, **Levi Little** and **Dave Hollister** in tow, he started BLACKstreet as a return to classic soul. Although he called his new style "Heavy R&B", the first, self-titled, BLACKstreet album was little different to previous Guy material, and tracks like "Before I Let You Go" and "Booti Call" were virtually indistinguishable from the deluge of swingbeat singles that followed in Guy's wake.

Little and Hollister left to pursue solo careers in 1995, and were replaced by **Mark Middleton** and **Eric Williams**. The following year, the second BLACKstreet album, *Another Level* – anchored by "No Diggity", one of *the* singles of the 90s – finally moved R&B away from the Guy and Babyface models. Despite occasionally straying into the same overwrought territory as Guy's lead vocalist **Aaron Hall**, the harmonies were more Earth Wind & Fire than New Edition, while the leads owed more to Luther Vandross than Teddy Pendergrass. *Another Level* was smooth without being too smarmy or too nasal, the beats had the funk but never slammed with hip-hop attitude; in fact, it sounded like an SWV album, but with guys singing.

Judging by the samples on "Don't Leave Me" and "The Lord Is Real (Time Will Reveal)", Riley seemed to have taken his lead from DeBarge. While not exactly as angelic or pristine as DeBarge, on *Another Level* Hannibal, Middleton and Williams injected some falsetto levity into the he-man parameters laid out by Hall, and Riley's production floated more than it bumped. Absorbing both DeBarge and Stevie Wonder – check out the synth solo on "Don't Leave Me", imitating Wonder's harmonica – Riley finally made peace with the slow jam, and largely jettisoned the frenetic synthscapes of old. Tracks like "I Can't Get You (Out Of My Mind)", "Never Gonna Let You Go" and "I Wanna Be Your Man" could be early 70s quiet storm numbers, right down to their narrative interludes, squishy Fender Rhodes licks and Grover Washington Jr. samples. All that's missing are thunderclaps and rain sounds. Where *Guy* broke with soul by embracing hip-hop and urban noise, *Another Level* was a retreat to the make-out couch of The Chi-Lites, far away from the stress and strife of the city.

On "Fix", Riley even managed to turn one of the hallmarks of hip-hop's engagement with ghetto chaos (the keyboard riff from Grandmaster Flash and the Furious Five's "The Message") into an instrumental chat-up line promising a night of essential oil rubdowns, scented candles and athletic sex. Elsewhere, on "This Is How We Roll", Riley took Montell Jordan's "This Is How We Do It", slowed down the pace to a crawl, added some Barry White keyboards and after-hours saxuality, and morphed an over-excit-ed, hip-hop dry hump into a slow and steady eargasm.

The reason *Another Level* went quadruple platinum, though, was "No Diggity". With its brilliant Bill Withers sample, melismatic come-ons and head-nodding beats, "No Diggity" was everything the merger of hip-hop and soul promised. Quite possibly Riley's finest moment, it's also, ironically, just what Guy would have sounded like if they had indeed reformed in the mid-90s.

Though, in a sense, it was hardly surprising that it took Riley three years to follow *Another Level*, when the finished product was finally delivered in 1999 you had to wonder what had taken so long – apart from simply assembling all the guest appearances from the likes of Jay-Z, Mary J. Blige, Stevie Wonder and Janet Jackson. *Finally* followed *Another Level* almost note for note, except with more up-to-date production values, and **Terrell Phillips** replacing Mark Middleton. This time around, there was no energy, no spark; it was the sound of one of R&B's most important and talented producers getting left behind. In 2003 *Level II* was similarly lifeless and behind the times. With his old protegés The Neptunes now dominating the R&B charts, Riley was left to imitate old glories – "She's Hot" – or jump on passing bandwagons – "Wizzy Wow".

Another Level
1996, Interscope

Sure, there's a little too much of the overwrought melisma that has blighted R&B since the dawn of the 90s, but Teddy Riley's production chops and songwriting flair make this probably the best male-led soul album of recent years. It would be worth buying for the definitive "No Diggity" alone.

Bobby "Blue" Bland

B obby "Blue" Bland was born **Robert Calvin Brooks** in Roseland, Tennessee, on January 27, 1930. He started out in the very early 50s as a member of the fabled **Beale Streeters**, a group of Memphis bluesmen that included **BB King**, Johnny Ace and **Rosco Gordon**. Although Ike Turner and **Sam Phillips** lent their typical intensity to his earliest solo records, Bland's heart was closer to the mellow blues styles of T-Bone Walker and Ace than to the brimstone and fire approach of the Sun Studio. The irony, however, is that Bland's success came from the tension between these two approaches – the smooth big-band blues sound and hard gospel testifying. It was brought to the fore by arranger/trumpeter **Joe Scott** from 1955 onwards, when Bland returned to music after a three-year stint in the army.

With the exception of Sam Cooke, no other secular singer was as obviously influenced by gospel as Bland. As his career progressed, Scott gradually harnessed Bland's vocal power – which he'd learned by listening to the Dixie Hummingbirds and Reverend C.L. Franklin – by encouraging him to learn Nat King Cole-style phrasing. The ensuing combination of pop economy and gospel force, stately grace and down-on-his-knees pleading, made Bland a crucial forerunner to Otis Redding, Percy Sledge, James Carr, Wilson Pickett and Joe Tex.

Joe Scott not only taught Bland pop vocal techniques, he also surrounded his cavernous voice with arrangements that dragged the blues kicking and screaming through Tin Pan Alley. Scott used strings, countrypolitan choirs, bizarre organs, massed brass and, later on, rumbas to create the blend of the blues, gospel, country and pop that was to coalesce as soul. Of course, there were still out-and-out blues touches on Bland's records – stinging guitar runs by **Pat Hare** and **Clarence Hollimon**, shuffling tempos and protagonists who were always hard done by their women – but the blend that Scott and Bland achieved was clearly something else.

"Little Boy Blue" from 1958 epitomized Bland's approach. It sounded as though it took all the antipathy between blues musicians and gospel practitioners and packed it into two and a half minutes of the fiercest catharsis on vinyl. Bland's churchy squall is doubled the entire way by strafing axe licks from Pat Hare, creating one of the most intense records ever and making soul's supplanting of the blues inevitable. "I'm Not Ashamed" followed in 1959, with the kind of 50s rock'n'roll piano holdover and guitar comping that later characterized Arthur Alexander's records, while "Lead Me On" had Bland crooning on top of a flute obligato, warbling Nelson Riddle strings and the kind

of singers Ray Charles would use on *Modern Sounds In Country And Western Music.*

Starting off as a fairly typical BB King urban blues shuffle, 1960's "Cry Cry Cry" built in intensity as Bland's melisma got stronger and more pronounced. After Bland testified his broken heart out, the arrangement shifted focus to a tinkling cocktail piano riff, only to speed up again to another exorcism of the demon of unrequited love. This was followed in 1961 by the seriously sinister "I Pity The Fool", which predated Mr. T by some two decades.

Bland retreated into the blues in 1962 for "Stormy Monday Blues" and his huge hit "That's The Way Love Is". "I'm Too Far Gone (To Turn Around)" existed in some strange netherworld between jazz, blues and soul, but it was one of Bland's best performances. As was "Good Time Charlie", which found him preening and strutting and getting downright nasty. His 1967 single "Shoes" became a Northern soul favourite, even though it was reminiscent of "Sunny" and Bland didn't quite sound comfortable at that tempo.

By the 1969 release of "Chains Of Love", a country-ish but bluesy end-of-the-night ballad, Bland had defined what became stock-in-trade for Southern soul artists like Z.Z. Hill and Latimore in the late 70s and early 80s. That formula paid dividends in 1974 on Bland's last two R&B top-ten hits, "Ain't No Love In The Heart Of The City" and "I Wouldn't Treat A Dog (The Way You Treated Me)".

After flirting with Perry Como blandness throughout much of the 80s, Bland returned to his signature combination of urban blues and gospel in the 90s. A member of both the Rock & Roll and Blues Halls of Fame, he remains one of the great practitioners of American music.

Two Steps From The Blues
1962, Duke

While Ray Charles generally gets most of the credit, if one record marks the transition from R&B to soul, it's *Two Steps From The Blues*, to all intents and purposes a great-est-hits collection of Bland's 1957–1961 singles. The title says it all. With its horn-fuelled arrangements, gospel shouting and classic pop phrasing, this album is a couple of rungs up the evolutionary ladder from the traditional delta blues, and represents the sharp right turn from the blues continuum that characterized Southern soul.

Turn On Your Love Light: The Duke Recordings, Vol. 2
1994, MCA

While the earlier *I Pity The Fool: The Duke Recordings, Vol. 1* collected his best blues tracks from the 50s, this 2-CD set, offering 50 tracks from 1960 to 1964, compiles Bland's best-known material. Forging a synergy between straight blues, a country influence and horn-driven soul, this was an outstanding period in Bland's career.

Mary J. Blige

Mary J. Blige is the undisputed "Queen of Hip-Hop Soul". Unlike the original Queen of Soul, Aretha Franklin, Blige's destiny as *the* female singer of her generation wasn't predetermined from childhood. As soon as Aretha Franklin started singing in her father's church in Detroit, everyone knew she would be a superstar; Blige, on the other hand, was a high-school dropout from the housing projects of Yonkers, New York, whose rough demo tape somehow found its way to **Andre Harrell**, the boss of Uptown Records.

Unlike Franklin, Blige was not blessed with a gorgeous instrument. She often sings with a rasp that's not so much coarse as corrosive, sounding like she's doing irreparable damage to her vocal chords every time she opens her mouth. Where Franklin's soaring voice matched the lofty aspirations of the Civil Rights era, Blige's modest vocal gifts make her evocations of pain sound una-dorned, a perfect match for a climate that demands that its artists "keep it real". It's this "realness" that makes Blige a star.

Unlike, say, Lauryn Hill, who is just so damned perfect that she seems like the air-brushed creation of some Madison Avenue advertising executive, Blige is true ghetto fabulous: a tough chick from the streets, with a plausible figure and a penchant for garish leather and ornate fingernails.

After Harrell heard her demo tape, a version of Anita Baker's "Caught Up In The Rapture", the 21-year-old Blige was signed immediately and paired with producer **Sean "Puffy" Combs**. Her 1992 debut album, *What's The 411?*, sold three million copies. Featuring guest raps from Brand Nubian's Grand Puba and the first sighting of Combs' karaoke-machine production style, it marked the transition away from New Jack Swing to the fuller integration of elements that was hip-hop soul.

Blige's second album, 1994's *My Life*, perfected the formula, and followed her debut to triple-platinum status. While it included no raps – beyond a 22-second interlude from Keith Murray – the music was hip-hop, pure and simple. "You Bring Me Joy" rode on top of large chunks of Barry White's "It's Ecstasy When You Lay Down Next To Me"; there were classic hip-hop breaks like Roy Ayers' "Sunshine" and Isaac Hayes's "Ike's Mood"; and the snares really snapped even when they were played by Chucky Thompson rather than sampled. Like most of Combs' productions, the sampling wasn't subtle or innovative and the covers of Rose Royce's "I'm Goin' Down" and Aretha Franklin's "Natural Woman" added nothing to the original versions. The point wasn't originality, however, but "real-ness", and on that score the song choices and the production could not have been better.

Share My World, on the other hand, came as a bit of a damp squib in 1997. A lifeless, paint-by-numbers album, it sounded good only in comparison to the wretched material that Blige's former producer was forcing on the world. Her 1999 album, *Mary*, was a more purist examination of her 70s roots, without being an exercise in boho chic *à la* Lauryn Hill. Instead Blige embraced the breadth of the decade's styles, from grits to glitter. She duet-ted with Aretha Franklin on "Don't Waste Your Time", hit below the Mason-Dixon line with "Your Child" and covered First Choice's Paradise Garage disco classic, "Let No Man Put Asunder". Despite an appearance from

The ghetto-fabulous Mary J. Blige on stage

Elton John, *Mary* wasn't merely a 70s pastiche, but perhaps the strongest album from the most important soul diva of the 90s.

No More Drama in 2001 found Blige working with **Dr. Dre** on the infernally catchy "Family Affair", and **Missy Elliott** on the surprisingly elegant "Never Been". Like most contemporary singers she was still overly dependent on her producers, but very few of her contemporaries could even come

close to pulling off a song like "PMS", about exactly what you think it is. *Love & Life* saw her reunite with **P. Diddy** in 2003, but the expected fireworks failed to materialize, with Blige sounding distant and uninterested.

My Life
1994, Uptown/MCA

The "realness" of Blige's excellent second album isn't that of grim, hip-hop verité, but in the album's portrait of the pain and vulnerability concealed beneath the street sass

and hypersexuality that has, for better or worse, become the image of urban femininity. *My Life*'s feel is summed up by the title track, a plea for people to look beyond the street attitude and get rid of all that "negative energy".

Mary
1999, MCA

Blige recalls the classic soul style of the 70s on this classy, elegant and coherent album, which includes material written by the likes of Stevie Wonder and Lauryn Hill. Less hip-hop and more soulful than her earlier albums, it still showcases her trademark grit and powerfully emotive voice. In no way just an imitation of 70s standards, *Mary* is a superior album from a first-rate soul diva.

Bloodstone

One of the very few soul acts to find Stateside success after going to Europe in search of fame, **Bloodstone** combined the doo-wop harmonies of The Dells with the soft-focus penthouse touches pioneered by **Thom Bell**. Having enjoyed several hits in this vein in the mid-70s, they later resurrected their career in the early 80s.

Bloodstone started out in Kansas City, Missouri, in the early 60s as an a capella group called The Sinceres (**Charles McCormick**, **Harry Williams**, Charles Love, Roger Durham and Willis Draffen, Jr.). Moving to Los Angeles in 1968, they soon created a stir, but relocated to England the following year on the advice of their management team. After wowing crowds opening for Al Green, Bloodstone was signed to Decca/London and teamed up with producer **Mike Vernon**.

The biggest of the whirlpooling sweet soul epics Vernon created for the group was the first, 1973's "Natural High". McCormick sang lead on that track, a retrogressive faux doo-wop ballad mixed with a touch of the Delfonics' stratospheric harmonies, while Williams took over on their other huge hit, the sitar-fuelled cheating ballad "Outside Woman".

Although Bloodstone tried to adapt to disco and funk in the mid-70s on tracks like "My Little Lady" and "Do You Wanna Do A Thing", uptempo was clearly not their forte. Thanks in part to their shockingly awful 1975 vanity movie, *Train Ride To Hollywood*, they disappeared from the charts after the United States Bicentennial.

After a 1978 album on Motown went nowhere, McCormick left the group and was replaced by **Ron Wilson**, just in time to sign to the Isley Brothers' T-Neck label. The doo-wop-style "We Go A Long Way Back" reached the Top 5 on the R&B chart in 1982, thanks to black radio's conservative dismissal of hip-hop and dance music, and Bloodstone charted a couple more times in a similar vein before T-Neck shut up shop in 1984.

Bloodstone lay dormant until the nostalgia boom prompted them back into action in 1994. They have performed steadily ever since, with **Donald Brown** replacing Draffen, who died in 2002, and they released *Now That's What I'm Talkin' About* in 2004.

The Very Best Of Bloodstone
1997, Rhino

This sixteen-track compilation, containing pretty much all of their hits from "Natural High" to "We Go A Long Way Back", proves Blackstone to have been a solid, if not stellar, sweet soul harmony group.

Blue Magic

In many ways the vocal group **Blue Magic** should have been the apotheosis of the Philadelphia sound. In lead tenor **Ted Mills**, they had a singer who could ascend the dreamy heights of The Delfonics and The Stylistics, while in working with Norman Harris, Bobby Eli, Gwen Woolfolk and Vince Montana, the group had the assistance of some of the finest dance music producers, writers and arrangers the city had to offer. However, this combination of elements only produced one surefire commercial success, and the uniting of the City of Brotherly Love's two main soul strands often proved why they should stay apart.

During the early 70s, Keith Beaton (tenor), Richard Pratt (bass) and Vernon and Wendell Sawyer (both baritone) were in a group called Shades of Love, who auditioned for the WMOT production team. Lacking a solid lead singer, they were matched with Ted Mills, who had previously sung with **The Topics**. As Blue Magic, the new group signed to Atco and hit the R&B Top 30 in 1973 with their first single, "Spell", written by Mills.

Their follow-up, "Look Me Up", was a sublime proto-disco confection with superb production, but Mills' ethereal voice didn't quite work on top – it needed the grit of The O'Jays to rub against it. Nevertheless, it was a big hit in the early discothèques in New York. That same year, "Stop To Start", a gurgling Jacuzzi of soft-soul clichés, did even better. In 1974 "Sideshow" out-wimped The Stylistics' Russell Thompkins, and its smooth-as-laxative sound made it Blue Magic's only R&B #1.

"Three Ring Circus" continued the circus theme in 1974, while the flip, "Welcome To The Club", was another favourite at early discos. The title track of the group's second album, *Magic Of The Blue*, was a wah-wah-heavy uptempo number, but the synth riffs made it unbearably cheesy, even for discos. Ironically, despite their early popularity, the emergence of disco stalled Blue Magic's rise. Even though they managed top-20 R&B chart success with ballads like "Chasing Rainbows" and "Grateful", their brand of soft soul was outdated. Mills was distinctly uncomfortable singing something like 1976's "Freak-N-Stein", and the group soon fell out of the charts.

The Sawyer brothers were temporarily replaced by Michael Buchanan and Walter Smith in 1978, but they soon returned to the fold. Although they didn't recapture their chart success, Blue Magic remained a popular live act, with their trademark sky-blue tuxedos and matching homburg hats.

Blue Magic had a couple of minor hits in the early 80s with "Land Of Make Believe" and "Magic #", before Richard Pratt left the group in 1985. Three years later, they bizarrely signed to Def Jam. Their 1989 album, *From Out Of The Blue*, featured two fairly substantial R&B hits – "Romeo & Juliet" and "It's Like Magic". Mills was replaced by Rod Wayne in 1991 and the group continued to soldier on, playing the lucrative nostalgia circuit.

Blue Magic
1974, Collectables

Only recently reissued on CD by Collectables, Blue Magic's debut album is a cult soft soul classic thanks to its willingness to embrace disco's pace, even if Ted Mills doesn't always sound at home at such breakneck tempos.

The Best Of Blue Magic: Soulful Spell
1996, Rhino

Only devoted fans and soft soul freaks will need anything more than Blue Magic's first album, but this 20-track compilation is the easiest album to track down. Blue Magic's combination of Philly strut and schoolboy purity didn't always work, but when it did it was pretty glorious.

Eddie Bo

Edwin Joseph Bocage is little more than a footnote in most histories of soul and funk. However, with well over a hundred singles to his name as either artist, producer or sideman, **Eddie Bo** has assembled a legacy as rich and deep as that of any of the acknowledged titans of funk. Sadly, most of his records appeared only on tiny independent labels that rarely made it out of his hometown New Orleans, but the joy, effervescence, electricity and sheer weirdness of his rhythmic palette enabled his grooves to escape the shackles of poor distribution and be championed by a wider audience. Perhaps the greatest contribution of the "rare funk" movement to the understanding of soul and funk has been the rediscovery of Eddie Bo.

Bo was born in New Orleans on September 20, 1930. Taught piano by his mother, he played in the "Junkers" style popularized by **Professor Longhair**. After being released from the army in the early 50s, he formed the Spider Bocage Orchestra and toured with Lloyd Price, Smiley Lewis and Ruth Brown. He released his first record, "Baby", on Johnny Vincent's Ace label under the name Little Bo in 1955. "I'm Wise" followed on Apollo in 1956, and became "Slippin' And Slidin'" in the hands of Little Richard a few months later.

Bo became the house producer and songwriter for Joe Ruffino's Ric label in 1959, and had a big local hit with the dance-craze-starting "Check Mr Popeye" in 1961. Moving to the AFO and Rip labels, he recorded "Te Na Na Na Nay" in 1962, an utterly delightful slice of early New Orleans soul distinctly reminiscent of Ray Charles.

After becoming the in-house arranger for Joe Banashak's new Seven B label in 1965, Bo's first single was Roger & The Gypsies' "Pass The Hatchet", which represented the missing link between the greasy R&B instrumentals of old and the *nastay* funk of the future. Other Bo classics recorded for Seven B included "From This Day On", a favourite hip-hop beat, and the almighty "Lover And A Friend", a duet with the overexcited **Inez Cheatham**. Oh my gosh, did it groove! It had the drum beats that were Bo's gift to the world, as well as classic Southern soul uplift.

Over the next few years, for labels like Scram, Power, Orbitone and his own Bo-Sound, Eddie Bo released some of the funkiest records ever, including "Hook And Sling", "If It's Good To You (It's Good For You)", David Robinson's "I'm A Carpenter", and Chuck Carbo's "Can I Be Your Squeeze" in 1969; "Check Your Bucket" and Marilyn Barbarin & The Soul Finders' "Reborn" in 1970; and "Getting To The Middle" and "Thang (We're Doin' It)" in 1972.

By the mid-70s Bo was concentrating on session work, with occasional releases like "Disco Party" in 1977 and his first album, *The Other Side Of Eddie Bo*, in 1979. He continues to tour and record new material, most recently on *We Came To Party* in 2001.

⊙ **The Best Of Eddie Bo**
1997, Hubbub

Bo may be a pianist, but he is also one of the best drum arrangers ever. This 14-track compilation is his testament, taking the New Orleans Mardi Gras and second-line traditions as far as anyone ever has.

Bob & Earl

Both **Bobby Day** and **Earl Nelson** were members of the West Coast vocal group **The Hollywood Flames**, who had a big R&B hit with "Buzz-Buzz-Buzz" in 1957. As Bobby Day & The Satellites they achieved minor success with a version of "Little Bitty Pretty One"

in 1957, while Day enjoyed a huge solo hit with the irresistible "Rockin' Robin" in 1958. That same year Day was also recording with Nelson as **Bob & Earl**, and they, in turn, achieved a regional hit with "Gee Whiz". Day then decided to go solo, and was replaced with the second "Bob" – **Bob Relf.**

Relf and Nelson's first record together as Bob & Earl, "Don't Ever Leave Me", was a small hit. In 1963, however, they released the definitive dance-craze disc, "Harlem Shuffle". After one of popular music's most iconic intros, Relf and Nelson got soulful – very soulful for 1963 – atop a richly textured shuffle rhythm. The record's brilliant, ahead-of-its-time production was confirmed in 1969, when it finally made the British pop chart.

After the duo failed to score a follow-up hit with "Everybody Jerk" in 1964, Nelson signed with Mirwood in 1965 and released "The Duck" as **Jackie Lee** (Lee was his middle name, and Jackie was his wife). Despite being produced by Fred Smith, who was also responsible for "Harlem Shuffle", "The Duck" wasn't quite as distinctive or original, but it still reached #14 on the pop chart. Neither "Do The Temptation Walk", a brazen Motown rip-off, nor "Oh My Darlin'", an overwrought Northern soul favourite, could recapture that success. Around the same time, Relf got his own solo deal, and released the fabulous "Blowin' My Mind To Pieces", a brilliantly orchestrated stormer that eventually became a Northern soul smash.

Earl Nelson was then paired with yet another Bob, **Bobby Garrett**, who had released the uptempo stomper "My Little Girl" in 1965. The reconstituted Bob & Earl had their biggest hit with "Baby It's Over" on Mirwood in 1966. The flip side, "Dancin' Everywhere", another great uptempo dance-craze number, was even better. After "I'll Keep Running Back" the next year, the duo released several records on small, mostly LA-based labels before fading away in the early 70s.

Nelson also enjoyed solo R&B chart success again, as Jackie Lee, with the funky "African Boo-Ga-Loo" and "The Chicken", and as **Jay Dee**, with "Strange Funky Games And Things", written and produced by Barry White.

○ **Dancetime USA**
1995, Goldmine

This split CD, combining ten Bob & Earl tracks with eight by LA-based group The Olympics, is far from perfect, but it's the best you can do at the moment. It features the Bobby Garrett version of the duo, and a re-recorded "Harlem Shuffle", but it does hold the excellent "Dancin' Everywhere", as well as Garrett's own "My Little Girl".

Bohannon

Hamilton Frederick Bohannon, who was born in Newman, Georgia, on March 7, 1942, has to be one of the most single-minded performers in the history of recorded music. No one has taken "groove" as literally as Bohannon – there are no peaks, no builds, no intensities anywhere in the records he made for Dakar/Brunswick from 1974 to 76. Bohannon churned out dance music like an assembly-line worker – his hypno-trance rhythms were so monotonous you could get RSI just from listening to them. But more so than anyone, except James Brown, Bohannon understood the power of the bump, and his records just bounce, skate and rock'n'roll all over the place.

After graduating from Clark College with a degree in music education, Bohannon taught high school in Georgia before moving to Detroit in 1964. He started drumming in Stevie Wonder's touring band the following year. He also served as either tour drummer or music director for several other Motown acts, including The Temptations, The Supremes, Gladys Knight & The Pips and The Four Tops.

When Motown ditched Detroit for the West Coast, Bohannon stayed behind and signed to the Chicago-based Dakar subsidiary of Brunswick in 1972. The next year, "Stop And Go", a wah-wah heavy vamp, featuring guitarists Leroy Emanuel and Melvin "Wah-Wah" Ragin, set in motion what became Bohannon's signature formula: a monstrous syncopated beat anchored by an unmovable kick drum and bass and an almighty guitar or keyboard riff (two if you were lucky). The follow-up single, "Pimp Walk", was even more emphatic and declarative. The rest of the releases from his 1973 album *Stop And Go* were more varied, particularly the eerie "Save Their Souls" – one

of the great rewrites of the **Bo Diddley** beat – and the gorgeous "Song For My Mother".

Keep On Dancin' in 1974 largely eliminated any of its predecessor's accents. Apart from the ballad "Have A Good Day", it consisted of nothing but pile-driver grooves like "Truck Stop", "Red Bone", "South African Man" and the title track. His next album, *Insides Out* (1975), featured his two biggest hits to date, "Footstompin' Music" and "Disco Stomp", another Bo Diddley rewrite that climbed to #6 in the UK. Bohannon claimed this beat as his own in 1976, with "Bohannon's Beat" and "The Bohannon Walk" from *Dance Your Ass Off*.

Leaving Dakar for Mercury in 1977, Bohannon scored a small hit with "Bohannon Disco Symphony". He then put his ego aside and enjoyed his biggest US hit in 1978, with the eternal "Let's Start The Dance", a slicker version of his signature style with killer diva vocals from **Carolyn Crawford**, whom he later produced. The follow-up "Me & The Gang" boasted an equally monstrous groove, but featured the band members introducing themselves instead of Crawford wailing.

Bohannon continued to plough the same furrow throughout the 80s, with the occasional additional touch, such as Philadelphia DJ Dr. Perri Johnson's rap on 1981's "Let's Start II Dance Again". In 1989 he released his final album, *Here Comes Bohannon* – featuring vocals from Altrinna Grayson and another rap, this time from Thomas Hearns – and retired to Atlanta shortly after.

○ **Footstompin' Music**
1998, Edsel

Although Bohannon's best studio album is his first, 1973's *Stop And Go*, this compilation of his work at Dakar collects most of the highlights of all his four albums for the label. With all the choked guitar riffs, shuddering basslines and syncopation allied to rock-steady kick drums, it's a sure-fire party starter.

Booker T. & The MG's

Booker T. & The MG's were rivalled as soul music's greatest instrumental group only by The Meters in New Orleans and the **Funk Brothers** at Motown. As the house band of the Memphis-based Stax label, they not only backed such gifted singers as Otis Redding, Sam & Dave, Wilson Pickett, **Carla Thomas** and Eddie Floyd, but were also largely responsible for crafting the label's signature sound. In addition, unlike other such house bands, Booker T. & The MG's were not physically tied to the studio. As the musicians on the touring Stax Revues, their multiracial line-up served as visual and aural proof that integration could work in the Mid-South.

Like most of the best things in life, Booker T. & The MG's got their start by accident. Guitarist **Steve Cropper** was in charge of Stax's early recording sessions. During a session with rockabilly singer Billy Lee Riley, the band – Cropper, keyboardist **Booker T. Jones**, bassist **Lewis Steinberg** and drummer **Al Jackson Jr.** – started jamming around a slow blues riff called "Green Onions". Introducing itself with perhaps the most memorable Hammond organ chords ever, "Green Onions" contained all the elements that would characterize the Stax sound: simple organ patterns, instantly memorable guitar punctuations and a deceptively basic, but incredibly swinging, rhythm courtesy of one of the most fabulous drummers who ever lived. "Green Onions" eventually sold 700,000 copies, and reached #3 on the US pop charts.

While the MG's enjoyed further moderate success with instrumentals like the searing "Tic-Tac-Toe" and "Soul Dressing", they failed to repeat the commercial success of "Green Onions" until 1965's "Boot-Leg". Benefiting from added horns provided by **Wayne Jackson** and **Charles Axton** and a dirtier, bouncier bottom end, "Boot-Leg" championed an altogether funkier sound and was the group's first R&B top-ten hit since "Green Onions". Part of the new sound was due to new bassist **Donald "Duck" Dunn**, who introduced a higher level of rhythmic sophistication and swing compared to Steinberg's rather pedestrian walking basslines.

Despite the incomparably *nastay* "Red Beans And Rice" (featuring the wildest, rawest drums of Jackson's career), the MG's had to wait until 1967 for their next big hit. Much like "Soul Finger" by The Bar-Kays, "Hip Hug-Her" featured a monstrous organ

PLAYLIST
Booker T. & The MG's

1 GREEN ONIONS from **The Very Best Of Booker T. & The MG's**
Perhaps the definitive greasy soul instrumental.

2 TIC-TAC-TOE from **The Very Best Of Booker T. & The MG's**
Booker T. at his wildest on the Hammond organ.

3 BOOT-LEG from **The Very Best Of Booker T. & The MG's**
Primal Memphis funk.

4 RED BEANS AND RICE from **The Very Best Of Booker T. & The MG's**
Snarling organ and guitar vamp.

5 HIP HUG-HER from **The Very Best Of Booker T. & The MG's**
Booker T. gets all the attention for that organ riff, but the star of the show is Al Jackson.

6 BOOKER-LOO from **The Very Best Of Booker T. & The MG's**
Another wildly creative Al Jackson beat.

7 SOUL LIMBO from **The Very Best Of Booker T. & The MG's**
Generations of cricket fans can't be wrong.

8 HANG 'EM HIGH from **The Very Best Of Booker T. & The MG's**
Mean and moody bass and organ from the big gundown.

9 TIME IS TIGHT from **The Very Best Of Booker T. & The MG's**
Old-school Memphis collides head-on with blaxploitation.

10 MELTING POT from **The Very Best Of Booker T. & The MG's**
Funk epic with breaks for days.

hook, and its pimp-strutting groove took the record into the pop Top 40. "Soul Limbo", a more modern-sounding production featuring marimbas and overdubbed cowbells, followed it into the Top 40 in 1968.

A spaghetti western cover, "Hang 'Em High", was the follow-up. Its stop-time dynamics and moody, bass-heavy sound were a big influence on Jamaican producers such as **Lee Perry**, who concocted dub a few years later. With its chase-scene feel and adrenaline-fuelled bassline, the group's second biggest hit, "Time Is Tight", was originally intended for a James Coburn movie, but its melody and rhythm worked just fine without the visuals.

After a couple of ill-advised moves like the *Abbey Road* cover album, the group's Stax swansong was the *Melting Pot* album. The title track, an eight-minute funk epic, might be the MG's' finest moment; it became a favourite among b-boys in The Bronx and earned an enduring status in the hip-hop community. Booker T. Jones went on to release a variety of strictly pro-forma records

Stax Records

The greatest of the Southern soul labels, Stax had a sound that was every bit as recognisable as Motown's, a studio band every bit as good as Motown's **Funk Brothers** and singers every bit as good as **Marvin Gaye**, **Eddie Kendricks** or **Stevie Wonder**. However, no matter how hard Stax tried, the label remained the sound of the South, not the "sound of young America". Even the label's most famous singer, **Otis Redding**, had only one top-twenty pop hit – and that was after he died.

Stax started life in Memphis in 1959 as a country record label called Satellite owned by **Jim Stewart** and **Estelle Axton**. Their country records weren't doing well from the beginning, so in 1960 they took a chance on an R&B record, "'Cause I Love You", by Memphis DJ **Rufus Thomas** and his daughter Carla. The record made some noise nationally and got them a distribution deal with Atlantic Records. **Carla Thomas**'s ingenue "Gee Whiz" then became Satellite's first national hit, even though it came out on Atlantic. The label's session band **The Mar-Keys** – bassist **Donald "Duck" Dunn**, guitarist **Steve Cropper**, trumpeter **Wayne Jackson**, pianist Smoochie Smith, saxophonist **Don Nix** and drummer Terry Johnson – had a huge hit the following year with the funky instrumental "Last Night".

Satellite changed its name to Stax in 1961 in honour of owners Jim Stewart and Estelle Axton. The first record of any significance on the new label was **William Bell**'s "You Don't Miss Your Water (Until Your Well Runs Dry)", a record that became a cornerstone of the country soul style. When Booker T. & The MG's (pianist **Booker T. Jones** plus several members of The Mar-Keys) hit #3 on the pop chart with "Green Onions" in 1962, the label truly arrived on the national scene. Stax went on to define Southern soul with such great artists as Otis Redding, Sam & Dave, Eddie Floyd, **Albert King**, Johnnie Taylor, Judy Clay, The Staple Singers, The Bar-Kays, **Jean Knight**, The Emotions and **The Soul Children**.

Stax was one of the very few Southern soul labels to record vocal groups. The best of these groups were **The Mad Lads** (Julius Green, John Gary Williams, William Brown and Robert Phillips) from Detroit, who had hits with "Don't Have To Shop Around" and "I Want Someone" in 1965. Memphis-based groups **The Astors** ("Candy") and **Ollie & The Nightingales** ("I Got A Sure Thing") also had hits at Stax in the vocal group format in the mid- to late 60s.

Mable John was one of the few artists to record for both Motown and Stax (not to mention her stint as a member of **Ray Charles**' backing group **The Raelettes**). Her best Stax record was 1966's deep, double-sided single, "Your Good Thing Is About To End/It's Catching". **Deanie Parker**, who would eventually move into the Stax boardroom, had a modest hit with "Each Step I Take" in 1964. It didn't sound particularly Stax-ish, but Parker sang it in a downtempo, gloomy sort of Raelettes style and the way the backing vocals blended with the sparse arrangement was a thing of subtle joy.

With the death of Redding and the departure of Sam & Dave to Atlantic after a contract dispute, Stax's fortunes took a turn for the worse. **Al Bell**, a radio DJ who became the head of A&R in 1966, moved the company away from its Southern soul roots by adding Black Power rhetoric and trying to compete with Motown. Although initially these efforts were enormously successful, the label suffered by trying to expand too quickly and alienated their core audience. **Isaac Hayes** symbolized the company's change in direction as he went from being the producer-songwriter of Sam & Dave's hard-driving Southern soul classics to the prophet of upwardly mobile quiet storm R&B. In 1972 Stax tried to stage an African-American Woodstock with a day-long concert called Wattstax, featuring nearly all the Stax artists and MC'd by Jesse Jackson at the Los Angeles Memorial Coliseum. Although the event was a symbolic triumph, Stax was unable to recover from a series of bad business deals and bad signings and the company was forced into bankruptcy on December 19, 1975.

Various Artists: The Complete Stax-Volt Singles 1959–1968
1991, Atlantic

This phenomenal collection includes every soul A-side – plus plenty of B-sides – released by Satellite, Stax and Volt during their golden age. At nine discs and 244 tracks, this may be a complete luxury, but it's also the greatest body of recorded soul music this side of Motown.

like "Sticky Stuff" and "I Want You" for labels like Asylum and A&M in the late 70s and early 80s, while both Cropper and Dunn joined the Blues Brothers. Al Jackson Jr., meanwhile, joined the house band at crosstown rivals Hi, where his finesse and delicate swing were a perfect match for singers like Al Green.

Jackson's career was sadly cut short in 1975 when he was murdered in his Memphis home after interrupting an attempted burglary. However, the remaining original members got back together in the late 80s and started touring again, famously backing the likes of **Bob Dylan** and Neil Young in the early 90s.

Green Onions
1962, Stax

This instrumental album was ahead of its time in 1962 and it now serves as an iconic example of the seminal Stax sound. While the smooth organ leads can sound a bit dated now, the brilliant guitar licks and the tightness of the rhythm section made The MG's' debut a suitable introduction to the great things to come when it was released – and it is still well worth a listen today.

Melting Pot
1971, Stax

The last album by the original line-up features all original tracks, unlike *Green Onions* which was mostly covers. When this was recorded in 1971, the band had adjusted to the times with extended jams that were FM radio friendly with solid playing throughout. It's great to hear what they could do when they spread out a bit, which made this their most listenable studio album.

The Very Best Of Booker T. & The MG's
1994, Rhino

Sadly, Stax's back catalogue is divided between Atlantic/ Rhino and Fantasy, so this is the only single-disc MG's collection to contain material from their entire Stax career. Although studio albums like *Soul Dressing*, *Green Onions* and *Melting Pot* are well worth chasing down, this has none of their filler and it is organized chronologically so you can trace the group's evolution.

Boyz II Men

It might make you cringe to read this, but, by almost any measure, **Boyz II Men** are the most successful R&B group of all time. They've released eight platinum singles in the US – only **Elvis** and Michael Jackson can boast more – and have spent a grand total of fifty weeks atop the US pop chart, a feat bettered only by Elvis, The Beatles and Mariah Carey. Two of their albums, *II* and *Cooleyhighharmony*, rank among the fifty best-selling albums ever. However, while you can't knock their hustle, theirs has been pretty much exclusively a commercial achievement; they've exercised no lasting influence, started not a single trend – all right, aside from copycats All-4-One – pioneered no new sound and are as faceless as any jingle singer.

Nathan Morris, Marc Nelson, Wanya Morris (no relation), **Shawn Stockman** and **Michael McCary** first hooked up in 1988 at Philadelphia's High School of the Creative and Performing Arts. They were originally called Unique Attraction, but soon renamed themselves Boyz II Men after a song by their favourite group, New Edition. In 1989 they finagled their way backstage at a **Bell Biv DeVoe** concert and sang for the group's Michael Bivins, who had just started his own production company. He signed them on the spot.

Trimmed to a quartet after Nelson left the group due to personality clashes, Boyz II Men released their debut album *Cooleyhighharmony* on Motown in 1991. On top of Bivins' contemporary, but not very interesting, New Jack Swing backing, they crooned smoothly and in a very clean-cut fashion. They may have called their sound "hip-hop-doo-wop", but no doo-wop group ever whined as piercingly or used melisma so excessively. Nevertheless, the upbeat "Motownphilly" and the ballads "It's So Hard To Say Goodbye To Yesterday" and "Uhh Ahh" were top-five R&B hits.

Although their debut album sold nine million copies in the US, the Boyz II Men juggernaut didn't really start rolling until 1992, when they recorded a ballad written by Babyface for the soundtrack of *Boomerang*. The mawkish "End Of The Road" broke Elvis' 36-year-old record by spending thirteen weeks at #1 – though Whitney Houston swiftly outdid them by keeping the equally saccharine "I Will Always Love You" at #1 for fourteen weeks later that year.

In 1994, "I'll Make Love To You", the first single from *II*, tied Houston's record, before being replaced by their follow-up "On Bended Knee" – a feat only managed previously by Elvis and The Beatles. That spent a further six weeks at the top of the charts, as *II* raced to blockbuster sales of twelve million. Even if *II* did feature state-of-the-art production from Jimmy Jam & Terry Lewis and the usual MOR schmaltz from **LA** and **Babyface**, it was merely a slightly hipper Céline Dion album. Their cover of "Yesterday" didn't help matters any.

To ensure that they weren't off Top 40 radio for more than three songs, Boyz II Men teamed up with Mariah Carey for the blockbuster single to end all blockbuster singles, "One Sweet Day". The song hit #1 on December 2, 1995, and stayed there for four months. Unfortunately for Motown, the record was released on Carey's label, Columbia; despite the group's objections, Motown rushed out a remix album, *The Remix Collection*, to take advantage of the single's staying power.

The relationship between Boyz II Men and Motown worsened in 1997, when *Evolution* was not given the kind of promotion they were used to, and probably deserved. The lead single, "4 Seasons Of Loneliness", spent a measly week at #1, and the album only sold two million copies. The group left Motown for Universal in 2000 and released *Nathan Michael Shawn Wanya*, yet another album that applied the power ballad approach to R&B, but without the commercial nous and (blissfully) quite as much histrionics.

They switched to Arista for the utterly ignorable *Full Circle* in 2002, before moving to Koch, home of over-the-hill rappers, in 2003 following McCary's departure from the group. Now a trio, the remaining members of Boyz II Men released the pointless covers album *Throwback* in 2004, and are likely to continue touring and recording for some time to come.

Legacy: The Greatest Hits Collection
2001, Universal

This hits compilation has all the group's mega-hits, including "Motownphilly", "End Of The Road", "I'll Make Love To You" and "One Fine Day". "Legacy" is a pretty big word to apply to your best-of album when you've only got four real albums to your name, so presumably this is "legacy" in the sense of their grandkids' college funds. If you need to relive the torture of mid-90s MOR pop-soul, get this; if not, they don't need your money.

Brandy

I n many ways the perfect contemporary R&B star – she's young and hip enough to use hotshot producers, but wholesome enough to please conservative urban radio programmers – **Brandy** was one of the biggest crossover successes of the last half of the 90s.

Born **Brandy Norwood** in McComb, Mississippi, on February 11, 1979, but raised in California, Brandy was groomed to be a child star. She appeared in *Arachnophobia* in 1990, but her big break came at age 14, when she landed a role on the short-lived TV series *Thea*. Her debut album, *Brandy*, appeared in 1994 with production from **Keith Crouch** and Somethin' for the People. Borrowing **Dr. Dre**'s whiny synths and a slow swingbeat from the East Coast, the single "I Wanna Be Down" showcased a surprisingly accomplished singer, even if it was relatively faceless. Still, it was an R&B smash and a pop top-ten hit. The follow-up, "Baby", did even better, and became one of the fastest-selling platinum singles in history. "Sittin' Up In My Room" from **Babyface**'s blockbuster *Waiting To Exhale* movie soundtrack followed at the end of 1995, and ensured Brandy's status as a superstar in waiting.

Brandy then went back to TV to star in her own sitcom, *Moesha*, before returning in 1998 with her second album *Never Say Never*. It featured the enormous hit duet with **Monica**, "The Boy Is Mine", which spent thirteen weeks at #1, despite neither singer doing anything more than low-level whining. It was followed to #1 in 1999 by the Bryan Adams-styled power ballad "Have You Ever?".

After a noxious reality TV series that documented her pregnancy and the birth of her daughter, *Brandy: Special Delivery*, she released her third album, the snorefest *Full*

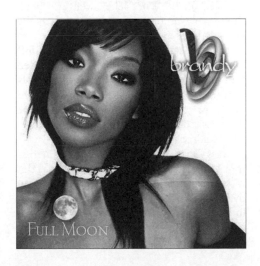

Moon, in 2002. However, in 2004 *Afrodisiac* became her best album by some distance. The lead single, "Talk About Love", ranks among producer **Kanye West**'s best tracks, while most of the rest was crafted by über-producer Timbaland, after Brandy ditched the originally slated beatsmith, Rodney Jerkins.

⊙ **Afrodisiac**
2004, Atlantic

The beats are by turns hypnotic and invigorating, bringing out the best in Brandy the vocalist, while the intriguing lyrics are often explicitly autobiographical, relating to her divorce and her occasional desire to leave the music industry.

Brass Construction / Skyy

Along with their neighbours **Crown Heights Affair**, **Brass Construction** were largely responsible for streamlining the horn-heavy funk of Kool & The Gang for the disco dancefloor. The group was the brainchild of **Randy Muller**, who was born in Guyana in 1956, but moved to Brooklyn, New York to live with his grandmother in 1964. A flautist and keyboardist, he formed The Dynamic Souls with drummer Larry Payton and bassist Wade Williamson in high school. The group soon added Jesse Ward and Mickey Grudge on sax, Wayne Parris and Morris Price on trumpet, Joseph Arthur Wong on guitar, and Sandy Billups on percussion, and changed their name to Brass Construction.

Their 1972 single "Two Timin' Lady", released on the Docc label, went nowhere, though it was funkier and rawer than the group's later trademark sound, with more Caribbean-style percussion. Producer **Jeff Lane** noticed Muller's talents and invited him to work on other projects, most notably as the string arranger on BT Express's 1975 hit "Express". Muller's arrangement became the classic disco string sound, heard on literally hundreds of records.

Brass Construction signed to United Artists in 1975, toned down some of their jazzier moments, and added basic chants to flesh out their instrumentals. The result was the absolute dancefloor perfection of "Movin'", from their platinum-selling debut album *Brass Construction I*. The Caribbean-by-way-of-

Kool-&-the-Gang horn charts, the guitar riff, the "got myself together" chants, the stomping rhythms, the bassline – oh that bassline – all made for a record that could leap funk and disco in a single bound. The equally pulsating "Changin'" followed in 1976, blessed with another bassline for the ages.

"Ha Cha Cha (Funktion)" pursued the same formula later that year, with a little added Spanish spice, while "The Message (Inspiration)" made a vague stab at social awareness in 1977. The group's 1977 album *Brass Construction III* contained the upbeat "Happy People" and the slower, but still driving, "Top Of The World", while "L-O-V-E-U" provided the group's last top-20 R&B hit in 1978. This lack of subsequent chart success is mind-boggling considering that the devastating in-the-pocket grooves "Celebrate", "Get Up" and "Music Makes You Feel Like Dancing" were released over the next two years. However, part of their poor chart showing was due to the label's insistence that outside songwriters be brought in.

Around this time Muller also started to concentrate on his own outside projects, working on records like Spider Webb's "I Don't Know What's On Your Mind", Garnett Mimms' "What It Is", Charles Earland's "Let The Music Play", Morning, Noon & Night's "Bite Your Granny" and Tamiko Jones's fabulous "I Can't Live Without Your Love". His most successful side project, though, was **Skyy**, a group from Brooklyn led by vocalist and guitarist **Solomon Roberts**, and including vocalists **Denise Crawford** and Dolores and Bonnie Dunning, guitarist Annibal Sierra, keyboardist Larry Greenberg, bassist Gerald LaBon and drummer Tommy McConnell.

Skyy's first single, "First Time Around" in 1979, rode a bouncy groove that was similar to the Brass Construction blueprint, but was more downbeat with a sinister, sleazy air perfect for the last days of disco. The group's best album was probably their third, *Skyyport* from 1980, boasting huge grooves like "Here's To You", "Superlove" and the breakbeat classic "No Music". Their biggest hit, however, came with the synth-funk of "Call Me" in 1981, a record that defined the post-disco sound of New York. "Let's Celebrate" followed the next year, adorned with that strange disembodied guitar sound that was so big in NYC discos in the early 80s, and squishy keyboards that just screamed 1982.

With the rise of hip-hop, both Skyy and Brass Construction started to fizzle out in 1983, even though Brass Construction scored a club classic that year with "Walkin' The Line". Skyy had a hit with "Givin' It (To You)" in 1986, then re-emerged in 1989 with a strange, out-of-nowhere R&B #1, "Start Of A Romance", which was a clever rapprochement between hip-hop and more traditional R&B. The ballad "Real Love" swiftly followed it to the top of the R&B charts, but the group hasn't yet been able to follow it up. Randy Muller still produces records and runs his own Plaza Records label.

 Skyy – Skyyport
1980, Salsoul

Even though it is only available on vinyl at the moment, Skyy's third album is their bounciest and most consistent. *Skyyport* includes most of their finest tracks, except for their biggest hit "Call Me", but it is a better bet than their many clumsily assembled greatest hits packages.

Brass Construction – The Best Of Brass Construction: Movin' And Changin'
1993, EMI

This decent single-disc career retrospective holds pretty much all the Brass Construction a non-obsessive could want, although why "Music Makes You Feel Like Dancing" isn't included is a mystery. Deep, in-the-pocket grooves, streamlined horns and simple chants make for dance-floor bliss.

Toni Braxton

Capable of spanning the R&B, pop and Adult Contemporary charts in a single bound, **Toni Braxton** more than held her own in the diva battles of the 1990s. Her stock-in-trade was the extra-slick, corny, over-the-top ballad beloved of both waiting rooms and Hollywood producers.

Braxton was born on October 7, 1968, in Severn, Maryland, and was raised in the Apostolic faith by her minister father and operatically trained mother. Although her religion forbade any contact with popular culture, she and her sisters (Traci, Tamar, Trina and Towanda) would sneak peaks at *Soul Train* whenever they could. Braxton was discovered singing to herself at a gas station by songwriter **Bill Pettaway**, and, with his help, the sisters signed to Arista as **The**

Braxtons. They notched up a minor R&B hit with "The Good Life" in 1990, before Toni was poached by **LA Reid** and Babyface for their LaFace label in 1991.

Braxton's coming-out party was the unfeasibly successful *Boomerang* soundtrack in 1992. Both the tracks on which she sang, "Give U My Heart" (with Babyface) and "Love Shoulda Brought You Home", were #2 R&B hits. Her debut solo album, 1993's *Toni Braxton*, presented her husky voice in cavernous synth-washed settings rife with drum machines purloined from an **Enigma** record. Inevitably, it was a huge success, selling some eight million copies and scoring enormous hits with "Breathe Again", "Another Sad Love Song", "You Mean The World To Me" and "Seven Whole Days".

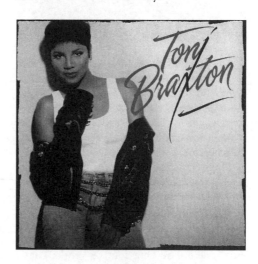

In 1996, *Secrets* matched the debut album's numbers thanks to the almost sexy "You're Making Me High" and the monster hit, "Un-Break My Heart", written by the queen of MOR balladry **Diane Warren**, which spent eleven weeks at #1. Braxton sued LaFace in 1997 and tried to escape her contract, declaring bankruptcy when the label countersued her. Eventually they kissed and made up, and she released *The Heat* on LaFace in 2000. Although on tracks like "Gimme Some" and "The Heat" she sounded like she was chasing the Timbaland supersonic-syncopation bandwagon (especially with the cameo from TLC's Lisa "Left Eye" Lopes), the overwrought "He Wasn't Man Enough" and "I'm Still Breathing" kept her middle-management fans happy, although only to the tune of double platinum.

More Than A Woman in 2002 again found Braxton unsure of her direction and chasing R&B's tail, calling in tracks from hip-hop producers like Mannie Fresh, Irv Gotti and The Neptunes. However, by now she sounded as though she was biding her time, waiting for Vegas to call.

Toni Braxton
1993, LaFace

In the early to mid-90s LA and Babyface's productions were all but interchangeable, with their grandiose synth washes, the Michael-Jackson-clone backing vocals and the whine. The only thing to set this album apart from any of their others was Braxton's husky voice, which added the merest hint of gravity to their wimpy, overstated balladry.

Brenda & The Tabulations

B renda Payton, Eddie Jackson, Maurice Coates and Jerry Jones got together in 1966, under the wing of Philadelphia DJ Georgie Woods. Although they were ultimately to dabble in all sorts of styles, **Brenda & The Tabulations** initially made their name with teen heartbreak ballads filled with innocence.

Their first single, the dreamy "Dry Your Eyes", was co-written by Payton and Coates and released on the Dionn label in 1967. It was their biggest hit, reaching the pop Top 20. Although later successes in that vein included "Just Once In A Lifetime", "Hey Boy", "To The One I Love" and "That's The Price You Have To Pay", their second single was a cover of The Miracles' "Who's Lovin' You". They became known for inventive covers, including versions of the Beach Boys' "God Only Knows" and Big Maybelle's "Oh Lord, What Are You Doing To Me", which were both on their very fine debut album, *Dry Your Eyes* (1968). Most of their records were arranged by **Richie Rome**, who later worked with The Three Degrees and, ahem, The Richie Family.

Moving to the Top & Bottom label in late 1969, Brenda & The Tabulations continued to release sweet soul ballads like "The Touch Of You", "And My Heart Sang (Tra La La)" and "Right On The Tip Of My Tongue". By this time, the group had become an all-female trio of Brenda Payton, **Pat Mercer** and **Deborah Martin**. Their 1971 album, *Brenda & The Tabulations*, was produced and arranged by **Van McCoy** in the lush orchestral style popularized by Philly producers like Gamble & Huff, Thom Bell and Vince Montana. While Payton was at her best on slower numbers, the extremely funky "Scuse Uz Y'All" – the B-side to 1971's "A Child No One Wanted" – pointed the Tabulations in their future dancefloor direction.

After one more tear-stained ballad, "One Girl Too Late", for Epic in 1973, Brenda & The Tabs moved to the Casablanca subsidiary Chocolate City. There they enjoyed some final dancefloor success in 1977 with "(I'm A) Superstar" and the amazing "Let's Go All The Way Down", on which the formerly virginal Payton outsexed both **Eartha Kitt** and Donna Summer.

Right On The Tip Of My Tongue
2000, Jamie/Guyden

This ultra-lush 15-track album collects almost all of Brenda & The Tabulations' output for the Top & Bottom label from 1969 to 1971. Produced and arranged by Van McCoy, it also features the cream of Philadelphia's session musicians.

The Brothers Johnson

T hanks in large part to their association with **Quincy Jones**, the Brothers Johnson were one of the biggest R&B acts of the late 70s, playing a streamlined, pop-oriented brand of lite funk, which strangely never crossed over as successfully as might have been expected.

Guitarist **George** and bassist **Louis Johnson** – born May 17, 1953, and April 13, 1955, respectively – got their start in the mid-60s with their older brother Tommy and cousin Alex Weir as the **Johnson Three Plus One**, gigging around Los Angeles. George and Louis joined Billy Preston's band in 1971, and featured the next year on his *Music Is My Life* album and its #1 hit, "Will It Go Round In Circles".

While auditioning for Stevie Wonder in 1973, the brothers caught the ear of Quincy Jones, who was in the adjacent studio. He recruited them to work on his own *Mellow Madness* album, which came out in 1975. With Jones's help, the two signed to A&M

as the **Brothers Johnson** in 1976, and scored an immediate R&B #1 with the breezy funk ballad "I'll Be Good To You". That was followed into the R&B Top 5 by the popping, percolating "Get The Funk Out Ma Face", from their 1976 debut *Look Out For #1*.

In 1977 the group's second album, *Right On Time*, included their second-biggest hit, a version of **Shuggie Otis**'s "Strawberry Letter 23". On their version, in an object lesson on how to update psychedelia for the 70s, the Brothers Johnson took Sly Stone's calliope funk-rock and gave it a disembodied sheen, plus a bridge that wouldn't be out of place on a Kansas record.

Their next album, *Blam*, from 1978, included "Ain't We Funkin' Now", which, even though it barely made a dent on the charts, marked the moment when Quincy Jones perfected the funk-pop sheen formula that was to make him the biggest producer in the business in the 80s. The formula was writ large in 1980 on the Brothers' *Light Up The Night*, which featured input from Jones, **Rod Temperton** and Michael Jackson – the team that would go on to make *Off The Wall* and *Thriller*. The album's foremost track was the irresistible "Stomp!", which featured the best use of strings in the service of the dance-floor this side of Chic.

In 1981 Jones split with A&M, who forbade the Brothers Johnson from working with him. That year's self-produced *Winners* album suffered as a result, and their subsequent albums, such as *Out Of Control* in 1984, were either desultory or five years out of date, and the group broke up soon after *Kickin'* in 1988. Louis Johnson returned to session work (often with Jones), while George briefly joined Graham Central Station. The two continue to reunite every so often, whenever Louis can take time off from running his bass academy in California.

Strawberry Letter 23: The Best Of The Brothers Johnson
2003, A&M

This 20-track greatest hits package has just about all you could want from these consummate professionals. That is, of course, the problem with their music: they're so damn competent they never allow in any of the freakishness that makes funk truly enjoyable. They definitely had their moments though.

Charles Brown

An unsung giant of American music, Charles Brown combined the relaxed jazzy approach of Nat King Cole with a pronounced blues feel. He influenced a whole generation of vocalists – most particularly Ray Charles – and his brand of urbane swing and late-night torch songs did much to shape the emergence of rock'n'roll.

Brown was born on September 13, 1922, in Texas City, Texas. Moving to Los Angeles in 1943, he began working as an elevator operator, before winning a talent contest at the Lincoln Theatre, much to his surprise. Guitarist **Johnny Moore**, who was in the audience, was so impressed that he asked Brown to replace pianist Garland Finney in **The Three Blazers**.

Rounded out by bassist Eddie Williams, the trio signed to the Philo label and released the epochal "Drifting Blues" in 1945. Featuring Brown's slick-backed vocals and Moore's jazzified blues licks, the record redefined "smooth" and spent 23 weeks on the R&B chart. It also spawned a host of imitators, including **Amos Milburn** and Ray Charles. Moving to the Exclusive and Modern labels, the group released a series of gently swinging records in a similar style throughout the late 40s, among them "Sunny Road", "New Orleans Blues" and "More Than You Know". The biggest of all, 1947's "Merry Christmas Baby", was one of the best-selling Christmas records ever, and became a Yuletide standard.

Brown opted to leave the group in 1949. Taking Eddie Williams with him, and recruiting guitarist **Charles Norris**, he formed his own trio, which recorded several sides for Aladdin. "Trouble Blues", a #1 R&B hit for fifteen weeks, introduced a significantly bluesier and darker direction than before. Brown sounded less like a hipper Nat King Cole and more like a Chicago blues singer. He briefly experimented with an eight-piece combo called The Smarties in 1950, but as another huge hit, "Black Night", demonstrated in 1951, he was far more effective as a trio singer.

By the end of 1952, Brown's hits had largely dried up, but he remained a popular draw on the live circuit. The onslaught of rock'n'roll cut even further into his popularity and he became largely known for his seasonal recordings, the eternal "Merry Christmas Baby" and "Please Come Home For Christmas", a #21 R&B hit in 1960. He persevered playing live dates throughout the 60s, even though his recording career was going nowhere, and played with Johnny Otis's R&B revue during the 70s.

In the mid-80s, however, Brown returned with a bang. The 1986 album *One More For The Road* proved that Brown was still a superb singer, and **Bonnie Raitt** picked him as her live opening act. The follow-up, *All My Life*, found Brown returning to old standards like "Trouble Blues" in 1990, with guest appearances from **Dr. John** and **Ruth Brown**. Following his successful comeback, the influential pianist and singer continued to tour and record, and released countless albums throughout the 90s, until he died from heart failure on January 21, 1999.

Driftin' Blues: The Best Of Charles Brown
1992, EMI

If your budget doesn't quite stretch to the excellent 5-CD Mosaic box set, this single-disc collection is the next best thing. This album's chief advantage over that massive anthology is that it includes the original recording of "Merry Christmas Baby".

The Complete Aladdin Recordings Of Charles Brown
1994, Mosaic

Mosaic makes the best box sets around and this lavish collection of Brown's 109 sides for the Aladdin and Philo labels is no exception. This is a beautiful compilation of utterly graceful and elegant blues recordings, including the epochal "Driftin' Blues", "Trouble Blues" and "Black Night", that helped pave the way for both rock'n'roll and Ray Charles.

James Brown

James Brown is one of the great icons of American music. As with Louis Armstrong or Jimmy Rodgers, it would be impossible to overstate his importance or overestimate his influence.

With James Brown the tiniest gesture – an "unnh", a "Good God", an off-the-cuff vamp – meant everything. No one else has packed as much stuff – timbres, forward motion, sparkle, intensity, unnh – into every single bar. Even when Brown started to economize in the 70s, he always retained a keen sense of

what made pop music great in the first place: an immediacy and momentum that steamrollered any obstacles in their path. With this simplicity, Brown is at once the most superficial musician in history and the most profound: there is nothing below the surface of any of his performances, yet his links to a tradition a millennium old are glaringly obvious. On top of that, he remains the "Godfather of Soul" for the simple fact that whether he was rocking a two-foot afro or showing off a super-sleek processed 'do, Brown was the most assertively *black* personality ever to be accorded mainstream acceptance in America. The great esteem in which he was held both within and beyond the African-American community was exemplified on the day **Martin Luther King** was assassinated in 1968. Television stations in cities with large black populations aired a live concert in the hope that it would prevent rioting; it worked.

James Brown was born in a shack on the outskirts of Barnwell, South Carolina on May 3, 1933, and took his first steps as an entertainer dancing for pennies in his adopted hometown of Augusta, Georgia. He was arrested for breaking into a car to steal a coat when he was 15 years old, but after he was paroled in 1952, he joined lifelong sidekick **Bobby Byrd** in the **Gospel Starlighters** (who were also called the Avons when they played secular gigs). Unable to afford horns, Byrd and Brown would whistle during their **Wynonie Harris** and **Joe Turner** imitations. Changing their name to **The Flames**, the band took over **Little Richard**'s local gigs when he hit the big time. Brown's irrepressible energy and acrobatics soon garnered attention, and they recorded "Please Please Please" at a local radio station in 1955. Signed to **Syd Nathan**'s King/Federal label, Brown and The Flames re-recorded the song at the label's studio in February, 1956, creating an R&B top-ten success which eventually sold over a million copies.

Before rewriting every rule about the role of rhythm in Western music, James Brown laid waste to the standard notion of a ballad singer – a feat arguably even more important than his mutations of rhythm. Like that other funky megalomaniac, George Clinton, Brown always wanted to be a crooner – in his fantasies he was a camel-walking cross between Louis Jordan and **Billy Eckstine**. However, as

James Brown – an icon of American music and the Godfather of Soul

much as he longed to be as urbane and smooth as Charles Brown, James was more like a rasping Roy Brown. If Ray Charles introduced the sound of gospel into R&B, then Brown brought the speaking-in-tongues *possession* – exhibited by such shouters as The Five Blind Boys of Mississippi's Archie Brownlee and The Swan Silvertones' Claude Jeter – into popular music.

Brown released nine duds in a row after "Please Please Please", before 1958's equally prostrate supplication "Try Me" firmly established him as "Soul Brother Number One". When Brown applied his scorched-earth vocals to standards like "Bewildered" and "Prisoner Of Love" and actually made the pop charts, smarmy love men like **Johnny Mathis** must have been running for cover. Indeed, by

the end of 1963, when Brown's godchildren **Otis Redding** and **Wilson Pickett** were right around the corner, Mathis was banished from the charts for fifteen years.

Monumental as Brown's ballads were, the greatest moment, both artistically and historically, of his early career was *Live At The Apollo*. Convinced that his fans would want a document of his electrifying live show, Brown approached label boss Syd Nathan about recording some concerts at Harlem's Apollo Theatre. Nathan steadfastly refused, but Brown went ahead and paid for the recording himself. Recorded on October 24, 1962, *Live At The Apollo* was shelved until May 1963, but, once released, it made #2 on the American album charts. This was pure physicality transposed to vinyl: flash, coruscating motion, bravado, urgency. The only problem with *Live At The Apollo* – or, indeed, any of his live albums – was that when you heard the crowd screaming, you knew that you were missing Brown doing the mashed potato or good-footing it across the stage or throwing his cape off to come back one last time. Not only was *Live At The Apollo* a commercial and artistic triumph, but thanks to Brown's financing and business acumen, the album served, along with Ray Charles's growing independence, as a high-profile symbol of the viability of African-American self-sufficiency.

Starting with *Live At The Apollo*, Brown embarked on an unparalleled period of world-changing creativity that continued until "Funky President (People It's Bad)" ended its R&B chart run at the end of 1974. During those eleven years, Brown and his band orchestrated a tectonic shift in the foundation of music. In a manner resembling the compositional methods of Charles Mingus or Duke Ellington, Brown sang and hummed the drum-like guitar lines, the walking basslines that used double-jointed limbs, and the hard-bop horn charts and rhythm patterns that later begat funk, disco, hip-hop, house, techno and drum'n'bass, to band leaders **Nat Jones** and **Pee Wee Ellis**. They then transcribed them for the other band members.

In 1964, with one ear on the street picking up the latest slang and the other on Jesse Hill's 1960 proto-funk classic "Ooh Poo Pah Doo", Brown crafted "Out Of Sight", a sinuous and sinewy groove that was as taut and lithe as his own dancing. As far away from Sam Cooke and Motown as "Out Of Sight" was, nothing could have prepared the world for 1965's "Papa's Got A Brand New Bag". The bone-rattling effect of the record was largely due to the fact that the master tape was sped up, giving "Papa" a claustrophobic feel which rendered the blaring horns, piercing guitar and ricocheting rhythm section all the more intense. At the same time as being all about glare and flamboyance – the horns, Brown reducing the gospel vocal tradition to nothing but falsetto shrieks and guttural roars, the "chank" of the guitar which was probably one of the building blocks of reggae – "Papa" also positioned the once anonymous bottom end as the be-all and end-all of music.

Brown followed "Papa's Got A Brand New Bag" with the equally marvellous "I Got You (I Feel Good)", "Money Won't Change You" and "Let Yourself Go". With the call-and-response interplay between guitarists **Jimmy Nolen** and **Alphonso "Country" Kellum** and the horn section on 1967's "Let Yourself Go", the guitar began to supplant the horns as the main instrumental focus in Brown's music. Nolen and Kellum were brought even further up front on the two records that definitively kick-started the shift away from soul towards funk, "Cold Sweat" and "There Was A Time". With the exception of the incomparably *nasty* Dyke & The Blazers, "Cold Sweat" sounded like nothing else that was around at the time: the "give the drummer some" interlude, where drummer **Clyde Stubblefield** and bassist **Bernard Odum** invented most of the next thirty years' worth of music; the catchiest horn hook ever; and Brown using his own voice like he used the rest of the band – as a percussion instrument.

In March, 1970, Brown's entire band, except for Bobby Byrd and drummers **Jabo Starks** and Clyde Stubblefield, walked out – although he was a tremendous bandleader, Brown ran his band like a US Marine drill sergeant, fining band members if they missed a note or if their shoes weren't shiny enough. They were replaced by **The Pacesetters**, a band of Cincinatti, Ohio teenagers who hung around the King studios. The core of the group, now renamed The J.B.'s, were two brothers, bassist **William "Bootsy" Collins** and guitarist **Phelps "Catfish" Collins**. Quickly recognizing them as stellar rhythm players, Brown forever banished the horns to the background. The first record cut with the new band, "Get Up (I Feel Like Being A) Sex Machine", ranks alongside "Papa's Got A Brand New Bag" and "Cold Sweat" as Brown's most influential. Only two things about it mattered: Bootsy's bass, which had more popping, slithering, sliding, strutting gangster lean than a hustlers' convention on Lennox Avenue, and Catfish's tersely angular chicken scratching. With almost nothing else but Starks' drums for company, the tension built up by the liquid bass and rawboned guitar was staggering.

Brown left Syd Nathan's King label for Polydor after 1970's *Sex Machine* album. His first Polydor album, *Hot Pants*, released in 1971, was also his first after Bootsy and Catfish left to form their own band, **The House Guests**. His finest funk-era album – principally because it wasn't a double and had only four tracks – *Hot Pants* was James Brown's greatest testament to the power of the vamp, and inaugurated his reign as the "Minister of the New, New Super Heavy Funk". As minimal in their way as anything by Steve Reich, "Blues & Pants", "Can't Stand It", "Escape-ism" and "Hot Pants (She's Gotta Use What She's Got To Get What She Wants)" relished the fact that they went nowhere fast – they hit their groove from the get-go and stayed there for an average of seven and a half minutes.

The new sound, which became Brown's signature until the dawn of disco, was based around droning but nevertheless fearsome guitar comps cum solo runs from **Hearlon "Cheese" Martin**, and rudimentary pulses from bassist **Fred Thomas**. Despite Jabo Starks' incomparable rhythmic patterns and Fred Thomas's increasing fluidity, early-70s singles like "There It Is", and albums like *The Payback* (1973) and *Hell* (1974), hung almost entirely on the choked riffs of Cheese and Jimmy Nolen. *The Payback*, in particular, explored the deepest regions of mantric wah-wah funk with cuts like "The Payback" and "Stoned To The Bone". Brown's last significant single of the funk era came in 1976 with the furious "Get Up Offa That Thing (Release The Pressure)", but by that point "The Original Disco Man" was eclipsed by a genre that took the concept of "Sex Machine" far more literally than the man who invented it.

Brown went on churning out single after single. Though nothing was as epochal as anything from his golden age, his late-70s and early-80s releases "The Spank", "For Goodness Sakes, Look At Those Cakes", "It's Too Funky In Here", "Rapp Payback (Where

---

PLAYLIST
James Brown

1 PLEASE PLEASE PLEASE from **Star Time**
Before rewriting every rule about the role of Western music, Brown laid waste to the standard notion of a ballad singer.

2 I'LL GO CRAZY from **Live At The Apollo**
One of the most brilliant performances of his incandescent career.

3 PAPA'S GOT A BRAND NEW BAG from **Foundations Of Funk: A Brand New Bag 1964–1969**
Reducing the gospel vocal tradition to falsetto shrieks and guttural roars, this is Brown's most revolutionary record.

4 I GOT YOU (I FEEL GOOD) from **Foundations Of Funk: A Brand New Bag 1964–1969**
"I feeeeeeeeel nice…": one of the most glorious moments in pop history.

5 IT'S A MAN'S MAN'S MAN'S WORLD from **Star Time**
Preposterous, grotesque, over-the-top: pure James Brown with one of the great all-time intros.

6 COLD SWEAT from **Foundations Of Funk: A Brand New Bag 1964–1969**
Brown uses his own voice like he uses the rest of his band – as a percussion instrument.

7 GET UP (I FEEL LIKE BEING A) SEX MACHINE from **Star Time**
With nothing but Jabo Starks' drums for company, the tension built up by Bootsy Collins's liquid bass and Catfish Collins's rawboned guitar is staggering.

8 HOT PANTS (SHE'S GOTTA USE WHAT SHE'S GOT TO GET WHAT SHE WANTS) from **Hot Pants**
Relishing the fact that it goes nowhere fast, this hits the groove from the get-go and stays there.

9 THE PAYBACK from **The Payback**
A Tantric cut exploring the deepest regions of mantric wah-wah funk.

10 GET UP OFFA THAT THING (RELEASE THE PRESSURE) from **Star Time**
Brown's last fast-and-furious record before he was eclipsed by the genre he helped create.

Iz Moses)" and the duet with Afrika Bambaataa, "Unity", all had their moments. In 1985, "Living In America", from the *Rocky IV* soundtrack, became, disgracefully, Brown's second-biggest pop hit, while in 1988 "I'm Real" and "Static" brought the Godfather into the hip-hop age.

In the late 80s and 90s Brown's constant run-ins with the law, well-publicized personal problems and erratic behaviour started to turn the most important pop music figure since World War II into nothing more than a caricature. However, the resilient and dynamic performer has continued to release new material and to bring his irrepressible energy to the stage. With the renewed interest in funk prompted by both hip-hop and Britain's rare groove movement, James Brown's tremendous legacy has recently been rediscovered and his music sampled on countless contemporary hip-hop and rap records. No major musical figure has been treated better after the end of their peak than Mr. Dynamite, and he is once again being recognized as one of the most influential figures in popular music.

Live At The Apollo
1963, Polydor

Over the years, live albums have gotten a bad rap as a mark of indulgence and fan exploitation. This, however, is one of the most electric recordings ever – and it's the record upon which James Brown's reputation was built. His energy and the ecstatic screams of the audience make the album – with no small amount of help from his hard-working and uniquely talented band – but it might also be Brown's finest vocal performance. Recorded on October 24, 1962, *Live At The Apollo* is almost certainly the greatest live album ever.

Star Time
1991, Polydor

No box set has been better received than this 4-CD anthology of James Brown's career, which is probably the greatest album ever released. If there is one single-artist

African Soul/Funk

The history of African popular music in the twentieth century is the history of re-Africanization. From the Western military marches that became all the rage among the colonial elite in the early 1900s and the Cuban son montuno and Trinidadian calypso that swept across the continent in the 1940s to the contemporary hip-hop craze, Africa has welcomed all the music from its worldwide diaspora as its own. As much as the "world music" industry would like to deny it, this was particularly true of soul and funk in the 60s and 70s.

The first major figure of African soul was **Geraldo Pino** from Sierra Leone, who took West Africa by storm in the mid-60s when he recorded his own endearingly hyper versions of American soul records. Another important early figure was Nigeria's Orlando Julius, who composed his own Afro-soul songs and later helped **Lamont Dozier** arrange his disco masterpiece "Goin' Back To My Roots".

Although his first love was jazz, the undisputed Afro-Soul Brother Number One was **Fela Kuti** from Nigeria. While in Los Angeles, Kuti was turned on to *The Autobiography Of Malcolm X* and the philosophies of Eldridge Cleaver, developing a pan-African philosophy that could only have been born outside of Africa. Combining the sounds and rhythms of jazz, James Brown and the indigenous highlife and sakara styles, Fela Kuti created a churning funk with dark drum vortices (largely thanks to one of the world's truly great drummers Tony Allen) and extreme pattern repetition that was one of the most single-minded and impressive oeuvres in popular music.

The other titan of syncretic African soul and funk was Cameroon's **Manu Dibango**. A popular saxophonist since the late 50s, Dibango blended jazz and roots music, until his conversion to soul in the early 70s led to his recording "Soul Makossa", which was one of the very few African records to make the charts in the West. The mesmerizing rhythms of "Soul Makossa" made it a huge hit in the early discotheques in New York, and it became so popular that it eventually made the Top 40 a year after it was released. Dibango's recordings from 1973 to 1975 remain some of the finest and funkiest African soul recordings.

Thanks largely to colonial and linguistic ties, soul and funk were most popular in English-speaking countries, but the music also made inroads into Ethiopia (where the great **Mulatu Astatqé** made several astonishing jazz-soul-Afro hybrids) and Zaire (home of Afro-funk-sters Dackin Dackino, Super Mambo 69 and Orchestra Lissanga). By the early 80s, though, soul and funk were dead as forces in popular African music, and reggae and Congolese soukous swept the continent.

Fela Kuti: Zombie
1976, MCA

The title track is unquestionably Fela's greatest record: a groove so intense, so vibrant, so militant that it could rouse a whole army of the undead – which is exactly box set every man, woman and child should own, this is it. Not only is it a near-perfect selection of the man's music, featuring revelations such as the original take of "Papa's Got A Brand New Bag" and the first appearance of material scheduled for the aborted *Love Power Peace* album, but it is also one of those rare anthologies that makes an undeniable argument for the greatness of its subject. Out of 70-something tracks, there's only one dud.

Love Power Peace
1992, Polydor

Originally recorded in 1971, but not released until 1992, this live tour de force captures Brown and The J.B.'s at their funkiest. If the earlier *Live At The Apollo* made his reputation as a live performer, this set, which includes performances of both older hits and newer jams, is an essential 70s update.

Foundations Of Funk: A Brand New Bag 1964–1969
1996, Polydor

This 2-CD compilation captures all that is essential from Brown's late-60s recordings. Many of the tracks here are the unedited extended versions that give a real flavour of how hot and innovative his band was. Often imitated, never equalled, this music was ground-breaking then and Is still fresh today.

JB40: 40th Anniversary Collection
1996, Polydor

If a single disc "best of" isn't enough – and it isn't – and the excellent 4-CD *Star Time* box set is, for some unknown reason, more than you're looking for, this is the compilation for you. Capturing the high points of his career from 1956 to 1979, this 2-CD collection will introduce you to, and impress you with, a whole range of Brown's hits.

Maxine Brown

Maxine Brown has regularly been hailed by British commentators as the greatest female soul singer of them all, while in the US, she's remembered, if at all, as a second-tier practitioner of unfashionable New

what it did. Appended to Allen's most direct, yet funkiest, drumming, stirring horn charts and percolating guitar riffs, the song's unrelenting mockery of the military regime and its foot soldiers bore deep into the Nigerian consciousness. People would take on the mannerisms of a George Romero or *Scooby-Doo* character – putting on a blank stare and marching with their arms outstretched in front of them – whenever they saw a soldier on the street.

Various Artists: Nigeria 70
2001, Strut

Sadly, the label is no longer around, but this is not just a wonderful compilation: it is a portrait of a time and place in sound and scholarship. Other superb African soul-funk collections worth tracking down are *Money Be No Sand* (1995, Original Music), *Afro-Rock* (2001, Kona) and *Ghana Soundz Volume 2* (2004, Soundway).

🔊 PLAYLIST

1 JIN-GO-LO-BA **Babatunde Olatunji** from **Drums Of Passion**
The record that popularized African music in the West.

2 ZOMBIE **Fela Kuti** from **Zombie**
Is this the greatest groove of all time?

3 SOUL MAKOSSA **Manu Dibango** from **Soul Makossa**
An utterly mesmerizing Afro-funk record that became one of the unlikeliest pop hits ever.

4 IJO SOUL **Orlando Julius** from **Super Afro Soul**
According to legend, this was the influence for James Brown's "I Got You (I Feel Good)". In truth, it sounds more like Sam & Dave, but it's pretty great no matter what.

5 LA LA LA **Segun Bucknor** from **Poor Man No Get Brother**
Menacingly funky take on the dark psychedelic soul of the early 70s.

6 HEAVY HEAVY HEAVY **Geraldo Pino** from **Afro Rock Vol. 1**
Never has a song's title been more appropriate – this is an absolute monster.

7 TALKIN' TALKIN' **Matata** from **Africa Funk Vol. 1**
These Kenyans groove harder than anyone, except perhaps Geraldo Pino.

8 KASALEFKUT HULU **Mulatu Astatqé** from **Ethiopiques Vol. 4**
Dark, otherworldly funk from the Ethiopian jazz master.

9 TLAHOUN GESSESSE **Aykedashem Lebe** from **Ethiopiques Vol. 17**
A strangely affecting astringent groove from one of Ethiopia's greatest singers.

10 N'GAROKOMO **Bembeya Jazz** from **The Sylliphone Years**
Perhaps the least soul-like of these tracks, this features spellbinding guitarist Sekou "Diamond Fingers" Diabate.

York soul. The truth, as always, lies somewhere in the middle. While Brown undeniably possessed a breathtaking voice, it was often undone by an overstatement accentuated by overblown arrangements.

Born in Kingstree, South Carolina, on April 27, 1932, Brown grew up singing in church. After moving to New York in the 50s, she was a member of several gospel groups including The Manhattans – not the ones who made "Kiss And Say Goodbye" – The Royaltones and The Treys before signing as a solo artist with the Nomar label. Her recording debut, 1960's "All In My Mind", is often cited as one of the first soul singles. The backing was that of a fairly typical tick-tocking rock'n'roll ballad, albeit with a great trombone line, but Brown was fantastic, creating a tremendous amount of tension and simmering emotion by restraining her gospel chops and then letting them out sparingly. "Funny" followed in a similar style in 1961, and Brown was signed by ABC-Paramount on the back of the two songs' R&B chart success.

Brown recorded eight singles for the label, but with little success. Her fortunes changed when she moved to Wand and worked with more sympathetic producers and songwriters on tracks like "Since I Found You", "Little Girl Lost" and "It's Gonna Be Alright". Her most famous Wand release was 1964's "Oh No Not My Baby". This David Goffin/Carole King classic only got to #24 on the pop charts – possibly because the arrangement lilted and dragged a bit too much – but Brown was sensational, especially on the chorus. Nonetheless, she remained in the shadow of the label's main asset, Dionne Warwick.

Brown teamed up with labelmate Chuck Jackson in 1965 for a series of duets that reached back to their roots south of the Mason-Dixon Line. The best of these was a version of "Something You Got". Although perhaps a slight caricature of Southern soul, it was affecting and compelling nevertheless. The following year, her solo single "One In A Million" became a Northern Soul favourite, despite sounding like a thousand other records from the era. Brown left Wand when the label ran into problems in 1967, and was due to work with Otis Redding at Stax/Volt before his untimely death left her label-less.

Signing to Epic and then to Commonwealth United in 1969, Brown hit the R&B charts a couple more times with "We'll Cry Together" and "I Can't Get Along Without You". She moved to Avco in 1971, but her records there, like "Treat Me Like A Lady" and "Picked Up, Packed And Put Away", failed to find an audience.

Although her fame has faded, Maxine Brown has since become a big favourite on the European revival circuit, and still appears at US music festivals. She has also continued to record a few albums, mainly thanks to her supporters in the UK, the most recent of which was 2005's *From The Heart*.

⊙ 25 All-Time Greatest Hits
2002, Varese Sarabande

Although it doesn't include any of Brown's duets with Chuck Jackson, this greatest hits package deserves recommendation over the rest because it includes the original versions of her two Nomar hits, "All In My Mind" and "Funny". If you really need the duets, opt for *Greatest Hits* (1995, Tomato) instead.

Nappy Brown

He may not have enjoyed a great deal of chart success, but **Nappy Brown** was a key, if unsung, figure in the transition from R&B to soul. He was born **Napoleon Brown Culp** on October 12, 1929, in Charlotte, North Carolina. Brown began his music career singing in numerous gospel groups, including The Golden Bells and The Selah Jubilee Singers. He was with The Heavenly Lights when he was approached by Savoy Records to record secular material.

Brown brought the intensity derived from his gospel training to R&B on early tracks like "That Man" and "Is It True – Is It True" in 1954. While he reached the R&B and pop charts in the mid-50s with novelty numbers like "Don't Be Angry" and "Piddly Patter Patter", he was far better on rocking records like "Open That Door (And Walk Right In My Heart)" and the Coasters-like "Little By Little".

In 1957 "The Right Time" marked a radical departure from Brown's previous rock'n'roll-style material. Swooping and hollering like he was at the pulpit with a choir behind him, he so successfully fused church and dance hall on "That Right Time" that

Ray Charles covered the song two years later. Some of Brown's records, like "Baby-Cry-Cry-Cry-Baby", continued to have a more rock'n'roll feel – not to mention searing guitar work – but he continued to pursue secular gospel in the late 50s and early 60s on records like "Down In The Alley", "Baby I Got News For You", "What's Come Over You" and "Didn't You Know".

After failing to score significant chart success, and feeling that he was being cheated out of royalties, Brown left Savoy in 1963, and returned to gospel music. However, in the mid-80s, spurred by renewed interest in his original R&B records, he returned with the very strong blues album, *Tore Up* (1984). He has since recorded several blues albums in that distinct revival style, and remains a popular draw on the circuit.

Night Time Is The Right Time
2000, Savoy Jazz

A long-overdue CD compilation for a singer whose blend of gospel intensity and blues phrasing made him an important bridge between R&B and soul, this 36-track album collects all of Nappy Brown's strongest sides for Savoy.

Roy Brown

Combining that characteristic, rollicking New Orleans swing with shrieks and squeals, **Roy Brown** has been called "the first singer of soul" by Crescent City R&B scholar John Broven. While certainly of the same jump-blues school as **Louis Jordan** and **Wynonie Harris**, Brown was less restrained – both musically and vocally – than any of his contemporaries, and his style provided a direct link to both rock'n'roll and soul.

Though born in New Orleans in 1925, Roy Brown spent a lot of time in both Texas and Los Angeles, trying to start a boxing career. It was after returning to New Orleans in 1947 that he recorded his most famous song, "Good Rocking Tonight", for the DeLuxe label. Although Wynonie Harris's faster, less jazzy version stole some of his thunder, Brown's superior performance was almost as popular, and charted in both 1948 and 1949. Although still characterized by the restraint typical of the period, there was something approaching gospel melisma in his phrasing. Brown introduced shrieking into the blues

shouter's vocabulary, and his vocals influenced everyone from Little Richard and **Elvis Presley** to BB King, **Bobby "Blue" Bland** and **James Brown**. His 1949 follow-ups "Rockin' At Midnight" and "Boogie At Midnight" upped the swing quotient. With their hand-clapping rhythms and killer sax solos, they were as assuredly rock'n'roll as anything that came after.

From 1949 to 1951, nearly all of Brown's records were big R&B hits. By this point DeLuxe had been bought by King Records,

PLAYLIST
Roy Brown

1 GOOD ROCKIN' TONIGHT from **Good Rockin' Tonight: The Best Of Roy Brown**
A little restrained, but pretty damn close to being the first great rock'n'roll record.

2 ROCKIN' AT MIDNIGHT from **Good Rockin' Tonight: The Best Of Roy Brown**
Churchy handclaps and phrasing enter the rock'n'roll vernacular.

3 BOOGIE AT MIDNIGHT from **Good Rockin' Tonight: The Best Of Roy Brown**
More of the same, but faster and more wailing.

4 BUTCHER PETE from **Good Rockin' Tonight: The Best Of Roy Brown**
Swinging single entendre.

5 HARD LUCK BLUES from **Good Rockin' Tonight: The Best Of Roy Brown**
One of the great urbane blues records.

6 BIG TOWN from **Good Rockin' Tonight: The Best Of Roy Brown**
So hep you can smell the pomade from here.

7 BAR ROOM BLUES from **Good Rockin' Tonight: The Best Of Roy Brown**
Another proto-rock'n'roll classic.

8 CADILLAC BABY from **Good Rockin' Tonight: The Best Of Roy Brown**
The lyrics are a bit more restrained than "Butcher Pete", but the band sure isn't.

9 LET THE FOUR WINDS BLOW from **Good Rockin' Tonight: The Best Of Roy Brown**
Brown finally acknowledges his hometown and makes one of the best records of his career.

10 SATURDAY NIGHT from **Good Rockin' Tonight: The Best Of Roy Brown**
Another swinging Crescent City stomp for those Saturday-night fish fries.

and Brown recorded his hot and blue "Butcher Pete" at King's Cincinnati headquarters in November, 1949. Despite the relocation, "Butcher Pete" was as frenzied and as swinging – not to mention as filthy – as anything concocted in New Orleans, and although the song was a comedy, it displayed Brown's commanding presence as a vocalist.

On 1950's "Hard Luck Blues", a straightforward slow blues number, Brown was equally at home, while 1951's "Big Town" saw his cosmopolitan-meets-downhome phrasing and mellow glissandi at their consummate best. He may not have had the range of the singers who followed his lead, but the urban blues style of **BB King** and Bobby Bland started right here. Roy Brown was the most committed singer outside of the church or the Mississippi Delta, and his passion and technique made a substantial contribution towards the birth of soul.

By the end of 1951, Brown had been usurped by BB King and the Northern harmony groups **The Clovers** and **The Dominoes**, who made the gospel connection explicit. Brown's records not only sounded too similar to each other, but more importantly, they sounded old compared to the new electrified blues and the excitement generated by the vocal groups. His 1954 single, "Ain't No Rocking No More", seemed to sum up his career at this point.

After a few years cutting solid, but old-fashioned, material for King, Brown returned to New Orleans. Working for the Imperial label under the auspices of the great producer/arranger **Dave Bartholomew**, he recorded

the original version of "Let The Four Winds Blow", a classic New Orleans shuffle that dented the American pop charts in 1957. However, his other quintessential New Orleans rock'n'roll record, "Saturday Night", failed to sell. Brown was clearly too old to be successful in the young person's world of rock'n'roll; after 1957's embarrassing version of Buddy Knox's "Party Doll", his career was effectively over. He made a brief and well-regarded comeback as part of Johnny Otis' revue in the early 70s, but died of a heart attack in Los Angeles in 1981, aged 56.

Good Rockin' Tonight: The Best Of Roy Brown
1994, Rhino

In some ways Roy Brown was more of an influence on rock'n'roll than on soul, but his urbane phrasing and melismatic, occasionally angst-ridden ballad style paved the way for singers like Bobby "Blue" Bland, Little Richard and Jackie Wilson. Spanning his records from 1947 to 1957 for both Deluxe and Imperial, this compilation showcases Brown at his prime.

Ruth Brown

In the years immediately preceding rock'n'roll, **Ruth Brown** was unquestionably the leading female R&B singer. Dubbed "Miss Rhythm", she was equally adept at rollicking uptempo numbers and slow and moody torch songs. Her jaunty swing and expressive, bluesy voice helped to lay the groundwork for the rock'n'roll that ultimately drove her from the charts. In her prime, though, she was so successful that her label, Atlantic Records, has been cheekily called "the house that Ruth built".

Brown was born **Ruth Weston** in Portsmouth, Virginia on January 30, 1928. The "Brown" came from her boyfriend (and later her husband), trumpeter Jimmy Brown, with whom she ran away from home at age 17 to try her luck on the music circuit. She briefly landed a gig with **Lucky Millinder**'s band, but was fired after a month. Singing some club dates in Washington DC, she was heard by **Duke Ellington**, who recommended her to Herb Abramson who had just started Atlantic Records.

After recovering from injuries suffered in a car accident en route to her first recording session, Brown recorded "So Long" with jazz guitarist **Eddie Condon** in 1949. "So Long" spent ten weeks on the R&B charts, peaking at #4, but it was Brown's seventh record for Atlantic, in 1950, that confirmed her position as "Miss Rhythm". "Teardrops From My Eyes" was a leaner-than-usual jump blues with Brown's cosmopolitan vocal style on top – despite the obvious jazz stylings, rock'n'roll was clearly right around the corner. A huge hit, it lasted eleven weeks at #1 on the R&B charts, and firmly established Atlantic as a rising force in the R&B world.

In 1952 "5-10-15 Hours" was even bigger in sales terms and became Atlantic's first gold single. Bluesier and sparer than "Teardrops", it featured a vaguely comedic bassline that soon became a rock'n'roll hallmark. With her squeals and hip-shaking sass, Brown herself was outrageously sexy for the 50s. She sounded equally voluptuous on 1953's "Mama (He Treats Your Daughter Mean)", another huge hit that would have been pure rock'n'roll were it not for the urbanity of the arrangement.

Both the bluesy ballad "Oh What A Dream" and the dance craze novelty "Mambo Baby" followed "Mama" to #1 on the R&B charts the following year. With the rock'n'roll revolution in full swing, Brown finally got some airplay on pop radio with records like "Mom Oh Mom" and "Lucky Lips". The latter was one of the rare examples of a black artist's original doing better on the pop chart than the white cover version (by Gale Storm). Its success persuaded Atlantic to push Brown in a more pop oriented direction, with predictably disastrous results both commercially and artistically.

Brown left Atlantic in 1961 and recorded a few jazz albums, but by the mid-60s she was raising her family on Long Island and making ends meet by working as a bus driver and a cleaning lady. Although she recorded the odd record, such as "You're A Stone Groovy Thing" in 1968, trying to keep up with the times, she wasn't exactly comfortable with the huge drums and new rhythms.

Brown worked her way back into mainstream showbiz in the late 70s with roles on sitcoms like, gulp, *Hello Larry* and later in Broadway musicals like *Black And Blue* – for which she won a Tony Award in 1989 – as well as films like John Waters' *Hairspray*.

She has since been a tireless crusader for the preservation of America's R&B heritage on her radio shows for NPR, and helped to establish the Rhythm & Blues Foundation. Brown was inducted into the Rock & Roll Hall of Fame in 1993 and, although she is now well into her 70s, she continues to perform regularly for her many fans.

Miss Rhythm: Greatest Hits And More
1989, Rhino

Covering Brown's heyday from 1949 to 1960, this 40-track anthology of both rollicking rockers and bluesy ballads makes essential listening for anyone interested in the development of R&B, and American music in general. Brown has never really received the credit she deserves as a pioneer and a performer, but this superb compilation goes some way towards re-establishing her reputation as one of the titans of post war pop music.

R+B = Ruth Brown
1997, Bullseye

If you're familiar with all the hits from Ruth Brown's classic Atlantic period, close your eyes and imagine that same great, sassy voice backed by a sharp, professional, sympathetic band 40 years later. The surprise here is that there's no surprise. Brown hasn't changed much, she's still one of the greats and this certainly doesn't disappoint.

Peabo Bryson

The career trajectory of **Peabo Bryson** amply illustrates the stones that lie in the pathway of the modern balladeer. Bryson was blessed with a silky voice that could caress the contours of just about any song, but when paired with the production styles predominant in the 80s and 90s, his voice too often became bland, blending in with all the synth washes in the background. When he tried to compete with the big production values, he simply sounded mawkish.

Born in Greenville, South Carolina on April 13, 1951, Bryson first made a name for himself while still in high school, with a band called Al Freeman & The Upsetters. He joined **Moses Dillard** and the Tex-Town Display in 1968, and sang with them until 1973 on tracks like "I've Got To Find A Way (To Hide My Hurt)" and "I Promised To Love You". Bryson then moved to Atlanta, where he signed with Bang and released the unremarkable "Disco Queen" in 1975. Working with another Bang artist, **Michael Zager**, he then released a series of so-so disco singles, including "Do It With Feeling" and

"Underground Music", and recorded his debut solo album, 1976's *Peabo*. Featuring backing vocals from **Luther Vandross**, *Peabo* provided the first indication that Bryson's future lay in slow jams, rather than the uptempo dancefloor numbers.

Signing to Capitol in 1978, Bryson released *Reaching For The Sky*, a minor classic of modern soul crooning. *Crosswinds* followed in a very similar style later that year, and scored a big R&B hit with "I'm So Into You". In 1979, Bryson recorded a duet album with **Natalie Cole** called *We're The Best Of Friends*; it wasn't an enormous hit, but it pointed the direction in which he was to make his name in the 80s.

Peabo replaced Donny Hathaway as **Roberta Flack**'s duet partner of choice in the early 80s, on records like "Make The World Stand Still", "Love Is A Waiting Game" and the monster hit "Tonight, I Celebrate My Love". As a solo artist, he also struck gold with such ickily sentimental ballads as "If Ever You're In My Arms Again" in 1984, although his theme song to the Mr. T flick *DC Cab* didn't fare quite as well.

In due course, Hollywood generated some hits for Bryson. Duetting with **Regina Belle**, he scored with "Without You" from *Leonard pt. 6* in 1987 and earned his first pop #1 with "A Whole New World" from Disney's *Aladdin* in 1992. Meanwhile, his fine solo remake of Al Wilson's "Show & Tell" was, surprisingly, his first R&B #1 in 1989, followed two years later by "Can You Stop The Rain". Bryson has since continued to record, achieving a minor hit with "On And On" from his 1999 album *Unconditional Love*.

I'm So Into You: The Passion Of Peabo Bryson
1997, EMI

This collection includes the best of the silky-voiced soul singer's early career, before he descended into the maudlin world of power ballads in the late 80s and 90s. It also has the finest of his duets with both Natalie Cole and Roberta Flack.

BT Express

Along with **Brass Construction** and **Crown Heights Affair**, **BT Express** was part of the "Brooklyn sound" that streamlined Kool & The Gang-style ensemble funk into

disco gold. Guitarist **Richard Thompson**, tenor saxophonist **Bill Risbrook** and alto saxophonist **Carlos Ward** had previously played together in the King Davis House Rockers, who released one single in 1972, "Rum Punch". Taking the name **Brooklyn Trucking Express**, they then teamed up with bassist Jamal Risbrook – Bill's brother – drummer Orlando Woods, percussionist Dennis Rowe and vocalist **Barbara Joyce Lomas**. One final addition, saxophonist and guitarist **Billy Nichols**, wrote their first single "Do It ('Til You're Satisfied)" which the group released on Scepter in 1974. Remixed by mixer extraordinaire **Tom Moulton**, the record became an early disco standard and eventually reached #2 on the pop chart.

Another simple vamping groove, "Express", soon followed, and did even better, thanks to the string arrangements by Brass Construction's **Randy Muller**. Muller had never written for strings before; his action in essentially transferring horn charts to the string section created the prototypical disco sound. Other songs from their 1974 debut album, also entitled *Do It ('Til You're Satisfied)*, were more straightforwardly funky, with tracks like "This House Is Smoking" following the Kool & The Gang blueprint more closely.

Non-Stop, from 1975, featured the driving wah-wah-infested love and harmony plea "Peace Pipe", which rode another Tom Moulton mix into the disco sublime. The cover of The Carpenters' "Close to You", however, was no one's idea of sublime. For their third album, *Energy To Burn*, in 1976, **Leslie Ming** replaced Woods on drums, and keyboardist **Michael Jones** joined up. The hit single from that album, "Can't Stop Groovin' Now, Wanna Do It Some More", was another relentless wah-wah groove that burned up dancefloors.

After the commercial and artistic failure that was 1977's *Function At The Junction*, the group started to slowly disintegrate, and Lomas left for a solo career. *Shout! Shout It Out!* offered a brief reprieve in 1978, with the title track reaching #12 on the R&B chart, but Ming, Jones and Nichols left soon afterwards. The remaining members of BT Express released two more albums, but their early disco-funk blend had fallen out of favour. Bandwagon-jumping such as 1980's

"Does It Feel Good"– perhaps the most brazen Chic rip-off in a long, long line of Chic larceny – failed to win them any new fans, and they finally broke up in 1982.

Billy Nichols, meanwhile, had a solo hit with the disco classic, "Give Your Body Up To The Music". He then went on to form the production team **Mighty M** with Paul Lawrence Jones and Morrie Brown. Together they crafted hit records for Whitney Houston, Evelyn "Champagne" King, Melba Moore and **Howard Johnson**.

Taking the name **Kashif**, Michael Jones achieved the biggest solo success after signing to Arista in 1982. He made his debut with the boogie classic "Just Gotta Have You", one of the singles that defined the sound of R&B for the next five years. He continued the synth-heavy techno-funk throughout the 80s on records like "Baby Don't Break Your Baby's Heart", "Love The One I'm With" with Melba Moore and "Love Changes" with **Mel'isa Morgan**.

Golden Classics
1991, Collectables

Their debut, 1974's *Do It ('Til You're Satisfied)*, is included in its entirety on this collection, alongside the two hits – and two best cuts – from 1975's *Non-Stop*. They were never really able to repeat the success of their first two albums of Brooklyn funk, so this gives you pretty much everything you need to know about BT Express.

The Best Of BT Express
1997, Rhino

A decent, if not perfect, greatest hits package, this has all the hits that made funk safe for disco dancefloors. It lacks some of the gems that are hidden away on the band's studio albums, but the streamlined funk sound of tracks like "Do It ('Til You're Satisfied)", "Express" and "Peace Pipe" will get any party started.

Leroy Burgess

You'd be hard pressed to find even a mention of **Leroy Burgess** in any traditional history of soul music. Check with disco aficionados or club mavens, however, and the falsetto Burgess would come near the top of their list of influential figures.

New Yorker Burgess first came to prominence as the lead singer of vocal trio **Black Ivory**. Emerging from a group called the Mellow Souls, they consisted of Burgess, **Stuart Bascombe** and **Russell Patterson**, and were marketed as a combination of the

Jackson 5 and sweet soul groups like The Delfonics. Signed to the Today label and teamed with cult producer and songwriter **Patrick Adams**, Black Ivory recorded Adams' pleading ballad "Don't Turn Around" in 1971. The next year, the seven-minute, slow-jam puppy-love epic "You And I" became their biggest hit.

While the group specialized in sappy teen ballads like "I'll Find A Way (Loneliest Man In Town)" and "Time Is Love", uptempo numbers like the very Jacksons-style "Surrender" and "What Goes Around (Comes Around)" hinted at Burgess's future direction. Despite their skill at dance numbers, Black Ivory were seen primarily as a ballad group and couldn't catch a break during the early days of disco. When Burgess went solo in 1977, Bascombe and Patterson carried on, releasing a couple of albums that went nowhere, although it was their soaring arrangement that turned the Burgess song, "Mainline", into a bona fide disco classic in 1979.

That same year Burgess hooked up with twin brothers who lived in his apartment building to produce a definitive New York disc of the era, **The Fantastic Aleems'** "Hooked On Your Love". Burgess was among the most distinctive, influential vocalists of the post-soul era, and "Hooked On Your Love" shows why: his voice defined the tightrope walk between ecstasy and despair that was the essence of the disco experience, and he was among the first singers to have that tight, slightly nasal quality that has defined R&B and dance music vocals since the 80s. Burgess was *the* voice of very late-70s and early-80s New York, heard almost non-stop at the Paradise Garage and over the airwaves of KISS on records like The Fantastic Aleems' "Get Down Friday Night" and "Release Yourself", **Logg**'s "I Know You Will" and "You've Got That Something", and his own "Heartbreaker".

As a producer and songwriter Burgess was almost equally influential. Aside from "Mainline", Burgess was responsible for the all-time disco classic "Weekend", recorded by Phreek in 1978 and Class Action in 1983, as well as Convertion's boogie standard "Let's Do It", Fonda Rae's "Over Like A Fat Rat" and countless other disco tracks throughout the 80s. Burgess has continued to produce, albeit at a slower pace than in his

80s heyday, and, since getting back together with Black Ivory in the mid-90s, to perform on the revival circuit.

Anthology Volume 1: The Voice
2001, Soul Brother

Even if his material never really made it out of the East Coast, Leroy Burgess defined the sound of New York in the early 80s. This excellent collection of the best material from his post-Black Ivory period serves as a fitting testament to a key figure in the transition from disco to house.

Solomon Burke

Dubbed the "King of Rock'n'Soul" by Baltimore DJ Round Robin, **Solomon Burke** ranks as one of the finest singers in soul music – as well as one of its greatest characters. Along with James Brown and Ray Charles, Burke made the influence of gospel on soul both unmistakable and inescapable, while, like Charles and Ivory Joe Hunter, he also exposed the truth, uncomfortable as some may have found it, that soul and country were flip sides of the same coin.

Born on March 21, 1940, in Philadelphia, Solomon Burke, more so than probably any other soul singer, was raised in the church. Legend has it that his grandmother set up the House of God for All People – also known as Solomon's Temple – in anticipation of his birth, and he was made a bishop on the day he was born. Burke was giving sermons by the age of 7 and was the lead singer in the church choir by 9, while at 12 "The Wonder Boy Preacher" was hosting his own radio programme, "Solomon's Temple".

Burke signed to Apollo in 1954 and recorded several gospel singles modelled on Roy Hamilton's "You'll Never Walk Alone" while still a teenager, before deciding to ditch music in favour of mortuary school. When he returned to the industry several years later, he cut a couple of singles for Singular before joining Atlantic in 1961.

His first Atlantic release, "Keep The Magic Working", was a total flop, so the label didn't have high hopes for his second. On the face of it, "Just Out Of Reach (Of My Two Open Arms)" may have been a hokey, cornpone country tear-jerker, but Burke's magnificent crooning, poised somewhere between Nat King Cole and Sam Cooke, made it a #7

R&B hit. "Cry To Me", on the other hand, drew its arrangement straight off a Drifters record, but Burke's phrasing was straight gospel and it earned him another big hit in 1962. Even more of an influence on Otis Redding, and Southern soul in general, was the follow-up, "Down In The Valley", which saw Burke move to full-throated, down-on-his-knees pleading and shouting.

Over the next few years, Solomon Burke released a series of records that not only defined soul, but established him in many

PLAYLIST
Solomon Burke

1 JUST OUT OF REACH (OF MY TWO OPEN ARMS) from **The Very Best Of Solomon Burke**
Proof of the affinity between country and gospel.

2 CRY TO ME from **The Very Best Of Solomon Burke**
The Drifters drift into a storefront church in south Philadelphia.

3 DOWN IN THE VALLEY from **The Very Best Of Solomon Burke**
The roots of Otis Redding.

4 IF YOU NEED ME from **The Very Best Of Solomon Burke**
The Bishop preaches to the non-converted.

5 YOU'RE GOOD FOR ME from **The Very Best Of Solomon Burke**
One of the definitive soul singles.

6 EVERYBODY NEEDS SOMEBODY TO LOVE from **The Very Best Of Solomon Burke**
Easily Burke's best sermon.

7 THE PRICE from **The Very Best Of Solomon Burke**
The practising minister and mortician gives his marriage its last rites.

8 GOT TO GET YOU OFF MY MIND from **The Very Best Of Solomon Burke**
The king of rock'n'soul summons up all the various strands that comprise soul.

9 SIDEWALKS, FENCES AND WALLS from **Sidewalks, Fences and Walls**
Polished, preachy and nearly perfect late-70s Southern soul.

10 A CHANGE IS GONNA COME from **A Change Is Gonna Come**
Some twenty years after his peak, Burke is still as powerful as ever.

Solomon Burke – the King of Rock'n'Soul

further. On early-70s records like "The Electronic Magnetism (That's Heavy Baby)" and "Shambala", he sounded ever more mannered, drifting aimlessly amid the changing production and cultural values.

After his final chart appearance – "Please Don't You Say Goodbye To Me" crept up to #91 in 1978 – Burke seemed to have been forgotten. However, he continued to tour, and his rehabilitation was triggered by the 1984 live album *Soul Alive!*, released on Rounder. The gospel fervour he picked up preaching back home in Philadelphia shone through and helped the album to sell 75,000 copies, almost entirely down South. A 1986 studio set, *A Change Is Gonna Come*, then proved that his voice was still near peak power, particularly on the fine title track.

Burke's downhome style continued to appeal to old soul fans and roots music enthusiasts on albums such as *The Definition Of Soul* (1996)

people's minds as the greatest soul singer of them all. Among them were a cover of Wilson Pickett's "If You Need Me" and the definitive version of Horace Ott and Don Covay's "You're Good For Me"; his own peace-and-love sermon "Everybody Needs Somebody To Love" and "The Price", which he allegedly improvised after being served with divorce papers; and his only R&B #1, "Got To Get You Off My Mind".

After 1965, however, Burke started to take his mock title seriously. He insisted on performing in a crown and robe – and the hits started to dry up. Burke's last hit for Atlantic was the expressly political and fairly mawkish "I Wish I Knew (How It Would Feel To Be Free)" in 1968. He left the label for Bell in 1969, and enjoyed moderate success with "Up Tight Good Woman", an answer to Laura Lee, and a cover of "Proud Mary", recorded in Muscle Shoals. When he moved to MGM, he saw his chart fortunes fade even

and *The Commitment* (2001), but it was 2002's *Don't Give Up On Me* that finally brought the legendary soulman back into the limelight. Released on Fat Possum Records and produced by **Joe Henry**, the album featured songs by **Bob Dylan**, Brian Wilson, **Van Morrison**, Tom Waits and **Elvis Costello**, many of them written specifically for Burke. Critics raved about the tremendous but unexpected return to form of one of soul's finest vocalists and awarded him with his first Grammy. The album caused such a sensation that Burke went on tour with **The Rolling Stones** and recorded with the likes of Junkie XL and Zuchero.

Make Do With What You Got, produced by **Don Was** in 2005, only intensified the spotlight. However, it faltered upon closer examination, largely because Was's production was too glossy. Was seemed to be in the crossover mode of his albums for Algerian superstar Khaled, when it was precisely the anti-crossover approach of producer Joe Henry that had made *Don't Give Up On Me* so appealing three years earlier.

The Very Best Of Solomon Burke
1998, Rhino

Earlier greatest hits collections may have had more tracks, but this 16-track compilation of his biggest hits from 1961 to 1968 makes the best and most concise argument for Solomon Burke's adoration by legions of soul fanatics. Heard at length, Burke's taste for showbiz BS and histrionics can grate; this is the perfect dose.

The Definition Of Soul
1997, Pointblank/Virgin

This self-produced gem represented a concerted effort at a comeback. People forget that Burke was a writer as well as singer, and nearly all the material here is original. Dipping more into his gospel than his country roots, the effort to modernize here is Burke's own, resulting in a hybrid contemporary soul classic.

Proud Mary: The Bell Sessions
2000, Sundazed

If you've already got a compilation of his best Atlantic tracks – 1998's *The Very Best Of Solomon Burke* recommended above – this reissue of 1969's *Proud Mary* (with bonus tracks) is the next place to turn. It was recorded in Muscle Shoals, the perfect place for Burke to update the country and gospel influences in his deep Southern soul. The hits had dried up, but the quality of material was just as good as anything on Atlantic.

Don't Give Up On Me
2002, Fat Possum

Burke may have remained as mannered as ever on his high-profile "comeback" album, but the songwriting credits, from the likes of Bob Dylan, Brian Wilson and Elvis Costello, had the critics and PR people frothing at the mouth. It's hardly surprising that fans were elated to find that classic deep soul albums were still being made in the twenty-first century.

Philadelphia International

No one had more impact on music during the 70s than producers, songwriters and **Philadelphia International** head honchos **Kenny Gamble** and **Leon Huff**. Perhaps the reason Philly International was so successful – in the mid-70s it was America's second most successful black-owned business after Motown – was that Gamble and Huff embodied the contradictions that were threatening to tear black America apart: Kenny Gamble was a cultural nationalist, but his music helped pave the way for the disco crossover; they preached about "cleaning up the ghetto", but aimed their records at the new hi-fi systems of the emerging African-American middle class; and they wrote paternalistic message songs that often criticized masculinity.

Gamble and Huff met in the early 60s as aspiring songwriters who collaborated on material for the Philadelphia vocal group **The Volcanos**. In 1966 they formed Excel Records, soon to be renamed Gamble Records, and released "(We'll Be) United" by the local soul group, **The Intruders**. The lushest, most extravagant record yet from Philadelphia's burgeoning assembly line of sweet, jazzy confections, "(We'll Be) United" established the Gamble & Huff sweet soul formula that would later prove successful for groups like The Delfonics.

Jerry Butler's "Only The Strong Survive", arranged and produced by Gamble & Huff in 1969, saw the blend of a richly upholstered musical bed and a Motown-based propulsive groove writ large. It had the sharpest instrumental definition of any soul record up to that point. Instead of recording the guitars through amplifiers, they were plugged directly into the soundboard, producing a deep, resonant sound that achieved almost the exact opposite effect to Motown. Where Motown mastered its records with lots of high end, geared towards the transistor radios and car audio on which most teenagers listened to music, Gamble and Huff used a more naturalistic sound, perfectly in tune with expensive new stereo systems.

While these arrangements and production values left the roadhouse and chicken shack behind once and for all, they were topped by either raggedy voices – Jerry Butler's voice fraying at the edges, straining to reach the notes on "Only The Strong Survive"; The Intruders' **Little Sonny** walking the tightrope of pitch; The Ebonys' tenor singer **David Beasley** adding a heap of gravel to the soft-soul mix on "You're The Reason Why" and "It's Forever" – or defiantly patriarchal, preaching, ruggedly masculine singers like **Wilson Pickett**, **Eddie Levert**, Joe Simon and **Teddy Pendergrass**. It was a sound struggling to come to grips with itself, constantly pulling and pushing against its own edges in a vain attempt to resolve its own contradictions; a sound that was desperately trying to move forward and aspire to something greater yet, at the same time, clinging onto the familiar to maintain a sense of rootedness. It was a sound of resolute, patriarchal masculinity and staunch classicism – the reliance on jazz licks and chords, the orchestral arrangements – wrestling with petticoat pop and vanguard technology.

Jerry Butler

The links between doo-wop, gospel and soul were made flesh in the person of **Jerry Butler**, whose cool exterior and impeccable suavity earned him the nickname "The Iceman". Born December 8, 1939, in Sunflower, Mississippi, Butler spent his childhood and adolescence singing with the Northern Jubilee Gospel Singers in Chicago. After meeting Curtis Mayfield in church, Butler began to perform secular music with him in doo-wop groups like The Quails and The Roosters.

The Roosters mutated into The Impressions, and signed to a subsidiary of Vee-Jay in 1958. Billed as Jerry Butler and The Impressions, which irked Butler's bandmates, they released "For Your Precious Love" that year, a dragging doo-wop-styled ballad with strong gospel overtones that became a huge hit. After the release of "Come Back My Love", also from 1958, Butler went solo.

His first few singles were awkward marriages of pop fluff and gospel gravity. In 1960, though, he reunited with Curtis Mayfield, who became his touring guitarist and collaborator. Their first record together, "He Will Break Your Heart", became an R&B #1 that year, thanks to its breezy Latinate arrangement and the sensational interaction on the chorus between Butler's stentorian baritone and Mayfield's angelic

These irreconcilable differences not only made for the most fascinating music of the early 70s, but also helped Philadelphia International to take over from Motown as the most visible and representative symbol of black capitalism. The label was formed in 1971 after a distribution deal with Chess for their Neptune label collapsed. Gamble & Huff approached CBS president **Clive Davis**, who was looking for a way to gain a foothold in the black music market (the only two contemporary artists of colour on their roster at the time were Sly & The Family Stone and **Santana**). They signed a modest independent production deal and had some moderate success on the R&B chart in 1971 with The Ebonys' "You're The Reason Why" and "Determination". In addition to his production duties, Kenny Gamble found himself working directly with CBS's promotions department to help them understand the world of black music.

Gamble & Huff's vision of the tension between the candy-coated sweetening and rootsy, churchified pleading fuelled most of the label's big hits: The O'Jays' "Back Stabbers", "Love Train", "I Love Music" and "Use Ta Be My Girl"; **Harold Melvin & The Blue Notes**' "If You Don't Know Me By Now", "The Love I Lost", "Bad Luck" and "Wake Up Everybody"; Billy Paul's "Me And Mrs. Jones"; The Three Degrees' "When Will I See You Again"; The Intruders' "I'll Always Love My Mama"; and Lou Rawls' "You'll Never Find Another Love Like Mine". Where other practitioners of symphonic soul like Barry White and Van McCoy gorged on sweet

strings and syrupy horn fanfares, Gamble & Huff often used the most unctuous elements of the arrangement to drive the track forward.

When the disco behemoth that the Phily label had largely created emerged in the mid-70s, the label's crossover hits dried up. Part of this was due to Gamble's insistence on message songs at a time when no one wanted to be preached at; part was due to many members of the house band **MFSB** (drummer Earl Young, bassist Ronnie Baker, vibist Vince Montana, guitarists Bobby Eli and Norman Harris, keyboardist Ron Kersey, string section leader Don Renaldo and vocalists Barbara Ingram, Evette Benton and Carla Benson) jumping ship to join upstart disco label Salsoul; and part due to Gamble & Huff turning the musical reins over to people like **Bunny Sigler** and **Dexter Wansel** who lacked their vision. Even so, while no longer the commercial juggernaut it had been, the label continued to have success until the mid-80s with acts like **Wansel**, The O'Jays and **The Jones Girls**.

○ **The Philly Sound: Kenny Gamble, Leon Huff & The Story Of Brotherly Love**
1997, Epic/Legacy

An absolutely essential purchase – this is three CDs and 48 tracks of some of the best soul music ever made. Starting with Gamble & Huff's first productions – The Intruders' "(We'll Be) United" from 1966 and The Soul Survivors' "Expressway To Your Heart" from 1967 – this album goes right through to 1976, when the label began to decline in influence and quality.

falsetto. The duo had two more hits together in 1961, "Find Another Girl" and "I'm A Telling You", before Mayfield turned his attention back to the re-formed Impressions.

The next couple of years saw Butler drifting in a strange wilderness, as on his bizarre but affecting versions of "Moon River" and "Make It Easy On Yourself". A sublime recording of Mayfield's "Need To Belong" knocked some soul back into him in 1963, and he followed it in 1964 with the haunting "Giving Up On Love". Later that year, "Let It Be Me", a classic "last dance" duet with Betty Everett, became Butler's first top-five pop hit. His momentum was stalled, however, by the financial troubles of Vee-Jay, and he switched to Mercury in 1966.

Butler's first year at the label was another awkward marriage of pop and soul on records like "Mr Dream Merchant", where, despite the awful song, his baritone was at its richest. In September 1967 Butler started working with Philadelphian producers **Kenny Gamble** and **Leon Huff**, a teaming that marked an epochal moment in soul history. On the records "Never Give You Up", "Hey Western Union Man" and "Are You Happy" the duo allowed a bit of grit to creep into Butler's voice and set it off against textures that were either shimmering or frothy, creating a compelling tension that changed the face of African-American music.

With its creamy, Wes Montgomery-style guitar licks, resonant vibraphone, prominent string section and a kick drum that sounded like a timpani purloined from the Philadelphia Philharmonic, 1969's "Only The Strong Survive" was like slipping on a smoking jacket and relaxing in front of the fire with a snifter of brandy. "Moody Woman" and "What's The Use Of Breaking Up" followed that same year, before Gamble and Huff left Mercury in 1970.

Nevertheless, the hits kept coming for Butler. His duet with **Brenda Lee Eager**, "Ain't Understanding Mellow", sold a million copies, while his version of The O'Jays' "One Night Affair" became an early disco favourite. However, after **Johnny Bristol** produced "Power Of Love" in 1973, the hits started to fade. He moved to Motown and had a hit with "I Wanna Do It To You" in 1976, but duets with **Thelma Houston** and a reunion with Gamble & Huff at Philly International couldn't stop the slide.

Butler moved into politics in the 1980s. He was elected as Cook County Commissioner in Illinois in 1985, a post he occupied for four terms. However, he didn't give up music for politics entirely; he still tours and records sporadically and his musical achievements were recognized in 1991 when he was inducted into the Rock & Roll Hall of Fame.

Iceman: Mercury Years Anthology
1992, PolyGram

This excellent 44-track compilation covers Butler's Mercury years, from 1966 to 1975. The highlights are the records he made with Kenny Gamble and Leon Huff between 1967 and 1970, which, with their warmth, pinpoint instrumental definition and gently uplifting momentum, heralded the Philadelphia sound as the new direction for African-American music.

The Philadelphia Sessions
2001, Mercury

Included in their entirety on this remastered reissue CD, 1968's *The Iceman Cometh* and 1969's *Ice On Ice* feature Jerry Butler at his creative peak in collaboration with Gamble & Huff. The production duo went on to create the Philadelphia International sound in the 70s, but it was these two albums that opened that door. "Only The Strong Survive" is the big hit, but it's all slick, sophisticated, and great.

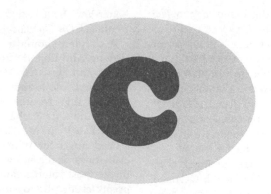

Cameo

Although they will probably only be remembered for their one truly transcendent moment, the 1986 single "Word Up", Cameo deserve to rank among the most innovative groups of the 80s. Taking funk in hitherto unimagined directions, both lyrically and musically, they were one of the very few bands to acknowledge the influence of hip-hop and respond to it without pandering to lowest-common-denominator commercial instincts. Bands like **Kraftwerk**, **Yellow Magic Orchestra**, **Depeche Mode**, **The Human League**, P-Funk, and **Afrika Bambaataa & The Soul Sonic Force** had all previously explored the possibilities of the synthesizer. However, with their angular and splintered soundscapes, Cameo were almost certainly the first group truly to appreciate the synthesizer's effect on how rhythm tracks would be put together in the future.

Cameo's main man, **Larry Blackmon**, began the 70s as a Juilliard School student who played drums on sessions for the cult proto-disco group, **Black Ivory**. He then joined the funk troupe **New York City Players**, who were heavily influenced by the Parliafunkadelicment Thang. After cutting the disco single "Find My Way" for Casablanca's Chocolate City imprint in 1976, the group was renamed Cameo. Later that year they released the compellingly minimalistic "Rigor Mortis", which was considerably more interesting than most funk of the period – and it wasn't afraid of disco. Even so, Cameo's early output didn't stray too far from the model of most funk bands: long,

mostly instrumental vamps based around a serpentine bassline and chicken-scratch guitar that masked the cloying, smarmy sweetness of their wretched ballads.

After Blackmon and other key members of the group had a brief foray recording under the name **East Coast** – achieving minor hits with "The Rock" and "Meat The Beat" – Cameo came into their own in 1979 with the release of "I Just Want To Be". Thanks to its clever use of synthesizers, original guitar sound, almost robotic backing singers and cryptic sociopolitical commentary, the single became one of the blueprints for black music in the 80s: some of its sound effects featured on the early hip-hop single "Jazzy Sensation" by **Afrika Bambaataa**.

With synth maestro **Gregory Johnson** on board, Cameo continued to push dance music towards a future of jagged edges and sharp contours. The squiggles, wiggles and farting basslines of 1980's "Shake Your Pants" further refined the vision of P-Funk's keyboard player, **Bernie Worrell**, but it was the 1982 release "Flirt" that firmly set much of 80s R&B in Cameo's musical image. Borrowing a guitar line from Prince, "Flirt" remade funk as a chopped-up groove with shards of synth effects flying around the mix. It was as though Jamaican dub pioneer King Tubby had remixed a P-Funk track using one of UTFO's drum machines.

Under this hip-hop influence, Cameo really hit their stride when they pilfered a synthesized **Ennio Morricone** riff from Jonzun Crew's 1983 single, "Space Cowboy", using it on "Single Life" and "She's Strange" (the group's first R&B #1 and one of the most original singles of the decade). On both tracks, the famous whistle from the soundtrack to *The Good, The Bad And The Ugly* lent a sense of ghost-town menace to Cameo's ultramodern sound – an implicit indictment of Reagan's abandonment of the inner city to outlaw gangs of thieves and drug dealers. The politics was writ even larger on "Talkin' Out The Side Of Your Neck", a vicious rant that once again borrowed Prince's post-Hendrix guitar to heap scorn on the powers that be.

Whittled down to a trio of Blackmon, **Nathan Leftenant** and **Tomi Jenkins,** Cameo created their lasting anthem in 1986. A top-ten single across the world, "Word Up" featured Blackmon uttering oblique lyrics like "We don't have time for psychological romance" in an exaggerated, nasal vocal style that was created using a battery of filters. Like its almost-as-good follow-up, "Candy", "Word Up" was a brittle synth-dub that created the snare sound that later defined the second half of the 80s. They continued along the same path with the records "Back And Forth", "You Make Me Work", "Skin I'm In" and "I Want It Now". Unfortunately, as their name suggested, Cameo's peak period was all too brief. Even though the early-90s singles "Emotional Violence", "Slyde" and "You Are My Love" continued to place in the lower reaches of the R&B chart, their innovations were to be perfected elsewhere.

The Best Of Cameo
1993, PolyGram

The Best Of Cameo is an excellent overview of the group's prime, when their funk was perfectly in tune with the sharper, more angular sensibilities of the 80s. The only unfortunate decision was to include the far inferior rap version of "She's Strange", one of their best and most outlandish records.

Tevin Campbell

This younger, more adenoidal Babyface clone made a splash when he burst onto the R&B scene in the early 90s. Born in Waxahachie, Texas on November 12, 1978, **Tevin Campbell** was plucked from his local church choir in 1988 for the television show *Wally & The Valentines.* He then firmly established himself as a pre-adolescent sensation by singing the show's title track and featuring on the #1 R&B hit "Tomorrow (A

Better You, Better Me)" from Quincy Jones' 1990 *Back On The Block* album.

A couple of soundtrack contributions – "Round And Round" from Prince's *Graffiti Bridge* and "Just Ask Me To" from *Boyz N The Hood* – followed before his own solo debut, *T.E.V.I.N.*, was released in 1991. On the album's R&B chart-topper, "Tell Me What You Want Me To Do", Campbell was a dead ringer for Whitney Houston, especially towards the end when he over-emoted in the most rote fashion and let rip with a preposterous falsetto shriek.

His second album, 1993's *I'm Ready*, featured the pop top-ten title track and the hook-laden Babyface ballad, "Can We Talk", another R&B #1, on which Campbell sounded exactly like Babyface and, by extension, Michael Jackson. 1996's *Back To The World* was afflicted by the child star disease, with Campbell trying to prove he was an adult talent and not just a cute teenage prodigy. Even if his mock dreadlocks on the cover didn't put you off, the "sexy" love man bumping and grinding inside was sure to, and the album flopped.

After yet more vocal grandstanding on *Tevin Campbell* in 1999 failed to ensure chart success, the former child star quickly faded from the scene.

The Best Of Tevin Campbell
2001, Qwest

If you want to revisit the early 90s, when cloying Babyface ballads blighted the airwaves, or marvel at the impressively developed pipes of a teenager, then this is a must. Just remember that age ain't nothing but a number.

Mariah Carey

Only **The Beatles** and **Elvis Presley** have had more American #1 singles than **Mariah Carey**… and she's gaining fast. Carey has actually spent more weeks at #1 than The Beatles! It may be shocking to some to put Carey in such illustrious company, but she dominated the 90s in the same way that Elvis and the Fab Four dominated the 50s and 60s, racking up no less than seven gold and an astonishing eight platinum or double platinum singles during a decade in which singles almost stopped selling. On top of that, she also wrote nearly all of her own material. Of course, she was more than just a commercial juggernaut – Carey defined the female voice in both contemporary R&B and pop.

Mariah Carey was born in Long Island, New York, on March 27, 1970. Her mother was a singer with the New York City Opera, and that unrestrained sensibility certainly rubbed off on her daughter. The day after Carey graduated from high school she moved to New York City to pursue a career in music. She got a job as a back-up singer for Brenda K. Starr, who invited her to a music industry party that Columbia president **Tommy Mottola** was also attending. Carey handed him her demo tape and he listened to it in the limo on his way home. According to legend, he loved it so much that he immediately turned the car around and went back to the party in search of her. She wasn't there, but he eventually tracked her down and signed her to Columbia.

Her debut single, "Vision Of Love", was a modern take on Minnie Riperton baroque and went to #1 on both the pop and R&B charts in 1990. Her next four singles – "Love Takes Time", "Someday", "I Don't Wanna Cry" and "Emotions" – all went to #1 on the pop chart, setting a record for a new artist. Her winning streak was stalled in 1991 by "Can't Let Go", which only made it to #2, but the sensational start to her career landed her a slot on MTV's *Unplugged* – the accompanying EP included a sixth #1 in the shape of a cover of The Jackson 5's "I'll Be There".

Mariah Carey married Tony Mottola in 1993, the same year she released her next album, *Music Box*, which was another huge smash. "Hero" and "Dreamlover" were both enormous hits, but most of *Music Box* was taken up with Carey trying to prove to the critics that she could actually sing rather than just belt. She wasn't very successful. Her 1995 album *Daydream* was bigger still – and not because of her ill-advised cover of Journey's "Open Arms". The lead single "Fantasy", with its sample of Tom Tom Club's "Genius Of Love", set all kinds of records for radio airplay in its first week and became only the second record to debut at #1 on the US pop chart. "Fantasy" was just the tip of the iceberg, however. Carey then teamed up with the whining nasal singing of Boyz II Men for the unlistenable "One Sweet Day". Although, apparently, plenty of people didn't agree – "One Sweet Day" stayed atop the pop chart for a record sixteen weeks.

Carey and Mottola divorced in 1997, and Carey reacted by releasing *Butterfly*, an album that ditched her Adult Contemporary R&B image of old in favour of full-on street R&B, featuring guest appearances from **P. Diddy** and Krayzie Bone. The demographic shift didn't hurt any, as the album contained three more #1 singles. The single "When You Believe", from the *Prince Of Egypt* soundtrack, followed in 1998. It was a duet between the two most successful female artists of all time, Carey and Whitney Houston. Their voices clashed as much as their egos and it was not the blockbuster the marketing executives were dreaming of.

The following year's album release, *Rainbow*, was a bit of a commercial dud. Only "Heartbreaker", in which Carey piggybacked on Jay-Z's charisma, and the violently awful cover of **Phil Collins**'s already unspeakable "Against All Odds (Take A Look At Me Now)" with British teenyboppers **Westlife** (who were to the UK charts what Carey was to the US charts), achieved any real success.

The wheels started to come off in 2000, after Carey signed the biggest contract in history with Virgin. She had a complete meltdown in 2001 – making strange personal appearances while wearing very little and rambling cryptically and morbidly – right around the time of her catastrophic film debut, *Glitter*. The accompanying soundtrack, her first record for Virgin, barely made it to gold status, and that was probably only down to rubbernecking; although, to be fair, it was released on 9/11.

Virgin dumped Carey and she signed with Island/Def Jam, releasing the terrible *Charmbracelet* in 2002. However, in 2005 she released *Emancipation Of Mimi*, a shockingly good album on which she finally proved that she is actually a singer. The hip-hopped Minnie Riperton vibe of "Stay The Night" suited Carey and was one of her most restrained performances. "We Belong Together", on the other hand, was an anonymous contemporary R&B production, although the by-the-numbers feel did rein in her excesses. She often still sounded like mutton dressed as lamb, with all that hopelessly outdated and forced bling-bling grandstanding, but the album – much to everyone's surprise – wasn't all just fireworks and became her best performance to date.

Mariah Carey's Greatest Hits
2001, Sony

Emancipation Of Mimi is her most – possibly only – listenable album, but this 28-track extravaganza has just about all the records that made Mariah Carey the third most successful chart act in American history. Anyone who listened to the radio from 1990 to 1999 probably has every one of these tracks scorched into their brain forever and never needs to hear any of them again, but it serves as a good primer nevertheless. British fans may be disappointed, however, that it does not include the nauseating duet with Westlife, "Against All Odds".

Carl Carlton

Born in 1952 in Detroit, R&B journeyman **Carl Carlton** began his recording career as a pre-adolescent on the Motor City's Golden World label. Dubbed "Little Carl Carlton the Twelve-Year-Old Wonder", he released the Richard "Popcorn" Wylie track "Nothin' No Sweeter Than Love" in 1965, and then two sides on the ultra-obscure Detroit label Lando in 1966, "I Think Of How I Love Her" and "So What".

Signing to Don Robey's Back Beat label as **Little Carl Carlton** in 1968, Carlton released the superb, driving Northern soul favourite, "Competition Ain't Nothin'", followed by the magnificently sleazy "46 Drums – 1 Guitar". It was only after "Drop By My Place" in 1970 that the "Little" was finally dropped. Carlton's last record for Back Beat,

1974's "Everlasting Love", fused early disco rhythms, Northern soul melodies and Europop sing-along cheesiness to provide his first and only pop top-ten hit.

During the mid-70s Carlton churned out a few minor disco hits, including "Smokin' Room" and "Ain't Gonna Tell Nobody (About You)", on ABC and recorded a solid album with producer **Bunny Sigler**, *I Wanna Be With You*, in 1976. However, nothing really stuck until Carlton moved to 20th Century and started working with singer/songwriter **Leon Haywood**. His collaboration with Haywood gave Carlton his one truly sublime moment: 1981's "She's A Bad Mama Jama (She's Built, She's Stacked)". Full of hooks – largely ripped off – and instantly memorable descriptions of female anatomy, the song was written by Haywood, but will always be remembered for its synth bassline, played, believe it or not, by **James Ingram**. It spent eight weeks at #2 on the R&B chart, languishing behind **Lionel Richie** and **Diana Ross**'s "Endless Love".

Carlton's 1982 single, "Baby I Need Your Lovin'", was a strange, Euro-stomp cover of **The Four Tops**' classic – in a similar style to Amii Stewart's version of "Knock On Wood" – featuring synthesizers from the great **Patrick Cowley**. It appeared on that year's *The Bad CC* album, which was a favourite amongst the roller-skating crowd thanks to boogie tracks like "Swing That Sexy Thang" and the fattest synth bassline ever on a version of "Groovin'". A move to the rapidly sinking Casablanca label in 1986 produced the single "Slipped Tripped (Fooled Around And Fell In Love)" – not to be confused with the Elvin Bishop song of almost the same name – which was another pastiche of just about every mid-80s keyboard sound you care to mention.

Carl Carlton largely disappeared from the scene after that, only to re-emerge in 1994 with *Main Event*, another collaboration with Leon Haywood. That album also failed to have any real impact on the charts or excite the critics, and Carlton vanished from the music scene once again.

Drop By My Place
1988, Charly

This excellent survey of Carlton's career until 1976 unintentionally shows the links between Northern soul and disco. While it doesn't include "She's A Bad Mama Jama", very fine records such as "Competition Ain't Nothin'" and "Everlasting Love" show that, when given decent material and arrangements, Carlton was a more than capable singer who could really move a dancefloor.

James Carr

B lessed with a voice so cavernous that you could never find the bottom, **James Carr** was the epitome of "deep soul". His greatest records – with their cry-in-your-beer country-style lyrics and mostly white backing musicians topped off by the booming gospelese style in which Carr begged, pleaded and confessed the blues – stand at the point where soul meets country. Despite their magnificence, however, Carr's name seems doomed to remain obscure, and, in a genre littered with unhappy endings, his personal saga remains among the saddest stories of all.

Carr was born in Mississippi in 1942, but moved to Memphis with his family soon afterwards. He got his musical training in church and his timbre from listening to **Julius Cheeks** belt out hosannahs with The Sensational Nightingales. While singing with the gospel group The Harmony Echoes in the early 60s, Carr met his future manager and lifelong ally **Roosevelt Jamison**. Jamison convinced Carr to go secular and brought him to Quinton Claunch's Goldwax label.

Despite his gospel credentials, Carr's first record, 1964's "You Don't Want Me", was an urban blues in the style of **BB King** and Bobby "Blue" Bland, albeit with more gravel and more drive in his voice. A few more lacklustre records followed until 1966's "You've Got My Mind Messed Up". Though the record was a complete Stax derivative, from its tick-tocking drum track and hungover horns to Carr's Otis Redding mimicry, Carr's sheer presence dominated proceedings. Carr may have been a dead ringer for Redding in the opening passage, but as the song built he exerted an imposing authority, and his breakdown shrieks as the song faded out had an intensity only matched by hard gospel singers Julius Cheeks, **Solomon Womack** of the Swan Silvertones and **Archie Brownlee** of the Five Blind Boys of Mississippi.

If "You've Got My Mind Messed Up" became a top-ten R&B hit because of its resemblance to Redding, "Love Attack", on which Carr copied Redding's mannerisms as well as his timbre, should have done even better. Instead, it stalled just outside the R&B Top 20. After Carr's next single, however, it would be Redding borrowing from him. With "Pouring Water On A Drowning Man", Carr became his own man and the song remains a Southern soul classic. Although Percy Sledge had recorded the song previously and Otis Clay would later, Carr imbued it with a power that no one else could approach. He may have been submerged, but his foghorn vocals, backed up by horn echoes, served as a warning call to anyone following the same course. Conjuring both baptism and the womb, the song's prevailing immersion metaphor wasn't all pain, and, with his laugh towards the end, Carr seemed to understand this.

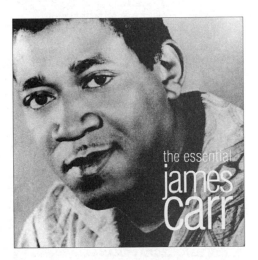

Great though "Pouring Water On A Drowning Man" was, Carr's masterpiece was his version of **Chips Moman** and **Dan Penn**'s "The Dark End Of The Street" – surely one of the greatest songs ever written. While most of Carr's records were dominated by the unremitting power of his voice, here he was restrained, almost defeated, resigned to the fact that his love affair could never be made public. From Carr's performance to the echoplexed cathedral of sound by the house band at Chips Moman's American Sound Studio, the record was near-perfect, with not a detail out of place.

Although "Dark End Of The Street" only reached #77 on the pop chart, it has since been covered by everyone from Clarence Carter to the Flying Burrito Brothers. Its legacy was secure, but unfortunately Carr's was not. Throughout his brief career, he was beset by emotional problems that were exacerbated by drugs. Both in the studio and on stage, he would go into near-catatonic states. After vanishing from sight when a 1971 single with Atlantic went nowhere, Carr re-emerged in 1977 with a single on Roosevelt Jamison's River City label. The single led to a 1979 tour of Japan, but he fell into a motionless trance while performing on stage in Tokyo. After disappearing from the public eye for most of the 80s, Carr released a couple of so-so albums in the early 90s – *Take Me To The Limit* (1991) and *Soul Survivor* (1994) – but his return was again beset with health problems. Lung cancer eventually took his life on January 7, 2001.

You Got My Mind Messed Up
1966, Goldwax

James Carr's debut album, recorded in Memphis, is a slice of deep Southern soul that critics mention in the same breath with the best records by Otis Redding and Percy Sledge. Carr's pleading vocal delivery on these early tracks, including the quintessential "Dark End Of The Street", is authentic and compelling.

The Essential James Carr
1995, Razor & Tie

This collection was the first time that James Carr's Goldwax singles were made available in his home country since they were originally released, and it went some way towards building the reputation of one of soul's unknown greats. His intensity may be too much for some, but there can be little doubt that there are few singers around who can match Carr's command of the tear-soaked ballad.

PLAYLIST
James Carr

1 YOU'VE GOT MY MIND MESSED UP from **The Essential James Carr**
One of the most intense gospel breakdowns in soul history.

2 LOVE ATTACK from **The Essential James Carr**
If you like Otis Redding, you'll love this.

3 I'M A FOOL FOR YOU from **The Essential James Carr**
A swaying duet that has all the things that make Southern soul eternal.

4 POURING WATER ON A DROWNING MAN from **The Essential James Carr**
Perhaps the most powerful record in the Southern soul canon.

5 THE DARK END OF THE STREET from **The Essential James Carr**
The definitive version of what is perhaps the definitive soul song.

6 A MAN NEEDS A WOMAN from **The Essential James Carr**
A splendid version of an OB McClinton standard.

7 FREEDOM TRAIN from **The Essential James Carr**
James Carr excels in The Staple Singers' territory.

8 LET IT HAPPEN from **The Essential James Carr**
Very fine end-of-the-night ballad.

9 TO LOVE SOMEBODY from **The Essential James Carr**
Right up there with Al Green's version of "How Can You Mend A Broken Heart?".

10 THAT'S THE WAY LOVE TURNED OUT FOR ME from **My Soul Is Satisfied**
After "Pouring Water" and "Dark End", this is Carr's most powerful performance.

Clarence Carter

In many ways **Clarence Carter** embodied the changes that African-American music underwent during the soul era. Having started out as an acoustic blues guitarist, the blind Carter has ancestral links to itinerant bluesmen like **Blind Willie McTell** and **Blind Willie Johnson**. Like Johnson, Carter was a sermonizer with a particularly dark vision of the human condition. On the other hand, he also had a sense of disengagement from his texts, singing in a put-on mannered fashion and often punctuating his songs with a deep chuckle – thus he recorded a version of Etta James's "I'd Rather Go Blind", as well as a song called "I Can't See Myself" – and a sense of self-reflexivity that had previously been wholly alien to soul.

Carter was born in Montgomery, Alabama, on January 14, 1936. He taught himself to play guitar from **John Lee Hooker** records, and earned a degree in music from Alabama State University. Around 1963 he began singing with schoolfriend **Calvin Scott**. They recorded a few singles for Fairlane and Duke as both Calvin and Clarence and the CL Boys. In 1965 they recorded a wonderful slice of country soul, "Step By Step", at Fame

Studios in Muscle Shoals. Soon afterwards, Scott was injured in a car crash and Carter carried on as a solo artist.

The uptempo burner "Tell Daddy" gave Carter his first solo hit in 1966, and was subsequently remade into a huge smash by Etta James. "Looking For A Fox", a bald-faced rip-off of both Them's "Gloria" and Sam & Dave, was his first Atlantic release in 1968, but he continued to record in Muscle Shoals. "Slip Away", a magnificent spare cheating blues, became his first entry into the pop Top 10 in 1968.

"Back Door Santa" offered the first glimpse of Carter's lascivious streak, but his personality was so forceful that he was just as adept as putting his stamp on non-novelty tracks. The following year's "Snatching It Back" was a typical by-numbers Southern soul side, but its B-side "Making Love (At The Dark End Of The Street)", was one of the weirdest records in the soul pantheon. A comic homily based loosely on James Carr's "Dark End Of The Street", it fused absurdity and profundity in a way only matched by George Clinton.

Carter continued to be a significant presence on the R&B chart in the late 60s and early 70s, with records like the faintly absurd "The Feeling Is Right", "I Can't Leave Your Love Alone" and "Slipped, Tripped And Fell In Love". His biggest hit, however, came with the totally absurd "Patches" in 1970, a corny story song that reached #4 on the pop chart. After a fabulously dirty version of "Sixty Minute Man" in 1973 and the sly "I Got Caught" in 1975, Carter drifted from the scene, a victim of disco and funk.

He made a small comeback with "Workin' (On A Love Building)" in 1977, before returning more prominently to the limelight on Ichiban Records in 1986, with the lewd novelty hit "Strokin'". Since then, Carter has released several albums and a steady stream of adult novelty records, including "Grandpa Can't Fly His Kite" in 1987 and, inevitably, "Still Strokin'" in 1989.

Snatching It Back: The Best Of Clarence Carter
1992, Rhino

At times, Carter can be a little too mannered and unhinged for many straight soul fans, but here, on a collection of the records that made his reputation, he's closest to the classic Southern soul mode – even if his bawdiness and irony still creep in here and there.

Alvin Cash

Had **Alvin Cash** started out in the 80s, he would probably have wound up like Kenny G or Kitaro. Thankfully, however, he came up in the 60s, when you could still specialize in instrumentals without resorting to schmaltzy love man saxuality or New Age nonsense. His prime 60s records for George Leaner's One-derful, Mar-V-Lus and Toddlin' Town labels remain delightful combinations of heat, hucksterism and hoodoo.

Born **Alvin Welch** in St Louis on February 15, 1939, Cash attended the city's legendary Sumner High School, a veritable R&B breeding ground that produced talent like Tina Turner, **Billy Davis**, Luther Ingram and **Chuck Berry**. While still in school Cash formed a dance troupe with his brothers Arthur, George and Robert called **The Crawlers**. They eventually tried their hand at music and built up a local following. Moving to Chicago in 1963 in search of a record deal, they were spotted by Andre Williams, who brought them over to Mar-V-Lus.

Alvin Cash & The Crawlers' first record, the truly marvellous "Twine Time" in 1964, was basically a sleazy Hammond B-3 vamp with interjections from a horn section that predated Junior Walker. "The Barracuda" followed in much the same style in 1965, though with a different line-up of Crawlers.

Changing their name to The Registers in 1966, the group released the ridiculously funky "The Philly Freeze", which was way ahead of its time with its distorted guitar riffs. "Alvin's Boo-Ga-Loo" was another funky groove with added dance instructions, in the same vein as Andre Williams and their cross-town rival **Jerry-O**. "Keep On Dancin'", which was released under Cash's name, was a neat harmony between the minimal guitar funk of James Brown, then on the ascendant, and the horn-heavy boogaloo that was fading out. "Funky Street" was another dance craze disc, adorned by a strange guitar riff that anticipated the sound of downtown New York avant-gardist **Robert Quine** by a good decade.

Cash left Leaner's stable after the fairly generic single "Funky '69" and released "Stone Thing", his only single for Westbound. One of the rawest funk cuts ever recorded, "Stone Thing" has since become a cult item on the

Southern Soul

Aside from Motown, the churning grooves, country piano lines, moralistic stories and gospel vocal styles of Southern soul are what nearly everyone thinks about when they think of soul music. The story of Southern soul is the story of integration and miscegenation, of hillbilly crackers working with the grandsons and grand-daughters of freedmen, of a tectonic shift in the faultline between Appalachia and the Delta.

All soul fans know about the sounds of New Orleans, Muscle Shoals in northern Alabama and the Stax and Hi labels in Memphis, but great soul music was made all across the South, even in Nashville, Texas and Virginia. **John Richbourg**'s Nashville-based Sound Stage 7 label may be one for the connoisseurs, but it released several exceptional Southern soul records in the 60s, including the deep soul classics "The Chokin' Kind" by Joe Simon, "There's A Heartbreak Somewhere" by Roscoe Shelton, "He Called Me Baby" by Ella Washington and "What Made You Change Your Mind" by Bobby King, as well as **Ann Sexton**'s rare groove favourite, 1973's "You're Gonna Miss Me".

Shelby Singleton's Nashville-based SSS International and Silver Fox labels scored with remarkable country soul recordings such as Johnny Adams' "Reconsider Me" and Bettye LaVette's "He Made A Woman Out Of Me". Meanwhile, in 1970 the House of the Fox label released "I'll Be Your Fool Once More" by **Big**

Al Downing and *Doin' Their Own Thing* by The J.B.'s' refugees **Maceo & All The King's Men**.

Texas is perhaps best known in soul circles for giving the world the great Bobby "Blue" Bland, but it also gave us the deep-throated balladeer **Joe Hinton**, whose 1964 version of Willie Nelson's "Funny" was one of the great country soul songs. Texas was also the home of **Bobby Patterson**, a journeyman with a couple of great moments: 1969's "TCB Or TYA" and 1972's "How Do You Spell Love?" – the answer was, inevitably, "M-O-N-E-Y".

Virginia may be one of the centres of contemporary R&B thanks to **Timbaland** and **The Neptunes**, but during the soul era Virginia was notable only for **Gary "US" Bonds** – who had hits in the early 60s with rollicking records like "New Orleans", "Quarter To Three" and "Dear Lady Twist" – and **Jimmy Soul**, who had an R&B #1 in 1963 with the calypso-fied "If You Wanna Be happy". The upbeat lightness of the Virginia sound was influenced by the state's proximity to the Carolinas where Beach Music was the ruling sound and homegrown act **Maurice Williams & The Zodiacs** had a big hit in 1960 with the post-doo-wop record "Stay".

Various Artists: Sweet Soul Music: Voices From The Shadows
1992, Sire

This 15-track compilation is the essential audio counterpart to Peter Guralnick's book *Sweet Soul Music:*

---

rare funk circuit – it's almost worth the Godfather's ransom you'll have to pay for it. Cash also recorded the fabulous "Funky Washing Machine" for the Sound Stage 7 label that same year, before returning to the theme he'd started in 1967 with "Doin' The Ali Shuffle". Just about every time **Muhammad Ali** had a big fight, Cash came out with a tribute song, including 1977's "Ali Shuffle", a fairly generic funk-disco offering on which he sang as though the 60s were still in full swing.

Alvin Cash remained a popular draw in Windy City clubs throughout his life, and appeared in several movies, including 1977's *Petey Wheatstraw* during the blaxploitation boom. He died in Chicago on November 21, 1999 after suffering from stomach problems.

Twine Time
1998, Mar-V-Lus

An excellent 25-track compilation that covers most of Cash's output for Mar-V-Lus. There's no attempt at profundity, just greasy grooves and a couple of hepcat phrases to keep the dancefloor moving.

Jimmy Castor

Despite having a career that extends back to the days of doo-wop, **Jimmy Castor** is one of the most underappreciated figures on the soul continuum. His position on the sidelines of soul history may owe something to his penchant for novelty numbers that have been marginalized as the modern-day equivalent of hokum jive. Or it may be because, by laying the breakbeat foundation of hip-hop on his 1972 single "It's Just Begun", he unwittingly sowed the seeds for the demise of classic soul. Even so, "The Everything Man" remains one of funk's finest practitioners; the undisputed king of the mastodon bassline thoroughly deserves a place in the soul/R&B pantheon.

Jimmy Castor was born on June 2, 1943 in Harlem, where he went to school with **Frankie Lymon**. As a nasal lead vocalist,

Rhythm And Blues And The Southern Dream Of Freedom. It's not exclusively Southern soul, but it focuses on great unheralded Southern soul cuts by artists such as Judy Clay, Don Covay, James Carr and Arthur Alexander. It also includes George Perkins & The Silver Stars' beautiful eulogy "Cryin' In The Streets".

▣ PLAYLIST

1 YOU BETTER MOVE ON Arthur Alexander from **The Ultimate Arthur Alexander**
The next decade of Southern soul and the coming of Mick Jagger unfold before your eyes.

2 RULER OF MY HEART Irma Thomas from **Crescent City Soul: The Sound of New Orleans**
Otis Redding re-recorded this as "Pain in My Heart" and took it into the pop charts, but Thomas still cuts him – perhaps the only time that ever happened.

3 TRAMP Otis Redding & Carla Thomas from **Dreams to Remember: The Otis Redding Anthology**
Otis Redding re-recording Lowell Fulsom and cutting him – not the only time that ever happened.

4 WHEN SOMETHING IS WRONG WITH MY BABY Sam & Dave from **The Very Best Of Sam & Dave**
One of the truly great soul ballads.

5 POURING WATER ON A DROWNING MAN James Carr from **The Essential James Carr**
The epitome of the Southern art – the music romps while the singer tears his guts out.

6 CALL ME (COME BACK HOME) Al Green from **Call Me**
The ultimate expression of the simplicity of the Southern blueprint.

7 HOLD WHAT YOU GOT Joe Tex from **His Greatest Hits**
Downhome country preaching set to a marvellously spare background.

8 I'D RATHER GO BLIND Etta James from **The Essential Etta James**
Etta James may be from LA, but it doesn't get any more Southern – or any better – than this.

9 I NEVER LOVED A MAN Aretha Franklin from **Queen of Soul: The Very Best of Aretha Franklin**
Why is it that singers from Michigan (see Al Green) make the best Southern soul?

10 STEAL AWAY Jimmy Hughes from **The Muscle Shoals Sound**
The archetypal cheating song.

Castor fronted **Jimmy & The Juniors**, who recorded a couple of sides for the Mercury subsidiary Wing in 1956. Their debut single, Castor's "I Promise To Remember", stalled when it was covered by Frankie Lymon & The Teenagers and taken into the Top 10. The following year, Castor took over from Lymon as lead vocalist for the Teenagers. After a stint with them, he worked as a session saxophonist in the New York area, most famously on Dave "Baby" Cortez's 1962 roller-rink organ classic, "Rinky Dink".

Castor's reign as the clown prince of Harlem began in earnest with the boogaloo craze of the mid-60s. Combining Latin percussion with soul's driving basslines, boogaloo took over America's dancefloors, and nowhere more so than in New York, with its huge Hispanic community. Castor's contribution was an inspired piece of jive called "Hey, Leroy, Your Mama's Callin' You". With a timbale groove to die for (played by Castor), and a mambo piano vamp, "Hey, Leroy" was more explicitly Latin in feel than most boogaloo records. Thanks largely to its enormous popularity in New York, it reached #31 in the American Top 40. More Latin soul records, like "Southern Fried Frijoles" and "Leroy's In The Army", followed, but failed to chart.

Six years later, Castor re-emerged with a record that made **Larry Graham**'s fuzztone bass with Sly & The Family Stone sound tame. "Troglodyte (Cave Man)" by The Jimmy Castor Bunch had a brontosaurus bass groove that fitted perfectly with its theme and title. Combining the most bottom-heavy bottom end ever with distorted guitar riffs, the most-sampled intro of all-time ("What we're going to do here is go back, way back…") and a stupid tale about Neanderthal sexuality, "Troglodyte" was Castor's biggest hit, reaching #6 in the US.

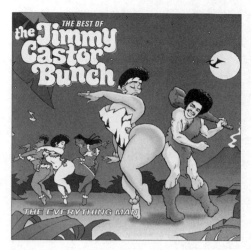

The Chairmen Of The Board / The Showmen

Modelled on the great gospel vocal groups, **The Showmen** formed in Norfolk, Virginia in the late 50s. Featuring Gene Knight, Dorsey Knight, Leslie Felton and Milton Wells, the group was led by one of soul's great unsung heroes – **Norman Johnson** (born May 23, 1943).

In addition to penning many of The Showmen's singles, Johnson was a prolific writer for the legendary production team of Holland-Dozier-Holland. He crafted hits for **Freda Payne**, **Laura Lee**, **Honey Cone** and **100 Proof Aged in Soul**, all of whom recorded for Holland-Dozier-Holland's post-Motown labels. Changing his name to **General Johnson**, he was also the leader of **The Chairmen of the Board**, who had several major R&B hits in the early 70s. A unique performer, Johnson conjured strange and wonderful sounds from his mouth and throat to match any scat singer.

The Showmen occupied an awkward position somewhere between doo-wop's last falsetto warble and soul's first assertive grunt. Their first record, 1961's "It Will Stand", may have been the best record ever made about music, although it only charted on its re-release in 1964. While it was strangely subdued for a celebratory record, "It Will Stand" succeeded musically, if not commercially, precisely because it was not hysterical – Johnson was such an original singer that any more embellishment would have over-egged the pudding.

The group's follow-up "39-21-46 (You)" eventually became an all-time slow dance classic. With its music-box piano part, vaguely Caribbean guitar line, cascades of flute and brass, and Johnson's astounding lead, the record was as unlikely as the proportions it celebrated. It was so strange that it didn't chart until four years after it was originally released, and then only at #101. "The Wrong Girl" had a real leaden beat, but included Johnson at his most soulful, while "Our Love Will Grow" offered a piston-

Even better and much more important was "It's Just Begun", a killer funk groove with lyrics about the energies of youth. The record was made by its "break", where all the instruments dropped out except for the timbales and wah-wah guitar. Played to death by DJs Kool Herc and **Afrika Bambaataa**, this section became one of the cornerstones of hip-hop.

"It's Just Begun" was Castor's greatest moment and it ensured his immortality, but his popularity on the streets, especially in New York, continued with "Say Leroy (The Creature From The Black Lagoon Is Your Father)" (a sublime piece with a spacy Latin soul groove), "Bertha Butt Boogie" (a reprise of the character from "Troglodyte"), the proto-disco of "Potential", and the devastating clavinet riff of "King Kong". Castor's hits dried up in the late 70s, just as the genre he unintentionally helped to create started to make its own noise. However, as the embodiment of post-war New York music, he will remain one of the titans of soul.

ⓞ **The Everything Man: The Best Of The Jimmy Castor Bunch**
1995, Rhino

Castor is too peripatetic a talent and has too bizarre a sense of humour to ever be considered a truly great artist, but his breadth is impressive and his commitment to both grooves and laughs will never fail to bring a smile to your face. This 17-track collection is a fine distillation of his career, even though his stupid jokes tend to undermine his prodigious talent.

pumping rhythm and dangling string fills. "Our Love Will Grow" later became a favourite on the UK's Northern soul scene, but Stateside success continued to elude the group, and they broke up in 1967.

Holland-Dozier-Holland were big fans of The Showmen and, after the group broke up, persuaded Johnson to come to Detroit to work with their new Invictus label. Teamed with Danny Woods, Eddie Curtis and Harrison Kennedy, Johnson formed **The Chairmen of the Board** in 1969. Their first single, "Give Me Just A Little More Time" was a smash hit in 1970 and helped to create the blueprint for the crossover between pop, easy listening and soul. However, none of the records that followed could duplicate Johnson's simultaneously lachrymose and optimistic vocals.

The next year's "Pay To The Piper" had a clumsy arrangement, but **Danny Woods'** lead was intense and assertive, and a great foil for Johnson's tearful wails. Although the group had further sizable hits with "Chairman Of The Board" and "Finder's Keepers", HDH's hit-making touch began to falter. Johnson's voice was perhaps too singular to sustain a long chart career. He abandoned his signature sound in favour of a so-so Al Green imitation on "Only Time Will Tell" in 1973, but to no avail.

A final album, 1974's *Skin I'm In*, saw the group shift tack entirely to a hard funk sound recorded with Funkateers **Eddie Hazel** and **Bernie Worrell**. "You've Got Extra Added Power In Your Love", a by-the-numbers disco track with an utterly bizarre guitar line that sounded as though it had been lifted wholesale from *Frampton Comes Alive*, was the group's last single before they broke up in 1976.

After a solo deal with Arista merely resulted in a string of half-hearted disco records, Johnson retreated to the Carolinas beach music circuit and formed Surfside Records with Mike Branch. He reformed The Chairmen of the Board with Woods and **Ken Knox** in 1980, and they recorded a series of beach standards throughout the 80s: "On The Beach", "Down At The Beach Club", "Carolina Girls", "Lover Boy" and "Gone Fishin'". The Chairmen are still performing live and remain enormously popular among the "Shaggers" in the Carolinas.

The Showmen – It Will Stand
1990 Collectables

This 16-track collection can't be called complete – it doesn't include the Northern soul favourite "Our Love Will Grow" and it is padded out with unnecessary alternate takes. However, it is the only available collection of the work of this terminally underrated vocal group.

The Charmen Of The Board – Everything's Tuesday: The Best Of Chairmen Of The Board
2000, Invictus

A fine 22-track compilation that covers all the stages of the Chairmen's career before their more recent beach-music renaissance. It includes not only all their chart hits, but gems like the original version of "Patches", as made famous by Clarence Carter, and a couple of tracks from the underrated *Skin I'm In* album.

Gene Chandler

In the popular imagination, **Gene Chandler** will forever be associated with the nostalgia favourite "Duke Of Earl", which is a shame, because there's much more to him than that. Although perhaps not blessed with a great instrument, Chandler approached soul singing with subtlety and nuance, and, along with Jerry Butler and The Impressions, helped to define what we think of as classic Chicago soul.

Chandler was born **Eugene Dixon** in Chicago on July 6, 1937, and grew up singing in street-corner doo-wop groups. He first made a name for himself as a member of **The Dukays**. They released two singles, "Girl Is A Devil" and "Nite Owl", for the Nat label in 1961 that were caught in the netherworld between doo-wop and soul. Switching to Vee Jay, they recorded "Duke Of Earl" in 1962, which was released under Dixon's *nom de guerre*, Gene Chandler. With its comic "Duke, Duke, Duke, Duke of Earl" chant, the record was a huge hit among teenage rock'n'roll fans, reaching #1 on both the pop and R&B charts. However, Chandler's soaring falsetto vocals also marked it as a soul record of the highest order.

Chandler went solo in 1963, and firmly established his soul credentials on the magnificent "Rainbow". Employing every trick in the book on this virtual catalogue of the soul man's art, Chandler delivered one of the most impressive vocal performances of early soul music. He followed later that year with the Curtis Mayfield number "Man's Temptation", which showcased his lovely falsetto at its very best.

Moving to the Constellation label, Chandler worked with producer **Carl Davis** on a series of classic Chicago ballads, including "Just Be True", "Bless Our Love", "What Now" and "You Can't Hurt Me No More". The uptempo "Nothing Can Stop Me", a total Impressions rip, became a top-five R&B hit in 1965, a feat soon matched by "Rainbow 65", a live version of his classic "Rainbow". Chandler's last record for Constellation, 1966's lightweight "Mr. Big Shot", became a huge hit at the Wigan Casino in the 70s.

In 1966 "I Fooled You This Time", a classic Chicago soul arrangement that turned into a dog's dinner on the chorus, became yet another big R&B hit, this time for Checker Records. Moving to Brunswick, Chandler recorded the lilting ballad "There Goes The Lover", before cutting a couple of excellent duets with Barbara Acklin in 1968, "Show Me The Way To Go" and "From The Teacher To The Preacher".

When production styles changed in the late 60s and early 70s, Chandler initially fared well, floating on top of wah-wah riffs on "In My Body's House" and swinging like crazy on the very groovy "Groovy Situation", which provided his biggest hit since "Duke Of Earl". By the release of "Don't Have To Be Lying" in 1972, however, Chandler was sounding distinctly uncomfortable, even if the production itself was a real proto-disco classic. Little was heard from Chandler for most of the disco era, though he did come bursting back in 1978 with the fabulous disco track "Get Down", released while he was in jail on drug-related offences. "When You're #1" and "Does She Have A Friend?" briefly kept the momentum going, but Chandler's chart career soon fizzled out. His swansong came with a version of **Lionel Richie**'s "Lucy" in 1986.

 Live At The Regal
1986, Charly

This may not be the equal of James Brown performing at the Apollo or Sam Cooke at the Harlem Square Club, but it is, nevertheless, a superb concert recorded on home territory in 1965 that shows why Chandler was such a big draw on the soul circuit. Chandler simply oozes charisma and his energy is breathtaking, which is surprising coming from a performer noted for his unruffled exterior.

Nothing Can Stop Me: Gene Chandler's Greatest Hits
1994, Varese Sarabande

This 20-track compilation spans Chandler's career from The Dukays' "Nite Owl" in 1961 to the disco-oriented "Does She Have A Friend?" in 1980, and includes all of his biggest and most popular hits. An excellent overview of a very underrated singer.

Ray Charles

Ray Charles is justly credited with changing the course of music history by incorporating gospel vocal techniques and instrumentation into the small-combo R&B style of the late 40s and early 50s, and thereby inventing soul. Even though Billy Ward & The Dominoes, The Clovers and The "5" Royales had all released records that bore the influence of gospel before Ray Charles, it's not always who got there first that matters. Unquestionably, Charles's records were the most startling and had the most impact. **Clyde McPhatter** of The Dominoes, **Buddy Bailey** of The Clovers and **Johnny Tanner** of The "5" Royales were all good singers, but Charles was one of the half a dozen greatest singers in popular music, and he practically created its post-war lexicon.

What's more, while his nimble swing and suggestive grunts and groans liberated libidos throughout the world, his country recordings of the 60s exposed another secret – that the nasal twangs and weepy timbres of country music were based on, and developed in close contact with, the black American music of the early twentieth century. Whether you consider him merely an important formal stylist or an epochal figure in American cultural history, Ray Charles more than deserves his epithet, "The Genius".

He was born in Florida on September 23, 1930 as **Ray Charles Robinson**, but later changed his name to avoid confusion with the well-known boxer Sugar Ray Robinson. After going blind at the age of six, he was sent to the St. Augustine School for the Deaf and Blind, where he received his musical training. After cutting several records that were largely derivative of the piano trio style of Nat "King" Cole and Charles Brown, Ray Charles signed with Atlantic Records.

Ray Charles at the keys

Charles's early releases for Atlantic consisted of fun, jivey material, until a 1954 session in Atlanta proved a turning point both in his own career and in the history of popular music. Working with his own band, Charles arranged and produced the session himself: the result was one of the two or three most important singles ever released, "Come Back Baby"/"I've Got A Woman". With the galloping, Holy-Roller rhythm track and vocal swoops of "I've Got A Woman" and the pleading singing and churchy piano figures of "Come Back Baby" – lifted straight from the gospel standard "Move On Up A Little Higher" – the single marked the true beginnings of soul music.

Charles continued to push the gospel elements to the fore. His arrangement of "Drown In My Own Tears" could have been drawn from any Southern Baptist church, while his stunning vocals lead the assembled congregation of saxes and backing voices towards the secular baptism of the title. "Hallelujah I Love Her So" began with a piano that was a dead ringer for **Mildred Falls**, Mahalia Jackson's long-time accompanist, while "Leave My Woman Alone" featured a rhythm lifted wholesale from the gospel standard "Old Landmark". That song's flip, "Lonely Avenue", marked the first appearance of vocal group The Cookies (who soon became **The Raeletts**) as background vocalists to enhance the Sunday-morning feel of Charles's recordings. The vocal interplay between Charles and lead Raelett, **Margie Hendrix**, became the defining characteristic of Charles's greatest record, 1959's "What'd I Say", and the almost-as-good "Tell The Truth".

PLAYLIST
Ray Charles

1 I GOT A WOMAN from **Genius & Soul: The 50th Anniversary Collection**
This is the genesis of soul.

2 WHAT'D I SAY from **Genius & Soul: The 50th Anniversary Collection**
Lust as a revival meeting – one of the most influential records ever.

3 DROWN IN MY OWN TEARS from **Genius & Soul: The 50th Anniversary Collection**
Perhaps not as epochal as "What'd I Say" or "I've Got A Woman", but every bit as good.

4 TELL THE TRUTH from **Genius & Soul: The 50th Anniversary Collection**
Call and response the way it was meant to be.

5 GEORGIA ON MY MIND from **Genius & Soul: The 50th Anniversary Collection**
Not his best record, but surely his most remarkable.

6 HIT THE ROAD JACK from **Genius & Soul: The 50th Anniversary Collection**
That rarest of records: a charming and delightful break-up song.

7 UNCHAIN MY HEART from **Genius & Soul: The 50th Anniversary Collection**
Another wonderful break-up song, but this is perhaps even more insidiously catchy.

8 I CAN'T STOP LOVING YOU from **Genius & Soul: The 50th Anniversary Collection**
In many ways this is as revolutionary as "What'd I Say" or "I've Got A Woman".

9 LET'S GO GET STONED from **Genius & Soul: The 50th Anniversary Collection**
When he had decent material like this, Charles was as good as anyone in the mid-60s.

10 I DON'T NEED NO DOCTOR from **Genius & Soul: The 50th Anniversary Collection**
The Genius's last moment of genius.

After shocking and delighting the world in equal measure with his heretical singing, sexual frankness and creation of a new genre, Charles set out to lay waste to the songbook of American standards. His stunning version of Hoagy Carmichael's "Georgia On My Mind" became his first pop #1 in 1960, a remarkable feat considering the racial unrest of the time. His incredibly emotive vocal performance imbued a piece of Dixie nostalgia with a complexity and power that were never there before, and a meaning that was certainly never intended.

Charles found further, albeit lighter-weight, pop success in 1961 with his loungey version of "One Mint Julep", the breezy "Hit The Road Jack" and the swinging "Unchain My Heart". That same year the album *Ray Charles & Betty Carter* teamed the two idiosyncratic vocalists with mixed results, though they did create the definitive version of "Baby, It's Cold Outside".

In 1962 Charles shocked the musical establishment even more deeply with *Modern Sounds In Country & Western Music*. The album featured versions of country standards, including the epic "I Can't Stop Loving You", which was a pop #1 for five weeks. The album proved to be the most popular of his career and had a wide appeal that sent it to the top of the pop charts. Just a few months later Charles released *Modern Sounds, Vol. 2*, which included the swinging "You Are My Sunshine" and the smoky "Your Cheating Heart".

Many of Ray Charles's mid-60s recordings had very fine qualities, but by that time other artists had taken up – and were advancing – the mantle of soul, and he was starting to become little more than a cabaret act. As his records drowned in treacle and Mantovani strings, he made more of an impact on the easy-listening scene than he did on the soul charts. During the ensuing years, his only record to have any relevance for the emerging soul scene was the bluesy "Let's Go Get Stoned" in 1966, though the chugging "I Don't Need No Doctor" displayed Charles and The Raelettes in fine form, and became a hit on the Northern soul scene despite its muddy sound.

In the late 60s "Sweet Young Thing Like You" and "Let Me Love You" found Charles getting funky in a slightly dated style, but at least they were better than the **Swingle Singers** schlock he had peddled for most of the decade. Quincy Jones stepped in to stop the rot in 1972, arranging Charles's *A Message From The People* album. While hardly perfect – check the John Denver and Melanie covers – it, nevertheless, featured better material than Charles had been producing for quite some time. Charles sounded like he wasn't just churning the album out to fulfil his contract, especially on his remarkable version of "America The Beautiful".

The similar album, *Renaissance*, from 1975 held great renditions of Stevie Wonder's "Livin' For The City", Randy Newman's "Sail Away" and, oddly, **Kermit the Frog**'s "It's Not Easy Being Green". Charles then flirted with disco for the next few years – a really bad idea – churning out genre exercises that, every so often, had a spark of inspiration. He returned to the top of the R&B charts once more in 1989, singing with **Chaka Khan** on Quincy Jones's version of the **Brothers Johnson**'s "I'll Be Good To You".

Ray Charles spent the bulk of the 90s touring, shilling for Pepsi and recording the occasional album. His final record was the unfortunately drab and predictable duets album, 2004's *Genius Loves Company*. On June 10, 2004, the Genius finally succumbed to liver disease at his home in Beverly Hills, but his profile remains as high as ever, largely thanks to Jamie Foxx's superb portrayal in the biopic *Ray*.

Modern Sounds In Country And Western Music
1962, ABC-Paramount

Having already expanded his sound by incorporating big-band and string arrangements into his gospel-tinged R&B, Charles's ground-breaking 1962 album applied all of the same techniques to country standards. He took the twang out and put the soul in and, in the process, synthesized a new, fresh kind of popular American music.

Anthology
1990, Rhino

This collection includes the very best of his 60s hits for ABC-Paramount. From the country sounds of "I Can't Stop Loving You" and "Crying Time" to the soul stomp of "Hit The Road Jack" to the anthemic "Georgia On My Mind", this album displays the many varying styles that were always so uniquely Ray Charles.

The Best Of Ray Charles: The Atlantic Years
1994, Rhino

On a single disc you get the cream of Ray Charles's singles from the 50s, including the classic "What'd I Say?" and "Lonely Avenue" and earlier hits like "I Got A Woman" and "Fool For You". This is prime stuff: vintage Atlantic R&B and vintage Ray Charles. Culled from a much greater body of work, there isn't a dud here.

Genius & Soul: The 50th Anniversary Collection
1997, Rhino

This 5-CD set is far too heavily weighted towards Charles's post-1966 career – a full forty percent – but it's still a fabulous collection that documents pretty much the entirety of one of the most important bodies of work in popular music. As the only set to include his epochal records for both Atlantic and ABC-Paramount, it's an essential purchase for anyone interested in the development of not only soul, but popular music as a whole.

Cherrelle

Cherrelle was a prime R&B hitmaker in the mid- to late 80s, thanks to the interaction between her girlish, innocent voice and the synthscapes crafted for her by producers **Jimmy Jam** and **Terry Lewis**. She was born Cheryl Norton in 1958 in Los Angeles, but earned the nickname Cherrelle while working as a bank teller. Her family moved to Detroit in the 70s, and it was there that she was discovered by singer/bassist **Michael Henderson**, who was her parents' neighbour.

Cherrelle sang back-up for Henderson in the late 70s and early 80s on his *In The Night Time*, *Do It All* and *Wide Receiver* albums, and also accompanied him on tour. She eventually decided to step out on her own, and signed to Tabu in 1983. Working with house producers Jam & Lewis, she immediately achieved a big R&B hit with 1984's "I Didn't Mean To Turn You On", which was later covered by **Robert Palmer**, the 80s equivalent of Pat Boone. While Cherrelle was fine, it was the production – the trademark Minneapolis stomp and skidding keyboards – that made the record.

In 1985, "Saturday Love", a duet with labelmate Alexander O'Neal, went to #2 on the R&B charts. Even though it had a great hook, it was less appealing than her earlier hit, being in the MOR style that Jam and Lewis were to perfect on their 1986 record with **Human League**, "Human". Another duet with O'Neal, "Never Knew Love Like This", replicated its success in 1988, with its over-processed production and sanitized growling and squealing.

The postmodern nightclub ballad "Everything I Miss At Home" gave Cherrelle her only #1 R&B hit in 1988, although the similar "Affair" went into the Top 5 the following year. Cherrelle was never quite able to attract a crossover audience and, once Jam and Lewis moved their concentration to Janet Jackson instead of her, Cherrelle's records sank, receiving little interest even from urban radio.

○ **The Best Of Cherrelle**
1995, Tabu/Motown

There's too much filler on Cherrelle's original albums, so this compilation is the obvious choice. She doesn't put a foot wrong, but the stars of the show are undoubtedly Jam & Lewis, who defined the sound of the late 80s with these recordings.

Chic

Rock fans used to talk about disco denizens as if they were lemmings marching to the cliffs, while soul patrons lampooned them as robots who were faking the funk. Chic were criticized for offering escapist music even though pop music is meant to be all about escape in the first place; and why these same people didn't say the same thing about Marvin Gaye and Tammi Terrell singing "If I Could Build My Whole World Around You" while Detroit was burning around them remains a mystery.

In any case, the mid- to late 70s cried out for that kind of music, and nowhere more so than in New York. In a climate of stagflation, when the city owed fealty to the bond-issuing robber barons who had bailed it out of bankruptcy, when the mercenary laissez-faire capitalism of the 80s was just starting to take hold, and when Reagan and the rollback of Civil Rights legislation was just around the corner, the only possible reaction was escapism. But Chic were about more than escape. While they enjoyed shaking their groove thing as much as anybody, they also recognized the limitations of hedonism, and saw its dangers.

For all their smarts and oddball touches, though, it was the grooves that everyone listened to. Nile Rodgers was one of the greatest rhythm guitar players of all time and Bernard Edwards was certainly one of the five most creative bassists ever. With drummer Tony Thompson, "the human metronome", behind them, the two distilled and updated Motown, James Brown, Stax and Miles Davis into the most lethal rhythmic attack of the last quarter century.

Rodgers and Edwards had gone through numerous bands and musical styles – including both punk rock and a ferociously metallic brand of Miles Davis-esque jazz-fusion, either of which would have cleared the floor at Studio 54 in the blink of an eye – before settling on the graceful funk of Chic. In 1976, with the disco boom in full swing, they recruited Thompson along with vocalists Alfa Anderson and Norma Jean Wright to produce a sardonic dancefloor anthem called "Dance, Dance, Dance". After a string of rejections, the record was finally picked up by Atlantic. Over a galloping rhythm, Anderson and Wright intoned the title phrase like deer caught in the headlights. To drive the point home, they borrowed Gig Young's catch phrase ("Yowsah, yowsah, yowsah") from the film *They Shoot Horses, Don't They?*, Sidney Lumet's attack on the American psyche set during a dance marathon. Typically of the mind-set that these art-rockers-at-heart were lampooning, no one got the joke, and "Dance, Dance, Dance" reached #6 on the American charts in 1977.

While their record was riding high in the charts, Rodgers and Edwards were invited to attend a party at Studio 54 by Grace Jones. Even though their record was being played inside, the duo couldn't get in. Returning to the studio to work out some aggression, they came up with a snarling, popping funk vamp that even James Brown wouldn't have touched, and, with Studio 54's bouncers in mind, called it "Fuck Off". A few days later, after they had calmed down, the chant "Aaahhh, fuck off!" became "Aaahhh, freak out!", and one of the best-selling singles of all time was born. While the words may have changed, the attitude was still there. With Luci Martin replacing Wright, the disembodied vocalists, who served as narrators, mocked the disco-as-liberation ethic with odd, deadpan lyrics that had no place in a song about a dance craze: "Night and days, uhhh, stomping at the Savoy/Now we freak, oh what a joy", "Big fun to be had by everyone/It's up to you, surely it can be done". Yet again, Chic had it both ways: they treated their audience with as much scorn as the Sex Pistols, but still managed to sell some six million copies of "Le Freak".

The success of "Le Freak" allowed Rodgers and Edwards to produce for outside artists. The music on Norma Jean Wright's 1978 *Norma Jean* is as good as any Chic album, even if the songwriting isn't quite up to par. The pair also managed to turn journeywomen Sister Sledge into superstars and to coax great records out of Diana Ross. However, the less

Chic's Nile Rogers – the genius of his guitar playing was transparent

said about **Debbie Harry**'s 1981 *KooKoo* album, the better.

In 1979 Chic's third album, *Risqué*, kicked off with disco's crowning achievement, "Good Times". A brilliant single that worked perfectly in the context of the album, "Good Times" was also one of the most influential records of the time, helping to kick off hip-hop with its use on **Sugar Hill Gang**'s "Rapper's Delight" and **Grandmaster Flash**'s "The Adventures Of Grandmaster Flash On The Wheels Of Steel", and was ripped off almost note for note by **Queen**'s "Another One Bites The Dust".

As with all of their best work, Chic had it both ways on "Good Times". With Bernard Edwards' stunning bassline and Nile Rodgers' seething guitar work, the record bumped like a real mother. However, the scything strings and ghostly piano gave the game away. As vocalists Alfa Anderson and Luci Martin intoned catch phrases like they were in a valium haze, the pep rally that "Good Times" at first seemed to be, gradually grew harder and harder to believe. Evocations of the good life such as "Clams on the half shell and roller-skates, rollerskates" were so absurd that not even Carly Simon could have sung the lyrics

seriously. Then, with the repetition of the second chorus, the song's sense of impending doom became clear: "A rumor has it that it's getting late/Time marches on, just can't wait/The clock keeps turning, why hesitate?/You silly fool, you can't change your fate".

Throughout the album's second half, sadism kept cropping up in the lyrics ("Love is pain and pain could be pleasure", "The way you treated me, you'd think I were into S&M"). Perhaps even more revealing were the lines, sounding like slogans from a political rally or extracts from the Iran-Contra trial transcripts, that leapt out fully formed from the disembodied vocals: "Now you've got yours, what about me?", "That sinister appearance and the lies/Whew, those alibis".

The 1980 album *Real People* also championed dance music as a way of shaking the heebie-jeebies, but with disco in its final death throes and in-fighting between the band and the record label, its venom was more direct and less cryptic. *Take It Off* followed in 1981, *Tongue In Chic* in 1982 and *Believer* in 1983, all serving up a similar, spare, angular post-disco/post-funk style, but without the spite of *Real People* or the eerie detachment of the earlier records.

PLAYLIST
Chic

1 DANCE, DANCE, DANCE (YOWSAH, YOWSAH, YOWSAH) from **Chic**
The first record that didn't remove sub-bass tones, so you can feel the bottom end in your bowels.

2 LE FREAK from **C'est Chic**
Maybe the archest, most ambiguous dance-craze disc ever.

3 AT LAST I AM FREE from **C'est Chic**
Who says a dance band can't move you to tears?

4 GOOD TIMES from **Risqué**
Hands down the greatest disco track and one of the most influential records of the last 30 years.

5 MY FORBIDDEN LOVER from **Risqué**
Yet another of Chic's remarkable explorations of fate and dancefloor fatalism.

6 CHIP OFF THE OLD BLOCK from **Real People**
Oedipal rage never sounded so good.

7 LOST IN MUSIC Sister Sledge from **We Are Family**
Chic provided everything but the lead vocals on this perfect ode to the power of music.

8 SATURDAY Norma Jean from **Norma Jean**
A cult disco classic that features one of Bernard Edwards' most outlandish basslines.

9 I'M COMING OUT Diana Ross from **Diana**
Not since The Supremes' heyday had Diana Ross sounded this good – and again it's Bernard Edwards and Nile Rodgers we have to thank.

10 WHY Carly Simon from **Soup For One**
Perhaps Chic's greatest feat – making Carly Simon listenable.

dalliance with his production of Robert Palmer's *Riptide* in 1985, and his work on **Mick Jagger**'s *She's The Boss* that same year. Thompson, meanwhile, was the drummer for the supergroup **Power Station**.

Rodgers and Edwards re-formed Chic in 1992 with vocalists **Sylver Logan Sharp** and **Jenn Thomas**, and drummers Sonny Emory and Sterling Campbell. The resulting album, *Chic-ism*, was a fine nostalgic blast, but it was somewhat dated by the drum machine programming and early 90s house tempos. *Chic Freak And More Treats* from 1995 was an album of re-recorded old hits made exclusively for the Japanese market, where they remained huge stars.

The group toured Japan in 1996 with an entourage that included Sister Sledge, Simon Le Bon, Slash from **Guns'n'Roses** and Steve Winwood. Sadly, however, after the show on April 18, 1996, Edwards died suddenly from pneumonia. A recording of this final concert, *Chic Live At Budokan*, was released as a tribute to Edwards in 1999. Thompson, who had spent part of the 90s playing with **Nine Inch Nails**, died of cancer of the kidney in 2003. Despite these tragedies, Rodgers remains a vital presence in the music scene. His Sumthing Else distribution company is the only African-American owned distribution channel, a potent reminder that this former Black Panther's music was never just about a facile disco groove.

Risqué
1979, Atlantic

From the unsurpassed "Good Times" onwards, *Risqué* focuses on the impossibility of changing your fate and rails against sadistic lovers. A more perfect metaphor for the Thatcher-Reagan era could not be found. The filler fluff of "Warm Summer Night" provides the one breath of fresh air.

Dance, Dance, Dance: The Best Of Chic
1991, Atlantic

If you just want the hits, this is the Chic compilation to go for. For subtle, nuanced dance music that makes you respond with your mind as well as your muscles, the records compiled here have never been bettered.

The Chi-Lites

The Chi-Lites were perhaps the quintessential 70s vocal group. Excelling at both the forlorn falsetto ballads that were the speciality of The Delfonics and The Stylistics, and the

Even after Chic broke up in 1983, they still reigned over contemporary music. In the UK, groups like **Duran Duran** (whose stated aim was to combine the Sex Pistols and Chic), ABC, Spandau Ballet and Haircut 100 all owed their sound and looks to Chic and **David Bowie**. So it was no surprise when Rodgers was enlisted to produce the Thin White Duke's *Let's Dance* in 1983 and Duran Duran's finest record, "Notorious", in 1986. Rodgers was also partially responsible for turning **Madonna** into the world's most famous woman with his production of *Like A Virgin* in 1984. Edwards had a briefer chart more assertive, uptempo declarations of pride and betrayal exemplified by The O'Jays and The Temptations, they blended the two dominant strains of 70s soul into a single package.

The Chi-Lites emerged from Chicago's deep doo-wop tradition. Key members of two struggling doo-wop groups – **Eugene Record**, **Robert "Squirrel" Lester** and **Clarence Johnson** from The Chantours, and **Marshall Thompson** and **Creadel "Red" Jones** from The Desideros – combined to form The Hi-Lites in 1960. Signing to Mercury, the group released "Pots And Pans" in 1961, but the only attention it attracted came from another set of Hi-Lites. Changing their name to The Chi-Lites, they released a couple of singles on the Daran label – including the most local hit "I'm So Jealous" – before Clarence Johnson left the group in 1964.

After The Chi-Lites signed to Brunswick in 1968, lead singer Eugene Record started working as a songwriter and producer with Barbara Acklin, whom he would later marry. The Chi-Lites finally achieved their first national hit in 1969 with "Give It Away", a fine midtempo ballad on which Record featured prominently. The loping follow-up "Let Me Be The Man My Daddy Was" had more of a group sound, while the much more uptempo "Are You My Woman? (Tell Me So)" was a minor classic among the paranoid soul songs that dominated the airwaves at the time. Its fabulous intro was later pilfered by **Beyoncé Knowles** of Destiny's Child for her massive solo hit "Crazy In Love" in 2003.

The more assertive "(For God's Sake) Give More Power To The People" and "We Are Neighbours" followed in a similar fiery style in 1971, but the group changed tack for their biggest hits, the lachrymose ballads "Have You Seen Her" and "Oh Girl", which both made #1 on the R&B chart. Another beautiful ballad came in the shape of "The Coldest Days Of My Life", which didn't sink to the bathetic lows of "Have You Seen Her". With the exception of the so-so "We Need Order" and the superb "Stoned Out Of My Mind", The Chi-Lites largely abandoned uptempo funk in the early 70s in favour of ballads: "A Letter To Myself", "Homely Girl" and the mawkish "Toby".

Although "Toby" proved to be the group's last entry into the R&B Top 10 for almost a decade, unlike many of their contemporaries The Chi-Lites excelled during the disco era, even if they didn't sell as many records as they deserved. "You Don't Have To Go", a pleasant midtempo groover, marked Eugene Record's final outing with the group in 1976. After he left for an unsuccessful solo career, The Chi-Lites (now featuring a line-up of Thompson, **David Scott**, **Danny Johnson** and **Doc Roberson**) released their finest disco record. The burning "My First Mistake" from 1977 must be one of the most intense dancefloor exorcisms ever recorded.

The Chi-Lites re-formed in 1980 with all of the original members, except Clarence Johnson, and scored surprising success with such post-disco dance tracks as "Hot On A

PLAYLIST
The Chi-Lites

1 GIVE IT AWAY from **20 Greatest Hits**
One of Eugene Record's finest performances.

2 ARE YOU MY WOMAN? (TELL ME SO) from **20 Greatest Hits**
Does this record have the funkiest intro ever?

3 (FOR GOD'S SAKE) GIVE MORE POWER TO THE PEOPLE from **20 Greatest Hits**
Not exactly The Temptations, but very fine paranoid soul nevertheless.

4 HAVE YOU SEEN HER from **20 Greatest Hits**
That guitar!

5 OH GIRL from **20 Greatest Hits**
The harmonica is so cornpone, but it sums up early-70s AM radio perfectly.

6 THE COLDEST DAYS OF MY LIFE from **20 Greatest Hits**
Peter Nero meets doo-wop.

7 STONED OUT OF MY MIND from **20 Greatest Hits**
This is perhaps a bit over-arranged, but Eugene Record is at his best here.

8 YOU DON'T HAVE TO GO from **20 Greatest Hits**
A fine midtempo disco groove.

9 MY FIRST MISTAKE from **The Fantastic Chi-Lites**
Intense disco floor-filler that's been sampled dozens of times since.

10 HOT ON A THING (CALLED LOVE) from **Me & You**
Nifty early-80s dance track.

Disco

While many contemporary commentators thought that the D-word was, as one-hit wonders **Ottawan** might have put it, "D – distasteful, I – insipid, S – superficial, C – crap, O – *oy vey*", the reality was that disco posed as much of a challenge to the status quo as punk, hiphop, rock'n'roll or any other "revolutionary" genre of music. Attempting both to banish the veneer of naturalism and authenticity ascribed to black music once and for all and to be the embodiment of the pleasure-is-politics ethos of the emerging Gay Pride movement, disco was a celebration of the fantastic in which flash, overwhelming melodrama, sex, surface and fabulousness were all that mattered.

It's true that disco's political thrust may have been largely apprehended only "in the mix". That is to say, as a participant in marathon, nocturnal trance sessions, in which poppers, strobe lights, tight trousers and a seamless mix of hysterical diva vocals, African and Latin American polyrhythms, unintentionally camp English-as-foreign-language songs from Spain and Italy and a relentless machine beat created a ritual of outlaw desire and physical abandon that existed outside the straight and narrow. However, disco was also capable of making political statements that even the most die-hard modernist could understand.

Take, for instance, **Machine**'s "There But For The Grace Of God Go I". Written and produced by **August Darnell** (the man responsible for both **Dr. Buzzard's Original Savannah Band** and **Kid Creole & The Coconuts**), the record was a morality play set to a throbbing electro-bassline, glittering keyboard licks and a four-to-the-floor beat. With dramatic piano chords introducing the action, the song told the story of Carlo and Carmen Vidale, who moved to the suburbs "with no blacks, no Jews and no gays" to raise their kid. With perhaps predictable irony, their daughter eventually turned into a rock'n'roll-loving "natural freak" and ran away from home aged 16. At a time when American inner cities were being ravaged by white flight, the song's message was clear, particularly to a dancefloor full of blacks, Jews and gays.

Admittedly, though, "There But For The Grace Of God Go I" was a rarity – great songwriting was never disco's strong point. Groove was. Disco's rhythmic impetus was created in the newly liberated gay clubs of New York in the very early 70s by early DJs such as **Francis Grasso**, **David Mancuso** and **Nicky Siano**, who

all homed in on records whose rhythms either slowly surged or grabbed you by the neck from the get-go. Disco's fierce rhythmic focus was part of a tribal celebration for gay men, who were beginning to throw off the shackles of centuries of oppression. Just as the Civil Rights Movement was the model for the Gay Pride Movement, so too was soul music the foundation for disco.

Disco's strict 4/4 beat was probably created by producer **Norman Whitfield** in 1973 on **The Temptations**' apocalyptic funk record "Law Of The Land". The skipping hi-hats, the subtle but crucial conga fills, the hand claps, the dubbing effects that Whitfield put on the horns, the hooky string lines and the uprooted gospel keyboards encompassed almost the whole of disco in one five-minute microcosm.

The disco beat, though, was created by the battery that played on almost all of the classic Philadelphia International records, drummer **Earl Young** and bassist **Ronnie Baker**. On **Harold Melvin & The Blue Notes**' "The Love I Lost", Ronnie Baker wrapped a rubber band around his bass strings at the bridge in order to get a thumpy sound that propelled the music forward, while Young unleashed a war dance on the kick drum with a shuffle on the snare, accenting the off-beats using an open hi-hat. The result was the hissing hi-hat sound that has dominated dance music since the record was first released in September 1973.

Unfortunately Young's new rhythm was quickly appropriated by seemingly every drummer and producer in the business and rather too liberally applied across thousands of records. When the record industry – reeling from years in the doldrums – realised that they could have hits with records that followed this formula, Young's disco beat was hastily thrown behind every singer from Rod Stewart to Ethel Merman. It all became a bit too much and disco was villified as the antithesis of soul music and the enemy of rock'n'roll.

While disco undoubtedly became utterly formulaic, it was at its most revolutionary when it sought to explore new spaces in between the notes. One of disco's great space cadets was **Arthur Russell**, a peripatetic eccentric of the kind that seem to be unique to New York. Russell studied under the great Indian sarod player, Ali Akbar Khan, was a key player in the Big Apple's "new music" scene and collaborated with the likes of **Philip Glass**, **John Cage** and

Laurie Anderson. He brought all this to the table when he created his deconstructionist disco. Working with DJ **Steve D'Acquisto**, Russell sculpted a crucial underground disco cut, **Loose Joints'** "Is It All Over My Face?". Featuring a bass-heavy, but simultaneously airy, groove, an almost out-of-tune guitar, abrupt edits and one of the just plain weirdest vocals ever – check out the guy mumbling at one point – "All Over My Face" was unique and one of the building blocks of house music. Recorded under the name Dinosaur L, Russell's "Go Bang!" was even weirder and, in the classic **François Kevorkian** mix, was even more of an influence on subsequent dance music producers.

Whatever its critics may have decreed at the time, disco has had a profound influence on popular music from the way it is produced to the way it sounds. House, techno, trance, drum'n'bass and garage wouldn't exist without disco, and it's entirely possible that hiphop wouldn't either. Contemporary production techniques like remixing, editing and mash-ups were all pioneered by disco producers and DJs. While America may now be dominated by hiphop – disco's evil twin – some seventy percent of the European charts would sound completely different if it were not for disco. Whether you think disco is part of the soul continuum or that it should be banished forever from the church of African-American music, the truth is that disco is as much an extension and continuation of the soul tradition as funk, R&B or anything else you care to mention.

Various Artists: Jumpin'
1997, Harmless

While hundreds of disco compilations offer tracks such as "I Will Survive" and "Got To Be Real?", *Jumpin'* is one of the few to feature the underground die-hards – Loose Joints' "Is It All Over My Face", Machine's "There But For The Grace Of God Go I", Dinosaur L's "Go Bang" and Wood, Brass & Steal's "Funkanova" – and not just the bandwagon-jumpers.

Various Artists: Give Your Body Up: Club Classics And House Foundations Vols. 1–3
1995, Rhino

This well-compiled and brilliantly annotated three-volume series amply demonstrates disco's profound influence on popular music. Volume 3 is the pick of the bunch, featuring Eddie Kendricks' "Girl You Need A Change Of Mind" – another contender for title of first disco record – Dan Hartman's anthemic "Vertigo/Relight My Fire" and Phreek's proto-garage classic "Weekend", but Volumes 1 and 2 are quite crucial too.

PLAYLIST

1 LAW OF THE LAND The Temptations from **Masterpiece**
The relentless 4/4 beat marks this as perhaps the first disco record.

2 TEN PERCENT Double Exposure
The first commercially available 12" single is also one of the best, thanks to a decadent mix by Walter Gibbons.

3 DON'T LEAVE ME THIS WAY Thelma Houston from **Any Way You Like It**
Contains nearly every element of classic disco: the skipping hi-hats, the popping bassline, the slicing strings and the erotic, over-the-top, gospel-charged vocals.

4 I FEEL LOVE Donna Summer from **I Remember Yesterday**
The cocaine chill of the "Me Decade" in a nutshell.

5 WEEKEND Phreek from **Disco Connection (Authentic Classic Disco 1976–81)**
A surging, percolating record that is all about dancefloor exorcism.

6 YOU MAKE ME FEEL (MIGHTY REAL) Sylvester from **Step II**
With its synth licks, mechanized bassline and drum-machine beats, this is the genesis of Hi-NRG and one of the most glorious, uplifting records in the disco canon.

7 I WILL SURVIVE Gloria Gaynor from **Love Tracks**
Moan and groan if you want, but 12 million hen parties haven't ruined the best disco record not made by Chic.

8 DISCO CIRCUS Martin Circus from **Martin Circus**
Conclusive proof that daft European novelty records aren't necessarily the scourge of the earth.

9 VERTIGO/RELIGHT MY FIRE Dan Hartman from **Relight My Fire**
A record so good not even Take That could mess it up.

10 GO BANG #5 Dinosaur L from **24>24 Music**
Crafted by the great disco maverick Arthur Russell, this is seven minutes of inspired dancefloor lunacy.

Thing (Called Love)" and "Bottom's Up". Creadel Jones left in 1983, followed by Eugene Record in 1988. Record was replaced by new face **Anthony Watson**, and the group continues to perform as a very popular trio on the oldies and soul circuit.

(For God's Sake) Give More Power To The People
1971, Brunswick

Their strongest album for Brunswick, *(For God's Sake) Give More Power To The People* offered the yin and yang of The Chi-Lites. Away from their sweet harmony smash, "Have You Seen Her?", and the power funk track, "Give More Power To The People", is an entire album of non-hits of top-notch quality. This is The Chi-Lites at their peak.

20 Greatest Hits
2001, Brunswick

Including all The Chi-Lites' major hits from "Give It Away" to "You Don't Have To Go" and some decent album tracks, arranged in chronological order, this is an excellent compilation. It showcases the impressive range of this archetypal 70s group from fiery protest songs to sweet ballads.

Dee Clark

B orn Delecta Clark on November 7, 1938 in Blytheville, Arkansas, **Dee Clark** was an important transitional figure between the worlds of rock'n'roll, R&B and soul. He first recorded at the age of 13 as one of the Hambone Kids – the Chicago trio's 1952 release "Hambone", on the Okeh label, was among the first to feature what became known as the **Bo Diddley** beat.

The following year Clark joined John McCall, Doug Brown, Teddy Long and John Carter in vocal group The Golden Tones. Renamed **The Kool Gents** in honour of a popular local DJ, the group signed to Vee Jay in 1955. Their second single, "I Just Can't Help Myself" from 1956, featured Clark on lead, but it was a flop. After another single that went nowhere, label boss **Ewart Abner** persuaded Clark to go solo, but the result, "Kangaroo Hop", was again poorly received.

While the remainder of The Kool Gents went on to become The El Dorados Mark II, Clark finally scored that elusive first hit in 1958, at the ripe old age of 20, with the rather wonderful "Nobody But You". The arrangement was a rock'n'roll shuffle with a prim female chorus in the background, but Clark sang like a low-key **Sam Cooke**. The next year's "Just Keep It Up" was much cheesier,

like a Disney version of rock'n'roll with its chirpy flute flourishes and "bom-b-b-bom-b-b-bom" backing, but, inevitably, was an even bigger pop hit. The far better "Hey Little Girl" returned Clark to the hambone/Bo Diddley beat and became the basis for The Strangeloves' and Bow Wow Wow's "I Want Candy".

The 1960 single "How About That" found Clark back amid the schmaltz, though his vocals served to alleviate the song's Lawrence Welk tendencies. Clark's biggest hit of all, 1961's "Raindrops", was one of the definitive early Chicago records. Clark sang in a bizarre combination of **Johnny Mathis**, **BB King** and, on his final falsetto shriek, **Prince**, on top of incredibly zingy orchestration.

Abner took Clark with him when he left Vee Jay in 1963 to found Constellation, but apart from "Crossfire Time", Clark failed to achieve any more hits. The mid-60s records "That's My Girl", "Come Closer", "Warm Summer Breezes" and "TCB" pitted his warm tenor against classic Chicago arrangements, while "In These Very Tender Moments", recorded in New York with Seymour Stein, featured big orchestration and a guitar figure lifted from **The Monkees**' songbook. After it too failed to chart, Clark slowly faded from the scene. He died of a heart attack on December 7, 1990.

Raindrops
1994, Charly

While it doesn't hold any of Dee Clark's records with Constellation, or even "How About That", this is the best Clark retrospective available, if only because it includes his very fine Kool Gents recordings. Among them is the gorgeous "When I Call on You", which was left on the cutting room floor until this release.

Judy Clay

J udy Clay was blessed with one of the most powerful voices in the history of soul music. Filled with gospel intensity and pure physical force, that voice may just have been too potent for the general public; sadly, she never enjoyed the success she deserved, and remained obscure to all but the most committed soul fans.

Born **Judy Guions** on September 12, 1938 in St Paul, North Carolina, she moved to New York as a young child. There she joined the gospel group **The Drinkard Singers**, who counted **Cissy Houston** and **Dee** and **Dionne Warwick** among their members. Judy Guions featured on two albums with the Drinkards – *The Drinkard Singers And The Back Home Choir At Newport* in 1957 and *A Joyful Noise* in 1958 – before departing for a solo secular career.

Taking the name Judy Clay, she recorded a couple of singles for the Ember label – "More Than You Know" and "Do You Think That's Right" – before moving to Scepter, where Dionne Warwick was already enjoying success. Clay's first single there was the fiery "You Busted My Mind" in 1963, which she re-recorded in 1966. The 1966 version's combination of a Motown stomp that almost reached escape velocity with Stax horn charts, made it a favourite with the UK's Northern soul aficionados. In 1966, "He's The Kind Of Guy" was the deepest imaginable deep soul, featuring Clay in stentorian, Mahalia Jackson-style form over a gospel-esque arrangement.

After Clay signed with Atlantic in 1967, **Jerry Wexler** sent her to Memphis to record at Stax. From her first record, the sterling double-sided "You Can't Run Away From Your Heart/It Takes A Lotta Good Love", it was evident that Clay felt at home. She finally got her first taste of chart success with two duets with **Billy Vera**, "Storybook Children" and "Country Girl – City Man". More important than their commercial success, however, was their symbolic force: Billy Vera was white, and this was the first interracial duo in American history to attain any kind of mainstream impact. The sight of the two singing love songs to each other was deemed so hard to take in those dark days that they were effectively banned from television.

Clay achieved more duet success with William Bell in 1968, on the lovely "Private Number". With the orchestra backing and a cymbal crash far too assertive to be Al Jackson, it was hard to believe that the song came from Memphis, but both Bell and Clay were defiantly Southern. A second duet with Bell, "My Baby Specializes", followed it into the R&B charts later that year. Clay's 1968 solo release "It Ain't Long Enough/Give Love To Save Love", another quintessential Southern soul record, failed to make an impact. She did, however, reach the charts on her own in 1970, with a cover of **Lee** Dorsey's "Greatest Love", a gut-wrenching slice of deep soul recorded at Muscle Shoals.

Judy Clay spent much of the 70s as a back-up vocalist for soul greats **Aretha Franklin** and **Ray Charles**. She also released a live version of **The Bee-Gees'** "Stayin' Alive" in 1978, but suffered a brain tumour the following year. Clay eventually recovered and returned to singing exclusively on the gospel circuit up until her death on July 19, 2001.

◉ **Private Numbers**
1993, Stax

This split disc with Veda Brown is sadly the only decent Judy Clay album on the market. It includes her duets with William Bell, as well as the solo recordings "It Ain't Long Enough" and "Give Love To Save Love". The stark gospel cut, "Children, Get Weary", represents Clay at her absolute best.

Otis Clay

Bridging gospel, urban blues and soul, **Otis Clay** was, in many ways, the perfect Chicago soul singer. Of course, that definition would also make him the perfect Southern singer, and on the material he recorded in Muscle Shoals and Memphis, he very nearly was.

Clay was born on February 11, 1942, in Waxhaw, Mississippi, where he became a member of the family gospel group, The Morning Glories, at age 4. After moving with his family to Chicago in 1957, he continued to sing in gospel groups The Golden Jubilaires and The Blue Jays. In 1964 he recorded "Jesus I Love To Call His Name" with **The Gospel Songbirds**, and was tapped to become the lead singer for **The Sensational Nightingales**. However, a year later, he decided to cross over and signed to the One-derful label.

Clay's first few secular records from 1966 – including the killer blues ballad "Flame In Your Heart" and the more uptempo, James Brown-style "I Testify" – captured him at his intense best. When the label tried to plug him into standard Chicago formulae, however, as on the awkward "A Lasting Love" or the uptempo, Motown-style "Showplace", his strident, assertive Southern voice sounded out of place.

On Clay's biggest One-derful hit, 1967's "That's How It Is (When You're In Love)", the band was all over the place and at times out of tune, while Clay was occasionally ridiculously overwrought, but it was strangely affecting nonetheless. "I'm Satisfied", on the other hand, was perhaps the most effective of his One-derful records because the arrangement was the least typically Chicago in style. The background choir and the piano gave things a nice country tinge, eschewing the singsong horns that typified Windy City soul.

With One-derful in financial straits, Clay signed to Atlantic's Cotillion subsidiary, whose first release was his blistering 1968 version of **Sir Douglas Quintet**'s "She's About A Mover", recorded in Muscle Shoals. The sizzling, almost out of control "Baby Jane" and frighteningly intense "Pouring Water On A Drowning Man" followed the next year, before Clay signed with **Willie Mitchell**'s Hi label in 1971.

Clay and Hi proved a perfect fit, because Clay was no longer battling busy arrangements. Mitchell's trademark minimalism allowed Clay's bluesiness to shine through on tracks like the fabulous uptempo "Trying To Live My Life Without You" and the string-led ballad "You Can't Keep Running From My Love". However, Clay was dropped from Hi, after disappointing sales, in 1974.

He then moved back to Chicago and started his own Elka label, releasing the similar "Turn Back The Hands Of Time/Good Lovin'" in 1974, before moving to Brad Shapiro and Henry Stone's Kay-Vette label, where he charted with "All Because Of Your Love" in 1977, and recorded the fine, pleading ballad "Let Me In" in 1978.

Despite achieving few chart hits, Clay was an electrifying performer. He also remains especially popular in Japan, where he cut two fantastic live albums, 1981's *Live In Japan* and 1984's *Soul Man Live In Japan*. He continues to record sporadically and release incendiary live albums, most recently 2005's *Respect Yourself*, which he cut in Switzerland with **Tyrone Davis**' band.

 The Complete Otis Clay On Hi Records
2000, Hi

Like most of Hi's artists, Otis Clay suffered commercially because he wasn't Al Green. Artistically, however, he thrived under the label because Willie Mitchell's sparse arrangements framed his sanctified intensity perfectly, something this overdue retrospective highlights over its 26 tracks.

Testify!
2003, Fuel 2000

Clay was essentially a singles artist during his brief tenure at Chicago's One-derful label from 1965 to 1968. This 22-track collection is "the album that never was" of that material. The uptempo funky cuts recall vintage Wilson Pickett, while the ballads show off Clay's gospel roots to great effect.

The Clovers

While the western half of postwar America was jumping to the hepcat blues of Louis Jordan, **Wynonie Harris**, and **Ella Mae Morse**, folks east of the Mississippi were grooving to the smoother sounds of the vocal groups inspired by The Ink Spots and The Charioteers. The best of these new vocal groups were **The Orioles**, whose gorgeous 1948 single, "It's Too Soon To Know", is a perennial choice as "the first rock'n'roll record". While The Orioles moved away from the classic pop stylization of their mentors, lead vocalist **Sonny Til** still sang in the "cool" style, even if it was more emotional than anything that had come before.

Largely inspired by The Orioles, **The Clovers** were one of the first vocal groups to incorporate influences from the blues and Southern gospel as well as classic pop. What might be called their defiled choirboy purity opened the floodgates for rock'n'roll, and laid the groundwork for soul. As Nick Tosches put it in *Unsung Heroes Of Rock'n'Roll*, "they became the first of the traditionally born vocal groups to make the leap across the Jordan to the chicken shack that transcends all knowing."

Formed as a trio in Washington DC in 1947, by **Harold Lucas**, **Billy Shelton** and **Thomas Woods**, The Clovers started out performing the usual ballads in a style derivative of The Orioles and The Ravens. However, when their manager Lou Krefetz brought them to Atlantic Records in 1950, the production team of **Ahmet Ertegun** and **Jesse Stone** persuaded them to sully their refined sound with blue-note slurs, Southern grit and gospel melisma.

With a new line-up of **John "Buddy" Bailey**, Harold Lucas, **Harold Winley**, **Matthew McQuater** and guitarist **Bill**

only made #14 on the R&B chart. Although they released some great singles, including the Elmore James-inspired "Down In The Alley", they went nowhere and the group parted company with Atlantic. Ironically, The Clovers' swan song, "Love Potion No. 9" for United Artists, became their biggest pop chart hit, reaching #23 in 1959.

The Very Best Of The Clovers
1998, Rhino/Atlantic

Despite lacking their best-known record, "Love Potion No. 9", this is a near-perfect chronicle of the career of the most successful R&B act in Atlantic's storied history. From "Don't You Know I Love You" – the first R&B record to feature a saxophone solo – to "Love, Love, Love", it holds some of the most revolutionary R&B material ever recorded.

Harris, The Clovers' first recording for Atlantic was "Don't You Know I Love You". A gently rolling Southern blues number with dirty sax runs in the background and Buddy Bailey singing in a more urgent, gutsy and bluesier voice than Sonny Til, this was a whole new thing. An unprecedented melding of Northern sophistication with Southern earthiness, The Ink Spots with The Golden Gate Quartet, and vocal harmonies with sax solos, "Don't You Know I Love You" was a #1 R&B hit throughout the spring of 1951.

Over the next two years The Clovers dominated the R&B charts with "Fool, Fool, Fool" (#1), "One Mint Julep" (#2), Ting-A-Ling" (#1), "I Played the Fool" (#3) and "Hey, Miss Fannie" (#2). "I Played the Fool" was particularly noteworthy, not only as the group's first successful ballad, but also because it set the stage for the doo-wop groups that were to follow in a few years' time. In 1953 Bailey was called up for military service, but despite losing their distinctive voice, The Clovers continued to enjoy R&B success.

With the less urbane lead singer **Charlie White**, who had previously sung with The Dominoes, the group's "Good Lovin'", "Lovey Dovey" (featuring the immortal line, "I really love your peaches, I'm gonna to shake your tree") and "Little Mama" all reached the Top 5. White was then replaced by **Billy Mitchell**, who sang lead on the great "Your Cash Ain't Nothin' But Trash". By the time Bailey returned to the fold in 1955, however, The Drifters and **Elvis** had made R&B safe for white teenagers, and The Clovers' definitive version of "Blue Velvet"

Nat "King" Cole

During the 40s and 50s, every black male singer wanted to be Nathaniel Adams Coles. Along with **Louis Armstrong**, James Brown, **Chuck Berry** and **Miles Davis**, Nat "King" Cole was one of the most important African-American musicians in terms of socio-cultural impact. His achievements were extraordinary: he was one of the most accomplished pianists of the late swing era; his trio was the first successful small jazz group and inspired the legendary trios of Art Tatum and Oscar Peterson; he was one of the most successful pop singers of the immediate post-war period, becoming America's most popular crooner after **Frank Sinatra**, Bing Crosby and Perry Como; he was the first black performer to be accorded his own TV programme; and, perhaps most impressively of all, he managed to elevate a Christmas song above schmaltz.

Cole was born on March 17, 1917, in Montgomery, Alabama. He started out playing in his brother's Chicago-based jazz band, **Eddie Cole's Solid Swingers**, before moving to Los Angeles, where he played in a revue band and then formed a trio with guitarist **Oscar Moore** and bassist **Wesley Prince**. The group originally concentrated on Earl "Fatha" Hines-style swing instrumentals and some hipster jive, novelty vocal numbers, but during their first sessions in 1940 for Decca they recorded "Sweet Lorraine" featuring Cole's creamy vocals.

Although he was all too often drowned in violins, treated "Those Lazy Hazy Crazy Days of Summer" seriously in 1963 and sang "Mr. Cole Won't Rock & Roll" in 1960, Nat "King" Cole wasn't a giant just because he was the first true crossover star of American popular music. He also largely invented the notion of "cool". Years before Miles Davis gave birth to cool jazz, Cole repressed his feelings and his church roots behind a veneer of classic pop artifice, hip lingo and sharp suits. Like other great crooners, his smoothness suggested intimacy, but it was the sense that he was holding something back that gave his performances another dimension and, paradoxically, made his records more emotional. Everyone from Charles Brown to Ray Charles was influenced by Cole's style and, despite gospel's ultimate victory in the 60s, Cole's coolness still has its adherents, albeit in very different clothes.

Cole's first major hit was his first side for Capitol in 1943, "Straighten Up And Fly Right", a jivey, little Louis Jordan-style cut, but it was his remake of "Sweet Lorraine" that same year that established his style and made his name. A restrained, bluesy ballad, "Sweet Lorraine" showcased Cole's mixture of classic pop and blue notes. On "Gee, Baby, Ain't I Good To You", he allowed a hint of churchiness into his repertoire, but his other hits "It's Only A Paper Moon", "(Get Your Kicks On) Route 66" and "(I Love You) For Sentimental Reasons" featured his more familiar combinations of finger-snapping propulsion and emotional reticence.

Nat "King" Cole and friends smile for the camera

The turning point in Cole's career was his 1946 version of **Mel Tormé**'s "The Christmas Song". Marrying pop's stylization and good-life fantasies with faint echoes of jazz rhythms and blue notes, Cole's first record with orchestration, like Louis Armstrong's "What A Wonderful World", transcended its origins by sheer force of personality. The song – best known by its first line "Chestnuts roasting on an open fire" – made it to #3 on the pop chart and has since become a perennial Christmas favourite. Records like "Nature Boy" and his stunning version of "Lush Life" followed with masses of strings – Cole was becoming a pop star. Perhaps his most saccharine recording, 1950's "Mona Lisa" put him over the top and Cole became one of America's biggest pop singers.

With the exception of sides like the Billy May collaboration, "Walkin' My Baby Back Home", and some inspired jazz recordings, Cole mostly abandoned any hint of R&B throughout the 50s in favour of mainstream pop arrangements. Although his short-lived television series in 1956–57 was of tremendous symbolic importance, Cole's best work was behind him and his innovations and role had been taken over by **Johnny Mathis**. After a series of novelty-ish, easy-listening records in the early 60s that were beneath a man of his great talent, Cole died of cancer on February 15, 1965.

After Midnight: The Complete Session
1956, Capitol

If you've already got the hits and you want a little more of the essence of Nat "King" Cole, this is a great place to start. Eschewing larger orchestral arrangements, this album was heralded as Cole returning to his jazz roots upon its release. He sings a number of standards in his usual smooth vocal style backed up with a small jazz combo and his own exquisite piano.

Nat King Cole
1992, Capitol

This 4-CD box set is still the best Nat "King" Cole anthology available and its one hundred tracks include such hits as "Route 66" and "Straighten Up And Fly Right", as well as some of his finer jazz sides. Spanning his two decades with Capitol, this contains all the records that made Cole one of the greatest pop singers *and* one of the most important African-American icons.

The Billy May Sessions
1993, Capitol

This 2-CD set is made up primarily of sessions recorded in 1957 and 1961 that were arranged by the great Billy May. The style is neither small combo nor syrupy strings, but a big-band sound that falls subtly in between. The album has a good range of ballads and uptempo numbers, all of which are vintage Nat "King" Cole performances.

Natalie Cole

When she burst on the scene in 1975, **Natalie Cole** was hailed as the new queen of R&B. She sounded like Aretha lite and was the daughter of Nat "King" Cole, so she seemed to be destined to become music royalty. While it didn't quite work out that way, Cole has, nevertheless, been one of the most successful artists on the R&B charts.

Natalie Cole was born on February 6, 1950, in Los Angeles. She first tried to enter the music business in the early 70s, but everyone wanted her to be a carbon copy of her father, while she wanted to sing soulful rock music. A fateful meeting in 1974 with Chuck Jackson and Marvin Yancey, both formerly in The Independents, changed her luck. Jackson and Yancey wrote and produced Cole's 1975 debut, "This Will Be". It reached #1 on the R&B charts thanks to its peppy cod-gospel feel and an impressive, but somewhat florid, vocal performance from Cole that was reminiscent of a less forceful Aretha Franklin. It was followed to the top of the R&B charts by the classically styled ballad "Inseparable" and the Ellington-inspired "Sophisticated Lady (She's A Different Lady)". "I've Got Love On My Mind", a somewhat mannered ballad, gave her a fourth R&B #1 in 1977, while later that year, "Our Love" made it five #1s out of seven.

Thereafter, however – with the exception of a 1979 duet with Peabo Bryson, "Gimme Some Time" – Cole didn't make the Top 10 for a decade. Her staggering fall from grace was largely due to a growing cocaine dependency. After divorcing from Yancey, she checked herself into a rehab clinic and finally emerged, clean, in 1984. The huge-selling 1987 album *Everlasting* secured her comeback. On its three hit singles – the electric "Jump Start", the schlocky ballad "I Live For Your Love" and a synth-heavy cover of "Pink Cadillac" (seek out the excellent house remix) – she proved that the more angular, brittle R&B production styles of the 80s suited her voice to a T.

The definitive 80s power ballad "Miss You Like Crazy" returned Cole to the top of the R&B chart in 1989, while the faintly ridiculous "Wild Women Do" from the *Pretty Woman* soundtrack provided another big hit the following year. Although it didn't do so well on the charts – even though it went gold – "Unforgettable", a digital duet from the grave with her father, was little short of a sensation in 1991. That year's *Unforgettable: With Love* album won three Grammys.

Since then, Cole has become the queen of Adult Contemporary radio and traditional pop by positioning herself as the inheritor of her father's mantle with recordings of "Cry Me A River" and the Grammy-winning posthumous duet, "When I Fall In Love". After releasing a couple of Christmas albums, she re-emerged in 2002 on *Ask A Woman Who Knows* as a torchy jazz singer covering Dinah Washington and her father again with a group that included Joe Sample, Roy Hargrove and Christian McBride.

The Collection
1987, Capitol

There's no consistently satisfying collection of Natalie Cole's hits because they were recorded across a series of labels, but this 15-track package compiles her biggest hits from 1975 to 1981. While it features an awful lot of Aretha-isms, these recordings are less of an acquired taste than her later material.

Mitty Collier

Chicago's **Mitty Collier** was among the most old-fashioned of the many gospel singers who managed to cross over to secular soul. While she had a fabulous voice, it was perhaps a bit too starchy to communicate soul's emphasis on pleasure and loss, and she never achieved the commercial success she deserved.

Born June 21, 1941 in Birmingham, Alabama, Collier spent much of her youth singing with gospel's **Hayes Ensemble**. When she switched to secular music in 1960, she was discovered by producer/talent scout Ralph Bass, who had recently joined Chess Records. Her first release on the label, "I've Got Love", went nowhere, as did subsequent follow-ups until 1963's "I'm Your Part Time Love". That fiery answer to **Little Johnny Taylor**'s "Part Time Love" reached the R&B Top 20. The single "Pain", on the other hand, showed why her records had trouble connecting with audiences: her stentorian contralto simply eviscerated the breezy, mambo-style backing.

Collier's biggest hit, "I Had A Talk With My Man", from 1964, aroused controversy for being a straight secular remake of **James Cleveland**'s "I Had a Talk With God Last Night". Both her Mahalia Jackson-style delivery – slightly stilted but with huge power – and the prim arrangement undercut its fleshiness, but it didn't please the church ladies. "No Faith, No Love", another

Cleveland rewrite – this time of "No Cross, No Crown" – was similarly drowned in treacle by producer Billy Davis to forestall controversy.

The more conventional soul record "Sharing You" gave Collier her final hit in 1966. After "Everybody Makes A Mistake Sometime", recorded at Muscle Shoals, she left Chess for William Bell's Peach Tree label. In many ways the Southern soul style suited her better, but none of her Peach Tree records, not even a fine rendition of "Mama, He Treats Your Daughter Mean", sold well.

In 1972, after a final single on Entrance, "Is This Our Last Time", Collier returned to the gospel world with *The Warning* album, which ironically featured a recording of "I Had A Talk With God Last Night". Collier has since released several gospel albums, including *Hold The Light* in 1977, *Gospel Roots* in 1979 and *I Am Love* in 1986, and she continues to sing on the gospel circuit.

Shades Of A Genius
1965, Chess

Collier's only non-gospel album is a very fine collection of slow, stately soul. She covers both Ray Charles and bluesman Little Walter, but definitely makes the songs her own with her almost magisterial delivery.

The Commodores

Long before becoming Motown's second most successful act (after Stevie Wonder) during the 70s, and before lead singer Lionel Richie became one of the biggest pop stars of the 80s, The Commodores were a hard funk band that instilled fear in any group that had to share a stage with them. Instead of following the groove, however, The Commodores pursued the path of least resistance with a series of sappy ballads and commercial club tracks.

The Commodores first took shape at the legendary Tuskegee Institute in Tuskegee, Alabama, in 1967. As some members of the leading campus band, The Jays, were graduating, those who remained (keyboardist Milan Williams, drummer Andre Callahan and bassist Michael Gilbert) asked guitarist Thomas McClary and keyboardist/saxophonist/vocalist Lionel Richie from another group, The Mighty Mystics, to merge with them. Calling themselves The Commodores,

the new group started to make a name for themselves around Alabama. In 1969 Callahan and Gilbert were replaced by Walter "Clyde" Orange and Ronald LaPraed respectively.

Successful gigs in New York and Europe earned the group a one-off deal with Atlantic, and 1971's "Keep On Dancing", a faithful cover of the Alvin Cash classic produced by Swamp Dogg, showed their badass side. Unfortunately, it went nowhere and the group learned their lesson about funk. However, during this period Suzanne De Passe, a Motown executive, caught one of the group's gigs in New York and was so impressed that she asked them to open for the Jackson 5. Two singles, "The Zoo (The Human Zoo)" and "Don't You Be Worried", followed on Motown's MoWest subsidiary. The reggae-ish "Are You Happy" appeared on the main Motown label in 1973 before the group achieved their breakthrough with "Machine Gun" the next year, a synth-heavy track that merged Sly Stone with novelty groups like Hot Butter and The Peppers.

"Slippery When Wet", a slab of ensemble funk reminiscent of Kool & The Gang and The Ohio Players, became the group's first R&B #1 in 1975, but "Sweet Love", an R&B #2 and their first pop top-ten hit later that year, set the template for the future. A standard MOR ballad punctuated by little R&B flourishes, "Sweet Love" featured Richie's nasal tenor lead over a midtempo groove. That same blueprint was followed throughout the 70s on "Just To Be Close To You",

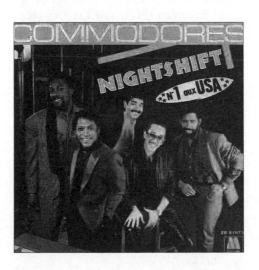

"Easy", "Three Times A Lady", "Sail On" and "Still". The bouncy club tracks "Fancy Dancer", "Too Hot Ta Trot", "Lady (You Bring Me Up)" and the seriously bumping "Brick House", on the other hand, recalled their early days, but it was the run of well-crafted ballads that made the group a commercial juggernaut.

In 1980 Lionel Richie wrote and produced "Lady" – not the same song mentioned above – for **Kenny Rogers**, which stayed at the top of the pop charts for six weeks. That success, and the subsequent nine-week sojourn at #1 of "Endless Love", his duet with Diana Ross, persuaded Richie to embark on a solo career in 1982. The Commodores struggled on without him for a couple of years before scoring a big hit – and winning their only Grammy – with "Nightshift", a tribute to Marvin Gaye and Jackie Wilson, in 1985. The record could have been by **Mr. Mister** but for the vocals, which came, in the main, curtesy of **J.D. Nicholas** (Richie's replacement and former member of the group Heatwave). The group then had a modest hit with the dance track "Goin' To The Bank" before settling down to a comfortable career, with various line-up changes, on the nostalgia circuit.

Richie, of course, went on to become the biggest thing since striped toothpaste, scoring huge hits throughout the 80s with crassly commercial pop records such as the schlocky ballads "Truly", "Hello", "Say You, Say Me" and "Ballerina Girl", and the airheaded peppy numbers "You Are", "All Night Long (All Night)" and "Dancing On The Ceiling". Richie disappeared from the limelight after 1987, but made a comeback with "Do It To Me" and "My Destiny" in 1992. He has continued to have modest hits ever since, including the 2003 duet with **Enrique Iglesias**, "To Love A Woman", and 2004's "Just For You" from the album of the same name.

The Ultimate Collection
1997, Motown

A no-fuss, no-muss, 15-track collection of The Commodores' biggest hits. It short-changes the group's funk side in favour of their sickly ballads, but there are still enough dance numbers to ensure that this is more than just a make-out album.

Con Funk Shun

Thanks to their clean lines and easily digestible grooves, **Con Funk Shun** – formed in Vallejo, California, in 1968, by guitarist/vocalist **Michael Cooper** and drummer **Louis McCall** – became one of the most successful ensemble funk bands of the late 70s and early 80s. Originally called Project Soul, the band was filled out in 1969 by keyboardist **Danny Thomas**, trumpeter **Karl Fuller**, saxophonist **Paul Harrell** and bassist **Cedric Martin**. From 1971 onwards, the group, with the addition of keyboardist/horn player **Felton Pilate**, regularly backed the Stax act The Soul Children, and they also backed Rufus Thomas at the Wattstax festival in Los Angeles.

In 1974, with Stax in disarray, Project Soul changed their name to Con Funk Shun (after a song by The Nite-Liters) and signed to Stax founder Estelle Axton's Fretone label. After a few singles – "Bumpsomeboody", "Mr Tambourine Man", "Clique" and "Now And Forever" – they signed to Mercury. Their first single for the label, "Sho Feels Good To Me", boasted a singsong hook, tight wah-wah guitars and an approach reminiscent of The Ohio Players, which was also writ large on 1976's *Con-Funk-Shun*. However, the group defined their own style on their second Mercury album, 1977's *Secrets*.

Produced by **Skip Scarborough**, who had worked with the likes of L.T.D. and Earth Wind & Fire, *Secrets* tempered the funk with the streamlined jazz-fusion that Scarborough had learned from **Donald Byrd**. The album's big hit, "Fun", was based heavily on the hit single "Dazz" by Atlanta group **Brick**, and featured that characteristically clean late-70s funk sound. While "Confunkshunizeya" had slightly more bounce, the players still sounded polished and methodical, as though they squeezed their toothpaste tubes from the bottom every time.

Con Funk Shun's next album, 1978's *Loveshine*, was even more well-groomed. The tracks "Shake And Dance With Me" and "So Easy" just about managed to be funky and were complemented by slick ballads, such as "Make It Last". *Candy*, in 1979, was a bit nastier, thanks to the uptempo funk of "Chase Me" with its Fat Albert vocals and

Larry Graham-style bassline, but tracks like "(Let Me Put) Love On Your Mind" were part of the trend of updating the old sweet soul sound with sleazier arrangements.

Despite the distinctly pop-funk flavour of the early-80s records "Got To Be Enough", "Too Tight", "Ms Got-The-Body" and the classic ballad "Love's Train", the group failed to dent the pop charts. **Kool & The Gang's** producer **Eumir Deodato** was brought in for Con Funk Shun's 1983 album *Fever*, which produced a big R&B hit with the ballad "Baby, I'm Hooked (Right Into Your Love)", but still no crossover success. By 1985, when Whodini's Larry Smith and pop svengali Maurice Starr were brought in to work on "Electric Lady" and "I'm Leaving Baby" respectively, the band was in turmoil. Pilate left in 1986 and the remaining musicians barely played on their own albums.

The group finally disbanded in 1988, after the release of *Burnin' Love*. Cooper enjoyed some solo success in the late 80s with the ballads "To Prove My Love", "Should Have Been You" and "My Baby's House", while Pilate became a successful producer and the musical force behind **MC Hammer**. Con Funk Shun reunited in 1993 and are still performing live all over the world – they even managed to achieve a small R&B hit in 1996 with "Throw It Up, Throw It Up".

The Best Of Con Funk Shun
1993, Mercury

Kool & The Gang they weren't, but Con Funk Shun still managed to produce agreeable, if not exactly challenging, funk jams. Their instrumental polish inevitably translated into too many ballads, but at least they were never sappy. This is as good a collection as you could hope for.

Arthur Conley

Born April 1, 1946, in Atlanta, Georgia, Arthur Conley was a sadly underrated stylist of Southern soul. He became Otis Redding's protégé – indeed it has often been said that he was a naive newcomer who hung on Redding's every word – after Redding heard his demo tape backstage at a concert in 1965. Conley signed to the new Jotis label (distributed by Stax), which Redding and **Joe Galkin** had formed that same year. Conley fell apart after Redding died at the end of 1967, and decided to relocate to Europe.

Ironically, however, Conley's biggest hit, 1967's "Sweet Soul Music", outsold any of the records Redding himself released before his death.

Redding is believed to have signed Conley because of his uncanny vocal resemblance to **Sam Cooke**. Along with nearly every other black singer of their generation, both Redding and Conley idolized Cooke. This was evident from the start of Conley's career as the leader of **Arthur & The Corvets** in the late 50s and early 60s. Their first record was 1959's "I'm Going To Cry", but by the release of "Aritha" in 1964, Conley was mimicking Cooke's style almost note for note.

"I'm A Lonely Stranger", the demo that Redding heard in 1965 and Conley's first release for Jotis, was a slow, creeping ballad strangely reminiscent of Aaron Neville. Another spine-tingling ballad, "There's A Place For Us", followed the next year, before Redding took Conley to Fame studios to record "In The Same Old Way" and "I'm Gonna Forget About You Baby".

Even though "Sweet Soul Music" amounted to little more than Conley giving namechecks to **Lou Rawls**, **Sam & Dave**, **Wilson Pickett**, Otis Redding and **James Brown**, it's easy to see why it soared to #2 on the pop chart in 1967. With a groove that managed to be both smoking and soothing at the same time, it was one of the few Southern soul records to be accessible to a broad audience. Even better, though, was that year's "Let Nothing Separate Us", a truly dark deep soul ballad that was Conley's finest performance, although it did have a very strong resemblance to Redding's records.

The success of "Sweet Soul Music" was to weigh heavily on Conley's career. He was then saddled with dreck like "Funky Street", which was, admittedly, his second-biggest hit, and uptempo fluff like "Aunt Dora's Love Soul Shack". On the other hand, that single's flip, "Is That You Love?", found Conley at his best on a slow ballad. Another record from the period, "Get Yourself Another Fool", showed how good he could be in classic Stax ballad style. The moving "Otis Sleep On", his 1969 tribute to Redding, was the flip side to an appalling version of "Ob-La-Di Ob-La-Da".

In 1971 Conley recorded for the Capricorn label with **Swamp Dogg** producing. While he was in fine voice on the classic Southern soul records "I'm Living Good" and "Walking On Eggs", he was still burdened with "More Sweet Soul Music" in 1972. His last single was 1976's "Another Time", a slow aching cover of a Leo Sayer song that showed off his voice to great effect.

Conley then moved to the Netherlands and changed his name to Lee Roberts. He continued to be involved in the music biz there and released *Soulin'*, a recording of a 1980 concert with The Sweaters, in 1988. Conley died of cancer in Ruurlo, Netherlands on November 17, 2003.

Sweet Soul Music: The Best Of Arthur Conley
1995, Ichiban

While it doesn't include some of Arthur Conley's best ballads, and focuses too much on uptempo fluff, this is the best compilation currently available, replete with fabulous performances of "Get Yourself Another Fool" and "In The Same Old Way", as well as his best-known hit "Sweet Soul Music".

Sam Cooke

That **Sam Cooke** was one of the greatest singers in the history of recorded music is undeniable. Unfortunately, Cooke's glorious voice was all too often buried beneath some of the least sympathetic production imaginable. While the standard explanation for this is that Cooke was the puppet of white pop Svengalis, the truth is that even if he didn't arrange them, Cooke wrote most of his own songs. Even if his determination to court as wide an audience as possible only produced a handful of good pop records, his efforts must be placed in the context of the 1957 American pop market. When Cooke crossed over to pop, America was still a place where Pat Boone out-sold Little Richard. In starting his SAR label – on which he produced artists like Bobby Womack, **The Soul Stirrers**, **The Simms Twins**, Billy Preston and **Johnnie Taylor** – he became of the first African-American entrepreneurs in the music business.

Sam Cook (the "e" came later) was born the son of a minister in Clarksdale, Mississippi, in 1931. After moving with his

family to Chicago in 1933, and spending his youth singing in church, he joined **The Highway QCs**, a group affiliated with the legendary Soul Stirrers. In 1950 he was picked by The Soul Stirrers to replace their enormously influential lead singer R.H. Harris. Like his predecessor, Cooke set about changing the rules of gospel – his pin-up good looks and sweet voice also helped to attract legions of swooning teenage girls. Gospel had never seen anything like it. The very earthly metaphors of Cooke's composi-

1 WONDERFUL from **Sam Cooke With The Soul Stirrers**
Practically every soul singer can trace their style and technique to this record.

2 TOUCH THE HEM OF HIS GARMENT from **Sam Cooke With The Soul Stirrers**
Cooke at his most intense.

3 YOU SEND ME from **Portrait Of A Legend 1951–1964**
What melisma should be – effortless and soaring.

4 CHAIN GANG from **Portrait Of A Legend 1951–1964**
For once, the overproduction of Cooke's secular records actually works with his voice.

5 WONDERFUL WORLD from **Portrait Of A Legend 1951–1964**
Kind of daft and ridiculous, but Cooke elevates it above the greeting card lyrics.

6 ANOTHER SATURDAY NIGHT from **Portrait Of A Legend 1951–1964**
Another transcendent Cooke performance.

7 BRING IT ON HOME TO ME from **Portrait Of A Legend 1951–1964**
Straight from the church – Sam Cooke and Lou Rawls go head to head.

8 TWISTIN' THE NIGHT AWAY from **Portrait Of A Legend 1951–1964**
This turns any room into a dance party.

9 SHAKE from **Portrait Of A Legend 1951–1964**
This isn't the most convincing dance craze disc, but it's better than being drowned by strings.

10 A CHANGE IS GONNA COME from **Portrait Of A Legend 1951–1964**
One of the few soul records of the period to address civil rights head on.

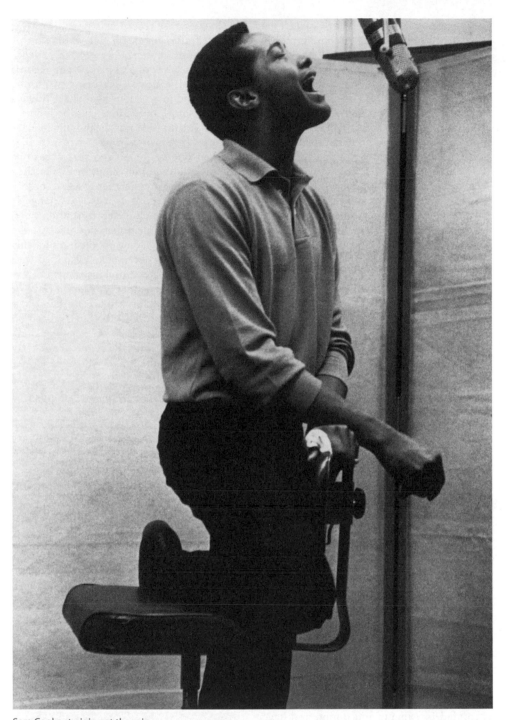

Sam Cooke straining at the mic

tion for The Soul Stirrers, "That's Heaven To Me", revealed that his conversion to the devil's music was inevitable. In 1956 he recorded secular material at a secret session and released it under a pseudonym. The record-

ings failed to sell, but they estranged Cooke from his record label, the rest of The Soul Stirrers and the bulk of the gospel community. He left the fold in 1957, never to return.

When Cooke went secular, he went all the way: sickly strings, cumbersome arrangements too clunky even for a Las Vegas singer and chorales straight from the Mormon Tabernacle Choir songbook. His breakthrough came with "You Send Me" in October 1957. Ray Charles had already rocked the world with "I've Got A Woman", but no one was quite prepared for Cooke's floating "whoooaaahhh". Nothing approaching the sensuality of his singing and his description of ecstasy had been heard outside of the gospel community. Far removed from the puppy love sentiments of the doo-woppers, "You Send Me" topped both the pop and R&B charts and set in motion a string of 29 hits in the Top 40 over the next eight years.

Were it not for Cooke's voice, these records – "(I Love You) For Sentimental Reasons", "Everybody Loves To Cha Cha Cha", "Only Sixteen" and the 1959 album of **Billie Holiday** covers, *Tribute To The Lady* – might have seemed like throwbacks to the days before rock'n'roll. When Cooke left the Keen label for RCA in 1960, the Italian-American duo **Hugo & Luigi** took over production duties. Their overwrought and unswinging arrangements were perfectly suited to trifles like "Frankie And Johnny" and "Tennessee Waltz", but Cooke was always capable of transcending his material. Even on a record as lame as "Chain Gang", the pure beauty of Cooke's voice rose above the arrangements and rescued the song from complete insignificance. Among all the rubbish, there were some genuinely sublime pop moments: "Wonderful World", "Twistin' The Night Away", "Soothe Me", "Bring It On Home To Me" and "Another Saturday Night". The last two, in particular, profoundly influenced the direction of soul after Cooke's death.

Sam Cooke was killed in mysterious circumstances outside a prostitute's motel room in Los Angeles on December 11, 1964. The particulars of Cooke's death are still shrouded in rumour and doubt, and have generated almost as many conspiracy theories as the murder of Tupac Shakur. What is certain, however, is that popular music lost one of its finest voices on that date in 1964, even if it was often wasted on trifles.

Cooke's best record as a pop singer was released after his death. The A-side of his posthumous top-ten hit was "Shake", a dance novelty that was one of his few pop records that actually moved, featuring a rhumba rhythm and instructions like "Shake it like a bowl of soup" and "Move your body like a whip". The flip side was the monumental "A Change Is Gonna Come", a record that marked one of the all too rare occasions when Cooke the pop singer truly matched the profundity of his earlier gospel records.

As great a record as it is, "A Change Is Gonna Come" is ultimately frustrating, however, because it demonstrates what Cooke could have been had he not died so suddenly at such a young age. Cooke was gifted with perhaps the greatest vocal instrument of any male soul singer – not even Marvin Gaye or Al Green could approach his effortless grace – but his talent was all too often wasted on the crossover market. "A Change Is Gonna Come" shows why everyone from Otis Redding to **Muhammad Ali** called Cooke the greatest of them all.

Live At The Harlem Square Club, 1963
1985, RCA

While perhaps not the equal of James Brown's *Live At The Apollo*, this set, recorded in front of a hardcore R&B crowd in Miami, nevertheless showcases the "real" Sam Cooke, liberated from the teen-schlock arrangements and sermonizing to his own flock. Cooke sounds amazing, although he is slightly let down by clumsy big-band arrangements that try too hard to smoke.

Sam Cooke With The Soul Stirrers
1991, Ace

This is a fine compilation of the bulk of Cooke's gospel material with The Soul Stirrers, recorded from 1951 to 1956. Cooke's voice is as wonderful here as it is on his secular records, but the material and the arrangements are far better.

Portrait Of A Legend 1951–1964
2003, Abko

Portrait Of A Legend is the best Cooke collection on the market, despite only containing one of his gospel records. In addition to brilliantly remastered tracks, it also includes excellent liner notes from blues/soul scholar Peter Guralnick. An essential purchase.

Don Covay

While **Don Covay** was a talented singer and an even more talented songwriter, and showed himself abundantly capable of making great records, he was never quite able to craft a persona, either as a performer or a recording artist, that stuck with the public. As a result, he has, unfairly, remained a second-tier artist for most of his career.

Born on March 24, 1938, in Orangeburg, South Carolina, Covay grew up in Washington DC. As a teenager he joined the legendary **Rainbows**, a group that included **Billy Stewart** and, according to legend, Marvin Gaye. After recording a couple of singles for the Red Robin and Pilgrim labels, Covay met **Little Richard** and started recording with his backing band. The result, "Bip Bop Bip", was a blistering piece of rock'n'roll fire-and-brimstone released in 1957 under the name Pretty Boy.

With his group **The Goodtimers**, Covay released a series of dance-craze records throughout the early 60s, including "Pony Time", "The Popeye Waddle" and "The Froog". Moving to New York, he got a job at the Brill Building and wrote "You're Good For Me" and "Tonight's The Night" for Solomon Burke, "You Can Run (But You Can't Hide)" for Jerry Butler and "I Don't Know What You Got (But It's Got Me)" for Little Richard.

Covay started to gain attention for his own recordings in 1964 with the release of "You're Good For Me" and "Mercy, Mercy". "You're Good For Me" was a screaming ballad reminiscent of The Falcons' "Found A Love" with some wonderfully silly lyrics: "Like sugar is good for the teeth/Girl, you're good for me". However, it was the follow-up, "Mercy, Mercy" – one of the first soul records to prominently feature a guitar rather than a horn section – that really had heads turning, particularly in Britain. Its stripped down feel, along with Covay's brash and bluesy delivery, was also a huge influence on **The Rolling Stones**.

The 1965 single "See-saw" was even better. The rhythm was quite complicated for what sounded like a Southern soul record – and what on earth was that bizarre voice accompanying Covay at points in the song? – but it was totally irresistible. The follow-ups, the proto-funk single "Sookie Sookie" and "Shingaling '67", showed that Covay's gruff voice was also perfect for uptempo dancefloor numbers.

Covay was at his best on "Soul Meeting", the underrated **Soul Clan** record he produced in 1968, which featured Covay, Solomon Burke, Arthur Conley, Ben E. King and Joe Tex. However, while Covay continued to create hits for other artists, including "Chain Of Fools" for Aretha Franklin, his own hits started to dry up – and his stab at blues-rock with the Jefferson Lemon Blues Band didn't help.

Covay returned to the charts in 1973 with a #6 R&B hit, the classic cheating song "I Was Checkin' Out She Was Checkin' In". "It's Better To Have (And Don't Need)" followed in a similarly preachy 70s Southern soul style, but "Rumble In The Jungle", an account of the Muhammad Ali/George Foreman fight, and "No Tell Motel" indicated that his best days were behind him.

Covay disappeared from the scene for a number of years, before re-emerging doing some backing work on The Rolling Stones' *Dirty Work* album in 1986. He suffered a stroke in 1992, the year before a tribute album, *Back To The Streets: Celebrating The Music Of Don Covay*, was released. He slowly recovered and finally returned to the studio to record the album *Adlib* in 2000 – his first album in a quarter-century – which featured cameos from Wilson Pickett, Ann Peebles, Syl Johnson and **Huey Lewis**.

Mercy Mercy: The Definitive Don Covay
1994, Razor & Tie

Covay's recordings spanned nearly all of the post-war African-American music from rock'n'roll to funk, and so, too, does this excellent collection. Ranging from "Bip Bop Bip" to "No Tell Motel", *Mercy Mercy* shows Covay to be an expressive singer capable of bringing out the best in his occasionally wonderful songs.

Deborah Cox

Often compared to Whitney Houston, if not boasting such a distinctive voice, **Deborah Cox** is Canada's most successful R&B singer. Like Houston, she specializes in the big-haired, big-throated, wailing power ballads that have blighted urban radio.

Born July 13, 1974, in Toronto, Cox spent her teenage years singing commercial jingles. In 1992 she appeared at President Clinton's inauguration as a back-up singer for fellow Canadian blowhard **Céline Dion**. That same year Cox hooked up with songwriter **Lascelles Stephens** – later to become her husband – and made a demo that found its way to Arista president **Clive Davis**. Signing to Arista, Cox moved to Los Angeles in 1994 and started recording her debut album with some of the biggest names in the business: **Dallas Austin**, **Babyface**, **Diane Warren** and **Keith Crouch**. Despite the cast list, the biggest hit on 1995's *Deborah Cox* was theself-penned "Sentimental", a solid, if generic, record that was as in tune with the street as it was with the office radio. Elsewhere, though, the album was largely indistinguishable from a Céline Dion record, featuring big belters like "Where Do We Go From Here" and utterly generic mid-90s production numbers like "Who Do U Love".

The mawkish, Stylistics-sampling "Things Just Ain't The Same", from the *Money Talks* soundtrack, was a moderate R&B hit in 1997, but was reborn when a dance remix by **DJ Hex Hector** became a big club hit. Arista tried to repeat the same trick for Cox's second album, 1998's *One Wish*. Thanks to several Hector remixes, the ridiculously over-the-top ballad "Nobody's Supposed To Be Here" spent fourteen weeks at the top of the R&B chart and eight weeks at #2 on the pop chart. The horribly cloying duet with **R.L. Huggar**, "We Can't Be Friends", was the album's second R&B #1.

When Clive Davis left Arista in 1999, Cox was unable to capitalize on the momentum of her recent hits and her career faltered. For the next few years she concentrated on acting, with roles in *Nash Bridges*, *Soul Food* and *Love Come Down*. By the time her third album *The Morning After* finally came out in 2002, no one remembered who she was. Not even a cameo from rapper **Jadakiss** on the remix of "Up & Down (In & Out)" could help matters. *Remixed* from 2003 was a collection of the remixes that had helped to make her one of the most successful club artists of recent years, but it couldn't disguise the fact that she was no Whitney Houston.

The Ultimate Deborah Cox
2004, BMG

If you just can't get enough bathetic Dianne Warren-style ballads or don't have enough Whitney Houston in your collection, then get this album. It offers Cox's biggest hits, plus a hint of gospel to lend some weight to all the over-emoting. The inclusion of a few dance remixes might woo some of her more casual fans.

Crown Heights Affair

Crown Heights Affair were largely responsible for paring down the early Kool & The Gang sound into a streamlined groove that was perfect for disco dancefloors, as well as European charts afraid of full-on funk bounce.

The group formed out of the ashes of **New Day Express** in the Crown Heights area of Brooklyn in the early 70s. Initially consisting of **William "Bubba" Anderson** (guitar), **Philip Thomas** (vocals), **Stan Johnson** (keyboards) – later replaced by Howie Young – **Arnold "Muki" Wilson** (bass) and **Raymond Rock** (drums), the group signed to RCA in 1974, and released a self-titled album that had some regional success with the singles "Leave The Kids Alone" and "Super Rod".

In 1975 they decided to add a horn section, made up of **Bert Reid** (saxophone), his brother **Raymond** (trombone) and **Tyrone Demmons** (trumpet). After signing with De-Lite, they were paired with producers Freida Nerangis and Britt Britton, who crafted a sound for the group that was more in tune with the emerging disco sound. The title track of their second album, *Dreaming A Dream*, gave Crown Heights Affair their first hit single, reaching #5 on the R&B chart on the strength of its mellow propulsion. However, it was the seven-minute "Goes Dancin' Mix" of the song that attracted attention on the dancefloor, thanks to its guitar riff and synth interjections.

Do It Your Way followed a similar template in 1976, though the hooks on tracks like "Far Out" and "Searching For Love" weren't quite as memorable. The title track of 1977's *Dancin'* was a blatant rip-off of Isaac Hayes's "Theme From Shaft", but it was the group's biggest American pop hit, stalling just outside the Top 40.

The 1978 single "Galaxy Of Love" was perhaps Crown Heights Affair's cheesiest release, sung in an absurdly high falsetto and featuring in-flight announcements during the intro, but it reached the Top 30 in the UK. Its flip, "Say A Prayer For Two", was a huge disco hit Stateside despite the at-times clumsy arrangement – it was so loaded with hooks, and the hi-hats were so over-mixed, that it couldn't fail to be a floor-filler.

After 1979's *Dance Lady Dance*, whose title track was a lush rapprochement between funk bounce and disco bump, the group started working with producer **Bert De Coteaux**. The immediate result was "You Gave Me Love", a top-ten hit in the UK that was largely ignored in the US. The Affair's final American R&B hit came in 1982, with "Somebody Tell Me What To Do", but by now the Reid brothers and William Anderson were concentrating more on production, and the group slowly dissolved.

Bert Reid went on to become an important figure in crafting the early-80s New York disco sound, most notably on Unlimited Touch's "I Hear Music In The Streets" and "Searching To Find The One", Raw Silk's "Do It To The Music", Denroy Morgan's "I'll Do Anything Tor You" and France Joli's "Gonna Get Over You". He continued to stay active on the dance scene throughout the 80s and 90s, working with **Barbara Tucker**, for example, on the house hit, "Stay Together".

○ **Crown Heights Affair: 100% Essential New York Disco**
2003, Union Square

This fine 13-track collection features most of the Brooklyn band's disco classics, including their biggest hits "Dancin'" and "Dreaming A Dream", as well as dancefloor favourites like "Say A Prayer For Two". Plenty of Crown Heights Affair CDs have been released over the years, but this is probably the best introduction to their particular brand of funk-oriented, floor-filling dance music.

The Crusaders

One of the most successful of all the jazz-fusion groups, **The Crusaders** began life in Houston, Texas as The Swingsters, a band formed by high-school friends pianist **Joe Sample**, saxophonist **Wilton Felder** and drummer **Nesbert "Stix" Hooper**. The Swingsters soon evolved into The Modern Jazz Sextet with the addition of trombonist **Wayne Henderson**, flautist **Ronnie Laws** and bassist **Henry Wilson**. The group moved to Los Angeles in 1960 and changed their name to **The Jazz Crusaders**.

Over the next ten years, The Jazz Crusaders (with rotating bass and guitar chairs) recorded some sixteen albums for the Pacific Jazz label that blended hard bop and soul-jazz. In 1971 they dropped the "Jazz" from their name, switched labels and recorded the album *1*, which was one of the landmarks of fusion. With Sample playing the Fender Rhodes, Felder occasionally joining **Chuck Rainey** on electric bass and the inclusion of three guitarists (Larry Carlton, Arthur Adams and David T Walker), The Crusaders created one of the most successful unions of jazz and funk. The lean groove of "Put It Where You Want It" became the group's first chart hit, stalling just outside the pop Top 50.

The Crusaders' 1972 album *The 2nd Crusade* was more straightforward and more commercial, particularly with Felder, a less expansive player, replacing Rainey as bassist. However, 1974's *Southern Comfort* contained their most successful fusion of funk and jazz yet – "Stomp And Buck Dance", which was one of the few fusion cuts where the musicians' chops didn't get in the way of the groove. In 1975 *Chain Reaction* erred on the side of pleasing palatability, while *Those Southern Knights* included the group's biggest hit to date, the very **Steely Dan**-ish track "Keep That Same Old Feeling".

Henderson left the group in the mid-70s to concentrate on producing – most notably for jazz-funkers **Pleasure** who had dancefloor hits with "Joyous" and "Glide" – and The Crusaders suffered as a result, becoming more streamlined and dull. However, they did have their biggest ever chart success

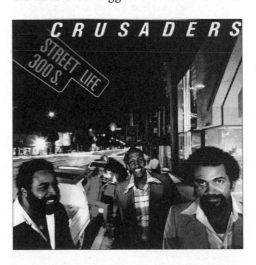

without Henderson, on 1979's "Street Life", a fairly generic disco-jazz groove with a fine vocal by **Randy Crawford**. The Crusaders released a few more desultory albums, but soon fizzled out. Sample went on to have a successful solo career, while the rest of the group remained highly sought-after session men. There have been various reunions over the years with Sample, Hooper and Felder using The Crusaders name, while Henderson uses the group's earlier name The Jazz Crusaders.

The Golden Years
1992, GRP

This 3-disc, 32 track compilation chronicles The Jazz Crusaders' transition to The Crusaders and their commercial apotheosis as fusion's headline act. It perhaps gives short shrift to their fine 1 album in favour of the ruthless professionalism of their later work, but as a testament to the peculiar virtues of bloodless competence it can't be beat.

Cymande

Cymande labelled their own music as "nyah-rock", in reference to the nyabinghi drumming and chanting of Rastafarianism. However, their blend of Afro-Caribbean percussion, Santana-style guitar runs and spaced-out trance chants – not to mention flutes poised somewhere between The Soulful Strings and Jethro Tull – made them under-acknowledged kingpins of psychedelic soul. That their most famous song, "Bra", was lifted hook, line and sinker by **The Stone Roses** in the aftermath of Britain's "Second Summer of Love"in the 80s only proves the point.

Cymande was formed in London in 1971 by Jamaican and Guyanese immigrants **Patrick Patterson**, **Steve Scipio**, Sam Kelly, Pablo Gonzales, Desmond Atwell, Mike Rose, Derek Gibb and Joey Dee. Influenced by both **Osibisa** and **The Equals** (who featured fellow Guyanan Eddy Grant), Cymande hooked up with producer John Schroeder and released "The Message" on the American Janus label. A fey plea for brotherhood based on Ghanaian highlife guitar lines, salsa timbales, waterdrop percussion and a loping, stoned groove, "The Message" crawled into the US Top 50.

On their 1972 self-titled debut album, *Cymande*, the group dedicated a song to Jah, "the world's first hippie", slowed down and drew out the guitar solos of **Carlos Santana** and Jorma Kaukonen and improvised like a slow-witted **Grateful Dead**. While the pace, chanting and guitar sounds sent out vibes like aural joss sticks, Cymande's psychedelia resided mostly in the basslines of the woefully underrated Steve Scipio. Lacking the force of a pure funk contemporary like **Bootsy Collins** or **Larry Graham**, Scipio compensated with odd melodic ideas and crazy patterns. On tracks such as "Bra" and "Dove", Scipio's bass was both anchor and space cadet – it grounded the records but it also floated off at weird angles.

Cymande's 1973 album *Second Time Round* was less psychedelic. The group played up the Afro side of their Afro-funk and were reminiscent of Nigerians **Fela Kuti** and Victor Olaiya on the tracks "Anthracite", "Trevorgus" and "Fug". Unfortunately, they also started to sing more, and the arrangements were often clumsy. In 1974 *Promised Heights* saw more of the same, though great nyabinghi-bass grooves "Pon De Jungle", "Breezeman" and "Sheshamani", and the Curtis Mayfield rip "Brothers On The Slide", kept things from becoming too oily. However, Cymande failed to replicate their initial success in the US. All but ignored in Britain, they inevitably broke up soon after *Promised Heights* was released.

The Message
1999, Sequel

A double-disc collection that features all three of Cymande's albums plus a few unreleased tracks, although you probably really only need the first album. The great bassist Steve Scipio shines throughout, his lines elevating their sub-par material above the mystical schlock.

D Train

In the early 80s, when disco mutated into boogie and house, no group better illustrated the transition than D Train. Built on ferocious, tech-savvy grooves and husky, assertive post-gospel male vocals, D Train epitomized the sound of New York at the dawn of the Reagan era.

Vocalist **James "D-Train" Williams** (a nickname earned from his speed and power on the football field) and keyboardist/producer **Hubert Eaves III** first met and started writing songs together while in high school in Brooklyn. After signing with Prelude, one of disco's true powerhouse labels, they released one of the all-time great dance singles in 1981, "You're The One For Me". Based on a monstrous keyboard riff and huge hand claps, and featuring a great performance from Williams, it was a club smash and a top-thirty pop hit in the UK. The album *You're The One For Me* followed in 1982, with two more killer dance tracks: an inventive cover of "Walk On By" and the surging, inspirational "Keep On".

Their 1983 album *Music* featured more state-of-the-art dance grooves and gospel-inspired messages, such as "Keep Giving Me Love". The title track, one of the definitive 80s keyboard workouts, also reached the UK Top 30. The duo's final album, *Something's On Your Mind*, was released in 1984. Its lightweight title track proved to be their biggest hit, reaching #5 on the R&B chart and further defining the sound of R&B over the next few years.

After D Train broke up in 1985, Eaves, with his characteristic keyboard sound, became an in-demand session player and helped craft hits for Whitney Houston, Aretha Franklin and Luther Vandross. Williams, meanwhile, signed with Columbia. He had some moderate success on the R&B charts with the records "Misunderstanding", "Oh How I Love You (Girl)" and "In Your Eyes", but none of his solo material was as original or as energizing as his D Train material.

The Best Of D Train
1989, Unidisc

This short but sweet collection includes all the big D Train dance hits that helped define the sound of post-disco New York. Buyer beware, however: the version of "You're The One For Me" on this album is an inferior remix. Despite that one poor decision, this is an album of exemplary early 80s dance music.

The Best Of The 12" Mixes
1992, Unidisc

The best choice for true dance aficionados, this album features D Train remixes by the great François Kevorkian and Paul Hardcastle. Many of these are the versions that tore up the dancefloor at clubs like Paradise Garage and The Roxy, making the group the favourites of New York's dance community.

D'Angelo

Michael D'Angelo Arthur was born the son and grandson of preachers in Richmond, Virginia on February 11, 1974. Like the very best soul singers, D'Angelo transferred gospel's religious ecstasies to their real-world equivalent – the pleasures of the flesh. While old gospel albums were his inspiration during the making of his 1995 debut album *Brown Sugar*, D'Angelo was also keenly aware of soul's own traditions.

D'Angelo first gained attention for his role in the hip-hop group **IDU** and then as part of **BMU** (Black Men United), together with anyone who's anyone in contemporary R&B. He was often lumped in with retro-soulsters like **Maxwell**, Lauryn Hill, Erykah Badu, **Raphael Saadiq** (who co-produced *Brown Sugar*'s "Lady") and **Tony Rich**, but D'Angelo was more than just a Marvin Gaye fetishist. Reproaching the new school of R&B for its overwhelming narcissism, D'Angelo – along with Hill – stood as a champion for soul's ability to communicate more complex ideas than knocking boots with a groupie in the backseat of a Lexus.

Not to say that D'Angelo's music wasn't sexy; just that it didn't pant or mawl you like some overexcited 14-year-old. Thus *Brown Sugar*'s sexiest, and best, song was a smouldering ballad dedicated not to a lover, but to smoking the kind bud. Co-produced by A Tribe Called Quest's **Ali Shaheed Muhammad**, "Brown Sugar" blended late-night Jimmy Smith-style organ, atmospheric percussion and snapping snares to create *the* soul song of the decade. Where Jodeci and their ilk were counting the notches on their bedposts, on "Brown Sugar" D'Angelo was extolling the pleasures of pot-fuelled solipsism ("Always down for a ménage à trois/But I think I'ma hit it solo/Hope my niggaz don't mind") and intimating that love, or at least love of the herb, leads to insanity ("Brown sugar babe/I gets high off you love/Don't

know how to behave"). On "Jonz In My Bonz", D'Angelo compared love to addiction and buried his moans and falsetto flights in an array of studio trickery reminiscent of Prince circa *Sign O' The Times*.

The metaphors weren't all weed-inspired, however. "Me And Those Dreamin' Eyes Of Mine" was about a man stuck in a fantasy, and featured D'Angelo singing in a quartet with all the voices in his head to reinforce the vibe. The tick-tocking drum-frame beat of the track led right into the nastiest cheating song since that hoary old standard of 60s rock, "Hey Joe". "Sh*t, Damn, Motherf*ckcr" found the singer walking in on his best friend and his wife in bed together, but instead of a narrative, the song was just a string of exclamations and rhetorical questions that ended with D'Angelo wondering, "Why the both of you's bleeding so much?/Why am I wearin' handcuffs?" The punchy drums and biting wah-wah guitar riff drove the point home as the singer replayed the scenario over and over again in his mind.

D'Angelo was just as good on the straight-up love songs. His cover of Smokey Robinson's "Cruisin'" was as good as, if not better than, the original and asked an important question in the age of downsizing: when was the last time you heard a real string section on an album? "Lady" brought a touch of paranoia to a plea to go public with their love, using the jazzy hallmarks of bohemian soul to emphasize the singer's insecurity. But however great the production was (all of it produced or co-produced by D'Angelo), what you really noticed was that D'Angelo was the finest singer since Prince.

The 1998 album *Live At The Jazz Cafe* was a fairly pointless stopgap measure while D'Angelo was reeling from follow-up pressure, the restructuring of his record label and problems with his management. He finally re-emerged with *Voodoo* in 2000. Although hailed in some quarters as a masterpiece, it sounded like the much-delayed album it was. Characterized by loose playing and bohemian self-indulgence, *Voodoo* drifted all over the map in a blunted haze, inviting rappers Method Man and Redman to get stoopid (and stupid) here, covering "Feel Like Making Love" there and invoking Prince just about everywhere. On the monotonous "Talk Shit 2 Ya" in 2001, D'Angelo reprised his fascination with hip-hop; even if he served as little more than falsetto flava in the background behind the mealy-mouthed Marlon C, D'Angelo's punctuations made the track work. However, apart from his contributions to some recent soundtracks and the intermittent rumours about the D'Live project, that was the last we've heard from him in some time.

Brown Sugar
1995, EMI

Aside from Prince, the best soul of the 80s and 90s was soul that dared to engage with hip-hop. The reason

D'Angelo's *Brown Sugar* was the best soul album since Prince's *Sign O' The Times*, however, was that its hip-hop-invigorated R&B was anchored by the most traditional of soul virtues – a solid grounding in the church.

Betty Davis

Long before there was a **Madonna** or a Lil' Kim, there was **Betty Davis**, perhaps the first of the "fuck me feminists", who used sex as a weapon, in the early 70s, to destroy lotharios with her own sexual power.

Neo-Soul

Even more than pop subgenres dreamed up by music critics, you have to be wary of terms credited to record label executives. Such is the case with "neo-soul", a term coined by Motown executive **Kedar Massenburg** in the late 90s. Neo-soul refers to all those bohemian types who thought that rehashing Donny Hathaway records was somehow more progressive than coming to terms with hip-hop.

Artists such as Maxwell, Erykah Badu, Macy Gray, **India Arie** and **Jill Scott** were not starting an honest revival of soul music, but were instead trying to set themselves apart from all those girl groups wearing knee pads and black Timberland boots. These larger-than-life prima donna superstars, Mary J. Blige hip-hop-soul wannabes and futuristic funkateers inspired by **Timbaland** got themselves crazy hairstyles and vintage threads and appropriated sounds, mannerisms and styles from the early 70s – and claimed it was a revolution. The greatest irony is perhaps that one of the best of the neo-soul records was made by a hip-hop artist, Lauryn Hill.

This putative subgenre was probably started by D'Angelo's *Brown Sugar* in 1995, although the roots had already been laid by the revivalist band led by **Raphael Saadiq** Tony! Toni! Toné! in the early 90s. Kedar Massenburg was already D'Angelo's manager, and when he discovered Erykah Badu in 1995, the marketing idea of neo-soul hit him like a ton of head wraps. After D'Angelo and Badu came a deluge of similarly bohemian artists all pledging to have received inspiration from their heroes of early-70s soul: Lauryn Hill, Macy Gray, India Arie, **Musiq Soulchild**, Jill Scott, **Lucy Pearl**, **Angie Stone**, Alicia Keys, Sunshine Anderson, etc, etc.

Lauryn Hill: The Miseducation of Lauryn Hill
1998, Columbia

Most neo-soul artists are little more than pouting poseurs with unconventional haircuts and Afro-centric wraps, but Lauryn Hill made the best crossover album of the era. On this album she makes hip-hop signify in the same way that vintage soul did in the 70s, and the soaring music transmits the album's message even more potently than the lyrics.

PLAYLIST

1 THE BLUES Tony! Toni! Toné! from **The Revival**
A marriage of jeep beats, P-Funk and a blues guitar lick that was the clarion call of neo-soul.

2 BROWN SUGAR D'Angelo from **Brown Sugar**
The subgenre's finest record is a smouldering ballad dedicated to smoking reefer.

3 ON & ON Erykah Badu from **Baduizm**
Badu's first R&B #1 showed her potential as the archetypal neo-soul singer.

4 EVERYTHING IS EVERYTHING Lauryn Hill from **The Miseducation Of Lauryn Hill**

The string stabs, upful drums and motorvational scratches transmit the song's message more potently than the lyrics.

5 GREEN GRASS VAPORS Angie Stone from **Black Diamond**
Neo-soul's second-best song about the kind bud.

6 JUST FRIENDS (SUNNY) Musiq Soulchild from **Aijuswanaseing**
The pleasantly jazzy backing makes the adenoidal warbling bearable.

Born **Betty Mabry** in Pittsburgh in 1945, she was a model, aspiring songwriter (responsible for the Chambers Brothers' "Uptown") and singer when she met, and then married, **Miles Davis** at the age of 23. She appeared on the cover of Miles' 1968 album *Filles De Kilimanjaro*, which included the composition "Mademoiselle Mabry". They were divorced a year later, but not before she introduced Miles to Sly Stone and **Jimi Hendrix**, with whom she was allegedly (though she denies it) having an affair, and thus helped to change the direction of jazz forever.

After recording an abortive session with The Commodores in 1971, Betty Davis linked up with some of the finest musicians in the Bay Area – **Greg Errico**, Larry Graham, **Michael Carabello**, The Pointer Sisters, Sylvester, **Merl Saunders**, **Neal Schon** and the Tower of Power horns. The resultant 1973 album, *Betty Davis*, was as flamboyant and over the top as any in the soul/funk lexicon. While Davis was not a great singer by any means – she depended on pure attitude rather than any melodic or technical gifts – tracks such as "Anti Love Song", "Game Is My Middle Name" and "If I'm In Luck I Might Get Picked Up" were seriously funky, nasty jams (thanks to the tight rhythm section of Errico and Graham) on which Davis was more predatory than **Mick Jagger** and Andre Williams combined. Her live performances were often even more outlandish than her lyrics, and her concerts regularly attracted legions of protesters.

They Say I'm Different from 1974 was even more ribald, with its songs about bondage and prostitution, but the musicianship (with a different band including Saunders, Buddy Miles, Mike Clark and Pete Escovedo) wasn't as good. Instead of offering a funky counterpoint to Davis's blustery vocals, on this album – with Davis producing rather than Errico – the backing was as blowsy as she was. *Nasty Gal* in 1975 offered more snarling flanged guitars and popping bass grooves, but the growling Davis was again more mannered and stilted than any Black Metal vocalist, even though the tracks "F.U.N.K.", "Dedicated To The Press" and "Nasty Gal" were pretty damn, well, nasty.

Davis recorded a session in 1979 that wasn't released until 1995, when it appeared as *Hangin' Out In Hollywood*, and again a year

later as *Crashin' From Passion*. The tracks from the session were smoother and jazzier than her earlier records and, unfortunately, highlighted her vocal deficiencies. Aside from being the inspiration for Miles Davis' "Back Seat Betty" in 1981, she's been out of the limelight ever since, taming her trademark Afro and laying low in Pennsylvania.

⊙ Betty Davis
1973, Just Sunshine

This is the sound of a woman scorned, exorcizing her demons with the help of one of the best funk bands in the universe. Sure, the sex is ridiculous and the singing even more so, but the album flat-out smokes.

Tyrone Davis

The undisputed master of confessional soul, **Tyrone Davis** was like a black working-class singer-songwriter minus the grotesque self-absorption of certain of his white counterparts. Marrying the eternal verities of the blues with smooth Chicago soul, Tyrone Davis was a soul giant throughout the 70s, even though he remained largely out of sight of the mainstream record-buying public.

Born in Greensville, Mississippi, on May 4, 1938, Davis moved to Chicago during the 50s, where he worked in a factory during the day and hit the blues clubs at night. In 1960 he began a two-year stint as blues guitarist Freddie King's valet. Discovered by Harold Burrage, he started out singing in the vein of Bobby "Blue" Bland on "I Need It (Over And Over Again)" for the Sack label in 1965, and on several records for the Four Brothers label. He subsequently mellowed out, hitting on his signature style with Carl Davis's Dakar label. Tyrone Davis's first Dakar release was both his biggest hit and his definitive record – "Can I Change My Mind", on which Davis followed the lead perfectly with a seemingly oxymoronic mix of vulnerability, wistfulness and assertiveness. The formula was so good that his follow-up, 1969's "Is It Something You've Got", was virtually the same record.

"Turn Back The Hands Of Time", a #3 pop hit in 1970, was an absolutely classic ballad crafted by some of the biggest names of Chicago's second wave: Davis, Barbara Acklin, **Eugene Record**, drummer Quinton

Joseph, pianist Floyd Morris, guitarist Carl Wolfolk and producer **Willie Henderson**. The records "Let Me Back In", "You Keep Me Holding On" and "I Had It All The Time" saw Davis playing a role alien to most soul men: that of the penitent lover abjectly grovelling to be allowed back home.

The superb "Without You In My Life" was more urgent and driving than usual, while "I Wish It Was Me" showed Davis to be just as good on midtempo ballads. He returned to the pumping tempo in 1974 with the great "What Goes Up (Must Come Down)", before settling back down as a midtempo love man on records like the R&B #1 "Turning Point" and the fine ballad "So Good (To Be Home With You)".

Leaving Dakar for Columbia, Davis released the excellent *Love And Touch* album in 1976. However, as the decade wore on, he was forced to conform to trends like disco and funk, with mixed results. The odd gem, such as "In The Mood" – a favourite of mid-90s crate-diggers thanks to its creeping tempo – appeared every once in a while, but Davis's stint at Columbia was characterized by junk like "Get On Up (Disco)" and "How Sweet It Is (To Be Loved By You)".

After scoring a major R&B hit with the bluesy "Are You Serious" in 1982, Davis continued recording for Future and Ichiban. However, he made his living for much of the 80s and 90s from touring the contemporary "chitlin' circuit" of small black nightclubs with his bluesy love man schtick. He then started recording for Malaco in 1996, releas-

ing the so-so album *Simply Tyrone Davis* – his later albums were sometimes marred by banal tracks such as 2000's "Tribute To Johnnie Taylor", a mawkish remembrance of the late soul singer. Still going strong on the touring circuit, Davis continued to release albums throughout the 90s and early 00s, before he suffered a stroke in September 2004 and, sadly, never regained consciousness.

Greatest Hits
1992, Rhino

This 17-track collection provides an excellent overview of Davis's Dakar years, the pinnacle of his career. Despite omitting the great "What Goes Up (Must Come Down)", it's a superb retrospective for an often forgotten titan of soul.

The Dazz Band

Not to be confused with Brick's "Dazz" – although many people do – the **Dazz Band** were one of the groups responsible for developing the synth-funk of the 80s. Thanks to their numerous early-80s hits, that distinctive fat synth-bass sound became one of the defining characteristics of funk during the Reagan/Thatcher era.

The Dazz Band was born from the merger of two Cleveland, Ohio funk units, **Bobby Harris'** Bell Telefunk and **Pierre DeMudd**'s Brain Tree. After several line-up changes the group united around Harris (saxophone), DeMudd (trumpet/vocals), **Skip Martin** (trumpet/vocals), **Kevin Frederick** (keyboards), **Eric Fearman** (guitar), **Kenny Pettus** (percussion) and **Michael** (bass) and **Isaac** (drums) **Wiley**. The group was originally called **Kinsman Dazz** after the *Kinsman Grill* – a club owned by Harris's father – and a contraction of the phrase "danceable jazz". Signing to 20th Century, the group had a couple of small R&B hits with "I Might As Well Forget About Loving You" and "Catchin' Up On Love" in the late 70s.

Moving to Motown in 1980 as the Dazz Band pure and simple, they hit big with the very fine slap-bass post-disco of "Shake It Up", but the record that finally gave them their rep was 1982's "Let It Whip". Riding one of the best basslines of the decade, it was an R&B #1 for five weeks, and went on to plague old women at Bar Mitzvahs and weddings for years to come.

More storming party records followed, including the bouncy "On The One For Fun", the more angular "Joystick" and the almost proto-house "Let It All Blow". However, by 1985 – with Fearman replaced by **Marlon McClain** and hip-hop coming to the fore – the hits began to dry up. The Dazz Band left Motown first for Geffen and then for RCA. Following "Single Girls" and "Open Sesame" in 1988, they dropped from the R&B charts and quietly disbanded after Skip Martin left the group to join Kool & The Gang.

Bobby Harris and McClain assembled a new Dazz Band in 1993, featuring vocalist Terry Stanton, keyboardists Michael Norfleet and Niles McKinney, bassist Nate Phillips and drummer Derek Organ. Primarily geared for the nostalgia circuit, the newfangled Dazz Band nonetheless made the lower reaches of the R&B chart with "Ain't Nuthin' But A Jam Y'All" in 1997, an old school throwdown with **George Clinton**.

Funkology: The Definitive Dazz Band
1994, Motown

This collection is all the Dazz Band anyone really needs. Although it has too many ballads, there's enough of the group's prime synth-funk to please all but the most committed fan, plus the bonus of their two hits as Kinsman Dazz.

DeBarge

A group of young Midwestern siblings singing sweet, ethereal falsetto ballads were hailed as the saviours of Motown's next generation – unfortunately for the **DeBarge** family from Grand Rapids, Michigan, their trajectory never quite followed the path set by The Jacksons.

The DeBarge story began with a mellow late-70s R&B group called **Switch**. Vocalist Phillip Ingram (brother of James), horn players Greg Williams and Eddie Fluellen, drummer Jody Sims, keyboardist **Bobby DeBarge** and bassist **Tommy DeBarge** got together in Mansfield, Ohio in 1975. They were soon discovered by **Jermaine Jackson** and signed to Motown in 1977. While they enjoyed hits with the softly bumping "There'll Never Be", the hideous puppy-love smarm of "I Call Your Name" and the Earth Wind & Fire rip of "Love Over And Over

Again", the group's real claim to fame is that the DeBarge brothers introduced Jermaine Jackson to the rest of their family, and Jackson promptly introduced them to the Motown brass.

Desperate for young hitmakers, Motown signed DeBarge (vocalists **Eldra** and **Bunny**, trumpeter **Mark**, keyboardist **James** and bassist **Randy**) and allowed them to have complete creative control. The family's 1981 debut album, *The DeBarges*, featured Eldra and Bunny singing together on high-flying falsetto ballads. Although the brother and sister brought a new twist to the sweet soul format, it went nowhere.

On 1982's *All This Love* – which spawned the R&B hits "I Like It" and "All This Love" – Eldra (also known as El) sang more like Michael Jackson, while the production found a middle-of-the-road pocket, which is where Babyface got a lot of his ideas. *In A Special Way* perfected the formula in 1983 with "Time Will Reveal" – #1 on the R&B chart for five weeks – which floated on gossamer wings and a Michael McDonald-style keyboard sound. Stevie Wonder also made a guest appearance on the album's hit single "Love Me In A Special Way". *Rhythm Of The Night* (1985) featured the group's biggest hit – the Diane Warren-penned title track, which aped **Lionel Richie**'s mid-80s hits and was used as the theme song to Berry Gordy's movie *The Last Dragon* – and the utterly sappy "Who's Holding Donna Now".

Around this time the group – and other members of the DeBarge family – became embroiled in turmoil and began to fall apart. James eloped with Janet Jackson in 1984, but their marriage was subsequently annulled. Bobby and younger brother **Chico DeBarge** – who scored a moderate solo hit with "Talk To Me" in 1986 – were convicted on cocaine trafficking charges in 1988. Meanwhile, El pleaded no contest to assaulting a woman in Grand Rapids. He also went solo, achieving an R&B #1 from his 1986 debut album *El DeBarge* with the soundtrack schlock of "Who's Johnny?", the theme song from *Short Circuit*. El's second solo album, *Gemini* (1989), found him a bit less wimpy and naive, but the music was as ignorable as ever. Bunny tried her hand at a solo career in 1987 and had a small R&B hit with "Save The Best For Me (Best Of Your Lovin')", but her voice was just too grating on its own. Randy, Mark and James soldiered on as DeBarge and released *Back On Track* in 1987. It went nowhere, and the group finally disbanded in 1989.

El scored a couple of big R&B hits in the 90s, first along with Barry White, James Ingram and Al B. Sure as part of Quincy Jones's "The Secret Garden (Sweet Seduction Suite)", and then with **Fourplay** on a cover of Marvin Gaye's "After The Dance". El also recorded "Where Is My Love?" with Babyface – who owes him more than a small debt – in 1994, which is often sampled by hip-hop artists. Bobby died from AIDS in 1995, but the rest of the family have carried on recording in one capacity or another.

Ultimate Collection
1997, Motown

Compiling the best not only of DeBarge's hits, but also of El, Bunny and Chico's solo careers, this is the best DeBarge family collection available. El and Bunny were blessed with amazing instruments, and listening to them alongside Chico's "Talk To Me" makes you wonder what a real producer could have done with DeBarge had they not been left to come up with shoddy MOR material on their own.

Sam Dees

A fine songwriter and excellent ballad singer, **Sam Dees** was one of those under-acknowledged American talents who managed to attract a devoted cult following in Britain. He may not have been the genius his supporters claim, but cults often have a point – and in the case of Sam Dees, the fans shone a spotlight on an artist who should be far more widely known.

Dees was born in Birmingham, Alabama on December 17, 1945, but raised in Rochester, New York. He made his first recording in 1968 for **Shelby Singleton**'s SSS International label: "Need You Girl". The song was an outmoded ballad, but the flip, "Lonely For You Baby", was an unheralded masterpiece on which the cod-Motown stomp of the day was subdued and slowed down like a creeping realization, while the big, blocky piano chords were a dark and foreboding accompaniment to Dees's singing as he moved from preacher-man begging to gentle resignation.

After recording a couple of solid deep soul sides on Lola Records – "It's All Wrong (It's All Right)" and "Easier To Say Than Do" – Dees moved to Chess and released a classic deep soul cut, the self-penned "Maryanna", in 1971. The following year's "I'm So Very Glad" proved him to be as good on uptempo numbers as he was on emotive ballads.

Dees enjoyed his greatest success, both artistically and commercially, with Atlantic. He debuted on the label in 1972 with the aching ballad "Just Out Of My Reach". Even more lachrymose, but also brutally frank, was that year's "Signed Miss Heroin", a grim, realistic musical portrait of drug abuse. His first album, 1975's *The Show Must Go On*, remains one of the holy grails for soul collectors, thanks to deep soul cuts like "Worn Out Broken Heart" – his biggest hit – and more political tracks like "Child Of The Streets". Though written and recorded for *The Show Must Go On*, "Heritage Of A Black Man" was not released until 1998 because of its political nature. It had a terribly overwrought intro, but when Dees actually sang, the chain-gang arrangement was quite harrowing.

Around the time of *The Show Must Go On*, Dees also started to attract attention for his songwriting, particularly on "Homewreckers" for Tyrone Davis, "Cry To Me" for **Loleatta Holloway** and "Just As Soon As The Feeling's Over" for Margie Joseph. He also had a small hit with "Storybook Children", a duet with Bettye Swann. In 1978 Dees recorded a couple of sides, "Say Yeah" and "In My World", at Malaco studios, which were his last releases for several years. Instead he concentrated on songwriting: "One In A Million You" for Larry Graham, "Love All The Hurt Away" for George Benson and Aretha Franklin, "Special Occasion" for Dorothy Moore, "Keep Your Pants On" for Denise LaSalle, "Where Did We Go Wrong" for L.T.D. and "Lover For Life" for Whitney Houston.

Dees later returned to his own material and released *Secret Admirer* on his own Pen Pad label in 1989 – both the title track and "After All" were fine contemporary soul cuts – followed by *The Homecomings* in 1990. Dees fans at European re-issue labels then started releasing his demos and unreleased tracks, including "Heritage Of A Black Man", during the 90s.

This Japanese import is hard to find, but certainly easier
to get hold of than Dees's masterpiece, *The Show Must
Go On*. Thankfully, this collection does include much of
that outstanding original album, but it is still a far from
perfect collection because it doesn't include any of his
brilliant early records.

The Delfonics

Under the guiding hand of producer/
arranger **Thom Bell**, The Delfonics pioneered the art of soft soul. Moving with ease
between ethereal falsetto ballads and airy
uptempo grooves, The Delfonics epitomized
Philadelphia soul. Bell took that tradition
and transformed it into the most extravagant
vision of the good life soul ever produced.

Randy Cain, **Ritchie Daniels** and brothers
William and **Wilbert Hart** were a four-piece
vocal group called The Four Guys when they
came to the attention of former **Del-Viking**
Stan Watson in the mid-60s. When Daniels
was drafted into the military, the remaining
trio were renamed first The Orphonics and
then, with Watson wanting to honour his
old group, The Delfonics. **Stan Watson**
introduced the group to Thom Bell, who
produced their first single, "He Don't Really
Love You", for the Moon Shot label in 1967.

Moon Shot promptly folded, so Watson
started his own soul label, Philly Groove, in
order to release The Delfonics' second single, "La-La Means I Love You", in 1968. Like
most of the group's songs, it was co-written
by William Hart and Thom Bell, and produced and arranged by Bell. At the time
nothing else was as opulent – Bell used
upwards of 40 musicians, playing woodwinds, strings, kettle drums, French horns
and even glockenspiels. No male singer ever
got as stratospheric as The Delfonics on "La-
La Means I Love You", which remains an
extraordinary record.

Bell upped the tempo a bit for "Ready Or
Not Here I Come", which featured one of
the most dramatic intros in pop history.
However, the group – and, in particular, lead
tenor William Hart with his pinched, nasal
falsetto – truly excelled at desperately pleading ballads such as "Didn't I (Blow Your

Mind This Time)", a shockingly frank
admission of male failure. Two more
midtempo tracks, "Trying To Make A Fool
Of Me" and "When You Get Right Down To
It", continued the group's streak of hits in
1970, and helped to make them the most
imitated group of the time; The Moments,
The Stylistics and Blue Magic all tried to
copy their formula.

Cain left the group in 1971, to be replaced
by **Major Harris**, a former member of The
Jarmels and Nat Turner's Rebellion who
later had a solo hit with the steamy "Love
Won't Let Me Wait". Around the time
Harris joined The Delfonics, Bell stopped
producing their music in order to concentrate on The Stylistics. Although William
Hart became the producer and had immediate success with the spacey and haunting
"Hey Love", the group's hits started to grow
less frequent. By the release of "Think It
Over" and "I Don't Want To Make You
Wait" in 1973, the electric sitar had worn
thin and their records were all sounding the
same. The uptempo "I Told You So", a
minor hit in the discos in 1974, was the
group's last record of any significance.

When Harris left the group to go solo in
1974, he was replaced by the returning
Cain, but, with the loss of Bell's production, the group's hit-making days were
effectively over. The Delfonics finally broke
up in 1979. The group split up and regrouped with various line-ups a number of
times over the next several years, before re-
forming again in the mid-90s – partly due
to the renewed interest created by Quentin
Tarantino featuring two of their hits in the
movie *Jackie Brown*. Since then, there have
been two competing Delfonics line-ups.
One, featuring William Hart, Randy Cain
and **Frank Washington** (a former member
of The Futures), released the album *Forever
New* in 2000; the other includes Wilbert
Hart and Major Harris and is a regular on
the touring circuit.

The Delfonics
1970, Philly Groove

This, The Delfonics' fourth album, was their final collaboration with producer Thom Bell. It's got a handful of
hits that are duplicated on *La-La Means I Love You: The
Definitive Collection*, but it also includes the exquisite "I
Gave To You" and other non-hits of equal quality. Quite
simply the group's best original album and a forerunner
to the great Philadelphia sound of the 70s.

1 LA-LA MEANS I LOVE YOU from **La-La Means I Love You: The Definitive Collection**
Hundreds of records tried to copy this, but it remains sui generis.

2 READY OR NOT HERE I COME from **La-La Means I Love You: The Definitive Collection**
Musical mise-en-scène at its best.

3 DIDN'T I (BLOW YOUR MIND THIS TIME) from **La-La Means I Love You: The Definitive Collection**
The diametric opposite of Wilson Pickett.

4 TRYING TO MAKE A FOOL OF ME from **La-La Means I Love You: The Definitive Collection**
Perhaps the most preposterous use of the sitar ever.

5 WHEN YOU GET RIGHT DOWN TO IT from **La-La Means I Love You: The Definitive Collection**
Probably the squishiest record of their career.

6 HEY LOVE from **La-La Means I Love You: The Definitive Collection**
Spacey soul psychedelia.

7 I DON'T WANT TO MAKE YOU WAIT from **La-La Means I Love You: The Definitive Collection**
So wispy it threatens to float out of existence.

8 I TOLD YOU SO from **La-La Means I Love You: The Definitive Collection**
The Delfonics don their flares and rhinestone jackets for a trip down to the disco.

La-La Means I Love You: The Definitive Collection
1997, Arista

The Delfonics were the embodiment of soft soul. Despite the helium highs of William Hart, they were more soulful than just about every group who followed in their wake, as these twenty tracks amply show. The bulk of these were produced by Thom Bell, the man who created the sound and one of soul's true originals. Many other collections have largely the same tracks, but this gets the nod because of its superior annotation.

The Dells

With a chart career that stretched all the way from the golden age of doo-wop to the early 90s, **The Dells** were among soul's most important and venerable vocal groups.

Their mix of the doo-wop and gospel traditions and their combination of assertive baritone lead with sweet falsetto counterpoint were enormously influential on groups like Harold Melvin & The Blue Notes.

Marvin Junior, Johnny Funches, **Verne Allison**, **Chuck Barksdale** and Lucius and Mickey McGill first got together in 1952 at Thornton Township High School in Harvey, Illinois. Originally known as The El-Rays, they recorded one single for the Chess subsidiary label Checker, the rough and ready "Darling I Know" in 1953. Lucius McGill left soon afterwards, and the group came under the wing of Chess's great doo-wop group **Harvey & The Moonglows**, who helped The El-Rays to improve their harmony chops.

Changing their name to The Dells, they signed to Vee-Jay and released "Tell The World" and "Dreams Of Contentment", neither of which attracted much interest. However, 1956's "Oh What A Nite" was a stone-cold classic. A perfect doo-wop record filled with melodic and harmonic hooks, it became a huge R&B hit. The group couldn't follow up on their success, however, and after a car accident hospitalized most of them in 1958, they decided to take a break.

The Dells re-formed in 1960, with former Flamingo falsetto singer **Johnny Carter** replacing Funches. The tension between Carter's falsetto and Junior's baritone was to become the group's trademark, but not before a jazzier period backing **Dinah Washington**. The Dells had a minor local hit with the rather silly "The (Bossa Nova) Bird" and sang backing vocals on Barbara Lewis's R&B smash "Hello Stranger", but much of their material during the early 60s was loungy, jazz-flavoured stuff like "My Baby Just Cares For Me" and "It's Not Unusual" – yes, the **Tom Jones** song.

They returned to Vee-Jay, and to soul, with "Stay In My Corner" in 1965, a slow grind, last-dance classic. Back at Chess in 1966, midtempo records, such as the Martha & The Vandellas-clone "Run For Cover" and the soulful "Thinking About You", made no impression on the charts, though they later became favourites on the UK's Northern soul scene.

In 1967 The Dells were paired with budding producer **Bobby Miller** and arranger extraordinaire **Charles Stepney**, and the group's career took off. The rich ballad "O O I Love You" harked back to their doo-wop days, but their breakthrough tracks were "There Is" and "Wear It On Our Face", which were both driving uptempo numbers featuring Junior in full-throated gospel mode with honeyed harmonies in the background. A lush, six-minute remake of "Stay In My Corner" – an unheard-of length for urban radio at that time – gave them their biggest hit yet, thanks to a sumptuous arrangement from Stepney and a remarkable display of virtuosity from Junior, who held a single note for sixteen seconds. All of these tracks were brought together on their masterpiece 1968 album, *There Is*.

The 1969 version of "Oh What A Night" was a monster remake of their first hit and was, perhaps surprisingly, far superior to the original. The Dells hadn't lost any of their vocal chops and the arrangement was fantastic, especially the string stabs and the wild guitar runs buried in the background, while changing styles and mores allowed them to get far more passionate than the buttoned-down 50s would have ever allowed. An equally outlandish rave-up version of Otis Redding's "(Sittin' On) The Dock Of The Bay" followed that same year.

Stepney was left to both arrange and produce, with mixed results, after Miller moved on to other projects in 1970. Old hand **Don Davis** then started producing the group in 1973, and hit immediately with the mawkish, schmaltzy "Give Your Baby A Standing Ovation", which might have made The Stylistics proud. By the time they were recording "My Pretending Days Are Over", "I Miss You", "I Wish It Was Me You Loved" and "Learning To Love You Was Easy", Junior was imitating Teddy Pendergrass rather than vice versa.

Although the collapse of Chess in 1975 and the rise of disco had a terrible impact on The Dells' career, they did achieve minor hits for Mercury in the latter half of the 70s with the sleazy downtempo ballad "Slow Motion" and the retro ballad "Betcha Never Been Loved (Like This Before)". Thanks to their timeless balladeering – and also to conservative black radio programmers – The Dells continued to have the odd small hit through the late 70s and early 80s.

The Dells were the inspiration for Robert Townsend's 1991 film *The Five Heartbeats*. They recorded "A Heart Is A House For Love" for the soundtrack and it became their first top-20 R&B hit in eleven years. That success led them to sign with Philadelphia International where they worked with songwriting and production team **Gamble & Huff** on their 1992 album, *I Salute You*, which marked the group's fortieth anniversary together.

There Is
1968, Chess

This breakthrough album marked The Dells' transition from their doo-wop roots to contemporary soul. It features the long version of their classic ballad, "Stay In My Corner", as well as the upbeat "There Is", which was one of their biggest hits. Produced by Bobby Miller and arranged by Charles Stepney, this fine CD is classic Chicago soul harmony from start to finish.

PLAYLIST
The Dells

1 OH WHAT A NITE from **Anthology**
Doo-wop perfection.

2 STAY IN MY CORNER from **Anthology**
The Dells invented soft soul with this record.

3 THINKING ABOUT YOU from **Anthology**
The Dells at their most ardently soulful.

4 O-O I LOVE YOU from **Anthology**
Retro doo-wop at its most ethereal.

5 THERE IS from **Anthology**
Northern chugger reminiscent of The Four Tops.

6 WEAR IT ON OUR FACE from **Anthology**
Charles Stepney's rather avant-garde arrangement opens up an amazing sound world.

7 STAY IN MY CORNER from **Anthology**
Another stunning arrangement from Stepney and Marvin Junior's most acrobatic performance.

8 OH WHAT A NIGHT from **Anthology**
Even better than their 1956 original.

9 GIVE YOUR BABY A STANDING OVATION from **Anthology**
The fabulous, the insurmountable, the incomparable, the mighty, mighty Dells give it up for their lady loves.

10 A HEART IS A HOUSE FOR LOVE from **Anthology**
A pleasant bit of nostalgia that returned the group to the charts nearly 40 years after they started.

Early Vocal Groups

African-American vocal harmony is just about as old as America itself. The first groups of slaves to perform work chants or sing spirituals in the cotton fields were not only the beginning of black harmony singing, but the very root of soul music. Early gospel and jubilee singing groups, such as **The Silver Leafs, The Norfolk Jazz Quartet** and **The Golden Gate Quartet**, may be closer antecedents to soul, but the secular harmony groups of the 30s, 40s and 50s are almost as important to the development of soul as gospel itself.

Picking up a trick from gospel quartets The Silver Leafs and The Golden Gate Quartet, **The Mills Brothers** introduced the sound of the human voice mimicking horns and kazoos to popular music on records like "Tiger Rag". The Mills Brothers were something of a novelty act, though, fitting too closely alongside Bing Crosby and "How Much Is That Doggie In The Window?". **The Ink Spots**, on the other hand, featured smooth lead singer Bill Kenny and comedic talking bass man Orville "Hoppy" Jones, and they managed to incorporate swing into their brand of classic pop.

The Ink Spots were hugely successful and spawned hundreds of imitators. The most important of these groups were **The Ravens** and **The Orioles**. The Ravens' bass singer Jimmy Ricks took Jones's innovations one step further by pushing the bass even more prominently into the mix, and the group's "Count Every Star" laid the foundations for doo-wop in 1950.

The Orioles were probably the most influential of all the early vocal groups: they were rougher in tone than the others, and **Sonny Til**'s wordless falsetto leads spawned doo-wop. Their 1948 release "It's Too Soon To Know" is considered, by some, to be the first rock'n'roll record. While it certainly didn't swing like rock'n'roll, Til's vocal was more emotional than anything in classic pop and was one of the early precursors to soul. The Orioles' 1954 "Crying In The Chapel" is another popular choice for the first rock'n'roll record, largely because it was the first of the new wave of R&B vocal records to cross over to the pop chart. Til's voice was even closer to **Sam Cooke**'s on "Crying In The Chapel" than on any of The Orioles' earlier records.

Meanwhile, **The Spaniels**, from Gary, Indiana, were the bridge between doo-wop and the early vocal groups. In their lead singer, James "Pookie" Hudson, The Spaniels had one of the most elegant singers of all, and their "Baby, It's You", "Goodnite Sweetheart Goodnite" and "You Painted Pictures" were some of the finest of all the vocal group records.

⊙ **The Dawn Of Doo-Wop**
2002, Proper

Four discs and one hundred tracks may be a little much for anyone except the most avid collector, but this is an excellent collection of doo-wop and early vocal group singing. It places The Orioles, The Ravens and The Spaniels in context and follows the thread from The Mills Brothers onwards.

⊙ **Anthology**
1999, Hip-O

This excellent, 2-disc, 37-track retrospective spans virtually all of The Dells' recording career, from 1953's "Darling I Know" to 1991's "A Heart Is A House For Love". As such, it's the entire history of soul balladeering in miniature.

Destiny's Child

B lessed with great looks, vocal chops and seemingly bottomless resources, **Destiny's Child** were, at the turn of the millennium, the only challengers to TLC's R&B throne. By 2001 the trio of female vocalists from Houston, Texas had become the biggest group in the world, and it doesn't look like they'll be relinquishing that position any time soon.

Named after a phrase from the *Book Of Isaiah*, the group began to take shape when

Beyoncé Knowles and LaTavia Roberson met at an audition in 1990, when they were both just 9 years old. With the addition of Knowles' cousin **Kelly Rowland**, Knowles' father began to shape the young girl group into a polished stage act that incorporated rap into their vocals. After their unsuccessful appearance on the American TV programme *Star Search*, on which they rapped rather than sang, they were joined by **LeToya Luckett** in 1993 and became a quartet.

Having built a buzz on the Houston club scene, Destiny's Child signed to Columbia in 1997 and debuted with "Killing Time", which also featured on the *Men In Black* movie soundtrack. The group's debut album, *Destiny's Child*, followed in 1998, bursting out of the gate with the **Wyclef Jean**-produced lead single, "No, No, No", which became an R&B #1 and pop #3. Subsequent

Michelle, Beyoncé and Kelly ask: "Can you handle this?"

singles, however, fell flat and Destiny's Child seemed doomed to follow the usual 90s R&B girl-group trajectory from supernova to quickly forgotten.

Nevertheless, in 1999 the group somehow managed to cobble together the kind of production values you thought only Whitney Houston and TLC could command, and an army of producers that would make even Michael Jackson envious. With such a line-up of mixing-board talent, the resulting album, *The Writing's On The Wall*, showcased state-of-the-art juvenile zing, teen longing and adolescent sass. Producer Kevin "She'kspere" Briggs contributed the album's two calling cards – "Bills, Bills, Bills", an R&B #1 for nine weeks and a pop chart-topper into the bargain, and "Bug A Boo", which only made the pop Top 40. Though Rodney Jerkins' "Say My Name", another #1, and Missy Elliott's "Jumpin' Jumpin'" were the finest tracks. While Beyoncé

hammed it up just as you'd expect from a contemporary R&B diva, she wasn't nearly as over-declamatory or as adenoidal as her peers. Definitive fin-de-millennium R&B.

At the end of 1999 Luckett and Roberson accused Knowles' father, who managed the group, of dodgy royalty practices and of favouring his daughter and niece at their expense. Two new members, Farrah Franklin and Michelle Williams, were quickly drafted in for the "Say My Name" video, prompting a high-profile lawsuit from Luckett and Roberson. The line-up changes continued in 2000 with Farrah Franklin also departing amid controversy, but all of this merely served to make Destiny's Child bigger than ever – a fact cemented by the success of *Survivor* in 2001. Until its final few tracks, where it descended into that special circle of hell that Dante reserved for over-produced, overwrought ballads, the *Survivor* album proved Destiny's Child to possess the

1 NO, NO, NO from **Destiny's Child**
A star is born.

2 BILLS, BILLS, BILLS from
The Writing's On The Wall
This cut all the competition in 1999, including TLC's
"No Scrubs".

3 BUG A BOO from **The Writing's On The Wall**
The first time Destiny's Child remade R&B as an
aerobic workout.

4 SAY MY NAME from
The Writing's On The Wall
Perhaps the closest contemporary R&B has got to
the verities of classic soul.

5 SURVIVOR from **Survivor**
Breathless and hysterical, but also inevitable.

6 INDEPENDENT WOMEN PART I
from **Survivor**
Not exactly the empowerment anthem feminists
have been looking for, but it'll do in a pinch.

7 BOOTYLICIOUS from **Survivor**
Everybody's ready for this jelly.

8 WORK IT OUT Beyoncé Knowles from
Austin Powers: Goldmember
Beyoncé channels the spirit of Betty Davis.

9 DILEMMA Kelly Rowland from **Simply Deep**
A sappy ballad not entirely without charm.

10 CRAZY IN LOVE Beyoncé from
Dangerously in Love
Uh-oh. Uh-oh. Uh-oh.

"Work It Out", from the soundtrack to *Austin Powers: Goldmember* (in which she also starred), was a Betty Davis-style throwback that bumped like crazy. Rowland, meanwhile, took the opposite tack with "Dilemma", a duet with Nelly, and the by-the-numbers #1 R&B album, *Simply Deep*, in 2002.

After a guest appearance on Jay-Z's "03 Bonnie & Clyde", Beyoncé established her iconic status with the monster hit "Crazy In Love", which launched a Chi-Lites sample into the stratosphere. Her 2003 solo album, *Dangerously In Love*, however, was nowhere near as delirious, as it tried to make Beyoncé an "artist", and not just a pop star.

Surprisingly, the group reunited in 2004 for *Destiny Fulfilled*, with its two great dance cuts – "Lose My Breath" and "Soldier" – and loads of lousy ballads that suffered from the same problem as *Dangerously In Love*. Perhaps someone needs to tell Beyoncé that she's more a force of nature than a singer. Inevitably, Destiny's Child decided to go their separate ways after a farewell tour and a greatest hits album falsely titled *#1s*.

⊚ The Writing's On The Wall
1999, Sony

Although almost anyone could have sounded good on the beats created by *The Writing's On The Wall*'s all-star line-up of producers, the real star of the show was Beyoncé, who redefined the sound of contemporary R&B vocals on this album. Taking the breathlessness of Latin freestyle (which suited the hyper-speed beats), but adding the personality and power of more traditional soul, Beyoncé changed the face of R&B much as Mary J. Blige had done almost a decade earlier.

eye of the tiger. The title track may have been too busy and too hysterical, but it broke down your defences, as all great pop singles do. The theme song to *Charlie's Angels*, "Independent Women Part I", on the other hand, whooped your ass just like Michelle Yeoh would have done, had she been in *Charlie's Angels*. The real highlight, though, was the amazing "Bootylicious" which rode a Stevie Nicks sample to pop and dancefloor heaven.

Although Michelle Williams became the first Child to go solo – with the 2002 gospel album *Heart To Yours* – the real solo action came from Beyoncé Knowles and Kelly Rowland. Beyoncé's Neptunes-produced

The Detroit Emeralds

With typical soul logic, **The Detroit Emeralds** vocal group actually hailed from Little Rock, Arkansas. **Abrim** and **Ivory Tilmon** sang with their brothers Cleophus and Raymond in various gospel groups around the Little Rock/Memphis area in the 60s, before trying their hand at secular music with school friend **James Mitchell**.

Signing to Detroit label Ric-Tic, the trio scored a modest hit with their 1968 debut single, the Junior Walker-styled "Show Time". After "Take Me The Way I Am" that same year, they moved across town to the Westbound label. Their 1970 releases, including "If I Lose Your Love" and "I Can't See Myself Doing Without You", were solid if unspectacular vocal fare, but 1971's very fine "Do Me Right", with its cowbell intro, showed the group's ear for novel arrangements.

The next year's midtempo groover, "Baby Let Me Take You (In My Arms)", proved that while The Detroit Emeralds were not the best singers in the world, their mic technique was superb, and the song's production was simply sublime. It was followed by "Feel The Need In Me", a fairly typical proto-disco slow-burn that was reminiscent of the Hi Rhythm Section – the house band at Hi Records – with strings punctuated by tight harmonies. It was a modest hit in the US, but a top-five smash in the UK.

Their 1973 release "You're Gettin' A Little Too Smart" was the Emeralds' best record yet: a calliope stolen from Sly Stone, proto-disco strings, a neat guitar vamp, the guys indulging in how rich their voices sounded with newfangled mics, a cowbell that bore into your skull and one of hip-hop's favourite drum loops.

After group turmoil from 1973 to 1977, which saw two versions of the group touring at the same time and eventually led to James Mitchell and Ivory Tilmon leaving the group, Abrim Tilmon reorganized the Emeralds as a quartet with Paul Riser, Maurice King and Johnny Allen. The new line-up of Detroit Emeralds returned in 1977 and had their last chart success with an extended seven-minute version of "Feel The Need". By that time disco was everywhere, and the idea was to capitalize on the record's standing on the early disco scene. They also recorded "Set It Out", a vocal version of Melvin Sparks' "If You Want My Love" from two years earlier.

By the release of their final album, *Let's Get It Together*, in 1978, the group was aiming directly for disco success, with very mixed results. Various incarnations of the group continued to perform on the oldies circuit during the 70s and 80s, though Abrim Tilmon died of a heart attack in 1982.

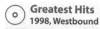

Greatest Hits
1998, Westbound

The Detroit Emeralds were no Temptations, but with the right production they were fabulous. This 20-track best-of album has all of those moments, including their three British top-40 hits, "Feel The Need In Me", "I Think Of You" and "You Want it, You Got It".

Dr. Buzzard's Original Savannah Band

Cloaking themselves in the suavity, élan and romantic-realist style of the age of Cab Calloway and Lorenz Hart, disco's most extraordinary revivalists, if you can call them that, were **Dr. Buzzard's Original Savannah Band**. The group was the brainchild of two mixed-race half-brothers from the Bronx hung up on George Raft and James Cagney movies. Pianist/vocalist **Stony Browder, Jr.** was the musical mastermind, while bassist/vocalist Tommy Browder, aka **August Darnell**, who was fresh out of drama school, was the wordsmith. Allegedly inspired by Dr. Carrash Buzzard – an itinerant musician who had a minstrel show in the 40s – and the multiculturalism of their home (a French-Canadian mother and Dominican father), the two started toying with the conventions of "race music". They formed Dr. Buzzard's Original Savannah Band with singer **Cory Daye**, percussionist **Andy Hernandez** and drummer **Mickey Sevilla** in 1974, to explore things further.

Unlike the legions of hapless artists who were attempting, at the time, to mix disco dazzle with Jazz Age pizzazz, the fraternal co-conspirators constructed a fantasy world in which show tunes actually swung, the ghetto was filled with golden-age Hollywood glamour and heartbreak could be exorcized with a witty turn of phrase. Granted, on paper it sounded like the most regressive, retrograde, revisionist kind of music, but on the turntable the group's self-titled debut album was one of the most fully realized, dazzling artefacts from the black bohemian intelligentsia.

The first words to be heard on 1976's *Dr. Buzzard's Original Savannah Band* were

"Zoot suit city"; the first couplet rhymed "if that would get me ovah" with "equivalency diploma"; the first sounds were the rum-tum-tum of the tom-tom and some **Glenn Miller** (not even Count Basie) brass razzle-dazzle. Stony Browder laid the penguin-suit-ed-big-band schmaltz on thick, with help from veteran Four Seasons arranger **Charlie Calello**. Vocalist Cory Daye displayed a winning combination of Broadway razzmatazz and uptown soul: rolling her tongue à la Billy Stewart and Jackie Wilson while giving the lyrics some Rita Moreno sass or oo-poo-pah-dooing like Betty Boop. So far, so tacky. No wonder the album went gold.

Once you got used to the Cotton Club shtick, though, you started to notice the Latin rhythms and consistently fantastic bassline, and discovered that beneath the children's chorus on "Sunshower" was a skeletal Nigerian Juju track complete with Hawaiian guitar and talking drums. That's when you remembered that the phrase "Zoot suit city" doesn't just refer to some idealized beau monde, but recalls the Zoot Suit Riots in Los Angeles in 1942–43, when military personnel clashed with Mexican-American youths. Instead of wallowing in rhinestone kitsch or indulging in disco escapism like their contemporaries, the brothers Browder used the Busby-Berkeley glitz both to interrogate the present and rehabilitate the past. This was glamour as defiance. Browder and Darnell were daring to dream of a world that locked them out as a matter of course – unless they wanted to be Butterfly McQueen or Stepin Fetchit – but they were equally locked out of the world traditionally ascribed to them because of their mixed race and light skin. Caught in between two worlds, they chose the path that would alienate both.

The group's second album, 1978's *Dr. Buzzard's Original Savannah Band Meets King Pennett*, was even sharper and more acerbic than their first, filled with brittle sarcasm and occasionally discordant jazz arrangements. While obviously smart, it was way too ambitious, and it went over the heads of just about everyone, including possibly the band members themselves. However, 1979's *James Monroe H.S. Presents Dr. Buzzard's Original Savannah Band Goes To Washington* was closer in spirit and sound to the debut. It indulged in rococo mambo and rhumba fantasies and was filled with the mock travelogues that were to characterize Darnell's post-Dr. Buzzard work as Kid Creole.

After their third album once again fell on deaf ears, the group, inevitably, broke up. Darnell became Kid Creole, while Cory Daye recorded the very underrated solo album, *Cory And Me*, in 1979 with Dr. Buzzard's producer **Sandy Linzer**. Daye's album was a minor disco success thanks to the tracks "Pow Wow" and "Green Light", but no follow-up was ever recorded. In 1984 Daye rejoined Stony Browder and drummer Mickey Sevilla to record the underwhelming *Calling All Beatniks!*, released under the name of Dr. Buzzard's Savannah Band.

Dr. Buzzard's Original Savannah Band
1976, RCA

To put it simply, this is the first great single-artist disco album. For all the industry name-dropping, internal rhymes and posing on *Dr. Buzzard's Original Savannah Band*, what matters most is that these fashion-mag wannabes transcended the crowd to create a record as moving and as smart as any other album in the history of soul.

Bill Doggett

Although his heart always remained devoted to jazz, pianist/organist **Bill Doggett** ranked among rock and soul's greatest instrumentalists. Born in the north side of Philadelphia on February 16, 1916, Doggett represented the city's long tradition of blending jazz with the popular R&B sounds of the day.

Doggett formed his first band, The Five Majors, at age 13, before graduating to the Jimmy Gorman Orchestra – the house band at the Nixon Grand vaudeville theatre – while still in high school. He was then a member of **Lucky Millinder**'s big band from 1938 until 1942, before, as both arranger and pianist, helping to craft the records that made **The Ink Spots** the biggest of the early vocal groups.

After leaving The Ink Spots in 1944, Doggett arranged and recorded for everyone from **Helen Humes** and **Lionel Hampton** to **Coleman Hawkins** and Johnny Otis, and then spent three years with Louis Jordan's Tympany Five. Wracked with guilt over the instrument's association with the church, but realizing he needed a new sound, Doggett switched to the Hammond organ in 1951, while working with **Ella Fitzgerald**. Forming his own small combo, he signed to King Records the following year.

Doggett recorded a dozen singles for King in a mellow lounge swing or slow blues style before finally hitting on the archetypal rock'n'roll and soul instrumental in 1956 with "Honky Tonk". A #1 R&B hit for thirteen weeks, and a #2 pop hit, "Honky Tonk" was at the very root of the lexicon of contemporary popular music. Its chugging organ-driven rhythm, **Billy Butler**'s guitar licks and **Clifford Scott**'s honking sax solo have been copied in one way or another by just about every group that have ever jammed together.

His follow-up records "Slow Walk" and "Leaps And Bounds" were more driving, but Doggett's signature sound became the greasy, wink-wink, nudge-nudge sound of "Ram-Bunk-Shush", a remake of a number he used to do with Lucky Millender. Doggett continued to have moderate hits in this vein with records such as "Hold It", "Rainbow Riot" and the Halloween novelty "Monster Party" throughout the late 50s, and he also provided backing for many of King's vocalists, including Little Willie John and **Annie Laurie**.

After leaving King in 1960, Doggett recorded for a succession of labels, including Warner Bros, Columbia, ABC-Paramount and Sue. Both Edwin Starr and Howard Tate fronted his band for a time in the early 60s, before going on to solo stardom. In the mid-60s Doggett signed to Roulette and released big chunky, stinkingly dirty grooves like "Ko-Ko" and "C'mon Git It". His biggest hit during this period came with 1968's "Funky Whistler", a terribly cheesy organ instrumental made wonderful by the sheer unabashed joy in the playing. However, Doggett's finest achievement of the 60s was his very active campaigning contribution to the civil rights movement.

Doggett largely returned to jazz in the 70s and 80s, and continued performing and recording into the 90s. He died of a heart attack in New York on November 13, 1996, having played his final session the year before as a member of **Bluesiana Hurricane** with Chuck Rainey, Lester Bowie and Bobby Watson.

 28 Big Ones
2000, King

Although it doesn't have much in the way of annotation, this collection includes all of Doggett's major hits and wacky one-offs for King Records. These are the early instrumentals that defined not just the instrumental genre, but much of the sound of rock and soul as well. Fans of funkier instrumentals should seek out his *Honky Tonk A-La Mod!* (1966, Roulette).

The Dominoes

Of all the early rock'n'roll vocal groups, **The Dominoes** had perhaps the most profound impact on the direction of soul music. Blessed with the two finest vocalists of the era, **Clyde McPhatter** and Jackie Wilson, and aided by the talent-spotting and commercial instincts of group leader **Billy Ward**, they were a hit-making machine during the 50s.

By the time he formed The Dominoes, Los Angeles native Billy Ward had already been a classically trained soprano singer, a member of his church choir, a boxer, a soldier, a journalist and a voice teacher. In 1950 29-year-old Ward persuaded Clyde McPhatter, who was then singing tenor with the gospel group The Mount Lebanon Singers, to ignore the wishes of his very religious parents and join The Dominoes. Second tenor **Charlie White** (later to join The Clovers), baritone singer **Joe Lamont** and bass singer **Bill Brown** were also recruited. That same year the group's first release on King Records' new R&B subsidiary label Federal, "Do Something For Me/Chicken Blues", rose to #6 on the R&B charts, thanks largely to McPhatter's sinfully beautiful voice.

It was The Dominoes' third single, however, that forever enshrined them in the annals of popular music. "Sixty Minute Man" was not only the biggest R&B hit of 1951, but it also reached #17 on the pop charts, making The Dominoes the first of the new breed of vocal groups to cross over the secular River of Jordan. The irony was that "Sixty Minute Man" wasn't sung by McPhatter, but by the group's bass singer, Bill Brown. Arranged by Ward, the song helped to establish the tradition of soul music that combined the utterly salacious (the lyrics, Brown's comic vocals) with the heavenly (the high harmonies, the churchy hand claps, McPhatter's "ooo"s during the intro).

More great proto-rock'n'roll followed in the shape of the wailing "That's What You're Doing To Me" and "The Deacon Moves In" featuring **Little Esther Phillips**. However, it was 1952's "Have Mercy Baby" that stood as The Dominoes' true legacy to soul. The first secular record to rock with all-out sanctified frenzy, it featured McPhatter not only singing with obviously gospel melisma, but also doing so with Holy Roller fervour, before breaking out in sobs at the end.

"The Bells", by contrast, sounded like a slow, mournful hymn of the kind that **Mahalia Jackson** made her own. This was no age-old spiritual, however. Instead, McPhatter broke into histrionics and sobbed his way through the tale of his own funeral. "The Bells" could only have been further from Jackson's stately grace if it had been sung by **Ozzy Osbourne**. On the gorgeous "Don't Leave Me This Way" and several other records, McPhatter shelved his over-the-top emotionalism in favour of a piercing tenor that was later imitated on countless doo-wop records. Meanwhile, his nasal shouting on "I'd Be Satisfied" laid the groundwork for Jackie Wilson.

In fact, when McPhatter left the group to join The Drifters in 1953, he was replaced by Jackie Wilson. Wilson's first record with the group – now billed as Billy Ward & His Dominoes and featuring Ward, Wilson, **James Van Loan**, **Milton Marle** and **Cliff Givens** – was "You Can't Keep A Good Man Down".

While his slightly astringent sound was obviously influenced by McPhatter, Wilson also brought an operatic range and an even greater sense of melodrama, which Ward exploited by moving away from the rousing R&B of the group's earlier releases. Even though records such as "I'm Gonna Move To The Outskirts Of Town" were sufficiently bluesy and showed off Wilson's stunning range and crystal falsetto, it was only a short step from them to the over-ripe cover versions that characterized the group's final period after Wilson left in 1957 to pursue a solo career.

PLAYLIST
The Dominoes

1 DO SOMETHING FOR ME from **Have Mercy Baby**
Clyde McPhatter brought sanctified intensity to R&B on this remarkable record.

2 SIXTY MINUTE MAN from **Have Mercy Baby**
Perhaps the ultimate conflict between gospel and perdition.

3 THAT'S WHAT YOU'RE DOING TO ME from **Have Mercy Baby**
Gospel meets wailing R&B to create the blueprint for rock'n'roll.

4 THE DEACON MOVES IN from **Have Mercy Baby**
Maybe even more shocking than "Sixty Minute Man".

5 HAVE MERCY BABY from **Have Mercy Baby**
As close to the birthplace of what we now consider popular music as any other record.

6 THE BELLS from **Have Mercy Baby**
A ridiculous, but strangely affecting, sobbing deathbed ballad.

7 DON'T LEAVE ME THIS WAY from **Have Mercy Baby**
Clyde McPhatter's piercing tenor at its best.

8 YOU CAN'T KEEP A GOOD MAN DOWN from **Have Mercy Baby**
Jackie Wilson's first record with the group was a jukebox hit.

9 I'M GONNA MOVE TO THE OUTSKIRTS OF TOWN from **Have Mercy Baby**
Wilson displays his mindboggling range.

10 STAR DUST from **Have Mercy Baby**
Completely overwrought and not in the least bit soulful, but compelling nonetheless.

Wilson was replaced by **Eugene Mumford**, former member of Los Angeles vocal group The Larks, and The Dominoes moved to Liberty Records. With Mumford as their new lead vocalist, they had their last significant hit in 1957 with "Star Dust" before starting to fizzle out. In decline, The Dominoes moved on to the supper-club circuit in the 60s and continued performing, trading on the names and reputations of former members McPhatter and Wilson.

Have Mercy Baby
1985, Charly

Avoiding the overwrought renditions of already sickly sweet standards that characterized their final years and instead containing all of their truly important records, this 16-track disc is probably the best collection of The Dominoes' output. It focuses on the records the vocal group made with Clyde McPhatter and Jackie Wilson as lead singers, including epochal songs such as "Sixty Minute Man" and the title track.

Lee Dorsey

Called "the hidden jewel of soul" by Joe Strummer, **Lee Dorsey** toured with **The Clash**, recorded with Southside Johnny & The Asbury Jukes and was name-checked by the **Beastie Boys** ("Everything I do is funky like Lee Dorsey", from "Sure Shot"). The reason for Dorsey's minor celebrity is simple: he was just about the hippest cat to ever shake his sacroiliac on vinyl. With his lazy drawl, comic timing, sly Ray Charles rips and Cajun *je ne sais quoi*, Dorsey was *the* voice of post-**Fats Domino** New Orleans. Combined with arrangements from **Allen Toussaint** and grooves from the best of the Crescent City's seemingly limitless talent pool, Dorsey's records were some of the crucial building blocks of "the fonk".

Born on Christmas Eve, 1924, Dorsey was an old man in pop music terms when he first burst on the scene in 1961. Prior to that he'd been a boxer, calling himself Kid Chocolate – though he wasn't the famous Kid Chocolate – and worked in a junkyard. Under the auspices of local legend **Joe Banashak**, he recorded a couple of small singles, such as "Lottie Mo", which didn't get out of the bayou. However, the singles were heard by New York R&B men **Marshall Sehorn** and **Bobby Robinson**, who sensed that Dorsey was a special talent.

Based on a schoolyard chant, Dorsey's first and biggest hit, "Ya Ya", was written in half an hour in a New Orleans bar by Robinson and Dorsey. Arranged by Allen Toussaint and Harold Battiste, it rode Toussaint's infectious piano line and subtle second-line swing all the way to #7 on the American pop chart in 1961. Moving from sublime melisma to a ridiculous whoop in the span of a few notes, Dorsey's unaccompanied intro encapsulated his basic vocal approach.

Dorsey followed up "Ya Ya" on Robinson's Fury label with the almost as good "Do Re Mi", which reached #27 in the Top 40. By 1963, however, Robinson and his labels were in financial trouble, and Dorsey disappeared back to New Orleans' Ninth Ward. Two years later he re-emerged on Toussaint and Sehorn's new Amy label with "Ride Your Pony", which was another top-forty hit. The single re-established the importance not only of the singer and producers, but of New Orleans as a whole. Suffering from a talent drain, New Orleans had lost its status as America's capital R&B city to Detroit and Memphis, but "Ride Your Pony" – stealing a riff and a groove from Motown's Junior Walker – helped reclaim the funk for its rightful home.

The following year Dorsey released the even more crucial "Get Out Of My Life Woman". With the hottest of drumbeats (played by jazz skinman June Gardner) and a vocal that oozed Southern attitude, the record inspired countless cover versions by everyone from Joe Williams to Bill Cosby, and became one of the most sampled records in history. While most of that single's impact came in hindsight – it only made the lower reaches of the Top 100 – Dorsey's next single was an instant pop smash. "Working In The Coalmine" boasted another outrageously funky beat, but this time it was the great vocal arrangement and Dorsey's almost camp asides that pushed the record into the pop Top 10.

The pop hits dried up after 1966's "Holy Cow", but with Toussaint and The Meters, Dorsey continued to release great records. "Love Lots Of Lovin'" was a sweet duet with Betty Harris with great percussion, while "Everything I Do Gohn Be Funky" more than lived up to its title, as Dorsey and organist Art Neville got mighty loose. "Give It Up" was the perfect union between Dorsey's back-porch drawl and The Meters' wobbly funk.

On his underrated album *Yes We Can* from 1970 Dorsey was somewhere below his vocal peak, but on tracks such as "Sneakin' Sally Through The Alley" and "Yes We Can" he was more than compensated for by some of the *nastayest* instrumental tracks ever recorded. Toussaint tried to ease Dorsey into the disco era on the 1977 *Night People* album, but with mixed results. He continued to tour through the 70s and early 80s, supporting James Brown as well as The Clash and many others, but sadly he succumbed to emphysema in 1986.

Wheelin' And Dealin': The Definitive Collection
1997, Arista

This great 20-track collection could never quite be called perfect because it doesn't include anything Dorsey recorded after 1969. However, it represents not only Dorsey's finest work, but also the very pinnacle of New Orleans funk – and that point's higher than anywhere else, barring wherever James Brown happens to be at the moment.

The Dramatics

Like so many vocal groups that emerged during the late 60s and early 70s, **The Dramatics** were profoundly influenced by Motown, especially The Temptations and The Contours. Unlike many such groups, however, The Dramatics managed to carve out a niche of their own and became one of the most popular soul acts of the 70s.

Originally known as **The Dynamics**, the group first got together for a talent show in the early 60s at Detroit's Pershing High School. **Ron Banks, Elbert Wilkins**, Larry Reed, **Larry "Squirrel" Demps** and Roderick Davis then signed to the local Wingate label in 1965, and released two Temptations-style singles, "Bingo" and "Inky Dinky Wang Dang Do", the next year.

Changing their name to The Dramatics in 1967, the group passed up a chance to sign with Motown and instead moved to the Sport label, where they made the lower reaches of the R&B chart with "All Because Of You". Detroit-based producer Don Davis then signed them to Stax-Volt. With a new line-up of Banks, Wilkins, Demps, **William**

"Wee Gee" Howard and **Willie Ford,** the group released "Your Love Is Strange" on the label in 1969, to little attention.

In 1971, working with songwriter/producer **Tony Hester**, The Dramatics swiped a catch phrase from comedian Flip Wilson and scored a huge hit with the midtempo "Whatcha See Is Whatcha Get". That success was followed by "Get Up And Get Down", on which, after a truly dramatic intro, The Dramatics did their best Temptations impersonation yet; that said, as Temptations rip-offs go it was pretty great. The quivering ballad "In The Rain" (complete with quiet storm sound effects) featured Ron Banks's lead vocals at their best, and became an R&B #1 for a month in 1972.

Another ballad, the unusually titled "Hey You! Get Off My Mountain", went into the R&B Top 5, and anchored their 1973 *A Dramatic Experience* album. Fitting in perfectly with the paranoid soul of the era, the album included three tough anti-drug songs – "The Devil Is Dope", "Beware Of The Man With Candy In His Hand" and "Jim, What's Wrong With Him?" – which was ironic because Tony Hester later became a casualty of long-term drug abuse.

Wilkins and Howard left the group in 1973 and formed their own version of The Dramatics. They released just one single, "No Rebate On Love", on Mainstream in 1975, although Howard had some limited solo success in the late 70s, under the nickname "Wee Gee". Meanwhile, the real Dramatics – now featuring **Lenny Mayes** and former Chocolate Syrup singer **Larry "L.J." Reynolds** – moved to Chess. They recorded one album for the label, a collaboration with The Dells, in 1974 before signing with ABC. There they scored immediate success with a version of Billy Paul's "Me And Mrs Jones". Unlike many older vocal groups, The Dramatics continued to have hits during the disco era, with ballads such as "Be My Girl" and "I Can't Get Over You", and uptempo dancefloor tracks such as "Shake It Well".

Though they didn't leave The Dramatics, Banks and Demps started to take on other projects. They both began working with **George Clinton**'s Parliafunkadelicment Thang in 1978, most notably as singers with The Brides of Funkenstein, and Banks also wrote and produced the R&B top-ten hit "Why Leave Us Alone" for his brother Bryan's group, **Five Special**. Although The Dramatics continued to ride high on the R&B chart with the ballad "Welcome Back Home" in 1980 for new label MCA, both Demps and Reynolds left the group later that year, and the rest of the band split in 1982.

That was not the end for The Dramatics, however. Banks, Reynolds, Mayes, Ford and Howard got back together in 1986 for *Somewhere In Time (A Dramatic Reunion)*, and the group continued to record new material on occasion throughout the 80s and into the 90s. They provided a smooth 70s vibe on **Snoop Dogg**'s "Doggy Dogg World" in 1993. The Dramatics remain a popular draw on the nostalgia circuit, especially following the 2002 release of their well-received, but poorly distributed, *Look Inside* album, but Lenny Mayes sadly died on November 8, 2004, after a long battle with lung cancer.

Ultimate Collection
2000, Hip-O

This 20-track collection is the only one that spans The Dramatics' career from Stax-Volt to MCA. It holds most of the highlights of their career, including "Whatcha See Is Whatcha Get", "Hey You! Get Off My Mountain" and "In The Rain", but sadly doesn't have any of their very fine drug trilogy from 1973. For that seek out *The Best Of The Dramatics* (1976, Stax), which is still in print and is an excellent survey of their Stax years.

The Drifters

Quite simply the greatest of all of the R&B vocal groups, **The Drifters** were, more than any of their peers, responsible for the transition from R&B to soul. Despite counting two quintessential R&B stylists – **Clyde McPhatter** and Ben E. King – among their ranks, their biggest and most enduring hits were made with vocalists who were little more than journeymen. Ultimately, what truly made the various incarnations of The Drifters so wonderful was that from their inception they were blessed with some of the most accomplished songwriters, arrangers and producers that popular music has ever known.

As soon as Clyde McPhatter, a tenor blessed with an angelic voice and pin-up looks, left The Dominoes in 1953, **Ahmet Ertegun** of Atlantic Records snapped him up. He was put together with former gospel singers **Bill Pinkney** and **Andrew** and **Gerhart Thrasher** to create The Drifters, who were to dominate the R&B charts for the better part of a decade. That year, their first single, "Money Honey", hit #1 on the R&B charts. While "Money Honey" is often cited as one of the first rock'n'roll records, it is also a clear ancestor of soul. Written by **Jesse Stone**, the song concerned itself with the realities of living in a material world. Though comic in tone, it was an obvious predecessor of records by Barret Strong, The Silhouettes, Otis Redding, Gwen Guthrie and countless others. McPhatter's gospel-esque flights of fancy fuelled further hits, including "Honey Love", "Such A Night" and "What'cha Gonna Do", before he left the group in 1955 to pursue a solo career.

That The Drifters survived the loss of McPhatter was largely down to the production of **Jerry Wexler** and Ahmet and Nesuhi Ertegun, as well as musicians like saxophonist **Sam "The Man" Taylor**, guitarist **Mickey Baker** and drummer **Panama Francis**. With the smoother, less nasal (read: less distinctive) Bill Pinkney and **Johnny Moore** taking over as leads, The Drifters had hits with "Adorable", "Steamboat" and "Ruby Baby". However, after 1956 they were plagued by line-up changes and infighting, to the extent that manager **George Treadwell** sacked the entire group in 1958.

Treadwell chose a local group called The Five Crowns, led by Ben E. King, to become the new version of The Drifters and to fulfil their scheduled gigs at the Apollo Theatre. The debut recording of the new Drifters, 1959's "There Goes My Baby", was one of the most significant records in the history of soul and R&B. Produced by **Jerry Leiber** and **Mike Stoller**, it was the first R&B record to feature strings, but more importantly it was the first to elevate studio alchemy above a more natural sound. "There Goes My Baby" definitively moved R&B groups away from both the street corner and the church towards what would become known as soul. The song's vaguely Latin feel grew more pronounced on the next year's "This Magic Moment" and "Save the Last Dance For Me", two more classics of downtown soul.

King left The Drifters in 1960 and was replaced by **Rudy Lewis**, but the hits didn't

The Drifters performing on British TV

stop. Over the next few years, on the tracks "Sweets For My Sweet", "Up On The Roof" and "On Broadway", The Drifters – with some help from Leiber & Stoller, Phil Spector, **Bert Berns**, **Gerry Goffin** and **Carole King** – continued to make heaven a place on earth. When Lewis died of a heart attack at age 27 in 1964, Johnny Moore rejoined the group. He took the lead on that year's "Under The Boardwalk", which proved to be the group's last major hit. However, records such as "Saturday Night At The Movies", "At The Club" and "Baby What I Mean" kept The Drifters on the R&B charts until their contract with Atlantic ended in 1972.

The Johnny Moore-led Drifters experienced a mild rebirth on the Bell label in the mid-70s with a string of nostalgia records:

"Like Sisters And Brothers", "Kissin' In The Back Row Of The Movies", "Down On The Beach Tonight", "There Goes My First Love" and "You're More Than A Number In My Little Red Book", some of which dented the pop Top 10 in the UK. However, even their UK chart success soon fizzled out, and Moore left the group in 1982.

Moore was replaced by none other than Ben E. King, who led The Drifters during their reign on the nostalgia circuit and brought them back to Atlantic, where they recorded a couple of albums of new material during the 80s. The Drifters may have been ridiculously lucky to have some of the greatest producers and songwriters in history at their disposal, but their legacy is, nevertheless, inviolate. Their records gave birth to downtown/New Yok soul and inspired

123

countless lonely, disaffected teenagers to escape their suburban squalor through the power of music.

Rockin' And Driftin': The Drifters Box
1993, Rhino

The 3-CD *Rockin' And Driftin': The Drifters Box* is the only package to feature all of the incarnations of The Drifters and their best work with the consummate talents of Jesse Stone, the Erteguns, Jerry Wexler, Leiber & Stoller, Bert Berns, Goffin & King, Doc Pomus and Mort Schuman. It

---

PLAYLIST
The Drifters

1 MONEY HONEY from **Rockin' And Driftin': The Drifters Box**
Clyde McPhatter invents rock'n'roll yet again.

2 HONEY LOVE from **Rockin' And Driftin': The Drifters Box**
It's amazing to think that back in the day this was so lewd it was banned from the airwaves.

3 WHAT'CHA GONNA DO from **Rockin' And Driftin': The Drifters Box**
Another killer proto-rock'n'roller from McPhatter's gospel-inflected tenor.

4 THERE GOES MY BABY from **Rockin' And Driftin': The Drifters Box**
Quite simply one of the most important records in soul music.

5 THIS MAGIC MOMENT from **Rockin' And Driftin': The Drifters Box**
The swirling Bollywood-style massed strings and Spanish guitar make for an epic of teen lust.

6 SAVE THE LAST DANCE FOR ME from **Rockin' And Driftin': The Drifters Box**
One of Ben E. King's finest performances on top of a lovely Latinate rhythm.

7 UP ON THE ROOF from **Rockin' And Driftin': The Drifters Box**
Produced by Leiber & Stoller and written by Goffin & King – what more do you need?

8 ON BROADWAY from **Rockin' And Driftin': The Drifters Box**
Beautifully urbane pop-soul with a cinematic sweep and feel.

9 UNDER THE BOARDWALK from **Rockin' And Driftin': The Drifters Box**
Bert Berns gives a model lesson in production.

10 AT THE CLUB from **Rockin' And Driftin': The Drifters Box**
The whole team had passed their peak, but the mariachi-cowbell production still raises a grin.

---

remains an absolute classic of New York soul and a great overview of the development of early R&B/soul.

Up On The Roof / Under The Boardwalk
1998, Collectables

If the box set is more than you're after, this single CD pairing two original Atlantic albums from 1963 and 1964 is a great introduction to The Drifters' excellent vocal group sound. It collects the very best of their early 60s hits, with a few non-hit Brill Building gems thrown in. This classic era of The Drifters is uniquely great American music.

Dru Hill

Overwrought, oversung, oversexed and all over the radio, the vocal quartet **Dru Hill** represent the nadir of contemporary R&B. Combining the unrestrained sexuality and excitability of Jodeci with the adenoidal balladeering of Boyz II Men, Dru Hill embodied almost everything that is unappealing about R&B's reaction to hip-hop.

Sisqo (Mark Andrews), **Jazz** (Larry Anthony), **Nokio** (Tamir Ruffin) and **Woody** (James Green) started singing together in high school in Baltimore, Maryland. Naming themselves after the local Druid Hill Park housing complex, Dru Hill began life as a gospel group before turning to secular music while entertaining the customers at a fudge shop where they all worked. Music executive **Hiram Hicks** noticed them in 1995 and signed them to Island.

"Tell Me", the group's debut single – and part of the soundtrack to the 1996 Whoopi Goldberg film *Eddie* – became a top-five R&B hit thanks to a fairly restrained slow bump'n'grind come-on and an appealing gospel-style chorus. However, this was to be the last time "restraint" and "Dru Hill" could figure in the same sentence. Their 1996 debut album, *Dru Hill*, was largely produced by Keith Sweat. He crafted the unctuous love-gone-wrong ballad "In My Bed", which spent an astonishing 63 weeks on the R&B chart, and the R&B #1 "Never Make A Promise", which sounded virtually indistinguishable from a Babyface-produced Boyz II Men record.

Dru Hill's second album, 1998's *Enter The Dru*, was another blockbuster, featuring "How Deep Is Your Love?", a rather racy collaboration with rapper **Redman**, and the sickly MOR ballad "These Are The Times".

The pop #1 "Wild Wild West", a collaboration with **Will Smith** from the 1999 movie of the same name, was a vile interpolation of a Stevie Wonder riff. It wasn't Dru Hill's fault that the record stank – that was strictly on Smith's shoulders.

Sisqo went solo in 1999 with *Unleash The Dragon* and perhaps the most ridiculous song in the history of recorded music, "Thong Song". The record was preposterous, but also perhaps the perfect fin-de-millennium R&B crossover – R&B audiences were used to such over-the-top depictions of the singer's sexcapades, but the focus on underwear gave it a novelty appeal that made it a huge hit. *Return Of The Dragon* followed in 2001 and included a couple of moderate hits, such as "Can I Live", but caused nowhere near the sensation.

Sisqo hadn't entirely cut his ties with the rest of the group by going solo and Dru Hill returned in 2002. Expanded to a quintet by the addition of new member **Skola** (Rufus Woller), Dru Hill released *Dru World Order* in 2002, and proved that their harmonies were still smooth, their appetites for rampant sex remained undiminished and their tastes were as baroque as ever.

Dru Hill
1996, Island

Sometime between the apotheosis of Aretha Franklin and the rise of Whitney Houston, R&B singing became nothing but vocal acrobatics. Dru Hill are among the worst offenders, particularly as they do it on top of some of the dullest beats this side of Babyface. If adenoidal melisma is your thing, look no further than this 17-track collection of Dru Hill's and Sisqo's solo hits.

Dyke & The Blazers

When it comes to sheer "unnnhhh", only one man could rival James Brown – **Arlester "Dyke" Christian**. Knowing that his primal funk grunt transcended all language, Dyke even titled one of his songs "Uhh", and in Dyke & The Blazers he fronted what was probably the greasiest, *stankin'*-est band ever. Born in Buffalo, New York, in 1943, Dyke joined a local soul troupe called Carl LaRue and His Crew in the early 60s. Taken under the wing of Ohio DJ **Eddie O'Jay** (who was also responsible for kick-starting the career of The O'Jays), LaRue and crew moved to Phoenix, Arizona, in 1964. When the group disbanded a year later, Dyke chose sun over snow and stayed in Phoenix.

Dyke formed a new band in Phoenix called **The Blazers**, with himself on vocals and bass, **Alvester "Pig" Jacobs** on guitar, organist **Richard Cason**, drummer **Rodney Brown** and saxophonists **Bernard Williams** and **J. V. Hunt**. In 1966 the group recorded their first single, "Funky Broadway (Parts 1 And 2)", for a local label called Artco. Its combination of Brownian motion on the bottom end and Stax grease on top made "Funky Broadway" an immediate regional hit, and attracted the attention of LA label Original Sound. With national distribution, this incredibly primitive slab of wax – so raw and unpolished as to be almost abstract – reached #65 on the pop charts and stayed on the R&B chart for six months. The first pop song with "funk" in its title, "Funky Broadway" was a harbinger of the revolution in black music – even James Brown would have to wait another year to come up with a record as *nastay* as this.

Although Wilson Pickett's version of "Funky Broadway" took the song all the way to the pop Top 10 in 1967, Dyke & The Blazers' momentum couldn't be curtailed by the major labels and they had another R&B hit with the extremely fonky, but admittedly messy, "So Sharp". With a couple of hits on their hands, the group went out on the road. Bassist **Alvin Battle** joined them, apparently to allow Dyke to slide, shimmy and drop to his knees during their shows. 1968's "Funky Walk (Parts 1 And 2)" began with a guitar line that presaged **Led Zeppelin**'s "Whole Lotta Love" and bumped and strutted its way to the R&B Top 30 with some of the meanest James Brown-style drums and chicken scratch guitar riffs this side of Clyde Stubblefield and Jimmy Nolen, not to mention wild organs that must have given Sly Stone an idea or two.

The Blazers' next big hit, 1969's "We Got More Soul", was a typically sparse funk vamp so crude that Motown's producers probably held their noses whenever it came on the radio. Listing African-American musicians like Ray Charles, James Brown, Johnnie Taylor and Aretha Franklin, "We Got More Soul" was a black pride anthem as only Dyke could do it – it was even open-minded enough to give a shout out to supper-club chanteuse **Nancy Wilson** and, umm, Pearl Bailey. "We Got More Soul" snuck into the pop Top 40, but the follow-up, "Let A Woman Be A Woman, Let A Man Be A Man", did even better. Another cryptic political ditty, espousing funk prophet Dyke's unique kind of philosophy, "Let A Woman..." was a top-five R&B smash and boasted one of *the* great breakbeats, which has featured on countless records ever since.

Although Dyke and the Blazers released a few more singles, including an outrageous cover of "You Are My Sunshine" and the string-soaked, **Norman Whitfield** rip-off, "Runaway People", by early 1971 funk seemed to be getting too sophisticated for a musician like Dyke. He never got the chance to develop in a different direction and prove us wrong. On March 30, 1971 he was shot outside a bar in Phoenix – his killer has yet to be found.

⊙ **Funky Broadway: The Very Best Of Dyke And The Blazers**
1999, Collectables

Funky Broadway is a towering collection of classic proto-funk that's every bit as essential as James Brown or The Meters. Like Brown, Dyke Christian used every instrument in his band as a percussion device, and his single-mindedness enabled him to create the funkiest music this side of the godfather.

Earth Wind & Fire

If funk was a TV programme, then **George Clinton**'s P-Funk Thang would have been the mustachioed evil twin of **Earth Wind & Fire**'s clean-cut hero. Where P-Funk had mad-scientist plans to conquer the world, EW&F played by the rules; where P-Funk read comic books and watched sci-fi flicks, EW&F read African history textbooks and listened to motivational tapes; where P-Funk sang about sex and the evil that men do, Earth Wind & Fire sang about love and spirituality; where P-Funk played only vamps and grooves, EW&F played traditional, radio-friendly songs. Unsurprisingly, EW&F were the most commercially successful black group of the 70s.

Earth Wind & Fire was the brainchild of **Maurice White**. White had been a session drummer for the fabled Chicago label, Chess (his first session for the label was Betty Everett's "You're No Good" in 1963), and part of the Ramsey Lewis Trio. In 1969 White started a production/songwriting partnership with singer Wade Flemons, who had a few solo R&B hits in the late 50s and early 60s, and keyboardist Don Whitehead. With White's brother Verdine on bass, the group called themselves **The Salty Peppers**, and had a regional hit with "La La Time", released in 1969 on their own Hummit label. The single got the group signed to Capitol, who brought them to Los Angeles to record, but, after one more single, "Uh Huh Yeah", the group was dropped.

Recruiting horn players Leslie Drayton, Alex Thomas and Chet Thomas, guitarist Michael Beale, percussionist Phillard Williams and vocalist Sherry Scott, the group renamed themselves Earth Wind & Fire after Maurice White's astrology chart. Their self-titled debut album was perhaps their heaviest and funkiest. It was released on Warner Bros in 1971 and featured the small R&B hit "Love Is Life", but the real action on the album was elsewhere. The vaguely psychedelic funk number "Bad Tune" featured the group's trademark kalimba at its most prominent, while "Moment Of Truth" has since become favourite sample fodder among hip-hop artists. In the same year, EW&F were also responsible for the soundtrack to **Melvin Van Peebles**' original blaxploitation flick *Sweet Sweetback's Baadasss Song*.

After the so-so, meandering *The Need Of Love* was released in 1972, most of the group left. However, after meeting falsetto singer **Philip Bailey** on tour in Denver, Colorado, Maurice White decided to reorganize the band around him. Recruiting keyboardist Larry Dunn and saxophonist Andrew Woolfolk from Bailey's band, as well as guitarist Al McKay from the Watts 103rd Street Rhythm Band, guitarist Johnny Graham from the Friends of Distinction, and drummer Ralph Johnson, the White brothers started **Earth Wind & Fire Mark II**.

Arranged by **Charles Stepney**, their fourth album, *Open Our Eyes*, was the group's breakthrough. The album's two singles, "Mighty Mighty" and "Kalimba Story", were fairly standard funk tracks, but with lyrics about positivity couched in vaguely mystical, Afro-centric metaphors. The Egyptian symbolism gave the band their signature shtick, but it was their optimism that made them a commercial juggernaut. "Mighty Mighty"

127

Earth Wind & Fire's lead singer Philip Bailey

and "Kalimba Story" were both top-ten R&B hits and made some noise on the pop charts.

By the release of their next album, *That's The Way Of The World* (the intended soundtrack to Sig Shore's film of the same name), EW&F were superstars. Riding a nasty chick-en-scratch guitar lick, the self-actualization lyrics of "Shining Star" worked so well that it reached the summit of the pop chart, while the mellower, Philip-Bailey-showcase title track stalled just outside the Top 10. More saccharine self-sufficiency lyrics – which would be enough to make even Maya Angelou blush – followed in the form of "Sing A Song" in 1975, but the groove was so sweet and uplifting that even the most hardened of cynics couldn't ignore it. "Saturday Nite" and "Getaway" were similarly galvanizing grooves, but their lyrics didn't make you cringe.

Featuring two of Earth Wind & Fire's best singles, "Serpentine Fire" and "Fantasy", 1977's *All 'N All* album was their best yet. "Serpentine Fire" was just what its title said it was – a sinuous bassline wrapping itself around slithering guitar licks – while "Fantasy", with its Burt Bacharach-like horns, soaring strings and seriously funky bassline and guitar riff, was pure pop bliss. Popping rhythms and zinging horns combined with Bailey's angelic chorus to make "September" even more perfect than "Fantasy", and a top-ten hit.

Not even disco could put a stop to the band's hits. Teaming up with Philly girl group The Emotions in 1979, EW&F created one of the most enduring records of dance-floor escapism, "Boogie Wonderland". They then managed to score their second-biggest hit in the age of the beat that never stopped with, of all things, a ballad – "After The Love Has Gone". Although it was not as good as the version on the album *I Am* (where it emerged from the lingering sax solo of the preceding song, "Can't Let Go"), "After The Love Has Gone" would become, thanks to its arrangement and vocal style, one of the most influential ballads of the decade.

Unfortunately, by the turn of the 80s, the group just couldn't keep up with the changing shape of R&B. They only had one more significant hit, "Let's Groove" – a magical pairing of Bailey's falsetto and a flatulent synth-bass riff – before breaking up in 1984. Philip Bailey went on to have a huge hit with Phil Collins on 1985's "Easy Lover", while Maurice White had his own R&B success with a cover of "Stand By Me", before producing for **Barbra Streisand** and Neil Diamond, but none of the group's solo careers really took off.

The White brothers, Bailey, Woolfolk, Johnson, guitarist Sheldon Reynolds and drummer Sonny Emory regrouped to form **Earth Wind & Fire Mark III** in 1987. They had a smash hit with their reunion album *Touch The World*, and managed to accom-modate the new techno-funk style on their R&B #1 single "System Of Survival". They continued to sporadically release albums throughout the 90s, but their subsequent efforts to remain in vogue – recording with The Boys, MC Hammer and Sunz of Man – just haven't been as stylish. Their 2005 album *Illumination* was no exception; although the guest appearances were of substantially better quality – OutKast, Raphael Saadiq, Brian McKnight and Black Eyed Peas – the mannered neo-soul settings just didn't make sense for a group that practically invented back-to-Africa bohemianism.

All 'N All
1977, Columbia/Legacy

Beautifully crafted and spirit-lifting, *All 'N All* is arguably Earth Wind & Fire's finest work. The sounds of Brazil effortlessly blend with African rhythms, coated in layers of silky smooth funk. Philip Bailey's falsetto shines on the tender "I'll Write A Song For You", and the brilliantly orchestrated "Fantasy" will live forever. A stunning album from one of the world's true supergroups.

The Eternal Dance
1992, Columbia

You probably won't often listen to the last half of disc three, which covers their 80s material, but this well-annotated 3-CD collection is easily the best Earth Wind & Fire package on the market. Covering the group's entire history from 1971 to 1989, *The Eternal Dance* makes a strong case for EW&F's membership of the funk and soul canon.

Missy Elliott

Missy "Misdemeanor" Elliott is the closest thing R&B's had to an iconic presence since Prince and Michael Jackson fell off. It's not just the eye-boggling, gargantuan rubbish bag she wears in "The Rain" video, though. With the exception of Mary J. Blige and Lauryn Hill, every other female R&B act is putty in the producer's hands. Elliott, on the other hand, is clearly her own woman. Showing why hip-hop has more or less killed off soul music, Elliott is pure attitude. She'd be buried in the back row of the church choir and she wouldn't be welcome in most hip-hop ciphers either, but she's upfront and in your face in an age when no one but the fiercest gangsta rapper has got any 'tude to speak of.

Elliott was born **Melissa Arnette Elliott** in Portsmouth, Virginia on July 1, 1971. She first gained attention as part of a vocal group called **Sista** that was signed to Jodeci member

DeVante Swing's Swing Mob label. She soon hooked up with Swing associate **Timbaland** as part of his production crew Da Bassment. Elliott came to prominence with her rap on the Bad Boy remix of Gina Thompson's "The Things That You Do" in 1996, but it was her debut album, *Supa Dupa Fly* (1997), and her extraordinary wardrobe in her videos that set her on the road to doing Gap ads with **Madonna**. With Elliott playing the bold supa hero up front and Timbaland the brainy producer who's got her back, the pair were a tag team that could have competed with the Road Warriors and the Freebirds. Their submission hold was the track that made Elliott a star,

"The Rain (Supa Dupa Fly)". With a sample of the weirdest R&B track until Timbaland came along, Ann Peebles' "I Can't Stand The Rain", a freaky, off-kilter bassline and Elliott rapping lines like, "Beep, beep, who's got the keys to the jeep/Vrrrroom", "The Rain" was the most crunching calling card since Ric Flair's figure-four leg lock.

While her 1999 album *Da Real World* was just as good, Elliott was fast becoming the premier singles artist of her generation. "She's A Bitch", "Hot Boyz" and "All N My Grill" dominated urban radio with the combination of Timbaland's digital breakbeat freakery and Elliott's take-no-prisoners persona. *Miss E… So Addictive* followed in 2001 with one of the most important singles of the new millennium, "Get Ur Freak On". The track's tabla and zither beat inaugurated the fad of hip-hop orientalism and launched a hundred records that used a similar beat (or sampled Asha Bhosle). "One Minute Man" and "Lick Shots" weren't bad either.

Under Construction, Elliott's 2002 love letter to hip-hop, featured another stone-cold classic in "Work It", an energizing take on the drums from Blondie's "Heart Of Glass" with dentist-drill synth stabs, siren effects, elephant noises and Elliott speaking in tongues because she's so horny. However, *This Is Not A Test!* (2003) found her and Timbaland in a holding pattern. Perhaps making her third album in three years had sapped her creative juices or maybe the rest of the world had finally caught up to Timbaland.

Indeed, 2005's *The Cookbook* finally relegated Timbaland to bit-part status as Elliott started working with beatmakers **The Neptunes** and **Scott Storch**. She also produced several tracks herself, including the lead single "Lose Control", another of her utterly infectious party jams, this time based largely on **Cybotron**'s electro classic "Clear". Elsewhere, "My Struggles" recalled the halcyon early 90s when New York ran the urban music world, while "Bad Man" was a pan-global grooveathon featuring British-Sri Lankan art rapper **MIA** and Jamaican dancehall don **Vybez Cartel**.

Supa Dupa Fly
1997, Elektra

Although the inevitable greatest hits package is probably your best bet, you can't really go wrong with any of Elliott's albums (except perhaps *This Is Not A Test!*). There

PLAYLIST
Missy Elliott

1 THE RAIN (SUPA DUPA FLY) from **Supa Dupa Fly**
A remarkable track that's even weirder than Elliott's costume in the video.

2 HIT 'EM WIT DA HEE from **Supa Dupa Fly**
The beat is incredible and the guitar that sounds like a rubber band thwacked across a cake tin hits you with the hah.

3 SHE'S A BITCH from **Da Real World**
An unfairly disregarded statement of purpose from the best singles artist in a generation.

4 HOT BOYZ from **Da Real World**
Hugely influential cinematic R&B.

5 ALL N MY GRILL from **Da Real World**
Timbaland ignores futurism in favour of an enlightenment parlour.

6 GET UR FREAK ON from **Miss E… So Addictive**
Is this the best single of the new millennium?

7 ONE MINUTE MAN from **Miss E… So Addictive**
Fifty years later, Elliott gives The Dominoes the answer song they deserved.

8 LICK SHOTS from **Miss E… So Addictive**
Absolutely crazy sci-fi-dancehall-techno that the rest of the world might never catch up with.

9 WORK IT from **Under Construction**
Yet another mind-boggling Timbaland beat.

10 LOSE CONTROL from **The Cookbook**
Elliott liberates Cybotron's "Clear" from all the techno trainspotters.

isn't a producer currently working in hip-hop or R&B who hasn't lifted ideas from this album. Elliott's strong personality, taking the place of the usual R&B eye candy, is much, much more than just the icing on the cake.

Under Construction
2002, Elektra

Missy Elliott goes back to the old skool with the 14-track *Under Construction*. This is a twenty-first-century take on 80s hip-hop and street soul – all unruly drums, flatulent synthesizers and Prince-style harmonies.

Shirley Ellis

Perhaps unfairly, **Shirley Ellis** will forever be remembered as the perpetrator of "The Name Game", that ridiculous novelty song ("Shirley, Shirley bo Birley, Banana fana fo Firley, Fee fi mo Mirley") that your parents probably sing when they get too drunk. While Ellis was the indisputable queen of the playground chant, when given the opportunity she was also a pretty decent soul singer.

Of West Indian heritage, **Shirley Marie Elliston** was born in The Bronx, New York in 1941. By the time she was a teenager, Elliston was singing with the doo-wop group **The Metrotones**. She was soon writing for other doo-wop groups, including **The Heartbreakers**, for whom she wrote "One, Two I Love You" in 1957. The manager of The Heartbreakers was her future husband Alphonso Elliston. In 1961 she recorded her first solo single, "Love Can Make You Know", for the Shell label.

Two years later and now calling herself Shirley Ellis, she signed to the Kapp subsidiary Congress label and released the wonderful "The Nitty Gritty". The huge piano line, chunky beats and riotous playground feel made it an instant classic. The song reached the pop Top 10, thus compelling Ellis to release the rather lame "(That's) What the Nitty Gritty Is" as a follow-up the next year. The infernal "The Name Game" firmly established Ellis as the savant of novelty soul when it reached #3 on the pop charts. Far better was the no less novel, but significantly more groovy, "The Clapping Song (Clap Pat Clap Slap)", which also made the Top 10.

Ellis's most straightforwardly pop single was "The Puzzle Song (A Puzzle In Song)", but it failed to climb past #78 on the pop chart, despite its rather wonderful rhythm. "Ever See A Diver Kiss His Wife While The Bubbles Bounce About Above The Water?", on the other hand, was an attempt at a postmodern calypso of sorts and it remains an endearing curio. It was also her last record for Congress.

Signing to Columbia, Ellis recorded "Soul Time" in 1967. It was a smoking tune that was the closest to a bona fide soul single that she ever released. After a couple more unsuccessful singles for Columbia, Ellis signed to Bell in 1968. However, nothing new was ever released and she retired from show business shortly after.

The Complete Congress Recordings
2001, Connoisseur Collection

Although this collection does not include the very underrated "Soul Time", it does have all of her novelty dance hits. Aside from all the unfalteringly effervescent pop-soul, it also features Ellis's surprisingly decent versions of Sam Cooke's "Bring it On Home To Me", Lloyd Price's "Stagger Lee" and Leiber & Stoller's "Kansas City".

Lorraine Ellison

Vocalist **Lorraine Ellison** had one of the most powerful instruments in soul history. She could outbelt anyone and soar with the birds. Unfortunately, just as often, that majestic sweep could become a piercing shriek because of her utter lack of restraint.

Born in Philadelphia in 1943, Lorraine Ellison started singing in church before joining her family's gospel group, **The Ellison Singers**, in her teens. She moved to another gospel group, the Golden Chords, in 1963, before deciding to record secular music the following year. Under the wing of former Enchanters' singer **Sam Bell**, she signed with Mercury and had her first R&B hit in 1965 with "I Dig You Baby" (which also became a hit for Jerry Butler two years later).

Ellison then signed to Warner Bros and made her most famous record, "Stay With Me". A 48-piece orchestra had been booked for a **Frank Sinatra** session, but he was ill and unable to perform, so it was used for Ellison's session instead. The musicians must have been shocked when they heard Ellison tear the paint off the studio walls with her hysteria on this emotionally ravaged soul record. However, either because of her excruciating performance or Warner's unfamiliarity with the soul market, the record only made #11 on the R&B chart, and Ellison spent the rest of her career feeling discouraged.

The following year's "I Want To Be Loved" was churchier and more Southern in style than "Stay With Me", and Ellison's performance was certainly more restrained, but it too failed to have any significant chart impact. Her next release, "Heart Be Still", was a secular rewrite of James Cleveland's "Peace Be Still". It proved to be her last chart appearance. The follow-up, "Try (Just A Little Bit Harder)" – which may have been her best record – was all but ignored until it was covered by **Janis Joplin** a couple of years later.

All of these singles were brought together in 1969 on one of the most intense soul albums ever recorded, *Stay With Me*, which was followed in 1974 by *Lorraine Ellison*. Her eponymous album included covers of Irma Thomas's "Time Is On My Side", **Jimmy Cliff**'s "Many Rivers To Cross" and **Duke Ellington**'s "Caravan", but her performances were again too overwrought for mass consumption. Excluding greatest hits collections, *Lorraine Ellison* was to be her last record.

(⊙) **Stay With Me: The Best Of Lorraine Ellison**
1995, Ichiban

Nearly definitive (it doesn't include "I Dig You Baby" or the two tracks she recorded with Oliver Nelson for her first album, 1966's *Heart And Soul*), this 23-track collection is easily the best Ellison retrospective available. Even on the very fine unreleased tracks taken from an aborted recording session in Muscle Shoals, Alabama, Ellison's almost baroque emotionalism can be too much for some, so approach with caution.

The Emotions

One of the most popular of all the female vocal groups, **The Emotions** (sisters **Wanda**, **Sheila** and **Jeanette Hutchinson**) started in Chicago in the mid-50s when they were just 3, 4 and 5 years old. Originally a gospel group called the Heavenly Sunbeams, and then the Hutchinson Sunbeams, they performed with the great Mahalia Jackson, **The Soul Stirrers** and The Staple Singers before the latter recommended them to their new secular label, Stax-Volt.

Signing with Stax in 1969, The Emotions worked with producers/songwriters **Isaac Hayes** and **David Porter** and hit immediately with their first single, the organ-heavy "So I Can Love You". While they had moderate success in the early 70s with records like "Show Me How" and "My Honey And Me", the Hutchinson sisters' airy vocals didn't always work with Stax's downhome sound. The most artistically satisfying records from their Stax period were often B-sides. Rapper Ol' Dirty Bastard may have sounded a lot better on the beat of "I Like It" when he sampled The Emotions' 1969 B-side on his hit "Shimmy Shimmy Ya" in 1995, but the sisters' breathy innocence worked perfectly on the original chorus. The flip side to "My Honey And Me", "Blind Alley", had an intro that has since become one of hip-hop's most famous loops, and the Hutchinsons were finally gritty enough to cope with the Stax grits-'n'-gravy backing.

After some personnel changes – Jeanette left in 1970 to get married and was replaced by her cousin, **Theresa Davis**, who was then replaced by the youngest Hutchinson sister, **Pamela**, in 1974 – and the collapse of Stax, The Emotions signed to Columbia, where they worked with Earth Wind & Fire's **Maurice White**. White's smooth funk sound suited the Hutchinsons perfectly and they had immediate hits with "I Don't Wanna Lose Your Love" and "Flowers" in 1976. Reprising a vocal trick from "Flowers" the following year, they had an R&B and pop #1 with "Best Of My Love". The single was the group's one transcendent moment, largely thanks to White's decision to get Wanda to sing the song one octave higher than her normal range.

Jeanette rejoined the group in 1978 and the quartet continued to have modest hits with "Smile" and "What's The Name Of Your Love?", as well as appearing on Earth Wind & Fire's "Boogie Wonderland". After a few more albums with White's ARC label, the Red label and Motown, The Emotions called it quits in the mid-80s, although Wanda and Jeanette continued to sing occasional back-up for Earth Wind & Fire throughout the late 80s and early 90s.

Best Of My Love: The Best Of The Emotions
1996, Columbia/Legacy

This 16-track retrospective covers The Emotions' five years at Columbia/ARC, their most fertile hit-making period. Since their sound was virtually interchangeable during the late 70s, if you like Earth Wind & Fire, odds are you'll like this. As well as "Best Of My Love", "Flowers" and their other pop chart hits, this also includes the collaboration "Boogie Wonderland".

En Vogue

The late 80s and early 90s were not a good time for soul/R&B. Teddy Riley's New Jack Swing mixture of hip-hop and soul had opened the floodgates for a whole heap of smarmy love men who had more self-regard than ability – many were graduates of New Edition whose voices had dropped and pecs had developed. This deluge of glorified Chippendales caused hip-hop crews like De La Soul to refer to R&B as "rap and bullshit". With the spectres of Mariah Carey and Whitney Houston looming over everything, female artists weren't offering much of a reprieve from all the garish over-singing and ego-tripping either. Then came En Vogue. They may have been as much the product of Svengalis as The Boys or Another Bad Creation; they may have been as cynically MTV-friendly as TLC, and used beats as tired as MC Hammer; but no other artists of the era did pop-soul so well.

The En Vogue concept was masterminded by producers **Denzil Foster** and **Thomas McElroy**, who also worked with Tony! Toni! Toné. Foster and McElroy had been responsible for Club Nouveau's pop #1 cover of Bill Withers' "Lean On Me" in 1987, and this crossover savvy came to the fore with En Vogue.

The group was formed in Oakland, California, after **Cindy Herron**, **Dawn Robinson**, **Maxine Jones**, **Terry Ellis** and one other singer showed up for an audition in 1988. The other singer was ruled out and 4-U was born, though they soon changed their name to Vogue and then En Vogue. Having made their debut on Foster and McElroy's *FM2* album in 1989, they released their first album, *Born To Sing*, in 1990. It featured the brilliant singles "Hold On" and "Lies", but little else of interest. Their second album, 1992's *Funky Divas*, was a more fully realized affair, although you still had to fast-forward through the painful cover of The Beatles' "Yesterday".

Designed to appeal to both men and women, En Vogue's success can be attributed, in part, to the fact that they seemed to be less of a constructed male fantasy than most of the girl groups that were their stylistic ancestors. It's hard to imagine another female harmony group – aside from perhaps TLC – singing songs as political as "Free Your Mind" or as tough as "My Lovin' (You're Never Gonna Get It)". Foster and McElroy also dared to set En Vogue against arrangements as varied as the rock guitars of "Free Your Mind", the grinding James Brown funk of "My Lovin'", the supper-club jazz of "Giving Him Something He Can Feel" and the po-mo exotica of "Desire".

Of course, the other big reason for their success – let's be frank – was their videos. It's impossible to listen to *Funky Divas* without images running through your mind of the group strutting their funky stuff on the catwalk in their futuristic LaBelle outfits or crooning to an audience of sweating men in their crushed red velvet get-ups. It wasn't just that they looked damn good, but that their videos created the blueprint for all subsequent diva clips: that almost digital blue lighting, the stretched film, the high contrasts, and so on. Luckily, though, Foster and McElroy were as talented as the make-up artists, and the musical language was as strong as its visual counterpart. The resultant pop-soul vernacular was to become unbiquitous over the next few years.

The stop-gap 1993 EP, *Runaway Love*, released as the group was drifting apart, featured collaborations with Foster and McElroy's FMob (the title track) and **Salt 'N' Pepa** (a remake of Linda Lyndell's "Whatta Man"). Terry Ellis then cut a yawner of a solo album, *Southern Gal*, in 1995 before the group reconvened in 1996 for one last great moment, "Don't Let Go (Love)" from the *Set It Off* movie soundtrack.

Dawn Robinson left En Vogue in 1997 to pursue a solo career that never took off, but she landed on her feet as part of **Lucy Pearl** with Raphael Saadiq and Ali Shaheed Muhammad. The remaining trio recorded *EV3* that same year, which was blessed with heavy-handed production from Babyface ("Whatever") and **David Foster** ("Too Gone, Too Long") and the godawful racial tolerance plea "Eyes Of A Child". *Masterpiece Theatre* was a terrible name for a terrible album in 2000. It featured the mock-classical "Love U Crazay", which may have been the worst idea for an R&B song ever.

Maxine Jones left the group in 2001, to be replaced by **Rhona Bennett**. Their 2004 album *Soul Flower* was an improvement on *Masterpiece Theatre*, but still failed to scale the heights of *Funky Divas*.

◎ **Funky Divas**
1992, East West

Funky Divas is one of the best pop-soul albums of the 90s. It includes "My Lovin'", which was largely a remake of "Hold On", but with even more hooks and horn stabs, "Free Your Mind", which borrowed ideas from both George Clinton and Michael Jackson's "Beat It", and "Giving Him Something He Can Feel", a verbatim reading of Aretha's 1976 record. However many second-wave girl groups follow in their wake, none of them seems to be able to get it together as well as En Vogue.

The Esquires

B ased around brothers **Gilbert** and **Alvis Moorer**, underrated Chicago soul group The Esquires was largely a family affair. They began as a doo-wop group in Milwaukee in 1957, made up of the Moorer brothers and their sister Betty (who later scored a solo hit with "It's My Thing", her response to the Isley Brothers' "It's Your Thing"). Betty left the group and moved to Los Angeles long before they hit the big time, and was replaced by **Sam Pace**, who eventually married into the Moorer family. **Shawn Taylor**, who lived with the Moorers when he moved to Milwaukee, completed the line-up.

Hooking up with producer **Bill "Bunky" Sheppard**, The Esquires released their debut single "Get On Up" in 1967 on his Bunky label. With its sweet harmonies, gently propulsive bassline, almost imperceptible conga fills and clean horn lines, "Get On Up" was archetypal Chicago soul and it reached #11 on the pop chart. Although the record was packed to bursting point with detailed percussion, guitar riffs, horn fanfares and piano lines, the catchiest hook on "Get On Up" was the bass singer intoning the title like an old bullfrog. Despite being crucial to the song, it was added almost as an afterthought – the original version only had the falsetto vocals and sky-high harmonies.

The bass refrain was included only after Sheppard consulted a friend, who told him the song was missing something. Conveniently, Sheppard's friend was **Millard Edwards**, who sang with a moderately successful Chicago doo-wop group. Edwards and Sheppard agreed on a mutually beneficial deal: Edwards sang the bass part on "Get On Up" and, in exchange, The Esquires backed Edwards on his single "Things Won't Be The Same".

The single "And Get Away" followed in very similar style, but the formula was still popular enough for it to make the charts. Their 1968 release "You Say" was a bit busy and didn't fare as well. Neither did "Why Can't I Stop", a should-have-been-bigger Chicago ballad that demonstrated the group's debt to The Impressions. After the doo-wop-style song "I Know I Can", The

Esquires moved to Wand and recorded the bright "You Got The Power" and "I Don't Know", but achieved limited chart success.

They updated their sound slightly – to something very much like **The Rascals** – in 1969, on "(That) Ain't No Reason" on the B&G label and the upbeat "Reach Out" on Capitol. The smooth "Girls In The City", released on Lammar in 1971, reached #18 on the R&B chart – their last chart appearance until 1976's disco remake of "Get On Up" on Ju-Par. Featuring various line-ups, the group remained active until the mid-90s, performing in and around Milwaukee.

○ **Get On Up…And Get Away With The Esquires**
1998, West Side

This 23-track collection has all The Esquires anyone would ever want, well almost. It has just about everything they ever recorded, although "Girls In The City" is a regrettable exclusion. They may not have been The Impressions, but The Esquires certainly made superb Chicago soul.

Betty Everett

E qually at home with the blues and gospel, Betty Everett was one of the great female soul singers. Born November 23, 1939, in Greenwood, Mississippi, Everett was brought up in a strict baptist household. Like so many soul singers of the period, she started singing in church, but when she moved to Chicago to live with her sister in 1957, she was immediately discovered by none other than **Muddy Waters**. He took Everett on tour with him, but she was too inexperienced for the road and was sacked within a week.

Back in Chicago, she impressed **Magic Sam** (who had seen her sing with Waters) so much that he got her signed to the Cobra label. She recorded three blues records for Cobra, including "I'll Weep No More", which featured Ike Turner's Blues Band. Turner invited Everett to record in St Louis, where he was based, but the two clashed over moral issues and she returned to Chicago. After a few singles that went nowhere for the CJ label, Everett started working with **Leo Austell** and **Milton Bland** (aka Monk Higgins) and released "Your Love Is Important To Me" – an excellent lover's lament that beautifully fused the blues and gospel – on Austell's Renee label.

Betty Everett then signed to Vee-Jay, for whom she recorded her first national hit, "You're No Good", in 1963. Everett's plain-speaking vocals worked in counterpoint to the sweet Chicago arrangement, but she really let him have it towards the fade-out. She followed up with her most famous single, "The Shoop Shoop Song (It's In His Kiss)", which went to #6 on the pop chart thanks to her exuberant vocals. Even better, although far less commercially successful, was "Getting Mighty Crowded" – a slice of definitive Chi-Town soul, with Everett modulating between relaxed midtempo singing and full-throated belting.

Everett had another huge hit in 1964 courtesy of a duet with Jerry Butler, "Let It Be Me", and a rather less successful version of Charlie Chaplin's "Smile". After the so-so "Too Hot To Hold", on which she tried to copy The Supremes with varying results, and the unjustly ignored "Trouble Over The Weekend", Everett moved to ABC-Paramount. There she was teamed up rather unsuccessfully with producer/arranger **Johnny Pate** on tracks like "Bye Bye Baby", which sounded very Aretha-ish but had the production of a pure Northern stomper. Moving again, this time to the Uni label, Everett scored an R&B hit with "There'll Come A Time" and recorded many fine records – "1990 Yesterday", "It's Been A Long Time" and "Unlucky Girl" – before her lack of sustained commercial success caused her to leave.

Signing with Fantasy, Betty Everett went on to have moderate success in the early 70s with the Donny Hathaway-arranged "I Got To Tell Somebody" and "Ain't Gonna Change Me", and the great two-sided single, "Sweet Dan/Who Will Your Next Fool Be", produced by **Johnny "Guitar" Watson**. After recording "True Love (You Took My Heart)", Everett grew increasingly disillusioned with the music biz and retired to Beloit, Wisconsin, where she died in 2001.

○ **The Shoop Shoop Song (It's In His Kiss)**
2000, Collectables

Hardly definitive, this 25-track collection is, nonetheless, an excellent overview of Betty Everett's Vee-Jay years. It includes several early Chicago soul classics, including the much-covered title track, her first big hit "You're No Good" and the often overlooked "Getting Mighty Crowded".

The Falcons

In many ways the greatest of the early vocal groups, Detroit's **Falcons** encapsulated the history of soul's formative days. The group was far more than a thumbnail sketch of soul history, though, and it gave soul music some of its greatest talents: Wilson Pickett, Eddie Floyd, **Joe Stubbs** and **Mack Rice** were all members of The Falcons at one time or another.

Formed in 1954, The Falcons were, along with **The Del-Vikings**, one of the very few integrated doo-wop groups. The original line-up of Eddie Floyd, Mack Rice, Tom Shelter and Bob Marando recorded their first two singles for the Flip label, followed by the Latin-flavoured "Baby That's It" on Mercury in 1956. Marando and Shelter left soon afterwards because of army commitments.

The group was then reorganized with **Joe Stubbs**, Willie Schofield and guitarist Lance Finnie joining the remaining original members. Featuring motivational guitar from Finnie, their 1957 release "Sent Up" appeared on manager **Robert West**'s Silhouette label, but it was "You're So Fine" that became the group's first hit. Boasting a soaring lead from Joe Stubbs, "You're So Fine" is often cited as the first soul record, but while Stubbs was all gospel heat and flourish, the backing and harmonies were pure rock'n'roll. Call it the perfect transition record.

Their next release, "Just For Your Love", was considerably less striking, but it followed "You're So Fine" onto the R&B chart. Wilson Pickett joined the group in 1960, debuting

on "Pow! You're In Love", and gradually replaced Stubbs as The Falcons' lead singer. With backing supplied by the Ohio Untouchables (who would soon become the Ohio Players), 1962's "I Found A Love" featured Pickett singing an amazing tenor lead that was so powerful it sounded like they had to record him in another room. "Lah-Tee-Lah-Tah" was Floyd's last record with the group, and Pickett also left in 1962 after the release of "Let's Kiss And Make Up".

The remaining Falcons disbanded in 1963, but manager Robert West transformed **The Fabulous Playboys** into the new Falcons. With a line-up consisting of Carlis Monroe, James Gibson, Alton Hollowell and Johnny Alvin, the new Falcons came up with the doo-wop-styled "Oh Baby" and the crudely recorded "Lonely Nights" for West's Lupine label in the early 60s. The new group's records for Big Wheel, epitomized by "(I'm A Fool) I Must Love You" and "Standing On Guard", were midtempo falsetto tracks that owed more to Chicago than Detroit. Their penultimate record as The Falcons was 1967's "Love Look In Her Eyes" – a rapprochement between Motown and Chicago that, inevitably, became a big hit on the UK's Northern soul scene. The group then morphed into **The Firestones** and began recording for Ollie McLaughlin's Moira label.

 I Found A Love
1986, Relic

Relic's excellent three-volume Falcons retrospective is probably becoming as rare as some of The Falcons' original recordings. Still, they're the only ones available right now. This, the second volume, concentrates on the Wilson Pickett era when the group helped to define the sound of vocal group soul, and it is probably the best introduction if you're new to the band.

The Fantastic Four

With a sound halfway between The Temptations and The Four Tops, The Fantastic Four were one of Detroit's most successful vocal groups outside of the Motown empire.

Formed by **James Epps** (a cousin of The Detroit Emeralds' Tilmon brothers), William Hunter and **Ralph** and **Joseph Pruitt**, The Fantastic Four signed to the Ric-Tic label and released "Girl Have Pity" in 1966. Hunter was replaced by **Wallace Childs** for their next single, the midtempo Northern soul favourite "Can't Stop Looking For My Baby", which was a dead ringer for a Motown record thanks to the moonlighting Funk Brothers who played on the record. Their first hit "The Whole World Is A Stage" followed in 1967. The song's mock Shakespearean metaphor was extended way beyond breaking point, but the quartet did a credible Temptations imitation.

Over the next couple of years The Fantastic Four were Ric-Tic's most successful act – they had more chart hits than either Edwin Starr or J.J. Barnes, both of whom they provided backing vocals for. Their biggest tracks were "You Gave Me Something (And Everything's Alright)", "To Share Your Love" (a cover of Bobby "Blue" Bland's "Share Your Love With Me") and "I've Got To Have You".

The wonderful 1968 release "I Love You Madly" was the group's last record for Ric-Tic because the label, and many of its artists, were bought by Motown that same year. The Fantastic Four recorded several sides for Motown's Soul label, but their harmonies became wimpified, perhaps because the label brass didn't want them to compete with either The Temptations or The Four Tops, and were instead looking for another Motor City Delfonics. Disillusioned, the group split in 1970.

The Fantastic Four were coaxed out of retirement by **Armen Boladian** of the Eastbound/Westbound labels in 1973, but with **Ernest Newsome** and **Cleveland Horne** replacing Wallace Childs and Ralph Pruitt. With an updated funk-disco sound, the new line-up released the very fine *Alvin Stone (The Birth And Death Of A Gangster)* in 1975, which included the great post-blaxploitation title track, as well as a couple of pretty decent ballads in "Words" and the surging "My Love Won't Stop At Nothing".

Dennis Coffey produced their disco cult classic "I Got To Have Your Love" in 1977, but, as with most soul vocal groups, the disco era wasn't kind to The Fantastic Four. After the lacklustre "BYOF (Bring Your Own Funk)", again produced by Coffey, The Fantastic Four stopped recording. They remained a popular draw in Detroit and in the UK, however, and James Epps recorded a few singles – "Love At First Sight", "High On The Hill" and "Working On A Building Of Love" – in the 80s and early 90s for the Northern soul market.

⊙ **Best Of The Fantastic Four**
1969, Motown

Luckily this isn't a collection of their very disappointing Motown sides, but rather their earlier Ric-Tic records, which made The Fantastic Four the best of the second-tier vocal groups from the Motor City. For the best of their Westbound years, seek out the double CD set that pairs *Alvin Stone* with *Night People* (2001, Westbound).

The Fatback Band

Although not one of their singles ever cracked the American Top 100 and they enjoyed only a handful of sizeable R&B hits, **The Fatback Band** are one of soul/funk's most popular and longest-lasting bands. This is largely because they have been more adept than any other group, except perhaps Kool & The Gang, at adapting to shifting trends.

The group was founded by drummer **Bill Curtis**, who moved from North Carolina to New York City in 1950. After seventeen years of session work and playing in bands with the likes of Bill Doggett and **King Curtis** (no relation), Bill Curtis decided to form his own label. Named after Curtis's shuffle-beat drumming style, Fatback Records kicked off in 1967 with a single by Brooklyn-based singer **Mary Davis**, "Stop Pretending/Get Up And Dance". More significantly, 1968's "The Cat Walk/Little Bit Of Soul", a huge hit on the UK's Northern soul scene for Gerry & Paul & The Soul Emissaries, consisted of two instrumentals

Detroit Soul

Detroit's soul legacy remains unequalled: Motown, Aretha Franklin, Jackie Wilson, The Falcons, Hank Ballard, sixty to seventy percent of all Northern soul records, Parliament-Funkadelic, Andre Williams, Little Willie John, etc, etc. While in the popular imagination the sound of Detroit is permanently fixed as the sound of Motown, the Motor City has actually produced a staggering range of soul, both well known and still largely undiscovered.

Soul in Michigan was born in 1954 with the doo-wop record "The Wind" by **Nolan Strong & The Diablos.** The backing was pro forma doo-wop, albeit more minimal than usual, but Strong's ethereal voice was unlike anything else at that time – an amazingly wimpy falsetto that paved the way for both Smokey Robinson and Michael Jackson. The Diablos recorded for Jack and Devora Brown's Fortune label, which also released wonderful R&B records by **The Five Dollars, The Don Juans,** Andre Williams (who sang with both of the previous groups) and **Nathaniel Mayer & The Fabulous Twilights,** whose "Village Of Love" was among the best records of the retro doo-wop craze of the early 60s.

The Anna and Check-Mate labels were outposts of the Chicago-based Chess empire, but they released some crucial early Detroit recordings by Lamont Anthony (aka **Lamont Dozier**), **Barrett Strong** and **David Ruffin.** Many of these records were written and produced by **Harvey Fuqua** and featured a young session musician by the name of Marvin Gaye. When these labels folded Fuqua founded his own labels, Harvey and Tri-Phi, which were home to The Spinners, **Shorty Long,** Junior Walker and **Eddie Burns.**

During the 60s the main Detroit labels, aside from Motown, were Robert West's Lupine, Contour and Flick labels, Ed Wingate's Golden World and Ric-Tic labels and Ollie McLaughlin's Karen/Moira/Carla complex. On records by The Falcons, **Eddie Floyd, Sir Mack Rice** and even **The Primettes** (who were about to metamorphose into The Supremes), Robert West's labels specialized in a harder, less polished brand of soul than would become the norm for Detroit. Golden World and Ric-Tic often used moonlighting Motown session musicians on a series of records that have become the canon for Northern soul aficionados. Ollie McLaughlin, meanwhile, was perhaps even more focused on pop acceptability than Berry Gordy. He discovered **Del Shannon,** and his mainstream sensibility could be found on records by Barbara Lewis, **Deon Jackson, The Capitols, Jimmy "Soul" Clark, Jimmy Delphs** and **Richard "Popcorn" Wylie** (whose "Rosemary What Happened" is said to have inspired the movie *Rosemary's Baby*).

Ollie McLaughlin's label also recorded **The Fabulous Counts,** whose "Jan Jan" and "Lunar Funk" were some of the funkiest records ever to come out of Detroit. However, the funk was at its strongest on Armen Boladian's Westbound label and, perhaps strangely, on Holland-Dozier-Holland's Invictus and Hot Wax labels. Aside from Funkadelic's shenanigans, Westbound dropped the bomb with records by The Detroit Emeralds, The Fantastic Four and Denise Lasalle, while Holland-Dozier-Holland gave us Laura Lee, Freda Payne, **Flaming Ember** and **The Politicians.**

---

that featured crunching Motown-style back-beats and wistful keyboards.

The Fatback Band emerged from the label as an entity in its own right with two singles for Curtis's new BC Project II label. In 1968 **Johnny King** and the Fatback Band's "Keep On Brother Keep On" served up a heavy fuzz bassline, Isley Brothers-style keyboards and very funky drums. Along with Curtis and vocalist/guitarist King, the line-up included keyboardist **Gerry Thomas,** bassist **Sam Culley** and saxophonist **Warren Daniel.** The same group recorded the slightly less well-realized "Put It In" in 1971.

In 1972 The Fatback Band signed to Perception Records and released their debut

album, *Let's Do It Again*, with a new line-up of Curtis, King, bassist **Johnny Flippin,** keyboardist **Saunders McCrae,** percussionist **Wayne Woolford** and a horn section of **Earl Shelton, George Williams** and **Richard Cromwell.** With monstrous tracks such as the festive "Street Dance" and the moody and minimal "Goin' To See My Baby" – both featuring killer flute solos by underground jazz legend George Adams – the album was a true funk classic, though it could have done without the cover of Bread's "Baby I'mA Want You". *People Music* followed in a similar vein in 1973 with stone-cold groovers like "Fatbackin'" (written by Weldon Irvine) and "Njia (Nija) Walk (Street Walk)".

Various Artists: Detroit Gold Vol. 1
1988, Solid Smoke

Unfortunately, this collection of recordings from Ollie McLaughlin's Karen/Moira/Carla labels has never been released on CD. It is, nevertheless, a superb overview of the very polished sweet soul sound that almost thrived in Motown's immense shadow. It includes such tracks as Deon Jackson's delightful Smokey Robinson-styled "Love Makes The World Go Round", Barbara Lewis's classy "Hello Stranger" and Jimmy "Soul" Clark's hand-clappy "If I Only Knew".

Various Artists: The Soul Of Detroit
1992, Relic

The Soul Of Detroit concentrates on Robert West's Lupine label. West had a much rawer sound than his Motor City contemporaries and, as a result, this 15-track collection of records by The Primettes, Mack Rice, Eddie Floyd, Joe Stubbs and The Conquerors often sounds more like Southern soul.

PLAYLIST

1 THE WIND Nolan Strong & The Diablos from **Mind Over Matter**
An extraordinary doo-wop record that marked the birth of the wimp in soul music.

2 I FOUND A LOVE The Falcons from **I Found A Love**
Wilson Pickett at his most powerful.

3 COOL JERK The Capitols from **Dance The Cool Jerk**
The bassline, piano and utterly charming vocals make this a sheer fingerpoppin' delight.

4 25 MILES Edwin Starr from **The Very Best Of Edwin Starr**
Starr re-enacts the story of The Little Train That Could.

5 HELLO STRANGER Barbara Lewis from **Hello Stranger: The Best Of Barbara Lewis**
The greatest supper-club R&B record since Dionne Warwick.

6 LOVE MAKES THE WORLD GO ROUND Deon Jackson from **Golden Classics**

Diabetes-inducing sweet soul that is, nevertheless, impossible to resist.

7 PLEASE LET ME IN J. J. Barnes from **The Groovesville Masters**
A gritty and impassioned Northern soul landmark.

8 CRUMBS OFF THE TABLE Laura Lee from **Women's Love Rights: The Hot Wax Anthology**
The best and least gimmicky of Lee's string of militant feminist soul singles for Holland-Dozier-Holland.

9 GIVE JUST A LITTLE MORE TIME Chairmen Of The Board from **Everything's Tuesday: The Best Of Chairmen Of The Board**
One of the records that created the blueprint for the pop-easy listening-soul crossover.

10 (I WANNA) TESTIFY Parliament from **I Wanna Testify: A Historic Compilation Of Vintage Soul**
This classic fusion of rock and soul proved that Clinton and his group had the vocal chops to compete with anyone.

After 1974's *Feel My Soul* and the great "Dance Girl", the group signed to Event/Spring. On the same year's *Keep On Steppin'*, their street funk had more of a jazz flavour, particularly on "Wicki-Wacky" and the title track. In 1975 *Yum Yum* followed in a very similar style, with the title track reaching the Top 40 in the UK, while *Raising Hell* added more disco to the mix, particularly on "(Are You Ready) Do The Bus Stop" and "Spanish Hustle", both of which were British top-twenty hits. *Night Fever* (1976) and *NYCNYUSA* (1977) followed with an even more pronounced disco feel.

The group changed its name slightly, to **Fatback**, with the release of 1977's *Man With*

The Band. The next year "I Like Girls" from *Fired Up 'N' Kickin'* became their biggest US hit, reaching the R&B Top 10 on the strength of a huge bassline and sing-along chorus. "King Tim III (Personality Jock)" from 1979's *XII* beat **The Sugarhill Gang** to the punch by a couple of weeks and was the first record to feature rapping – yet again, the group was on top of a new dancefloor trend. With Gerry Thomas's synth programming paying dividends on the tracks "Gotta Get My Hands On Some (Money)" and "Backstrokin'", 1980's *Hot Box* became the band's most successful album.

Unfortunately, Fatback then spent much of the early 80s in an overproduced rut.

However, they continued to have some moderate R&B hits – "Take It Any Way You Want It", "On The Floor" and "The Girl Is Fine (So Fine)". The one track that rose above the formulaic during this period, "Is This The Future?", was a political song with a sort of rap by Gerry Bledsoe that was reminiscent of some of **Gary Byrd**'s message records. Although Fatback disappeared from the American charts after 1985's "Spread Love" (with **Evelyn Thomas** on vocals) and "Girls On My Mind", 1987 saw their biggest hit in the UK. A remix of their mid-80s record "I Found Lovin'" reached #7 on the UK pop charts that year and became a dance standard. With much the same line-up, the group continues to tour, and remains enormously popular in the UK. They haven't recorded anything new for some time, but they still show up at the Jazz Cafe in London once a year – and they always sell it out.

Hustle!: The Ultimate Fatback
2004, Ace

A 2-CD retrospective that covers most of The Fatback Band's career, from 1968's "Keep On Brother Keep On" to 1987's "I Found Lovin'". Inevitably, some key tracks are missing, but this is by far the best Fatback compilation on the market, and it comes with the quality packaging you expect from Ace.

The 5th Dimension

Blending easy listening, pop and soul into a mellifluous package destined for St Peter's waiting room, **The 5th Dimension** were the pre-eminent commercial soul group of the late 60s and early 70s. Between 1968 and 1973, the group had five platinum singles and racked up Grammy after Grammy. However, outside of their commercial achievements, their influence on the soul community is negligible.

The 5th Dimension began life as **The Hi-Fis**, a group formed by former fashion model **Marilyn McCoo**, fashion photographer LaMonte McLemore, Harry Elston and Floyd Butler, who performed as part of the Ray Charles Revue. In 1966 Elston and Butler left to form Friends of Distinction, and gospel singer **Billy Davis Jr**, Ron Towson and Florence LaRue were brought in to replace them. This new group was called **The Versatiles** and signed to Johnny

Rivers' Soul City label. The Versatiles' first single was "I'll Be Lovin' You Forever", but of more interest to soul fans, particularly Northern soul fans, was the flip side, "Train Keep On Movin'".

Rivers thought that "The Versatiles" sounded old-fashioned, so the group changed their name to The 5th Dimension for their next single, a cover of **The Mamas & The Papas'** "Go Where You Wanna Go". The record laid out the formula that created The 5th Dimension commercial juggernaut: the Bacharach-lite arrangement, the airy harmonies, the jaunty horns and the sprightly rhythm. Significantly, while the record went to #16 on the pop chart, it didn't even place on the R&B chart. Again, of more interest was the flip side, "Too Poor To Die", another Northern soul chugger with that characteristic plinking keyboard sound.

Starting in 1967 with "Up-Up And Away", a pop top-ten that again failed to make the R&B chart, the group became a vehicle for the then unknown songwriter Jimmy Webb, who also wrote "Paper Cup" and "Carpet Man" for them. With "Stoned Soul Picnic", written by **Laura Nyro**, the group finally reached the R&B chart by allowing the minutest hint of funk to creep into their wispy sound. Fusing two songs from the hippie musical *Hair*, the group had their biggest hit in 1969 with "Aquarius/Let The Sun Shine In (The Flesh Failures)", a pop #1 for six weeks. The way too chipper follow-up "Wedding Bell Blues", another Laura Nyro song, stayed at #1 for three weeks. In 1970 "One Less Bell To Answer" was a strange combination of easy listening, torch song and the blues, but it was another definitive Adult Contemporary record and went to #2 on the pop chart. The group's last mega-hit was "(Last Night) I Didn't Get To Sleep At All", their schmaltziest, most Broadway record yet.

After dominating the supper-club circuit and playing for **Richard Nixon** at the White House, The 5th Dimension found themselves two members down when McCoo and Davis (who were now married) left the group. The duo had one monster hit in 1976 with the schlock disco of "You Don't Have To Be A Star (To Be In My Show)", before McCoo went on to host the pop music show *Solid Gold* in the early 80s. The remainder of the group struggled on for a few more years, releasing two rather unsuccessful albums under Motown, and finally split in 1980. However, that was not the last to be heard from them. The 5th Dimension re-formed in the 90s, with Greg Walker and Phyllis Battle replacing Davis and McCoo. Their 1995 release *In The House* proved that things don't always improve with age, especially not a cover of the **Bee-Gees'** "How Deep Is Your Love".

Up, Up & Away: The Definitive Collection
1997, BMG

Northern soul fans will probably be disappointed by the lack of "Too Poor To Die" and "Train Kept On Movin'", but this 30-track greatest hits package contains all the hits that made The 5th Dimension one of the most commercially successful soul groups ever.

First Choice

Although they never had commercial success commensurate with the quality of their records, Philadelphia's **First Choice** were probably the finest female vocal group of the disco era. Originally formed by **Rochelle Fleming** and **Annette Guest** at Overbrook High School, the group went through various names (including The Debronettes and The Silver Rings) and personnel changes before settling on First Choice and the line-up of Fleming, Guest, **Wardell Piper** and **Mulaney Star**. Working with Philly mainstays **Norman Harris** and **Alan Felder**, the group recorded their debut single, the frantic "This Is The House Where Love Died" on Scepter/Wand in 1972.

Star left the group shortly after, and the remaining trio recorded "Armed And Extremely Dangerous" for Philly Groove. It was their biggest pop hit, thanks to one of the definitive proto-disco beats, but Fleming wasn't at her best with the awkward melody or the somewhat camp lyrics. Despite the record's success, Piper left the group (she later had solo success with the disco hits "Captain Boogie" and "Super Sweet") and was replaced by **Joyce Jones** on "Smarty Pants", which went to #9 in the UK. It was hardly the best lyric in the world, but Fleming was at her best on the track, and the rhythm from drummer **Earl Young** and bassist **Ronnie Baker** was soon to become the definition of disco.

In 1974 "The Player" was classic Philly sound, with that hissing hi-hat and deep, watery Fender Rhodes, as well as great vocals from Fleming, while "Guilty" – a cover of The Pearls' record – suffered by not having Fleming on lead. First Choice signed with Warner Bros in 1976, but their stay there only lasted for one lacklustre album, *So Let Us Entertain You*.

With Jones replaced by **Ursula Herring**, the group signed to Salsoul's Gold Mind subsidiary and proceeded to record some of disco's greatest records. "Doctor Love" was a pumping dancefloor classic, while "Double Crossed" may have been pretty uninspiring for the most part – by-numbers Salsoul/late Philly disco – but the string intro was one of disco's most sublime moments. Most sublime of all, however, was "Let No Man Put Asunder". Originally recorded in 1977, the 1982 remix by **Shep Pettibone** turned it not only into one of the greatest disco records, but also into one of the building blocks of house music.

It was "Love Thang", First Choice's 1979 dancefloor stormer, that finally established Rochelle Fleming as one of the great disco divas. The group split up after the release of the album *Breakaway*, but Fleming continued to record club anthems, including "Love Itch", "Danger" and "Suffer (The Consequences)", into the 90s.

Greatest Hits
1993, Salsoul

This 23-track collection is a superlative survey of the development of the disco sound from its Philly roots to its stripped-down New York pinnacle. Moving from "Armed And Extremely Dangerous" to "Love Thang" and "Let No Man Put Asunder", it proves that Rochelle Fleming is one of the soul continuum's most unheralded vocalists.

The Five Du-Tones / South Shore Commission

Despite having one of the definitive R&B names, **The Five Du-Tones** are remembered, if at all, for one single and one single only. Of course, that single is so pure, raw and transcendent that they would belong in this book even if they had never released another record. An utterly joyous ode to watching girls shake their asses, 1963's "Shake A Tail Feather" was co-written and produced by Andre Williams, whose salaciousness and recorded-in-a-broom-closet quality burst from the record's every groove. "Shake A Tail Feather" is such a rollicking good time that it has been covered by James & Bobby Purify, Ike & Tina Turner and Ray Charles (in *The Blues Brothers* movie).

The Five Du-Tones – Frank McCurrey, Andrew Butler, Leroy Joyce, Jim West and Willie Guest – formed in high school in St. Louis in 1957, but moved to Chicago in 1962. They recorded two singles for the One-Derful label, "Please Change Your Mind" and "Come Back Baby", before the planets aligned for their biggest hit "Shake A Tail Feather" (though it only made #51 on the pop chart and #28 on the R&B chart). They continued to work with One-Derful and Williams for the next few years, releasing singles such as "The Gouster", "The Cool Bird", "Sweet Lips" and "Mountain Of Love", without any chart success. Even forming a review with two female singer/dancers, The Du-Ettes, failed to attract enough attention, and the group disbanded in 1967.

When The Du-Tones broke up, McCurrey joined Sidney Lennear, Sheryl Henry, David Henderson, Eugene Rogers and Warren Haygood in a Washington DC vocal group called The Exciters (not the New York group that recorded "Tell Him"). Changing their name to The South Shore Commission, they recorded one single for Atlantic – "Right On Brother" – and another for Nickel – "Shadows" – before signing to Scepter/Wand in 1974. The group's 1975 12" version of "Free Man", produced by Bunny Sigler and mixed by Tom Moulton, was one of the first 12" singles and a huge disco hit on the East Coast. Punchy and assertive, yet simultaneously smooth and gently uplifting, "Free Man" was textbook early disco. A self-titled album followed later that same year, and produced two more disco favourites, "We're On The Right Track" and "Train Called Freedom", but the group soon faded into glitterball obscurity.

The Five Du-Tones
1996, Ring Of Stars

Even though you really only need one single by The Five Du-Tones – "Shake A Tail Feather" – this 21-track compila-

tion has nearly everything the group ever recorded. If you can get hold of this album, you're sure to agree that it's all rollicking good fun.

Free Man: The Very Best Of The South Shore Commission
1998, Collectables

This 8-track collection is essentially the album the group recorded for Wand in 1975, plus the extended disco versions of both "Free Man" and "Train Called Freedom" (as well as the original album versions). It is the best, and for that matter the only, South Shore Commission collection on the market.

The "5" Royales

Perhaps more than any other vocal group, The "5" Royales epitomized the pre-history of soul music. The roots of The "5" Royales lay in a gospel group called The Royal Sons, which was formed by Lowman Pauling, Clarence Pauling (who later became a session director at Motown), Windsor King, William Samuels and Anthony Price in Winston-Salem, North Carolina, in 1938. In 1951 the group – with only Lowman Pauling left from the original line-up – recorded two singles for the New York-based Apollo label in the style of the Soul Stirrers: "Bedside Of A Neighbour/Journey's End" and "Come Over Here/Let Nothing Separate Me". By the end of 1951, the group had moved to New York, where Apollo began recording them as a secular group.

Compared to The Royal Sons' gospel recordings, the newly minted "5" Royales sounded like they came from another century. The Royal Sons were raggedy and rough and sang over primitive instrumentation, while The "5" Royales were smooth and polished and sounded like anything but the country bumpkins they were. For their first single, "Too Much Of A Little Bit/Give Me One More Chance", The "5" Royales' line-up was Pauling, Johnny Tanner, Jimmy Moore, Obadiah Carter and Otto Jeffries. Recorded in 1951 and released the following year, "Give Me One More Chance" could very well be the Rosetta Stone of soul. Even more obviously than The Dominoes' "Have Mercy Baby" and "Sixty Minute Man", "Give Me One More Chance" was a secular lyric sung with a holy feel. Over an instrumental backing

that was pure devil's music, and borrowing the odd flourish from **The Orioles**, The "5" Royales crooned like angels.

The group's big commercial breakthrough came with "Baby, Don't Do It" in 1953. With its rollicking R&B backing and gospel soars, whoops and pleads, "Baby, Don't Do It" was a #1 R&B hit and started a chart run of five top-ten R&B hits over the next year. By this time, **Eugene Tanner** had replaced Jeffries to form the classic "5" Royales line-up. Even bigger than "Baby, Don't Do It" was their two-sided follow-up smash, "Crazy, Crazy, Crazy/Help Me Somebody", which also hit #1 in 1953. The single was everything 50s R&B was all about: one side ("Crazy, Crazy, Crazy") was all honking sax rolling piano, relaxed vocals and throwaway jive, while the flip was a gospel testifying of very secular blues.

With the exception of "Laundromat Blues", all of The "5" Royales' hits were written by Lowman Pauling. His standing as one of the truly great R&B songwriters came to the fore when the group moved to King in 1955 following a royalties dispute with Apollo. Pauling's stinging guitar style also became prominent on their King recordings and was a huge influence for both Stax guitarist **Steve Cropper** and the British blues movement. Despite their success with Apollo, The "5" Royales didn't hit the charts again until 1957. Laden with guitar reverb, Holy Roller hand claps and one of Johnny Tanner's best performances – setting the stage for **Bobby "Blue" Bland** – "Think" was the finest record of their career and another crucial influence on the future of soul. They followed it up with "Dedicated To The One I Love" in which

Tanner's lead connected together the entire ancestry of soul, from the blues to gospel.

Unfortunately, it fell to other artists to make the public appreciate The "5" Royales' King material. "Think", "Dedicated To The One I Love" and "Tell The Truth" all became bigger hits for James Brown, The Shirelles, **The Mamas & The Papas** and Ray Charles. Meanwhile, unique Pauling compositions like "Monkey Hips And Rice" and "Slummer The Slum" were completely ignored. The "5" Royales gradually faded into oblivion after a lawsuit between the group and King over James Brown's 1960 recording of "Think", finally breaking up in 1965.

Monkey Hips And Rice: The "5" Royales Anthology
1994, Rhino

Two discs may seem like overkill for a group you've never heard of, but time and scholarship have granted The "5" Royales a critical standing well beyond their general reputation – it's well worth finding space for this anthology in your CD collection. The "5" Royales truly were one of the greatest, most influential vocal groups of their time; if not for them, we might still be listening to "The Tennessee Waltz" and "Mairzy Doats".

The Five Stairsteps

Long before the Jacksons from Gary, Indiana came to prominence, the **Burkes** from Chicago were "the first family of soul". Groomed by their father, Clarence, to be singers from the time they uttered their first words, **Alohe**, **Clarence Jr**, **Dennis**, **James** and **Kenneth** were the epitome of virginal innocence, puppy-love longing and slick choreography until Michael and his brothers stole the limelight.

In 1965 The Impressions' Fred Cash noticed The Five Stairsteps and, with his help, they signed to Curtis Mayfield's Windy C label. Their self-titled debut album was a minor sensation in the R&B community when it was released in 1966. It yielded five charting singles and created the foundation for every teen group from The Jackson 5 and **The Osmonds** to Menudo and N'Sync. Although lead singer Clarence Jr was, at times, a bit mannered and stilted, the group had their biggest success with the album's ballads: "You Waited Too Long", "World Of

Fantasy", a remake of The Miracles' "Oooh Baby Baby" and "Danger! She's A Stranger". The latter featured Clarence's best singing and the group's best production.

The brothers' third album, *Love's Happening*, for Mayfield's Curtom label, was their best. No longer doe-eyed balladeers, the group now excelled at uptempo groovers and proto-funk tracks. "Don't Change Your Love" had really raw drums, JB-style guitar licks, great dangling strings and fab vocals, while "Stay Close To Me" was a surging, uptempo track in the best Chicago style. More bizarre was "The New Dance Craze" which featured baby (literally) brother **Cubie** trying to sing along to a smoking instrumental.

The group moved to New York in 1970, where they started recording for the Buddah label. Working with producer **Stan Vincent**, they had their biggest hit with "O-o-h Child", a hippy dippy anthem with a lot of Mike Curb Congregation to the vocals. By now, though, the Jackson 5 had stolen their groove. With Alohe leaving the group to go to college in 1972, The Stairsteps (as they were now called) began to imitate the Jacksons on tracks like "I Love You – Stop". After a three-year hiatus, the Burkes returned with "From Us To You", a top-ten R&B hit, and "Lifting 2nd Resurrection", an awkward, busy, overly jazzy gospel with syntheist Robert Margouleff's hands all over it.

Clarence Jr (guitar and vocals), James (vibes), Dennis (guitar) and Kenneth (bass) re-emerged in 1980, with keyboardist Dean Gant, as **The Invisible Man's Band**. Their self-titled debut album featured a couple of cult disco and boogie hits, such as the bouncy "All Night Thing" and the Latinate "Love Can't Come Will Come", but the group split in 1983 after the strange but affecting "Sunday Afternoon". Meanwhile, Kenneth (now known as **Keni**) scored a cult hit as a solo artist, with one of the great bass grooves of all time, "Risin' To The Top", and Cubie set boogie dancefloors alight with "Down For Double".

Love's Happening
1968, Curtom

Produced by Curtis Mayfield, this fine album moved The Five Stairsteps away from archetypal kiddie pop to a more fully developed soul sound. It could probably do without the Impressions covers, but otherwise this ranks as one of the finest of all the family group albums.

The First Family Of Soul: The Best Of The Five Stairsteps
2001, Buddha

This 17-track collection gives short shrift to their excellent *Love's Happening* album, but is still the best overview of The Five Stairsteps' prime years from 1966 to 1970, when they excelled at giving the breezy Chicago sound a youthful gloss.

Roberta Flack

Urbane, genteel and jazzy, **Roberta Flack** was, in many ways, the perfect soul act of the early 70s. Her pretty, sensuous ballads appealed to the **Burt Bacharach**/5th **Dimension** crowd, while her shimmering keyboards and flawless diction made her the poster child of the penthouse soul crowd.

Born February 10, 1939 to a church organist in Asheville, North Carolina, Flack started playing piano at a very early age. At just 15 years old she won a music scholarship to Howard University. One of her classmates there was **Donny Hathaway**, and the pair later developed a lifelong working partnership. After a stint as a music teacher, Flack started working in Washington, DC, accompanying opera singers during the day and singing and playing piano at an R&B club at night. Word started to get out and, in 1968, she was discovered by pianist/vocalist **Les McCann**, who got her signed to Atlantic.

With the exception of her rousing version of "Compared To What", a song that McCann had made famous, her 1969 debut *First Take* sounded more like a folk album than a soul record. Produced by Joel Dorn and featuring a jazz-leaning line-up of guitarist John Pizzarelli, bassist Ron Carter and drummer Ray Lucas, the album focused on folk material: Ewan MacColl's "The First Time Ever I Saw Your Face", Leonard Cohen's "Hey, That's No Way To Say Goodbye" and the traditional "I Told Jesus". The folky bent continued on *Chapter Two*, which featured versions of **Bob Dylan**'s "Just Like A Woman" and Buffy Sainte-Marie's "Until It's Time For You To Go".

Flack's first hit was a duet with Donny Hathaway – a cover of **Carole King**'s "You've Got A Friend" – but it was the inclusion of "The First Time Ever I Saw Your Face" on the soundtrack to *Play Misty For Me* that suddenly made Flack a household name. The record became a sensation and stayed at #1 for six weeks. Another MOR classic – and another duet with Hathaway – "Where Is The Love" was a top-five hit before "Killing Me Softly With His Song" became her second blockbuster, spending five weeks at the top of the pop chart. 1974's "Feel Like Making Love" had a bit more of a groove and it became her biggest R&B hit, spending five weeks at #1.

After a performing hiatus, Flack returned to the top of the charts in 1978 with another duet with Hathaway, "The Closer I Get To You". Hathaway committed suicide shortly after, and their final recordings together were released as *Roberta Flack Featuring Donny Hathaway* in 1980. More contemporary in style and more uptempo than her previous records, the album showed that Flack could hold her own with the dancefloor divas on tracks like "Back Together Again" and the very underrated "God Don't Like Ugly".

Later that year Flack chose **Peabo Bryson** as her new duet partner. They had immediate success with "Make The World Stand Still" and later with "Tonight, I Celebrate My Love". By now, though, Flack's days of superstardom were over. She settled comfortably into a lite jazz vein, recording with **Miles Davis**, Sadao Watanabe and **Luther Vandross**. She made a brief return to the charts in 1991 with "Set The Night To Music", a minor hit recorded with pop-reggae singer Maxi Priest, but, aside from a couple of Christmas albums, her last album was 1995's *Roberta*, a collection of interpretations of standards.

First Take
1969, Atlantic

It's hard to pick the best Roberta Flack album because her early releases are all uniformly good. This, her first, is extraordinary in the power of its understatement. The laid-back jazzy backing and light strings leave plenty of room to embrace the earnest honesty and soulful vocal stylings of this great talent – an outstanding debut.

Softly With These Songs: The Best Of Roberta Flack
1993, Atlantic

If you just want Flack's hits, this is the album to go for. However, it is a far from perfect collection, omitting several important records. *First Take* is probably her best original album, especially for fans of her soothing voice, but soul and R&B traditionalists should probably give *Roberta Flack Featuring Donny Hathaway* (1980, Atlantic) a shot.

Eddie Floyd

Somewhat unfairly categorized as a second-tier talent, singer-songwriter **Eddie Floyd** was doomed to work in the shadows of his peers at Stax. Without the presence of **Otis Redding** or the chops of **Sam & Dave**, Floyd was a workmanlike singer and a very accomplished songwriter, who showed occasional flashes of brilliance.

Born on June 25, 1935, in Montgomery, Alabama, Floyd was raised in Detroit where he co-founded **The Falcons** in 1954. After The Falcons broke up Floyd recorded a couple of solo singles for his uncle **Robert West**'s Lu Pine label, "Will I Be The One?" and "I'll Be Home". In 1963 he moved to Washington DC where he worked with DJ **Al Bell**. The two formed the record label Safice, for whom Floyd recorded the **Sam Cooke**-style ballad "Never Get Enough Of Your Love".

When Bell became the head of promotions at Stax, Floyd went with him to Memphis. Floyd became a staff writer there, working with William Bell, Carla Thomas and Steve Cropper, and writing "634-5789" for his old bandmate **Wilson Pickett** in 1966. That same year Floyd released the unremarkable "Things Get Better", but the follow-up was far more significant. "Knock On Wood" was one of the all-time great Memphis grooves, with **Al Jackson** pounding the heck out of the snare. Nearly anyone would have sounded good on top of it, but Floyd's forceful, back-of-the-throat vocals worked perfectly.

The infectious "Raise Your Hand" and "Love Is A Doggone Good Thing" were both thoroughly generic Southern soul records, but Floyd proved that he was more than just restrained power. "I've Never Found A Girl (To Love Me Like You Do)" and a cover of Sam Cooke's "Bring It On Home To Me" were his biggest hits, aside from "Knock On Wood", and perhaps his second-best records as well. "Big Bird" – perhaps the loudest record ever to come out of Stax – somehow never made the charts, even though both Floyd and the band absolutely smoked.

From 1969 onwards, Floyd's records became increasingly generic and his chart placings increasingly modest. After the fairly funky "Soul Street" and the collapse of Stax, Floyd went on to record the disco-fied *Experience* for Malaco in 1977. A couple of ill-advised disco records for Mercury followed, before Floyd moved to England and worked with Mod revivalists **Secret Affair**. Returning to the US in the 80s, Floyd worked with New Orleans greats Marshall Sehorn and Wardell Quezergue on the disappointing album *Try Me!* that featured a fine ballad in "Our Love Will Survive". His subsequent reunion with William Bell on *Flashback* in 1988 failed to fan the flames, and his appearances at George Bush Senior's inaugural ball and in the film *Blues Brothers 2000* are probably best left unmentioned.

Chronicle: Greatest Hits
1979, Stax

Eddie Floyd hasn't been served very well in the CD era, but this compilation is the best of a bad bunch. Inexcusably, it includes neither the storming "Big Bird" nor the fine ballad "I've Just Been Feeling Bad", but it does have all of his biggest hits, which is something no other Floyd CD can claim.

King Floyd

Although he was known almost exclusively for his monster hit "Groove Me", **King Floyd** was far too good a singer to be merely a novelty artist. His best records from the early 70s combined the loping funk of his hometown, New Orleans, with the horn charts and textures of Memphis – and it made perfect sense that they were largely recorded in Jackson, Mississippi, a city halfway between the two.

Floyd was born on February 13, 1945, in the Crescent City and, after being discharged from the army in 1963, he moved first to New York, and then to Los Angeles, hoping to make it as a soul singer. In LA he recorded his first single, "Walkin' And Thinkin'", for the Original Sound label in 1965, before falling in with a coterie of New Orleans musicians, including Harold Battiste, Jesse Hill and **Mac Rebennack** (aka Dr John). Floyd formed a moderately successful songwriting partnership with Rebennack that enabled him to record the single "Times Have Changed" and the album *A Man In Love* on Mercury's Pulsar subsidiary.

Moving back to New Orleans in 1969, Floyd started working with producer **Wardell Quezergue**, who took him to Malaco Studios in Jackson to record "Groove Me", a song that Floyd had written sometime in the late 60s. You could tell that the song was written in the 60s because of the dated lyrics and the bassline (reminiscent of **Fontella Bass**'s "Rescue Me"), but the minimal arrangement and playing by the battery of **Vernie Robbins** and **James Stroud** made it irresistible. The follow-up "Baby Let Me Kiss You" was essentially the same record as "Groove Me", but more low-down and salacious, and not quite as successful.

Floyd's 1972 release "Woman Don't Go Astray" was a similar rapprochement between that off-kilter New Orleans swing and more traditional Southern soul, but it proved that he was a more than capable singer and not a one-trick pony. "Do Your Feeling", on the other hand, went straight for the jugular with Floyd's grunts and Stroud's monstrous beats, although the horns were straight from Memphis. His funk records stopped selling, so he went smooth on records like "We Can Love", a duet with **Dorothy Moore**, in 1975. Lacking the spunk of his earlier releases, these were simply generic mid-70s Southern soul records and they got lost. Floyd even tried to get a disco makeover on "Body English" in 1976, but the wah-wahs didn't suit him. Like many Southern singers, he was blinded by the glitterball of the disco years, but he managed to re-emerge in the 90s on the blues circuit.

Choice Cuts
1994, Waldoxy/Malaco

This 15-track collection has all of Floyd's hits and is the only decent CD of his music available. It does, however, miss out on some of his more obscure funky gems, like "Do Your Feeling", which can be found on his surprisingly solid original albums on Atco and Cotillion Records.

The Four Tops

One of the great fallacies surrounding soul music (perpetrated by both aficionados and Philistines) is that Motown is a diluted version of black music. It's a patently racist assumption, but you can almost see what they're getting at: the deportment lessons, the strings and celestes, the melodrama, the sing-song melodies, the blind crossover ambition. They may even have a point when it comes to **The Supremes**, but how on earth do these nay-sayers explain **The Four Tops**? With arrangements based around rhythms developed from prayer-meeting hand claps and tambourines and the Pentecostal bluster of lead singer **Levi Stubbs**, The Four Tops were the most gospel-grounded Motown act. For all the sweetened production **Holland-Dozier-Holland** might have layered on, and for all the supper-club blandness of backing vocalists **Renaldo "Obie" Benson**, **Abdul "Duke" Fakir** and **Lawrence Payton**, Stubbs' testifying of the torment of love never let the group leave the gospel firmament for the purgatory of pop.

The Four Tops, originally called the Four Aims, formed in Detroit in 1953. They started off imitating local groups like **The Falcons**, before mutating into a nightclub act. The group recorded largely unnoteworthy material for several local labels, as well as Chess, Columbia and Riverside, before joining Motown in 1963. Paired with producers/songwriters Brian Holland, Lamont Dozier and Eddie Holland, The Four Tops first made their mark with 1964's "Baby I Need Your Loving". While HDH became famous for their work with The Supremes, their records with The Four Tops made them perhaps popular music's greatest production team. "Baby I Need Your Loving" had all of their familiar elements: the urgent, tumbling rhythm and overwhelming brass charts mirroring Stubbs' anguish and matched with a simple, cheery melody and finger pops, suggesting that all is not doom and gloom.

The Tops' follow-up hit was "Ask The Lonely", produced by **Ivy Hunter** and **William Stevenson**, but it was their next single that made the group superstars. "I Can't Help Myself" remains perhaps the definitive pop single: no matter how much you resist its almost irritating rhythm, cheesy sax solo and relentlessly corny "Sugar pie, honey bunch" refrain, "I Can't Help Myself" evades your defences and crawls under your skin.

The Four Tops keeping everything crossed for a good show

PLAYLIST
The Four Tops

1 BABY I NEED YOUR LOVING from **Anthology**
The Holland-Dozier-Holland formula in a nutshell.

2 I CAN'T HELP MYSELF from **Anthology**
Like most of HDH's records with The Supremes, you want to hate this, but you just can't do it.

3 IT'S THE SAME OLD SONG from **Anthology**
It may be the same old song, but its a damn great formula.

4 SOMETHING ABOUT YOU from **Anthology**
The Four Tops at their most gospelesque.

5 REACH OUT I'LL BE THERE from **Anthology**
Forget Phil Spector, this is the real "Wall of Sound".

6 STANDING IN THE SHADOWS OF LOVE from **Anthology**
A masterpiece of unrequited love.

7 BERNADETTE from **Anthology**
Possibly bassist James Jamerson's finest record at Motown.

8 DON'T BRING BACK MEMORIES from **Anthology**
A stomping Northern soul favourite.

9 STILL WATER from **Anthology**
Majestic soft soul with a reggae-ish lilt.

10 AIN'T NO WOMAN (LIKE THE ONE I'VE GOT) from **Anthology**
Catchy, retro harmony group soul.

The clip-clop rhythm from "Reach Out" continued in 1966 on "Standing In The Shadows Of Love". Firmly establishing the Tops as the troubadours of the desperately lovelorn, the record was another masterpiece of towering emotion, this time carried by the insistent percussion that later became the hallmark of **Norman Whitfield**'s productions with The Temptations and, by extension, disco. "Bernadette" completed this trilogy of brilliant singles, which established the blueprint for the paranoid soul that would mark the end of the 60s and early 70s. On "Bernadette", HDH took all of the Motown conventions – liquid bassline, pounding drums, strings, saccharine choruses – and rearranged their pop affirmations to make them downright scary.

After a couple of singles that followed the same path, but with less successful results, HDH left Motown, and The Four Tops were saddled with wretched material like 1968's "Walk Away Renee". The Northern soul favourite "Don't Bring Back Memories" was far better, while "Still Water" had a proto-quiet storm arrangement, with creamy guitar licks and a portentous clavinet riff, and might have been their best post-HDH Motown record. After a dismal cover of "MacArthur Park", a strange medley of Latinate hits, "Medley (Hey Leroy)" and the early disco hit "(It's The Way) Nature Planned It", The Four Tops finally left Motown for ABC-Dunhill.

Their first record for their new label was "Keeper Of The Castle" in 1972, which began promisingly enough with an almighty wah-wah riff, before devolving into a preachy, sanctimonious message track. The insanely catchy "Ain't No Woman (Like The One I've Got)" was a huge improvement the following year, as was their contribution to **Johnny Pate**'s Shaft In Africa soundtrack, "Are You Man Enough". By the mid-70s, however, the group had run out of steam. Their impressive hit-making prowess eluded them and their producers, and they left ABC in 1978.

After spending a couple of years without a recording contract, The Four Tops were picked up by Casablanca in 1981. Their first record for Casablanca was "When She Was My Girl", a nostalgic throwback with a wistful melodica solo that became their first R&B #1 in fifteen years. It was all downhill from

The record was so effective (it was an American #1) that the follow-up was exactly what it said it was, "It's The Same Old Song", and reached the Top 5.

After a classic blend of Holy Roller intensity and orchestral grandeur ("Something About You") and some OK pop singles, The Four Tops had their second #1 single, "Reach Out I'll Be There". Holland-Dozier-Holland and the Tops hit their peak with the song's Grand Canyon echo, eerie flute melody, surging drums, seismic bass, galloping percussion and Stubbs' overwhelming voice. With his borderline hysterical vocals, Stubbs was always almost too much, but here his dominating presence was perfect.

there, though, and the group finally settled into a comfortable existence performing on the oldies circuit throughout the 80s and 90s. Their first personnel change in 43 years followed the death of Lawrence Payton in 1997, but the remaining members didn't let The Four Tops end there; instead they hired **Theo Peoples** to continue touring with them.

Anthology
1974, Motown

The Four Tops' 1997 compilation, *The Ultimate Collection* (Motown, 1997), is more concise at 25 tracks, whereas *Fourever* (Hip-O, 2001) is more complete with 85, but no one really needs "Loco In Acapulco". Therefore, this 40-track, double-disc collection is the perfect compromise, with all the hits plus enough charming lesser-known tracks to make anyone happy.

Four Tops / Second Album
2001, Universal

This is a 1-CD reissue of the group's first two albums, which were both released in 1965 and produced by Holland-Dozier-Holland. It's full of hits, such as "Baby I Need Your Loving", "Ask The Lonely", and "It's The Same Old Song", balanced with non-hit ballads and uptempo numbers. The Four Tops' later albums were usually filled with weak covers of other people's hits, but this is almost all original Motown material and essential 60s soul.

Inez & Charlie Foxx

Sadly, **Inez Foxx**'s legacy is forever attached to one track – "Mockingbird" – the charming novelty record she made with her brother **Charlie**. She was, however, a fine soul vocalist of protean talents, who made a number of good records across a variety of soul styles.

Born **Inez Fox Fletcher** in Greensboro, North Carolina, on September 9, 1942, Foxx began singing in church as a young girl. By the time she was 7 years old, she was a member of The Gospel Tide Chorus along with her two sisters, but it was with her older brother Charlie (born October 23, 1939) that she would really make her name. The two started making music together in high school and, in the late 50s, they moved to New York to try to make it big in the music biz.

Recording as **Inez Johnston**, the duo released two singles, "A Feeling (That I Can't Explain)" and "Change Of Heart", for Brunswick that went nowhere. In 1963 they took a nursery-rhyme song they had written to **Juggy Jones** at Sue Records. He loved what he heard. "Mockingbird" became a huge hit, thanks to its instantly memorable lyrics and the interaction between Charlie the straight man and Inez the overreaching gospel shouter.

More kiddie lyrics followed on Inez's solo release "Hi Diddle Diddle", but she proved her adroitness with adult themes – and tore her voice box asunder like **Tina Turner** – on the bluesy chug-along "Hurt By Love". Back again with Charlie in 1966, their record "Come By Here" was a breathy, very secular version of "Kumbaya", with great guitar work.

The duo then moved to Dynamo where they were produced by **Luther Johnson**, who wrote and produced for **The Shirelles**, **Chuck Jackson** and **Maxine Brown**. Inez & Charlie's "Tightrope" became a Northern soul favourite, thanks to its relentless momentum and Foxx's sexy vocals, but the duo's biggest hit at Dynamo was the infectious "(1-2-3-4-5-6-7) Count The Days". They peppered their special brand of jaunty, light soul with a couple of gospel testifiers, including a version of **Jerry Butler**'s "I Stand Accused" and the controversial "Fellows In Vietnam".

Inez Foxx and Luther Johnson eventually married, and together they wrote and produced "I Love You 1,000 Times" for **The Platters**. Meanwhile, Charlie produced **Gene Pitney**'s "She's A Heartbreaker". After releasing her excellent solo track, "You Shouldn't Have Set My Soul On Fire", in 1970, Inez left Dynamo for Stax. There she released a couple of excellent Southern soul sides, "You Hurt Me For The Last Time" and "The Lady, The Doctor And The Prescription", and the funk burner, "Circuits Overloaded". She vanished from the limelight soon afterwards, but Charlie continued to produce records for other artists.

The Dynamo Duo
2001, Kent

The only version of "Mockingbird" contained here is a later version recorded with strings, but this is a very good overview of Inez & Charlie Foxx's years at Dynamo. What these recordings lack in gravitas, they more than make up for in sheer spunk and delightful energy.

Aretha Franklin

It's an article of faith among popular music fans that **Aretha Franklin** is, if not *the* greatest, then one of the two or three best female singers ever. Although her records have all too often failed to live up to her vocal cords, it's hard to disagree that Aretha is the undisputed "Queen of Soul" and that her voice is one of the glories of modern music.

As the daughter of one of America's most famous Pentecostal preachers, Franklin spent her childhood as a gospel singer with a remarkably precocious talent. In 1956, at the age of 14, she recorded a version of "Precious Lord" that heralded her arrival as one of the greatest singers of the twentieth century.

Four years later, she moved to New York to become a pop singer and was signed by **John Hammond** to CBS/Columbia Records. Hammond, who was one of the major figures behind the blues revival of the 60s, was a died-in-the-wool purist, incapable of understanding and responding to the musical changes going on around him. He saw Franklin as the successor to **Billie Holiday** and tried to fashion her into a melancholy torch singer, with mixed results. Although the "standards" format showcased Franklin's protean talents as a pianist more obviously than her subsequent material would, her voice lumbered along with trite material like "Over The Rainbow" and "Love For Sale". Typical of her material during this period was 1965's "One Step Ahead": Franklin soared, but the stiff arrangement and prim strings restricted her voice.

She made some decent records at Columbia, like her 1964 tribute to **Dinah Washington**, but while James Brown was belting out "Papa's Got A Brand New Bag", Franklin was shackled to material like "Misty" and "If I Had A Hammer". At one point, she worked with **Mitch Miller** – the leader of the "Sing-Along Gang" and one of the titans of middle-of-the-road music – who saddled her with lumbering orchestras and extravagant production. Despite this troubling experience, Franklin was given singing lessons and she learned the "textbook" phrasing and control demanded by pop compositions that would later serve her

so well during her more fruitful relationship with Atlantic. By combining the fire of her gospel roots with the economy of a classic pop singer, Aretha Franklin became pop music's greatest vocalist.

In 1966 Atlantic bought Franklin's contract and paired her with **Jerry Wexler**, a former customs inspector who was one of the most important producers in popular music. Wexler detected her discomfort with Hammond's urbane style and, in January 1967, brought Franklin to Fame studios in Muscle Shoals, Alabama where a white house band made the toughest soul music outside of Memphis. With guitarist Jimmy Johnson, organist Spooner Oldham, drummer Roger Hawkins, bassist Tommy Cogbill and guitarist **Chips Moman** creating a secular cathedral out of gospel elements, Franklin felt right at home and produced the exquisite "I Never Loved A Man (The Way I Love You)", her first real hit and an R&B chart-topper for seven weeks.

With many of the same musicians in New York a month later, she came up with her towering achievement. Otis Redding would complain that Franklin stole "Respect" from him, but she did more than steal it, she made it completely her own. Evolving out of Aretha and her sister, **Carolyn Franklin**, fooling around with Redding's hit in the studio, Franklin's "Respect" may have been impromptu, but the details are so perfect they seem as though they came out of one of da Vinci's notebooks. With her sisters backing her up – "woo" and "Just a little bit" –

Aretha Franklin – the undisputed Queen of Soul

most enduring records. "Baby, I Love You", "Chain Of Fools", "Since You've Been Gone (Sweet Sweet Baby)" and "Think" had all raced to the top of the R&B chart by the summer of 1968, while "(You Make Me Feel Like) A Natural Woman" was kept from the top only by Sam & Dave's "Soul Man". It was a staggering run that made Franklin the irrefutable "Queen of Soul".

By 1969 Franklin was one of the biggest names in popular music. Instead of continuing to push boundaries, however, she was content to become the finest pop vocalist on the planet. Her subsequent hits were nowhere near as epochal as those of 1967 and 1968. They were merely the sound of the world's greatest voice relaxing and doing stuff that turned her, or her producer, on. In other words, making the kind of records for which just about every other singer would gladly give their first-born. During a period that saw her record covers of "Eleanor Rigby", "Bridge Over Troubled Water" and "Spanish Harlem", Franklin managed to make even **Elton John** and **Bernie Taupin** sound good on her version of "Border Song (Holy Moses)".

Aretha Franklin's most significant post-60s recordings were from 1972. Her gospel album, *Amazing Grace*, featured not only spine-tingling moments of vocal acrobatics, but also the swinging rhythms and soaring emotions that made gospel the foundation of all modern popular music. *Young, Gifted And Black*, and its two brilliant singles, "Rock Steady" and "Day Dreaming", found her successfully navigating the divide between the pop recognition she sought and the funkier, more streetwise music bubbling up from the cities.

Throughout the mid-70s she continued to have R&B hits galore – "Angel", "Until You Come Back to Me (That's What I'm Going To Do)" and "I'm In Love" all reached #1 – but the inspiration had started to wane. The title of her 1976 album *La Diva* didn't exactly win her any fans, but producer Van McCoy helped her craft one of her better mid-career albums, with the help of a glittering support cast, which included backing singer Zulema, Cornell Dupree and Richard Tee.

At the beginning of the 80s, Franklin ditched Atlantic for Arista, where she was teamed up with producers **Luther Vandross** and **Narada Michael Walden**. Most of her

the moment where Franklin breaks it down – "R-E-S-P-E-C-T" – is more than just an undeniable hook. It's also a stunningly effective political statement: "What, do I have to spell it out for you?"

While "Respect" was fixed at the top of the R&B charts for most of the summer of 1967, Franklin continued to record some of soul's

Gospel

In terms of influence, popularity and endurance, black gospel was the most significant musical form of the twentieth century. Unfortunately, for most gospel practitioners and record buyers, that triumph was purely formal, as gospel's innovations were brought to the mainstream secular world by soul singers. Gospel was crystallized as a genre around the same time as jazz and blues, but it has outlived both as a presence on the contemporary music scene. While jazz has been increasingly forced into a tiny ghetto of intellectuals and die-hards, and the blues influence on rock has more or less faded away, the vocal techniques, physicality and intensity of gospel remains the lingua franca of popular music.

That the lexicon of gospel became the language of love, sex, desire, heartbreak and ecstasy is mostly down to **The Soul Stirrers**, who were, unquestionably, the most influential of all the male harmony groups, secular or sacred. Formed in 1927 in Trinity, Texas, The Soul Stirrers changed the face of gospel music in the mid-30s when they changed their repertoire, and soon the repertoire of all harmony groups, from the traditional spirituals and jubilees to modern gospel compositions which were, until then, only sung in church. Even more revolutionary was the way the group shifted the vocal arrangements. Adding a second lead vocalist, The Soul Stirrers' brand-new style gave the first lead space for extended solo passages without abandoning the traditional harmony. This setup also created a contrast between the two lead voices, which enabled the group to crank up the emotional intensity and would soon become the stock-in-trade of every vocal group from **The Swan Silvertones** to The Temptations.

In gospel terms, The Soul Stirrers, most influential lead vocalist was **R.H. Harris**. Joining the group in 1936, he was responsible for most of the group's paradigm shifts in harmony group singing. Harris was a one-man quartet: he was perhaps the first sanctified falsetto singer, yet he could also growl with the best of them. On songs such as "By And By", Harris's timing was impeccable: there was not a "whoa" or "Lord" out of place and, despite his awesome stylistic range, most of the song's force came from his emphasis and phrasing. Freed from the traditional harmony constrictions, Harris introduced blues-style ad-libs and jazzy syncopations to gospel singing, thus creating the archetype of the swooping, soaring, freestyling, sermonizing gospel singer. Singers **Claude Jeter**, **Archie Brownlee** and **Julius Cheeks** followed in Harris's footsteps, providing the models for soul singers **Eddie Kendricks**, James Brown and Wilson Pickett respectively.

Religion was often considered a "woman's concern", and, within the church, women have been allowed to develop as singers largely protected from the male prejudices and vampirism that haunt the less salubrious corners of the music industry. So, it's hardly surprising that many of gospel's greatest singers were women. Perhaps the best, and certainly the most well-known, is **Mahalia Jackson**, who brought a bluesy quality and an improvising gift – not to mention the most ferocious set of pipes ever – to the stately manner of female gospel singing and influenced practically every singer who came after her.

The most famous gospel singer after Jackson was, probably, **Sister Rosetta Tharpe**. Tharpe was raised in the Pentecostal Church and was the bluesiest of all the female gospel singers. With an expressive voice full of character and a gift for showbiz, Tharpe quickly became the most commercially successful gospel artist of the day, and her influence and esteem were such that she was Elvis' favourite gospel singer.

Along with Jackson and Tharpe, **Clara Ward** is considered one of the greatest female gospel singers. With her slightly nasal voice, slurred notes and potent vibrato, Ward was an individualistic stylist. She teamed up with Reverend C.L. Franklin in the 1950s, and the debt his daughter, Aretha Franklin, owes to her is obvious. **The Ward Singers** were the most influential group of the 40s and 50s, introducing soloists such as **Frances Steadman** and **Marion Williams**. More than one critic has called Williams the greatest singer ever, and it's hard to disagree. Too demonstrative to settle safely into pop's constraints, Williams revelled in the gospel tradition and she exploited this freedom with some of the most amazing flights ever captured on vinyl.

With the commercial success of soul in the 60s and, even more importantly, the changes in the African-American community in the 70s, the tables turned and gospel gradually became nothing more than a pale imitation of secular music. Even though gospel is now in the hands of bandwagon jumpers like Kirk Franklin, gospel's glories still live on in every singer who can bend a note or sing glissandos into a higher register.

Various Artists: Jubilation! Great Gospel Performances Vols. 1 And 2
1992, Rhino

The two volumes that concentrate on black gospel artists in the superb *Jubilation! Great Gospel Performances* series are the best introductions to gospel music currently available. Covering just about all of the major figures, including Mahalia Jackson, The Swan Silvertones and The Soul Stirrers, and some truly spectacular recordings, these compilations stand as a fine testament to what may be America's greatest style of music.

Aretha Franklin

Arista records were stable, well-crafted affairs in that bland, functional, big-budget style the 80s are famous for. However, 1985's *Who's Zoomin' Who?* was a great pop album – and, remarkably, Franklin's first platinum album in the US. Since then, her voice has been used as little more than a flavour enhancer to be sprinkled liberally on everything from wretched movies (*Jumpin' Jack Flash*) and worse TV shows (*Wheel Of Fortune*) to the launches of Stateside solo careers (George Michael and Annie Lennox). It's a tragic end to the career of the greatest vocal genius popular music has produced.

I Never Loved A Man The Way I Love You
1967, Atlantic

Aretha's debut for Atlantic, brilliantly produced by Jerry Wexler, paired her with Muscle Shoals' deep Southern soul backing with immediate and overwhelming results. Perhaps even more than the hits, it's the album tracks and the covers of Ray Charles's "Drown In My Own Tears" and Sam Cooke's "Change Is Gonna Come" that truly distinguish this flawless effort.

Lady Soul
1968, Atlantic

All of Aretha's first four Atlantic albums are outstanding, so this, her third, is a case where more of the same is a good thing. It includes several of her big hits, but, once again, it's the album tracks, such as the bluesy "Good To Me As I Am to You" and her version of Curtis Mayfield's "People Get Ready", that lift things up a notch and dignify this as her best original album ever.

Young, Gifted And Black
1972, Atlantic

Young, Gifted And Black found Aretha at the peak of her popularity, when she was updating her records with a funkier and more sophisticated sound. Here, self-penned hits like "Rock Steady" and "Day Dreaming" are joined by decent covers of well-known songs. Aretha was becoming a great song interpreter and her deft command of gospel allowed her to make familiar records all her own.

Queen Of Soul: The Very Best Of Aretha Franklin
1994, Rhino

If you can afford to spring for it, the box set *Queen Of Soul: The Atlantic Recordings* (1993, Rhino) is the way to go because you can't have too much Aretha in your collection. However, despite not having any of her gospel recordings, this single-disc distillation of that 4-CD box set has nearly all of the finest tracks from her Atlantic years and is the best single-CD Aretha Franklin compilation currently available.

154

The Gap Band

Cameo may have had bigger hits, and The Time may have spawned master producers Jam & Lewis, but **The Gap Band** were the quintessential funk band of the 80s. From the sheen of their production values to their godawful ballads, these natives of Tulsa, Oklahoma, epitomized funk's journey from the backwoods to the suburbs. More successfully than anyone else, The Gap Band managed to update the Parliafunkadelicment Thang sound for the Reagan era.

In their hands, P-Funk's afronautic futurist soundscape was brought down to earth to become the sound of upward mobility; **Bootsy Collins**'s comedic smarm became a po-faced come-on and the comic-book narratives became boudoir poetry. That said, while the Wilson brothers may have dumbed down **George Clinton**'s vision, at their best they streamlined his complexity and made his sound more immediately booty-shaking. The Gap Band also borrowed extensively from Stevie Wonder, especially on the ballads, and lead vocalist **Charlie Wilson**'s combination of croon and yowsah has become the definitive R&B vocal style of the last twenty years.

Charlie and his brothers, **Robert** and **Ronnie**, began singing as choirboys in their father's church. However, they abandoned the Pentecostal melisma in favour of a slicker style by the time they formed The Gap Band, naming their group after three streets in Tulsa: Greenwood, Archer and Pine. They recorded their first album, *Magician's Holiday*, in 1974 for the Shelter label owned by Okie rock star **Leon Russell**, in whose band they had served as musicians.

The band's breakthrough only came when they signed to Mercury and released *Gap Band II* in 1979. Both the album's big hits were distillations (read: complete rip-offs) of formulas created by the two biggest R&B bands of the time, P-Funk and Earth Wind & Fire. "Shake" was a barely reworked version of **Maurice White**'s trademark jazziness, while "I Don't Believe You Want To Get Up And Dance (Oops)" (aka "Oops Upside Your Head") borrowed the giggles, nursery rhymes and the lines, "The bigger the headache, the bigger the pill" and "It's funkin' habit forming" from P-Funk. It didn't do the group any harm, though, as "Oops" became a dancefloor sensation and hit the British Top 5.

The Gap Band started to stake their own turf with 1980's "Burn Rubber (Why You Wanna Hurt Me)" which became a #1 US R&B hit on the strength of Robert Wilson's crunching adaptation of Bernie Worrell's synth-basslines. Like all The Gap Band's hits, "Burn Rubber" was produced by **Lonnie Simmons**, one of the main instigators of the synthification of 80s funk. It was another glossy Simmons production, Yarbrough & Peoples' "Don't Stop The Music", that replaced "Burn Rubber" at the top of the R&B charts in February 1981.

Simmons and the Wilson brothers really dropped the bomb, though, with 1982's *Gap Band IV* album. Charlie's Stevie Wonder impression on "Stay With Me" made the group a favourite with the Luther Vandross crowd, while "You Dropped A Bomb On Me" took the bassline from "Burn Rubber"

The Gap Band shake their funky stuff

and magnified it a thousand times. "Outstanding", the ultimate MOR funk ballad, transcended sentimental schmaltz thanks to Simmons' glistening production; his percussion hooks have since formed the basis of at least ten hip-hop records. However, "Early In The Morning" was the catalyst for the album's platinum success. Cruising on top of a similar synth-bass riff and an almost identical drum track to "Burn Rubber", while borrowing the melody and cadence from Stevie Wonder's "I Was Made To Love Her", "Early in the Morning" was the tale of the next day in the life of the jilted lover in "Burn Rubber".

Although The Gap Band continued to have hits throughout the 80s, with records like "Party Train", "Beep A Freak" and "All Of My Love", the synth-bass novelty progressively wore off, and vocalists like Guy's **Aaron Hall** stole Charlie Wilson's fire.

Ultimate Collection
2001, Hip-O

A 19-track collection of just about all The Gap Band's synth-funk hits you could want, plus a few of the over-wrought ballads that followed in their wake. The funk's the fun stuff for parties, even if the ballads strangely have the weight of history behind them.

Marvin Gaye

Born **Marvin Pentz Gay, Jr.** in Washington DC on April 2, 1939, **Marvin Gaye** was one of the four or five greatest singers in the history of popular music. Blessed with a gorgeous voice, impeccable phrasing bequeathed to him from his father's storefront church, and a square jaw and long lashes, Marvin Gaye was perhaps the quintessential pop star. He was an iconoclast who railed against both the machinery of stardom and social injustice – and, unlike other great pop stars, he was also a peerless duet singer. This combination of arrogance and openness made Gaye extremely versatile and helped him to create a staggering recorded legacy.

Gaye dropped out of high school in the mid-50s to work with doo-wop legends **Harvey & The Moonglows** and, at around the same time, added the "e" to his stage name. The Moonglows' leader **Harvey Fuqua** brought Gaye to Detroit, where he met **Berry Gordy** and joined the Motown staff as a session drummer. After marrying Gordy's sister Anna in 1961, he made his first solo Motown recordings as a Nat "King" Cole-style balladeer, but they were hopelessly out of date. Once he began to combine croon with rasp, though, the results were little short of magical. Gaye's earliest hits, 1962's "Stubborn Kind Of Fellow" and "Hitch Hike", featured some of the gutsiest vocals Motown would ever record.

While 1963's rollicking "Can I Get A Witness" continued to showcase Gaye's abilities as a secular gospel shouter, 1964's "How Sweet It Is (To Be Loved By You)" proved he could be just as effective when singing with seemingly effortless ease. After splendid records like "Ain't That Peculiar" and "I'll Be Doggone", Gaye began his series of remarkable duets in 1966 with **Kim Weston**. Perhaps the slightest of his duets, "It Takes Two" was, nevertheless, pure pop bliss conjured from one of Motown's most complex and awkward arrangements. It was with **Tammi Terrell**, however, that Gaye cut his finest duets. Helped in no small part by **Harvey Fuqua** and **Johnny Bristol**'s dramatic arrangement, 1967's soaring "Ain't No Mountain High Enough" began a string of epochal hits for the two, which included "Your Precious Love" and "If I Could Build My Whole World Around You" in 1967, and "Ain't Nothing Like The Real Thing" and "You're All I Need To Get By" in 1968.

1968 was Gaye's year. Not only did he have monumental hits with Terrell, but he recorded one of the definitive soul singles of all time, "Heard It Through The Grapevine". On top of mind-bogglingly detailed production from **Norman Whitfield** and perhaps the best strings ever to be heard on a pop record, Gaye delivered the opening salvo in the subgenre of paranoid soul that was to characterize the best records of the next several years. Gaye's next couple of releases, 1969's "Too Busy Thinking About My Baby" and "That's The Way Love Is", were comparative retreats, but he was just preparing for his full-on onslaught of Motown's business as usual.

Tammi Terrell's death from a brain tumour drove Gaye into seclusion for several months, during which he spent a lot of time talking to his brother, Frankie, who had served in Vietnam. After writing and producing "Baby I'm For Real" and "The Bells" for **The Originals**, Gaye re-emerged with what most people consider to be the greatest soul album ever, 1971's *What's Goin' On*. At this point, Gaye was battling for creative control over his career and was further distancing himself from the almost tyrannical reins of Motown's quality control department by growing a beard and ditching the dapper suit. With his new threads and a socially aware attitude, which was in part precipitated by his brother's return from Vietnam, Gaye was seeking (like Sly Stone out in San Francisco) to unite the hippy vision of the world with the moral and stylistic authority of soul music. When Gaye approached Motown head Berry Gordy with the idea of an entire album based around protest songs, Gordy effectively responded, "Over my dead body". Despite that rebuff, Gaye went ahead and recorded *What's Going On* anyway. On first hearing the album, Gordy allegedly called it "the worst thing I've ever heard in my life".

When it was finally released almost a year after it was recorded, *What's Going On* became a landmark in the history of pop music. From the voices and soprano sax in the opening to the multi-tracked vocals in which Gaye sang a duet with himself, *What's Going On* was unlike anything Motown had ever done before. Capitalizing on the fact that many of the label's session

Marvin Gaye, having ditched the dapper suit for 1971's *What's Going On*

musicians were slumming jazz players, Gaye's arrangements were dense and complex, completely unlike the standard Motown beat – or, indeed, what anyone else was doing. Combining the stylistic innovations of Isaac Hayes' lush soul masterpiece, *Hot Buttered Soul*, with the technological innovations of psychedelic rock, Gaye created a vision of the world that united dystopia with hope.

At the same time as he was decrying injustice, his gorgeous, easy falsetto, the cocooning bass groove from **James Jamerson**, the gently percussive congas and the smooth horns all suggested that Eden was just around the corner if we could all just love each other. It might have been a platitude that not even someone like folk singer Melanie would have been comfortable voicing, but coming from a soulman that kind of

PLAYLIST
Marvin Gaye

1 HITCH HIKE from **Anthology**
Gaye may be young and callow, but his power is all there.

2 CAN I GET A WITNESS from **Anthology**
Motown's greatest secular gospel record.

3 AIN'T THAT PECULIAR from **Anthology**
Gaye has learned the art of restraint, making him perhaps the greatest male soul singer.

4 AIN'T NO MOUNTAIN HIGH ENOUGH from **Anthology**
Motown at its most soaring and dramatic.

5 YOU'RE ALL I NEED TO GET BY from **Anthology**
Ashford & Simpson's masterpiece.

6 HEARD IT THROUGH THE GRAPEVINE from **Anthology**
Journalist Dave Marsh thinks this is the greatest record ever made – it's hard to disagree.

7 WHAT'S GOING ON? from **Anthology**
It may be overrated by people who don't really like soul and don't understand the power of metaphor, but, gosh, it's an awfully good record.

8 INNER CITY BLUES from **Anthology**
A potent gospel graffiti haiku.

9 LET'S GET IT ON from **Anthology**
The ultimate makeout record.

10 GOT TO GIVE IT UP from **Anthology**
Gaye goes disco with an impossibly fat bassline and wicked cowbells.

1973 with the definitive quiet storm record, "Let's Get It On" – it was so sexy and such a great come on that you could ignore lines like "We're all sensitive people", and the awful pun, "stop beating around the bush". The album of the same name was an occasionally dazzling, sometimes muddled, conflation of God and sex, which seemed to characterize the bulk of his work in the 70s.

Before recording *Let's Get It On*, Gaye's relationship with Anna Gordy had begun to sour – though the album's finale, "Just To Keep You Satisfied" was dedicated to, and co-written with, her – and, as a result, his relationship with Berry Gordy, and Motown as a whole, also got worse. A 1973 album of duets with Diana Ross, *Marvin And Diana*, was an absolute disaster – there was so much ego involved that the two couldn't even record in the same studio.

Although Gaye's creative peak was over, he still emerged every so often with sublime records like 1976's "I Want You" and "After The Dance" (both made with producer and songwriter **Leon Ware**) and 1977's "Got To Give It Up" (does this have the greatest cowbell playing of all time?). By this point Gaye was in the process of divorce and, as part of the settlement, he had to give Anna Gordy the proceeds from his next album. The result was *Here, My Dear*, a raw, ravaged record that was a towering monument of megalomaniacal bullshit ("Somebody tell me please/Why do I have to pay attorney fees?") and, at the same time, Gaye's best singing (on the track "Sparrow").

Divorce wasn't Gaye's only problem, however; he also owed millions to the tax man, was suffering from bouts of depression and was in a pharmacological haze – songs like 1979's quasi-rap "Ego Tripping Out" were directed at himself. Gaye's last album for Motown, 1981's *In Our Lifetime*, was another maddeningly eccentric album that hinted at greatness, but was too often nothing but sketches of ideas. In the early 80s, Gaye moved to Belgium and released his last great single, "Sexual Healing", for Columbia. He returned to the US a star, but his personal problems still plagued him and any comeback was halted on April 1, 1984, when Gaye was murdered at the hands of his father, following a heated argument. Seemingly like too many of his relationships, Gaye's relationship with his father (a deeply

"love" was a statement as powerful as anything **Bob Dylan** could deliver. The album almost ended with "Wholy Holy", its most spiritual and optimistic track, but Gaye knew that would have been trite. Instead, he ended it on "Inner City Blues (Makes Me Wanna Holler)", a tough, dramatic chain of catch phrases that read like graffiti, but, in Gaye's hands, became a staggering union of the blues and gospel that remains as potent today as it was then.

After *What's Goin' On* changed the shape and direction of pop music, Gaye retreated into his falsetto and framed it with sketchy, but effective, funk vamps on records such as "You're The Man" and "Trouble Man", both from 1972. He emerged from his funk in

Motown

Saying that Motown belched out prefabricated product with the same regularity that Ford's Red River plant churned out Fairmonts is to neglect the divergent styles of, for example, **Smokey Robinson**'s simple, singsong arrangements for **The Temptations** and **Holland-Dozier-Holland**'s whirlpools of sound for **The Four Tops**. Certainly, General Motors never sent its workers to charm school or hired choreographers to orchestrate their routines. What Motown did have was an instantly recognizable sound, inch-perfect craftsmanship and a seemingly endless repertoire of hooks and catch phrases.

Whatever similarities with the neighbouring automobile production lines it may have had, however, Motown was far more than just an unlikely commercial juggernaut. Motown was the ultimate symbol of black economic self-sufficiency. Conversely, the label also represented the integrationist ideal: articulating the black bourgeoisie's claim on the American Dream by courting a white audience without diluting African-American culture. Of course, let's not forget that the music also spoke on its own terms as perfectly crafted pop. As a mediator in countless romances, as a new rhapsodic language, as the voice of unarticulated pleasure and loss, it was, as the label claimed, "the sound of young America".

However divergent the styles of its main artists and producers may have been, Motown is still the only record label that can be considered a genre unto itself. While Motown had some of the greatest singers in soul history – **Marvin Gaye**, Smokey Robinson, **The Temptations'** **David Ruffin** and **Eddie Kendricks**, **The Four Tops'** Levi Stubbs, **Martha Reeves**, **Stevie Wonder** – they would have been nothing without the label's exceptional producers and songwriters – Holland-Dozier-Holland, Smokey Robinson, **Norman Whitfield**. With the aid of the Motown studio band, **The Funk Brothers**, Holland-Dozier-Holland defined the Motown sound. They made huge, crashing records that, although filled with detail and nuance, relied on sheer force for their effectiveness. Crucially, HDH understood the link between cars, freedom, teenage lust and music. As a result, their enormous sound was EQd, tweaked and finely honed to make a big impact on the tiny, tinny speakers of car radios where much of the emotional life of young America was played out. These were the records that fulfilled **Berry Gordy, Jr.**'s dream of the ultimate crossover.

Gordy, a former boxer, had turned his attention to R&B after his jazz record store closed down. He started peddling songs to the New York publishing houses and labels in the mid-50s and caught his first big break when

Brunswick bought his "Reet Petite" for **Jackie Wilson**. After writing a few more hits for Wilson, Gordy decided to produce records himself. **Marv Johnson** was the first artist to take a Berry Gordy production into the charts – the first artist to articulate "the sound of young America". Johnson's 1959 single "Come To Me" had a style very similar to that of Gordy's earlier records with Jackie Wilson. However, Johnson's later songs, such as "Happy Days" and "Merry Go-Round", introduced the broader palette and stronger production values that would later become Motown's hallmarks.

After leasing Johnson's "Money" to his sister **Gwen Gordy**'s Anna label, Berry Gordy, Jr. founded his own Tammie label, before quickly changed the name to Tamla Records. Tamla's first hit was **The Miracles'** "Way Over There" in 1960, which was followed later that year by their "Shop Around". Over the next two years, Gordy added Motown and Gordy to his stable of record labels.

The Contours – Billy Gordon, Sylvester Potts, Billy Hoggs, Joe Billingslea and Hubert Johnson – were the second million-sellers on Motown. Their wonderful "Do You Love Me" was a huge smash in 1962 and it helped put the label on the map. Sadly, The Contours' brand of high-energy dance records never again found favour with the public. Aside from The Contours, the funkiest artist ever to record at Motown was **Shorty Long**. He had hits in the mid- to late 60s with "Devil With The Blue Dress", "Function At The Junction" and "Here Comes The Judge".

The first group to go gold on the label were **The Marvelettes** – Gladys Horton, Wanda Young, Katherine Anderson, Juanita Cowart and Georgeanna Tillman – with 1961's "Please Mr Postman". They recorded several other hits in the standard bouncy girl group vein, including "Beechwood 4-5789" and "Strange I Know", before moving into more sophisticated **Martha & The Vandellas** territory with "Too Many Fish In The Sea", "Danger Heartbreak Dead Ahead" and "Don't Mess With Bill".

While **The Supremes** were far and away the most successful Motown act on the pop chart, it was **Martha & The Vandellas** that truly heralded what would become the trademark Motown sound. They did so with "Heat Wave" in 1963, an epochal Holland-Dozier-Holland production that exploded out of speakers and laid the foundation for the Motown formula: the sibilant cymbals, booming bass, pentecostal tambourines and the constant repetition of the hook. With various permutations of this formula, Motown racked up a massive 240 Top 40 hits between 1962 and the move to California in 1971.

Of course, it wasn't just the superstars that struck gold for Gordy's empire. Aside from their duets with Marvin Gaye, **Tammi Terrell** and **Kim Weston** both recorded several fine singles as solo artists. Terrell had recorded with Scepter/Wand and James Brown before signing to Motown. She was an excellent, sensuous singer, which was displayed to full effect on 1966's "Come On And See Me" and her 1969 version of "This Old Heart Of Mine (Is Weak For You)". Weston, meanwhile, recorded the original version of the enduring "Take Me In Your Arms (Rock Me A Little While)" in 1965 and "Lift Ev'ry Voice And Sing" in 1969, which has since become "the black national anthem".

Even before Motown abandoned Detroit to move to LA in 1971, they already had a presence on the West Coast. The Supremes had recorded several of their records there, as had **Brenda Holloway**, Motown's first West Coast signing. Many soul cultists have suggested that she was the best of all the Motown singers. While that assessment is very hard to agree with, it's also hard to disagree with wonderful performances such as "Every Little Bit Hurts", "When I'm Gone" and the 1967 original version of "You've Made Me So Very Happy". Sadly, when Motown finally left Detroit for good in 1971, it spelled the death of the label as a commercial juggernaut and the end of the golden age of soul.

Although there had been dissention in the ranks before the move to California (most notably the departure of Holland-Dozier-Holland in 1967), the West Coast trek was the final nail in the coffin for the old studio system. Perhaps just as importantly, the move signalled a shift of the fream. No longer, it seemed, was Motown content with success on its own terms, it now wanted to buy fully into mainstream American culture – with plush LA offices and movie deals for its stars. Inevitably, both the vision and the music became less and less dinstinctive. Motown continued to have success, most notably with **The Commodores**, and later with the bland, watered-down R&B of **Shanice**, but the label was largely left behind by Gamble & Huff's Philadelphia revolution, disco, funk and hip-hop. Motown had become just another label.

○ Various Artists: The Complete Motown Singles
2005–2009, Hip-O Select

In 2005 Hip-O Select launched this extraordinary 12-part series that will cover every single released by Motown and its subsidiaries from 1959 to 1971. There is obviously going to be a lot of filler on these sets, which are only available to buy online, but this is a fitting testament to the greatest record label of all time. Only the first three volumes, covering 1959–1963, are available at the time of writing and they are fantastic and revelatory – and Motown's music only got better from then on.

🔊 PLAYLIST

1 DO YOU LOVE ME The Contours from **The Very Best Of The Contours**
This utterly electric record is light years away from the Motown of deportment lessons and taffeta gowns.

2 NOWHERE TO RUN Martha & The Vandellas from **Live Wire!**
Reeves really did have nowhere to run on this record – the Vandellas backing sounds as though they're stalking her.

3 LOVE IS LIKE AN ITCHING IN MY HEART The Supremes from **The Ultimate Collection**
If you want to know why Motown was the sound of young America, listen to those drums.

4 HEARD IT THROUGH THE GRAPEVINE Marvin Gaye from **Anthology**
The greatest performance of Gaye's career, unifying all of his gospel training and earthly sensuality in one sustained cry of desperate passion.

5 THE TRACKS OF MY TEARS Smokey Robinson & The Miracles from **Anthology**
A lesson in how craftsmanship turns schoolboy doggerel into a grand poetic exposition on the human condition.

6 REACH OUT I'LL BE THERE The Four Tops from **Anthology**
Holland-Dozier-Holland channel the spirit of Phil Spector in three overwhelming minutes.

7 PAPA WAS A ROLLING STONE The Temptations from **Anthology**
Did people really dance to this?

8 LIVIN' FOR THE CITY Stevie Wonder from **Innervisions**
Hip-hop producer Prince Paul calls this the greatest hip-hop skit of all time.

9 THIS OLD HEART OF MINE Isley Brothers from **It's Your Thing: The Story Of The Isley Brothers**
Archetypal singsong melody with a beat that will change your life.

10 GIRL YOU NEED A CHANGE OF MIND Eddie Kendricks from **People...Hold On**
Criminally underrated record by the Temptations' best singer that is often considered the first disco record.

conservative minister and practising transvestite) had long been torn by jealousy, fear and resentment – the very demons that often made Gaye's music so great.

⊙ What's Going On
1971, Motown

Soul's first, and greatest, concept album, *What's Going On* wasn't about the travails of an alienated rock star. Instead, it applied soul's core theme – love – and its cultural context – the gospel feel of the black church – to the real world. Previously, soul had channelled its rage, its frustration, its hope into love songs, but here, on the title track and on "Mercy Mercy Me (The Ecology)", Gaye does the reverse.

⊙ Anthology
1995, Motown

As is too often the case with the Motown catalogue, the only time that the entirety of Gaye's work has been properly collected is on this superb 2-CD collection that is now out of print. At 47 tracks this is a near-definitive collection – only "Sexual Healing" is missing – of the work of one of soul's true titans. It was replaced by *The Very Best Of Marvin Gaye* (2001, Motown) which has 13 fewer tracks, so opt for this one if you can find it.

⊙ Moods Of Marvin Gaye / In The Groove
2001, Motown

Moods Of Marvin Gaye from 1966 is quite simply one of the best soul albums ever released, and 1968's *In The Groove* is only a notch or two behind. Beside the hits, this reissue CD is filled with Motown originals from the label's entire stable of producers. Gaye's ultimate cool is on display throughout this single-disc tour de force.

⊙ Marvin Gaye & Tammi Terrell – United / You're All I Need
2001, Motown

Marvin Gaye also sang duets with Mary Wells and Kim Weston, but the records he made with Tammi Terrell were special. This single-disc reissue of their two duet albums from 1967 and 1968 captures their very best material, including "Ain't No Mountain High Enough", "You're All I Need To Get By", "Ain't Nothing Like The Real Thing".

Gloria Gaynor

Crowned the "Queen of Disco" by the International Association of Discotheque Disc Jockeys in 1975, **Gloria Gaynor** was, in reality, never much more than a modestly gifted singer who had the good fortune to be in the right place at the right time.

Gaynor was born **Gloria Fowles** on September 7, 1949 in Newark, New Jersey. By the time she was 17, she was singing on the "chitlin' circuit" with a variety of nightclub bands, including Eddie McLendon & The Pacesetters, The Soul Brothers, The Soul Satisfiers and The Unsilent Majority. In 1966, under the name Gloria Gaynor, she recorded "She'll Be Sorry", a midtempo Northern dancer with a salsa-ish piano line, for **Johnny Nash**'s Jocida label.

Gaynor was discovered in 1972 by **Jay Ellis**, while she was working at the Wagon Wheel Club on Manhattan's 45th Street. Ellis became her manager and got her signed to Columbia, where she released "Honeybee", a strange mix of trademark Philly soul and a buzzing fuzz guitar that imitated the insect of the title and sounded as though it was played by a 60s garage band. It was an uncomfortable mixture of sound and the record tanked. After the song's failure, the rights reverted back to Jay Ellis, who had recently set up DCA (aka Disco Corporation of America) with **Mcco Monardo**, former producer of Tommy James & The Shondells, and Motown engineer **Tony Bongiovi**. DCA decided to tinker with "Honeybee" and kept the buzzing guitar (but placed it way down in the mix), the strings and Earl Young's drums, but changed the bassline, added new instruments and generally smoothed the record out. The new "Honey Bee" record was released on MGM in April 1974, becoming a modest R&B hit and an enormous disco hit.

After her version of The Jackson 5's "Never Can Say Goodbye" became a disco and pop smash, it was weaved together with "Honey Bee" and "Reach Out, I'll Be There" to form a non-stop disco suite on her 1975 debut album *Never Can Say Goodbye*. Later that year, Gaynor struck disco gold again with the light and fluffy (aside from its great breakdown) "Casanova Brown" and a sultry remake of "Walk On By".

After she was crowned "Queen of Disco" in 1975, Gaynor's dancefloor hits started to dry up. But, on a fateful night in 1978, Studio 54 DJ **Ritchie Kaczor** decided to play the B-side to her most recent single "Substitute". When he put "I Will Survive" on the decks, nearly everyone left the dancefloor, but Kaczor persisted. Within a few more spins, "I Will Survive" was the biggest record at Studio 54 – and soon in all of New York. The buzz was so great that the record company re-released the single with "I Will Survive" as the A-side, and it eventually went to #1 in just about every country in the world. Its association with Studio

54 may have been why it initially became a dancefloor hit, but the record had everything a great disco record is supposed to have: full-throated gospel release complemented by a surging bassline, dramatic strings, hissing hi-hats and a hint of Broadway razzmatazz.

Again, despite being on top of the disco world, Gaynor's hits quickly dried up. "Anybody Wanna Party?" and "Let Me Know (I Have A Right)" were slight and they paled in comparison to "I Will Survive". At the end of the disco boom, Gaynor's covers became increasingly more ludicrous – "Stop! In The Name Of Love" – and unoriginal – "I Am What I Am" – and she suffered because of her inescapable association with disco.

After a long hiatus, during which time she rediscovered Christianity, Gaynor returned in 1995 with *I'll Be There*, an album that continued her fascination with inappropriate cover material, including "I Will Always Love You" and "Oh Happy Day". She has since continued to perform live all over the world and, in 2002, released *I Wish You Love*, which was an underwhelming bid at commercial dance flavours, but featured a fiery title track that was a notch above the run of the mill.

⊙ I Will Survive: The Anthology
1998, Polydor

This 25-track overview of Gloria Gaynor's career is probably far more "Queen of Disco" than you could ever need, but it has the edge over the *20th Century Masters: The Millennium Collection: The Best Of Gloria Gaynor* (2000, Polydor) because it includes her very underrated version of "Walk On By". As an added bonus, "Honey Bee", "Never Can Say Goodbye" and "Reach Out, I'll Be There" are presented in the original dancefloor suite format.

Ginuwine

Before exploding onto the music scene with his debut single as **Ginuwine**, R&B singer **Elgin Baylor Lumpkin** (born October 15, 1975 in Washington, DC) performed with several local hip-hop groups and worked as a Michael Jackson imitator. He was discovered by **Jodeci** in 1996, moved to New York and immediately had a smash hit with "Pony".

One of the first **Timbaland** productions to make a big impact, "Pony" had a remarkable vocoded bassline as well as ricocheting click beats – which were to become Timbaland's

trademark – that anchored Ginuwine's rather tawdry sex metaphor. "Pony" was an instant hit, going platinum and topping the R&B chart for two weeks.

The song was also the lead cut on Ginuwine's debut album, *Ginuwine…The Bachelor*. The album, which sold two million copies, was mostly produced by Timbaland, who gave Ginuwine a state of the art *mise en scène* for his contemporary love man shtick. Tracks such as "Tell Me Do U Wanna" and "I'll Do Anything/I'm Sorry" also did well on the R&B charts, but the most striking song on the album was an outlandish cover of Prince's "When Doves Cry".

Ginuwine provided "Same Ol' G" for the soundtrack to the movie *Dr. Doolittle*, before releasing his second album in 1999, *100% Ginuwine*. Again produced by Timbaland, the album was a marvel of sonic invention, even though Ginuwine's seductions couldn't live up to the music. *100% Ginuwine* included an audacious cover of Michael Jackson's "She's Out Of My Life", but the album's most inventive track was "So Anxious", a quiet, crawling, almost spectral come-on.

The 2001 album *The Life* was the first to be made without Timbaland – Big Dog Productions and Troy Oliver and Cory Rooney produced – and it was a big letdown. "Differences", a paint-by-numbers twenty-first century quiet storm track, was nevertheless Ginuwine's biggest pop hit, reaching #4 on the charts. After appearing in the film comedy *Juwanna Man* and duetting with P. **Diddy** on "I Need A Girl, Part 2" in 2002,

Ginuwine released the very lacklustre *The Senior* in 2003, which featured guest appearances from **Method Man** and **Solé**. No matter who he drags into his projects, however, it is quite clear that the collaborator Ginuwine really needs is Timbaland.

Ginuwine...The Bachelor
1996, 550/Epic

This album may not sound like a revolution now, but that's only because everyone who's anyone in R&B has borrowed from it since. *Ginuwine...The Bachelor* was the first big album that Timbaland produced and its sound still reverberates on the R&B scene. The cavernous architecture, plush synth beds and ultra-modern percussion made Ginuwine sound like a slick twenty-first century ladies' man even though he wasn't doing anything Teddy Pendergrass hadn't done two decades earlier.

Larry Graham

B orn August 14, 1946 in Beaumont, Texas, **Larry Graham** grew up to become, unquestionably, one of the most influential bassists ever to slap the roundwounds in anger. In fact, if it hadn't been for Graham, it's quite possible that no one would slap the bass at all – he invented the technique. Raised in the Bay Area, Graham started playing guitar in his mother's trio lounge act when he was 15 years old, but when the drummer left the group he picked up the bass. He developed his signature thumping sound as a way of compensating for the band's lack of a drummer.

Sly Stone heard the trio play one night in 1966 and immediately offered Graham a job in his band. With **Sly & The Family Stone**, Graham not only popularized slap bass, but also defined fuzz bass playing with a seemingly impossible combination of mastodon stomp and cat-like grace and agility. As was the case with all the members of the Family Stone, Graham's instrumental role was mirrored by his vocal role, and his leagues-deep baritone anchored many of their records in the same way as his basslines.

Graham left Sly & The Family Stone in 1972 and joined a group called Hot Chocolate (not the group led by Errol Brown that had a hit with "You Sexy Thing"), which was soon renamed **Graham Central Station**. The group – guitarist **David Vega**, keyboardists **Butch Sam** and **Hershall Kennedy**, drummer **Willie Sparks** and percussionist/

vocalist **Patrice Banks** – scored a big R&B hit with their debut single, "Can You Handle It", and Graham once again helped redefine bass playing on their self-titled debut album in 1974. Using an array of effects pedals that would have embarrassed even **Eddie Van Halen**, Graham attempted to turn the bass into a lead instrument that could compete with the guitar. The black rock approach continued later that year on *Release Yourself*, which included a reinterpretation of **The Detroit Emeralds**' "Feel The Need".

The 1975 album *Ain't No 'Bout-A-Doubt It* was the group's breakthrough. It included the R&B #1 "Your Love", which was largely based on the Family Stone's "Hot Fun In The Summertime" and featured Graham singing falsetto for the first time. The album also contained one of the all-time great funk tracks, the ludicrously heavy "The Jam". Banks and Sparks left the group in 1976 and, after releasing the monstrous, vocoder classic "Now Do-U-Wanta Dance", Graham Central Station released a few lacklustre singles and desultory albums before disbanding in 1979.

Larry Graham went solo in 1980, but he put away his Godzilla bass and refashioned himself as a smooth love man. "One In A Million You" was as sickly as any **Diane Warren** ballad and, inevitably, became a huge hit. Graham's version of The Intruders' "When We Get Married" and the record "Just Be My Lady" also made it into the R&B Top 10, but his subsequent fall from grace was just as sudden as his earlier reinvention and his next records got lower and lower chart placings. After his 1987 duet with **Aretha Franklin**, "If You Need My Love Tonight", only managed to squeak into the R&B Top 100, Graham concentrated on session work and production.

Graham Central Station reunited in the mid-90s and, most notably, became a regular opening act for **Prince**, one of Graham's most loyal supporters, on his 1997 Jam of the Year tour. The group then released an album of mostly new material, *GCS 2000*, in 1999 on Prince's NPG label.

The Jam: The Larry Graham And Graham Central Station Anthology
2001, Rhino

At two discs and 33 tracks, this exhaustive collection is probably more Larry Graham than most people need.

However, the excellent packaging – including fine liner notes from funk historian Rickey Vincent – and the fact that it covers all of his Graham Central Station days, as well as his solo years, make this anthology more than worth its weight.

Dobie Gray

Although he had some modest success on the R&B charts, **Dobie Gray**, with his weepy, hiccupping voice, was destined to be a country singer. He was born on July 26, 1940, with the name of either Laurence Brown or Leonard Ainsworth (sources vary), and was raised on country music in Texas. Gray's grandfather was a Baptist minister and he forbade any music, other than country and gospel, from being played in the house. It wasn't until he was a teenager that Gray moved to Houston and discovered **Bobby "Blue" Bland** and **T-Bone Walker**.

Gray moved to Los Angeles in 1960 to try to make it as a crooner. That same year he recorded his first single, "To Be Wanted", on the Stripe label as **Leonard Ainsworth**. However, it wasn't until 1962 that he had his first R&B chart success with the uptempo "Look At Me" on the Cordak label, released under the new name of Dobie Gray. He followed that up with the rather cheesy and awkward "Feelin' In My Heart", before moving to Charger Records in 1964. There Gray scored his second-biggest hit with "'The 'In' Crowd", which was surely the squarest ode to hipness ever recorded – but even poseurs deserve soaring horn charts and great hooks.

Dobie Gray continued in this high-energy dancefloor style with "See You At The 'Go-Go'", "Monkey Jerk" and "Out On The Floor", but none of them had any real chart impact. After cutting two singles for Capitol, which also flopped, Gray moved to the White Whale label and released the string-fuelled stomper "Honey, You Can't Take It Back". He then joined the group **Pollution** in the early 70s, sharing vocal duties with future disco chanteuse **Tata Vega** on two albums for Prophecy.

While appearing in the LA production of the musical *Hair*, Gray was rediscovered by producer **Mentor Williams**, who moved him to Nashville. In Music City, Gray recorded a series of albums that were closer to country

than they were to soul and included his biggest ever hit, the gold-selling 1973 single "Drift Away". The follow-up, "Loving Arms", was even more of a country track, and has since become something of a country standard. Gray's affinity for Nashville was finally announced once and for all by the title of his 1974 album – *Hey Dixie*; Gray became one of the few black artists to use that very loaded word.

In 1976 Gray signed to Southern rock stalwart Capricorn and had success with "Find 'Em, Fool 'Em And Forget 'Em". He had his last hit in this insipid country style with the disco-ish "You Can Do It" in 1978, and then started to concentrate on songwriting, penning hits for **Don Williams**, Charley Pride, **John Denver** and David Lee Murphy. Gray returned to recording in 1986 with the album *From Where I Stand*, but faded soon afterwards. He returned again in 1997 with the self-released *Diamond Cuts* album, which featured new recordings of old hits plus some brand-new compositions, and in 2001 he released a collection of Christmas records, *Songs Of The Season*.

Ultimate Collection
2001, Hip-O

This 20-track collection has the edge over Razor & Tie's 1996 greatest hits album, *Drift Away: His Very Best*, because it includes more of Dobie Gray's uptempo dancefloor material from the mid-60s – the great R&B hits he recorded before drifting away into a bland MOR version of country soul in the mid-70s.

Macy Gray

Sounding like **Dinah Washington**, if she had learnt to sing with Britney and Christina in the *New Mickey Mouse Club* and then started hanging out with **Lenny Kravitz**, **Macy Gray** has perhaps the most mannered voice in the history of popular music. Combine that with a "crazy" persona and a charmless insouciance that comes off as devil-may-care arrogance and you have one of the least appealing figures on the contemporary music scene.

Gray was born **Natalie McIntyre** in Canton, Ohio in 1970. While enrolled at a screenwriting class in Los Angeles, she wrote some lyrics to accompany a friend's music. When the singer failed to show up for the recording session, Gray ended up singing on the demo tape. With a voice that sounded like a combination of Selma Diamond, Carole Channing and Biz Markie sharing a joint, Gray started to attract attention as the tape made its way round the LA music scene. Taking the name Macy Gray from one of her neighbours back home in Canton, she started singing for a jazz/standards band that played in Los Angeles hotels.

After a false start with Atlantic Records, who decided not to release her album, she signed to Epic and recorded – and released – *On How Life Is* in 1999. Working with Fiona Apple's producer **Andrew Slater**, Gray created an adventurous but overreaching album that had many people labelling her as a hip-hop version of **Billie Holiday**. The album went on to sell over seven million copies, and her biggest hit, "I Try", won her a Grammy Award in 2000. Sure, "I Try" had a decent hook and "I've Committed Murder" was slightly eyebrow-raising to anyone who has never listened to the blues or hip-hop, but Gray had as much shtick as a Borscht Belt comedian.

If you chose to look beyond the hackneyed observations of her lyrics, her helium, stoned soul-girl vocals may have been a diverting novelty on *On How Life Is*. However, she was given a relatively free rein on 2001's *The Id*, after the commercial success of her debut, and her lack of original ideas and her excessive self-indulgence came into sharp focus. She tried desperately to sound like **Al Green**, stole vocal arrangements, inflections and beats from **Sly Stone** and **Allen Toussaint** and mostly just ended up sounding like a female Lenny Kravitz who grew up on **Cat Stevens** and **Janis Ian** as well as **Hendrix**, **Prince** and Memphis soul. The album also included the catastrophic carnival-esque track "Oblivion", which played up to her "crazy" persona more than ever and featured such lyrics as "In my underwear/Sometimes I visit there/Oblivion/Ignorance is bliss".

On 2003's *The Trouble With Being Myself*, Macy Gray wallowed ever deeper into her persecution complex. Strangely, though, she didn't seem very interested and neither did her band. Apparently, she was more concerned with her acting career by this point and, despite releasing a *Live In Las Vegas* album and DVD in 2005, acting seems to be where her focus has remained. Arrogant,

braindead, retrograde and bohemian is no way to go through life – listen to **Destiny's Child** instead.

On How Life Is
1999, Epic

Despite what the title may suggest, this 10-track debut is Macy Gray's least egotistical record and her freshest. Several years later, her unique raspy voice no longer surprises – though it still annoys – but Andrew Slater's hip-hopped Memphis soul production continues to hold its own.

Al Green

More than any other performer of his generation, **Al Green** symbolized the secular/sacred divide that gives soul music its emotional power. Unlike many of his contemporaries, however, Green's attempt to have it both ways with God and sex was the result of intense, quiet introspection. Some have complained that Green is a solipsist, which may very well be true – no one else has made such gorgeous music about being alone. But his is the sound not of someone wrestling with himself, but of someone wrestling with two different kinds of joy that threaten to tear his soul apart.

Al Greene (he later dropped the "e" from his surname) was born in Forrest City, Arkansas in 1946, and was introduced to gospel music at a very young age. His journey across the battlefield of sexual release and spiritual transcendence really began in 1960 as a member of his brothers' gospel quartet, **The Greene Brothers**. After he was kicked out of the group when his father caught him listening to the worldly Jackie Wilson, Green tried his hand at pop music. He formed an R&B group called **The Soul Mates**, who had an R&B top-ten hit with their debut single, "Back Up Train", in 1967. The group's next few releases failed to make any impression on the charts, but Green was fortunate enough to meet producer and label boss **Willie Mitchell** in 1969, who immediately got him signed to Hi Records.

Hi Records had previously been known for producing some decent instrumentals and country records, but Green and Mitchell worked together to create the composite portrait of the soul man: both funky and forlorn, assertive and acquiescent, greedy and generous. The formula proved to be so successful

Al Green singin' his heart out

that, between 1971 and 1976, Green had thirteen top-forty singles and sold some 30 million records. Even more than **Barry White** or **Teddy Pendergrass**, Green became the definitive 70s love man. Where other soft-soul icons were slightly wimpy and put upon, Green's falsetto was just plain sexy. Combining a gospel falsetto, **Sam Cooke**'s smooth phrasing, **Smokey Robinson**'s sweetness and an ear for country and western music, he managed to create a vulnerable yet assertive persona that was unique among male soul singers. Green's synthesis of Cooke and Robinson was also a combination of the Northern and Southern soul traditions: he fitted the stylization of the North into the more emotionally direct sound of the South.

Green's Hi Records debut, the muddled 1969 album *Green Is Blues* (with its subdued soft-soul textures highlighting his introspective tone) showed glimpses of the formula that would make him the most accomplished

soul singer of the 70s. However, it was when the sublime drummer **Al Jackson, Jr.** from rival label Stax began working with Mitchell, that Green's persona and music really began to take shape. On *Al Green Gets Next To You* in 1970, Green combined the Southern rawness of **Otis Redding** with smooth **Marvin Gaye**-style moves and the tenderness of **Smokey Robinson**. The album gave a composite portrait of the soul man, both funky ("I'm A Ram For You") and forlorn ("Tired Of Being Alone").

Green distilled all this emotional range into his next release, "Let's Stay Together", which was a perfect pop single conveying both the pain and joy of love and sex in one sing-along chorus. The 1972 album of the same name was weighed down by material that failed to live up to the single, although Green's version of the Bee-Gee's "How Can You Mend A Broken Heart?" was a remarkable redemption of the original. Green's other 1972 release, *I'm Still In Love With You*, was a deceptively simple album laden with unforgettable hooks. The gorgeous title track presaged his preoccupation with the bittersweet melancholy of love – a theme that would be writ large on his next album.

The 1973 album *Call Me* was Green's masterpiece. A sad, painful, but ultimately uplifting exploration of loss, it displayed the most generous view of love ever voiced by a male singer. Green may have been self-absorbed, but it was his openness that made *Call Me* such a great record: it was at once the best break-up, and the best make-out, record ever made. On "Call Me (Come Back Home)", Green sounded simultaneously ragged and warm, like he was caught between an exasperated sigh and an affectionate whisper. Elsewhere, his sensuous voice turned Willie Nelson's "Funny How Time Slips Away" from a cry-in-your-beer mourn to a warm embrace of good memories, and Hank Williams' "I'm So Lonesome I Could Cry" into a gospel hymn. Tailing Green's voice perfectly, Al Jackson's drumming sounded so simple; no one played the drums with as much finesse. Jackson managed to make his kit sound driving and floating at the same time, a combination that gave Green's records their substantial bottom, but never overwhelmed his silky voice.

He followed up in 1974 with *Al Green Explores Your Mind*, which suffered from weaker material and music that retreated back to the old formula of subtle drum figures and nearly acoustic instrumentation. The album's standout track was "Take Me To The River", a mixture of sexual and baptismal metaphors that was, perhaps, the ultimate expression of the conflict between the pleasures of the flesh and the ecstasies of the spirit. After the album was recorded, Green had a vicious fight with an ex-lover, who threw a bowl of boiling-hot grits over him, causing second-degree burns, and then killed herself. The incident pushed Green closer to God and created a musical fallout that resulted in three lacklustre and frequently bizarre albums on which he was constantly searching for his voice and his vision.

The turning point came when Green parted company with Willie Mitchell, whose formula had become particularly ossified after Al Jackson's death in 1975. Green's first self-produced album, *The Belle Album* (1977), made sense both of what had happened to him and of the body/spirit split that had created soul in the first place ("It's you that I want, but it's Him that I need", he sang on "Belle"). Featuring Green's most emotional and dynamic singing since *Call Me*, the album was boldly built around his often inspired acoustic guitar riffs. The same daring that led to Green making an acoustic soul album in the age of disco also saw him cover "I Say A Little Prayer" on his next album, *Truth 'N' Time*, in 1979.

That year also saw a turning point in Green's career when he fell off stage during a performance in Cincinnati. Interpreting the injury as a sign from God, he devoted himself to religion and became an ordained minister, founding the Full Gospel Tabernacle Church in Memphis. In 1980 Green defected to the gospel label, Myrrh. With a couple of exceptions, most notably *Tokyo...Live!* and *Higher Plane* (both 1981), this period saw Green descend into genre exercises that combined pop stylings with gospel lyrics. Although Green was undoubtedly still a great singer, he was past his prime, and his unforceful style didn't lend itself to gospel the way the stately, and no less subdued, style of **Mahalia Jackson** did.

Throughout the 90s, Green had an awkward time trying to fit in with the new production styles. His 1993 release *Don't Look Back* was disappointing and strangely conceived, and it saw him peculiarly paired with producer **Arthur Baker**, one of the founders of the electro sound. Green recently got back together with producer Willie Mitchell, and the reunion saw something of a return to form for the pair with the 2003 album *I Can't Stop*. Green was on fine form, if not quite as beautiful as he was during his prime, and the production was in classic Hi Records' style – although you can't help missing Al Jackson's magnificent drumming. The 2005 album *Everything's OK* was more

of the same, proving that time still hasn't ravaged Green's spectacular instrument.

Call Me
1973, Hi

One of the finest soul albums ever made, *Call Me* represents the creative apex of the most accomplished soul man of the 70s. Superbly assisted by Willie Mitchell's production and Al Jackson's drumming, *Call Me* exemplifies Al Green's tremendous emotional range, from the bawdy and salacious "Here I Am (Come And Take Me)" to the beautiful whispered intimacy of "Have You Been Making Out OK".

Al Green's Greatest Hits
1995, Right Stuff

Essentially 1975's *Al Green's Greatest Hits* with the five best tracks from 1977's *Al Green's Greatest Hits, Vol. 2*, this is the definitive single-disc compilation of this consummate soul singer. It doesn't have a lot in the way of notes and extras, but the music speaks for itself.

Everything's OK
2005, Blue Note

After many years of dividing his attention between straight gospel and his secular roots, Al Green reunited with producer Willie Mitchell in 2003 to stage a proper comeback. Both of the albums they've made since are high quality, but while 2003's *I Can't Stop* made a conscious effort to capture the sound and spirit of his best 70s material, *Everything's OK* is less reminiscent and is, because of its progress, a contemporary soul classic.

Garland Green

With a pleading baritone voice similar in style to that of **Tyrone Davis**, **Garland Green** was one of the finest exponents of Chicago soul. Unlike many of his Windy City contemporaries, Green sang soft soul as if he were singing the blues, undercutting the typical breezy lilt with downhome grit.

Green was born on June 24, 1942 in Dunleath, Mississippi, but he moved to Chicago in 1958 in search of work. His big break came in 1967, when he was spotted performing at the Sutherland Lounge by saxophonist **Mel Collins** and his wife songwriter **Joshie Jo Armstead**, who immediately signed him to her Gamma label. Working in Detroit with producer **Mike Terry** (who also produced for J.J. Barnes and Maxine Brown), Green recorded Armstead's "Girl I Love You" as his debut. The record became a small hit in Chicago, probably due to its resemblance to a Jerry Butler track, with its acres of strings and singsong melody, and MCA picked it up on their Revue subsidiary.

Green followed that up with a few more singles for Revue before recording his biggest hit, "Jealous Kind Of Fella", in 1969 for MCA's Uni label. The record's arrangement was a bit awkward, but Green's almost hysterical apology was quite affecting and the song became a top-ten R&B hit. Green released an album of the same name later that year, and then the similarly styled single, "Don't Think That I'm A Violent Guy", the next year, but he failed to replicate his earlier success.

In 1971 Green signed to Cotillion and had a reasonable hit with "Plain And Simple Girl", which was produced by Syl Johnson and arranged by Donny Hathaway. His other records for Cotillion, including "Love Is What We Came Here For" written by Bunny Sigler and arranged by Norman Harris, were commercial failures. Green's smooth baritone just didn't work with the lush Philly sound.

Garland Green finally found a home at Spring Records in the mid-70s. Less jazzy than the sound he was saddled with at Cotillion, Spring's rapprochement between penthouse and roadhouse suited Green to a T. His Spring records "He Didn' Know (He Kept On Talking)", "Let The Good Times Roll" and "Bumpin' And Stompin'" all charted, although modestly.

After a brief period recording at Muscle Shoals and with Leon Haywood in LA, Green signed to Ocean Front Records at the recommendation of Tyrone Davis. Green's bluesy version of Lamont Dozier's "Tryin' To Hold On", produced by Dozier himself, managed to creep into the R&B chart in 1983, where it stayed for a surprising ten weeks. Green's last recording was "Let's Keep It Simple", released on his own Love LA Music label in 1987. He has never been able to re-create the success of his one big hit, 1969's "Jealous Kind Of Fella".

Jealous Kind Of Fella
1969, Varese Sarabande

The 1995 CD reissue of Green's debut album is a great rediscovery of one of the Windy City's most underappreciated soul singers. Produced by Joshie Jo Armstead and Mel Collins, this album features all of Green's best tracks for MCA's Uni label. When the arrangement and singer gel, this is midtempo soul of the highest order.

Guy

The founder and producer of R&B trio Guy has become the most important figure in R&B of the past two decades. An accomplished multi-instrumentalist and a maestro of the sampler, Teddy Riley once and for all took R&B out of the hands of the vocalist and put it in the hands of the producer. After his apotheosis, the success of an R&B track depended almost entirely on the beats; the vocals were almost immaterial. Riley is often credited as the father of New Jack Swing (the combination of hip-hop and soul) and it's largely thanks to him that R&B and hip-hop became inseparable. What's often overlooked, however, is the part Riley played in making hip-hop attractive to R&B artists and producers in the first place. He was behind such classics as Doug E. Fresh's "The Show", Kool Moe Dee's "Go See The Doctor", Heavy D's "Mr. Big Stuff" and Rob Base & DJ E-Z Rock's "It Takes Two".

Despite Riley's behind-the-scenes work on so many of hip-hop's earliest pop successes, Guy was the project that really made his name. A trio of Riley plus brothers Damion and Aaron Hall, Guy permanently changed the face of R&B. Although traces of the church were still evident in his voice, lead vocalist Aaron Hall picked up where Charlie Wilson of The Gap Band left off, situating soul firmly in a strictly secular uptown where melodramatic melisma was as garish and over-the-top as the band's leather suits. While Hall, despite his he-man huskiness, unfortunately helped to create the adenoidal whine that dominates R&B these days, Riley forged the angular beatscape that defines contemporary "urban" music.

With its synth hooks, glossy vocals and shiny production values, the influential smash that was Guy's 1988 self-titled debut album was as upwardly mobile as anything by Luther Vandross or Anita Baker. Crucially, though, Guy were very much the product of the Harlem housing projects where they grew up – Guy never forgot the street. There were only two slow joints on the album; all the other tracks were uptempo funk jams that featured the crunching kick drums and smacking snares of mid-80s hip-

hop, with the added bounce of **Cameo** and The Gap Band. No one had ever achieved such a synthesis of the material good life with the vibes from the street, and every R&B producer from **Dallas Austin** to **Rodney Jerkins** has since tried to duplicate the Riley formula.

The Riley sound was rooted in the interaction between the brittle beats of his armoury of drum machines and the plasmic brio of his synth bass. *Guy*'s best tracks – "'Round And 'Round", "Groove Me", "Teddy's Jam" and "I Like" – were collages of ricocheting kick drums, stuttering snares, backwards beats and screaming, farting, belching, crooning synths that turned the vocals into just another synth colour. It's this quality, however, that revealed the ultimate problem: since Guy and **Whitney Houston**, R&B vocalists have aspired to a kind of digital lin-

earity that mimics the cathedral of machinery in which they're placed, rather than aspiring to the dirt and grit of a church made of earth and wood.

While Guy were a sensation in the R&B world, they made no impression on the pop charts. Strangely, 1989's "My Fantasy", from the soundtrack to Spike Lee's *Do The Right Thing* and featuring Riley's herky-jerky lead vocals, became the group's first R&B #1. Their second album, *The Future* (1990), may not have been as epochal as the first, but it was every bit as good, even though Guy split from their manager **Gene Griffin** mid-flow. The slamming club funk of album tracks such as "I Wanna Get With U" and "D-O-G Me Out" were equally as effective as the soft-focus boudoir ballads "Let's Chill" and "Do Me Right". Guy, however, broke up soon afterwards. Riley went on to form BLACKstreet, while the Hall brothers tried their hands at solo careers. Unfortunately, by the time the group re-formed in 2000 for *Guy III*, the R&B scene had long since moved on, and they sounded like has-beens.

⊙ Guy
1988, Uptown/MCA

Whatever the wheels it set in motion, this is one of the most innovative and important albums of the past two decades. Despite his innovations, Teddy Riley didn't forget where he came from. A child of hip-hop, he chopped, edited and reconstructed the original soul groove – mutating samples from Stevie Wonder, James Brown, Trouble Funk and The Mohawks – to make sense to a generation whose fantasies were shaped by technology rather than the church.

Donny Hathaway

A talented pianist, songwriter, arranger and singer who owed more than a little debt to Stevie Wonder, **Donny Hathaway** was hailed as one of the brightest stars of 70s soul. However, with the exception of his duets with Roberta Flack, here never really rose above the ranks of cult stardom. With an often appealing, but occasionally saccharine, combination of jazziness, traditional pop, gospel and a hint of old-fashioned soul and roots, his records embodied the dreams of the post-civil rights era. Unlike the aspirational records released by Philadelphia International, Hathaway's class fantasies were rarely accompanied by a groove that brought everyone along to the party.

Donny Hathaway was born on October 1, 1945 in Chicago, but was raised by his grandmother, a professional gospel singer, in St. Louis. As a young child, Hathaway performed as "The Nation's Youngest Gospel Singer" before winning a music scholarship to Howard University. At Howard he roomed with **Leroy Hutson** (who later became the lead singer of The Impressions) and was a classmate of Roberta Flack. In the mid-60s Hathaway started to play piano in classmate Ric Powell's jazz trio in and around the Washington DC area, but by 1968 he was a staff writer, arranger, producer and pianist for Curtis Mayfield's Curtom label.

Hathaway's first record was a duet with **June Conquest**, "I Thank You Baby", released under the name June & Donnie in 1969. After a stint playing with guitarist Phil Upchurch's group, Hathaway landed a record deal with Atco. His debut album, 1970's *Everything Is Everything*, was a critically acclaimed cult hit, largely thanks to "The Ghetto". With his most soulful ever vocals accompanied by the Fender Rhodes and Latin percussion, "The Ghetto" was Hathaway's masterpiece track. His 1971 release, *Donny Hathaway*, was a bizarre album full of sombre covers of contemporary hits such as "He Ain't Heavy, He's My Brother" and "Put Your Hand In The Hand". The album also included a version of "Magnificent Sanctuary Band", which had Hathaway marching with Jesus, although the song's real glories were to be found in the drum break that opened it.

In 1972 Hathaway teamed up with his former Howard University classmate to create an album of duets, *Roberta Flack & Donny Hathaway*, which included the hits "You've Got A Friend" and "Where Is The Love?". Later that year, Hathaway released *Live*, which was perhaps his most impressive album. Despite including an overly jazzy version of Marvin Gaye's "What's Goin' On", *Live* demonstrated not only Hathaway's vast musical skills, but also his great rapport with the audience. The album was not a big commercial success, however, and Hathaway received greater exposure for his theme song to the American sitcom *Maude*.

On his 1973 album *Extension Of A Man*, Hathaway indulged his worst instincts with overblown tone poems and fusiony, noodly tracks such as "Valdez In The Country", which later became a favourite with the jazz-dance crowd. Around this time, Hathaway started to suffer from severe depression, which sometimes called for hospital treatment. As his mood swings and depression worsened, his gigs and recording sessions became more sporadic. Hathaway continued to perform the odd club date and recorded the R&B #1 smash "The Closer I Get To You" with Flack. However, part way through the recording sessions for a second album of duets with Flack in January 1979, Hathaway was found dead, having apparently jumped from the window of his 15th-floor apartment in New York City.

◉ **These Songs For You, Live!**
2004, Rhino

Compiling tracks from *Live*, the posthumously released *In Performance* album and previously unreleased recordings, this excellent collection presents Hathaway at his best – performing live. Everything here was recorded between 1971 and 1973 when Hathaway was at his peak. Even if his sometimes florid compositions won't make a believer out of you, the audience certainly will.

Isaac Hayes

Often reduced to a caricature of a bald-headed, gold-chain wearing, hyper-masculine black love man, **Isaac Hayes** was, in fact, one of soul music's most versatile talents. He was a session pianist at the Stax studios where he played on sides by Otis Redding and Wilson Pickett; he wrote classics like "Hold On! I'm Comin'", "When Something Is Wrong With My Baby", "Soul Man" and "B-A-B-Y" with **David Porter**; and he scored the films *Shaft*, *Tough Gugs* and *Truck Turner*. Above all that, he was Stax's most successful artist – an amazing achievement considering the label also had Redding, Sam & Dave, Booker T. & The MG's, The Staple Singers, Eddie Floyd and The Bar-Kays.

Born August 20, 1942 in Covington, Tennessee, Hayes was raised by his grandparents after both of his parents died while he was an infant. While attending grade school in Memphis, Hayes and his sister performed **Perry Como** songs at a school talent competition. He is now the very incarnation of the husky love man, with his deep, overwrought and thick-as-molasses voice, but when Hayes first started to sing in public, he was teased for sounding like a girl. His voice was apparently even higher than his sister's,

and his classmates started calling him the "Swoon Crooner". Fortunately, by the time he was 15, Hayes's voice had become the rich bass that he's known for today and he had the last laugh on his classmates – girls were now swooning over him as he sang Nat "King" Cole songs at talent competitions.

After recording several singles for small local labels in the early 60s, Hayes was chosen to be the house pianist at Stax Records. While playing in the house band, he developed a friendship and eventually a strong songwriting partnership with **David Porter**. With over 200 compositions to their credit, the duo became one of the cornerstones of Stax's commercial and creative success.

Hayes's first album as a solo artist, 1967's *Presenting Isaac Hayes*, was a commercial flop recorded in an impromptu trio format with MG's' drummer **Al Jackson, Jr.** and bassist **Donald "Duck" Dunn**. To say that 1969's *Hot Buttered Soul* was a departure would be an understatement of gargantuan proportions. Seemingly featuring a cast of thousands, with a battery of effects pedals, *Hot Buttered Soul* had only four songs and they averaged over eleven minutes each. Unlike the famous, urgent, gospelese declarations he wrote for Sam & Dave, Hayes's voice on *Hot Buttered Soul* was deep, overwrought and thick as molasses. With even richer arrangements, an album has never been so appropriately named.

His soundtrack to the 1971 blaxploitation movie *Shaft* may have had the wah-wah riff of the gods, but *Hot Buttered Soul* was more influential. Just about all of 70s soul and disco owes a substantial debt to Isaac Hayes's second album – not to mention hip-hop (the piano riff that anchored **Public Enemy**'s "Black Steel In The Hour Of Chaos" was sampled from "Hyperbolicsyllabicsesquedaly mistic"). It was also remarkably successful. Simultaneously charting on *Billboard*'s R&B, jazz, pop and easy-listening charts, *Hot Buttered Soul* sold over a million copies, unheard of for an R&B album.

The first few minutes of the first track, "Walk On By", set the stage for the rest of the album and for the next decade: the organ and string intro was the blueprint for **Willie Mitchell**'s productions for Al Green, the blazing wah-wah solo sounded like what Funkadelic were doing up in Detroit, the

Isaac Hayes chained to his sax

abstract keyboard noodling and angular guitar figures must have given **Miles Davis** an idea or two, and everyone stole the string stabs and loping bass shuffle. The album's trademark cut was Hayes's eighteen-minute-plus version of **Jim Webb**'s "By the Time I Get To Phoenix". Beginning life as a way of getting the crowd's attention in a nightclub, Hayes' eight-and-a-half-minute rap intro became his signature shtick and inspired the likes of **Millie Jackson**. Milking the song for all it was worth, Hayes's vocals and the arrangement redefined the parameters of sweet soul and deconstructed and recreated a hoary pop standard.

Hayes's next album, 1970's *To Be Continued*, was even more over the top than *Hot Buttered Soul*, thanks to sickeningly unctuous tracks such as "Ike's Mood", although hip-hop producers have since rescued Hayes from his worst instincts by isolating sections of this baroque grotesquerie. *The Isaac Hayes Movement* (also 1970) was yet another syrupy string confection, this time with Hayes covering **Jerry Butler**'s "I Stand Accused" and **The Beatles**' "Something".

As ridiculous and over the top as Hayes's records often were, the single "Do Your Thing" was probably his most preposterous. He positively oozed with macho smarm, and the wink-wink nudge-nudge horns and organ backing were oilier than ever. The full twenty-minute version of the song was included on the 1971 *Shaft* soundtrack, his most commercially successful album, which was imitated as much as anything by The Beatles or **Velvet Underground**. Hayes's other great soundtrack was for 1974's *Truck Turner* (in which he also played the lead role). While the title track had a great arrangement, it was too similar to his earlier hit "Theme From Shaft". However, the rest of the tracks, including the chase theme, "Pursuit Of The Pimpmobile", and the love jam, "Buns O' Plenty", were definitive blaxploitation records.

By the mid-70s Isaac Hayes was both creatively and literally bankrupt following the failure of his own Hot Buttered Soul record label. He had a modest hit with "Don't Let Go" in 1979 and returned in the mid-80s with the top-ten R&B hit "Ike's Rap", before putting his famous baritone to use as a radio DJ. Hayes soon turned his attention exclusively to acting, appearing in a number of movies and TV shows from the mid-80s to the present, including a small role in the 2000 remake of *Shaft*. In 1997 Hayes became the voice of "Chef" on the animated comedy *South Park* and, as that character, had a UK #1 with the infamous novelty song "Chocolate Salty Balls".

Hot Buttered Soul
1969, Stax

Isaac Hayes's breakthrough album was a landmark in the history of soul – not bad for an album that's only got four tracks. Precedent-setting and hugely influential, *Hot Buttered Soul* single-handedly opened the doors for album-length statements by Marvin Gaye, Stevie Wonder, The O'Jays and Curtis Mayfield, while its production defined the sound of 70s soul by providing the blueprint for the likes of Philadelphia International, Barry White, Van McCoy and the Salsoul Orchestra.

PLAYLIST
Isaac Hayes

1 WALK ON BY from **Hot Buttered Soul**
Dionne Warwick is pre-digitally morphed into a smarmy lounge singer with a taste for expensive string arrangements.

2 BY THE TIME I GET TO PHOENIX from **Hot Buttered Soul**
This 18-minute marathon caused the drummer's hand to cramp.

3 HYPERBOLICSYLLABICSESQUEDALYMISTIC from **Hot Buttered Soul**
Hugely atmospheric mood music.

4 I STAND ACCUSED from **The Isaac Hayes Movement**
A hilarious oily remake of Jerry Butler.

5 NEVER CAN SAY GOODBYE from **Black Moses**
Another utterly preposterous epic remake.

6 THEME FROM SHAFT from **Shaft**
Can you dig it? You're damn right.

7 DO YOUR THING from **Shaft**
Quién es más macho? Nadie.

8 JOY from **Joy**
Ike cranks up the tempo for this come-on.

9 PURSUIT OF THE PIMPMOBILE from **Truck Turner**
The essence of blaxploitation.

10 BUNS O' PLENTY from **Truck Turner**
Wink-wink, nudge-nudge.

Black Moses
1971, Enterprise

Capitalizing on the success of his *Shaft* soundtrack, Isaac Hayes released this double album of his finest early 70s material. Filled with his trademark lush arrangements and extended jams, the album is punctuated by intimate "Ike's Raps" and it flows seamlessly. An outstanding talent, an enjoyable listen and quintessential Isaac Hayes.

Branded
1995, Pointblank

If you missed this – and many did – 1995's *Branded* was the only new music Hayes released in the 90s (other than the same year's instrumental album *Raw And Refined*). Although his sound is updated and this features a nod to rap courtesy of Chuck D., this is still classic Hayes all the way. A beautifully crafted work of mostly original material that leaves one wishing he'd find time to give us more.

Blaxploitation

Just as blaxploitation movies were a reaction against the letter-perfect morality of the roles given to **Sidney Poitier**, the musicians who composed the soundtracks for films such as *Slaughter!*, *Black Gestapo* and *Black Shampoo* were reacting against the mannered leitmotifs and cod-jazz of Quincy Jones's soundtracks to Poitier films like *In The Heat Of The Night* and *They Call Me Mister Tibbs!* Taking **Norman Whitfield**'s sweeping productions for The Temptations and The Undisputed Truth as their starting point, musicians as diverse as Isaac Hayes, Curtis Mayfield, Roy Ayers and War tried to work the funk, effects pedals, social commentary and a bit of ghetto fabulousness into the standard formulas of soundtrack construction.

Unfortunately, the recent elevation of the 70s black action film to cult status has tended to reduce the genre to a series of outrageous Afros, leather pimp coats, wah-wah licks, fantasies of the black super-stud, cathartic scenes of the Man getting what's coming to him and, maybe, if you're lucky, a celebration of Tamara Dobson and **Pam Grier** kicking serious ass. While there's a lot to be said for the pleasures of watching a neon violet, velour jumpsuit strut across the screen, such superfly fetishism diminishes the potency of the black style politics of the 70s to nothing more than content-free imagery.

The assertive camouflaging of grim inner-city realities using unfeasibly wide lapels and enormous hoop earrings had its parallel in songs like The Four Tops' "Are You Man Enough" (from the *Shaft In Africa* soundtrack). With its contribution to the "smiling faces sometimes tell lies" trope of 70s soul – "Can't turn your back on a smiling face" – the song was at once a bitter jibe at the ghetto's growing junkie culture and the failure of the Black Power movement, a cautionary tale against the happy-faced lies of the white establishment, and a warning that there's something lurking beneath the grotesque smiles of the long-standing pickaninny caricature. Meanwhile, unapologetic reality tales, such as Bobby Womack's "Across 110th Street", offered a different slant on political protest and set much of the agenda for the musique verité style of hip-hop.

Although an early incarnation of Earth Wind & Fire, along with **Melvin Van Peebles**, count as the first blaxploiters for their psychedelic, Ramsey Lewis-esque score for *Sweet Sweetback's Baadasss Song*, it is the wah-wah riff-of-the-gods from Isaac Hayes's "Theme From Shaft" that will forever be associated with the genre.

Various Artists: The Big Score
1998, EMI

While this calls itself the "definitive" compilation of blaxploitation soundtracks, it fails to include epic chase and fight themes like Isaac Hayes's "Pursuit Of The Pimp Mobile" or Roy Ayers' "Brawling Broads". However, any compilation hip enough to include Edwin Starr's fat, funky and fresh "Easin' In", the all-time great string stabs from Barry White's "Theme From Together Brother", James Brown going through the Zodiac on "People Get Up And Drive Your Funky Soul" and Joe Simon's 21-vocal-cord salute to *Cleopatra Jones* is well worth its weight in Afro Sheen.

PLAYLIST

1 SWEET SWEETBACK'S THEME Melvin Van Peebles/Earth Wind & Fire from **Sweet Sweetback's Baadasss Song**
Social-realist funk concrete.

2 THEME FROM SHAFT Isaac Hayes from **Shaft**
The wah-wah riff of the gods.

3 FREDDIE'S DEAD Curtis Mayfield from **Superfly**
Mayfield's bitter answer to blaxploitation's glorification of the worst of the ghetto.

4 PURSUIT OF THE PIMPMOBILE Isaac Hayes from **Truck Turner**
Even more definitive wah-wah than "Theme From Shaft".

5 THEME FROM TOGETHER BROTHERS Barry White from **Together Brothers**
The Walrus of Love sheds some weight for this sleek groover.

6 BRAWLING BROADS Roy Ayers from **Coffy**
The epitome of the minimal, hideously funky incidental music blaxploitation is famous for.

7 T PLAYS IT COOL Marvin Gaye from **Trouble Man**
Deceptively funky and very dark synth groove with chilling, chiming pianos.

8 THE BOSS James Brown from **Black Caesar**
The interaction between the horns and guitar riff turns everyone who listens to this into Fred "The Hammer" Williamson strutting down 125th Street.

9 EASIN' IN Edwin Starr from **Hell Up In Harlem**
Crazy funky bass and synth groove with Starr at his least stentorian.

10 TWO PIGS AND A HOG Freddie Perren from **Cooley High**
Percussive workout that was an early disco DJ favourite.

Leon Haywood

Journeyman **Leon Haywood**'s career spans R&B, soul and funk, but without any great distinction. As a producer, keyboardist and vocalist, Haywood has been content to drift along with the times, make an occasionally interesting record in whatever style was popular at the time, then disappear, only to emerge again a few years later with another genre exercise that nailed the conventions down cold.

Born in Houston, Texas on February 11, 1942, Haywood spent his teens working and touring with blues musician **Guitar Slim**. In the early 60s he moved to Los Angeles and supported saxophonist **Big Jay McNeely**. Haywood's first record, "Without A Love", was an instrumental that sold well when it was released in 1963, but Haywood never saw any royalties. Such bad luck and poor business deals came to characterize his early career.

In 1964 he joined Sam Cooke's band, but Cooke was killed a few months later. Under the auspices of LA DJ **Magnificent Montague**, Haywood then signed to Imperial and had a hit with "She's With Her Other Love". Unfortunately, the cheques were made out to Montague directly and, once again, Haywood didn't see any money. To add insult to injury, his name was misspelled as Hayward on his Imperial releases.

Moving to the small Fat Fish label, Haywood recorded "Baby Reconsider", a single that was reminiscent of The Temptations' "Ain't Too Proud To Beg". "Baby Reconsider" became one of the first records to be championed on the UK's Northern soul scene. Haywood then released the Beach Music classic "It's Got To Be Mellow" for Decca. The track was an effective pastiche of Motown and Chicago styles, but Haywood wasn't as graceful a singer as any of his sources. After session work for **The Romeos** and Dyke & The Blazers and a few singles released on Galaxy, Capitol and Atlantic, Haywood became a solid R&B hitmaker at 20th Century in the mid-70s.

With a streamlined but funky sound, Haywood was able to stay mellow during the funk and disco era. He had small hits in this vein with "Keep It In The Family", "Sugar Lump" and "Come An' Get Yourself Some" before he nailed the formula with his biggest hit, "I Want'A Do Something Freaky To You" in 1975. Based on a great groove that didn't drown in essential oils the way many of **Barry White**'s records did, this sleazy track ("Your love is like a mountain/I'd like to slide down your canyon") later became the basis for **Dr. Dre**'s "Nuthin' But A 'G' Thing".

Haywood continued to have moderate R&B hits throughout the late 70s and into the 80s with grinding, sexually suggestive material like "Strokin'", "Super Sexy" and "Double My Pleasure". "Don't Push It Don't Force It" rode one of the great synth basslines and a joyous breakdown all the way to #2 on the R&B chart. After releasing the novelty number "Tenderoni" in 1984, Haywood started to concentrate on production, first working for the Edge label and then producing several blues revival albums in the 90s on his own EveJim label.

The Best Of Leon Haywood
1996, Mercury

With the exception of 1967's "It's Got To Be Mellow", this 19-track compilation album focuses on Leon Haywood's 70s releases. The songs are mostly soft-porn come-ons, but Haywood always performed them with a sly wink, and the production is uniformly excellent.

Lauryn Hill

R&B circa 1997 was an ugly place to be. Sure, there was Missy Elliott and all that **Timbaland** ultra-futuristic, super-syncopated beat science. But for all of the changing production paradigms, the vocalists were still mirror-dancing prima donnas. Ever since the apotheosis of **Luther Vandross**, **Whitney Houston** and **New Edition** in the mid-80s, narcissism had ruled R&B and threatened to fritter away all of the moral and aesthetic capital that soul had accumulated. With vocalists as self-involved as Mariah Carey, Ginuwine and Jodeci, opera divas had nothing on R&B singers in the vainglory stakes. In this climate, **Lauryn Hill**'s first solo album was nothing short of a revelation.

Hill was born on May 25, 1975 in South Orange, New Jersey. Although she first came to the public attention as an actress, famously appearing in *Sister Act II: Back In The Habit*, Hill really came to prominence as a member of hip-hop crew the **Fugees**. Formed in New Jersey at the turn of the 90s, the Fugees were vocalist Hill, multi-instrumentalist **Wyclef Jean** and keyboardist **Prakazrel Michel**. Their 1996 album, *The Score*, had been that year's big breakthrough on the strength of covers of **Roberta Flack**'s "Killing Me Softly" and **Bob Marley**'s "No Woman No Cry", which heavily featured Hill's sung vocals.

Despite this success, the triumph of Hill's 1998 solo debut *The Miseducation Of Lauryn Hill* still came as a shock. Written, produced and arranged largely by Hill, it was a slap in the face to everyone who thought that women in R&B were little more than blank slates with whom male producers worked their magic. Looking back to 60s and 70s soul's age-old virtues, referencing 70s sitcoms, reminiscing about mid-80s hip-hop, dabbling in reggae and dancehall and digging in the crates like the best 90s beatfreaks, *The Miseducation Of Lauryn Hill* was the black bohemian equivalent of a **Beastie Boys** album, but from a woman's point of view. Replacing the wisecracks and cheap laughs of the Beasties with a sense of personal triumph, Hill made the ultimate crossover album of the hip-hop era.

Although it began with "Lost Ones", a tough warning to any pretenders to the throne Hill already knew was hers, *The Miseducation Of Lauryn Hill* was a beacon of warmth in a landscape dominated by crude, hopeless hip-hop and crude, compassionless R&B. Even if tracks like "Ex-Factor" and "I

Used To Love Him" were bitter break-up songs, the music and the overall feeling of the album were a warm antidote to the astringency and commercial gloss of so much black music of the decade. "Everything Is Everything" summarized the album's trick: like all the best soul, the soaring music – the string stabs, the uplifting drums, the motivational scratches, the grain of her voice – transmitted the album's message more potently than the lyrics, turning clichés into words that hit like the gospel truth.

Unfortunately, Hill followed *The Miseducation Of Lauryn Hill* with the ultimate car-crash of an album, 2002's *MTV Unplugged No. 2.0*. The album was two discs of Hill rambling on in twisted Oprah-speak platitudes and rasping her way through original songs about the political climate and how terrible fame was. She said that her old songs were nothing but lies – never a way to keep fans – and that she was now all about "reality". The 90s had brought a whole rash of stars whining about the celebrity spotlight, but this was the least fun, the least insightful, the most full-of-itself record in a singular ignominious genre.

Hill reunited with the Fugees in September 2004 and the group performed on stage together for the first time in years for the film *Dave Chapelle's Block Party*. The Fugees toured Europe in 2005 and are now back in the recording studio, so a new Lauryn Hill solo album seems unlikely to appear any time soon.

The Miseducation Of Lauryn Hill
Columbia, 1998

It was impossible to make R&B this late in the 90s without engaging with hip-hop, but Hill's triumph was that by half-singing and half-rapping and by enveloping the album in a patina of Stax horns, fatback beats and Kingston, Jamaica voodoo, she managed to make hip-hop personal, to make it signify in the same way that vintage soul did.

Z.Z. Hill

Although it doesn't have a happy ending, the story of **Z.Z. Hill** at least offers some hope in a genre littered with tales of tragedy. Hill toiled for 20 years at the margins of the music industry before hitting on a formula that not only saved his career, but also rescued the fortunes of a flagging record label and an entire group of artists who were being ignored by the mainstream.

He was born **Arzel Hill** on September 30, 1935 in Naples, Texas. Hill started singing in a gospel group called The Spiritual Five, but after listening to some **BB King** records, he crossed over to the devil's music. He began

performing in clubs in the Dallas area in the late 50s and moved to California with his brother Matt, a budding record producer, in the early 60s.

On his brother's MH label, Hill released "You Were Wrong" in 1964, which just barely dented the pop Top 100. He then signed to Kent Records and released dozens

Malaco Records

Funk, disco, hip-hop and new jack swing may have finished off soul in the popular consciousness, but die-hard fans will never let it vanish. Fittingly called "the last soul company" by writer Peter Guralnick, **Malaco Records** has stubbornly refused to change its ways since it first opened for business in Jackson, Mississippi in the late 60s. Even if classic soul might as well be cakewalking music to the new generation of urban R&B fans, soul still means something down in the American South.

Started by concert promoters **Tommy Couch** and **Mitch Malouf** in 1968, Malaco only survived the failure of its largely underwhelming early releases by recording advertising jingles. None of the masters it licensed to major labels went anywhere until it joined forces with New Orleans R&B stalwart **Wardell Quezergue** in 1970. His production nous payed immediate dividends when **King Floyd**'s "Groove Me" – simple, syncopated, slinky and full of "unnh" – rode its sublime bassline all the way to #6 in the pop charts. Floyd's "Baby Let Me Kiss You" was a funky, almost identical, follow-up, but the record that really established Malaco was released the following year.

With a bassline carbon copied from "Groove Me", **Jean Knight**'s "Mr. Big Stuff" was an adaptation of classic New Orleans R&B for the James Brown age. One of the sassiest tracks ever made, and that rarest of things, a great funk record fronted by a woman, it reached #2 on the pop charts in 1971. Although artists as diverse as **Paul Simon** and The Pointer Sisters went down to Jackson to record at the Malaco studios over the next few years, the label soon lost its momentum again. Malaco failed either to create a signature sound or to keep up with the changing musical climate.

The company's fortunes were ultimately revived in 1976 by a record that wouldn't have sounded out of place ten years earlier: **Dorothy Moore**'s "Misty Blue". With a shuffling rhythm and loping piano and guitar figures of the kind formerly found on **Joe Tex** records, Moore's 1976 hit was a country soul throwback that pretended that The J.B.'s, Sly & The Family

Stone and P-Funk had never existed. It became a pop #3 during the first year of the disco boom. Dorothy Moore became Malaco's biggest artist during the 70s, hitting the R&B chart thirteen times with a streak of string-drenched traditionalist records.

Even though classicism had rescued the company, Malaco still dabbled in dealings with traditional soul's sworn enemies. **Anita Ward**'s bubble-headed disco smash, "Ring My Bell", was recorded at Malaco and became a worldwide #1 when it was leased to TK Records in 1979. That same year, a track by funk group **Freedom** further inadvertently eroded soul's constituency. The kazoo intro and the trumpet bridge of "Get Up And Dance" later became favourite breaks with New York's hip-hop DJs, and they were looped the following year by **Grandmaster Flash & The Furious Five** for their epochal track "Freedom".

What Malaco did best, however, was to cater for the audience that hip-hop had left for dead. **McKinley Mitchell**'s slightly slick mid-70s blues recordings established the Malaco formula, and Z.Z. Hill perfected it. Featuring the hit singles "Down Home Blues" and "Cheating In The Next Room", Z.Z. Hill's *Down Home* (1981) became the best-selling blues album of all time. Malaco's modernized take on soulful blues attracted artists such as Latimore, Denise LaSalle, Little Milton and Bobby "Blue" Bland to the label in the 80s and 90s, and Malaco continues to achieve regional success to this day.

(o) **Various Artists: The Last Soul Company: Malaco, A Thirty-Year Retrospective**
1999, Malaco

Although this 6-CD box set is more than anyone but the most committed Malaco fan needs, it's also the kind of monument that such labels deserve for their perseverance. From one of the first records cut at Malaco's studios, Haran Griffin's absurd "Looking For My Pig", to stalwart Little Milton's 1998 regional hit "Big Boned Woman", this collection honours meat-and-potatoes soul and R&B created without fancy gadgets and computerized gizmos – the way it was meant to be made.

of fine singles that went nowhere. On records such as "What More", "No More Doggin'", "Baby I'm Sorry" and "Nothing Can Change This Love", Hill's laid-back, slightly nasal drawl was set against music that was halfway between Motown and Otis Redding, with a driving beat and distinctive Memphis-style horns. Z.Z. Hill had his biggest hit in seven years with "Don't Make Me Pay For His Mistakes" on his brother's Hill label, which prompted Kent to release "I Need Someone (To Love Me)". The song had been recorded back in 1964, but reached the R&B Top 30 in 1971.

In 1973 Hill signed to United Artists where he achieved some modest chart success with "Ain't Nothing You Can Do" and "I Keep On Lovin' You", and released the 1975 album *Keep On Loving You*, which included an excellent rendition of Johnnie Taylor's "Mr. Nobody, Somebody". Moving to Columbia Records, Hill had his biggest R&B hit with "Love Is So Good When You're Stealing It", but the label then spent the next two years trying to turn him into a disco artist – with predictably poor results.

Signing to the Mississippi-based Malaco label, Hill released "Please Don't Make Me Do Something Bad To You" in 1980, which had an old-fashioned arrangement reminiscent of an Arthur Alexander record and saw Hill modulating between soul and blues shouting. The record didn't sell that well, but it started the formula that would finally make Hill a minor star. A mix of Bobby Bland, Muscle Shoals, unabashed sweetening and that streamlined late 70s Southern groove, the following year's *Down Home* was nothing short of a sensation. It sold some 500,000 copies and revitalized the genre. The album's blend of soul and blues struck a chord with the mature Southern audience that had been ignored by the funk and disco pushers, while the great track "Cheating In The Next Room" broke in New York thanks to DJ Frankie Crocker.

The 1982 album *The Rhythm And The Blues* suffered from poorer material, but 1983's *I'm A Blues Man* was almost as good as *Down Home Blues* and firmly established Hill as a star down south. At the peak of his newfound success, however, Hill died suddenly of a heart attack on April 27, 1984.

Greatest Hits
1986, Malaco

While Z.Z. Hill was certainly in the right place at the right time, the secret to his success is that his producers consistently found great songs for him. This superb distillation of his Malaco albums shows that Hill was a fine, but not spectacular, performer blessed with great songs in an age when songwriting became secondary to production.

Holland-Dozier-Holland

Quite simply, **Eddie Holland** (born October 30, 1939), **Lamont Dozier** (born June 16, 1941) and **Brian Holland** (born February 15, 1941) were the greatest songwriting and production team in the history of popular music. During their stay at Motown, Holland-Dozier-Holland created many of soul's best and most enduring records: Martha & The Vandellas' "Heat Wave" and "Nowhere To Run"; The Four Tops' "Reach Out I'll Be There", "I Can't Help Myself" and "Standing In The Shadows Of Love"; Marvin Gaye's "Can I Get A Witness" and "You're A Wonderful One"; Junior Walker's "(I'm A) Road Runner"; The Isley Brothers' "This Old Heart Of Mine" and "Take Me In Your Arms (Rock Me A Little While)"; The Elgins' "Heaven Must Have Sent You" and "Darling Baby"; Mary Wells' "You Lost The Sweetest Boy"; and all of The Supremes' best records.

The three songwriters were all fine singers in their own right, and they all got their start in the business as performers. Eddie Holland was the most successful vocalist of the three and led a doo-wop group called The Fidelatones in the mid-50s. Eddie's voice bore a striking resemblance to Jackie Wilson's, so he was chosen as Wilson's demo singer. However, it was while recording these demos that Eddie met Berry Gordy. With Gordy producing, Eddie released "You" on Mercury in 1958, followed by several singles for United Artists. In 1961 Gordy signed him to his own Motown label and he released "Jamie", a falsetto ballad that sounded almost exactly like a Jackie Wilson record and reached #6 on the R&B chart. The delicate ballad "Just Ain't Enough Love" followed, but Eddie's finest solo record was "Leaving Here", a rollicking number that has

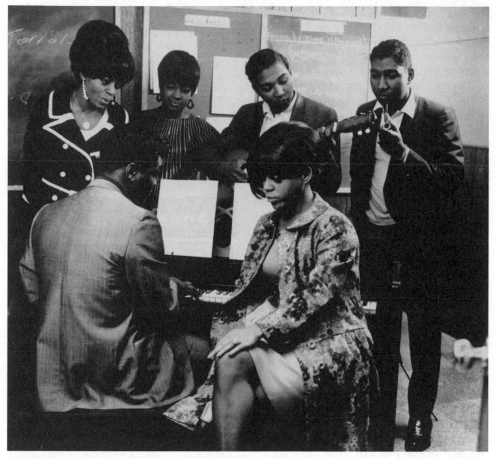

Holland-Dozier-Holland in the studio with The Supremes

since become something of a standard for rock groups like **Motörhead** and Motor City punkers **The Rationals**.

Meanwhile, Eddie's brother Brian Holland came into the Motown fold as part of the **Rayber Voices**, who provided backing vocals for Marv Johnson. Brian also performed on 1960's "Sugar Daddy", the first record ever released under the Motown name, as a member of **The Satintones** with Freddie Gorman. Lamont Dozier was originally a member of a vocal group called **The Romeos**, which also included future Motown stalwart Leon Ware. Dozier released a couple of singles on Berry Gordy's Anna label as part of **The Voicemasters** with David Ruffin and Freddie Gorman, before going solo (as Lamont Anthony) on "Let's Talk It Over" in 1960.

Lamont Dozier and Eddie Holland recorded the single "What Goes Up Must Come Down" together as Holland-Dozier in 1963 (but the record was largely ignored), before teaming up with Brian Holland to create countless huge hit records for Motown over the next five years. The songwriting and production team of Holland-Dozier-Holland brought the fervour, the apocalyptic play of light and dark and the tambourine of pentecostal gospel to Motown. The label's inviolate 4/4 time signature, which became so beloved of Northern soul fanatics, was also largely their creation. However, their sense of melody and phrasing was just as strong as their feel for rhythm.

When the trio left Motown in 1968 over a bitter royalty dispute, they moved to Los Angeles and formed their own HDH, Invictus, Hot Wax and Music Merchant labels. On their own record labels, they ditched the classic Motown stomp in favour of more straightforward pop craftsmanship on hit records by The Chairmen of the

Board, Freda Payne, 100 Proof Aged in Soul, Laura Lee and Honey Cone. They also found time amid their writing and producing to restart their own recording careers, releasing several records on Invictus.

Lamont Dozier sang the lead on 1972's "Don't Leave Me", which was a semi-classic of soft soul percolating into proto-disco, while the flip side, "Why Can't We Be Lovers", was far more successful (reaching the pop Top 30 in the UK) despite being saccharine and smarmy. However, the horn line on "Why Can't We Be Lovers" did introduce the breathy tone that became characteristic of quiet storm and later **Kenny G**. They also had success that year with Brian singing lead on "Don't Leave Me Starvin' For Your Love", while Eddie Holland and Dozier sang a duet on "New Breed Kinda Woman" in 1973.

With their Hot Wax and Invictus labels suffering from financial problems and falling into disarray, the Holland-Dozier-Holland partnership broke up later that year when Dozier split from the Holland brothers to concentrate on a solo recording career. The Hollands continued producing, most notably working on both **The Jackson 5**'s *Moving Violation* and **Michael Jackson**'s *Forever Michael* in 1975 – although their work on **Donny Osmond**'s *Winning Combination* is probably best forgotten.

Going solo, Lamont Dozier had great initial success with "Trying To Hold On To My Woman", "Let Me Start Tonite", the upbeat "Fish Ain't Bitin'" (one of the few songs to attack Nixon directly) and the early disco classic "Breaking Out All Over". His 1977 *Peddlin' Music On The Side* album featured the truly wonderful "Going Back To My Roots", which was later covered in a far inferior version by **Odyssey**. Dozier's singing career fizzled out in the late 70s, but he carried on producing and writing for Aretha Franklin, Z.Z. Hill, Ben E. King, **Eric Clapton** and **Phil Collins**. The songwriting trio had a well-publicized reunion in 2005 to write new material for the Broadway musical of the movie *The First Wives Club*.

(◉) **Why Can't We Be Lovers: The Invictus Sessions**
2000, Castle

This 2-CD, 28-track collection of Holland-Dozier-Holland's own recordings may be a tad excessive, especially as it includes both long and short versions of several of the

same songs, but it does show what fine performers they all were. The bulk of this album dates from 1972 and it is largely smooth, romantic soft soul that bubbles over into early disco rhythms.

(◉) **Heaven Must Have Sent You: The Holland-Dozier-Holland Story**
2005, Hip-O

If you put the Doobie Brothers and Simply Red tracks out of your mind, this 65-track collection of HDH's greatest hits is damn near essential – if you don't have all the tracks already. Even if you have got them all on other albums, check out the 26-page booklet, which includes an excellent essay on the trio's working methods. All in all, this is a fitting monument to their genius.

Honey Cone

Honey Cone were one of the most successful girl groups of the early 70s. They were discovered by **Eddie Holland** in 1969 singing back-up for **Burt Bacharach** on *The Andy Williams Show*. The trio recorded some great battle-of-the-sexes songs, mostly written by **Chairmen of the Board**'s General Johnson and Greg Perry, but the vocals were more showbiz than soulful and **Holland-Dozier-Holland**'s music merely sounded like a response to the **Jackson 5** sound that they helped invent in the first place.

Honey Cone (named after a brand of ice cream popular in the 50s) comprised **Edna Wright** (Darlene Love's sister), former Bob B. Soxx & The Blue Jeans singer **Carolyn Willis** and former Ikette **Shellie Clark**. Wright was an established background singer on the LA studio scene, and in 1965, under the name Sandy Wynns, she had a big Northern soul hit with the upbeat Philly-style "A Touch Of Venus". Wright then became one of **Ray Charles**'s Raelets for a brief period in 1967 and 68, before forming Honey Cone.

The group signed to Holland-Dozier-Holland's Invictus label in 1969 and had small hits with "While You're Out Looking For Sugar" and "Girls It Ain't Easy" before recording their first album, *Take Me With You*, in 1970. *Take Me With You* included the underrated "Sunday Morning People", an early example of the paranoid, bitter self-critical soul of the early 70s. This was followed by their mega-hit "Want Ads", on which they sang about finding lipstick and perfume on their boyfriends' shirts and set in motion the personal ad craze. Honey Cone had their second consecutive R&B #1 with "Stick Up", in which the narrator's virginity is "robbed" and she forces the lothario to marry her by having his baby. As awful as the song was, it was the best production the group got, balancing the pop imperative with music full of portent and meaning.

After Honey Cone released the utterly infectious "One Monkey Don't Stop No Show" and "The Day I Found Myself", on which a great lyric was undermined by a singsong melody and rather anodyne vocals, Holland-Dozier-Holland seemed to be losing their magic touch and their label was in financial crisis. "Sittin' On A Time Bomb (Waitin' For The Hurt To Come)" couldn't even break the R&B Top 30 in 1972 – the flip, "It's Better To Have Loved And Lost", would have been a far better choice – and after the weak "Innocent Til Proven Guilty", the group split up.

Carolyn Willis and Shellie Clark returned to session singing, while Edna Wright returned to solo recording. She released a solo album in 1976, *Oops, Here I Go Again*, which was a bit too busy and "jazzy", but the faded guitar intro of the title track was later sampled by **De La Soul**. That same year, a new Honey Cone line-up released one record, "Somebody's Always Messing Up A Good Thing", but to very little success.

○ **Soulful Sugar: The Complete Hot Wax Recordings**
2002, Castle

A massive 45 tracks by Honey Cone is probably too much for anyone, but this excellent package is nowhere near as compromised as their other greatest hits collections, especially since it has just about everything they ever recorded. It also includes some very fine tracks that were either commercial failures or never released as singles, such as "Sunday Morning People" and "Ace In The Hole".

Hot Chocolate

Before **Hot Chocolate** became nothing but a bland pop machine, the multiracial band from London blended rock, pop, soul, funk and Caribbean rhythms into one of the more interesting rewrites of the Europop formula.

Influenced by **The Equals**, who had a similarly politicized, geographically non-specific sound, Jamaican expatriate **Errol Brown** and his songwriting partner **Tony Wilson** first got together in 1969 and reworked **John Lennon**'s "Give Peace A Chance". Under the auspices of **The Beatles**' Apple organization, the duo, recording as The Hot Chocolate Band, released their version later that year.

The record got them the attention of famed producer **Mickie Most**, who signed them to his new RAK label. With guitarist **Harvey Himsley**, keyboardist **Larry Ferguson**, drummer **Tony Connor** and percussionist **Patrick Olive**, Hot Chocolate released the sing-along "Love Is Life" in 1970, which climbed into the UK Top 10. They had further pop success with "You Could Have Been A Lady", "I Believe (In Love)" and "You'll Always Be A Friend", before 1973's "Brother Louie" firmly marked them as a group worth watching. With a sound and lyrical approach similar to War's records, 'Brother Louie" tackled racism head-on. It was followed by the equally forceful "Rumours" and a chronicle of a lover's suicide, "Emma", which was more rock-oriented, but no less effective.

In 1975 Tony Wilson left the group and Patrick Olive took over as bassist. The group's sound became markedly lighter on subsequent records such as "Disco Queen", the infectious "You Sexy Thing" – which was their first US hit – the bass-heavy "Don't Stop It Now" and "So You Win Again", their only UK #1. Hot Chocolate were still capable of producing surprising oddities, however. On "Put Your Love On Me", they hitched a ride on the synth train (think **Donna Summer**'s "I Feel Love" or **David Bowie**'s *Low*) and produced a record that sounded like **Blondie** a couple of years early. The bombastic "Every 1's A Winner" was what Sly Stone and Larry Graham would have sounded like if they were still recording together. Their most original record was probably 1979's "Mindless Boogie", with its spacey synth shtick anticipating the pop of a few years later, although combining disco with the Jonestown Massacre was probably overdoing it a bit.

Hot Chocolate continued to have hits into the 80s in the UK, with "It Started With A Kiss" and "What Kinda Boy You Looking For Girl", before finally splitting up in 1985. The group's 1975 hit "You Sexy Thing" has since taken on a life of it own and revealed itself to be one of Britain's favourite records, making the Top 10 when it was reissued in 1987 and in 1997, after it featured in the hit comedy film *The Full Monty*.

○ **Essential Collection**
2004, EMI

Lacking any kind of clear or chronological order, this 36-track, 2-CD collection jumps all over the place in a particularly annoying way. However, it does have the best selection of tracks of any of the compilation albums available, and it shows what a fine pop group Hot Chocolate could be when they felt like it.

Thelma Houston

These days **Thelma Houston** is known for two things: her storming disco rendition of "Don't Leave Me This Way" and being Whitney Houston's aunt. Although this is unfair to Thelma Houston, who was a very good singer, it is indicative of her eclecticism and seemingly infinite adaptability.

Thelma Houston was born in Leland, Mississippi on May 7, 1946 and moved to Long Beach, California with her family when she was 10 years old. In the mid-60s she joined the gospel group the **Art Reynolds Singers**, and they had a small hit in 1966 with a version of "Glory Glory Hallelujah" on which Houston sang lead. Following the record's success, Houston was offered a solo contract with Capitol, who had released "Glory Glory Hallelujah", and recorded "Baby Mine", an eventual Northern soul classic with its singsong strings and churning backbeat.

In 1968 Houston was discovered singing at a club in Los Angeles by The Fifth Dimension producer **Marc Gordon**. He signed her to ABC-Dunhill where she recorded the 1969 album *Sunshower*, a cult classic of baroque soul produced by **Jimmy Webb**. The album was a commercial flop, but the string-fuelled version of The Rolling Stones' "Jumpin' Jack Flash" and the stirring "Everybody Gets To Go To The Moon" made it an artistic triumph. After her version of **Laura Nyro**'s "Save The Country" only reached #74 on the pop chart, Houston was dropped from the label.

After playing as part of the house band on *The Marty Feldman Comedy Machine*,

Houston signed to Motown's Mo West subsidiary and worked with **Gene Page** on a self-titled album that again went nowhere. Her first single to hit the R&B chart was "You've Been Doing Wrong For So Long", and it only reached #64, although it was nominated for a Grammy. In 1975 she recorded the very first direct-to-disc recording, *I've Got The Music In Me*, which was more of a technological feat than an artistic one.

The following year Houston was paired with producer **Hal Davis**, who decided to bring her back to her gospel roots – but in a disco setting. With 1976's "Don't Leave Me This Way", Davis crafted what was perhaps the ultimate disco record, containing almost every element of classic disco: the skipping hi-hats, the popping bassline, the slicing strings and the erotic, over-the-top, gospel-charged vocals. **Harold Melvin & The Blue Notes** may have recorded the original version of "Don't Leave Me This Way", but Houston made the song her own. It soared to the top of both the pop and R&B charts.

The title of Houston's next single, "I'm Here Again", said just about everything you need to know. It was almost exactly the same record as "Don't Leave Me This Way" and was another big disco hit. After recording a decent album of duets with **Jerry Butler** in 1977, Houston solidified her dancefloor diva status with "Saturday Night Sunday Morning" and a cover of The Miracles' "Love Machine".

Moving to RCA in 1980, Houston reunited with producer Jimmy Webb for the *Breakwater Cat* album, which featured a novel rendition of **Elvis Presley**'s "Suspicious Minds". Houston had a small club hit with a striking cover of ? & The Mysterians' "96 Tears", followed by "If You Feel It" and the Hi-NRG-style "Working Girl", while the subtle ballad "What For" from 1983's *Thelma Houston* album proved that she wasn't just a high-tempo belter. On *Qualifying Heat* in 1984, Houston worked with Jam & Lewis, who crafted the two R&B hits, "You Used To Hold Me So Tight" and "(I Guess) It Must Be Love".

Thelma Houston continued to hit the lower reaches of the R&B chart in the late 80s and early 90s, with records such as the 1989 duet with **The Winans**, "Lean On Me". Although she slowed down considerably in the mid-90s, Houston made a notable appearance in the 1998 Oprah Winfrey film *Beloved*. She continues to perform live all over the world and regularly performs her disco classic "Don't Leave Me This Way".

○ **Sunshower**
1969, ABC-Dunhill

Recently reissued in Japan, this cult collectable almost lives up to all the hype. Producer Jimmy Webb errs on the side of orchestral grandeur, but Thelma Houston sings beautifully and powerfully, particularly on the great cover of The Rolling Stones' "Jumpin' Jack Flash". Although this is undoubtedly her best album, if you're after her disco hits, try *The Best Of Thelma Houston* (1991, Motown).

Whitney Houston

For better or worse, **Whitney Houston** is the most successful and most influential R&B singer of her generation. Thanks to a style equally comfortable with the gospel-like flights of fancy required by R&B, the Hollywood theatrics of Adult Contemporary and the breeziness of dance-oriented pop, she is one of the biggest female pop singers ever. Her virtuosity has informed every R&B singer, male or female, who has followed in her wake. So, if you're looking for the Typhoid Mary of the oversinging plague currently blighting contemporary R&B, look no further.

The daughter of soul and gospel singer **Cissy Houston**, the niece of disco diva **Thelma Houston** and cousin of **Dionne Warwick**, Whitney Elizabeth Houston was born on August 9, 1963 in Newark, New Jersey. At age 11, she became the soloist for the New Hope Baptist Junior Choir and, a few years later, she was singing back-up for **Lou Rawls** and **Chaka Khan**, as well as her mother. Despite this early musical success, Houston initially turned to modelling and acting, appearing in *Glamour* and *Seventeen* magazines and on the dire sitcoms *Gimme A Break* and *Silver Spoons*. She first appeared as a featured vocalist in 1982 on eclectic experimentalist group Material's *One Down* album, singing on a beautiful version of Soft Machine's "Memories" alongside saxophonist **Archie Shepp**.

In 1984 Whitney Houston signed with Arista and released her self-titled debut album the following year. *Whitney Houston* was a slow-building sensation that eventually sold thirteen million copies, making it the best-selling debut album ever. Tracks such as the ballad "Saving All My Love For You", the effervescent "How Will I Know" and the cod-inspirational "Greatest Love Of All" demonstrated the breadth of her talent, as well as her lack of vocal restraint. The follow-up album, 1987's *Whitney*, was almost as big, selling nine million copies and scoring four #1 pop hits – "I Wanna Dance With Somebody", "Didn't We Almost Have it All", "So Emotional" and "Where Do Broken Hearts Go" – making her the first artist ever to have seven consecutive #1 singles.

Houston's third album, 1990's *I'm Your Baby Tonight*, was more mature and more R&B in flavour, and, inevitably, significantly less successful. Nevertheless, it also included two #1s: the title track and a version of Sister Sledge's "All The Man That I Need". The grotesque, jingoistic version of "The Star Spangled Banner" that she performed at the Super Bowl became a top-twenty hit on the back of Desert Storm zeal in 1991.

In 1992 Houston married R&B bad boy **Bobby Brown** and appeared in the Hollywood star vehicle *The Bodyguard* alongside **Kevin Costner**. The soundtrack, which featured six Houston tracks, went on to sell sixteen million copies, largely thanks to her overblown reading of **Dolly Parton**'s "I Will Always Love You". Houston's cover became one of the biggest singles in history, staying at #1 for an excessive fourteen weeks and going quadruple platinum.

Another movie, *Waiting To Exhale*, followed in 1995, along with another blockbuster soundtrack and the single "Exhale (Shoop Shoop)", produced by Babyface. Houston then appeared alongside **Denzel Washington** in 1996's *The Preacher's Wife*. Just when it seemed as though she was more interested in making movies than records, she released *My Love Is Your Love* in 1998. A surprisingly decent album of contemporary R&B, *My Love Is Your Love* had production help from hip-hop stars **Missy Elliott**, **Lauryn Hill** and **Wyclef Jean**, and included the R&B #1 "Heartbreak Hotel" and the very underrated "It's Not Right But It's OK".

Houston's relationship with Bobby Brown had long been tabloid fodder, but the gossip industry went into overdrive at the turn of the millennium, and a series of concert cancellations, erratic appearances and rumours of drug addiction left her career in tatters. She attempted a comeback in 2002 with *Just Whitney*, a superficially conservative but whiny, defensive and supremely self-indulgent album that was roundly ignored. Was she kidding with that cover of "You Light Up My Life"? If her recent appearances on her husband's reality TV show are anything to go by, she clearly wasn't. A new album was due at the end of 2005, but at the time of going to press, it still hadn't arrived.

Whitney Houston
1985, Arista

All of Whitney Houston's albums are calculated, commercial pop offerings blessed by her truly virtuosic voice singing whatever schlock and fluff her producers and handlers can come up with. On this, her debut album, however, she was still a fairly innocent talented young vocalist and hadn't yet become the full-blown diva she quickly metamorphosed into.

Whitney: The Greatest Hits
2000, Arista

This double-CD collection brings together 35 of Whitney's greatest songs. The first disc, *Cool Down*, runs through her catalogue of downtempo tracks, starting with the career-launching "Saving All My Love For You", while the second, *Throw Down*, contains her more upbeat dance-friendly numbers, plus some remixes – including a surprising disco version of "I Will Always Love You".

Ivory Joe Hunter

An urbane blues crooner somewhere between Nat "King" Cole and Charles Brown, **Ivory Joe Hunter** had a string of substantial R&B hits from the late 40s to the late 50s. Hunter's real contribution to the development of soul and R&B, however, was that he was probably the first African-American artist to make clear the links between R&B and country.

Ivory Joe Hunter was born on October 10, 1914 in Kirbyville, Texas. A fan of legendary jazz pianist **Fats Waller**, Hunter started his musical life as a boogie-woogie pianist in the 30s, making his first recording in 1933 for a Library of Congress folklorist. However, he was also equally fond of the country music that he had grown up with in Texas, and he wrote songs that tried to blend the two genres. Hunter was briefly a radio show host and station programmer for KFDM in Beaumont, Texas before moving to Los Angeles in 1942.

In 1944 Hunter's composition "Love Please Don't Let Me Down" was recorded by hillbilly singer **Jimmie Davis** and, by 1945, Hunter had established himself as a fixture on the LA R&B scene. He recorded "Blues At Sunrise" with backing from Johnny Moore's **Three Blazers** and released it on his own Ivory label – it became a #3 R&B hit. Another of Hunter's labels, Pacific, played host to his first big hit, "Pretty Mama Blues" in 1948, which topped the R&B chart for three weeks.

Later that year, Hunter moved to the King label, where he developed a smooth crooning style designed to cross over to a white audience. He sounded startlingly like Nat "King" Cole on 1949's "Guess Who", and the violin in the background, credited to Hunter's wife Beatrice, sounded as though it could have been recorded in either Nashville or Paris. His cover of **Tex Ritter**'s "Jealous Heart" was a bizarre combination of hayseed and city slicker, like Merle Travis and Bobby Short trying to share the same body.

Signing with MGM in 1949, Hunter released "I Almost Lost My Mind", an R&B #1 hit for five weeks. Perhaps his finest record, "I Almost Lost My Mind" was exactly the synthesis of Fats Waller and **Lefty Frizzell** that Hunter had been looking for. The success of the record's fusion was reaffirmed in 1956 when **Pat Boone** took it to #1 on the pop chart. In April 1950 Hunter had another R&B #1 with "I Need You So". That same month he won a lawsuit against a restaurant in Bakersfield, California that refused to serve him because he was black.

Hunter's hits started to dry up at MGM, so he signed with Atlantic in 1954, returning to the R&B chart almost immediately with "It May Sound Silly". In 1956 "Since I Met You Baby", which featured his slightly pinched voice wavering above a Floyd Cramer-style piano, became not only an R&B #1, but also his first pop hit, charting at #12. The even more country "Empty Arms" backed with "Love's A Hurting Game" followed in a similar style in 1957, but a cover version by **Theresa Brewer** and the onslaught of rock'n'roll soon ended his hit-making career.

Ivory Joe Hunter continued to record for Vee-Jay, ABC-Paramount and Capitol until the mid-60s, but without any significant success. In the late 60s, he played a regular gig at the Grand Ol' Opry in Nashville, Tennessee and spent a brief spell with the **Johnny Otis** revue, before dying of lung cancer in 1974.

⊙ **Since I Met You Baby: The Best Of Ivory Joe Hunter**
1994, Razor & Tie

This is an excellent 25-track compilation of Hunter's MGM and Atlantic years (1949–1958). It showcases all the facets of the velvet-voiced crooner's music, from countrypolitan strollers like the title track and "Empty Arms" to rollicking boogie numbers like "Shooty Booty".

Willie Hutch

Like many other soul artists, the multi-talented **Willie Hutch** was often shunted to the sidelines because of his versatility. A fine singer, songwriter and producer, Hutch never really found a sound or style that particularly suited him and drifted along, never really getting the attention he deserved.

Born **Willie Hutchinson** in Los Angeles in 1946, Hutch was raised in Dallas where he sang with a group called **The Ambassadors** (not to be confused with the group from Philadelphia) as a teenager. He recorded his debut solo single, "Love Has Put Me Down", in 1964, for the Soul City label. Hutch then released "Love Runs Out" on ABC, which has since become a favourite on the UK's Northern soul scene. Another uptempo track favoured by British dancers, "Your Love Has

Made Me A Man", followed on Modern in 1966.

Moving to Los Angeles, Hutch wrote songs for The 5th Dimension and co-produced their 1967 debut *Up, Up And Away*. During that same period, Hutch also worked as a songwriter and producer at the Venture label with **Calvin Arnold** and female vocal group **The Ballads**. In 1969 he signed to RCA and released the much sought-after *Soul Portrait*. Including the uptempo tracks "Lucky To Be Loved By You" and "You Can't Miss Something That You Never Had" that had Hutch modulating from his sandpaper Texas drawl to a honeyed falsetto, *Soul Portrait* was an album that successfully bridged the gap between the more traditional soul sounds of the 60s and the new styles of the 70s. His 1970 album, *Season For Love*, was less appealing, although it did include the very fine "Let's Try It Over Again".

Hutch's songwriting talents came to the attention of Motown producer **Hal Davis**, who called Hutch in to work on "I'll Be There" for The Jackson 5. Hutch went on to arrange the vocals for The Jackson 5's recordings of "Never Can Say Goodbye" and "Got To Be There", and was soon brought into the Motown fold. In 1973 Hutch produced *Smokey*, Smokey Robinson's first album without the Miracles. That same year Hutch was invited to compose the soundtrack to the blaxploitation flick *The Mack*. Perhaps the best blaxploitation soundtrack that wasn't produced by Isaac Hayes, *The Mack* featured the excellent main theme as well as the dramatic "Brothers Gonna Work It Out" and the fine ballad "I Choose You".

Hutch's first proper album for Motown was 1973's *Fully Exposed*, but his soundtrack for the movie *Foxy Brown* was more successful. The "Theme Of Foxy Brown" featured fantastic interaction between a ludicrously flanged guitar riff and strings, while "You Sure Know How To Love Your Man" was a bouncy Philadelphia International-style number with a killer bassline that became a favourite of the early discotheques. In the mid-70s Hutch had sizeable R&B hits with the very funky "Get Ready For The Get Down" and the perky "Love Power", and scored disco hits with "Party Down" and "Shake It, Shake It".

Hutch moved to **Norman Whitfield**'s Whitfield label for two albums backed by Rose Royce in 1978, one of which included the soul-boy classic "Easy Does It". Returning to Motown in 1982, he had a modest hit with "In And Out" and produced the soundtrack for the 1985 movie *The Last Dragon*. In 1994 Hutch formed his own GGIT label. He sporadically released new albums throughout the 90s and the early 00s, including *From The Heart* (1994), *The Mack Is Back* (1997) and *Sexalicious* (2002) before dying on September 19, 2005, at the age of 59.

The Very Best Of Willie Hutch
1998, Motown

This 14-track compilation is the best introduction to Willie Hutch's brand of 70s soul. It holds most of his biggest R&B hits, including "Brothers Gonna Work It Out" and the upbeat "Love Power", as well as covers of Barbra Streisand's "The Way We Were" and The Jackson 5's "I'll Be There". If you want the tracks that were big underground hits on the UK's Northern soul scene, check out *Try it, You'll Like It: The Best Of Willie Hutch* (2002, Expansion).

Phyllis Hyman

Part of the trend that saw light jazz musicians and smooth fusioneers slide into big-budget balladeering and easy dance tracks, **Phyllis Hyman** (born July 6, 1950 in Philadelphia) parlayed her jazz-honed vocal chops into a substantial R&B chart run during the late 70s, 80s and early 90s.

In between training to be a legal secretary and working as a model, Hyman sang with several R&B groups in the early 70s, including her own **P/H Factor**. Moving to New York from Florida in 1974, she started singing at clubs like Rust Brown's and Mikel's where she built a strong reputation with her lush vocal style. After singing back-up for **Jon Lucien**, she became the featured vocalist for drummer **Norman Connors** and had an R&B hit with a cover of The Stylistics' "Betcha By Golly Wow".

Hyman released her self-titled solo debut in 1977 on Buddah, but had her first big hit the following year on Arista with the Barry Manilow-produced schlockfest "Somewhere In My Lifetime". Far better was "You Know How To Love Me", which had fairly generic late disco backing, but provided a nice frame for Hyman's belting and gave her probably the best hooks of her career. Hyman's first R&B top-ten hit was 1981's "Can't We Fall In Love Again", a bland duet with **Michael Henderson**.

Hyma's 1982 release "Riding The Tiger" may have had one of the worst titles ever, but it showed that she should have been singing more uptempo dance tracks rather than drowning in the schmaltz that her producers saddled her with. Unfortunately, power ballads like "Old Friend" and slow-burn tracks like "Living All Alone" were what the urban contemporary radio programmers were looking for.

After indulging her jazz roots by singing with **Grover Washington Jr.**, Lonnie Liston Smith, **Joe Sample** and McCoy Tyner, Hyman got her first R&B #1 in 1991 with "Don't Wanna Change The World", an utterly generic track in that slightly housey early-90s R&B style. The equally faceless ballads "Living In Confusion" and "When You Get Right Down To It" followed it into the R&B Top 10 that same year. Around the time that she was achieving her biggest commercial successes, Hyman was also fighting a continuing battle with severe depression. Her demons finally caught up with her on June 30, 1995 when she tragically committed suicide, just hours before she was scheduled to play a gig at the Apollo Theatre.

Ultimate Phyllis Hyman
2004, BMG

From her breakthrough with Norman Connors to her 90s albums with Kenny Gamble at Philadelphia International, this 17-track compilation spans Phyllis Hyman's entire recording career. While there are way too many sleek, overproduced ballads and pillow-talk numbers, Hyman always brought a bit more to the table than most singers who specialized in the genre.

The Impressions

Although **The Impressions** never made the same mark on mainstream America as Otis Redding, Aretha Franklin or Smokey Robinson, it would not be stretching it to claim that they were the most influential of all the soul vocal groups. With a hit-making career that ran from 1958 to the early 70s, only James Brown spent longer at the top during soul's golden age. Working with arranger/producer **Johnny Pate**, The Impressions almost single-handedly created the blueprint for the softer sounds of Chicago soul, and did as much as anyone to secularize gospel. In their lead singer and chief songwriter Curtis Mayfield, The Impressions were also blessed with one of the most talented and likeable musicians America has ever produced.

The Impressions were formed in Chicago in 1957 by Mayfield, Jerry Butler, **Sam Gooden** and **Arthur** and **Richard Brooks**. Signed to Vee Jay, they had their first hit with 1958's "For Your Precious Love". Butler's lead vocals were closer to a sermon than the mannered doo-wop-inspired vocals of the time and the single reached #11 on the pop charts. But the fact that it was credited to "Jerry Butler & The Impressions" tore the band apart. Butler then launched a solo career, aided and abetted by Mayfield, who co-wrote and sang harmony, and played **Pops Staple**-style guitar on Butler's top-ten hit "He Will Break Your Heart". Ironically, the success of "He Will Break Your Heart" helped get The Impressions signed to ABC-Paramount in 1961.

With **Fred Cash** replacing Butler, the group released The Drifters-influenced "Gypsy Woman" that same year, reaching #20 on the *Billboard* chart. It was, however, to be The Impressions' only hit for the next few years, with several follow-up records failing to match its success. Disillusioned, the Brooks brothers left the group in 1962, just before their huge breakthrough hit – "It's Alright". The Impressions' first record with Johnny Pate, "It's Alright" virtually wrote the Chicago soul rulebook, with its horn charts, gentle propulsion, easy swing, mellow harmonies and Mayfield's falsetto vocals. The flip, "You'll Want Me Back", had a strained lyric, but was also home to one of Mayfield's finest vocal performances.

"It's Alright" peaked at #4 on the pop chart and was their first R&B #1, beginning a two-year chart run that included the feel-good gems "Talking About My Baby", "I'm So Proud", and "Woman's Got Soul". Two

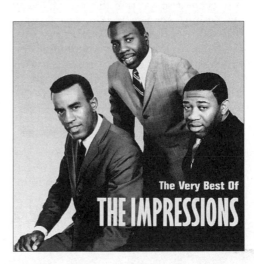

The Very Best Of
THE IMPRESSIONS

189

The Impressions, just being themselves

of their best songs from this period, "Keep On Pushin'" and "People Get Ready", were among the few soul records to engage with the Civil Rights struggle. Combining the timeless imagery of black spirituals with heavenly harmonies and arrangements so rich they were positively sinful, "People Get Ready" and "Keep On Pushin'" were great records not because of their righteousness, but because of their sublime craft.

This was borne out by 1965's *People Get Ready* album, perhaps the group's finest. Johnny Pate was at his best on the album, not just on well-known tracks like "Woman's Got Soul" and "You Must Believe In Me", but also on potential throwaways like "See The Real" (check out that brass intro) and

"Hard To Believe" (with its great string arrangement).

The group's last record for ABC-Paramount before moving to Mayfield's own Curtom label was 1968's "We're A Winner", which set the pattern for The Impressions' next few records with its earthy lyrics and its funky bottom. By that time Mayfield was no longer couching his politics in churchy metaphors and, although his politics were little more than NAACP platitudes, in the context of soul's development they were shockingly radical. "This Is My Country" was one of the first soul songs to dare to bring up slavery, and the way it staked a claim on American-ness on the grounds that the country was built on the back of "that peculiar institution" was nothing short of breathtaking. The #1 R&B hit, "Choice Of Colors", followed in a similar vein in 1969, while "Mighty Mighty (Spade & Whitey)" staked out the same turf with a nod to **Sly Stone**.

The Impressions' last hit with Mayfield as lead singer was 1970's "Check Out Your Mind". He left the group to devote more time to his solo career, so remaining members Cash and Gooden recruited **Leroy Hutson**, and later **Reggie Torian** and **Ralph Johnson**, to replace him. The new line-up would go on to have a couple of successes, most notably the 1974 R&B #1 "Finally Got Myself Together (I'm A Changed Man)", but by this time the group's best days were definitely behind them.

The group had hits in 1975 with "Sooner Or Later" and "Same Thing It Took", before Johnson left to become the lead singer of **Mystique**. With **Nate Evans** replacing Johnson, The Impressions left Curtom and started recording for Cotillion, but without much success. Another label move, this time to Chi-Sound, again resulted in little chart interest. Evans left the group just before the remaining trio recorded their final album, *Fan The Fire*, in 1981.

The Young Mods' Forgotten Story
1969, Curtom

This is worth checking out as a precursor to Curtis Mayfield's solo releases from the 70s. Mayfield had hit his stride by 1969, and he was getting ready to go out on his own, but he made this one last great album with The Impressions. Divided between songs of romance and socially conscious message songs, this material is uniformly strong.

The Very Best Of The Impressions
1997, Rhino

It may only have sixteen tracks, but what an impressive sixteen tracks they are! This hits compilation is a great first buy for any soul newcomer because it really does include the best The Impressions have to offer. It may include too many post-Curtis Mayfield records (3) but it is, nevertheless, the perfect distillation of the career of one of the pre-eminent soul groups.

James Ingram

What's a guy who performed with New Age musician **John Tesh** doing in a book about soul music? **James Ingram** may have been the king of the Adult Contemporary ballad, but his approach typi-

PLAYLIST
The Impressions

1 FOR YOUR PRECIOUS LOVE from **The Very Best Of The Impressions**
Jerry Butler's sermon-like vocals make this a contender for the title of first soul record.

2 GYPSY WOMAN from **The Very Best Of The Impressions**
Strangely mystical ballad with the imagistic quality of a Henri Rousseau painting.

3 IT'S ALRIGHT from **The Very Best Of The Impressions**
The blueprint of Chicago soul.

4 KEEP ON PUSHIN' from **The Very Best Of The Impressions**
Mayfield's falsetto is at its most glorious on this remarkable secular gospel record.

5 PEOPLE GET READY from **The Very Best Of The Impressions**
One of Mayfield's timeless civil rights spirituals.

6 WE'RE A WINNER from **The Very Best Of The Impressions**
The groove and production are as optimistic as Mayfield's lyrics and performance.

7 THIS IS MY COUNTRY from **The Very Best Of The Impressions**
Mayfield interrogates America's history of slavery in one of the most daring soul records ever.

8 CHOICE OF COLORS from **The Very Best Of The Impressions**
Mayfield's preachiest song and the group's most strident performance.

9 MIGHTY MIGHTY (SPADE & WHITEY) from **The Very Best Of The Impressions**
The Impressions at their funkiest.

10 FINALLY GOT MYSELF TOGETHER (I'M A CHANGED MAN) from **The Very Best Of The Impressions**
The group's best record without Curtis Mayfield.

fied the mainstream soul of the 80s: smooth, sophisticated soul with a hint of gospel, that was, above all, harmless.

Born on February 16, 1956 in Akron, Ohio, Ingram first came to attention as part of **Revelation Funk**, a group of Ohio Players wannabes from his home town. In 1973 Ingram moved to Los Angeles where he was a member of Ray Charles's touring band, played keyboards on Leon Haywood's

Chicago Soul

As wellsprings of American popular music, only New Orleans, Memphis and New York can rival Chicago. With records recorded by the likes of **Jerry Butler** and **The Impressions**, the Windy City was one of the first homes of the secular gospel sound and its influence on soul has been enormous. Chicago is best known for the soft, breezy soul sound of artists like Jerry Butler, The Impressions (in particular, the group's lead singer and songwriter **Curtis Mayfield**), **Gene Chandler, Tyrone Davis, Betty Everett, The Dells, The Five Stairsteps, The Chi-Lites** and **Major Lance**. As one of the centres of gospel, though, Chicago also produced plenty of harder vocalists, including **Etta James, Syl Johnson, Otis Clay, Harold Burrage** and **Johnny Sayles**.

One of the best and most underrated of Chicago's deep testifiers was **McKinley Mitchell**. He recorded for George Leaner's One-Derful and Mar-v-lus labels, which also had hits with records by Burrage, Sayles, Clay, The Five Du-Tones, The Sharpees, Betty Everett, Billy Emerson, Willie Parker and Alvin Cash. Mitchell's 1962 soul ballad "The Town I Live In" had a one-note roller-rink organ riff and drunken horns, over which Mitchell pleaded like a more urbane Bobby "Blue" Bland before unleashing bloodcurdling wails on the record's second half. His other records, such as "All Of A Sudden" and "Handful Of Sorrow", were more firmly in Southern soul style, but failed to find an audience. Mitchell ended up on Chimneyville and Malaco Records in the late 70s, recording in a bluesy style that suited him to a T.

Carl Davis ran Columbia's OKeh subsidiary in Chicago for its glory years, 1962–1965, when it helped define the sound of the Windy City with arrangements by Johnny Pate and songs by Curtis Mayfield. OKeh's biggest artist was Major Lance, but the label also had hits with records by Billy Butler & The Enchanters ("I Can't Work No Longer"), Walter Jackson ("Suddenly I'm Home"), **Ted Taylor** ("Stay Away From My Baby") and The Artistics ("This Heart Of Mine").

Equally successful but less stylistically consistent was the great Chess label. Moving from The Vibrations' pulsating dance hit "The Watusi", Billy Stewart's jazzy tongue-twisting rendition of "Summertime", Fontella Bass's Aretha Franklin blueprint "Rescue Me", Tony Clarke's soft soul standard "The Entertainer" and The Radiants' gorgeous "Voice Your Choice" to the blues soul of Little Milton's "Grits Ain't Groceries" and the avant-garde productions of Charles Stepney, Chess had all the bases covered. The label released a shockingly underappreciated corpus of soul.

Chicago's radio DJs also got into the action. Jerry-O (aka Jerry Murray) and the legendary E. Rodney Jones both released a series of records on which they talked over the top of some searing funk grooves. Worth searching out are Tom & Jerry-O's "Soul L-O-V-E-R" – another entry in the enduring "Tramp" saga – Jerry-O's "Karate Boogaloo", "Funky Four Corners" and "There Was A Time", and E. Rodney Jones's "R&B Time".

"Don't Push It Don't Force It" and Shalamar's "A Night To Remember", and sang lead on the group Zingara's modest R&B hit "Love's Calling". Ingram also worked as a demo singer and, in 1980, one of his tapes was heard by **Quincy Jones**. The song was "Just Once", and Jones asked Ingram to sing it on his 1980 album, *The Dude*. Released as a single in 1981, "Just Once" became a top-twenty pop hit and earned Ingram two Grammys, for Best Pop Male Vocal and Best R&B Vocal.

As well as signing to Quincy Jones's Qwest label, Ingram co-wrote both "PYT" and "We Are The World" for **Michael Jackson** with Jones. Ingram's duet with **Patti Austin**, "Baby Come To Me", was a quintessential 80s soul ballad with its unsubtle hook, breezy melody and

Hollywood soundtrack date-montage feel. He also recorded a duet with **Michael McDonald**, "Yah Mo B There", in which you couldn't tell where one voice began and the other ended. The production on the track was dire, it included every mid-80s cliché and the drum machine dictated the beat, rather than vice versa.

Ingram had several minor R&B hits on his own in the mid-80s, including "Party Animal", "There's No Easy Way" and "Always", but he was far more successful with his duets. "What About Me?" with **Kenny Rogers** and **Kim Carnes** was a top-twenty pop hit, while the sickly "Somewhere Out There" with **Linda Ronstadt**, from the 1986 Disney movie *An American Tail*, went to #2.

After releasing the shocking "(You Make Me Feel Like A) Natural Man", a male version

Various Artists: OKeh Soul
1995, Epic

Largely the product of Johnny Pate and Curtis Mayfield, the 24 tracks collected here represent Chicago soul at its very best. Included are eight tracks by Major Lance, six by Walter Jackson and four by Billy Butler & The Enchanters.

Various Artists: Windy City Soul
1999, Charly

This superb compilation collects 28 tracks recorded for George Leaner's One-Derful/Mar-v-lus stable, including very fine records from The Sharpees, Otis Clay, Betty Everett and Liz Lands.

PLAYLIST

1 FOR YOUR PRECIOUS LOVE Jerry Butler & The Impressions from **Soul Workshop**
With Butler's shuddering baritone, this lugubrious, dragging ballad is a masterpiece of early soul.

2 RAINBOW Gene Chandler from **Nothing Can Stop Me: Gene Chandler's Greatest Hits**
One of the most impressive vocal performances from Chandler, one of the avatars of Chicago soul.

3 THE MONKEY TIME Major Lance from **Everybody Loves A Good Time!: The Best Of Major Lance**
Perhaps the definitive Windy City arrangement.

4 I'D RATHER GO BLIND Etta James from **The Essential Etta James**
This may have been recorded down South, but the stunning voice belongs to Chicago.

5 IT'S ALRIGHT The Impressions from **The Very Best Of The Impressions**
A damn-near-perfect pop record.

6 STAY IN MY CORNER The Dells from **Anthology**
An ethereal combination of doo-wop and soft soul.

7 FREDDIE'S DEAD Curtis Mayfield from **Superfly**
Chicago's traditional swirling brass and wind arrangements become dark and claustrophobic on Mayfield's masterpiece.

8 DIFFERENT STROKES Syl Johnson from **Twilight & Twinight Masters Collection**
One of the stone-cold funkiest soul tunes ever.

9 CAN I CHANGE MY MIND Tyrone Davis from **Greatest Hits**
One of those gently upful grooves that are Chicago soul's gift to the world.

10 ARE YOU MY WOMAN? (TELL ME SO) Chi-Lites from **20 Greatest Hits**
Uptempo, paranoid soul at its best – just ask Beyoncé Knowles.

of "Natural Woman", Ingram appeared on Quincy Jones's ode to the quiet storm format, "The Secret Garden (Sweet Seduction Suite)", alongside Al B Sure!, El DeBarge and Barry White in 1990. That same year, Ingram finally got a solo #1 with "I Don't Have The Heart". However, despite that success and his remaining a favourite with soundtrack producers and quiet storm/smooth jazz radio programmers, Ingram's hits soon dried up. He now reappears on other artists' records as a guest vocalist from time to time and has formed his own Intering Records label.

Greatest Hits: The Power Of Great Music
1991, Qwest

The album's title is nauseating and so are many of the records inside, but at least here, unlike with his other compilation, *Forever More (Love Songs, Hits & Duets)* (1999, Private Music), you don't have to listen to his collaboration with John Tesh or his wretched version of "I Believe I Can Fly". This also includes most of the duets that made James Ingram one of the biggest Adult Contemporary stars of the 80s.

Luther Ingram

Luther Ingram is principally known as an early 70s Southern soul stylist and is largely remembered for just one song, the great "(If Loving You Is Wrong) I Don't Want To Be Right". However, his career extends back to the mid-60s when he made several records that combined the Southern elegance of Sam Cooke with the debonair élan of Chicago.

Ingram was born in Jackson, Tennessee on November 30, 1944, but he was raised in

Illinois. Credited to **Luther Ingram & The G-Men**, his first record was the original version of "I Spy For The FBI", released in 1965 on the Mercury subsidiary Smash. While almost anyone who could carry a tune would have sounded good on the brilliant finger-popping arrangement, Ingram sang it with real gospel conviction, bringing a hint of paranoia to what could have been a silly novelty song in lesser hands. The following year's "It's All The Same To You Babe" was a coronary-inducing uptempo number produced by **Richard "Popcorn" Wylie**, whose instrumental, "Exus Trek", was a big Northern soul number.

In 1967 Ingram signed to **Johnny Baylor**'s KoKo label and recorded "I Can't Stop". The record featured an instrumental backing that was like a ramshackle Muscle Shoals arrangement, but Ingram sang the rather banal lyric with a beautiful combination of Southern grit and Northern grace. After Baylor met **Al Bell** at an industry convention, KoKo became part of the Stax family, and, in 1969, Ingram had his first hit with "Pity For The Lonely", followed by the delightful "My Honey And Me".

Ingram's first big hit was the terribly arranged ballad "Ain't That Loving You (For More Reasons Than One)", which reached #6 on the R&B chart. Around this time, he also co-wrote "Respect Yourself", which would become a huge hit for **The Staple Singers**. Ingram had a few more modest hits – "To The Other Man" (an answer song to Doris Duke's "To The Other Woman"), "Be Good To Me Baby" and "You Were Made For Me" – before he cut his biggest record and, possibly, the most important ballad of the early 70s: 1972's "(If Loving You Is Wrong) I Don't Want To Be Right". One of the definitive cheating songs, the record itself was equally superb, with Ingram's gospel-influenced vocals, the surging horns, the slightly salacious guitar and the Echoplexed organ interjections. It spent a month at the top of the R&B chart and reached #3 on the pop chart.

The more uplifting "I'll Be Your Shelter (In Time Of Storm)" followed it into the R&B Top 10, but after releasing "Always" in 1973, Ingram's career suffered with the collapse of Stax. Baylor managed to rescue his KoKo label from the Stax rubble and, in 1976, Ingram had a modest hit with the funky "Ain't Good For Nothing". As the disco boom wore on, Ingram's records became increasingly humdrum. "Do You Think There's A Chance?" was a break-up song in that characteristically faceless Southern production style of the late 70s, where disco strings were added to really bland arrangements, while "Get To Me" was a saccharine midtempo ballad with a wretched guitar solo.

Ingram re-emerged in the late 80s as a singer of sickly, keyboard-heavy ballads, such as "Baby Don't Go Too Far" and "Don't Turn Around", which later became a hit for **Neil Diamond** and **Ace of Base**. He also appeared on *926 East McLemore*, the 1998 reunion of Stax artists, with a fine new recording of "How Sweet It Would Be".

Greatest Hits
1996, The Right Stuff

This well-chosen collection of sixteen of his KoKo/Stax tracks demonstates that Luther Ingram was one of the finest interpreters of Southern soul. Unfortunately, it doesn't include any of the excellent records he made above the Mason-Dixon Line that made his Southern records all the more remarkable.

The Isley Brothers

They will never be mentioned in the same breath as those titans of African-American music, **Louis Armstrong** and **Ella Fitzgerald**, but **The Isley Brothers** have maintained a career in the music biz for just about as long. Ever since 1957 when they released the mediocre doo-wop single, "Angels Cried", the Isleys, in one form or another, have kept pace with changing styles and stalked the American R&B chart – it's a good thing they've got a large and talented extended family to draw from. However, unlike some of their more illustrious contemporaries who burned brightly and then faded away as fickle tastes moved on, the Isley Brothers have never really been innovators. They are regarded, by some, as nothing more than survivors, but that is more than a little unfair given the quality and sheer energy of some of their records.

After recording a couple more doo-wop singles under the supervision of *the* impresario of street-corner harmony, **George**

Goldner, the Isleys (real-life brothers Ronald, Rudolph and O'Kelly) were signed to RCA and released their first hit, "Shout", in 1959. Recorded five years after Ray Charles's secular gospel megalith, "I've Got A Woman", "Shout" had all the gospel trademarks: over-the-top melisma, feverish handclaps, choral call and response and even the organist from the brothers' church. Aside from Ronald's falsetto "wooo", which launched a few dozen Beatles records, the most remarkable thing about this explosion of raw energy was that it was produced by those ham-fisted enemies of raw soul, Hugo & Luigi – the men responsible for chaining Sam Cooke to an army of strings.

Their next few singles were destroyed by Hugo & Luigi's routine suppression of swing, but when the Isleys moved to Wand and recorded with producer Bert Berns they struck gold again with "Twist And Shout" (famously covered by The Beatles), and the calypso-like original version of "Who's That Lady". With the Stax label making soul funkier, the group decided to set up their own label, T-Neck, which was an unheard-of step back then, especially for a black group. Realizing that they needed a guitarist, Ronald discovered some guy called James Hendrix playing in a bar in Harlem and immediately gave him a starring role on their first T-Neck singles. The question of who influenced whom comes to mind when listening to their strutting "Move Over And Let Me Dance" (the vocals of which sound an awful lot like Jimi's) and the amazing gospel harmony-garage band soundclash, "Testify".

After they failed to get any hits on T-Neck, the Isleys moved to Motown and had a major hit with the very Motownish "This Old Heart Of Mine" and a version of "Take Me In Your Arms (Rock Me A Little While)". The brothers weren't happy there, however, and left the label in 1969 to reform T-Neck, inviting younger brothers Ernie and Marvin and Rudolph's brother-in-law, Chris Jasper, to join the band. This was the beginning of a new era of sartorial magnificence, with the group resplendent in fur-lined Elizabethan coats and velvet trousers. They changed their musical direction too, heralded by that masterpiece of funk, "It's Your Thing", a song that began a string of almighty grooves,

PLAYLIST
The Isley Brothers

1 SHOUT from **It's Your Thing: The Story Of The Isley Brothers**
Pure Holy Roller dementia that drove 'em wild in *Animal House*.

2 TWIST AND SHOUT from **It's Your Thing: The Story Of The Isley Brothers**
The only version of this song you should have in your collection.

3 WHO'S THAT LADY from **It's Your Thing: The Story Of The Isley Brothers**
The beautiful Caribbean lilt makes this as mystical as any of their more explicitly psychedelic records.

4 TESTIFY from **It's Your Thing: The Story Of The Isley Brothers**
A garage gospel record with Jimi Hendrix on guitar.

5 THIS OLD HEART OF MINE from **It's Your Thing: The Story Of The Isley Brothers**
Featuring strings as weepy as Ronald Isley's lead.

6 IT'S YOUR THING from **It's Your Thing: The Story Of The Isley Brothers**
With a groove this *nastay*, no wonder thay had to leave Motown.

7 GET INTO SOMETHING from **It's Your Thing: The Story Of The Isley Brothers**
One of the cornerstones of hip-hop, thanks to Ernie Isley and Bernard Purdie's ferocious drumming.

8 THAT LADY from **It's Your Thing: The Story Of The Isley Brothers**
Ernie Isley's ultra-processed post-Hendrix guitar steals the show.

9 FIGHT THE POWER from **It's Your Thing: The Story Of The Isley Brothers**
This has a preposterously fat bassline, courtesy of synthesists Tonto's Expanding Headband.

10 LIVE IT UP from **It's Your Thing: The Story Of The Isley Brothers**
Producers Margouleff and Cecil strike again with the Stevie Wonder-styled ARP line.

like "I Turned You On", "Freedom", "Keep On Doin'" and the epochal "Get Into Something".

While still maintaining a commitment to the funk, 1973's re-recording of "Who's That Lady" shone a spotlight on Ernie's wah-wah guitar and highlighted the group's commitment to staying current. The Isleys started working with synth programmers and producers Malcolm Cecil and Robert Margouleff (who had previously assisted **Stevie Wonder**), and this partnership was responsible for "Fight The Power", "Live It Up" and "Harvest For The World". In response to the quiet storm phenomenon of the early 80s, The Isley Brothers covered their asses and became consummate purveyors of the saccharine ballad with a version of "Summer Breeze" and the original "Between The Sheets".

In 1984 younger brothers Ernie and Marvin left the band with Chris Jasper to become **Isley Jasper Isley** and had an R&B #1 with the saccharine "Caravan Of Love". O'Kelly died of a heart attack on March 31, 1986, but Ronald and Rudolph continued as The Isley Brothers until 1988 when Rudolph decided to join the ministry. Marvin and Ernie rejoined Ronald two years later, and The Isley Brothers continued to score R&B hits right through to the end of the 90s. Their remarkable career continued with *Taken To The Next Phase* in 2004, a surprisingly decent remix album that featured **Steven "Lenky" Marsden**, **Mos Def** and several others reconstructing the Isleys' classics.

⊙ It's Your Thing: The Story Of The Isley Brothers
1999, Sony Legacy

They don't always get the respect they deserve, but as this excellent, enlightening 3-CD anthology shows, The Isley Brothers have been responsible for some of the most electric soul music ever recorded. Sure, this includes too many of their icky ballads, but it is the only collection to provide a complete overview of their long career. When they wanted to be, the Isleys were as good as anyone.

The Jackson 5

From The Osmonds and The DeFranco Family to Boyzone and S Club 7, **The Jackson 5** has inspired more bands, or rather more Svengalis, than The Beatles, Velvet Underground and The Rolling Stones put together. While the blame for the demise of the gospel tradition of African-American singing has been put squarely on the shoulders of disco and funk, the combination of **Michael Jackson**'s prepubescent vocals, his tendency to oversing and his emulation of **Diana Ross**'s streamlined style have done as much to make the world safe for adolescent, adenoidal melisma as the precedence of rhythm over melody. What the "King of Pop" possesses, more than any other performer this side of **James Brown**, is dynamism and charisma. For all his faults, he is probably – alongside **Prince** – the best pure singer to emerge in the past three decades.

The Jackson 5's timing could not have been better. With the rhythmic innovations of James Brown and **Sly Stone**, soul's emphasis was changing and its attitude was becoming ever more assertive. By the end of 1969 **Sly & The Family Stone** was no longer the voice of a shiny, happy, integrated America. Sly turned to cataloguing the betrayals of the 60s dream and America needed a new black icon to make it feel good about itself. Instead of someone who still believed in the possibilities of the American experiment, this new icon was an 11-year-old boy who didn't know any better. The Jackson 5 were the first pop band of the 70s. With glam rock in the UK, the schlock shock antics of **Kiss** and

Alice Cooper in the US, and the teenybop of **The Osmonds** and **The Partridge Family**, the pop of the first half of the 70s was all about running away from the 60s into the safe confines of a naive innocence. The Jackson 5 epitomized this retreat.

Schooled in allegedly drill sergeant fashion by their controversial father Joe, the five eldest Jackson brothers – **Jackie**, **Tito**, **Marlon**, **Jermaine** and **Michael** – were moulded into a slick musical group by the time they were barely pubescent, or in Michael's case barely prepubescent. Despite his young age, Michael soon became the centre of the group as it was apparent to Joe, and pretty much anyone who heard them, that Michael was the real talent in the family.

Motown legend has it that the group were discovered performing in a Gary, Indiana nightclub by Diana Ross. They were soon signed to her Motown label and paired with

Michael leads his brothers on a Bob Hope television special

The Corporation, a team of producers that included **Berry Gordy**, **Freddie Perren** (who later defined mainstream disco with **Peaches & Herb**, Yvonne Elliman and **The Sylvers**), **Deke Richards** (Black Oak Arkansas) and **Alphonso "Fonce" Mizell** (responsible for records by Donald Byrd, Johnny Hammond and A Taste of Honey).

The Jackson 5 rode in on streamlined Sly Stone rhythms and vivacious melodies to redefine pop music. Their first four singles – "I Want You Back", "ABC", "The Love You Save", "I'll Be There" – all went to #1 in the US in less than a year. Only a spoilsport or a militant Maoist could have denied that they were some of the greatest radio songs ever. Bursts of energy, syncopation, buzzing fuzz guitars, bridges stolen from **The Meters**, upful strings and intense lead vocals from Michael that sounded like he was singing for his life – the first three records laid down the foundations not just for all subsequent teen pop, but for a good portion of 70s pop in general. The group proved so popular that

they briefly had their own animated series, *The Jackson 5ive*, in 1971.

After The Jackson 5's first singles, it was a series of diminishing returns – check out their awful version of **The Isley Brothers'** "It's Your Thing". With the exceptions of "Never Can Say Goodbye", "Get It Together" and "Dancing Machine", their ballads were so sickly that even prepubescent girls were probably turned off. Some of their album tracks, however, absolutely smoked, and you have to wonder why they were never released as singles.

Their 1973 album *Get It Together* included "Hum Along And Dance", which was probably the funkiest track any member of the Jackson family ever recorded: the organ sounded like Jon Lord from heavy-metal progenitors **Deep Purple**; Tito's guitar solo was somewhere between Dick Dale and obscure hard-rock legend Jordan Macarus; the Jacksons sounded like **The Temptations**; and the breakdown was sheer b-boy bliss. The beginning of "It's Great To Be Here", from 1971's *Maybe Tomorrow*, was one of the definitive b-boy breakbeats. In fact, it's now bizarre to listen to the song all the way through because you're so used to hearing it cut up by DJs. Meanwhile, the relentlessly robotic, galloping bassline of their version of The Supremes' "Forever Came Today", from 1975's *Moving Violation*, quickly became one of the hallmarks of disco.

In 1976, after a dispute about creative control, The Jackson 5 left Motown and signed with Epic. They changed their name to **The Jacksons** and replaced Jermaine (who stayed at Motown largely because he was married to Berry Gordy's daughter) with their youngest brother **Randy**. On the 1976 album *The Jacksons*, the brothers teamed up with legendary Philly producers **Gamble & Huff** with mixed results. However, the album did include the sizeable hits "Enjoy Yourself" and "Show You The Way To Go".

On 1978's *Destiny* the group were finally allowed to write their own material and produce themselves, and they created a minor masterpiece. How on earth did the pop disco gem "Blame It On The Boogie" only reach #54 on the US pop charts? Thankfully, it made it into the UK Top 10, and "Shake Your Body Down To The Ground" going platinum also helped make up for the blunder. Michael shined and his performance convinced him to return to solo recording after his awkward first stab at a solo career under Gordy's tutelage in the early 70s.

After Michael Jackson became the biggest thing since The Beatles, Jermaine rejoined the fold for *Victory* in 1984. The only album to include all six brothers, *Victory* only featured Michael on a few tracks. It was Michael's last album with the group and they effectively split up shortly afterwards, with Marlon trying an ill-advised solo career and Randy, Tito and Jackie becoming session musicians. The group reunited in 1989 for *2300 Jackson Street*, which was notable only for the appearance of the entire family, save LaToya, on the title track.

Destiny
1978, Epic

Following their departure from Motown and two albums recorded with Gamble & Huff for Epic, *Destiny* was the first album written and produced solely by the Jacksons. The funk is strong, the ballads are smooth and the new sophistication is their own. Michael's vocals are great throughout, previewing the talent that would explode the next year on his solo *Off The Wall* album.

The Ultimate Collection
1996, Motown

There are lots of holes that a more savvy compiler would have filled, and an extraneous remix of "It's Your Thing", but this single-disc, 21-track collection is the best available introduction to the Jackson family's brand of infectious pop-soul. It includes a few of Michael and Jermaine's early solo hits, as well as most of the very fine recordings that made The Jackson 5 one of the greatest pop groups ever.

Chuck Jackson

Although largely unknown these days, **Chuck Jackson** was, to many soul aficionados, one of the true greats, right up there with **Aretha Franklin**, **Otis Redding** and **Solomon Burke**. Jackson had a thunderous baritone filled with gospel torment, but he had trouble keeping it in check, and when combined with the ornate productions of early-60s New York soul, his records often slipped into melodrama.

Born July 22, 1937 in Latta, South Carolina, Chuck Jackson was raised in Pittsburgh. In 1955 he joined a gospel group called The Raspberry Singers and, two years later, became part of one of the many **Del-Vikings** line-ups. Impressed with his talent, Jackie Wilson asked him to leave the group and become his opening act. While performing with Wilson, Jackson drifted between several small labels, including Clock and Beltone, before being spotted by **Luther Dixon**, a producer for Scepter/Wand.

Jackson's first single for Wand, "I Don't Want To Cry", became an early soul classic. Jackson may have been from South Carolina, but "I Don't Want To Cry" was pure New York. **Carole King**'s flowery cod-Latin arrangement had Jackson doing a call-and-response with cellos, but his baritone lent weight to an arrangement that threatened to fly off at any moment. Jackson gave "I Wake Up Crying" one of his best readings, which wasn't all power, but the material itself was pretty weak. Jackson's biggest hit was 1962's "Any Day Now", a Burt Bacharach song that featured a wonderful contrast between Jackson's gravelly vocals and the twee rhythms. However, he was horribly inconsistent over the next few years. While he was absolutely great on "Beg Me", one of the most stereotypically soulful productions that he ever got at Wand, he was hideously over-wrought on "Hand It Over".

A series of duets with Maxine Brown in the mid-60s – "Something You Got", "Please Don't Hurt Me", "Hold On I'm Coming" and "Daddy's Home" – tempered his excesses and worst instincts. Several of his solo records from the same time, on the other hand, including "Good Things Come To Those Who Wait", were characterized by really over-wrought performances from both Jackson and his backing singers. The gem "What's With This Loneliness" was recorded in 1966, but was not released until the 90s. The song's production was the very definition of the pop soul of the late 60s and Jackson was at his huskiest and most soulful. However, "I've Got To Be Strong" was as close to the South as Jackson ever got. He sounded great in that environment, like a less subtle Otis Redding.

In 1968 Jackson signed to Motown on the recommendation of Smokey Robinson. He recorded seven singles for the label, but none of them was particularly noteworthy. When he moved to ABC in 1973, however, he had a modest R&B hit with "I Only Get This Feeling", which was reminiscent of late-period Jackie Wilson. Jackson then moved to the All Platinum label, where he recorded a series of rote disco records, including 1977's "I Got The Need". His last chart hit came in 1980 with a version of Bob Marley's "I Wanna Give You Some Love". Since then, Chuck Jackson has largely disappeared from the limelight, although he did release an album in 1992 with Cissy Houston and he remains a popular live act, particularly on the UK's Northern soul scene.

⊙ **Any Day Now: The Very Best Of Chuck Jackson 1961–1967**
1997, Varese Sarabande

This 16-track compilation represents the best of Jackson's peak period at Wand. While he often sounded like he wanted to burst out of his tuxedo and rough up the string section, when he kept his prodigious pipes in check the tension between his hoarse vocals and the prim arrangements made for some terrific soul music.

Freddie Jackson

Freddie Jackson (born October 2, 1956 in New York City) was one of seemingly dozens of sensitive balladeers who appeared in the wake of Luther Vandross. Without the grace of Vandross or the ability to carry off the he-man antics of Alexander O'Neal, Jackson largely imitated Marvin Gaye, but with a bit of jazzy overenunciation thrown in for good measure. He was, nevertheless, one of the biggest R&B stars of the 80s, clocking up ten #1s between 1985 and 1991.

Jackson started singing as a child at White Rock Baptist Church in Harlem. It was here that he met Paul Laurence, who later became his producer, and joined his group, LJE, when he finished high school. In the early 80s Jackson briefly fronted a group called Mystic Merlin before becoming a backing singer for Evelyn "Champagne" King and Melba Moore (he also co-wrote Moore's top-twenty hit "Keepin' My Lover Satisfed"). In 1984 Moore's manager helped Jackson get a contract with Capitol Records.

Jackson's first single, "Rock Me Tonight (For Old Times Sake)", was written by Paul Laurence, although its melody was straight off Gaye's Let's Get It On. It was an urban radio sensation, spending six weeks at #1 on the R&B chart in 1985. It was followed swiftly to the top of the charts by "You Are My Lady", which owed more than a little to Chicago's hit from the previous year, "You're The Inspiration".

His second album, Just Like The First Time (1986), dominated the R&B charts for the next year. "A Little Bit More" (an MOR duet with Melba Moore), "Tasty Love" (a Marvin Gaye-style tune), "Have You Ever Loved Somebody" (a ballad that was used heavily on the soap opera One Life To Live) and "Jam Tonight" (which didn't jam) all topped the R&B chart, while "I Don't Want To Lose Your Love" reached #2. "Tasty Love" replaced "A Little Bit More" at #1, making Jackson the first artist to have back-to-back #1s since Dinah Washington in 1960.

The 1988 album Don't Let Love Slip Away could only muster two #1s: "Nice 'N' Slow" and "Hey Lover". "Love Me Down" and "Do Me Again", from 1990's Do Me Again, also went to #1, but by this point it was nearly impossible to tell Jackson's records apart. His quiet storm thunder was also being stolen by more assertive love men who had grown up on hip-hop and were appending Jackson's oversinging to honest-to-goodness beats, rather than simpering keyboard washes. By 1995 Jackson had vanished from even the lower reaches of the R&B chart.

Jackson re-emerged in 2005 with *Personal Reflections*, a rather bizarre album of covers of Lite FM standards like Captain & Tennille's "Do That To Me One Last Time", Vanessa Williams's "Save The Best For Last", Paul Davis's "I Go Crazy" and The Spinners' "I'll Be Around".

⊙ The Greatest Hits Of Freddie Jackson
1994, Capitol

While it contains nearly all of Jackson's big hits, there are two problems with this compilation. One is the redundant remix of "Rock Me Tonight"; the other is that it substitutes a pointless Christmas track for Jackson's #1 duet with Melba Moore, whose voice would have at least provided a bit of contrast amongst the sheer monotony of Jackson's oily seductions.

Janet Jackson

Born on May 16, 1966 in Gary, Indiana as the youngest of the nine Jackson siblings, **Janet Jackson** began singing with her brothers, The Jackson 5, at a very young age in the mid-70s. From 1977 to 1984 she spent most of her time on television, appearing in *Good Times*, *Diff'rent Strokes*, *A New Kind Of Family* and *Fame*. Her father Joe strongly "encouraged" her to start a singing career and, in 1982, she released a self-titled album on A&M. It went nowhere and neither did the 1983 follow-up, *Dream Street*.

Only someone with the gargantuan Jackson ego could title their breakthrough album *Control* (1986) when it was little more than a showcase for producers Jam & Lewis. Janet Jackson's songs (all co-written with Jam & Lewis) helped to assert the youngest member of the Jackson clan's independence, but without Jam and Lewis's spiky beats, synth splinters and sharp basslines, *Control* would have fallen as flat as her two previous albums of weak-as-water teen-pop.

What Jackson did bring to the project was venom. Rebelling against her parents by marrying **James DeBarge** (from the family harmony group DeBarge that had superseded the Jacksons at Motown) in 1984, Janet Jackson was the only member of the family who seemed determined to make it on her own. When her marriage failed six months later, instead of running back to her family,

she went to Minneapolis and recorded her third album, *Control*, with Jam & Lewis. As members of The Time, Jam & Lewis had been part of Prince's crew and had helped to redefine soul at the start of the 80s. Since the group disbanded, the duo had become the hottest producers in R&B, crafting hits for The SOS Band, Cherrelle, Alexander O'Neal, Patti Austin and the Force MDs. Many of the backing tracks that were used on *Control* were actually already crafted by Jam & Lewis for an album they were working on with Atlantic Starr singer Sharon Bryant. She rejected the tracks, but when Janet Jackson showed up with her pissed-off lyrics, the tapes were recycled and the sound of 80s pop-funk was born.

Control would eventually sell some five million copies in the US, spawning one pop #1 and five R&B #1 singles (significantly, the pop #1, "When I Think Of You", was the only one of the album's singles not to reach the top of the R&B chart). The album's first single, "What Have You Done For Me Lately", shook the foundations of an R&B world dominated at the time by Whitney Houston and Freddie Jackson. Lewis's drum programming leaped from the speakers, while Jam's ferocious bassline and angular synth riffs had an attitude, a strut, a funk that was wholly missing from the R&B records of the day. Until **Teddy Riley** (who was surely listening closely) came along, this was the closest R&B would get to hip-hop. "Nasty" followed in quick succession with even bigger drums and Jackson's own keyboard line put together at such sharp angles that you could put your eye out if you listened too closely. Her toughest vocal ever only added to the aggression. Featuring the most intricate drum programming (the result of sequencing mistakes), "Control" was the album's third, and last great, single.

Rhythm Nation 1814 (1989) was a brave follow-up and it was even more commercially successful, selling six million copies. The album ham-fistedly tackled social issues, but the real rabble-rousing was committed by Jam & Lewis, who again redefined the sound of urban pop. They sampled **Sly Stone** on the ultra-percussive title track; set a pining lover's lament to a prickly, martial, almost industrial beatscape; and let guitarist **Vernon Reid** loose on "Black Cat". Janet Jackson became the first artist ever to score seven Top 5 hits from one album; her brother Michael only ever managed five.

After she moved to Virgin from A&M with a celebrated record deal, her 1993 album *janet.* became her biggest yet, selling seven million copies. Working again with Jam & Lewis, Jackson retooled her sound to focus more on slinkier, 70s-inspired grooves. "That's The Way Love Goes" sampled James Brown and spent eight weeks at #1, while "Any Time, Any Place" became one of the biggest R&B hits of the decade, spending ten weeks at the top of the chart.

By now it was Michael asking Janet for help. She appeared on "Scream" from his stillborn *HIStory: Past, Present And Future Book 1* album in 1995, helping him to ratchet up sales and deflecting attention away from his legal difficulties. Janet Jackson was now just calling herself "Janet", but despite putting herself in the single-name company of Elvis, Madonna, Brazilian footballers and Fabian, her next album, 1997's *Velvet Rope*, tanked. While most pop singers would never consider a triple-platinum album a failure, the bloated, overambitious *Velvet Rope* could only generate one #1 single, "Together Again", an elegy for AIDS victims.

The 2001 album, *All For You*, was similarly indulgent, if less socially conscious, focusing instead on sex and railing against the record industry, which was even more ludicrous than **George Michael**'s anti-music biz rants. *Damita Jo* (2004) was soft porn, pure and simple, and was even less titillating than the

real thing. Of course, by now Jackson was more famous for "Nipplegate" (the "wardrobe malfunction" during the 2004 Super Bowl half-time show) than her singing.

Control
1986, A&M

Control was a virtual manual for producers on how to overcome the vocal deficiencies of your client. In the dark ages before these things could be fixed with Pro Tools, Jam & Lewis's slashing keyboards and spiky beats camouflaged Jackson's little-girl whimpering. While this created the framework for the teen-pop explosion, you can't blame the messenger, and this is a great album.

Michael Jackson

It was with **Michael Jackson**, the biggest pop star of his generation, that soul's vision reached its goal and, effectively, ended. Jackson is the only African-American artist to seriously rival either **Elvis** or **The Beatles** – a feat he achieved through startlingly well-crafted pop that blended "white" and "black" music seamlessly. Of course, this came at an enormous cost, and the aftermath of Jackson's triumph was the surest delineation of the post-soul generation.

Michael Joseph Jackson was born on August 29, 1958 in Gary, Indiana as the fifth son in the Jackson family. He was only 5 years old when he started performing with his older brothers and he quickly became the lead singer of The Jackson 5, making history when the group's first four singles all shot to the top of the charts in 1970. Motown boss **Berry Gordy** immediately began grooming Michael for a parallel solo career. His first solo records worked the same terrain as his records with The Jackson 5 – dance novelties and lovelorn kiddie ballads. There was a certain amount of charm about the records "Got To Be There", his version of **Bobby Day**'s "Rockin' Robin", "Ben" and "Just A Little Bit Of You", but Jackson's rise to icon status didn't begin until he teamed up with **Quincy Jones** in 1979.

Jackson's first "adult" record was 1979's *Off The Wall*, which proved he was something more than a charming little kid with good pipes and great dance moves. The music was slick, big-budget disco-funk crafted by Quincy Jones with a band that included the **Brothers Johnson**, Greg Phillinganes, Phil Upchurch and Paulinho Da Costa, but Michael Jackson was the clear star. His grainy falsetto and his yelps, huffs and whoops brought an energy and visceral excitement that were missing from the utterly professional instrumental backing. If you want to know why singers don't sound like **Al Green** or **Aretha Franklin** anymore, listen to "Off The Wall", which is the next quarter-century of R&B vocals in microcosm.

Off The Wall was a huge hit, but 1982's *Thriller* was the most successful album ever made and it turned Jackson into a phenomenon. *Thriller* was straightforward pop's last gasp before **Prince** took it to the conceptual high ground and hip-hop dismantled its structure altogether. *Thriller* was the culmination of the soul experiment: it was the ultimate crossover album and one of the best examples of white and black musicians working together to produce a unified vision. After *Thriller* both the R&B and pop charts, and the black and white underground scenes, veered away from each other and wouldn't meet up again until the lack of decent rock music made hip-hop's commercial victory inevitable. Perhaps that is why *Thriller* remains so vital – or maybe it's just the craft.

Even if it is just the craft, however, the implications of the way the album was put together are unavoidable. With its hard-rock guitar solo from **Eddie Van Halen**, "Beat It" laid down the framework for the nest two decades' worth of R&B integration. "Beat It" may have been nothing but the Rod Stewart/Rolling Stones disco moves in reverse, but it was the biggest blow to narrow-casting radio segregation of the 80s and laid the groundwork for Prince's crossover. Stealing its hook from **Manu Dibango**'s Cameroonian disco classic, "Soul Makossa", "Wanna Be Startin' Somethin'" highlighted both disco's integrationist ideal and its love of world music,

The very "bad" Michael Jackson

thus giving the lie to disco's detractors by showing that it was more in tune with Africa than funk or any other form of "real" black music. The huge success of both "The Girl Is Mine" (recorded with **Paul McCartney**) and "Billie Jean" broke down MTV's colour barrier, forcing the network to play videos by black artists despite all of its costly market research and demographic projections.

Jackson's next album, 1986's *Bad*, was far less interesting. Again, it was impeccably crafted, but instead of subtext and allusion, Jackson indulged his ego and his stardom and shoved everything in your face. While R&B had moved on in leaps and bounds since *Thriller*, Jackson remained rooted in disco and Adult Contemporary hackery. Where *Thriller* seemed to have barely any filler, *Bad* was almost all filler with few notable hooks, melodies or rhythms.

For 1991's *Dangerous*, Jackson ditched Jones in favour of a producer with a bit more street

cred – **Teddy Riley**. Riley gave Jackson the hippest rhythms of his career and Jackson responded with his best songs since *Thriller*. "Jam" and "Remember The Time" found Jackson attempting a reconciliation with contemporary R&B; "In The Closet" was a confidence game with his image; and "Black Or White" was a hook-laden car-crash that only a megastar like Jackson could produce. This brave attempt to make "the King of Pop" relevant to a black audience again was laudable, but it backfired on the pop charts: Jackson was unceremoniously dumped from the top of the album charts by three nobodies from Seattle.

Embroiled in legal troubles, speculation about plastic surgery and hyperbaric oxygen chambers, and a shambles of a marriage to **Lisa-Marie Presley**, Jackson hoped that his 1995 album *HIStory: Past, Present And Future Book 1*, half new material, half greatest hits, would take the heat off. The problem was that the new material was horrendous: whiny, self-indulgent, saccharine, grooveless and overwrought. Things had gotten so bad that he had to call in his sister **Janet Jackson** for a favour, rather than vice versa.

In 2001 *Invincible* was the most expensive album ever made, although it wasn't quite the musical equivalent of *Waterworld* or *Heaven's Gate* that most people said it was. That's not to say that it was good, however, nor does it mean that whatever limited artistic success it achieved was due to the King of Pop. Never have Michael Jackson's vocal mannerisms sounded more annoying, more like a constriction than a matter of style (which wasn't helped by the use of the same rhythmic patterns he'd been using since *Dangerous*). On "2000 Watts" and "Heartbreaker" he even sounded more like **Justin Timberlake** than Michael Jackson. While his desperation and tightness, matched with the strangulated R&B minimalism of the uptempo tracks, might have been interesting in the early 90s, Jacko the icon was by now so overdetermined that the subtexts and implications of the music had long ceased to have any impact. What was left was competent but very rarely exciting contemporary R&B (although an EP of the instrumental tracks of "Unbreakable", "Heart breaker" and "2000 Watts" would destroy any club) sitting uneasily alongside some of the most overwrought ballads in the history of this most overwrought of ballad singers.

Things only went downhill after *Invincible*. Jackson took to wearing a surgical mask to conceal his plastic surgery disasters and caused a media storm by dangling his 11-month-old son, **Prince Michael II** (whom he calls Blanket), over the balcony of his hotel room in Germany while acknowledging crowds of fans in the street below. During a television interview in 2003, Jackson then revealed that he shared his bed with young children, and saw nothing wrong with that. A storm of controversy erupted, culminating in Jackson's Neverland Ranch in California

PLAYLIST
Michael Jackson

1 I WANT YOU BACK Jackson 5 from **The Ultimate Collection**
A simply perfect pop record.

2 ABC Jackson 5 from **The Ultimate Collection**
More of the same, only even more infectious.

3 HUM ALONG AND DANCE Jackson 5 from **Get It Together**
Absolutely killer funk/proto-disco.

4 ROCK WITH YOU from **Off The Wall**
Unthreatening exuberance – the bedrock of Jackson's appeal.

5 DON'T STOP 'TIL YOU GET ENOUGH from **Off The Wall**
Big-budget pop-funk-disco record that manages to groove despite all the professionalism.

6 BILLIE JEAN from **Thriller**
There will never again be a song as well crafted as this.

7 BEAT IT from **Thriller**
Eddie Van Halen gave us all a brief hope in the death of radio segregation – it didn't last long.

8 WANNA BE STARTIN' SOMETHIN' from **Thriller**
Lifting its hook from Manu Dibango, this is dance-floor perfection.

9 REMEMBER THE TIME from **Dangerous**
Thanks to producer Teddy Riley, this has Jackson's best beat since *Thriller*.

10 BLACK OR WHITE from **Dangerous**
For sheer vainglory alone "Black Or White" is a remarkable piece of work.

being searched by police and, later, a trial, in which he was acquitted by a jury of child molestation charges. Soon after his acquittal in 2005, Jackson moved to Bahrain.

Off The Wall
1979, Epic

Sure, it sounds like a Brothers Johnson album, but there's a reason why they never sold a billion albums – they didn't have Michael Jackson singing on top of their grooves. The breakthrough that made him a star in his own right, not just the cute little lead singer of The Jackson 5, *Off The Wall* is an album of professional, finely crafted, but fresh, vibrant and exciting, disco-funk. Michael Jackson is quite simply electric on the album that started his rise.

Thriller
1982, Epic

As they used to say in the days of Elvis, 40 million *Thriller* buyers can't be wrong. There is a reason – besides hype – why this is the biggest-selling album of all time. Unlike other "event albums", like Pink Floyd's *Dark Side Of The Moon* or Alanis Morissette's *Jagged Little Pill*, where buying the thing along with millions of others was as much a part of the record's meaning as the music it contained, *Thriller* is the only one that holds up long after the initial buzz has gone.

Dangerous
Sony, 1992

Though for some Jackson's glory days ended after *Thriller*, *Dangerous* still sold over 20 million copies and is home to a few classic tracks that will make it into the King of Pop's musical obituary. The angry "Black Or White" and the sickly campaign manifesto "Heal The World" are obvious candidates, but its the floor-fillers, such as "Why You Wanna Trip On Me" and "Jam", that really set the tone.

Millie Jackson

According to legend, **Millie Jackson**'s career began when she heckled a singer at the Harlem nightclub Small's Paradise. Challenged by the woman on stage to sing better, Jackson got up and sang a **Ben E. King** tune to rapturous applause. For Jackson – one of the most audacious, outlandish and ballsy performers in soul history – this creation myth makes perfect sense.

Jackson was born in Thomson, Georgia on July 15, 1944. She was raised by her preacher grandfather until she ran away to live with her father in New Jersey in 1958. After her raucous debut at Small's in the mid-60s, Jackson spent the next few years playing nightclubs in and around New York and touring as a backing vocalist before signing to MGM and recording "A Little Bit Of Something" in 1969. After moving to Spring Records, Jackson first gained attention for her controversial single, "A Child Of God (It's Hard To Believe)", a scathing attack on religious hypocrisy and a plea for tolerance.

"Ask Me What You Want" had newfangled production values, but could have been a classic Southern soul ballad and went to #4 on the R&B chart in 1972. That same year "My Man A Sweet Man" sounded like it had been recorded about six years earlier and hit not only with the Northern soul aficionados but also with the American record-buying public, becoming another top-ten R&B hit.

"Hurts So Good", from the soundtrack to *Cleopatra Jones*, highlighted her grainy voice and became her biggest hit.

In 1974 Jackson released the concept album *Caught Up*, which was about infidelity, with one side for the wronged wife's point of view and one for the "other woman". It was raunchy and forthright and it made Jackson a star in the African-American community. An eleven-minute version of "If Loving You Is Wrong I Don't Want To Be Right" was preambled by a rap that laid the foundations for what would become Jackson's signature shtick. Two more albums – *Still Caught Up* and *Free And In Love* – of cheating songs followed in 1975 and 76, the latter of which included a version of **Bad Company**'s "Feel Like Makin' Love".

Although it featured a fine, and straight, cover of **Merle Haggard**'s "If You're Not Back In Love By Monday", Jackson's 1977 record, *Feelin' Bitchy*, was filled with x-rated monologues and was her raunchiest album yet. With its ribald audience interaction and some really great performances from Jackson, 1979's *Live And Uncensored*, on the other hand, proved that she was more than just the female version of crude singer-songwriter **Blowfly**. Then again, it did include the delirious "Phuck U Symphony".

The 1980 rap parody "I Had To Say It" was as gloriously unhinged as anything in Jackson's catalogue – except, perhaps, for the moment when the KKK give her an honorary membership – but her shtick started to wear thin as the 80s progressed. After some success in the mid-90s with the musical *Young Man, Older Woman*, which she both wrote and starred in, Jackson recorded several decent, if uninspiring, albums of retro bluesy soul for Ichiban. Jackson now runs her own Weird Wreckuds label, on which she releases new material from time to time, and hosts a radio show in Dallas, Texas.

⊙ Caught Up/Still Caught Up
1999, Hip-O Records

None of the available greatest hits packages put her records in the proper context, so this reissue of Millie Jackson's two best studio albums, 1974's *Caught Up* and and 1975's *Still Caught Up*, is the logical choice. The disc's finale, in which she is dragged screaming to a mental hospital, is perhaps not to everyone's taste, but the other sixteen tracks are an interesting extended examination of soul's favourite subject, the love triangle.

Walter Jackson

I f you've ever wondered just what impact crooners like Nat "King" Cole and **Billy Eckstine** had on soul singers, look no further than the records of **Walter Jackson**. While Jackson's brand of Chicago soul was so uptown that it often crept into suburban supper-club schlock, his brand of smooth balladry was a major influence on later love men such as Luther Vandross.

Born March 19, 1938 in Pensacola, Florida, Walter Jackson was raised in Detroit. His first record, "Who Took My Girl", was as the lead singer of **The Velvetones** in 1959. After failing an audition at Motown, Jackson was discovered in a Detroit nightclub in 1962 by Chicago producer **Carl Davis** who brought him to the Windy City to record. Jackson released "I Don't Want To Suffer" on Columbia that same year, but it wasn't until he moved to the subsidiary label OKeh and started working with Curtis Mayfield that his career really took off.

Jackson's "That's What Mama Say" was a brassy answer record to another of Mayfield's songs, "Mama Didn't Lie", which **Jan Bradley and The Fascinations** had recorded a couple of years earlier. The very Impressions-styled "It's All Over" became Jackson's first hit in 1964, but big, string-laden records like "Suddenly I'm All Alone" and his covers of "Moonlight In Vermont" and "Where Have All The Flowers Gone" were more typical of his style. Jackson's best record with Mayfield was probably the glorious ballad "Welcome Home".

In 1966 Jackson started working with producer **Ted Cooper**, who kept the style that Mayfield had introduced, but made it even smoother. Jackson's Cooper-produced records "It's An Uphill Climb To The Bottom", "Tear For Tear", "A Corner In The Sun" and "Speak Her Name" were all lushly produced and featured massed woodwinds, fitting right in with the easy-listening tenor of the times. Jackson's best record of this period was 1966's "After You There Can Be Nothing" on which Cooper let him escape his button-down demeanour for a while.

Leaving OKeh in 1968, Jackson bounced around for a few years between several labels: Cotillion (1969's "Any Way That You Want Me"); USA (1971's "The Walls That Separate", an overwrought ballad with a cheesy arrangement and strangely over-miked drums); and Brunswick (1973's "It Doesn't Take Much"). He then reunited with Carl Davis at Chi-Sound in 1976, where his straight reading of Morris Albert's "Feelings" became his only entry into the R&B Top 10. An utterly bizarre cover of **Peter Frampton**'s "Baby, I Love Your Way" followed, but the hits quickly dried up again. Walter Jackson's final chart appearance was with "If I Had A Chance", just a few months before he died of a brain haemorrhage on June 20, 1983.

The Best Of Walter Jackson: Welcome Home – The OKeh Years
1996, Sony

This 15-track collection covers Walter Jackson's artistic peak, his tenure with OKeh Records between 1963 and 1967. Although these tracks are all examples of highly polished pop-soul, Curtis Mayfield and Carl Davis's production does not wallow in the gloss the way some of Jackson's later records did, and Jackson himself is at his most elegant and powerful.

Jam & Lewis

Along with **Teddy Riley**, **Jimmy Jam** (né James Harris III) and **Terry Lewis** were the most important R&B producers of the 80s. As much as anyone, they were responsible for the angular beats and sharp synth edges that defined the urban soundscape of the Reagan era.

Jam & Lewis first got together as the keyboardist and bassist of **Flyte Tyme**, a Minneapolis funk troupe, before being recruited by **Prince** to join funk group **The Time** in 1981. Within a few years, the duo were working on their own projects on the side, arranging and performing on Captain Rapp's electro classic "Bad Times (Can't Stand It") with synth player Rich Carson. Then, they produced The SOS Band's "Just Be Good To Me" and its ridiculous synth bassline. Following that song's success, Jam & Lewis accepted an offer to produce The SOS Band's next album. The only problem was that they were also supposed to be on tour with **The Time**. They tried to combine the two, flying back and forth between the recording studio and The Time's concerts until they finally missed a gig and Prince fired them from the band.

Free to concentrate on production, the duo created their first R&B #1, "Encore" for **Cheryl Lynn** in 1983. They then went on to work with **Klymaxx**, **Change**, **Alexander O'Neal**, **Patti Austin** and **Cherrelle**, before magnificently rescuing the career of **Janet Jackson** – and, ultimately, redefining R&B – with the huge 1986 album *Control*. Jam & Lewis created two more hit albums for Janet Jackson, 1989's *Rhythm Nation 1814* and 1993's *janet.*, before her brother **Michael Jackson** asked them to produce his single "Scream" in 1995.

Although their work with Janet Jackson may have been their defining moment, Jam & Lewis still found time to produce hits for many other artists during the 80s and 90s. The duo's work with **New Edition** on "If It Isn't Love" and "Can You Stand The Rain" helped to create the R&B sound of the early 90s – something they influenced all the more when they encouraged the formation of **Bell Biv DeVoe**. During this time, Jam & Lewis also managed the impossible: making both the **Human League** ("Human") and **George Michael** ("Monkey") funky.

As the 90s progressed Jam & Lewis's sound became less individual and more workmanlike, although their success didn't abate a jot. Their later hits included: Johnny Gill's "Rub You The Right Way", **Boyz II Men**'s "On Bended Knee", **Ralph Tresvant**'s "Sensitivity", **Mint Condition**'s "What Kind Of Man Would I Be?", **Mary J. Blige**'s "I Can Love You" and "Everything", and **Patti LaBelle**'s "When You Talk About Love". The new millennium found the two working with Mary J. Blige, **Mariah Carey**, Usher, Shaggy, Kelly Price and, umm, Westlife, but by this point the real innovations in R&B production were happening elsewhere.

Janet Jackson: Control
1986, A&M

Unquestionably one of the best albums of the decade, *Control* redefined R&B. Although Janet Jackson's voice wasn't exactly the best material for them to work with, Jam & Lewis used the jagged feel of synthesizers and drum machines to create tension and make her weak-as-water breathiness signify. Truly, one of the great production masterstrokes.

Jamaican Soul

Ever since Jamaican musicians, turned onto the American R&B of **Dexter Gordon**, created ska, and New Orleans musicians added a touch of Caribbean gumbo to R&B, there has been a dialogue between the grooves of Afro-America and the riddims of Jamaica.

As ska was developing into reggae in the late 60s, Jamaican artists started covering American soul records with great regularity. Often the covers were straight, note-for-note rip-offs, but with a slightly different rhythmic emphasis to give them that skanking feel. Perfect examples of this were: **Shell Alterman**'s version of **Solomon Burke**'s "Got To Get You Off My Mind"; **The Marvels**' cover of The Radiants' "Voice Your Choice" (not to mention their medley of doo-wop classics featuring The Moonglows' "Sincerely" and The Penguins' "Earth Angel"); and **The Techniques**' version of The Impressions' "You Don't Care".

Curtis Mayfield's impossibly sweet falsetto was a huge influence on **Bob Marley** and **The Congos**, and **The Temptations** were another favourite with Jamaican vocalists, particularly **Derrick Harriott** who covered "Born To Love You" and "Message From A Black Man" in 1970. Even instrumental groups like **The Meters** were influential in Jamaica. **Lloyd Charmers** covered their "Look-Ka-Py-Py", while legendary keyboardist **Jackie Mittoo** had an organ style derived from that of The Meters' Art Neville and often covered soul songs, such as "Summer Breeze", in a fairly straight fashion.

Many of the best early-70s Jamaican soul records were covers of songs that were quite downbeat, such as **Carl Bradney**'s cover of War's "Slipping Into Darkness". War were a big favourite with reggae musicians, possibly because of the Caribbean lilt in their grooves. The best reggae version of a War record was **Big Youth**'s "Streets In Africa". Meanwhile, Jamaica's love of falsetto received its best expression in **Junior Murvin**'s extraordinary cover of Curtis Mayfield's "Give Me Your Love".

While **The Harry J. All Stars**' 1969 reggae hit "The Liquidator" was a big influence on **The Staple Singers**' "I'll Take You There" and the jerky computerized riddims of Jamaican dancehall have made inroads into the US hip-hop scene in recent years, the only Jamaican soul record to have any real impact in America was **Boris Gardiner**'s 1973 version of **Booker T & The MG's**' "Melting Pot". More funky than the original, Gardiner's "Melting Pot" was an early classic in New York discotheques.

 **Various Artists: Darker Than Blue: Soul From Jamdown (1973–1980)**
2001, Blood & Fire

Blood & Fire is peerless as a reggae reissue label and their survey of Jamaican soul is no different. This expertly compiled and packaged 18-track album includes Junior Murvin's remarkable "Give Me Your Love", Alton Ellis's charming reading of The Spinners' "It's A Shame" and Tinga Stewart's resourceful remake of Timmy Thomas's "Why Can't We Live Together".

PLAYLIST

1 **GIVE ME YOUR LOVE Junior Murvin** from **Darker Than Blue: Soul from Jamdown 1973–1980**
The best Curtis Mayfield cover ever – it may even outdo the original.

2 **MESSAGE FROM A BLACK MAN Derrick Harriott** from **Uprising!: Reggae On The March**
Killer, militant version of a Temptations' track.

3 **IS IT BECAUSE I'M BLACK Ken Boothe** from **Darker Than Blue: Soul From Jamdown 1973–1980**
Boothe gives a performance as impassioned as Syl Johnson's original.

4 **AIN'T NO LOVE IN THE HEART OF THE CITY Al Brown** from **Darker Than Blue: Soul From Jamdown 1973–1980**
Again, a militant roots reggae viewpoint re-animates a rather standard blues record.

5 **STREETS IN AFRICA Big Youth** from **Natty Universal Dread 1973–1980**
Here the DJ talks over a chilling version of War's "The World Is A Ghetto".

6 **GET READY Delroy Wilson** from **Darker Than Blue: Soul from Jamdown 1973–1980**
A rather remarkable collision between skank and Motown.

Etta James

Although she is revered by soul aficionados and respected as an elder statesman on the R&B and blues revival circuit, it wouldn't be much of a stretch to suggest that **Etta James** is among the most underrated singers ever. She has modulated from sassy rock'n'roll spitfire to powerful soul mama to raucous, tongue-in-cheek performer over the course of four decades in the music biz, but she's far more than a mere survivor. While she has never had major commercial success, her recording career has been perhaps more consistent than **Aretha Franklin**'s; more dynamic than **Dionne Warwick**'s; more "soulful" than **Diana Ross**'s; less compromised than **Gladys Knight**'s.

James was born as **Jamesetta Hawkins** on January 25, 1938 in Los Angeles. Moving with her family to Oakland in 1950, she sang in her church choir before forming a secular girl group called **The Creolettes**. By 1954 she was back in LA where she was spotted at a talent show by **Johnny Otis**. Transposing her first name and ditching her surname, Otis gave Etta James her stage name and got her a contract with Modern Records. Her first single, 1955's "Roll With Me Henry", was later retitled "The Wallflower" because of the original title's risque implications. Nevertheless, the sprightly answer song to **Hank Ballard**'s "Work With Me Annie" spent four weeks at #1 on the R&B chart.

The slighter "Good Rockin' Daddy" also made the R&B Top 10, but it was to be James's last hit with Modern, despite her spending four years recording great records for the label, including "W-O-M-A-N", the bawdy retort to **Bo Diddley**'s "I'm A Man", the full-force "Tears Of Joy" and the rollicking "Tough Lover". Around this time, while touring with the Johnny Otis revue, James became addicted to heroin, a habit she wouldn't kick until the 70s.

In 1959 James signed with the Chess label and immediately had a hit with the stark "All I Could Do Was Cry". That was followed into the R&B Top 10 by the sensational, if a little old-fashioned, duet with her then-boyfriend **Harvey Fuqua**, "If I Can't Have You". However, most of James's early recordings with Chess were melodramatic, string-laden weepies like "My Dearest Darling", "At Last", "Trust In Me" and "Fool That I Am".

On 1962's "Something's Got A Hold On Me", her most churchy record that swung like something unholy, James unleashed the full fury of her squalling vocals for the first time. Her records then started to become more intense, as horns gradually replaced the massed strings and the beat became more driving. While James was absolutely fantastic on these records, they failed to strike much

of a chord with record buyers. James's drug problem was also getting the best of her around this time and, from late 1964 to 1967, her only charting single was "In The Basement", a duet with her old high-school friend **Sugar Pie DeSanto**.

In 1968 James went to the legendary Fame Studios at Muscle Shoals, Alabama and recorded the amazing *Tell Mama*. Just like Aretha Franklin, James sounded like she was born to sing Southern soul. James was simply stunning on the ballad "I'd Rather Go Blind", with producer **Rick Hall** sensibly adding the merest hint of horn and organ colouring. James was great once again on the album's hit title track, but the horns stole the show. On "Security", a fiery version of an **Otis Redding** tune, and "You Got It", James was at her absolute belting best.

James continued to issue sterling recordings on Chess in the late 60s and early 70s, including "Ms Pitiful", "Losers Weepers" and "I Found A Love", but the label's financial problems and her own heroin addiction made for a difficult decade. James returned in 1980 to record the underrated album *Changes* with **Allen Toussaint** in New Orleans, but her true rehabilitation began with a performance at the opening ceremony of the Los Angeles Olympics in 1984. She built on this resurrection with the two live *Blues In The Night* albums in 1986 and 1988, which highlighted her raunchy stage patter, and with the very solid album of contemporary Southern soul, 1988's *Seven Year Itch*.

Etta James's 1994 *Mystery Lady: Songs Of Billie Holiday* was that rarest of records: a

PLAYLIST
Etta James

1 **THE WALLFLOWER** from **Best Of Etta James**
One of the all-time great answer records.

2 **ALL I COULD DO WAS CRY** from
The Essential Etta James
The backing is a bit stiff, as is James herself, but her power is amazing.

3 **IF I CAN'T HAVE YOU** from
Best Of Etta James
Fabulous pre-Beatles rock'n'roll duet.

4 **SOMETHING'S GOT A HOLD ON ME** from
The Essential Etta James
Pure gospel fire.

5 **IN THE BASEMENT** from
The Essential Etta James
Joyous big mama proto-funk.

6 **I'D RATHER GO BLIND** from
The Essential Etta James
Stark, doom-laden, funereal – this may be the quintessential Southern soul track.

7 **TELL MAMA** from **The Essential Etta James**
Both James and the horns come on like sheer forces of nature.

8 **LOSERS WEEPERS** from
The Essential Etta James
A preaching, testifying cautionary tale in the finest Southern soul tradition.

tribute album that shed light on both singers. Since then, James has recorded several albums of torch songs and numerous live albums that prove she can still get down and dirty with the best of them, even after more than 40 years in the business. In 2003 she released an excellent album of new material, *Let's Roll*. Her first self-produced album, *Let's Roll* was more bluesy than her previous releases, while "Please No More" was in classic country soul style, but husky-voiced James was in fine form throughout.

 The Essential Etta James
1993, MCA/Chess

This double-disc, 44-track collection of Etta James's Chess years (1960–1975) represents the best of a singer who should probably be ranked right behind Aretha Franklin in the female soul hierarchy. James was a little ball of fire whose irrepressible energy could not be constrained and whose pure singing ability has very few equals.

Tell Mama
1968, Chess

When Chess sent Etta James to record at Muscle Shoals, just as Atlantic had done with Aretha Franklin the previous year, the result was this lasting artistic milestone. The distinctive Muscle Shoals' sound suited James to a T and this is an indispensable album of grit, funk and yearning blues. The 2001 remaster *Tell Mama: The Complete Muscle Shoals Sessions* includes five previously unreleased tracks.

Rick James

Long before he became the punchline to comedian Dave Chappelle's catch phrase, **Rick James** was one of the most talented funk musicians, songwriters and producers. Born **James Johnson** on February 1, 1948 in Buffalo, New York, Rick James spent the better part of a decade trying to make it – most notably as part of **The Mynah Birds**, who recorded for Motown in 1968, but never had their material released because James was AWOL from the navy at the time. James finally achieved his goal when he came up with a freaky funk formula in 1977.

James had been a staff writer and producer at Motown since the early 70s, but after hearing **Bootsy Collins**, he decided to record his own material. The immediate result was the ridiculously funky "You And I", which went straight to the top of the R&B chart and even managed to reach #13 on the pop chart at the height of the disco era. The equally nasty "Mary Jane" followed, and established James as one of funk's leading lights.

The smoking "Bustin' Out" continued James's hot streak, but he almost derailed his career completely with the 1980 ballad album *Garden Of Love*. Returning to his previous in-your-face funk formula, James hit his peak the following year with *Street Songs*. The best-selling album's "Super Freak" was preposterous, sexist and stupid, but utterly irresistible, while "Give It To Me Baby" bumped with macho brio. "Ghetto Life", "Mr Policeman" and "Below The Funk (Pass The J)", on the other hand, offered a more social-realist view of urban life.

James's party hardy songs and in-your-face attitude helped create a less subtle, less acid-fried funk than that pioneered by **Parliament-Funkadelic**. However, he was more than just hot basslines, leather trousers and carefree groupie sex. He produced albums for his then-girlfriend Teena Marie, his backing singers **The Mary Jane Girls** (who had a big hit with the magnificent "All Night Long") and even a fairly traditional record for **The Temptations**. James also proved his soul chops with "Ebony Eyes", a 1983 collaboration with **Smokey Robinson**. The cheapness of the keyboard sound let it down, but the dream-like ballad with its strong echoes of classic doo-wop ballads of yore was strangely affecting.

The 1982 hit "Cold Blooded" found James stripping down his music with the aid of a synthesizer. It still moved, though, and spent six weeks at #1 on the R&B chart. The records "17" and "Sweet And Sexy Thing" continued his trashy image, but his production of actor **Eddie Murphy**'s "My Girl Likes To Party All The Time" was far less appealing. James's last big hit was 1988's "Loosey's Rap", recorded with rapper **Roxanne Shanté** before his life started to spiral out of control. Drugs and legal problems, resulting from his desire to live up to his wild funk rocker image, severely disrupted his career during the 90s. Then, just as he was becoming a minor pop culture icon again thanks to Dave Chappelle's comedy routine, Rick James died of a heart attack on August 6, 2004.

The Ultimate Collection
1997, Motown

Streamlining the sound and hedonism of Parliament-Funkadelic, Rick James came up with a new brand of funk that laid the groundwork for the rise of pop-funk icon Prince. James's music was also pretty fabulous in its own right as this 13-track anthology of his prime hits – including a large number of tracks from his finest studio album *Street Songs* – shows.

The J.B.'s

The J.B.'s may "merely" have been James Brown's backing band, but the core of the group – drummer **John "Jabo" Starks**, horn players **Maceo Parker, Fred Wesley** and **St Clair. Pinckney**, guitarists **Jimmy Nolen** and **Hearlon "Cheese" Martin** and organist **Bobby Byrd** – were one of the greatest ever funk ensembles. On their own records, The J.B.'s concocted grooves that were every bit as vital as James Brown's. As emcee Danny Ray used to say when introducing them, "Ladies and gentlemen, there are seven acknowledged wonders of the world. You are about to witness the eighth."

James Brown was notorious for being a vicious taskmaster, but given the often hodge-podge nature of his band, he had to be. With drummers subbing for sick bassists, trumpet players saying they were sax players in order to land gigs and everyone having to record whenever and wherever it felt right and sometimes with less than a week to rehearse before going out on the road, the "Godfather of Soul" had to instil his troops with a sense of discipline and fear worthy of the Cosa Nostra. With Brown laying down the law and trombonist Fred Wesley arranging various riffs into vamps, 1972's *Food For Thought*, The J.B.'s' first album under their own name (but released on Brown's own subsidiary label, People), was easily as good as, if not better than, any of Brown's own funk-era albums.

Comprised of three different line-ups (one including such fusion luminaries as **Randy Brecker, Joe Farrell** and **Bob Cranshaw**) and recorded at six different sessions, *Food For Thought* made it on pure kinetics alone. "The Grunt", recorded when **Bootsy Collins**, his brother **Phelps "Catfish" Collins** and drummer **Frank Waddy** were still in the fold, was probably the rawest track James Brown had been associated with since "Cold Sweat". "The Grunt" sounded like it had been recorded in the studio bathroom, and it featured what may have been Bootsy's most swinging bassline alongside great maracas and horns that were pure Afro-beat call-and-response, while the boss's screams were replaced by a squealing sax.

Food For Thought was swiftly followed by 1973's *Doing It To Death*. Nearly as good as their debut, *Doing It To Death* featured two twelve-minute-plus jams – the title track (which had Brown rapping with the band) and "More Peas" (which had Cheese Martin and Jimmy Nolen's most atonal guitars). Brown's bizarre association with Richard Nixon reared its ugly head on the matter-of-fact "You Can Have Watergate, Just Gimme Some Bucks And I'll Be Straight", but their next album, credited to Fred Wesley & The J.B.'s, showed a better choice of political allies. *Damn Right I Am Somebody*'s theme was inspired by one of Jesse Jackson's catch phrases, while the music was undoubtedly inspired by **Herbie Hancock**. Brown's first

Rare/Deep Funk

Record collectors are a strange lot. Stories abound of people who have facsimile collections at different locations in case something should happen to their precious booty, or there's the guy in New York who goes into the Tower Records sale annexe every two hours to check if they've put out anything new. The rare doo-wop, garage rock, Northern soul, rare groove and "Killed By Death" punk scenes all have their cabals of celebrity record collectors and small, hopelessly devoted audiences. What sets apart the rare funk scene, however, is that many of its celebrity collectors are not only DJs and curators, but producers as well.

Hip-hop is largely built on the back of obscure (and not so obscure) funk and soul records. Legendary hip-hop producers and artists like **Afrika Bambaataa**, **Grandmaster Flash**, Pete Rock, Biz Markie, Q-Tip, DJ Shadow and Kenny "Dope" Gonzales are all connoisseurs of funk arcana and they use many of their discoveries in their own work. Hip-hop and the recent revivals of Northern soul and disco have created a whole new generation of soul and funk fans who passionately collect only the most outré of records. While this has led to the rediscovery of some scandalously overlooked music, it has also led, concomitant with the rise of Internet auction site eBay, to the emergence of the record collector with little knowledge of the mainstream canon. Whether or not this is a good thing for the development and longevity of the music remains to be seen.

For years the lifeblood of the scene were the dodgy rare funk bootlegs sourced by lunatic collectors willing to shimmy up drain pipes to get into boarded-up record warehouses in Harlem to rescue impossibly obscure records from the hungry mouths of rabid rats. This began to change when collectors like **Keb Darge** and **Gerald The Jazzman** started to release compilations on labels that tried to pay royalties to the original artists. Working under the umbrella of **Peanut Butter Wolf**'s Stones Throw label, **Eothen "Egon" Alapatt** has continued to up the ante with a series of superb compilations and reissues on the Now Again and SoulCal imprints.

⊙ **Various Artists: Keb Darge's Legendary Deep Funk Vol. 1**
1997, Barely Breaking Even

One of the first legit rare funk compilations and still one of the best, this begins with the ferocious instrumental "Zambezi" by The Fun Company. With its wailing Hammond clarion call and bubbling, strutting bassline, "Zambezi" is a blistering, hard funk tune that neatly sums up the kind of rare funk championed by DJ Keb Darge.

⊙ **Various Artists: The Funky 16 Corners**
2001, Stones Throw

Perhaps the best of all the rare funk collections, this 22-track album features great music from the likes of Bad Medicine, The Highlighters Band, Kashmere Stage Band and Carleen & The Groovers. It also includes detailed liner notes, group photos and absurdly meticulous scholarship from Egon Alapatt.

▣ PLAYLIST

1 DAP WALK Ernie & The Top Notes from **Keb Darge's Legendary Deep Funk Volume 1**
It may be a rip-off of Archie Bell & The Drells, but it's got so much vim and vigour that it's hard to be a spoilsport.

2 ZAMBEZI The Fun Company from **Keb Darge's Legendary Deep Funk Volume 1**
Who needs coffee when you've got this percolating jam?

3 TRESPASSER Bad Medicine from **The Funky 16 Corners**
Space-age bayou funk.

4 KASHMERE Kashmere Stage Band from **The Funky 16 Corners**
Embarrassingly good big-band funk from a bunch of high-school kids.

5 BUMPIN' BUS STOP The Playboys from **Funk Spectrum II**
Step up and get in line.

6 BABY DON'T CRY Third Guitar from **Funk Spectrum II**
Hands down the best breakdown ever.

7 HUNG UP Salt from **Saturday Night Fish Fry**
Messy, stank funk gumbo from New Orleans.

8 I TURN YOU ON Latin Breed from **Texas Funk**
What "96 Tears" by ? & The Mysterians might sound like as a funk record.

9 PSYCHO The Fabulous Mark III from **Texas Funk**
Wild freak-out funk straight out of the acid trip scene of an early Jack Nicholson movie.

10 GIVE EVERYBODY SOME Mickey & The Soul Generation from **Texas Funk**
Wah-wah and organ madness from the Lone Star state.

excursion into the world of synthesizers produced the landmark tracks "Same Beat" and "Blow Your Head", which had Moog riffs, played by the "Godfather of Soul" himself, that opened up street funk to the far less earthy regions being explored by jazz-funk fusion band **The Headhunters**.

The title track of 1974's *Breakin' Bread*, credited to Fred & The New J.B.'s, had Wesley rapping about his mother making cakes, while 1975's *Hustle With Speed* found the group trying to accommodate disco on "(It's Not The Express) It's The J.B.'s' Monaurail". The J.B.'s' final single was the following year's "Everybody Wanna Get Funky One More Time", but by this time Wesley and Parker had left the group to join P-Funk and there were few of the original band members left. Polydor pulled the plug on Brown's People imprint soon after the record was released, effectively putting an end to The J.B.'s' recording career.

○ **Funky Good Time: The Anthology**
  1983, PolyGram

When James Brown's loyal sidemen stepped out of the Godfather's shadow in the early 70s, they were given the chance to really shine. Across two discs and 30 tracks there are only a couple of duds – testament to The J.B.'s' remarkable ability to flesh out even Brown's most minimal sketches.

The Jive Five

The Jive Five were one of the few vocal groups to make the transition from doo-wop to soul. Their underrated lead singer, **Eugene Pitt**, had performed in several earlier groups, including The Top Notes, The Genies and The Akrons, before he formed The Jive Five with **Norman Johnson, Jerome Hanna, Thurmon "Billy" Prophet** and **Richard Harris** in Brooklyn in 1959.

Signing to Les Cahan's Beltone label, the group's 1961 debut single was the all-time doo-wop classic "My True Story". The song spent three weeks at the top of the R&B chart, and Pitt's soaring falsetto hook on the chorus was one of the most scintillating moments in early rock'n'roll. Pitt was less convincing, however, on the next year's "Hully Gully Callin' Time", a dance craze disc that included instructions like "Do The Frank Sinatra!/Put your hands in your pock-

et". The Jive Five returned to the pure doo-wop transcendence of their earlier hit on the singles "What Time Is It" and "These Golden Rings", which both showcased the impressive interplay between Pitt and bass singer Johnson. Pitt's falsetto was at its most piercing on 1963's "Rain", which was let down by an awkward arrangement. However, by that time, doo-wop was becoming increasingly unfashionable, and "Rain" was the group's last record for Beltone.

Pitt and Johnson replaced the rest of the group with three new members, **Webster Harris** (Richard's brother), **Casey Spencer** and **Beatrice Best**, and signed the new Jive Five to United Artists in 1964. The group moved into soul territory with their first singles for the label, "United" and "I'm A Happy Man", and unintentionally pitched their next release, "A Bench In The Park" – on which Pitt was superb – at the exact middle ground between the Northern soul and beach music scenes.

Moving to Musicor in 1968, The Jive Five had a minor hit with the loping Chicago soul-style single "Sugar (Don't Take Away My Candy)", but they seemed to be losing their way, drifting from style to style looking for a hit. In 1970 they renamed themselves **The Jyve Fyve** and had a small hit with "I Want You To Be My Baby". The group then briefly appeared as **Ebony, Ivory and Jade** on a couple of singles for Columbia that went nowhere, before returning to their original name. The Jive Five recorded several retro doo-wop albums for various labels throughout the 80s and 90s, and remain a popular draw on the oldies circuit.

○ **Our True Story**
  1983, Ace

This collection of their Beltone material is still the best Jive Five album, even though it excludes "Rain" and lacks the soul records they released on United Artists and Musicor. Doo-wop was rapidly going out of fashion when these records were originally recorded, but Eugene Pitt's gorgeous tenor remains irresistible.

Jodeci

The roughnecks to **Boyz II Men**'s clean-cut preppies, **Jodeci** dominated the R&B charts in the 90s with their histrionic combination of **Teddy Pendergrass** and The Gap

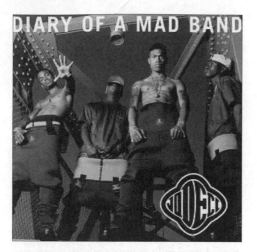

DIARY OF A MAD BAND

Band's **Charlie Wilson**. Despite their taste for concupiscence and their less than savoury off-stage reputation, **Joel "Jo-Jo" Hailey, Cedric "K-Ci" Hailey, Donald "DeVante Swing" DeGrate** and **Dalvin DeGrate** started their careers singing gospel in Charlotte, North Carolina. The two sets of brothers got together in 1990 and headed straight to New York to shop their demo tape.

After a string of rejections, Jodeci were signed by Uptown Records in 1991. While that same year's *Forever My Lady* contained plenty of testosterone-fuelled New Jack Swing, it was the love jams "Forever My Lady", "Stay" and "Come & Talk To Me" that took urban radio by storm, with their high-gloss retro-modernism and whining entreaties to the opposite sex.

By the release of *Diary Of A Mad Band* in 1993, the adulation had gone to their heads, and they became more interested in taking off their shirts and flexing their muscles than trying to seduce anyone. Jodeci's moaning ballad style was displayed on the tracks "Cry For You" and "What About Us", but mostly the album featured terrible rapping and overheated sex fantasies that would be laughed out of most high-school boys' locker rooms. After its release, both K-Ci and DeVante Swing pleaded guilty to sexual assault charges.

Following a too-slick version of Stevie Wonder's "Lately", Jodeci released *The Show, The After Party, The Hotel* in 1995, another dose of adolescent wet dreams, ridiculous vocal flourishes and keening melisma. The least offensive track on the album was perhaps "Freek 'N You", but it

still had its share of baroqueness – and they should leave the vocoder to Roger Troutman.

K-Ci and Jo-Jo joined **2Pac** for the double-platinum soft-porn epic "How Do U Want It" in 1996 and later had huge hits as a duo with the Bone-Thugs-N-Harmony-meets-Babyface "All My Life" and "Tell Me It's Real". DeVante Swing and Dalvin, meanwhile, started their own production company, and introduced the world to **Missy Elliott** and super-producer **Timbaland**. Although they haven't officially split up, the two sets of brothers haven't recorded together since 1995.

Forever My Lady
1991, Uptown

If you grew up listening to soul records made before 1986 or so, Jodeci's vocal style takes some getting used to. However, this album of new-wave street-corner harmonizing highlights the brothers' vocal chops – if only they could learn how to control them – before their egos took over.

Syl Johnson

Syl Johnson was born Sylvester Thompson on July 1, 1936, into a blues family in Holly Springs, Mississippi. His eldest brother, **Mac Thompson**, played bass for **Magic Sam**, while middle brother **Jimmy Johnson** has had a long career recording albums for Delmark and Alligator. The strong blues current running through Syl Johnson's music gives his vocals a unique, almost bittersweet quality.

Moving to Chicago with his family in the 40s, he was playing guitar and harmonica with Elmore James, **Jimmy Reed**, Billy Boy Arnold, Shakey Jake and **Junior Wells** by the mid-50s. He changed his name from Thompson to Johnson when he signed to Federal in 1959 and released "Teardrops". After touring with **Howlin' Wolf** and releasing several more Federal singles that went nowhere, Johnson started to record in a soul style. His local hit "Straight Love, No Chaser", released in Chicago on Zachron in 1966, got him signed to the Twinight label.

His first record for the label was the raw "Come On And Sock It To Me". That first hit was little more than a messy **James Brown** rip-off that never worked up the funk, but the incredible "Different Strokes", released later that year and featuring a tremendous intro, was one of the funkiest ever soul tunes. "I Can Take Care Of Business" was recorded in Memphis with producer **Willie Mitchell** in 1968, who re-Southernized Johnson's gritty vocal style. "Is It Because I'm Black?" gave Johnson his second-biggest hit in 1969, primarily because of his impassioned performance rather than the expressly political content, which was echoed in "Concrete Reservation" the next year.

Johnson was again in scintillating form on "One Way Ticket To Nowhere", though Tyrone Davis's version of the song became the big hit. Johnson's remake of The Temptations' "Get Ready", however, was nearly as low-down and funky as "Different Strokes". Around this time he also started producing records for Twinight, including **The Notations**' "I'm Still Here". His last record for the label, "Annie Got Hot Pants Power", may not have been his finest moment, but it grooved nicely nonetheless.

When Twinight went bust in 1971, Johnson joined Willie Mitchell's Hi label. Although the two had made some great records together at Twinight, Johnson just didn't fit easily with the signature Hi sound. On records such as "We Did It", he sounded as though he was struggling to keep up and, although that gave the tracks a unique quality, it didn't always work. Johnson was at his best either on uptempo material, such as "Back For A Taste Of Your Love" and the Beach Music classic "I Want To Take You Home (To See Mama)", or on slow, moody songs such as 1973's "Wind, Blow Her Back My Way". A little of Mitchell's production magic that worked so well for Al Green and Ann Peebles rubbed off on Johnson's original version of "Take Me To The River", a bluesier, more straightforward take than Green's later cover.

While at Hi, Johnson produced records for Garland Green ("Plain And Simple Girl") and The Drifters, and he also produced some of Otis Clay's biggest hits on his own Shama label in the late 70s. After leaving Hi in 1980, Johnson returned to his blues roots with that year's *Brings Out The Blues In Me* and 1982's *Ms. Fine Brown Frame*. The latter was a fusion of blues and disco fusion inspired by **The Rolling Stones**' "Miss You" and featuring harmonica player **James Cotton**. Although these were Johnson's last albums of any stature, he has continued to release several fine blues albums throughout

the 90s and into the 00s, including his 1994 comeback album *Back In The Game*, a reunion with members of the Hi Rhythm Section, *Bridge To A Legacy* (1998), and *Two Johnsons Are Better Than One*, a 2001 album recorded with his brother Jimmy Johnson.

Twilight & Twinight Masters Collection
1996, Collectables

Despite lacking the silly, but rather funky, "Annie Got Hot Pants Power", this is a near-perfect overview of the many fine recordings that made Syl Johnson's name. Far grittier and greasier than his Hi records, Johnson's Twinight material represents the dark underbelly of the breezy Windy City sound exemplified by Curtis Mayfield.

Glenn Jones

Born in Jacksonville, Florida, in 1961, **Glenn Jones** could have been one of the great soul singers of the 80s. He was blessed with a phenomenal range and a gorgeous falsetto, but he used these gifts to sound like blue-eyed soul singer **Michael McDonald**. Despite this attempt to seemingly cross over into the commercial mainstream, none of his singles ever charted higher than #66 on the pop charts.

Jones began his career singing gospel as a child with a group called Bivens Special. Then, after moving with his family to Philadelphia, he formed a group called **The Modulations**, who recorded three albums under the auspices of **Reverend James Cleveland** in the mid- to late 70s. In 1980 Jones hooked up with **Norman Connors**, who convinced him to try his hand at secular music. After touring with Connors and singing on two of his albums – *Take It To The Limit* and *Mr. C.* – Jones signed a solo deal with RCA. His first single, "I Am Somebody", was inspired by a famous speech by Civil Rights activist **Jesse Jackson**. Jones's vocals embodied the contemporary smooth gospel style, but it was the slithery keyboard riffs and great synth bassline that made the track.

The 1984 album *Finesse*, produced by **Leon Sylvers**, spawned Jones's first big hit, the syrupy ballad "Show Me", which went to #3 on the R&B chart. Jones was responsible for even more MOR schlock over the next few years, including the 1985 duet with Dionne Warwick, "Finder Of Lost Loves" (the theme song to the wretched TV show of the same name), the trite "Everlasting Love" and "Together", an overblown duet with **Genobia Jeter**.

Leaving RCA for Jive Records in 1987, Jones immediately had a smash hit with "We've Only Just Begun (The Romance Is Not Over)", a big-haired 80s ballad that was barely rescued by his vocal flights of fancy at the end. "Stay" followed in a similar style in 1990, before Jones moved to Atlantic and released 1992's *Here I Go Again*. The record was more whiny and melismatic than his previous albums, but he still enjoyed two big R&B hits with the title track and "I've Been Searchin' (Nobody Like You)". *Here I Am* followed two years later, but by that time his audience had moved on.

It's Time, released on the independent SAR label in 1998, became something of an underground hit and proved its staying power when "Baby Come Home" went to #5 on the R&B chart two years later. Jones has since continued to release new material in the new millennium, including 2002's *Feels Good*, another independently released album of slow jams and quiet storm tracks.

⊙ **Giving Myself To You: The Greatest Hits Of Glenn Jones**
1998, Razor & Tie

This 14-track best-of album includes Glenn Jones's big hits, from "I Am Somebody" to "I've Been Searchin' (Nobody Like You)". He looks an awful lot like Billy Ocean on the cover, but his impressive, gospel-honed pipes elevate this collection above the run-of-the-mill post-Luther Vandross balladry of his day.

Linda Jones

No one, not even **Lorraine Ellison** or **Jodeci**, has ever scaled the histrionic heights attained by **Linda Jones**. Although **Gladys Knight**, **Patti LaBelle** and **Aretha Franklin** all ranked her among their favourite singers, Jones is an acquired taste. Her utter lack of restraint meant that she was probably the first singer to turn gospel melisma into a show of athletic prowess, thus paving the way for contemporary blowhards like **Mariah Carey**.

Born on January 14, 1944, Linda Jones started singing at age 6 with her family's gospel group, **The Jones Singers**. She then went secular in 1963, under the name **Linda Lane**,

with a version of "Lonely Teardrops" on the Cub label. "Take This Boy Out Of The Country" and "You Hit Me Like TNT" followed over the next few years, but without much success.

Signing with Warner Bros' Loma subsidiary in 1967, she was paired with producer **George Kerr**, whose baroque downtown soul style allowed her to fully indulge her penchant for ornamentation. Their first record together, "Hypnotized", was not as volcanic as she could be – Jones mostly kept her emotions in check until the end when she laid the groundwork for the New Jack Swing vocal style and everything that came after – and it became her biggest hit. While Jones was blessed with pipes to rival Aretha's, her melodramatic instincts dragged down potentially great records like "My Heart Needs A Break", a surging New York soul production on which she sang about the perils of loving a younger man, and "It Won't Take Much (To Bring Me Back)", a desperation ballad that predated the quiet storm revolution of the 70s with both her over-the-top melisma and wailing and the string and horn arrangement.

In 1969 Jones moved to Neptune, where she recorded the classic Philly ballad "That's When I'll Stop Loving You" and the rather more over-the-top "Ooh Baby You Move Me". Moving again in 1971, this time to Turbo, she recorded the tortured and wracked "Stay With Me Forever" and "Your Precious Love". Tragically, Linda Jones died at the age of just 28, on March 14, 1972, a couple of days after she collapsed due to diabetes complications after a show at the Apollo Theatre.

⊙ **Hypnotized: 20 Golden Classics**
1994, Collectables

Hypnotized is the best available Linda Jones compilation, despite lacking both "My Heart Needs A Break" and "That's When I'll Stop Loving You". There is no doubt that her voice was incredible, but unless you think Liberace was too tasteful, her theatricality will probably prove a bit hard to take over the course of twenty tracks.

Quincy Jones

Michael Jackson once called him "the king of all music" and he has worked with everyone from Ray Charles to Frank

Quincy Jones in a shirt that was even funny back then…

Sinatra, from Aretha Franklin to Lesley Gore, from Sarah Vaughan to Billy Eckstine, from Count Basie to Miles Davis. As a producer, arranger, film composer and media executive, **Quincy Jones** was the master of the mainstream. As an artist in his own right, he has been somewhat less successful, but when you were responsible for the second best-selling album of all time, who cares?

Born **Quincy Delight Jones, Jr.** in Chicago on March 14, 1933, Jones was raised in Seattle. He began his music career in the late 40s, playing trumpet alongside Ray Charles. After completing a scholarship at the Berklee School of Music, Jones moved to New York and worked as an arranger for **Count Basie**, Cannonball Adderley, **Dinah Washington** and Tommy Dorsey. Then in 1953 he joined Lionel Hampton's big band as a trumpeter. A few years later, he recorded his first album, 1957's *This Is How I Feel About Jazz*, and joining **Dizzy Gillespie**'s all-star group for a European tour. When the tour ended, Jones decided to stay in Paris to study composition with the legendary **Nadia Boulanger**, who had also taught the likes of Stravinsky. During his time in Paris, Jones also worked as a producer and arranger for the Barclay label.

Upon returning to the US in 1961, **Quincy Jones** was named vice-president of A&R at Mercury, becoming the first African-American upper-level executive at a major record label. While continuing to record his own jazz albums, including *I Dig Dancers* (1961) and *Bossa Nova* (1962), which featured the popular "Soul Bossa Nova" that was famously sampled by The Dream Warriors, Jones ventured into pop music production. He most famously produced a series of pop hits for teen sensation **Lesley Gore**, such as "It's My Party" and "You Don't Own Me", in 1963. Around this time, Jones was also moonlighting as an arranger for his childhood friend Ray Charles.

In 1963 Jones composed the score to Sidney Lumet's movie *The Pawnbroker*, the first of some 30 film scores he has written during his career. He excelled at the kind of funky soundtracks that were so popular in the late 60s and early 70s. Tracks such as "It's Caper Time" from 1968's *The Italian Job* – a sort of Area Code 615's "Stone Fox Chase" meets the *Sanford And Son* theme (which he also wrote) – and his amazing theme for the 1971 movie *Ironside*, with its siren-like synth, highlighted his Oliver Nelson-style compositional skills.

Jones left Mercury in 1968 to try to resuscitate his solo career. The following year he released *Walking In Space*, a strange mixture of big band and fusion that really came together on the album's title track. In addition to producing and arranging for Aretha Franklin and **Paul Simon**, Jones put together a series of very commercial albums featuring all-star line-ups. *Body Heat* from 1974 was a smarmy, somewhat sleazy jazz-funk album featuring Herbie Hancock, Wah-Wah Watson, **Minnie Riperton**, Bob James, Billy Preston and Bernard Purdie, while 1976's *Mellow Madness* featured his latest discovery, the **Brothers Johnson**, getting mildly funky on the tracks "Just A Little Taste Of Me" and "Tryin' To

Find Out 'Bout You". The 1979 album *Sounds...And Stuff Like That!* included a track called "Stuff Like That", which featured **Ashford & Simpson** and **Chaka Khan** and became Jones' first R&B #1 under his own name. "Ai No Corrida" from 1981's *The Dude* began like an Italian disco anthem before becoming a stale Chic rip-off with an Al DiMeola arrangement and an awful chorus. However, it still reached the R&B Top 10.

While creating these sweeping all-star commercial albums, Jones also found the time to work with Michael Jackson on his 1979 smash *Off The Wall*. The pair then reunited in 1982 and 1987 to create *Thriller* and *Bad*, two of the biggest-selling records in history. Jones also founded his own record label, Qwest, a subsidiary of Warner Bros, in 1980, produced the film *The Color Purple* in 1985 and **Will Smith**'s TV series *The Fresh Prince Of Bel-Air*, and established Vibe magazine in 1990.

Jones's most successful album released under his own name was 1990's *Back On The Block*. Featuring three R&B #1 hits – "I'll Be Good To You", "The Secret Garden (Sweet Seduction Suite)" and "Tomorrow (A Better You, Better Me)" – *Back On The Block* saw Jones calling in favours from his biggest associates: Ray Charles, Miles Davis, **Barry White**, Sarah Vaughan, Ella Fitzgerald, Dizzy Gillespie, **James Ingram**, Chaka Khan, **Al B. Sure!** and **Tevin Campbell**. Unfortunately, Jones's 1994 album, *Q's Jook Joint*, failed to build on that success. *Q's Jook Joint* was an ill-conceived celebration of the African-American tradition that was, at the same time, too slick and too much of a mess.

For much of the ensuing time, Jones has busied himself with pet projects, such as 2000's *Basie And Beyond*, on which he teamed up with **Sammy Nestico** to play some vintage Count Basie charts. Despite the disappointments and mediocrity of much of his solo career, Quincy Jones's influence and accomplishments as a producer, arranger and film composer cannot be underrated. He remains one of the musical establishment's quintessential figures.

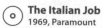

The Italian Job
1969, Paramount

Finally issued on CD in 2000, *The Italian Job* soundtrack may be Jones's finest record. Once you get passed the Matt Monroe number that starts the album, you get vintage Jones' quasi-bossa on "On Days Like These", a harpsichord remake of "Greensleeves", the very groovy "Something's Cookin'" and the almighty "It's Caper Time".

Ultimate Collection
2002, Hip-O

For a soul fan, Quincy Jones's best records are his film soundtracks. Unfortunately, a collection of that material has yet to be released and, until it is, this middling compilation album (which sadly includes none of his soundtrack material) will have to do. This collection gathers together his biggest and most commercial hits from 1974 to 1999, including his groovy fusion funk tracks from the mid-70s and his megalomaniacal all-star recordings of the 90s.

Louis Jordan

These days he may be remembered principally for providing the music for *Five Guys Named Moe*, but there was a time when **Louis Jordan** was so big that he duetted with **Bing Crosby**. Along with **Nat "King" Cole**, Louis Jordan was one of America's first crossover stars – he even had a #1 pop hit with "G.I. Jive" in 1944 – and his easy-swinging hepcat jive numbers made the mainstream safe for the coming of rock'n'roll. Even more significantly, **Louis Jordan and His Tympany Five** were the most important R&B group of the 40s, not to mention the most successful R&B group of all time, holding a never-to-be-broken record of 113 weeks at the top of *Billboard*'s "race chart".

Jordan was born in 1908 in a small town in Arkansas. His horn-playing father encouraged him to play the clarinet, and by the early 1920s he was touring with the legendary **Rabbit Foot Minstrels**. By the time Jordan's family moved to Philadelphia in 1930, he had switched to alto sax and joined various jazz bands, culminating in a stint with **Chick Webb**'s Savoy Ballroom Orchestra in 1936. After two years of playing second fiddle to **Ella Fitzgerald**, Jordan started his own group and landed a residency at Harlem's Elk's Rendezvous Lounge. **The Elk's Rendezvous Band** was a five-piece "jump" combo that played hot swing solos on top of shuffling boogie-woogie rhythms and, following their first 1938 recordings for Decca, this style was to dominate R&B for the next decade.

Renamed The Tympany Five in 1939, the band had their first hits in 1941 with "I'm Going To Move To The Outskirts Of Town" and "Knock Me A Kiss". Over the next nine years, Jordan reached the R&B charts a remarkable 57 times, and between 1946 and 1947 he was at #1 for a staggering 75 weeks, with hits including "Choo Choo Ch' Boogie", "Ain't That Just Like A Woman" and "Ain't Nobody Here But Us Chickens". Although the jump style varied from region to region, Jordan's singing style, like that of Nat "King" Cole, appealed throughout the US. Jordan also exuded a suave cosmopolitanism and, despite his comedic songs, a distance that was closer to classic pop than the blues.

Like the calypso for which he had an affinity, however, Jordan's humour and detached air masked lyrics that were subtle protests against racism and injustice. "Beans And Corn Bread" was a Leiber and Stoller-esque quasi-novelty song about racial conflict, while "Ration Blues" tackled poverty on the homefront during World War I. Jordan's last big hit, "Saturday Night Fish Fry", was a diatribe against racist cops camouflaged as a party tune.

Jordan's greatest gift, however, was his sense of swing. All of Jordan's Decca material grooves and parties as hard today as it did in the 40s. As Jordan himself would have said, if songs like "Caldonia", "Open The Door, Richard!" and "Ain't That Just Like A Woman" don't make you smile, then "Jack, You're Dead!". Jordan and the Tympany Five were far more than mere commercial hacks, and their blend of swing, humour and social commentary influenced nearly all who followed in their wake. Jordan was James Brown's favourite artist, while Ray Charles recorded some of his songs and signed him to his Tangerine label in the 60s. **Carl**

THE BEST OF LOUIS JORDAN

MCD04079

Hogan's guitar solo that introduces "Ain't That Just Like a Woman" was the influence for **Chuck Berry**'s "Johnny B. Goode", while Jordan's squeals when he calls his lover girl in "Caldonia" set the stage for **Little Richard**. Even artists who could barely walk when Jordan was in his heyday found elements to borrow: you can definitely hear **Junior Walker** coming down the road in Jordan's sax solo on "Early In The Mornin'".

Jordan was such a huge star that he declared his candidacy for the presidency on 1952's "Jordan For President" in 1952. Unfortunately, that came at the precise moment that his singles stopped selling, as rock'n'roll supplanted jump blues as the music of the day. In 1956, with **Quincy Jones** arranging, he recorded a blazing rock'n'roll album with the cream of New York's session musicians, including guitarist **Mickey Baker** and saxophonist **Sam "The Man" Taylor**, but the record-buying public thought he was just too old to rock'n'roll. Jordan recorded sporadically over the next twenty years and played plenty of lounge gigs, before dying of a heart attack on February 4, 1975 and leaving a legacy of some of the most joyous, slyest music ever recorded.

The Best Of Louis Jordan
1975, MCA

Although three decades have gone by since its release, this is still the best single-volume Louis Jordan collection. Holding most of his big hits, it's as delightful and swinging as any other album that exists today. Serious collectors will want to save up and get Bear Family's staggering 10-CD collection, *Let The Good Times Roll: The Complete Decca Recordings*.

Margie Joseph

Although she achieved fourteen R&B chart hits and occasionally flirted with pop success, **Margie Joseph** – like too many other female soul singers – was never able to establish a persona that stuck with the record-buying public. Born in 1950 on the Gulf Coast in Pascagoula, Mississippi, she was raised in New Orleans, where she has spent most of her life. Joseph was discovered by the DJ (and her future husband) **Larry McKinley** at Dillard University and he took her to Muscle Shoals in 1967. There she recorded "Why Does A Man Have To Lie",

which was eventually released by OKeh in 1968. The follow-up, "Matter Of Life Or Death", was released on the label later that same year.

Joseph then signed to Stax/Volt and released a couple of singles, "One More Chance" and "What You Gonna Do", produced by home-town semi-legend **Willie Tee**. She had her first hit with "Your Sweet Loving", produced by **Fred Briggs**, but she really made her name with a startling, slowed-down, countrified version of **The Supremes**' "Stop In The Name Of Love". Another fine, half-speed Supremes' cover, "My World Is Empty Without You", appeared on her 1972 album *Phase II*, but it was never released as a single.

Moving to Atlantic in 1972, Joseph worked with **Arif Mardin** on the self-titled album *Margie Joseph*. While spawning a modest R&B hit with a version of "Let's Stay Together", the album tried too hard to make Joseph into another **Aretha Franklin**, although the funky track "I Been Down" showed that she excelled at the sexier, slinkier New Orleans style. Her 1974 release *Sweet Surrender* provided her biggest hit, a cover of **Paul McCartney & Wings**' "My Love". For several years Joseph drifted between producers (Johnny Bristol, **Lamont Dozier**, Dexter Wansel) and labels (Cotillion, Atlantic, WMOT), occasionally producing minor R&B hits, such as "Hear The Words, Feel The Feeling" and her collaboration with **Blue Magic**, "What's Come Over Me".

After a few years in the wilderness, Joseph rebounded in 1982, proving her talent for dancefloor records with "Knockout", a #12 R&B hit released on the small HCRC label out of Houston. She moved back to the Atlantic family in 1984 for a rather dull record with **Narada Michael Walden**, *Ready For The Night*. Her last record of new material was the underrated *Stay*, released by Ichiban in 1988, and little has been heard of her since.

The Atlantic Sessions: The Best Of Margie Joseph
1994, Ichiban

It may not have either of her Supremes' covers or the bumping "I Been Down", but this 11-track collection of her R&B hits proves that Joseph was an underrated singer with plenty of skills and personality. She just never found a producer who knew how to get the most out of her.

KC & The Sunshine Band

Until *Saturday Night Fever* made **The Bee-Gees** superstars, **KC & The Sunshine Band** were the undisputed kings of disco. Their bouncy, bubble-headed enthusiasm and their slightly square approach to black slang (their records somehow recalled the atmosphere of a suburban swingers' party) were some of the things that gave disco such a bad name. While KC's (**Harry Wayne Casey**) background in the Pentecostal church may have had something to do with the group's singles-bar style straightness, it also gave him some honest-to-goodness vocal chops. It was clear that the band were not just Johnny-come-latelys trying to capitalize on a new trend. They loved this music and their enthusiasm, however ungainly, was infectious.

In 1973 Harry Wayne "KC" Casey (vocals, keyboards) and **Richard Finch** (bass) worked together at the warehouse of **Henry Stone**'s Tone Distribution company in a run-down Miami suburb. Casey heard the Bahamian Carnival music, junkanoo – similar to the music made by New Orleans' Mardi Gras Indians with its cow bell percussion, whistles and goat-skin goombay drums – and came up with the idea of integrating it with more straightforward R&B rhythms.

Henry Stone allowed them to use the studio above the warehouse at night and, along with members of the multiracial studio band (guitarist **Jerome Smith**, conguero **Fermin Coytisolo**, drummer **Robert Johnson** and horn players Ronnie Smith, James Weaver, Denvil Liptrot and Charles Williams), Casey and Finch recorded "Blow Your Whistle" in 1973 as KC & The Sunshine Junkanoo Band. "Blow Your Whistle" was a slightly strange mixture of drums and an out-of-date soul bassline with jingling percussion rolling underneath until the dams burst during the whistle-blowing breaks. Despite its awkwardness, the record's carnival vibe worked perfectly in a disco context and, thanks to this exposure, "Blow Your Whistle" reached #15 on the R&B chart. The similarly styled but funkier follow-ups, "Sound Your Funky Horn" and "Queen Of Clubs", which were released under the shorter name of KC & The Sunshine Band, were big hits in the UK.

Casey and Finch went on to write "Rock Your Baby" in 1974, which became a huge hit for George McCrae. "Rock Your Baby" helped kick off the mainstream disco craze in the US and paved the way for KC & The Sunshine Band's tremendous mid-70s breakthrough. And what a breakthrough it was. "Get Down Tonight", "That's The Way (I Like It)", "(Shake, Shake, Shake) Shake Your Booty" and "I'm Your Boogie Man" all made it to #1 on the pop chart, and "Keep It Comin' Love" reached #2. However, by 1978, just as The Bee-Gees were becoming the biggest group in the world, KC & The Sunshine Band collapsed in a heap of terrible material ("Boogie Shoes") and ill-advised covers ("It's The Same Old Song").

The 1978 single "Black Water Gold", which was credited just to The Sunshine Band, was a cover of an African Music Machine track and was as funky as the group ever got. KC, on the other hand, was preoccupied with becoming as big as the brothers Gibb and he released a string of dire pop ballads, including "Please Don't Go" and "Yes, I'm Ready", the latter with **Teri DeSari**. The group's swansong was 1983's "Give It Up", which became a #1 hit in the UK largely because it was based on the Euro soul format developed two decades earlier by **The Equals** and **The Foundations**. KC did make one final, bizarre, return to the R&B charts in 1998 alongside **2 Live Crew** on their "2 Live Party" single.

⊙ The Best Of KC & The Sunshine Band
1990, Rhino

It doesn't include their sublime cover of "Black Water Gold" or their fine version of "I Get Lifted", but this retrospective shows that beneath their goofy white guy exteriors KC & The Sunshine Band grooved like crazy. When you listen to this great album, the band's light-heartedness can't fail to put a smile on your face.

Kelis

The first psychedelic R&B sex queen of the new millennium announced herself with the most outrageous hook in living memory and the wildest haircut this side of the guy with the rainbow afro who held up the "John 3:16" signs at American sporting events in the 70s. However, as everyone from **Little Richard** to **Pete Burns** could tell you, such a combination of outrageousness and genius is almost impossible to maintain and **Kelis** has been caught in a downward spiral ever since her outlandish debut.

Born August 21, 1980 in Harlem, New York to a Pentecostal minister father and a clothes designer mother, **Kelis Rogers** grew up around jazz and immediately gravitated towards the unique vocal style of **Betty Carter**. As well as enrolling at the Fiorello H. LaGuardia High School for Music, Art and Performing Arts (yes, the same school on which *Fame* was based), she began modelling at the age of 13. She quit school and left home at 16 to pursue music full time. She landed a vocal spot on the second album by the shock rap supergroup **Gravediggaz** and was briefly one-third of an aborted girl group project called BLU (Black Ladies United), but her career finally took off when she met the up-and-coming hip-hop/R&B production team **The Neptunes**. Kelis sang the hook on their calling card, **Ol' Dirty Bastard**'s "Got Your Money" in 1999, and quickly bcame the duo's diva of choice, providing hooks for everyone from Foxy Brown to Noreaga.

It was the hook to her own debut single, however, that caught the ears of radio programmers the world over. "Caught Out There" (aka "I Hate You So Much Right Now") was a fairly typical, albeit excellent, R&B tune, but Kelis literally screaming the catch phrase made it one of the most original singles in a genre based almost exclusively on its stylization of love and heartbreak. It was perhaps the most direct expression of female rage this side of **Bikini Kill**. Her 1999 debut *Kaleidoscope* couldn't maintain the momentum of "Caught Out There", but tracks such as the rousing "Good Stuff", the pizzicato "Get Along With You" and "Mars", which in a better world would have been the love theme of *Logan's Run*, transcended the conventions of contemporary R&B.

Despite its shortcomings, *Kaleidoscope* was successful enough to allow Kelis to hobnob with **Moby** and jet set around Europe (where she covered **Nirvana**'s "Smells Like Teen Spirit" live) with **U2** and German trancemeister **Timo Maas**. Her 2001 album *Wanderland* suffered from her new-found celebrity, as well as that of The Neptunes who had seemingly produced every other song that had made it onto the radio since her debut. By this point The Neptunes signature sound had become a rote formula, with only the heavy-handed rock posturing of the lead single, "Young, Fresh 'N' New", sounding in the least bit original. Kelis insisted on writing most of the album herself (The Neptunes had written most of *Kaleidoscope*) and didn't do herself any favours by collaborating with **No Doubt** and Fieldy from nu-metal band **Korn**.

Kelis's third album, 2003's *Tasty*, was a marked improvement, largely because it included the fresh production blood of Dre 3000, Rockwilder, Dame Grease, Raphael Saadiq and Dallas Austin. Still, the album's best moment belonged to The Neptunes, who produced "Milkshake", her biggest hit to date. "Milkshake" was raunchy as hell, but that buzzing synth riff punctuated by a triangle hit would have made the song a hit even if Kelis was singing the phone book.

Kaleidoscope
1999, Virgin

It's not a perfect album by any means, but this is about as unconventional as R&B gets these days – and in a world of cookie-cutter, adenoidal girl groups, that means a lot. When Kelis and The Neptunes gel, it's a thing of weird beauty, producing tracks than run a close parallel to Betty Davis's vintage soul recordings of the early 70s.

Paul Kelly

An excellent songwriter and a strong vocalist in the mould of a more downhome **Curtis Mayfield**, **Paul Kelly** is one of soul's more egregiously underrated talents. Born on June 19, 1940, in Miami, he joined his brother's vocal group, The Superiors, in the mid-50s. After further stints in The Spades and The Valadeers, he joined Clarence Reid's group **The Del-Mires**, for whom he sang lead on "Sooner Or Later" in 1963 after Reid was stricken with laryngitis.

Continuing to work with Reid, Kelly recorded "The Upset" as a solo artist in 1964, inspired by Muhammad Ali's heavyweight championship victory over Sonny Liston. The track attracted the attention of **Buddy Killen**, who signed Kelly to his Dial label, where he released the poppy "Chills And Fever" and the grittier and more typically Southern soul-styled "Since I Found You" and "Call Another Doctor".

In 1967 Kelly moved to Brooklyn and began to write songs in earnest. These included his masterpiece, "Stealin' In The Name Of The Lord", recorded in Muscle Shoals in 1970. Featuring a straightforward gospel arrangement, a **Sister Rosetta Tharpe**-influenced guitar figure front and centre, a Holy Roller piano line and a rousing choir, "Stealin' In The Name Of The Lord" could easily have been the **Edwin Hawkins Singers**' follow-up to "Oh Happy Day" – except Kelly wasn't singing about a happy day and the song wouldn't have been played in any church in the world. Kelly sermonized against manipulative religious charlatans like Father Divine, who preyed upon the desperation and willingness to believe of the poorest members of society. The secular and sacred strains of African-American music have never seen eye to eye, especially after soul singers appropriated gospel's language of religious ecstasy to articulate the pleasures of the flesh, but the antagonism of "Stealin' In The Name Of The Lord" was unique.

The equally churchy, but far brighter, "Poor But Proud" followed later that year. While "Soul Flow" saw Kelly at his funkiest, with rocking organ and screaming guitar solos underpinning dirty wah-wah vamps, "(He Ain't Nothin' But) Dirt" was his most Curtis Mayfield-like track, but it had distinctly Southern-fried horns. Aside from the title track, Kelly's fine 1973 album, *Don't Burn Me*, didn't get much airplay, but it had the same relationship with Southern soul that **Robert Cray**'s 80s albums had with traditional blues records.

Kelly's 1974 album *Hooked, Hogtied & Collared* was essentially a concept album about the S&M aspects of relationships. After several of his self-produced singles, including "Get Sexy" and the terribly cheap-sounding "Play Me A Love Song", failed to chart significantly over the next few years, Kelly was paired with arch sweetener **Gene Page** for 1977's *Stand On The Positive Side*, but the album was too sickly, even for the disco era.

Paul Kelly gradually drifted away from music in the late 70s and early 80s, although **Karla Bonoff** had a hit with a cover of his "Personally". However, in 1989 the devastation wrought by crack on his Brooklyn neighbourhood inspired a comeback and he wrote and recorded "Crack (The Devil's Pipe)" that same year. Kelly also released a bluesy comeback album, *Gonna Stick And Stay*, in 1992, which was well received, but

223

his 1998 release *Let's Celebrate Life* was messy and featured an ill-advised remake of "Stealin' In The Name Of The Lord".

The Best Of Paul Kelly
1996, Warner Archives

A fairly solid 20-track selection, *The Best Of Paul Kelly* covers his years at Warner Bros from 1972 to 1977. Although this inexplicably omits "Soul Flow", it does include the original version of Kelly's best single, "Stealin' In The Name Of The Lord".

R. Kelly

R. Kelly spent the early days of his music career as a busker on the streets of Chicago, constantly being hassled by the police, which didn't exactly suggest he would become the biggest male R&B star by the turn of the millennium. However, that sort of street pedigree aligned him with the itinerant bluesmen of old, and it goes some way to suggest why he became such a huge star: he is perhaps the only male performer of his generation to explore the age-old soul dilemma of the sacred and the profane.

He was born **Robert Kelly** in Chicago on January 8, 1969. He first gained public attention in 1990 when his group **MGM** won the televised talent contest *Big Break*. They broke up soon after, however, and Kelly re-emerged the following year with a new group, **Public Announcement**. They had moderate hits with "She's Got That Vibe", "Honey Love" and "Slow Dance (Hey Mr DJ)", but attracted just as much attention for their penchant for wearing what looked like coal miners' lamps in their videos.

Kelly ditched Public Announcement in 1993 to record the solo album *12 Play*, which was one of the most salacious albums in R&B's fairly pervy history. Alternating between leering come-ons and downright sexist bullshit, Kelly dominated urban radio, particularly with the insidiously catchy "Bump 'N' Grind". Around that time Kelly also started working with **Gladys Knight**, **Michael Jackson** and 15-year-old **Aaliyah** (to whom he was briefly married in 1994, although the union was quickly annulled).

His second solo album *R. Kelly* went quadruple platinum in 1995 on the strength of the singles "You Remind Me Of Something" – which was perhaps the worst love song ever written, with lyrics such as "You remind me of my jeep/I wanna ride it" – and "Down Low (Nobody Has to Know)". On album tracks like "Religious Love", however, Kelly lost himself in a conflation of love, sex and faith. It wasn't exactly **Al Green**, but Kelly's exploration of carnality and spirituality was rare among contemporary R&B performers.

In 1996 Kelly traded in any sense of ambiguity for a Hallmark-card version of gospel on the truly wretched *Space Jam* movie theme "I Believe I Can Fly", which, nevertheless, made it to #2 on the pop charts and won several Grammys. The saccharine level became cavity-inducing on "I'm Your Angel", a duet with **Céline Dion**, from his 1998 double-disc *R.*, perhaps the only album to feature both Céline Dion and **Jay-Z**.

Jay-Z collaborated with Kelly again on "Fiesta", a hideously infectious, flamenco-flavoured semi-acoustic groover from 2000's *TP-2.com*, and they also recorded the disappointing album *The Best Of Both Worlds* together in 2002. That same year the *Chicago Sun-Times* newspaper reported that Kelly had been caught on videotape having sex with an underage girl. He was eventually charged with 21 counts of child pornography offences in Chicago and twelve in Florida, although some of the charges have since been dropped.

Despite controversies surrounding the law suits and his private life, Kelly released another new album, 2003's *Chocolate Factory*. He mostly played it safe with the album, which was a collection of ballads and fairly tame lust jams, including the hits "Ignition" and "Step In The Name Of Love". While he returned to the dilemma of sex and religion in 2004 on the double-album *Happy People/U Saved Me*, Kelly's apparent conversion looked to be one of convenience as he played on America's love of redemption and tried to portray himself as a pimp with a heart of gold.

TP-3 Reloaded was released just days before Kelly's trial on child pornography charges was due to start in 2005. It was his most over-the-top album yet, centred around the absurd and mind-boggling soap opera "Trapped In The Closet" that was equal parts *Footballers' Wives* and **Millie Jackson**'s *Caught Up* and centuries of tall tales and trickster myths. At the time of going to press, Kelly's trial was still caught up in a morass of pre-trial motions.

The R. In R&B Collection 1
2003, Jive

The title of this hits collection couldn't be any more arrogant, but as the most successful solo male artist of the 90s, R. Kelly has probably earned it. This has 23 tracks of middle-of-the-road beats, he-man come-ons and some of the worst metaphors in the history of doggerel – and it's only the first collection – but, hey, twenty million R. Kelly fans can't be wrong.

Alicia Keys

The eminently marketable **Alicia Keys** is one of those R&B divas that the industry just loves: she's young, classically trained, easy on the eye and owes fealty to an industry mogul. That she's got more pipes than soul only means that when she gets older she'll be perfect for those Hollywood-style show-stopper ballads so beloved of the Academy and she'll be bathing in Grammys by the time she's 30.

Keys was born **Alicia Augello Cook** on January 25, 1981, in New York City. Her musical aptitude became apparent when she was very young and she graduated from the Professional Performing Arts School at the age of 16. Keys briefly attended Columbia University, but soon dropped out in order to pursue a music career full time. She was signed to Arista by **Clive Davis** in 1998, but moved with him to his own J Records label in 2000.

Thanks to an unseemly amount of hype and the success of the lead single "Fallin'" (which owed much to **James Brown**'s "It's A Man's Man's Man's World"), Keys 2001 debut *Songs In A Minor* was a sensation, selling ten million copies. The strange thing was that, for a singer-songwriter specializing in confessionals, it seemed as though Keys couldn't care less whether anyone was actually listening – this was clearly a woman head over heels in love with the sound of her own voice.

Two years later, she released a second album, *The Diary Of Alicia Keys*, which was only rescued by the surprisingly superior lead single, "You Don't Know My Name". The track was produced by hip-hop artist **Kanye West**, who gave Keys the best setting she has ever had. Complete with a sample of **The Main Ingredient**'s "Let Me Prove My Love To You", "You Don't Know My Name"

was the kind of tribute to the mack soul of the early 70s that **Dr. Dre** and **Ice Cube** always wanted to make, but never could. However, the rest of the album was a dog's dinner of boring midtempo ballads and awkward attempts at keeping up with contemporary state-of-the-art R&B production.

Keys's 2005 follow-up *Unplugged*, recorded as part of the *MTV Unplugged* series on July 14, 2005, showed that, even away from the studio, she was still the cold and calculated music industry creation that all the critics feared she was. She has since turned to acting, starring alongside Ben Affleck and Andy Garcia in *Smokin' Aces* (2006), and she is currently working on her third studio album, tipped for release in 2007.

The Diary Of Alicia Keys
2003, J Records

Titles like this are usually sure indications of an album to avoid like the plague. That general rule is largely true of *The Diary Of Alicia Keys*. However, it does have the shockingly good "You Don't Know My Name", which is perhaps the only song in Keys's catalogue that isn't grotesquely self-important. The reason, of course, is that the song's success has more to do with Kanye West's genius production than with Keys's arrogant fireworks.

Chaka Khan

Great Lakes Naval Training Centre, Illinois, doesn't exactly resound with bluesy mythology or soulful passion, but it was the birthplace of one of African-American music's great voices. **Chaka Khan** was born there as **Yvette Marie Stevens** on March 23, 1953, into a musical family that also included future disco diva **Taka Boom** and jazz-fusion vocalist **Mark Stevens**. When she was 11 years old Yvette Marie Stevens joined a girl group called The Crystalettes and, a few years later, became a member of The Shades of Black, a group in tune with the revolutionary tenor of the times. Around this time she also became interested in her African ancestry, and changed her name to Chaka Adunne Yemoja Aduffe Hodarhi Karifi. "Chaka" was the name of a Zulu monarch, and the moniker, which means "fire warrior", perfectly suited her fierce vocal style.

Shortening her name to Chaka Khan after a short-lived marriage to Chicago musician Assan Khan, she started playing nightclubs around the Windy City as well as singing back-up for cult singer **Baby Huey**. On the circuit she often ran into a multiracial group called Ask Rufus that was formed by former members of the bland rock group American Breed. Ask Rufus had released a couple of singles on Epic in 1971 that went nowhere, but when they shortened their name to **Rufus** and Khan became their lead singer, the group's fortunes began to change.

Signing to ABC in 1973, Rufus – Chaka Khan, drummer **Andre Fischer**, keyboardists **Kevin Murphy** and **Ron Stockert**, guitarist **Al Ciner** and bassist **Dennis Belfield** – released a moderately successful self-titled album that included a cover of **Stevie Wonder**'s "Maybe Your Baby". Their version of his record impressed Wonder so much that he showed up unannounced at Rufus's next recording session and wrote their breakthrough, "Tell Me Something Good". The percolating, bouncy midtempo track went gold and established Khan as one of the strongest voices in pop. The song anchored their fine *Rags To Rufus* album in 1974, which also featured another midtempo funk killer, "You Got The Love", co-written by Khan and **Ray Parker Jr.** However, the fact that the album was credited to "Rufus featuring Chaka Khan" upset Belfield, Stockert and Ciner, who soon left the group.

Guitarist **Tony Maiden** and bassist **Bobby Watson** were brought in as replacements on 1975's *Rufusized*, and their funk chops paid dividends on "Once You Get Started". Khan was again the star, as cuts like "Please Pardon

---

PLAYLIST
Chaka Khan

1 TELL ME SOMETHING GOOD Rufus from **The Very Best Of Rufus Featuring Chaka Khan**
Hooks galore and a funk groove bordering on the comedic.

2 YOU GOT THE LOVE Rufus from **The Very Best Of Rufus Featuring Chaka Khan**
Who knew Ray Parker Jr (who co-wrote "You Got The Love") could be this funky?

3 DO YOU LOVE WHAT YOU FEEL Rufus from **The Very Best Of Rufus Featuring Chaka Khan**
Booty-bumping disco-funk courtesy of producer Quincy Jones.

4 AIN'T NOBODY Rufus from **Epiphany: The Best Of Chaka Khan**
Shimmering, rousing early 80s dancefloor funk.

5 I'M EVERY WOMAN from **Epiphany: The Best Of Chaka Khan**
A rousing disco cut written by Ashford & Simpson.

6 CLOUDS from **Epiphany: The Best Of Chaka Khan**
This Ashford & Simpson track demonstrates disco's affinity for gospel.

7 MOVE ME NO MOUNTAIN from **Naughty**
Chaka Khan at her fiercest.

8 WHAT CHA' GONNA DO FOR ME from **Epiphany: The Best Of Chaka Khan**
The arrangement is slightly overripe, but Khan cuts through it all.

9 I FEEL FOR YOU from **Epiphany: The Best Of Chaka Khan**
The first hip-hop soul track.

10 THROUGH THE FIRE from **Epiphany: The Best Of Chaka Khan**
A sickly, overproduced ballad with a killer chorus that later made a star out of Kanye West.

Me (You Remind Me Of A Friend)", "I'm A Woman (I'm A Backbone)" and "Stop On By" displayed the full range of her pipes and interpretive abilities. *Rufus Featuring Chaka Khan* swiftly followed that same year, featuring the group's biggest R&B chart hit, "Sweet Thing", a fairly dull, jazzy ballad on which Khan sounded great soaring over the noodly backing and watery keyboards.

Ask Rufus in 1977 included another R&B #1, "At Midnight (My Love Will Light You Up)", as well as the smooth "Hollywood"

and the fine ballad "Everlasting Love". However, the following year's disappointing *Street Player* was ruined by personnel changes and internal strife, and Khan finally decided to go solo. Rufus released the weak *Numbers* without her in 1979, but she was contractually obliged to return for *Masterjam* later that year. Producer Quincy Jones streamlined the group's bounce and added lots of disco zing, but thankfully didn't remove the cowbell on "Do You Love What You Feel". While Khan recorded a few more albums with Rufus in the late 70s and early 80s, her focus was definitely on her solo career. Her one sparkling moment with Rufus came in 1983 with the release of "Ain't Nobody", a modern funk track that exploded into fully fledged gospel fury on the chorus.

Khan's first solo album, 1978's *Chaka*, featured the cream of New York's studio players

Chaka Khan performing with Rufus on hit TV show *Soul Train*

– the Brecker brothers, Richard Tee, David Sanborn – as well as The Average White Band. The album's biggest track was the Ashford & Simpson disco classic "I'm Every Woman", which reached #1 on the R&B chart. Her second solo album, 1980's *Naughty*, was even better and it included "Move Me No Mountain" and "Clouds", which combined the unmistakable gospel stamp of Ashford & Simpson with Khan at her fiercest and most diva-like. The title track of 1981's *What Cha' Gonna Do For Me* was a sassy song that belied its unctuous arrangement, and became her second solo R&B chart-topper.

Chaka Khan (1982) included a fine cover of Michael Jackson's "Got To Be There", but it was *I Feel For You* (1984) that sealed Khan's reputation. The title track, "I Feel For You", was one of the definitive singles of the 80s: it was written by Prince, had a rap by Melle Mel from Grandmaster Flash & The Furious Five and featured harmonica from Stevie Wonder – Khan simply tore it up. The album also held another electro-funk number, "This Is My Night", produced by The System, and the slightly overproduced ballad "Through The Fire". The album elevated Khan to superstar status, and she went on to work with Robert Palmer (helping to arrange "Addicted To Love"), David Bowie and Steve Winwood (singing back-up on "Higher Love").

As her subsequent albums concentrated too heavily on sickly ballads, Khan soon began to lose momentum in the latter half of the 80s. Her focus should have centred on the fact that she was one of the few vocalists with a voice and delivery powerful enough to work with the harsher environments of contemporary production styles. She did manage to achieve a few more R&B hits, such as the 1989 duet with Ray Charles, "I'll Be Good To You", and her 1992 rapprochement with hip-hop, "Love You All My Lifetime". Khan continues to record – outshining wannabe diva Brandy on the 1996 collaboration "Missing You" and working with the London Symphony Orchestra on the 2004 album of standards, *Classikhan* – but her superbly controlled gospelese was showcased far more effectively on the funk records of old than on the jazzier music she has more recently veered towards.

 Rufus Featuring Chaka Khan – Rufusized
1975, ABC

The Very Best Of Rufus (1996, MCA) is an excellent compilation, but *Rufusized* is the group's best original album. Away from the hits, if you want to hear the band play and if you want to listen to Khan sing, album tracks are the way to go. This was Rufus's strongest album in terms of material and performance, and it includes their strongest funk tracks and sweetest ballads.

Epiphany: The Best Of Chaka Khan
1996, Reprise

Despite being the best currently available collection of Chaka Khan's solo work, this is an unsatisfying package, with no surprises, that has been put together in a hodgepodge fashion. Still, if you just want to listen to her delivering her biggest solo hits, whether fierce funky numbers or gentle ballads, in her superb and distinctive vocal style, this is the place to go.

Kid Creole & The Coconuts

It wouldn't be much of a stretch to suggest that Tommy Browder (better known as August Darnell or Kid Creole) is the greatest synthesist of disco, funk, salsa, Cab Calloway and Cole Porter the world has ever known. Just as his brother Stony tried to turn the ghetto into a glittering Broadway extravaganza with Dr. Buzzard's Original Savannah Band, Darnell suggested that style could transcend even the most brutal material reality. With their arch lyrics, Cotton Club horn charts, Broadway vocal mannerisms, chicken scratch guitars and bubbling basslines, Kid Creole & The Coconuts were simultaneously as fabulous as the Ziegfeld Follies and as abrasive as Johnny Rotten.

Paradoxically, the dawn of the Reagan/Thatcher era saw a convergence of black and white music that we will probably never see again. Post-punk groups such as The Gang of Four and The Pop Group appropriated the precision of funk as a metaphor for control, while avant-funksters ESG borrowed punk's discord and first-generation hip-hoppers were dancing to Kraftwerk and Thin Lizzy. Straddling New York's disco and new wave scenes, Kid Creole & The Coconuts adopted punk's main weapon – attitude – to make up for their lack of roots and singing ability. Continuing from where Dr. Buzzard's left off, Darnell and Andy "Coati Mundi" Hernandez dressed themselves up in zoot

suits, surrounded themselves with three European ice queens, read from Bobby Short's supper-club lexicon and played confidence games with racial stereotypes.

Kid Creole & The Coconuts debuted with the biting *Off The Coast Of Me* in 1980, an album that tackled the hoary stereotype of the tragic mulatto on tracks such as the snide "Calypso Pan-American" and the hilarious "Darrio", in which the narrator failed to get his girlfriend into Studio 54. Although well-received by critics, the album failed to sell.

The group's second album, 1981's *Fresh Fruit In Foreign Places*, was a Homerian epic that, while populated with sirens and sorceresses, was more concerned with cuckolds and cads than heroes and monsters. Instead of Cyclops and Lotus-eaters, the protagonist had to outwit fast-talking natives, cope with difficult Latin music and strange customs and fend off predatory Swiss ski instructors. Of course, our hero probably never even left New York – the entire world could be found in the Big Apple's five boroughs.

The next year's *Wise Guy* (or *Tropical Gangsters* in the UK) was a mock travelogue in which the band were "washed up on the shore of B'Dilli Bay – island of sinners ruled by outcasts where crime is the only passport and RACE MUSIC the only way out!" The pan-Caribbean vibe of *Fresh Fruit In Foreign Places* reappeared in the ersatz soca/salsa of "Annie, I'm Not Your Daddy", the trade-wind lilt of "No Fish Today" and in the synthesized steel drum and timbale fills of "I'm Corrupt", but *Wise Guy* was mostly straight-ahead, if slightly astringent, R&B. Well, as straight-ahead as can be

expected from a guy who called his backing musicians "The Pond Life Orchestra". *Wise Guy*'s deceptively simple light funk bottom streamlined the band's sound, reining in the big-band arrangements without neutering their effectiveness.

Doppelganger, which followed in 1983, was not quite as sharp or as hook-laden as its predecessors. It did have its moments, though, especially the Zouk-flavoured "There's Something Wrong In Paradise" (about Third World revolution) and the faux son montuno of "Survivors" (a cautionary tale about dead musicians). The 1985 album *In Praise Of Older Women And Other Crimes* was even more lacklustre and brittle, although it was redeemed by the wonderful "Endicott" and Coati Mundi's showcase, "Dowopsalsaboprock".

I, Too, Have Seen The Woods from 1987 was perhaps Darnell's weakest album yet, both structurally and musically. "Dancin' At The Bains Douches" might have been the closest he came to duplicating **Cole Porter**, but the remaining tracks sagged in comparison. Kid Creole's 90s and 00s albums – *Private Waters In The Great Divide* (1990), *You Shoulda Told Me You Were…* (1991), *Kiss Me Before The Light Changes* (1994), *To Travel Sideways* (1995), *The Conquest Of You* (1997) and *Too Cool To Conga!* (2001) – all hold a redeeming song or two, but the synthesis of vision and sound has long since eluded Darnell.

Wise Guy (aka Tropical Gangsters)
1982, Ze/Sire/Island

August Darnell's music may be too knowing and his image too unauthentic to gain mainstream acceptance, but you can't deny his singularity: only he could have staged the break-up invective of "Loving You Made A Fool Out of Me" to Chic-meets-Ellington razzmatazz or made a dance song about a "Stool Pigeon". Look out for the 2002 reissue, which includes six bonus tracks of remixes and previously hard-to-find B-sides.

Ben E. King

Born Benjamin Earl Nelson on September 23, 1938, in Henderson, North Carolina, **Ben E. King** is unquestionably one of popular music's greatest vocalists. Possessing both gospel fire and classic pop elegance, his baritone made him a crucial crossover figure in early soul.

As a teenager, King was briefly in a group called **The Moonglows**, and he then joined **The Five Crowns** in 1957. Two years later, that group became the new line-up of The Drifters in the post-Clyde McPhatter years; King sang lead on enduring Drifters' classics like "There Goes My Baby", "Save The Last Dance For Me" and "This Magic Moment".

King decided to go solo in 1961 with the ghostly but slightly overproduced "Spanish Harlem". However, it was the follow-up, "Stand By Me", co-written with **Leiber & Stoller**, that solidified him as the voice of bruised restraint and became his biggest hit, making #1 on the R&B chart and #5 on the pop chart. Assuming you're not bored to tears by it yet, King's signature tune remains one hell of a record, largely because of his impeccable performance, especially that piercing crescendo.

King's 1962 record "Don't Play That Song Again (You Lied)" was almost a note-for-note remake of "Stand By Me", but he again gave the song the crumbling-stiff-upper-lip pain that it demanded. He continued to enjoy chart success over the next few years with "I (Who Have Nothing)" and "Seven Letters", but more interesting were some of his commercial duds, such as the Latin-tinged pop trifle "Walking In The Footsteps Of A Fool", which King sung as though he actually meant it, the harrowing deep soul ballad "It's All Over" and "The Record (Baby I Love You)", which found him at his most soulful.

As soul grew rawer and more assertive, the urbane King was left behind. However, when he was allowed to get gritty on "What Is Soul?" in 1967 or as part of **The Soul Clan** (with Solomon Burke, Arthur Conley, Don Covay and Joe Tex), King proved that he was still a solid sender. As with most singers, his main problem was material. Early on he was saddled with trash like 1963's "Auf Wiedersehen, My Dear", while in 1970, for example, he cut a preposterously overwrought version of **The Beatles**' "Don't Let Me Down", trying to keep up with the times.

King's old boss at Atlantic Records, **Ahmet Ertegun**, rescued him from the ignominy of the oldies circuit in 1975, when "Supernatural Thing" became a disco smash thanks to a slow and sleazy arrangement and fabulous guitar riff and strings. King spent the rest of the decade attempting to duplicate that success on fine records with The Average White Band, including "Get It Up" and "A Star In The Ghetto", and on the solo 1980 record "Music Trance".

King returned to the oldies circuit in the early 80s, but his career was again resuscitated in 1986 when Rob Reiner's movie about childhood friendship *Stand By Me* returned his classic hit to the pop charts. Returning to the studio shortly after, Ben E. King has recorded steadily ever since, although he now pursues a more jazzy direction.

Anthology
1993, Rhino

Ben E. King has been poorly served by the reissue market, and, even with 2 CDs and 50 tracks, the compilers of this anthology still couldn't get it quite right. Though this remains the best King package thanks to its range and breadth and it does include all of his biggest hits, where are 1962's "Too Bad" and 1963's "Tell Daddy"?

Benny And Us
1977, Atlantic

If you own *Anthology* or any of Ben E. King's other "best of" compilations, you've already heard all of his biggest hits from the 60s, but this was his strongest 70s soul release. The third album from his 70s comeback, *Benny And Us* is a collaboration with The Average White Band, and their bright, slick funk makes this an interesting contrast to King's 60s material.

Evelyn "Champagne" King

Unlike many other disco divas, who were either too tainted by the glitterball or simply too wooden to sing anything else, **Evelyn "Champagne" King** had both the pipes and the sense of swing to make the transition from disco to 80s R&B with ease.

Born in the Bronx into a musical family on June 29, 1960, King moved to Philadelphia in 1970, where her parents worked at the legendary Sigma Sound Studios. One fateful night in 1976 she accompanied her mother to work and Philadelphia International producer **T. Life** overheard her singing Sam Cooke's "A Change Is Gonna Come" as she cleaned the bathroom. He immediately took King under his wing and got her a deal with RCA who released her debut album, *Smooth Talk*, in 1977. Her first single, "Shame", was an unimpeachable disco anthem and a sure-fire party starter that sold a million copies. The equally successful midtempo follow-up, "I Don't Know If It's Right", proved that King wasn't merely a belter and that she had both range and finesse.

King's second album, 1979's *Music Box*, was less impressive than her debut, although the title track and "Out There" set many dancefloors alight. The next year's *Call Me* suffered from the anti-disco backlash, but for 1981's *I'm In Love* she started working with producers **Kashif**, **Morrie Brown** and **Paul Lawrence Jones III**. They gave her a more bouncy, synthesized R&B sound and told her to sing in a higher register. The plan worked; the album's title track became King's first R&B #1, while "Don't Hide Our Love" showed that she could sing a ballad as well as any of her peers.

The 1982 album *Get Loose* was again produced by Kashif, Brown and Jones, and it featured King's other transcendent moment, "Love Come Down". This was what every freestyle record wanted to be, but none of the other singers had King's vocal chops or a groove this liquid. "Betcha She Don't Love You", meanwhile, was a classic early 80s midtempo femme synth stomp. Unfortunately, creative differences then split up the production team, leaving King to work with **Foster Sylvers** and **Andre Cymone** on *Face To Face* in 1983. The album's "Action" and "Shake Down" made King sound like a rather unconvincing Prince girl, while "Teenager" was an ill-advised new-wave number.

So Romantic marked a disastrous attempt to make King into a pop singer in 1984. Thankfully, she returned to the dancefloor in 1985 on *Long Time Comin'*, which featured the very fine slap bass groove of "Your Personal Touch". King then left RCA for EMI and released *Flirt* in 1988, which produced two funky R&B top-ten hits, the title track and "Hold On To What You've Got". The rise of hip-hop and new jack swing meant that King was quickly left behind thereafter, but she continues to perform on the disco oldies circuit.

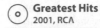 **Greatest Hits**
2001, RCA

This excellent 18-track collection makes a convincing case for King being one of the 70s' and 80s' most underrated singing talents. You know her for "Shame" and "Love Come Down", but her moderate hits are hardly dead weight on this pulsating dancefloor package.

Klymaxx

One day in the very near future a generation of hipsters will rescue this all-female funk troupe from the dustbin of historical neglect and restore them to their place as one of the finest groove bands of the 80s. Sure, they were little more than **Prince** and **Jam & Lewis** rip-off artists, but remaking the brittle funk of the Reagan era as tongue-in-cheek feminist war chants was an act of brilliant defiance.

Klymaxx was founded by drummer/vocalist **Bernadette Cooper** in Hollywood in 1979, together with bassist/vocalist **Joyce "Fenderella" Irby**, vocalist **Lorena Shelby**, guitarist **Cheryl Cooley**, keyboardist **Lynn Malsby** and vocalist **Robin Grider**. Signing to Solar Records, they released their debut album, *Never Underestimate The Power Of A Woman*, in 1981. Produced by **Lakeside**'s Otis Stokes and Stephen Shockley, it was full of solid, if unremarkable, poppy funk very much in the label's house style.

In 1982 *Girls Will Be Girls* – the first outside production work by Jam & Lewis – further proved that Klymaxx wasn't merely a novelty act or a bunch of groupies living out their fantasies of stardom. The lead single, "Wild Girls", was particularly effective, but it was only once the group left Solar for Constellation that they really hit their stride.

Klymaxx's 1984 album *Meeting In The Ladies Room*, co-produced by the band and Jam & Lewis, was a classic 80s synth-funk record. "The Men All Pause" may be one of the worst puns in history, but it grooved something fierce, had killer percussion, was a very rare song about female narcissism and may have been the first R&B track to give a shout out to **Gianni Versace**. The title track was an almost note-for-note remake with a little more instrumental detail and better singing. The rather terrible, but interestingly produced, ballad, "I Miss You", was the group's biggest pop hit, reaching the Top 5. *Klymaxx* (1986) lacked the spark of its predecessor, partly because the funk had become less brittle and the edges had been smoothed out. It sounded like a bad **Pointer Sisters** record. Despite two top-twenty pop hits, "Man Size Love" and "I'd Still Say Yes", the group broke up in 1987.

Bernadette Cooper became the Svengali behind **Madame X**, a feminist spin on Prince's **Vanity 6** girl group concept with vocalists Iris Parker, Alisa Randolph and Valerie Victoria. Madame X released the remarkable, but completely overlooked, "Just That Type Of Girl" in 1987. The percussion evoked both Jamaican dancehall with its skittering trigger beats and a balafon ensemble greeting the sun on a Malian plain – it was one of the great feats of drum machine programming. The girls themselves were sassy and sexy, skewering both sexism and consumerism in a single bound. Cooper moved on to release a solo album in 1990, *Drama According To Bernadette Cooper*, which found her making like a hip-hop version of **Madonna**, particularly on the single, "I Look Good (Interview)".

Joyce "Fenderella" Irby had one big hit after the demise of Klymaxx, 1989's "Mr DJ", a duet of sorts with **Doug E. Fresh**. Meanwhile, the remaining three members of the group, Cooley, Grider and Shelby, re-formed Klymaxx as a trio. Their comeback album, 1990's *Maxx Is Back*, found them sounding very much like **Soul II Soul** on the top-five R&B hit "Good Love". In the late 90s and the early part of the new millennium, two competing versions of Klymaxx emerged, one fronted by Cooley, the other by Cooper and Irby (who had given up on their solo careers) together with Malsby and Shelby (who was now using her maiden name of Lorena Stewart).

Greatest Hits
1996, MCA

The Klymaxx records you really want are *Meeting In The Ladies Room* and the first two Solar albums, but, at the time of writing, they're all out of print. This hits package gets the nod over *20th Century Masters – The Millennium Collection: The Best Of Klymaxx* (2003, MCA) because it includes decent solo records by Bernadette Cooper and tacks by the the trio version of Klymaxx.

Gladys Knight & The Pips

Detractors say that despite a 35-year string of hits, **Gladys Knight** has never settled on a distinctive style of her own. Though aesthetically this may be the case, her seemingly infinite malleability – she is equally comfortable singing bluesy ballads, gospel-esque stormers and big-haired MOR schmaltz – has made her and her family group one of the most durable presences on the R&B charts.

Born to two members of the Wings Over Jordan Choir in Atlanta on May 28, 1944, Gladys Knight was singing in her church choir at the age of 4. Aged 7 she won first prize on the TV talent show *Ted Mack's Amateur Hour* for her rendition of Nat "King" Cole's "Too Young". The following year Knight and her brother **Merald** (born September 4, 1942) formed a vocal group with their sister **Brenda** and their cousins **William** and **Eleanor Guest**. They performed gospel as The Fountaineers, but secular music as **The Pips**, taking their name from another cousin, **James "Pip" Woods**, who became their manager.

After touring with Jackie Wilson in 1957, The Pips signed to his label, Brunswick, and released "Whistle My Love" the next year. When the single failed to gain any attention, Brenda Knight and Eleanor Guest left the group, to be replaced by another cousin, **Edward Patten**, and **Langston George**. The Pips' version of Johnny Otis's "Every Beat Of My Heart", released on the local Atlanta label Huntom in 1960, became a regional hit, before being licensed to Vee-Jay and hitting #1 on the R&B chart the following year.

Legendary impresario **Bobby Robinson** then signed The Pips to his Fury label and re-recorded a more sedate version of the song. Credited to **Gladys Knight & The Pips**, it reached #15 on the R&B chart. The follow-up, 1961's "Letter Full Of Tears", was even better – a smokey ballad showcasing Gladys Knight at her bluesiest. After they released the upbeat "Operator", Langston George quit and the group temporarily broke up when Knight married and had a child.

PLAYLIST
Gladys Knight & The Pips

1 **EVERY BEAT OF MY HEART** from **Essential Collection**
Old-fashioned rock'n'roll ballad that shows what an excellent interpretive singer Knight really is.

2 **LETTER FULL OF TEARS** from **Essential Collection**
A superb, string-laden early soul ballad.

3 **GIVING UP** from **Essential Collection**
Haunting end-of-the-night ballad with a fog-horn undertow.

4 **TAKE ME IN YOUR ARMS AND LOVE ME** from **Essential Collection**
The harpsichord is a bit much, but Knight is at her sexiest.

5 **I HEARD IT THROUGH THE GRAPEVINE** from **Essential Collection**
Fiery gospelese version that's nearly as good as Marvin Gaye's.

6 **YOU NEED LOVE LIKE I DO (DON'T YOU?)** from **Essential Collection**
Killer uptempo horn-driven funk.

7 **FRIENDSHIP TRAIN** from **Essential Collection**
This is Knight at her most fiery and churchy.

8 **IF I WERE YOUR WOMAN** from **Essential Collection**
A gorgeous ballad displaying her extraordinary, expressive and technical range.

9 **MIDNIGHT TRAIN TO GEORGIA** from **Essential Collection**
This is perhaps the most underrated song in the soul canon.

10 **BEST THING THAT EVER HAPPENED TO ME** from **Essential Collection**
The epitome of craftsmanship.

The Pips returned to the Maxx label in 1964 with two superb ballads written by Van McCoy, "Giving Up" and "Lovers Always Forgive". After three more fine, but underappreciated, Maxx singles, they signed to Motown's Soul subsidiary in 1966. Their first two Soul singles, "Just Walk In My Shoes" and "Take Me In Your Arms And Love Me", were percolating numbers in the finest Motown style, but it was the doo-woppy "Everybody Needs Love" – a #3 R&B hit – that established the group as hitmakers, even though Knight sounded out of place on such a soft track.

Produced by the great **Norman Whitfield**, The Pips' fierce, churchy 1967 version of "I Heard It Through the Grapevine" was their breakthrough, and it stayed at #1 on the R&B chart for a month. Whitfield brought out the gospel fire in Knight's voice on the records "It Should Have Been Me", "The Nitty Gritty" and "You Need Love Like I Do (Don't You?)". Knight was at her most fiery on "Friendship Train", a strange intermingling of funky cowbell and searing guitar solos with some terribly showbiz horns.

In 1970 producer **Clay McMurray** refashioned Gladys Knight & The Pips as a ballad group and they recorded the gorgeous "If I Were Your Woman". Similarly emotional ballads followed – "I Don't Want To Do Wrong", "Make Me The Woman That You Go Home To", "Help Me Make It Through The Night" and "Neither One of Us Wants To Be The First To Say Goodbye" – and established the group on the pop charts.

Leaving Motown for Buddah Records in 1973, the group achieved their first pop #1 with the stunning "Midnight Train To Georgia". Three more top-five pop hits followed in quick succession: the pulsating "I've Got To Use My Imagination", the touching "Best Thing That Ever Happened To Me" and "On And On". The latter featured Knight at her gospel rawest and The Pips at their least demonstrative on top of a fierce funk backing.

With the exception of the defiant "I Feel A Song (In My Heart)" and an ill-advised cover of "The Way We Were", the group started to fall out of favour with the pop audience in the mid-70s. After the group had a somewhat successful season on their own variety television show on NBC, Knight made her acting debut in 1976 in the largely self-financed *Pipe Dreams*, a turkey of a movie that landed her heavily in debt. The group went on to have some moderate success in the disco era with the Van McCoy-produced "Baby Don't Change Your Mind" and "Come Back And Finish What You Started", a piece of haphazard disco tripe that embarrassingly gave them one of their biggest hits in the UK.

After legal wrangling with Buddah, during which time Knight signed to Columbia as a solo artist, she and The Pips were forced to perform separately for two years. In 1980 the reunited group signed to Columbia and released "Landlord", written and produced by Ashford & Simpson, which returned them to the R&B Top 3. Working with **Foster Sylvers** and Sam Dees, they subsequently had a huge R&B hit with the dancefloor classic "Save The Overtime (For Me)" in 1983. Perhaps more importantly, they helped define the 80s power ballad that same year with "Hero", now better known as "Wind Beneath My Wings".

After a best-forgotten TV role on the short-lived sitcom *Charlie And Company* and a cameo on Dionne Warwick's "That's What Friends Are For", Knight returned to the top of the R&B charts with The Pips in 1987 with "Love Overboard", an angular dance track produced by Midnight Star's Reggie and Vincent Calloway. Gladys Knight & The Pips finally split in 1990, with Knight carrying on as a solo artist. She reached #2 on the R&B charts with the forgettable "Men" in 1991, and had a small hit with a medley of Boyz II Men's "End Of The Road", "If You Don't Know Me By Now" and "Love Don't Love Nobody" in 1994. She continues to perform live all over the world and is currently appearing in semipermanent residence in Las Vegas.

Imagination
1973, Buddah

This groundbreaking album, released just after their "Neither One Of Us" finale for Motown, is a smooth, sleek, well-produced example of the best Gladys Knight & The Pips have to offer. It features several of their biggest hits, including "Midnight Train To Georgia", but the album tracks are also uniformly fine and well worth a listen. Look out for the 1995 Sequel reissue CD that pairs this with 1974's *I Feel A Song*.

Essential Collection
1999 Hip-O

This excellent 18-track overview is the only collection that documents every phase of Gladys Knight & The Pips' career, from 1960's "Every Beat Of My Heart" to 1987's "Love Overboard". Including material from Vee-Jay, Fury, Maxx, Soul, Buddah and MCA, it's the only single-disc package to buy.

Kool & The Gang

There is perhaps no greater compliment than being called "the second baddest out there" by James Brown. Before metamorphosing into funk's equivalent of used-car salesmen with their slick, smarmy pop hits in the late 70s and early 80s, Kool & The Gang mined a deep, polyrhythmic, jazzy groove that was so innovative and successful even the Godfather had to take notice.

Starting life as **The Jazziacs** in Jersey City, New Jersey, the band was founded in 1964 around bassist **Robert "Kool" Bell** and his multi-instrumentalist brother, Ronald (**Khalis Bayyan**). The Bells' father, Bobby, was a friend of Thelonius Monk and the boys were brought up with the sounds of Monk, John Coltrane and Horace Silver, which they took and blended with the rhythms of the street. With neighbours **Dennis "Dee-Tee" Thomas** (saxophone), **Charles Smith** (guitar), **George Brown** (drums), **Robert "Spike" Mickens** (trumpet), **Ricky West** (keyboards) and **Woody Sparrow** (guitar), The Jazziacs became The Soul Town Band, then The New Dimensions, then Kool & The Flames and, finally, when they signed to Gene Redd's De-Lite Records in 1969, Kool & The Gang.

PLAYLIST
Kool & The Gang

1 LET THE MUSIC TAKE YOUR MIND from **The Best Of Kool & The Gang (1969–1976)**
Funk as indomitable youthful exuberance.

2 NT from **The Best Of Kool & The Gang (1969–1976)**
Bouncing bass and killer horns.

3 FUNKY STUFF from **Wild And Peaceful**
Who knew a whistle could be so damn funky?

4 JUNGLE BOOGIE from **Wild And Peaceful**
A snarling guitar line played like Larry Graham plays the bass, plus Cookie Monster vocals.

5 HOLLYWOOD SWINGING from **Wild And Peaceful**
Something approaching an actual song appended to the bassline from Mandrill's "Fencewalk".

6 SUMMER MADNESS from **The Best Of Kool & The Gang (1969–1976)**
Is this the pinnacle of the Fender Rhodes?

7 CELEBRATION from **Celebrate!**
If REO Speedwagon had made a funk record, it would probably sound something like this.

8 LADIES' NIGHT from **Ladies' Night**
Crass and cynical, yet its sheer effervescence takes over.

The band's early records – "Kool And The Gang", "The Gang's Back Again", "Chocolate Buttermilk", "Let The Music Take Your Mind", "Love The Life You Live" – and the 1971 albums *Live At P.J.'s* and *Live At The Sex Machine* showcased a sound that was heavily based on James Brown, The Meters and Sly & The Family Stone. Combining clipped guitars, bumping bass runs, lots of effects pedals and jazz chops, these early releases achieved moderate chart success, but the group's sound wasn't all that different from the deluge of post-Sly bands. It wasn't until 1973's *Wild And Peaceful* that they finally emerged with their own identity.

From Harlem to Times Square to Soho, the biggest record in New York in 1973 was **Manu Dibango**'s "Soul Makossa". Recorded in Cameroon, "Soul Makossa" was a deep, hypnotic rhythm-mantra that combined American funk with African polyrhythms. It was a huge hit on both the funk and developing disco scenes and a hugely influential record. Their record label, De-Lite, wanted Kool & The Gang to do a cover version, but the band had their own ideas. Using "Soul Makossa" as a blueprint, they recorded the bulk of *Wild And Peaceful* in a single session in a studio built in a former morgue.

The album's first single, "Funky Stuff", kicked off with a party whistle and then settled into a bouncing groove that streamlined their previously meandering sound. While "Funky Stuff" reached the R&B Top 5 and the pop Top 30, the album's next two singles were even more successful. "Jungle Boogie", again influenced by "Soul Makossa", had an impossibly tight guitar figure fleshed out with a killer clavinet riff, Meters-style scat singing and Tarzan screaming. One of the funkiest records ever, "Jungle Boogie" reached #2 on the R&B charts and #4 pop. Their first R&B chart-topper, "Hollywood Swinging", borrowing the bassline from another massive 1973 record, **Mandrill**'s "Fencewalk", truly established Kool & The Gang as one of the most commercially successful of all funk bands.

"Rhyme Tyme People" and "Spirit Of The Boogie" both had a slightly harder, more direct sound, but it was the latter's B-side, "Summer Madness", that achieved immortality thanks to its jazzy Fender Rhodes and synth lines that have came to epitomize the R&B summer jam. In 1976 Kool & The Gang started to sound more like Earth Wind & Fire with the harmonizing horns and cod-spirituality of "Love & Understanding (Come Together)" and the silly *Arabian-Nights*-goes-disco fantasy of "Open Sesame".

The group went through a few tough years in the face of the disco juggernaut, before deciding that if you can't beat 'em you gotta join 'em. With the addition of **James "J.T." Taylor** on vocals and **Eumir Deodato** as producer, 1979's *Ladies' Night* was symptomatic of the same disease that afflicted The Rolling Stones and Rod Stewart during the late 70s: fitting an irreconcilable musical style into the parameters of disco in order to shift units. Although Kool & The Gang had their biggest hits with Deodato producing and Taylor's more pop-flavoured vocals – "Ladies' Night", "Celebration" and "Get Down On It" – all of these singles were little more than corporate disco and they sounded as though they were created with a sports highlight montage in mind.

Deodato stopped producing their records in 1983, but the hits kept on coming throughout the 80s in a similar teenage-perfume-advert style: "Fresh", "Joanna", "Cherish", "Victory" and "Stone Love". The group's most recent recruit, James Taylor, left in 1988 to pursue an ill-advised solo career, but the remaining band members continued to record, with almost no chart successes, into the 90s. Taylor was reunited with the rest of the gang in 1996 for the album *State Of Affairs* and, two years later, they formed their own record label KTFA Entertainment. The remaining band members continue to be a popular draw on America's burgeoning funk revival circuit.

Wild And Peaceful
1973, De-Lite

The first half of this fine album has all the monster Kool & The Gang funk jams you know, while the second features extended jazz jams crafted into message songs. With its mixture of groove and message, this album spent a year on the charts, becoming the band's most successful studio album and one of the pillars of funk.

Spirit Of The Boogie
1975, De-Lite

Much in the same vein as *Wild And Peaceful*, here's a case where more of the same is a good thing. There's a dud or two on every Kool & The Gang album, but, in the main, this is filled with the kind of brassy, show-stopping funk that made them famous before disco crept in. "Jungle Jazz" and "Spirit" highlight their tight, clean sound.

Patti LaBelle

W hile soul has always had its fair share of gospel-derived showmanship, the campy, overwrought virtuosity of **Patti LaBelle** – particularly when combined with the Starchild outfits of her group **LaBelle** – is far closer to Vegas than it is to vespers. The theatricality isn't just pure ornament, though. The group's breakthrough was the 1974 *Nightbirds* album, which featured her signature track "Lady Marmalade". The album's forcefulness and sexual forthrightness stood in sharp relief to the prissiness and cutesiness of so many girl groups.

That said, LaBelle started life as **The Bluebelles,** a typical 60s girl group in ludicrously frilly dresses who sang songs like "Down The Aisle (The Wedding Song)" and "Danny Boy". When original member **Cindy Birdsong** left to join The Supremes, they were down to a trio of Patti LaBelle (born **Patricia Holt** on May 24, 1944), **Nona Hendryx** and **Sarah Dash.** Then they met **Vicki Wickham,** who had previously produced the classic television show *Ready Steady Go* and managed Dusty Springfield. She metamorphosed them into a feminist rewrite of the girl-group blueprint.

On 1971's *LaBelle* and 1972's *Moon Shadow,* Wickham had the group singing rock songs such as The Rolling Stones' "Wild Horses", The Who's "Won't Get Fooled Again" and Cat Stevens's "Moonshadow". However, they were sent to New Orleans for the *Nightbirds* album to work with **Allen Toussaint** and The Meters, who concocted the best music of LaBelle's career. In addition to the irresistible "Lady Marmalade", they produced the fine Hendryx ballad, "Are You Lonely?", and the fiery, political "What Can I Do For You?"

Although both 1975's *Phoenix,* which featured the excellent "Messin' With My Mind",

PLAYLIST
Patti LaBelle

1 LADY MARMALADE Labelle from **Nightbirds**
Put the Christina Aguilera car-crash version out of your mind – this is the real deal.

2 WHAT CAN I DO FOR YOU? Labelle from **Nightbirds**
Rousing disco funk track with a political statement.

3 MESSIN' WITH MY MIND Labelle from **Phoenix**
A stomping early disco record.

4 FUNKY MUSIC from **Patti LaBelle**
A slice of popping, stomping, shouting funk from the disco era.

5 TEACH ME TONIGHT (ME GUSTA TU BAILE) from **Lady Marmalade: The Best Of Patti & LaBelle**
A great, sashaying Latin disco number.

6 SPIRIT'S IN IT from **Spirit's In It**
More dancefloor extravagance from perhaps the ultimate diva.

7 IF ONLY YOU KNEW from **Lady Marmalade: The Best Of Patti & LaBelle**
The monster ballad that revived her career.

8 NEW ATTITUDE from **Lady Marmalade: The Best Of Patti & LaBelle**
Aerobic MOR à la Pointer Sisters crossover hits.

and the next year's *Chameleon* were almost as good, none of the singles connected the way "Lady Marmalade" did, and the group soon disbanded. Nona Hendryx went on to record a number of decent, if challenging, avant-funk albums with **Bill Laswell**, the best of which was probably 1983's *Nona*. Sarah Dash had one moment of solo transcendence – 1979's cult disco hit "Sinner Man".

Patti LaBelle, however, went on to stardom. After recording several middling R&B chart entries for Epic, including the excellent "Teach Me Tonight (Me Gusta Tu Baile)", she moved to Philadelphia International. Her 1981 album *Spirit's In It* didn't deliver the crossover hit she was after, but the title track was very popular in New York discos. In 1983 the ballad "If Only You Knew" was a monster hit, topping the R&B chart for a month. With her outrageous wigs and equally over-the-top pipes, Patti LaBelle was a constant presence on the charts in the mid-80s with records like "Love Has Finally Come At Last", "New Attitude" and "Stir it Up".

A 1986 duet with **Michael McDonald** on Burt Bacharach and Carole Bayer Sager's "On My Own" became her first pop #1 without the rest of the group, and enshrined her as one of the voices of the glitzy 80s. Perhaps inevitably, she soon started to sing on *James Bond* film soundtracks. Her relevance as a pop singer started to wane in the 90s, although she still managed high R&B chart appearances with the ballads "Somebody Loves You Baby", "When You've Been Blessed (Feels like Heaven)" and "The Right Kinda Lover".

○ **Lady Marmalade: The Best Of Patti &
LaBelle**
1995, Sony/Legacy

It may hold little of the trio's early rockier material, but this 16-track collection of LaBelle's hits and Patti LaBelle's solo Epic records still stands as a testament to the audacity of their rewrite of the girl group format. With songs like "Lady Marmalade", "What Can I Do For You?" and "Messin' With My Mind", it demonstrates just how brassy, assertive and extraordinary they were in their heyday.

Major Lance

B orn in Winterville, Mississippi, on April 4, 1941, but raised in the Windy City, **Major Lance** was a true great of Chicago soul. His voice was simultaneously thin and warm, a perfect fit for the breezy but rich productions for which the city became famous. As a teenager Lance sang with the Five Gospel Harmonaires and with the secular group The Floats, as well as being a successful amateur boxer.

In 1959 he released "I Got A Girl" on Mercury, written and produced by high-school friend Curtis Mayfield. After a couple of years singing with The Ideals, Lance returned as a solo artist on OKeh in 1962. He had a small local hit with the piano-led "Delilah", but his next single, "The Monkey Time", was definitive Chicago soul. It had lyrics by Curtis Mayfield, an intricate, brass-heavy arrangement by **Johnny Pate**, production by **Carl Davis** and Lance's own wonderfully elastic vocals. "Hey Little Girl" followed in nearly identical style, while "Um, Um, Um, Um, Um, Um" was arguably Mayfield's catchiest song. It aslo featured Pate's jazziest arrangement, but Lance shined the brightest with his brilliantly pure falsetto.

Mayfield, Pate and Davis continued this formula into the mid-60s with "Rhythm", "Sometimes I Wonder", "Come See" and "Ain't It A Shame". Mayfield then stopped writing for Lance to concentrate on his own projects, and while 1965's "Too Hot To Hold" had a real nice slowed-down Motown feel, Lance's chart career went into decline. The following year's "Investigate" and "It's The Beat" were by-the-numbers uptempo Chicago soul, while 1967's very uptempo "You Don't Want Me No More" featured a heart-attack bass and the female backing singers becoming breathless as they tried to catch up. Lance also sounded a bit flat at such a breakneck speed.

Lance was reunited with Mayfield in 1970 and cut two fine singles for the Curtom label, "Stay Away From Me (I Love You Too Much)" and "Must Be Love Coming Down", and three singles for Volt that failed to go anywhere. He then lived in the UK between 1972 and 1974, where he made numerous appearances on the Northern soul circuit. Back in Atlanta in 1974, he released an awful disco version of "Um, Um, Um, Um, Um, Um" on Playboy.

Lance's career went into further decline. In 1978 he was arrested for selling cocaine and spent four years in prison. After his release, he became a popular draw on the Carolina Beach Music circuit. He died of heart failure on September 3, 1994.

Denise LaSalle

The vastly underappreciated **Denise LaSalle** was born Denise Craig in LeFlore County, Mississippi on July 16, 1939. Although she grew up listening to the Grand Ole Opry on the radio, and much of her youth was spent singing in the Zion Temple Choir and later with The Sacred Five, LaSalle was a ribald singer of rare quality who excelled at putting no-good men in their place. She was also a gifted songwriter and she wrote most of her debut album herself.

LaSalle moved to Chicago in the 50s where she was eventually discovered by Chess producer **Billy "The Kid" Emerson**. Her first single, "A Love Reputation", was released on Emerson's Tarpon label in 1967. It was a hit in the Windy City, but failed to break nationally. The following year, she split from Emerson and founded the Crajon label with her husband Bill Jones. LaSalle wrote "Get Your Lie Straight" and "When You Find A Fool Bump His Head", which were both modest hits for Bill Coday on Crajon in 1971, and she also wrote and produced "Hey Romeo" for The Sequins.

Around this time, LaSalle's 1970 release "Hung Up, Strung Out" reached the ears of **Armen Boladian**, who signed her to Westbound Records in Detroit. He sent LaSalle down to Memphis to work with **Willie Mitchell**, who was then also working with Westbound's The Detroit Emeralds. The result was LaSalle's "Trapped By A Thing Called Love", an earthy but relaxed gospel-blues groove that ranks among Mitchell's best productions. The 1971 album of the same name and the superb follow-up single, "Run And Tell That", were largely written by LaSalle herself, suggesting the emergence of a great talent.

LaSalle's next album, 1972's *On The Loose*, was a disappointment. It had too many covers (although her version of "Breaking Up

Somebody's Home" was pretty great) and less than inspired production. The album's highlight was the wonderfully lascivious "Man Size Job", a seriously funky ode to cradle robbing. *Here I Am Again* (1974) featured the fabulous Southern-style funk track "Get Up Off My Mind", which showcased LaSalle as one of the great female funk singers. After releasing the excellent cheating song "Married, But Not To Each Other" in 1975, LaSalle moved to ABC and became something of a Southern-fried disco diva.

"Freedom To Express Yourself" and "Workin' Overtime" managed to inject some blues gravitas into her generally flighty disco records. The 1979 album *Unwrapped* held an ill-advised cover of Rod Stewart's "Do Ya Think I'm Sexy", but LaSalle redeemed herself the following year with "I'm So Hot", a cult disco hit that was later covered by **Sugarhill** rapper Superwolf (aka her second husband, radio personality James Wolf).

In 1982 LaSalle was recruited by Malaco Records to write material for Z.Z. Hill. His "Someone Else Is Steppin' In" was the result and Malaco promptly signed her as a recording artist. Her debut for the label, "A Lady In The Street", was a combination of Betty Wright's "Clean Up Woman" and Marvin Gaye's "Sexual Healing". The following year's "Right Place, Right Time", a duet with Latimore, was an erotic take on the tick-tocking early soul ballads, while "Your Husband Is Cheating On Us" was a delicious sassy blues. LaSalle's biggest record with Malaco was "My Tu Tu", her 1985 spoiler version of Jean Knight's cover of Rockin' Sidney's zydeco novelty "My Toot Toot", which reached #6 in the UK.

LaSalle released a string of albums for Malaco in the 80s and 90s that alternated between classic soul, up-to-the-minute R&B and blues, the best of which were 1984's *Right Place, Right Time* and 1990's *Still Trapped*, which featured the wonderfully feisty tale of male dysfunction "Wet Match". Her latest offering, 2002's fine, bluesy *Still The Queen*, includes the rather wonderful ballad "Who Needs You".

ⓞ **On The Loose / Trapped By A Thing Called Love**
1992, Westbound

LaSalle's first two albums (from 1972 and 1973) released together on one CD, are some of the best Southern soul-funk recordings of the 70s. Even if *On The Loose* was disappointing in comparison to her debut, it does include two of her best records – "Man Size Job" and "Breaking Up Somebody's Home" – making this an effective précis of her Westbound years.

Latimore

B orn **Benjamin Latimore** in Charleston, Tennessee on September 7, 1939, Latimore was one of the biggest stars of the contemporary soul-blues scene that swept the South in the late 70s and 80s. With its deep resonance, Southern twang and laid-back delivery, Latimore's voice was as distinctive as his silvery mane.

After growing up on the blues, country music and gospel, Latimore joined The Hi-Toppers in the early 60s before joining **Joe Henderson**'s band as keyboardist. In 1964 Latimore became the organ player in **Steve Alaimo**'s band and sometimes served as his opening act. When Alaimo started producing for **Henry Stone**'s Miami-based music empire in 1965, Benny Latimore was among the first artists he recorded. The early tracks Latimore released on Stone's Blade label, such as "Rain From The Sky" and "I Can't Go On", were solid deep-soul records. Latimore's finest early record was his emotional version of **Doc Pomus**'s "The Power And The Glory", released on Stone's Dade label in 1969.

Dropping his first name, Latimore moved to sister label Glades, and his career surprisingly took off in 1973 with a mundane reading of "Stormy Monday". The following year's "If You Were My Woman" was a neat little answer record to Gladys Knight & The Pips' "If You Were My Man", but it was the self-penned "Let's Straighten It Out" that truly shot Latimore to prominence – and the top of the R&B chart. In the age of funk and disco Latimore and Alaimo had dared to make a record without a guitar, framing Latimore's voice with what would become his characteristic deep Fender Rhodes backing. The funkier but not quite as startling "Keep The Home Fire Burnin'" followed it into the Top 5 the next year.

Although the humorous but sympathetic "There's A Red-Neck In The Soul Band" suggested that Latimore had more pizzazz

than his unadorned style might have suggested, he settled for becoming a comfortable downhome version of Barry White for the rest of the decade, with records like "Ordinary Man", "Somethin' 'Bout 'Cha" and "Dig A Little Deeper". However, he really came to life in 1979 on the superb "Discoed To Death".

Unfortunately, the title "Discoed To Death" aptly summed up the state of Henry Stone's empire at the beginning of the 80s, and Latimore soon found himself without a label. Signing to Malaco in 1982, Latimore released *Singing In The Key Of Love*, a lusher and more straightforwardly R&B album than was the Malaco norm. His biggest hit for the label was 1986's "Sunshine Lady", an unrepentantly cheesy ballad written for him by Homer Banks. Latimore left Malaco after nine albums – the last being the very fine 2000 release *You're Welcome To Ride* – and reappeared on Brittney Records in 2003 with the tastefully synthesized *Latt Is Back*.

Straighten It Out: The Best Of Latimore
1995, Rhino

This excellent 17-track compilation album includes all of Latimore's R&B chart hits for Miami-based label Glades from the 70s. This is laid-back Southern soul at its finest, although the smarmy similarity can get a bit wearing after a while.

Stacy Lattisaw

B orn on November 25, 1966 in Washington, DC, **Stacy Lattisaw** helped define the sound of R&B during the 80s. A talent circuit veteran by the time she was 10, Lattisaw had her recording debut at age 12, making her perfect for the cutesiness that plagued R&B during the Reagan era. While her dance records were relatively effervescent, the ballads she was saddled with were clunkers that lent themselves to nothing but over-the-top belting, another hallmark of the 80s.

Aside from the forgettable "When You're Young And In Love", Lattisaw's 1979 debut album *Young & In Love* was mostly covers of oldies from the 60s and 70s produced by Van McCoy. The album tanked and Lattisaw was then paired with **Narada Michael Walden** who made her something of a star on 1980's *Let Me Be Your Angel*. Despite

Latin Soul

The first Latin soul records were made by Mexican-Americans living in Los Angeles. Teen groups such as The Velveteens, **The Romancers** and **Rene & Ray** blended doo-wop and Richie Valens-style rock'n'roll in the early 60s. **The Salas Brothers**' "Darling (Please Bring Your Love)" in 1963 was perhaps the first truly "soulful" Latin record made in the US. The Salas Brothers, Steve and Rudy, later became part of two of the best Latin rock bands, **El Chicano** and **Tierra**. The most successful of the Eastside LA Latin soul tunes were rockier versions of R&B records, such as **The Premiers**' 1964 rendition of Don & Dewey's "Farmer John" and **Cannibal & The Headhunters**' wonderful 1965 version of Chris Kenner's "Land Of 1000 Dances".

Meanwhile, on the East Coast, the blend of Cuban rhythms and jazz was some 20 years old by the time a new generation of Puerto Rican immigrants came of age in the 60s. Instead of turning to the jazz of their parents' day, they affirmed their Americanness by blending the sounds of their homeland with the rhythmically more aggressive soul music. This new genre would be called "boogaloo" or "shingaling". The very first boogaloo record was **Ricardo Ray**'s "El Señor Embajador" (1966), but *el rey del shingaling* (the king of shingaling) was unquestionably **Joe Cuba**, who had big hits with "Bang Bang" and "El Pito" that same year. **Pete Rodriguez**, who had an East Coast smash with "I Like It Like That", came a close second. Other boogaloo records to look out for are **The Latinaires**' smoking "Camel Walk" and **The Harvey Averne Dozen**'s "Micro Mini".

By the end of the 60s boogaloo was passé and Latin soul became psychedelic like its African-American cousin. Psychedelia entered the vernacular of Latin music with **Ray Barretto**'s monumental 1968 album, *Acid*. Soul-jazz rhythms and melodies had a big impact on Latin records thanks to **Pucho & The Latin Soul Brothers**' *Heat!*, released that same year, and **Eddie Palmieri**'s ground-breaking Harlem River Drive project.

The interlocked percussion of Latin music was a natural partner for funk and disco, and these two genres introduced Latin music to the mainstream in the 70s. **Joe Bataan**'s "Latin Strut" from his crucial 1973 *Salsoul* album and **Ricardo Marrero**'s 1975 record "Babalonia", released on Don King's label, were landmarks in this respect. Meanwhile **Louie Ramirez**'s seriously funky 1976 cover of "Do It Any Way You Wanna", the disco classic by People's Choice, proved that the influence went both ways. From here it was a short distance to the electronic clavés of Latin Freestyle in the 80s.

(o) **Various Artists: Nu Yorica!: Culture Clash In New York City: Experiments In Latin Music 1970–77**
1996, Soul Jazz

Although this isn't strictly a Latin soul compilation, it is one of the best overviews of the cross-cultural musical traffic of Harlem in the 70s, and it features the best of New York City's Latin musicians. This 2-CD, 16-track album includes Harlem River Drive's "Harlem River Drive Theme" and "Idle Hands", Joe Bataan's "Latin Strut" and Ricardo Marrero's "Babylonia".

Lattisaw's nasal, too-young vocals, which were an unholy meeting of Michael Jackson circa "Ben", Deniece Williams and a chaste Teena Marie, the uptempo disco-lite "Dynamite" and the horribly saccharine title track were top-ten R&B hits. The best track, though, was "Jump To The Beat", a Chic rip-off with a mean cowbell.

Lattisaw's third album, 1981's *With You*, featured her biggest hit yet, an utterly bizarre and somewhat inappropriate version of The Moments' "Love On A Two-Way Street". *Sneakin'* from 1982 included another big hit, "Don't Throw It All Away", as well as the charming "Attack Of The Name Game", a silly, electro update of Shirley Ellis's novelty classic that beared more than a resemblance to the Tom-Tom Club's "Genius Of Love".

In 1984 Lattisaw hooked up with her childhood friend **Johnny Gill** to record *Perfect Combination*, a teeny-bopper update of Marvin Gaye and **Tammi Terrell**'s duets. Moving from Cotillion to Motown, Lattisaw returned to cutting dancefloor records in 1986 with "Nail It To The Wall", a popular club track produced by **Jellybean Benitez**. In 1989 *What You Need* was racier and more sensual than any of her previous albums and it featured her only R&B #1, "Where Do We Go From Here", which was another duet with Johnny Gill. Soon after releasing this album, Lattisaw abandoned secular music for gospel, and she has made only sporadic appearances since.

The Very Best Of Stacy Lattisaw
1998, Rhino

It has neither "Jump To The Beat" nor "Where Do We Go From Here", but this 16-track summation of her career is just about all the Stacy Lattisaw anyone needs to own. Fans of teen pop will be delighted by the bubbly dance tracks, but soul fans should approach with a bit more caution – the ballads are probably best avoided by everyone.

Bettye LaVette

P ossessed of a remarkably powerful voice, **Bettye LaVette** is another in the tragically long line of female soul singers who, through a combination of bad luck, mismanagement and stones in her path, failed to gain the recognition she deserved.

Bettye Lavette in let me down easy in concert

Born **Betty Haskins** in Muskegon, Michigan on January 29, 1946, LaVette is one of the few soul singers who didn't grow up singing in the church. Discovered at the age of 16 by longtime Detroit presence **Johnnie Mae Matthews**, LaVette released her first single on Atlantic in 1962. "My Man – He's A Lovin' Man" was a swinging, sashaying early soul classic that reached the R&B Top 10. After releasing a couple more singles on Atlantic and Lupine that failed to go anywhere, LaVette returned on the Calla label in 1965 with the all-time great ballad "Let Me Down Easy". LaVette was at her scratchy, gritty best, and while the string arrangement was over the top, it was pulled back to earth by the bluesy guitar runs and the spooky percussion.

Although none of her Calla follow-ups made the charts, tracks such as the burning "I Feel Good All Over" and "Stand Up Like A Man" were big hits on the Northern soul circuit. LaVette's funked-up 1968 version of **The First Edition**'s "Just Dropped In (To See What Condition My Condition Was In)" was heard by the group's lead singer, **Kenny Rogers**, who suggested she went down to Nashville. There she signed to Shelby Singleton's Silver Fox label and recorded the wonderful country-funk record "He Made A Woman Out of Me".

After releasing nice versions of Joe South's "Games People Play" and **Erma Franklin**'s "Piece Of My Heart", LaVette signed to Atlantic again, releasing "Your Turn To Cry" in 1973. With the drums ticking down the seconds, the mourning strings bitter-sweetening the bluesy arrangement and LaVette on simply stunning form, "Your Turn To Cry" became a definitive break-up ballad. Her one-off 1978 release for West End Records, "Doin' The Best That I Can", became a disco classic thanks to the fabulous remixes of disco legend **Walter Gibbons**. When Gibbons actually allowed her to sing she sounded great, but the record was really all about his extraordinary dubby mix.

LaVette finally released her first studio album, *Tell Me A Lie*, for Motown in 1982, and returned to the R&B charts that year with the classic country soul of "Right In The Middle (Of Falling In Love)". Aside from a handful of lousy Stock, Aitken & Waterman-style records for Ian Levine's ill-fated Motor City project in the 80s and 90s, LaVette's recording career remained dormant until the release of *Souvenirs*. Originally recorded in 1973 at Muscle Shoals with producer **Brad Shapiro** (no relation), *Souvenirs* was shelved until 2001, when it was resurrected by the French Melodie label.

LaVette is still a popular live draw in Europe, as documented on her live 2001 album *Let Me Down Easy: In Concert*. She was a bit ragged on both 2003's *A Woman Like Me* and 2005's *I've Got My Own Hell To Raise*, but that only added poignancy and gravitas to her bluesy ballads.

Bluesoul Belles: The Complete Calla, Port and Roulette Recordings
2005, EMI

This 24-track split disc with soul-blues singer Carol Fran collects all the material that Bettye LaVette recorded for

Calla Records in the mid-60s, including the poignant ballad "Let Me Down Easy". Criminally neglected soul music of the highest order, this album is definitely not just for Northern soul obsessives.

Souvenirs
2001, Melodie

An album of prime country funk tracks finally released almost 30 years after they were originally recorded at Muscle Shoals. Although hampered by some poor material and strange choices, *Souvenirs* displays LaVette's deep affinity for country soul – and includes a fantastic cover of Free's "The Stealer".

Laura Lee

Now known almost exclusively for her gimmicky feminist funk tracks "Women's Love Rights", "Wedlock Is A Padlock" and "Rip Off", **Laura Lee**'s talents as a vocalist were obstructed by her choice of material. Born Laura Lee Newton in Chicago on March 9, 1945, she moved to Detroit in the 50s and started singing gospel with her adoptive mother's (Ernestine Rundless) group, **The Meditation Singers**. At the age of 13, Lee appeared with the group – alongside featured lead Della Reese – on 1958's *Amen*, as well as on several sides for the Hob and Gospel labels.

Lee's first secular recording came in 1966 with "To Win Your Heart", a vocal version of the San Remo Golden Strings' "Festival Time", released on Ed Wingate's Ric-Tic label. Although she sounded as though she couldn't keep up with the uptempo stomper, Lee was signed to Chess Records the following year. Recorded in Muscle Shoals, her Chess sides were certainly closer in spirit to the South than to anything coming out of Chicago. The lyrics of "Dirty Man", her first Chess single, were a bit silly, but the arrangement was great in that end-of-the-night Goldwax style. The follow-up, "Uptight Good Man", was even better. Also in a deep-soul vein, it featured midnight tremolo guitar and a great vocal performance from Lee. Further fine deep-soul cuts, such as "Need To Belong" and "As Long As I Got You", followed in 1968, before Lee began to assert herself on tracks such as 1969's uptempo, organ-led "Mama's Got A Good Thing".

Signing to Holland-Dozier-Holland's Hot Wax label in 1970, Lee began to apply her gusto to the feminist tracks with which she made her name. "Wedlock Is A Padlock" was perhaps the worst of them, because the production was just too chirpy, but "Woman's Love Rights" was funkier and less like a novelty record, adding a little gravitas to the lyrics. With her gritty, assertive voice and the vivid, popping production of its drums-along-the-Mohawk breakdown, "Crumbs Off The Table" ranked among the best militant soul.

Lee earned her biggest R&B hit in this style in 1972 with "Rip Off", while also proving that she was more than a gimmick on the superb Southern soul tune, "But You Know I Love You", which had been recorded in the 60s, but was released on Lee's 1972 Chess album *Love More Than Pride*. Her version of Buddy and Ella Johnson's "Since I Fell For You" featured a rap intro, while the sass continued on 1974's "I Need It Just As Bad As You". **Brian Holland**'s mock Southern soul production was a bit too linear, but Lee shone on this tom-tom-heavy funk track.

When HDH's Hot Wax label collapsed in the mid-70s, Lee moved to the Ariola label, where she had a final modest hit with the silly "Love's Got Me Tired (But I Ain't Tired Of You)" in 1976. Retiring her salty humour, Lee returned to her gospel roots with *Jesus Is The Light Of My Life* in 1983, which she co-produced with **Al Green**.

Women's Love Rights: The Hot Wax Anthology
2002, Castle

This 2-CD, 29-track collection includes just about everything Laura Lee recorded under the auspices of Holland-Dozier-Holland in the early 70s. She recorded some of her biggest hits with HDH and she's uniformly superb across this album, even though the material lets her down from time to time.

Barbara Lewis

The classy pop-soul singer **Barbara Lewis** was born in South Lyon, Michigan, on February 9, 1943. While her records, which she often wrote herself, had a tendency to veer perilously close to easy listening, her smooth, sensual voice elevated them above the lowest common denominator.

Lewis was one of the earliest signings on **Ollie McLaughlin**'s Karen label. Her first single for the label, 1961's "My Heart Went Do Dat Da", was picked up by Atlantic, who released all of her records until the end of the decade. Her first hit was the remarkable "Hello Stranger" in 1963. Its gentle, Latinate sway, roller-rink keyboards and "Seems like a mighty long time" hook made the record a pop chart #3, while Lewis's superbly controlled vocals and the sublime backing from The Dells pushed it to the top of the R&B chart.

The follow-up, "Puppy Love", was just too cutesy for words, but the next year's "Someday We're Gonna Love Again", a cheesy little chugger with what sounds like **The Swingle Singers** in the background, became a big Northern soul hit thanks to its irrepressible energy. Her next single, "Pushin' A Good Thing Too Far", was stilted and outdated, but Lewis returned to the pop charts in 1965 with "Baby, I'm Yours". One of the first soul tracks to make use of eight-track, "Baby, I'm Yours" featured Van McCoy overdubbing his backing vocals several times, but was just as notable for Lewis's affecting virginal innocence. "Make Me Your Baby" was a similarly constructed Bacharach-David-style cathedral of longing.

Several more singles, such as "I Remember The Feeling" and "Love Makes The World Go Round", failed to chart in the mid-60s, probably due to the tinkly arrangements and awkward phrasing. "Sho 'Nuff" was her funkiest track, but it was little more than a Supremes supper-club rip-off and it also tanked. Lewis moved to the Stax subsidiary label Enterprise in 1969, but she didn't sound very comfortable on top of the gritty but light 70s arrangements on tracks such as "Ask The Lonely".

After recording "Rock & Roll Lullaby" in 1972 for Reprise, Lewis quit the music business. She did, however, make a few appearances during the late 90s on the Beach and Northern soul circuits, where her records remain popular.

🔘 **Hello Stranger: The Best Of Barbara Lewis**
1994, Rhino

If you prefer Dionne Warwick to Aretha Franklin, this is the album for you. Twenty cool, smooth pop-soul sides, representing the best from the golden age of the mid-60s, performed in Lewis's classy, sensual voice, camouflage torrents of yearning beneath a gentle sway and a quivering upper lip.

Ramsey Lewis

Thanks to his winning combination of gentle post-bop, churchy feel, breezy funk and pop melody, **Ramsey Lewis** was the most commercially successful pop-jazz pianist of the 60s. That doesn't mean he was merely **Kenny G** before the fact, however. His blend of pop, gospel and jazz was, and remains, the epitome of soul-jazz.

Born on May 27, 1935, in Chicago, Lewis was a child piano prodigy who began his career at the Zion Hill Baptist Church before studying at the Chicago Music College. He quit school after a year and joined **The Clefs**, a popular local dance band. In 1956 he formed The Gentlemen of Swing trio with the rhythm section of The Clefs, bassist **Eldee Young** and drummer **Issac "Red" Holt**. From their debut album with Argo Records, 1957's *Ramsey Lewis And His Gentlemen Of Swing*, through 1964's *Pot Luck* and *Bach To The Blues*, the group (renamed **The Ramsey Lewis Trio**) specialized in a jaunty, lightweight, easy-on-the-ears brand of jazz. During this time Lewis also worked with jazz giants **Max Roach**, Sonny Stitt and **Clark Terry**.

When The Ramsey Lewis Trio grew a bit funkier in the mid-60s, they became a sensation. Their version of Chris Kenner's "Something You Got" was a minor pop hit and greatly expanded their audience in 1964. The next year's version of Dobie Gray's "The In Crowd" was the swinging quintessence of soul-jazz and it reached the Top 5. A similar treatment of The McCoys' "Hang On Sloopy" reached #11, while "Wade In The Water" took the opposite tack, toning down a spiritual for a pop audience, but was nearly as successful.

After an acrimonious split, Young and Holt left the group to form **The Young-Holt Trio** in 1966. Lewis reformed his own trio with **Maurice White** on drums and **Cleveland Eaton** on bass. Although Lewis's group had lost its commercial momentum, records such as "Party Time" – the blueprint for Bohannon's "Disco Stomp" and a neat little Bo Diddley swipe – kept the dancefloors swinging. On 1968's *Maiden Voyage* and 1969's *Mother Nature's Son*, The Ramsey Lewis Trio teamed up with producer **Charles**

243

Soul-Jazz

The jazz impulses of improvisation, redefinition and questioning within a tradition are part and parcel of all African-American music, and soul is certainly no different. However, in purely sonic terms, the sounds of soul and jazz started to merge almost as soon as soul itself was born.

While jazz and R&B are inextricably linked, the first explicit merger of the two forms was the hard bop movement of the late 50s. The hard bop style was born in late 1954 when pianist **Horace Silver** and **The Jazz Messengers** – Art Blakey, Kenny Dorham, Hank Mobley and Doug Watkins – recorded "The Preacher" and "Doddlin'", two cuts that tempered bebop's flurry of notes with a funky backbeat derived from gospel.

Following Silver's lead, scores of jazz musicians took inspiration from R&B and gospel, including organist **Jimmy Smith**, who brought jazz, gospel and R&B as close as they would ever come on "The Sermon" in 1958. The great bassist **Charles Mingus** also followed in Silver's footsteps and his 1959 records "Wednesday Night Prayer Meeting" and "Moanin'" may be the greatest jazz-gospel tracks.

Ramsey Lewis's version of "The In Crowd" was, in all likelihood, the most important record in terms of bringing jazz into soul, and his former bassist **Eldee Young** and drummer **Isaac "Red" Holt** came to epitomize soul-jazz with records like "Wack Wack" and "Soulful Strut". Another soul-jazz landmark was **Julian "Cannonball" Adderley**'s "Mercy, Mercy, Mercy", the track that started the vogue for the Fender Rhodes.

As soul metamorphosed into funk, jazz soon followed suit. With **Miles Davis** and **Herbie Hancock** leading the way, jazz musicians including **Donald Byrd**, Lou Donaldson, Charles Earland, Johnny Lytle, Melvin Sparks, Ruben Wilson and Sonny Stitt combined funk rhythms with jazz tones and improvisation. This sound quickly became ossified as "fusion" as artists such as The Crusaders, Ronnie Laws, Roy Ayers, Spiro Gyra, Grover Washington, Jr. and George Benson streamlined the sound, making it slick and sickly. The nadir of the union of soul and jazz was the jazz-funk style that emerged in the UK in the 80s led by the odious **Shakatak**.

Various Artists: Mod Jazz
1996, Ace/Kent

This very fine 25-track collection emphasizes the cool danceable jazz that drove 'em wild on the British Mod scene in the mid-60s. It includes great examples of the soul-jazz style by Cannonball Adderley, Shirley Scott, Brother Jack McDuff, Rusty Bryant, Boogaloo Joe Jones, Sonny Stitt, Cal Tjader and Mongo Santamaria.

PLAYLIST

1 THE PREACHER Horace Silver And The Jazz Messengers from **Horace Silver And The Jazz Messengers**
The first record to explicity combine jazz and R&B.

2 THE SERMON Jimmy Smith from **The Sermon!**
The roadhouse meets the pulpit meets the supper club.

3 WEDNESDAY NIGHT PRAYER MEETING Charles Mingus from **Blues And Roots**
All the complexity of the most experimental jazz with all the swing and fervour of a revival meeting.

4 THE IN-CROWD Ramsey Lewis from **The In Crowd**
Lewis adds a bit of gospel grit and gravitas to Dobie Gray's rather ridiculous original.

5 WACK WACK Young-Holt from **Wack Wack: The Best Of Young-Holt**
This track opens with one of the great uses of cymbals in recorded music followed by the funkiest piano riff ever.

6 MERCY, MERCY, MERCY Cannonball Adderley from **Mercy, Mercy, Mercy**
If you like the Fender Rhodes, you have this track to thank.

7 SOUL STRUTTIN' Shirley Scott from **Mod Jazz**
Sleazy, greazy Hammond workout.

8 SOOKIE, SOOKIE Grant Green from **Alive!**
An outlandish cover of Don Covay's proto-funk classic.

9 TURTLE WALK Lou Donaldson from **Hot Dog**
It's the drums, stupid.

10 BLACK JACK Donald Byrd from **Black Jack**
A radical reconstruction of the immortal "Get Out My Life Woman".

Stepney to create out-there beat-diggers' favourites, thanks to freaky, funky and very chunky tracks like "Back In The USSR".

Maurice White left the group in 1971 to form Earth Wind & Fire and Lewis soldiered on with shifting line-ups and dwindling commercial fortunes. The best of these new line-ups was with Eaton and **Morris Jennings**, who upped the funk quotient on 1972's *Upendo Ni Pomoja* and 1973's *Funky*

Serenity. In 1974 Lewis teamed up with Earth Wind & Fire for the cult classic *Sun Goddess*. After further, less effective, dalliances with synthesizers and Brazilian rhythms, Lewis settled into an MOR career working with vocalists like Nancy Wilson, Alice Echols, Morris Gray and Daryl Coley. Lewis's 2004 album, *Time Flies*, featured reworkings of some of his classic records and proved him to be as effervescent as ever.

Maiden Voyage (And More)
1994, Chess

This CD reissue is essentially 1968's *Maiden Voyage* and 1969's *Mother Nature's Son* – the two least typical of Lewis's albums, but also his best – on one disc. Producer Charles Stepney's lush psychedelia is slightly dated and a little too much for some, but it lends some meat to Lewis's frequently flighty work.

20th Century Masters: The Millennium Collection: The Best Of Ramsey Lewis
2000, Chess

Ramsey Lewis's easiest, breeziest hits from the mid-60s are all gathered together on this 12-track, 1-CD compilation album. Alongside his superior versions of Dobie Gray's "The In Crowd" and The McCoy's "Hang On Sloopy" are covers of The Beatles' "Julia" and "A Hard Day's Night".

Little Anthony & The Imperials

A crucial bridge between doo-wop and soul, **Little Anthony & The Imperials** were one of the few groups to manage to have hits in both eras. Born on January 8, 1941, **Anthony Gourdine** began his recording career for the legendary producer and record label boss **Paul Winley** in 1956 as part of The Duponts. After they recorded a couple more singles for Roulette and Royal Roost, Gourdine left the group to join another collection of Brooklyn street-corner singers, **The Chesters** (Tracy Lord, **Ernest Wright, Jr.**, Glouster "Nat" Rogers and **Clarence Collins**).

The Chesters then changed their name to **The Imperials** and signed to George Goldner's End label. Their debut single, 1958's ethereal "Tears On My Pillow", was a true doo-wop classic, despite being largely based on the records of Frankie Lymon & The Teenagers. At the suggestion of DJ Alan Freed, the group became known as Little Anthony & The Imperials and continued to

enjoy success in the doo-wop/rock'n'roll vein the following year with "So Much" and the wonderfully stupid "Shimmy, Shimmy, Ko-Ko-Bop". However, their next seven singles, including the dire dance-craze misfire "Limbo", tanked. The group broke up in 1961 when Gourdine was advised to go solo.

Gourdine released two solo singles on Roulette, and The Imperials recorded several singles without him, but they reunited in 1964 with former Chips' singer **Sammy Strain** replacing Lord and Rogers. Working with Don Costa and **Teddy Randazzo** at the DCP label, the group became practitioners of the lushest downtown soul ever recorded, starting with "I'm On The Outside (Looking In)". The follow-up, "Goin' Out of My Head", was produced, arranged and written by Teddy Randazzo and became a monument of easy listening. It was one of the most over-the-top productions in the excessive history of downtown soul, but Anthony Gourdine's helium vocals were strange enough – and his phrasing gritty enough – to overcome the cloying backing. No girl group record ever got as hysterical or as melodramatic as Little Anthony & The Imperials' "Hurt So Bad", and things only got worse with "I Miss You So", which featured orchestration from The 101 Strings.

Even after The Imperials moved from DCP to the Veep label in 1966, the extreme pathos continued. On "Better Use Your Head" Gourdine's nasal falsetto and Randazzo's stardust orchestration threatened to float off to the moon on gossamer wings. The group was renamed **Anthony & The Imperials** in 1966, but their baroqueness was now out of touch with the times. Moving to United Artists three years later, they had a couple of modest hits with The Fifth Dimension-style light-psych-soul record "Out Of Sight, Out Of Mind" and "Help Me Find A Way (To Say I Love You)".

Sammy Strain left the group to join The O'Jays in 1974, but thanks to 70s nostalgia for the 50s, The Imperials continued to enjoy modest hits with "I'm Falling In Love With You" and "Hold On (Just A Little Bit Longer)". While Anthony & The Imperials continued to record for Avco, Clarence Collins also left the group and formed his own version of The Imperials.

Taking advantage of their popularity on the Northern soul scene, Anthony & The Imperials cut a remake of "Better Use Your Head", and had a UK hit with "Who's Gonna Love Me" in 1977. In the 80s Gourdine recorded some religious material for Songbird and MCA, before finally reuniting with Collins, Wright and Strain in the early 90s to tour the oldies circuit.

25 Greatest Hits
1999, EMI

This excellent package is the only one to feature Little Anthony & The Imperials' material from End, DCP, Veep and United Artists. It is also, therefore, the only album to paint a complete portrait of one of the few groups that managed to straddle both doo-wop and soul with ease and grace.

Little Willie John

If any one person invented soul singing it was **Little Willie John**. While there were gospel influenced singers before him, no one previously, and perhaps only **James Brown** subsequently, sang with as much intensity. Certainly no one has ever sung with as much emotion – as much pure, abject misery – as Little Willie John without becoming mawkish and unlistenable. John blended the crooning ballad style of **Billy Eckstine** and **Nat "King" Cole** with the naturalism of the blues, the physical impact of gospel and a bit

Little Willie John during one of his more energetic dance routines

of showbiz pizzazz. He was also just about as sexy as it was legal to be in the 50s. Basically, he was the archetypal soul man.

He was born **William Edgar John** in Arkansas in 1937 and moved to Detroit in the 40s. After hooking up with Johnny Otis in 1951, he spent much of the next few years moving in and out of various bands, but never staying long thanks to his wild streak and street tough's version of the Napoleon complex. However, when King Records' **Henry Glover** heard him hustling for work in New York, he signed him on the spot.

In June 1955, John recorded "All Around The World", a novelty number that had just been released by **Titus Turner**. John's version blew Turner out of the water, and hit #6 on the R&B charts. Along with Ray Charles's "I've Got A Woman" and **Chuck Berry**'s "Johnny B. Goode", "All Around The World" helped create the lexicon of release in popular music. Ignoring the comic element of the lyrics, John sang the song like he really meant it: "All around the world, I'd rather be a fly/Alight on my baby, stay with her 'til I die/With a toothpick in my hand, I dig a ten-foot ditch/And run through the jungle fighting lions with a switch".

The follow-up, "Need Your Love So Bad", established John as one of the greatest singers ever to get on his knees in supplication. No soul man, not even Smokey Robinson, has ever sounded so miserable, but John's performance remained frighteningly intense. When he sang "Don't worry baby, we won't fuss and fight", he laid the foundations for James Brown's scorched-earth vocals on "Please, Please, Please". Brown was also the opening act at John's live gigs in 1956, and he recorded a tribute album to John after his death in 1968.

If John is known at all, however, it's for his original version of "Fever". **Peggy Lee** may have ripped off the arrangement and the phrasing note-for-note, but her Mae West come-on routine couldn't even begin to approximate John's vocals. His going-hoarse excitement propelled his definitive version of the record to #24 on the pop charts.

While John continued to have pop success with records such as "Talk To Me, Talk To Me" and "Let Them Talk", the arrangements grew increasingly string-soaked and pop-oriented. By the early 60s, he could still sing

circles around anyone, but the hits stopped coming and he became increasingly irascible. In October 1964, he stabbed someone in a fight at a house party and was sentenced to eight-to-twenty for manslaughter. He died in prison in mysterious circumstances on May 26, 1968; the cause of death was initially listed as pneumonia, but then changed to a heart attack.

Fever: The Best Of Little Willie John
1993, Rhino

One of the most dynamic performers in a genre whose *raison d'être* is energy, Little Willie John created the blueprint for fire-starters like James Brown and Prince – even though most of his material dredged the pits of despair. This excellent anthology highlights the toughness, wicked sense of humour and urban concerns that took R&B out of the chicken shack and into the corner shebeen.

Loose Ends

Peckham, South London, doesn't exactly ring with the mythopoeic force of Muscle Shoals or Motown, but it was the birthplace of **Loose Ends**, one of the best soul groups of the 80s. Keyboardist and trumpeter **Steve Nichol** was a student at the Guildhall School of Music and Drama when he met aspiring fashion model and sometime singer **Jane Eugene**. With session bassist **Carl McIntosh**, they formed the group Loose End in 1980 and signed to Virgin Records the following year.

Their debut single, 1982's "In The Sky", was written by Chris and Eddie Amoo of the

Liverpool group **The Real Thing**. For their first album, *A Little Spice*, in 1984 Nichol's group changed their name to Loose Ends and began working with American producer **Nick Martinelli**. They had some modest success that year with "Tell Me What You Want" and the Chic-like groove record "Emergency (999)".

Loose Ends' 1985 album, *So Where Are You?*, was again produced by Martinelli and marked the group's breakthrough. The track "Hangin' On A String (Contemplating)" remains, by some distance, the best British soul record ever released, aside from some of The Equals's best material. With its stereo panning, dubby effects, drum machine woodblock sounds, and deep proto-house keyboards, "Hangin' On A String" was a production masterpiece. The heavily accented vocals worked perfectly in the echo cathedral Martinelli built for them. The record was so good that Loose Ends became the first British act to have a #1 on the US R&B chart.

The following year they repeated that tremendous success with "Slow Down". The single was perhaps less startling than "Hangin' On A String", but it followed the formula perfectly and even added a **Maceo Parker**-style sax solo to the mix. The group achieved further hits with "Stay A Little While Child", "Watching You" and "Mr. Bachelor", before breaking up in 1989.

With singers **Linda Carriere** and **Sunay Suleyman**, bassist Carl McIntosh reconvened Loose Ends in 1990. Despite the new blood, that year's *Look How Long* album continued in the same midtempo vein on tracks such as "Love's Got Me" – seek out the great mix by David Morales – and "Don't Be A Fool". After label and personal problems caused rifts within the group, Loose Ends split up after the release of their greatest hits/remix project, *Loose Ends Tighten Up Volume 1* in 1992.

McIntosh went on to work with Beverley Knight, Omar and ex-Soul II Soul singer Caron Wheeler in the mid-90s, and reunited with Jane Eugene on Pete Rock's "Take Your Time" in 1999.

(◎) **The Best Of Loose Ends**
2003, EMI

This 15-track collection is by no means perfect – it features none of the group's early singles and doesn't include the modest 1987 R&B hit "You Can't Stop The Rain". However, since nearly all Loose Ends' records mined the same groove, it doesn't really matter – and the album does offer a great cover of David Bowie's "Golden Years".

L.T.D. / Jeffrey Osborne

Much like The Commodores, L.T.D. was one of those funk troupes who were equally comfortable with bumping party jams and florid lyrical ballads. As was unfortunately typical of such groups, however, the ballads eventually won out.

Originally called **Love Men Ltd**, the group was founded in Greensboro, North Carolina in the late 60s by keyboardist **Jimmie Davis** and saxophone player **Abraham "Onion" Miller**, both of whom had served time in Sam & Dave's live band. Moving to New York, they linked up with guitarist Johnny McGhee, bassist Henry Davis and a horn section of Carle Vickers, Lorenzo Carnegie, Toby Wynn and Jake Riley Jr. At a gig one night their drummer got into a fight outside the club and was arrested. Vocalist/drummer **Jeffrey Osborne** (born March 9, 1948 in Providence, Rhode Island), who happened to be in the audience, filled in. He was asked to join the group and they soon relocated to LA, where they were joined by Osborne's brother, keyboardist **Billy Osborne**, and drummer Alvino Bennet.

Changing their name to L.T.D. (Love Togetherness Devotion), the group signed to A&M and released the mediocre, faceless albums *Love Togetherness & Devotion* in 1974 and *Gittin' Down* in 1975. Bizarrely, L.T.D. hit their stride the next year with "Love Ballad", produced by the Mizell brothers. The record had no hook whatsoever, but Jeffrey Osborne helped establish the modern ballad style with his vocals and "Love Ballad" went to #1 on the R&B chart. The group then started working with Philly producer **Bobby Martin**, who helped craft their biggest hit, 1977's irresistible "(Every Time I Turn Around) Back In Love Again". While that was an utterly infectious dancefloor groove, middle-of-the-road ballads proved to be the group's calling card in the late 70s: "Holding On (When Love Is Gone)", "We

Both Deserve Each Other's Love" and "Where Did We Go Wrong".

The Osbornes left the group in 1980 when Jeffrey decided to pursue a solo career. The rest of L.T.D carried on until 1983 with vocalists Andre Ray and Leslie Wilson, but only achieved very modest success. Jeffrey Osborne, meanwhile, went on to define the crossover R&B ballad with sappy, stiff, thin, over-enunciated 80s records such as "On The Wings Of Love", "Don't You Get So Mad", "Stay With Me Tonight", "The Last Time I Made Love", "You Should Be Mine (The Woo Woo Song)", "Love Power", "She's On The Left" and "Only Human". His collaborators included **George Duke**, Michael Sembello, Dionne Warwick, Barry Mann, Cynthia Weil and David Wolinski.

◉ Greatest Hits
1996, A&M

Inevitably, this 15-track collection focuses on L.T.D.'s soft-soul ballads at the expense of their uptempo funk tracks, which were, admittedly, fairly tame anyway. However, L.T.D.'s version of MOR was better than the trash Osborne churned out as a solo artist, and this album does include the funky dancefloor groove "(Every Time I Turn Around) Back In Love Again."

Barbara Lynn

It is difficult to understand why **Barbara Lynn** didn't become one of the biggest stars in soul. Aside from the fact that she played guitar and wrote much of her own material, Lynn could flat out sing. Her emotional range – from coquettish teen balladry to strutting soul mama, from swamp pop to shuffling blues to gutbucket soul – was the equal of anyone, while her grace and economy were breathtaking.

Born **Barbara Lynn Ozen** in Beaumont, Texas on January 16, 1942, Lynn began her career as a backing singer for the Goldband label. However, when she recorded "Give Me A Break" in 1961, she came to the attention of producer **Huey P. Meaux**. Meaux took her to Cosimo Matassa's studio in New Orleans to record "You'll Lose A Good Thing". A true soul masterpiece, Lynn's self-written ballad became a huge hit and, perhaps even more importantly, played a vital role in moving female singers away from girl

groups and towards becoming fully fledged solo soul singers in their own right.

The next year's "You're Gonna Need Me" was a similarly classic, languid New Orleans-style record, but Lynn also showed her facility with the blues on "Oh Baby (We Got A Good Thing Goin')", which was covered by **The Rolling Stones** a year later. Flitting from teen pop ("I Cried At Laura's Wedding") to the blues and country soul ("Careless Hands"), Lynn was never allowed to develop a recognizable style, even though she excelled at them all, and she was dropped from the Jamie label in 1965.

Meaux then started to release Lynn's records on his own Tribe label. She frankly kicked ass on 1966's "I'm A Good Woman", a dark burner with horns that sounded like they came straight off a Nigerian highlife record. Her fabulous version of **Maurice & Mac**'s "You Left The Water Running" the following year earned her a deal with Atlantic. Her first record on the new label, "This Is The Thanks I Get", was a great vocal performance that ranged from sultry to pleading to strutting. It was recorded at the Grits'n'Gravy studio in Jackson, Mississippi, along with the scintillating "(Until Then) I'll Suffer", which made the R&B chart when it was eventually released as a single in 1971. Again, Lynn's adaptability was her undoing: her self-penned songs were mostly in the Southern soul style, but she was also made to sing lightweight Motown-style songs that did her no favours commercially. After releasing "I'm A One Man Woman", a nice but not thrilling Southern groover, and "It Ain't No Good To Be Too Good", a sloppily arranged confessional, in the mid-70s, Atlantic dropped her from the label.

Over the next few years Lynn recorded very little new material, all but retiring from the music business. However, her 1976 single "Movin' On A Groove" showed that even formulaic disco couldn't temper her individuality. Lynn returned in 1988, her voice as good as ever, with "Tryin' To Love Two", which featured a fine **Nile Rodgers**-style guitar background. Holding on to a devoted fan base, she toured regularly throughout the 90s and has released several albums over the past decade or so in a bluesy vein displaying her fine fretwork.

The Best Of Barbara Lynn: The Atlantic Years
1994, Ichiban

A fine compilation of Lynn's Southern style recordings for Atlantic dating from 1968 to 1973. Although Lynn was also made to sing some fairly pedestrian Motown-styled numbers, the highlights here are her own grittier compositions, such as "This Is The Thanks I Get", "(Until Then) I'll Suffer" and "You're Losing Me".

You'll Lose A Good Thing
1997, Bear Family

You'll Lose A Good Thing is a superb 28-track collection of Barbara Lynn's recordings with the Jamie label, cut between 1962 and 1965. Its wild stylistic diversity amply illustrates her adaptability and talent.

Cheryl Lynn

One of the great voices of the disco daze, **Cheryl Lynn** (born Cheryl Lynn Smith on March 11, 1957 in Los Angeles) was bizarrely discovered on Chuck Barris's ridiculous talent show mockery, *The Gong Show*. After executives at Columbia saw her tape in 1978, she was signed on the spot.

Lynn's staggering range was showcased on her first record, 1978's "Got To Be Real". Although it was written by **David Foster**, the master of the huge schlocky ballad, "Got To Be Real" was one of the brightest hits of the disco era thanks to Lynn's powerful vocals, the burning "to be real" hook and some stellar horn charts. The next year's "Star Love", with its bionic bassline and tortuous extend-

ed metaphor, bordered on Hi-NRG, but Lynn's extraordinary voice elevated it above the purely generic. It was followed in 1980 by the poppier and more effervescent "Shake It Up Tonight" produced by Ray Parker, Jr.

Lynn proved she was more than just a disco diva two years later with a fine cover of Marvin Gaye and **Tammi Terrell**'s "If This World Were Mine", which she sang as a duet with Luther Vandross. She then returned to the dancefloor in 1983 with "Encore", her second-biggest hit. The skidding synths and sparse drum machine matrix perfectly framed her over-enunciated vocals.

Although the 80s were the decade of the power ballad – a style that would have suited Cherly Lynn perfectly – she never found one that really worked for her, and her productions became increasingly faceless as the decade wore on. She found her way back into the R&B Top 10 in 1989 with a version of "Every Time I Say Goodbye", but soon returned to recording largely anonymous background vocals for the likes of Luther Vandross, **Lenny Williams** and **Richard Marx**.

Got To Be Real: The Best Of Cheryl Lynn
1996, Sony/Legacy

Holding all her Columbia hits, this 15-track compilation is more or less all the Cheryl Lynn anyone needs and it amply displays the sheer range of her powerful voice.As a bonus, this best-of album also includes her 1979 disco version of Toto's "Georgy Porgy", which is just about made bearable by her backing singing.

The Main Ingredient

Among the finest soft soul groups of the early 70s, **The Main Ingredient** originally formed in Harlem in 1964. **Enrique "Tony" Silvester, Luther Simmons, Jr.** and lead tenor **Donald McPherson** were originally known as The Poets (not to be confused with The Poets who had a hit with "She Blew A Good Thing" in 1966). After releasing "Merry Christmas Baby" on Red Bird, The Poets changed their name to The Insiders, and then, after a solitary single for RCA, "I'm Better Off Without You", they changed it again, to The Main Ingredient.

Working with producer **Bert DeCoteaux**, the group had a modest hit in 1970 with the pastoral and orchestral ballad "You've Been My Inspiration". The follow-up was a similar cover of The Impressions' "I'm So Proud", but it was the next year's "Spinning Around (I Must Be Falling In Love)" that became their first R&B top-ten record. The title of their 1971 album said it all: *Tasteful Soul*.

The Main Ingredient changed tack on the underrated, psychedelic Temptations style *Black Seeds* album in 1971. *Black Seeds* was a surprisingly political album for a group who were soon to be lampooned for their feyness by **George Clinton**. While they were touring the album, McPherson was suddenly taken ill with leukemia, and was replaced by back-up singer **Cuba Gooding**. When McPherson died on July 4, 1971, Gooding permanently took over as lead singer of the group.

McPherson had been blessed with a rich, creamy falsetto that could scale the same heights as The Stylistics' **Russell Thompkins**. Gooding, on the other hand, was more nasal and less ethereal. His voice and slightly stilted delivery stood out in the soft-soul market and their first record featuring his lead, 1972's "Everybody Plays The Fool", gave The Main Ingredient their pop breakthrough. The twee piano line worked against the seriously funky beat, while Gooding's spoken intro rendered the record instantly unforgettable. The hook sealed the deal.

"Just Don't Want To Be Lonely", with its buzz guitar and tinkly piano, was another crossover smash. Unlike most vocal groups, The Main Ingredient had their ears tuned to the disco scene, and their 1974 version of **Brian Auger**'s "Happiness Is Just Around The Bend" was an important early disco record. The piano groove was somewhere between early Earth Wind & Fire's records and War's "Flying Machine", the strings were amazing and Gooding's refrain of "There's something going on inside my head" was sampled endlessly by junglists twenty years later. The more straightforwardly funky track, "California My Way", was almost as big.

Silvester left the group to become a producer in 1975. Working with Bert DeCoteaux and **Patrick Adams**, and sometimes alone, he was responsible for hit disco records by Ace Spectrum, **Ben E. King**, Linda Lewis and **Sister Sledge**. Meanwhile, he was replaced in The Main Ingredient by **Carl Thompkins**, who sang on the group's final top-ten R&B record, "Rolling Down A Mountainside", in 1975. Silvester briefly formed his own group, **Tony Silvester & The New Ingredient**, and had a modest R&B hit with "Magic Touch".

Without Silvester, The Main Ingredient's success continued to wane and the group split when Gooding left to pursue a solo career at Motown. However, Simmons, Silvester and Gooding re-formed the group in 1980, recording "Think Positive" as their comeback single. The next year they released *I Only Have Eyes For You*, produced by the great **Patrick Adams**. The album featured the cult late disco track "Evening Of Love", but it failed to make much noise commercially and the group soon disbanded again. Gooding's solo 1983 remake of "Happiness Is Just Around The Bend" was fine, but is really only remembered for being the first record ever to feature digital sampling – producer/keyboardist **John Robie** constructed an entire chorus out of Gooding singing only one syllable, "bop".

The Main Ingredient reunited yet again in 1986 for "Do Me Right", and then once more in 1989, when a line-up of Gooding, Silvester and **Jerome Jackson** enjoyed a hit with the smooth "I Just Want To Love You". Various members of The Main Ingredient continue to reunite periodically, most recently to release *Pure Magic* in 2001.

Everybody Plays the Fool: The Best Of The Main Ingredient
2005, RCA

The Main Ingredient may not have been as unique as The Delfonics, but these sixteen tracks show them to rank alongside the best of the soft soul groups. The out-of-print *All-Time Greatest Hits* (1990, RCA) album includes more tracks, but this compilation is the better package and it has better sound.

Steve Mancha

Steve Mancha is one of soul's undersung heroes. He was born on December 25, 1945 in Walhall, South Carolina as **Clyde Wilson**, but took his cousin's name when he moved into the music business. He moved to Detroit with his family in 1954 and, five years later, began singing with **Wilbert Jackson** in a duo called **Two Friends**. In 1959 they recorded "Just Too Much To Hope For" on the HPC label.

Hooking up with **Don Davis**'s Groovesville empire as a songwriter in the mid-60s, he changed his name to Steve Mancha and recorded a series of singles that were later hailed as Northern soul classics: "Did My Baby Call", "Still In My Heart" (which was terribly mixed, but perhaps his best solo vocal performance), "I Don't Want To Lose You" and "Don't Make Me A Story Teller". His best record during this period was 1966's "Monday To Thursday", which was in the classic Groovesville style: a whole lot of Motown, a little bit of Parliament and a *soupçon* of Ric-Tic era Edwin Starr. Many of these singles were issued on a split album with J.J. Barnes, 1969's *Rare Stamps*, as part of the Stax in Detroit series.

In 1969 Mancha joined Holland-Dozier-Holland's Invictus/Hot Wax stable as part of a group called Aged in Soul, who soon changed their name to **100 Proof (Aged In Soul)**. The group was put together by Mancha and **Curtis "Sonny" Munro**, who used to be in the Fabulous Playboys and The Falcons. The changeable line-up included, at various times, Mancha, **Eddie Anderson** of The Holidays, **Don Hatcher** and Joe Stubbs, who had sung lead on The Falcons' "You're So Fine", helped form **The Originals** and had been a member of **The Contours**.

100 Proof's first release was Mancha's self-penned "Too Many Cooks (Spoil The Broth)" in 1969, but their finest moment was the next year's "Somebody's Been Sleeping (In My Bed)", a really driving Detroit beat with hard gospel vocals reminiscent of Wilson Pickett singing irresistible nursery-rhyme lyrics. "If I Could See The Light In The Window", a bouncy Detroit number with mean guitar comping, followed in 1970 as the flip side of the weaker record "One Man's Leftovers Is Another Man's Feast", which made the R&B chart. The bluesy but slightly cheesy "90 Day Freeze (On Her Love)" and "Everything Good Is Bad" were the group's last singles before the Hot Wax label folded in 1974.

While recording with 100 Proof, Mancha also provided the testifying lead vocals on the minor classic of funky soul, 1970's "She's Not Just Another Woman". Released under the name of **8th Day**, the track was cut by a cast of slumming Motown all-stars gathered together by Holland-Dozier-Holland. Mancha (using his real name, Clyde Wilson) then co-wrote and sang lead on Parliament's mighty funk-rock merger "Breakdown" and the elegiac "Come In Out Of The Rain".

100 Proof (Aged In Soul) made a brief comeback in 1977 with "I'm Mad As Hell (And I Ain't Gonna Take No More)", a discofied James Brown production with a lyric swiped from **Peter Finch**'s ageing anchorman in the 1976 film *Network* and backing vocals from obscure soul group **New York Port Authority**. However, Mancha's recording career all but ended with the demise of Holland-Dozier-Holland's empire. He switched to gospel music and reverted to his real name in the late 70s, and he is currently one of the leading contemporary gospel songwriters.

Detroit Soul Man: The Best Of Steve Mancha
2000, Connoisseur Collection

Collecting almost all of his solo singles, this is a fine 20-track compilation of Steve Mancha's 1965 to 1969 recordings with Don Davis. Fairly evenly split between ballads and Northern stompers, every one of these tracks is a collector's item and a testament to an underrated talent who seems finally to be getting the recognition he deserves.

Mandrill

Formed in Brooklyn's Bedford-Stuyvesant neighbourhood, **Mandrill** were one of the best purveyors of that politically charged Latin-rock-soul-funk thang that groups like **Santana**, War, Ocho, Barrio Band, El Chicano, The Ghetto Brothers and Malo were dabbling in during the early 70s. The core of the group were a trio of Panamanian brothers – **Carlos** (flute, trombone, guitar, vocals), **Ric** (saxophone, vocals) and **Louis** (trumpet, congas, vocals) – who performed as a combo called **The Wilson Brothers** in high school. They started jamming with local organist **Claude "Coffee" Cave**, Cuban guitarist **Omar Mesa**, Puerto Rican drummer **Charlie Padro** and bassist **Bundie Cenac** from the Virgin Islands. Naming themselves after a baboon they saw in the Central Park zoo, Mandrill signed to Polydor in 1970.

The 1971 *Mandrill* album was a dazzling blend of holy-rolling, hippy-jamming, tribal percussion, jazzy noodling and symphonic daydreams. The follow-up, 1972's *Mandrill Is*, was a tighter, more focused and even better exploration of the same territory, and it

spawned their first R&B chart hit, the Deep Purple-meets-Tower-of-Power "Git It All".

Fudgie Kae replaced Bundie Cenac for 1973's *Composite Truth*, Mandrill's most commercially successful album. Both the political psych-funk track "Hang Loose" and the slamming funk jam "Fencewalk" were minor R&B hits. **Neftali Santiago** replaced Charlie Padro on drums for *Just Outside Of Town* later that year, but rhythmically the group were as strong as ever on fierce funk cuts like "Mango Meat" and "Fat City Strut".

After releasing the slightly too slick and overambitious double album, *Mandrilland*, in 1974, the group moved to Los Angeles. Although they began to lose momentum in the mid-70s and had a host of personnel changes, they still had minor hits with "Funky Monkey" and "Can You Get It (Suzie Caesar)", which was a percolating Brass Construction-style groove with a more pronounced Caribbean feel.

The group's penultimate chart hit, 1978's "Too Late", proved that the increasingly sophisticated studio equipment only served to tame their sound, streamlining the Latinate swing and the rough edges into blandness. They signed to Montage in 1982, releasing "Put Your Money Where The Funk Is" and their final album, *Energize!*, but record buyers thought the funk was elsewhere. The label promptly went out of business, signalling the end for Mandrill.

Fencewalk: The Anthology
1997, Polygram

Until their ill-fated move out west, Mandrill were one of the great funk ensembles, as this 31-track, double-disc compilation proves. Their blend of Latin music, funk, soul, gospel and rock was the sound of New York City in the early 70s and it helped to lay the foundations for both hip-hop and disco.

The Manhattans

Calling their brand of vocal group harmonizing "progressive doo-wop", **The Manhattans** were one of soul's most venerable groups, with a chart career that extended over 25 years. Although The Manhattans had their roots in 50s street-corner doo-wop, unlike just about every other vocal group they had their biggest hits at the height of the disco era.

The Manhattans hailed from Jersey City, New Jersey, but their beginnings can be traced to an air force base in Germany, where Edward "Sonny" Bivins, Winfred "Blue" Lovett and Richard Taylor sang together in a group called The Statesmen. When their tours of duty were over, Lovett and Taylor returned home and formed The Dulcets with George Smith and Ethel Sanders. The group disbanded after just one single, but Lovett, Taylor and Smith went on to form Ronnie & The Manhattans with Bivins and Kenneth "Wally" Kelly. The quintet recorded one single for the Piney label in 1962, before shortening their name to The Manhattans when they signed to Enjoy the following year.

The Manhattans only hit their stride when they signed with Joe Evans's Carnival label in 1964. The jaunty harmonies of their Carnival single, "I Wanna Be (Your Everything)", written by Lovett, gave them their first R&B hit in 1965. "Call Somebody Please" had teenage lyrics, in which the narrator desperately asked everyone from newspaper editors to telephone operators to help him with his lovelorn quandary, but the song also found lead singer George Smith at his most churchy and intense.

The excellent double-sided single, 1965's "Searchin' For My Baby/I'm The One That Love Forgot", showed The Manhattans to be equally adept at lovelorn ballads and more traditional doo-wop singing. Over the next few years the group alternated between late-night doo-wop-style ballads, such as "When We're Made As One", and midtempo sweet soul tracks, such as "Baby I Need You".

Moving to the King subsidiary DeLuxe label, The Manhattans achieved immediate success in 1970 with "It's Gonna Take A Lot To Bring Me Back" and "If My Heart Could Speak". Sadly, George Smith died of spinal meningitis that December, and was replaced by former New Imperials singer Gerald Alston. The Manhattans had a #3 R&B hit with "One Life To Live" in 1972, but DeLuxe had got into financial trouble, and further success was delayed until the group signed to Columbia later that year.

Paired with Philadelphia producer Bobby Martin, The Manhattans hit pay-dirt with "There's No Me Without You". Using Philadelphia's pervasive sweet-soul high harmonies while avoiding the cloying orchestral accompaniment, Martin had managed to bring out the best in The Manhattans. The song also set in motion the formula of a bass monologue from Lovett set against Alston's slightly adenoidal tenor lead that became the group's hallmark. If you want to know where the whining, over-enunciated singing style that characterizes today's R&B came from, listen to this record.

After two somewhat extravagant pleading ballads, "Don't Take Your Love" and "Hurt", the group hit the big time in 1976 with "Kiss And Say Goodbye". It may have sounded like an old country weepy, but Martin's swirling production and Alston's most restrained performance made it a two-million seller and a pop #1 for two weeks. Although 1977 was the height of the disco era, The Manhattans somehow managed to have a hit that year with "We Never Danced To A Love Song", in which Alston begged "Please Mr DJ, slow the music down".

Around this time Taylor left the group and was never replaced. The Manhattans continued as a quartet and had another big R&B hit with "Am I Losing You" in 1978, but it was to be their last for several years. Leaving Martin, the group started working with Chicago-based producer Leo Graham, who had previously worked with Tyrone Davis, and they had an enormous hit in 1980 with the sappy country-flavoured song, "Shining Star".

Although they cut some fine records during the early 80s – "I'll Never Find Another (Find Another Like You)", "Crazy" and a surprisingly decent remake of Sam Cooke's

"You Send Me" – The Manhattans' commercial returns started to diminish. After they recorded "Where Did We Go Wrong?" with Regina Belle, Alston left the group to pursue a solo career in 1986. Considering that his singing style had helped to create contemporary R&B, Alston had no trouble fitting in with urban radio and he had top-ten R&B hits with "Take Me Where You Want To", "Slow Motion" and "Getting Back Into Love".

Roger Harris briefly replaced Alston in The Manhattans, but he left when Lovett and Kelly retired from the group to sing back-up for Alston. Bivins started his own version of The Manhattans in 1992, and a year later Alston and Lovett reunited to create their own Manhattans line-up. Both remain popular draws on the nostalgia circuit.

○ **Dedicated to You: Golden Carnival Classics**
1990, Collectables

This is a fine 12-track collection of The Manhattans' earlier sides from the 60s. Their early releases, such as "I Wanna Be (Your Everything)", with the Carnival label may not have been as commercially successful as their later Columbia records, but the group cut some great, pure soul tracks with George Smith as lead singer.

○ **Kiss and Say Goodbye: The Best of The Manhattans**
1995, Sony/Legacy

Although it contains nineteen tracks, this Manhattans' compilation is still missing some of the group's key songs, such as the mopey anti-disco number "We Never Danced To A Love Song". It remains, nevertheless, the best overview of The Manhattans' main hit-making period at Columbia, when Gerald Alston was singing lead.

Teena Marie

With her boudoir poetry, strained similes and overripe metaphors, **Teena Marie**'s "opening line might be a bit passé", but no one, with the exception of Prince, so perfectly encapsulated the 80s. The Reagan era saw R&B move out of the church and into the shopping mall, and Teena Marie was the ultimate transition artist.

Teena Marie began life as Mary Christine Brockert in 1957 in suburban Santa Monica, California, but she grew up in less salubrious Venice down the road. After fronting several local R&B bands and lying about her age so she could play the club circuit, she signed to Motown after graduating from high school.

She was paired with Rick James, who moulded her into Motown's most successful white artist and wrote and produced her debut album, 1979's *Wild And Peaceful*.

James crafted a string of hard funk R&B hits for Marie, including the hit "I'm A Sucker For Your Love", which they sang as a duet. Further albums and funky R&B hits, such as "Behind The Groove" and "I Need Your Lovin'", followed at the beginning of the 80s. However, by the release of her fourth album, 1981's *It Must Be Magic*, Marie was writing and producing all of her own material. The album included what must surely be the only top-five R&B hit ever to use the word "Kismet" – 1981's "Square Biz". The single was as angular and stilted as its lyrics, but the slap bass, rap interlude and water-drop effects punctuated the awkward groove to great effect.

Marie left Motown in a dispute over royalties in 1983. She signed to Epic where, thanks to the monster single "Lovergirl", her 1984 album *Starchild* became the most successful of her career. Ditching the slap-bass sound of Rick James's Stone City band in favour of the processed guitars and synth curlicues of Minneapolis, Marie found the ideal vehicle for her slightly astringent vocal style. *Starchild* was full of angular funk jams, shoulder-padded power ballads, Harold Faltermeyer synth arrangements and he-man guitar solos, and it boasted the ultimate Reagan-era couplet: "Looking out the window I can hear an engine roar [cue revving noises]/Cobalt blue Pantera dashes through the garage door".

Just like Prince, the architect of the Minneapolis sound, Marie was a multi-instrumentalist – as well as producing *Starchild* and writing and singing all the songs, she also played guitar, piano, synth, drums and percussion and programmed the drum machines. Also like Prince, she tried to have it both ways with sex and God. But where Prince was firmly convinced that paradise is earthly, Marie was not so sure. Although most of the slow numbers on *Starchild* were a disappointment, except perhaps for "My Dear Mr. Gaye", the uptempo tracks made the album: "Lovegirl" is the best non-Prince Prince song ever, while "Help Youngblood Get To The Party" epitomized 80s synth programming.

On Marie's next album, 1986's *Emerald City*, the Latin rhythms that subtly percolated beneath most of her music came to the surface. The album sounded like a female Prince in full **Hendrix** mode jamming with Gilberto Gil and Jade Warrior – kind of wonderful and horrendous. The 1988 record *Naked To The World* had a couple of big R&B hits in "Ooh La La" and "Work It", but with the dawn of the 90s Teena Marie's time was over. Not even signing with Southern rap label Cash Money for 2004's *La Doña*, or working with Common, MC Lyte, Levert and Mannie Fresh could revive her fortunes.

Starchild
1984, Epic

Starchild is so 80s that you probably need to wear parachute pants to fully appreciate it, but it is also one of the few 80s R&B albums to explore the tension between the spirit and the flesh. What the neon-lettered sleeve art makes clear is that Teena Marie's conception of spirituality goes a lot further than the biblical passages she cites: there is also a lot of the unicorn-stickered otherworldliness of pre-adolescent girls on display here.

Martha & The Vandellas

Although **Martha & The Vandellas'** records epitomized the **Motown** sound, **Martha Reeves** was probably the least typical Motown vocalist. She was certainly the punchiest, sassiest and most assertive of all the label's female singers, and while many of the male vocalists wore their gospel influences on their sleeves, they were all smoother and more polished than Reeves. Even though she was sometimes saddled with lame, lovelorn material, Reeves' gutsy voice meant it was impossible for her ever to sound demure.

Reeves was born on July 18, 1941 in Eufaula, Alabama, but grew up in Detroit, where she worked and sang in her grandfather's church. Before she joined Motown as an A&R secretary in 1962, Reeves had recorded the single "I'll Let You Know" with **The Del-Phis** for the Checkmate label. At Motown, she eventually talked her way into singing on a demo. When the label's usual troupe of female backing singers, The Andantes, couldn't make a studio date, Reeves and her Del-Phis bandmates, **Annette Beard** and **Rosalind Ashford**, stepped in. That record just happened to be **Marvin Gaye's** "Stubborn Kind Of Fellow".

Signed to Motown as Martha & The Vandellas in 1962, they had their first hit in February 1963 with the rather banal "Come And Get These Memories". Despite its awful lyrics, the group managed to inject a true sense of longing into the teddy-bear pap. A mere five months later, the group, together with their producers/writers **Holland-Dozier-Holland**, put their stamp on pop music history.

With its heart-attack beat, honking baritone sax riff, dizzy piano chords and tumbling guitar intro, "(Love Is Like A) Heat Wave" was simply bursting with relentless forward motion and visceral excitement. As Beard and Ashford urged her on with "Go ahead girl" and "Don't pass up this chance", Reeves shouted and whooped and could barely be contained by the constraints of vinyl. As intense as its title suggested, "Heat Wave" scorched that long, hot summer as it screamed out of speakers across the country. The formula was so good that the group's next two singles, "Quicksand" and "Live Wire", were virtual note-for-note copies.

Just as The Vandellas seemed to be getting into a rut, they hooked up temporarily with **Mickey Stevenson** and **Ivory Joe Hunter**. The result was another definitive pop single, 1964's "Dancing In The Street". As well as being one of the great songs about getting down, "Dancing In The Street" derived much of its force from subtle references to the Civil Rights struggle. Lyrics like "This is

Martha & The Vandellas on British TV's *Ready Steady Go*

an invitation across the nation, a chance for folks to meet", "Are you for a brand new beat?" and "Let's form a big strong line" sounded like canny double entendres, while that martial beat and whip-crack snare seemed to imitate the tramping of a million feet marching to the Capitol.

Early in 1965, Annette Beard was replaced by **Betty Kelley**, and The Vandellas returned to the Holland-Dozier-Holland fold. Once again, the result was one of pop music's greatest moments, "Nowhere To Run". Motown producer **Norman Whitfield** was to define "paranoid soul" in the late 60s/early 70s, but the subgenre started here. Ashford and Kelley shadowed Reeves' vocals, while **James Jamerson**'s bassline and that insistent tambourine propelled the music to almost

unbearable levels of intensity. The flip side, also made with Stevenson and Hunter, was one of Motown's strangest records. "Motoring" was a raunchy car metaphor straight out of the Robert Johnson songbook – in other words, just the kind of song that Motown boss **Berry Gordy** usually frowned upon. What made the record truly bizarre, though, was the weird backing track, which sounded slightly out of time, a result of Hunter running the tape backwards.

After "Nowhere To Run", Martha & The Vandellas continued to create fine pop hits throughout the mid-60s – "My Baby Loves Me", "I'm Ready For Love", "Jimmy Mack" – but nothing that was anywhere near as epochal as their earlier masterpieces. From 1967's "Honey Chile" onwards, the group was renamed Martha Reeves & The Vandellas, but they couldn't adjust to a changing era and their singles barely dented the R&B Top 40.

The group disbanded in 1969, and then re-emerged in 1971 with a new line-up of Reeves, her sister **Lois** and **Sandra Tilley**. Reeves signed a solo deal with MCA in 1973 and released her solo debut *Martha Reeves: Produced By Richard Perry* the following year, but she soon suffered a nervous break-down. A few more solo recordings followed in the 70s and 80s, before Reeves eventually resigned herself to the oldies circuit. She continues to perform regularly in the US and the UK, and has recently moved into poli-tics, becoming a member of the Detroit City Council in 2006.

ⓞ Dance Party
1965, Gordy

If the excellent hits "Dancing In The Street", "Nowhere To Run" and "Wild One" aren't enough to get your atten-tion, this album is bursting with classic mid-60s Motown tracks. The label often filled out albums with mediocre leftovers, but there's no padding on this great party album. Look out for the 2002 CD reissue that pairs this with 1966's *Watchout!* and three bonus tracks.

ⓞ Live Wire!
1993, Motown

Motown constantly shifts and changes its greatest hits packages, often leaving only haphazard collections in print. This 2-CD, 43-track collection of all singles from 1962 to 1972 contains all the Martha & The Vandellas you need, along with fairly decent packaging. It can be hard to find nowadays, but it is their best compilation by far.

The Marvelettes

Although they were the first Motown group to go gold, **The Marvelettes** were quickly eclipsed by The Supremes as the label's – and the world's – pre-eminent girl group. While The Supremes went on to become one of the most successful acts in the history of pop music, The Marvelettes, with their ragged harmonies, remained mired in the archetypal girl-group sound for several years before they were finally given material equal to that of The Supremes and Martha & The Vandellas.

The Marvelettes started to take shape in Inkster, Michigan as a group called The Del-Rhythmettes. That group, featuring **Gladys Horton** and **Juanita Cowart**, recorded "Chic-A-Boomer" for the JVB label in 1959, before disappearing into history. Horton and Cowart then hooked up with **Wanda Young**, **Katherine Anderson** and **Georgeanna Tillman** and became The Marvelettes. They managed to wrangle an audition at Motown while still in high school and released their first single for the label, "Please Mr Postman", in 1961. "Please Mr Postman" remains one of the classics of the girl-group sound thanks to its cha-cha feel (Marvin Gaye was on drums) and a fine delivery by Gladys Horton. The song went gold and, inevitably, inspired the girls to release the rather less good "Twistin' Postman" the next year.

"Playboy", "Beechwood 4-5789" and "Strange I Know" followed in traditional girl-group style. The honking saxophones and Wanda Young's lead on 1963's "Locking Up My Heart" marked their transition away from boilerplate material to something more original. They had modest success in 1964 with "He's A Good Guy (Yes He Is)" and "You're My Remedy", but it was "Too Many Fish In The Sea" – perhaps Motown's most high-energy record and easily The Marvelettes' best – that brought them back to prominence.

A string of fine records followed in 1965: "Danger Heartbreak Ahead", the closest they ever got to the breathless overload of Martha & The Vandellas; "I'll Keep Holding On", which didn't quite come together, but had that slightly spectral quality that marked the best Motown records of the period; and "Don't Mess With Bill", a superb Smokey Robinson production. Georgeanna Tillman left the group in late 1965 due to ill health and – as Juanita Cowart had already left, allegedly following a nervous breakdown – the remaining Marvelettes carried on as a trio. After 1967's dull "The Hunter Gets Captured By The Game", Horton also left the group and was replaced by **Anne Bogan**.

Although a hit, 1967's "My Baby Must Be A Magician" was gimmicky, jazzy, nightclub schmaltz that can't hold a candle to sister duo Heart's "Magic Man". Things improved slightly the next year with the slowburn funk of "Here I Am Baby", but The Marvelettes recorded less and less in the late 60s. They finally disbanded in the early 70s following the release of "A Breath Taking Guy", not long after Motown moved to LA.

The Ultimate Collection
1998, Motown

At 25 tracks, this compilation has just about all The Marvelettes a non-Northern soul freak could ask for (except for the chugging "Your Love Can Save Me"). They were not blessed with vocalists as distinctive as Diana Ross or Martha Reeves, or the best material, but every so often they struck gold, and when they did they were easily the equal of their more prestigious labelmates.

Barbara Mason

Born in the City of Brotherly Love on August 9, 1947, **Barbara Mason** was the first lady of Philadelphia soul. Although she recorded in 1964 for the Crusader label, her records for Johnny Bishop's Arctic label helped create the blueprint for the Philly sound. She first hit the R&B chart with "Girls Have Feelings Too" in 1965, but it was the self-penned "Yes, I'm Ready" that truly established her as an artist and Philadelphia as a soul centre. That torrent of virginal teen longing featured the musicians who became the backbone of Philly soul – guitarists **Norman Harris** and **Bobby Eli**, drummer **Earl Young** and bassist **Ronnie Baker** – and introduced the impossibly lush strings that became characteristic of the Philly sound.

Mason excelled at such first-love yearning, and went on to mine the genre throughout the 60s on records such as "Keep Him", the Motown-ish "Bobby Is My Baby" (it sounded almost like her voice was cracking) and "Ain't Got Nobody". Mason was at her best on her own self-written tracks, such as "Sad Sad Girl" and "Oh How It Hurts", which both sounded slightly less teen-beaty. "You Never Loved Me at All" was another standout record, filled with pregnant pauses and stuttering, halting anger.

Moving to the National General label in 1970, Mason recorded a series of woefully dated and awkward pop-soul tracks. She then signed to Buddah and scored an R&B top-ten with a fabulous cover of Curtis Mayfield's "Give Me Your Love", produced by the man himself. The singles "From His Woman To You" and "Shackin' Up" banished her teen persona of old and established Mason as a sassy, no-holds-barred chronicler of love affairs. However, on 1975's "Make It Last" with **The Futures**, Mason still tried to sound girlish and innocent.

After recording a couple of disco duets with **Bunny Sigler**, Mason returned to the cheating arena in 1978 with "I Am Your Woman, She Is Your Wife", complete with a sleazy sax that let you know that she certainly wasn't innocent anymore. She explored the same territory yet again on the semi-classic 1981 record "She's Got The Papers (But I Got The Man)" and on 1983's "Another Man", a bass-heavy sequel of sorts. Mason sounded great over her producers' electronic backing on these records, and it is strange that so few producers have tried to record older soul singers in the same way.

Yes, I'm Ready
1997, Bear Family

Barbara Mason's career spanned too many labels for there to be one definitive compilation of her work, but this is a superb collection of her early Philly soul sides with Arctic. This is aching sweet teen soul at its best. The second half of her Arctic tenure is covered on the equally good collection *Oh, How It Hurts* (1997, Bear Family).

Maxwell

Exploding onto the scene in the mid-90s with wild hair and extravagant cheekbones, **Maxwell** was on the leading edge of the neo-soul "revolution". Despite its prefix, neo-soul was a thoroughly retrograde movement, and Maxwell was among its most regressive artists.

Born in Brooklyn on May 23, 1973, Maxwell (he doesn't want anyone to know his real name) sang in church as a young child, but claims that he was shy and awkward and didn't start performing in earnest until he was 17. In 1994 he signed with Columbia and released his debut *Maxwell's Urban Hang Suite* two years later. With songwriter **Leon Ware**, who had previously worked with Marvin Gaye, Maxwell had created an overly mannered pastiche of early 70s soul that was all style and no substance. Inevitably, it was hailed as a masterpiece by people who don't really like R&B.

His 1998 album *Embrya* was just plain pretentious. Like way too many of his predecessors (step forward Terence Trent D'Arby and D'Angelo), Maxwell took his reviews too seriously – face it guys, none of you are Prince. There was the odd bright moment, such as "Luxury: Cococure", but the record was mostly as bad as its titles. The following year Maxwell scored his only real smash, the R. Kelly-penned "Fortunate" from the soundtrack to the Eddie Murphy and Martin Lawrence film *Life*, which spent eight weeks at the top of the R&B chart.

Now from 2001 was more of the same: lots of production tricks and sumptuous arrangements with absolutely nothing to hang it all on, with the exception of the **Kate Bush** cover, "This Woman's Work", which he had previously released on his live *Maxwell Unplugged* album.

⊙ Maxwell's Urban Hang Suite
1996, Columbia

Filled with empty posturing and boho stylization, this is not the masterpiece that it was called in some quarters, although it is, to date, Maxwell's best album. At its best, as on "…'Til The Cops Come Knockin'" and "Ascension (Don't Ever Wonder)", it is mildly diverting mood music. However, at its worst, it is the retrograde twaddle of Oasis and Blur with a nicer voice.

Curtis Mayfield

Like that other key falsetto voice of the 60s, Smokey Robinson, Curtis Mayfield was more than just a very good soul singer. Just as Robinson was the main architect of the Motown sound, Mayfield – as a member of The Impressions, songwriter, producer, label owner and focal presence – was the prime mover behind Chicago soul. Unlike Robinson, however, who remained a pop craftsman throughout his career and nothing else throughout his career (unless you count the wretched "Abraham, Martin and John" as social critique), Mayfield injected his music with not just the gospel sound, but also gospel's sense of moral authority and uplift. He was one of the first soul artists to incorporate messages of black pride and self-

Curtis Mayfield tries to remember the chords

was his 1972 soundtrack to the blaxploitation film, *Super Fly*. The film told the story of a drug dealer named Priest who managed to leave the game with bags of money and escape from the ghetto with a good woman by his side. With its glamorization of pushers and pimps, ridicule of community activists and message of "go out and get yours", the film has become one of the most influential cultural artefacts of the past thirty years. While Civil Rights activists, Malcolm X and Black Panthers tried to take the moral high ground, *Super Fly* presented a vision of the ghetto that was a dark, hopeless, mercenary inversion of the American Dream and people bought it by the bucketload.

Mayfield was one of the few who didn't. He saw that this glorification of the underworld was a dead end and he conceived his soundtrack as a riposte to the film's message. However, when the film showed in cinemas, it featured Mayfield's music, but not his vocals. As such it's possible to criticize Mayfield's work for making Priest, and the rest of the film's rogues' gallery, seem that much more heroic. Listen to the record, though, and his intentions become clear. Combined with Mayfield's lyrics, the Beatles-esque strings, the horns, flutes, detailed percussion, propulsive basslines and wah-wah guitar became a chorus of voices pleading for sanity.

The album *Back To The World* followed in 1973. Again explicitly political, it had a sharper edge both musically and lyrically than *Super Fly*, but it was also preachier and more heavy-handed. By 1974's *Got To Find A Way* and *Sweet Exorcist*, Mayfield sounded less inspired, and that trend continued until he let someone else produce for him. With 1979's *Heartbeat*, Philadelphia's **Bunny Sigler**, **Norman Harris** and **Ronnie Tyson** created a superb disco album for Mayfield. It may not have been as good or as important as his early 70s records, but tracks such as "You're So Good To Me" and "Between You Baby And Me" boasted grooves that would have made anyone sound good, let alone someone with a voice as sweet as Mayfield's.

Industry indifference and a radically changing climate soon made Mayfield yesterday's news. However, he tragically returned to the headlines on August 13, 1990 when a lighting tower fell on top of him at a concert in Brooklyn, leaving him paralyzed

determination into his music. Unlike James Brown, who couldn't have been any more strident on 1968's "Say It Loud – I'm Black And I'm Proud", Mayfield's messages were more gentle, built on the quiet righteousness of gospel rather than its more charismatic shrieks and hollers.

Mayfield was born on June 3, 1942 in Chicago and grew up listening to local gospel, blues and soul musicians. He taught himself to play the guitar as a child and was writing his own songs in his teens. By age 16, he had left school and formed The Impressions with Jerry Butler, **Sam Gooden** and **Arthur** and **Richard Brooks**. As lead singer and chief songwriter of the group, Mayfield was instrumental in their success. Inevitably, he left The Impressions in 1970 to concentrate on a solo career. Mayfield's music began to get tougher when he left the group, but as funk grew ever more minimal, his particular brand stayed as detailed and as uplifting as his music of the 60s.

His solo debut, 1970's *Curtis*, was an absolute classic that included the moody "The Other Side Of Town", the moving "We The People Who Are Darker Than Blue" and the uplifting "Move On Up". The highlight was "(Don't Worry) If There's A Hell Below, We're All Gonna Go". Mayfield's first solo hit basically created the template for blaxploitation: the vague psychedelic atmosphere, the socio-politics, the darkness, the string arrangements that acted as secondary horn charts and the wah-wah riffs.

While 1971's *Roots* represented a step backwards in terms of both engagement and arrangement, Mayfield's solo masterpiece

PLAYLIST
Curtis Mayfield

1 WE THE PEOPLE WHO ARE DARKER THAN BLUE from **Curtis**
One of Mayfield's most poignant hymns.

2 MOVE ON UP from **Curtis**
Optimism without airheadedness or preachiness, plus remarkable string arrangements.

3 (DON'T WORRY) IF THERE'S A HELL BELOW WE'RE ALL GONNA GO from **Curtis**
Dread-filled, psychedelic-funk inferno.

4 PUSHERMAN from **Super Fly**
One of the best-produced records of the 70s.

5 SUPER FLY from **Super Fly**
Mayfield struts with gangster lean.

6 FREDDIE'S DEAD from **Super Fly**
Mayfield takes on blaxploitation on its own turf – and wins.

7 LITTLE CHILD RUNNIN' WILD from **Super Fly**
Dystopic funk symphony.

8 YOU'RE SO GOOD TO ME from **Heartbeat**
Mayfield's falsetto sounds fantastic over a slow-burning disco groove.

9 IN MY ARMS AGAIN from **Give, Get, Take And Have**
Mayfield's best guitar riff since *Super Fly*.

10 MS MARTHA from **New World Order**
Mayfield's moving final record, made with hip-hop production team Organized Noize.

and doesn't let up. Further simplifying and refining the groove he had established with The Impressions, this masterpiece was a great introduction to Mayfield's long and respected solo career.

Super Fly
1972, Curtom

The music on *Super Fly* was perhaps the most challenging soul in an era marked by challenging soul. The arrangements are incredible: the sinister bass and guitar of "Freddie's Dead" are undermined by the heavenly strings that are ultimately drowned out by an acerbic flute; the cheery piano and horns of "No Thing On Me (Cocaine Song)" sound as unreal as the song's drug-fuelled fantasy; and the woodwinds challenge "Super Fly"'s pimp strut.

The Anthology 1961–1977
1992, MCA

While the bulk of this 2-CD, 40-track collection is taken up with records Mayfield cut with The Impressions, it also includes eight of his best solo recordings. Arranged chronologically, *The Anthology* charts the progress of his music and his social conscience and is a near-definitive overview of his career.

New World Order
1996, Warner Bros

Curtis's final album – recorded with much help years after the accident that left him paralyzed – is compelling, not just as a last word, but because, while modern and beautifully produced, it is filled with the spirit of his best 70s material. There is optimism, sadness and resolution in his message, and this is a most dignified farewell.

Maze Featuring Frankie Beverly

Maze was one of the last self-contained R&B bands to achieve commercial success before disco and hip-hop conspired to make African-American music nothing but a producers' medium. Led by **Frankie Beverly**, the group alternated between bumping funk and sleek, jazzy ballads.

Beverly was born Howard Beverly in Philadelphia on December 6, 1946, but loved **Frankie Lymon & The Teenagers** so much that he had changed his name to Frankie by the time he filled in for one of The Silhouettes on tour at the age of 12. As a teenager, Beverly was a member of doo-wop group The Blenders. In the 60s, as both a solo artist and frontman of **The Butlers** (alongside future Maze percussionist **McKinley "Bug" Williams**), Beverly recorded a series of records, including "She Kissed Me" and "Because Of My Heart", on labels such as Guyden, Liberty Bell, Gamble, Sassy,

from the neck down. Despite his paralysis and ill-health, Mayfield managed to record a final studio album, *New World Order*, in 1996. The album featured excellent collaborations with hip-hop producers **Organized Noize**, "Ms Martha" and "Here But I'm Gone", plus a wretched remake of "Darker Than Blue". Mayfield died on December 26, 1999, but as one of America's most talented singers, musicians and songwriters, and a key voice in the Civil Rights Movement, he left behind a tremendous legacy.

Curtis
1970, Curtom

A staggering, ground-breaking first solo album from this soul giant, *Curtis* sets out with the apocalyptic "(Don't Worry) If There's A Hell Below, We're All Gonna Go"

Soul and the Civil Rights Movement

On the surface, the soul music of the time seemed to have little to say about the Civil Rights Movement. All soul seemed to be concerned about was "Baby Love", "The Leader Of The Pack" and "The Chapel Of Love". The music of the movement was the forceful, implacable gospel of **Mahalia Jackson**: "Move On Up A Little Higher", "Walk In Jerusalem", "How I Got Over", "I've Heard Of A City Called Heaven". Even for the most literal-minded culture on earth, it was hard to miss the Civil Rights' metaphors in gospel songs.

When talking about soul music one must always keep in mind author **James Baldwin**'s classic put-down in *The Fire Next Time*: "White Americans seem to feel that happy songs are happy and sad songs are sad". Beauty and meaning are always in the ear of the listener, and it's no stretch to believe that, whatever **Berry Gordy**'s intentions, the metaphorical force of records such as Martha & The Vandellas' "Nowhere To Run" or "Dancing In The Street" was just as strong as Mahalia Jackson's "I've Heard Of A City Called Heaven".

Perhaps the first expressly political soul records were Sam Cooke's "A Change Is Gonna Come" and The Impressions' "People Get Ready", both from 1965. Both of these records moved gospel's communitarian, hopeful, redemptive urge to the secular world. The metaphorical force of soul was reinforced that summer when "Dancing In The Street" and **The Creators**' "Burn Baby Burn" became the soundtrack of the Watts riot in Los Angeles.

Aretha Franklin's 1967 version of Otis Redding's "Respect" may be the greatest political record ever made – not that that was her intention. However, it was James Brown's "Say It Loud – I'm Black And I'm Proud" the following year that made it fashionable to be political in black pop music. From that point until the mid-70s, soul music was perhaps even more political than the folk boom of the early 60s.

While there was a steady stream of records from James Brown, The Temptations, The Impressions, Curtis Mayfield, **The Last Poets**, Marvin Gaye, **The Voices of East Harlem**, Stevie Wonder and many others, the music was largely severed from a connection to the "movement", whatever that had become by this point. Responding to this was one of the great unsung soul records, **George Perkins & The Silver Stars**' "Cryin' In The Streets" from 1970, a eulogy for the beloved community of the Civil Rights Movement and one of the most moving records in soul's emotive history.

⊙ **Various Artists: Stand Up And Be Counted: Soul, Funk And Jazz From A Revolutionary Era**
1999, Harmless

Although this has more to do with the soul and funk music of the Black Power era than the Civil Rights era, this is one of the few soul collections with an expressly political bent. It includes tracks by James Brown, The Impressions, Eddie Kendricks, Nina Simone, The Last Poets and Gil Scott-Heron. George Perkins' "Crying In The Streets" can be found on the excellent *Down & Out: The Sad Soul Of The Deep South* (1998, Trikont).

Fairmount and Rouser. All of these early singles are now highly prized on the UK's Northern soul circuit. On Frankie Beverly & The Butlers' "Love (Your Pain Goes Deep)", recorded for Gamble in 1968, Beverly sounded undeniably overwrought, but the bass undertow and the slightly sinister strings provided a nice counterpoint.

Inspired by Sly Stone, The Butlers turned to funk in 1969 and changed their name to Raw Soul. Billed as The Raw Soul With Frankie Beverly, they recorded a few sides with producer Jimmy Miller for the Gregar label. While "Open Up Your Heart" and "Color Blind" were ferocious hard-funk tunes with snarling guitar solos and nasty drum breaks, it was 1971's "While I'm Alone", a two-step classic, that pointed out the future direction for the band. Just as

Philly soul was becoming a commercial juggernaut in the hands of **Gamble & Huff**, Beverly and Raw Soul decided to move to Oakland.

After a few rough years, Raw Soul's big break came when Marvin Gaye's sister-in-law caught one of their gigs and immediately fell in love with them. Gaye took them out on the road as his opening act, and helped them to land a deal with Capitol Records. Changing their name to Maze, a line-up of Beverly, Williams, bassist **Robin Duhe**, guitarist **Wuane Thomas**, keyboardist **Sam Porter**, percussionist **Ronald "Roame" Lowry** and drummer **Joe Provost**, recorded their album debut, *Maze Featuring Frankie Beverly*, in 1977. The album, which included their first R&B chart hit, a remake of "While I'm Alone", went gold, and suggested that soul groups could find a way to get out of the disco quagmire.

With **Ahaguna G. Sun** replacing Provost, 1978's *Golden Time Of Day* also went gold, this time on the strength of laid-back but funky cuts like "Workin' Together" and the title track. Their third album, 1979's *Inspiration*, included Maze's first major hit, "Feel That You're Feelin'", a loping, gospelly, keyboard-heavy ballad that featured Beverly's thick, but not necessarily rich, voice. Sun and Thomas left in 1980 and were replaced by **Ron Smith**, **Billy Johnson** and **Philip Woo** for the group's finest studio album, *Joy And Pain*. The title track could be considered Maze's signature record thanks to its generic post-Chic groove and facile lyrics. The album also included the funky instrumental "Roots", the spiritual "Changing Times" and the top-ten R&B hit "Southern Girl".

A combination of live and studio recordings, 1981's *Live In New Orleans* was Maze's masterpiece. The live portion was electric, while the studio segment featured "Running Away", a keyboard jam that anticipated the Minneapolis sound that was soon to take over the charts. Their next couple of albums were derailed by too many line-up changes and a lack of radio singles. However, "Love Is The Key" from 1983's *We Are One* was a big hit, making it to #5 on the R&B chart.

Maze had their biggest hit, and R&B #1, in 1985 with "Back In Stride", a track that funked up that syrupy 80s production vibe epitomized by **Steve Winwood**'s come-back singles of the period. The follow-up, "Too Many Games", was a top-five R&B hit, but the real action was on the flip, "Twilight", an abstract, moody, synth-heavy, mostly instrumental jam that evoked both outer space and dawn on the Serengeti.

Maze left Capitol in 1986 and signed to Warner Bros, where their most successful album was 1989's *Silky Soul*. Its title track, an ode to their former benefactor Marvin Gaye, borrowed heavily from his "What's Goin' On", while the intense break-up ballad "Can't Get Over You" was their second R&B chart-topper. With the rise of hip-hop, Maze slowly faded from the charts, as tracks such as 1993's "The Morning After" were too jazzy to appeal to record buyers accustomed to more assertive songs.

Greatest Hits
2004, The Right Stuff/Capitol

Although *Anthology* (1996, Capitol) holds two more tracks, this compilation includes material from both Capitol and Warner Bros, making it the definitive overview of Maze's career. Although none of their records reached higher than #67 on the pop chart, this is an excellent précis of the funk and balladry that dominated urban radio at a time when the R&B and pop charts did not see eye to eye.

Van McCoy

Forever remembered as the man who perpetrated "The Hustle", **Van McCoy** was, in fact, a presence on the R&B scene as a singer, songwriter, producer and label owner long before the heady days of disco.

Born on January 6, 1940 in Washington, DC, he sang in the Metropolitan Baptist Church choir as a child. In 1955 Van and his brother **Norman McCoy** formed a doo-wop group called The Starlighters and had modest success on the East Coast with "The Birdland", a jumping R&B tune written by Van McCoy. The group followed up with the similarly styled "You're The One To Blame", but soon broke up due to the draft.

Van McCoy then enrolled at Howard University to study psychology, but dropped out after a year to pursue music full time. He moved to Philadelphia and formed his own label Rockin' Records. In 1959 he released "Mr DJ", a slow late-night shuffle that caught the attention of **Florence Greenberg**, who hired him as a staff writer for her Scepter label. After writing 1962's "Stop The Music" for The Shirelles, McCoy moved to **Leiber & Stoller**'s Tiger label and wrote songs for Jackie Wilson, Betty Everett, Gladys Knight & The Pips, **Erma Franklin**, Ruby & The Romantics, Barbara Lewis, **Nina Simone**, Irma Thomas and Peaches & Herb.

In the mid-60s McCoy recorded a series of Northern soul classics under a variety of pseudonyms with **Kendra Spotswood**: The Pacettes' "You Don't Know Baby", Jack & Jill's "Two Of A Kind", The Fantastic Vantastics' "Gee, What A Boy", Kendra Spotswood's "Stickin' With My Baby", The Vonettes' "Touch My Heart" and Sandi Sheldon's "You're Gonna Make Me Love You". **The Van McCoy Strings'** "Sweet & Easy", a ridiculously cheesy Northern soul classic released on the Share label in 1967, proved that McCoy was up to no good as early as the 60s.

In the early 70s McCoy produced a series of middling soft-soul records for the likes of ex-Spinners singer GC Cameron, The Choice Four and girl group **Faith, Hope & Charity** (including the R&B #1 "To Each His Own"). He also produced **David Ruffin**'s comeback record, "Walk Away From Love", in 1975.

It was with 1975's "The Hustle", however, that Van McCoy became a household name. "The Hustle" (from the album *Disco Baby*) wasn't the kind of record that you would normally associate with a dance craze. After its great, almost mysterious intro, it devolved into something akin to The Starland Vocal Band's "Afternoon Delight". But thanks to the infernal flute line, "The Hustle" was inescapable and inevitable and it went to #1 on both the pop and R&B charts.

The follow-up, "Change With the Times", was the better record with its "Machine Gun"-style clavinet riff, but it stalled at #6 on the R&B chart and outside the pop Top 40. McCoy's subsequent records failed to catch fire, but he continued to write and produce material for some of soul's greatest artists before his sudden death from a heart attack on July 6, 1979.

The Hustle And The Best Of Van McCoy
1976, Amherst

A collection of fifteen tracks, mostly instrumentals, that Van McCoy recorded right around the time he crafted "The Hustle". This album isn't exactly the height of soul or disco or even McCoy's oeuvre, but as cheesy mood music it's hard to beat.

George and Gwen McCrae

The first couple of Miami soul, **George and Gwen McCrae** achieved a string of hits in the mid-70s that blended their honest-to-goodness gospel and vocal group chops with the loping Caribbean-inspired groove that was south Florida's gift to disco.

Gwen McCrae was born **Gwen Mosley** in Pensacola, Florida on December 21, 1943, while George was born on October 19, 1944 in West Palm Beach. Gwen sang in her Pentecostal church as a child and began per-

forming in local clubs in her teens. In 1964 she met George, who was stationed with the navy in Pensacola, and married him after a one-week courtship. After George left the navy, the couple performed together in George's vocal group, **The Jiving Jets**, before moving to Palm Beach and striking out on their own as George & Gwen. Discovered by producer **Brad Shapiro** at a club in Fort Lauderdale, they signed to Henry Stone's Alston imprint. Their 1969 debut was an awkward reading of Roy Drusky's classic country song "Three Hearts In A Tangle".

After some back-up work for Betty Wright, Gwen began a solo career in 1970, when her radically reworked version of Bobby "Blue" Bland's "Lead Me On" was leased to Columbia and reached #32 on the R&B chart. Another Bland cover, "Ain't Nothing You Can Do", followed the next year before her contract reverted back to Stone. She then recorded the sexy "Keep Something Groovy Going On" and the rather wonderful "For Your Love", in which she growled like Al Green on top of a classic Southern soul groove, for the Cat subsidiary in 1973. She was great on the Muscle Shoals-styled number, "It's Worth The Hurt", which charted in 1974, but the flip, "90% Of Me Is You", was her best record and it featured one of the all-time great flanged guitar riffs.

At around the same time, George began his own solo career when Betty Wright and Gwen both rejected "Rock Your Baby", a song written by Henry Wayne Casey and Richard Finch of KC & The Sunshine Band. The song's proto-drum machine beat – from Timmy Thomas's "Why Can't We Live Together" – underpinned the trade-wind lilt of a groove and George sang on top of it as though in a reverie. The record was a huge hit in the discotheques and eventually went to #1 on the pop charts in 1974. The follow-up, "I Get Lifted", with its ferocious bassline, was even better and reached the pop Top 40 that same year. George was a more limited vocalist than his wife, however, and he couldn't sustain this momentum. His records soon became increasingly formulaic and, despite releasing the occasional new album in Europe, he has all but disappeared from the scene.

Gwen recorded her own disco stormer, "Rockin' Chair", in 1975. The song was basically a remake of "Rock Your Baby" and it went into the pop Top 10. Unfortunately, her follow-up, the dated "Love Insurance", wasn't nearly as strong as her husband's "I Get Lifted". The two reunited in 1976 for *Together*, an album of duets that featured the fine minimal disco cut "Winners Together Or Losers Apart", but appearances were deceiving and they divorced soon after. Gwen tried to go all Millie Jackson, with mixed results, on 1976's "Damn Right It's Good", before turning traditional in 1978 for a remake of Latimore's "Let's Straighten It Out". Despite releasing an excellent cover of Mel & Tim's "Starting All Over Again" and the slow-burn rare groove anthem "All This Love I'm Givin'", she disappeared from the charts in the late 70s.

Moving to New Jersey in 1980, Gwen hooked up with producer **Kenton Mix**. He was responsible for her "Funky Sensation" in 1981, which was the perfect bridging record between disco and the hip-hop-inspired funk that was soon to take over. **Webster Lewis** produced the equally fine dancer "Keep The Fire Burnin'" in 1982. A bizarre version of Lee Michaels' "Do You Know What I Mean?" gave Gwen her final chart outing in 1984. She then retired from music, until 1979's "All This Love I'm Giving" was rediscovered and became a huge hit on the British rare groove scene in the late 80s. She was coaxed out of retirement for *Girlfriend's Boyfriend* in 1996 and released the gospel album *I'm Not Worried* in 2004.

The Best Of Gwen McCrae
2004, EMI

It may not include the vital "Funky Sensation", but this 19-track retrospective of Gwen McCrae's Cat recordings, including three duets with her then-husband George McCrae, proves that she was a fine singer in a variety of settings, and much more than just a disco dolly.

Eugene McDaniels

Singer-songwriter **Eugene McDaniels** was born in Kansas City on February 13, 1935. Recording as **Gene McDaniels**, he enjoyed two huge hits in 1961, "A Hundred Pounds Of Clay" and "Tower Of Strength", in a very clean-cut, quasi-**Ben E. King** uptown soul style. On 1963's "Point Of No Return" he sounded unpleasantly stiff on top of the most ridiculously overripe downtown soul ever recorded. McDaniels was such a part of the institution that he even had a role in the British rock'n'roll exploitation flick *It's Trad Dad*.

By 1965, though, McDaniels was fed up of the industry, the system and The Man. He started playing jazz clubs and wrote the scathing anti-Vietnam War/anti-establishment/anti-everything song "Compared To What" for **Les McCann**. In 1969 he appeared on **Bobby Hutcherson**'s dark *Now!* album and wrote the controversial "Reverend Lee" for Roberta Flack.

The next year McDaniels was courted by Atlantic thanks to the success of Les McCann and **Eddie Harris**'s performance of "Compared To What" at the Montreux Festival, and he decided to return to recording. He transformed himself first into a folky squatter living with the disenchanted freaks in New York's Lower East Side for 1970's *Outlaw*, and then into the firebrand liberation theologist "The Left Rev McD" for what was effectively psychedelic soul's Book of Revelation, 1971's *Headless Heroes Of The Apocalypse*. The album was so politically uncompromising that legend has it that Nixon's Vice President Spiro Agnew successfully pressurized Atlantic to withdraw it.

Unfortunately, McDaniels not only learned how to get far out from the hippies on St. Mark's Place, he also learned how to sing, as the suave urbanity of old was replaced by an overly declamatory style that made the doggerel of the lyrics even worse. As with those other deities in hip-hop's revisionist canon, **David Axelrod** and **Stark Reality**, there's an unappealing dryness, a disappointing straightness, an awkward marriage of jazz and rock on most of the grooves. That said, McDaniels' fusing of **Bob Dylan** and **Miles Davis** was a laudable attempt to skewer black essentialism, while his passion and commitment were undeniable – and those aren't qualities psychedelia was exactly known for.

McDaniels mellowed a bit with his group Universal Jones, who had a hit with "River" in 1972, and on his own 1975 album *Natural Juices*. The album included versions of "River" and "Feel Like Makin' Love" which he had written for Roberta Flack the previous year. However, by this point McDaniels had become mostly a producer and writer, working with Flack, Melba Moore, Nancy

Wilson, Merry Clayton, Jimmy Smith and The Voltage Brothers.

Headless Heroes Of The Apocalypse
1971, Atlantic

This politically charged album is at its best – and most psychedelic – when McDaniels is at his most restrained. "Jagger The Dagger" is a sly dig at The Rolling Stones' cultural tomb-raiding that works precisely because it is more cryptic than the sloganeering that characterizes much of the rest of the album. His backing group are also at their best here: their laid-back but quietly fierce groove with delicate shading stalks the alleys of the mind.

Harold Melvin & The Blue Notes

It wasn't just the fact that **Kenny Gamble** and **Leon Huff** were responsible for some of the greatest music of the 70s that made their label, Philadelphia International, so remarkable. It was also the fact that they made their best records with relative nobodies whom they rescued from obscurity. Then again, perhaps it wasn't that remarkable; Gamble & Huff worked to such a rigid formula that they needed artists who lacked fixed images or personas and wouldn't buck against their strictures. Just as they did with The O'Jays, Gamble & Huff turned struggling vocal group **Harold Melvin & The Blue Notes** into one of the premier R&B hit-making machines of the decade.

Harold Melvin (born June 35, 1939) formed The Blue Notes in Philadelphia in 1953 as a doo-wop group. Although Melvin was the group's leader and driving force, **Bernard Williams** was lead singer. After winning the Amateur Night at Harlem's Apollo Theatre five weeks in a row, they issued a stream of records on small labels like Josie ("If You Love Me"), Rama ("If You'll Be Mine") and Dot ("Darling Of Mine"). Their Value release, "My Hero", was a minor R&B hit in 1960, while "Get Out (And Let Me Cry)", recorded for Landa in 1965, became a Northern soul favourite. In the late 60s the group, who now had **John Atkins** as their lead singer, hired a local band called **The Cadillacs** (not the group who did "Speedo" and "Gloria") to be their backing band on tour. When Atkins left The Blue Notes mid-tour in 1970, Harold Melvin asked The Cadillacs' drummer to replace

him. That drummer was Teddy Pendergrass and the career of one of the great male soul icons was born.

The group was reorganized around Pendergrass in 1971 and a line-up of Melvin, Pendergrass, Jerry Cummings, Lawrence Brown, Bernard Wilson and Lloyd Parkes signed to Philadelphia International that year. Their first Philadelphia release, 1972's "I Miss You", created the group's formula: The Blue Notes' sweet harmonies backing Pendergrass as he delivered a gruff, baritone sermon on love. "I Miss You", which was originally written for another former doo-wop group from Philadelphia, The Dells, peaked at #7 on the R&B charts for Harold Melvin & The Blue Notes, and Pendergrass's melodramatic, straining vocals inspired a generation of soul singers.

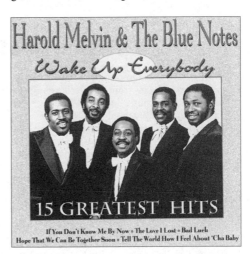

The follow-up single, also from the group's impressive 1972 debut *Harold Melvin & The Blue Notes*, did even better. Reaching the pop Top 3 and topping the R&B chart for two weeks, "If You Don't Know Me By Now" was one of the defining records of the 70s. Although "I Miss You" presaged the sound of black radio for the next two decades, it was too churchy for pop radio. "If You Don't Know Me By Now" streamlined and smoothed out the gospelese and added a mass of strings, becoming the model for the crossover hits of the next few years. Irrespective of its historical significance, the song was one of pop music's best evocations of a marriage breaking up. While Pendergrass attempted to overcome his frustration, begging, pleading and haranguing his wife, The Blue Notes and the string section exuded calm, patience and understanding.

The group's next big hit was 1973's "The Love I Lost". Originally intended as another ballad, it failed to work at a slow tempo. However, recorded with hissing hi-hats, a driving beat, string obbligatos and histrionic vocals, it became one of the building blocks of disco. "Bad Luck" was another dancefloor classic and its criticisms of the President showed that disco was more than just functional, robotic music. After a 1975 R&B #1 duet with **Sharon Paige**, "Hope That We Can Be Together Soon", The Blue Notes recorded another potent disco message, "Wake Up Everybody". It also went to the top of the R&B charts that year, on the strength of its slowly building momentum

and another rousing Pendergrass sermon. However, it was also the group's last significant hit. Pendergrass left The Blue Notes to launch a solo career in 1976.

Pendergrass was replaced by **David Ebo** and the group moved to ABC. Although they had an R&B top-ten hit with "Reaching For The World" in 1977 without Pendergrass, from then on their records never made much of an impact on the R&B chart. Various members of the group came and went over the next few years, but Melvin kept The Blue Notes alive. After 1984's "I Really Love You" and a final album, *Talk It Up (Tell Everybody)*, the group split up. Melvin continued to tour with various Blue Notes lineups throughout the 80s and into the 90s, before succumbing to a stroke on March 24, 1997.

New Orleans Soul

With a cosmopolitan population that included recent immigrants from the Caribbean, freed slaves and decommissioned soldiers with their marching band instruments, New Orleans at the turn of the twentieth century was the birthplace of modern popular music. From the jazz that developed out of this melting pot to the swinging rhythms of 50s, 60s and 70s R&B that the original Creole second-line beats evolved into, New Orleans has been the epicentre of the most ground-breaking developments in African-American music.

The decisive influence of the Crescent City's marching band heritage has already been celebrated in this book (see The Meters), but New Orleans' piano players played just as crucial a role in shaping the direction of soul and R&B. The most famous early New Orleans ivory tinkler was **Jelly Roll Morton** who was perhaps the most pivotal figure in the development of jazz. Morton's milieu was in the bordellos of the Storyville district, where dozens of piano players developed a syncopated, funky style that was miles away from the European tradition. In the hands of **Fats Domino** (and his arranger **Dave Bartholomew**) this Creole style became simultaneously more percussive and more loping. The lazy, easy swing of Fats Domino's records made him one of the biggest pop stars of any era, charting something like 63 singles in the pop charts from 1950 to 1964. Domino's piano triplets and his slyly rollicking rhythms (and the even funkier style of **Professor Longhair**) are at the root of that undefinable, but instantly recognizable, New Orleans swing.

The other great New Orleans pianist who changed the shape of R&B and soul was **Allen Toussaint**. As producer/arranger/A&R man/jack of all trades for the Minit label from 1960 until he was drafted in 1963, Toussaint was responsible for the records that made the period between **Buddy Holly**'s death and the emergence of **The Beatles** better than what preceded it or what came immediately after. Minit's first hit was **Jessie Hill**'s "Ooh Poo Pah Doo" in 1960. Pure New Orleans drawl, "Ooh Poo Pah Doo" combined Mardi Gras Indian chants, rhythmic guitar comping and an insistent horn riff into a swampy bayou of bass that just might be the first funk record. Toussaint followed "Ooh Poo Pah Doo" with a string of equally joyful, brilliant records that included **Ernie K-Doe**'s "Mother-In-Law" and "Te-Ta-Te-Ta-Ta", Jessie Hill's "Whip It On Me", Chris Kenner's "I Like It Like That" and "Land Of 1000 Dances", **Benny Spellman**'s "Lipstick Traces (On A Cigarette)" and "Fortune Teller", and The Showmen's "It Will Stand".

By the mid-60s much of New Orleans' finest talent had emigrated to LA (to work with Phil Spector, among others) and New York. In the Big Apple, Big Easy singer Alvin Robinson hit with the funkiest record ever to be cut so far away from the bayou, "Something You Got", while **The Dixie Cups**' version of the Mardi Gras chant, "Iko Iko", was easily the weirdest record of the girl group era. Perhaps the most New Orleans artist of all, though, wasn't even from Louisiana. **Little Richard** (from Macon, Georgia)

Wake Up Everybody
1975, Philadelphia International

All of the early Blue Notes' albums are probably worth listening to because even the filler was good stuff. On this, the final album they recorded with Teddy Pendergrass, the sound is classic Philadelphia International. In addition to the hit title track, this has their original version of "Don't Leave Me This Way", which has far more grit and soul than Thelma Houston's hit remake.

The Ultimate Blue Notes
2001, Sony Legacy

In the absence of a fully comprehensive Blue Notes retrospective, this 15-track compilation will have to do. Covering the period from 1972 to 1975 when Teddy Pendergrass was the group's lead singer, this has all their best-known tracks, including their first big hit "I Miss You" and their calling card, the classic break-up track "If You Don't Know Me By Now".

The Meters

Though not as well trained as the mixed-race Creole bands, the black bands of New Orleans developed a style of playing that was "hotter" and more rhythmically charged than the Creoles' more European style. Meeting up on Sundays in the city's Congo Square, their musically competitive gatherings were known as "cutting sessions". The band who played the "hottest" would march in victory, accompanied by a "second line" of people clapping, stomping and shouting along with the music. Rhythmically, this "second line" was a combination of **John Phil Sousa** with Latin American clavé patterns, and this syncopation is at the root of

cut rock'n'roll records that were New Orleans rhythms with their fingers in electrical sockets, and he recorded his most soulful record, the deep-soul ballad "I Don't Know What You Got (But It's Got Me)", in New Orleans.

When New Orleans' old guard left town in the mid-60s, they left a hole for an entire new generation of local musicians to fill. That new generation included such greats as Lee Dorsey, **Betty Harris**, The Meters, Eddie Bo, **Robert Parker**, **The Gaturs** and many, many others that have kept the Crescent City's remarkable musical tradition alive.

Various Artists: Crescent City Soul: The Sound of New Orleans
1996, EMI

It's not quite perfect, but this 4-CD, 119-track set is about as good an overview of the New Orleans R&B sound as you're going to get. A more concise history is provided by the double disc *The New Orleans Hit Story* (1997, Charly), while the funkier, more obscure side is covered by *New Orleans Funk* (2000, Soul Jazz) and *Saturday Night Fish Fry: New Orleans Funk Volume 2* (2001, Soul Jazz).

PLAYLIST

1 BIG CHIEF **Professor Longhair** from
'Fess: The Professor Longhair Anthology
Longhair's is the sound that defines the Crescent City's singular second-line rhythmic hoodoo.

2 LITTLE LIZA JANE **Huey "Piano" Smith** from
This Is Huey "Piano" Smith
As joyous and infectious as any record in popular music.

3 MOTHER IN LAW **Ernie K-Doe** from
Crescent City Soul: The Sound Of New Orleans
Only a New Orleans musician could pull off a trinket as endearingly daft as this.

4 OOH-POO-PAH-DOO **Jessie Hill** from
Crescent City Soul: The Sound of New Orleans
The beginning of funk music.

5 LIPSTICK TRACES (ON A CIGARETTE)
Benny Spellman from **Crescent City Soul:
The Sound Of New Orleans**
An utterly bewitching, cryptic record that is the essence of New Orleans soul.

6 GET OUT MY LIFE WOMAN **Lee Dorsey** from
Crescent City Soul: The Sound Of New Orleans
The greatest drum beat of all time and Lee Dorsey's fabulous lazy drawl – what more do you need?

7 HOOK AND SLING **Eddie Bo** from
The Best Of Eddie Bo
Pure stank – one of the funkiest records ever.

8 HERCULES **Aaron Neville** from **Treacherous:
A History Of The Neville Brothers**
The Meters plus Aaron Neville equals funk ecstasy.

In their heyday, no one was funkier than The Meters

just about every form of African-American music – especially funk.

For all of New Orleans' rich funk tradition, however, its finest exponents were **The Meters**. Comprising organist **Art Neville** – who also had a successful parallel career as one of **The Neville Brothers** – bassist **George Porter, Jr.**, guitarist **Leo Nocentelli**, and drummer **Joseph "Zigaboo" Modeliste**, The Meters were effectively **Allen Toussaint**'s house band from the mid-60s onwards, where they played on records by Lee Dorsey and **Betty Harris**. In 1969 The Meters started releasing their own instrumental material on the Josie label in 1969 and immediately hit the R&B Top 10 with their version of a popular local dance, "Sophisticated Cissy".

Probably the funkiest drummer ever to zing a Zildjian, Ziggy Modeliste brought both the New Orleans tradition and the James Brown beat – which came courtesy of Brown's drummer **Clayton Fillyau** – to hitherto unimagined levels of polyrhythmic dexterity. Modeliste was such a bad-ass because he kept time like a Swiss quartz – it's not for nothing the group were called

The Meters. But as their masterpiece, 1969's "Look-Ka Py Py", showed, The Meters were not just about syncopation: no funk troupe had as strong a sense of the space between the beats. The holes were not just created by Ziggy's outlandish grooves meeting Porter's bass precision, but by the unique comping of Neville and Nocentelli as well.

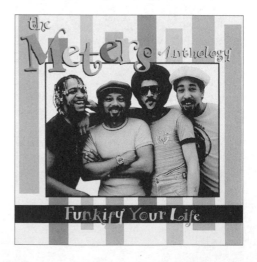

PLAYLIST
The Meters

1 SOPHISTICATED CISSY from **Funkify Your Life**
Lazy, loping, languid funk born of humid nights.

2 LOOK-KA PY PY from **Funkify Your Life**
The incredibly dexterous Ziggy Modeliste imitates an octopus behind a drum kit.

3 CISSY STRUT from **Funkify Your Life**
I ask you again, how great a drummer is Ziggy Modeliste?

4 EASE BACK from **Funkify Your Life**
Mellow and deceptively poly-percussive jam.

5 HANDCLAPPING SONG from **Funkify Your Life**
Not that Ziggy Modeliste needs any help, but the syncopation is bananas.

6 JUST KISSED MY BABY from **Rejuvenation**
New Orleans' finest at their stankiest and most accessible.

7 HEY POCKY A-WAY from **Funkify Your Life**
"Feel-good music that's good for your soul."

8 FIRE ON THE BAYOU from **Funkify Your Life**
Less compelling and singular than their early records, but awfully funky nevertheless.

The Meters had ten R&B hits with Josie, including "Cissy Strut" (a mind-boggling showcase for Zigaboo), "Ease Back" (which sounded like the Phantom of the Opera jamming with the canteen band from Star Wars) and "Chicken Strut" (featuring the funkiest organ playing this side of Jimmy McGriff and a monumental bass breakdown). In 1972 the group signed with Reprise and added vocals to the mix, courtesy of Neville, to appease the major-label mind-set. Even though none of these recordings matched the quality of their instrumentals, they still had plenty of gumbo flavour. Their best track from the period was the rare groove favourite, "Just Kissed My Baby", from 1974's *Rejuvenation* album.

The title of "Disco Is The Thing Today", recorded with vocalist **Cyril Neville** in 1976, is perhaps an indicator of why The Meters fell into a downward spiral in the mid-70s and broke up in 1977. However, the group reformed in 1989, with new drummer **David Russell Batiste, Jr.** replacing Modeliste, after an informal jam at that year's New Orleans and Jazz Festival. Various modified line-ups have continued to churn out New Orleans' standards to crowds of hippies and fans ever since, touring under the new name of The Funky Meters since 1994. Still, during their heyday, no one was funkier than The Meters.

Funkify Your Life
1995, Rhino

Although *Funkify Your Life* doesn't feature any of The Meters' session work – check out their phenomenal grooves on Dr. John's *In the Right Place* album – this is the best available collection of their material. One disc covers their Josie period, the other their Reprise days, and this does an admirable job of sorting the wheat from the chaff and demonstrating why The Meters were voted World's Best Instrumental Group for two years running.

Midnight Star

Despite forming at Kentucky State University in 1976, **Midnight Star** were the main architects of the so-called "Cincinnati Sound", an electro-funk sound that was closer to techno and electro hip-hop than the similarly synth-based "Minneapolis sound". The prime movers of Midnight Star were brothers **Reggie Calloway** (trumpet) and **Vincent Calloway** (trombone), who wrote and produced all their material.

With vocalist **Belinda Lipscomb**, vocalist/keyboardist **Bo Watson**, bassist **Kenneth Gant**, guitarist **Jeff Cooper** and saxophonist **Bill Simmons**, they signed to the Solar label and released *The Beginning* in 1980. Midnight Star enjoyed modest chart success with the singles "Make It Last", "I've Been Watching You" and "Hot Spot", but it was only after they embraced the synthesizer and added drummer **Bobby Lovelace** and vocalist **Melvin Gantry** that they really took off.

"Freak-A-Zoid" became a huge R&B hit in 1983 thanks to its Vocoded vocals and its streamlined electro flavour. The same year's "Wet My Whistle" was a more straightforward boogie track, although it was equally dependent on synths for its lush sound and squiggly hooks. The silly novelty track "No Parking (On the Dance Floor)" reached no higher than #43 on the R&B chart later that year, but became a Bar Mitzvah staple. The most important track on 1983's *No Parking On The Dance Floor* wasn't released as a single; the syrupy ballad "Slow Jam", written by Kenneth "Babyface" Edmonds of Midnight Star protegés **The Deele**, presaged the future shape of R&B.

In 1984 "Operator", which bore a lot of similarity to the early techno tracks coming out of Detroit, but with vocals, provided Midnight Star's biggest hit, spending five weeks at #1 on the R&B chart. It was followed in 1986 by three more hits, "Midas Touch", "Headlines" and "Engine No. 9". However, the Calloway brothers, who had produced The Deele, Klymaxx, **Levert**, The Whispers, Teddy Pendergrass and Natalie Cole, wanted to concentrate on production work and left the group in 1988. Midnight Star briefly carried on without the Calloways, achieving hits with "Don't Rock The Boat" and "Snake In The Grass", but they folded after *Work It Out* in 1990.

Reggie and Vincent recorded the smash "I Wanna Be Rich" as **Calloway** in 1990, but their success proved fleeting. Despite releasing two albums, 1990's *All The Way* and 1992's *Let's Get Smooth*, the brothers soon returned to behind-the-boards work with **Bootsy Collins**, Teddy Pendergrass and Pieces of a Dream.

The Anniversary Collection
1999, Capitol

While it doesn't have "Engine No. 9" and you can certainly do without the "Millennium Mix" of "Freak-A-Zoid", this 16-track CD is the best Midnight Star package. For the most part, it's breezy party music that won't offend anyone, although it won't truly excite anyone either.

Stephanie Mills

B lessed with a stunning voice but never quite able to connect with a pop audience, **Stephanie Mills** had a career typical of female singers in the late 70s and 80s. Part of her problem was that she moved too easily between her gospel roots and Broadway, without really settling on a single persona. Her breakthrough only came in the late 80s when urban radio programmers scared of

hip-hop flooded the airwaves with power ballads. That genre suited Mills perfectly, and she scored five R&B #1 hits, although none crossed over to the pop chart.

Born in Brooklyn on March 22, 1957, Mills began singing as a young child at her mother's Baptist church. After winning the Amateur Hour at the Apollo Theatre for six straight weeks aged 9, she appeared on Broadway in *Maggie Flynn*. In 1974 she released her debut single, "I Knew It Was Love", and album, *Movin' In The Right Direction*, on ABC-Paramount. The next year she embarked on a four-year stint in the starring role of Dorothy in *The Wiz*. Signing to Motown in 1976, she released *For The First Time*, an album of Bacharach/David songs. However, she left the label after she was passed over in favour of Diana Ross when **Berry Gordy** turned *The Wiz* into a movie in 1978.

Working with former **Miles Davis** band members James Mtume and Reggie Lucas for the 20th Century label, Stephanie Mills had two disco hits in 1979: "What Cha Gonna Do With My Lovin'" and the great Larry Levan remix of "Put Your Body In It". Her next releases, such as "Never Knew Love Like This Before", "Try My Love" and the title track from 1980's *Sweet Sensation*, were a classic meld of late disco and very early boogie. The following year Mills scored a big R&B hit with the gently uplifting "Two Hearts", a duet with Teddy Pendergrass.

Moving to Casablanca Records, Mills had several small dancefloor hits, including a very un-Prince-like version of the purple one's "How Come U Don't Call Me Anymore?" in 1983 and the strange, angular "The Medicine Song" in 1984. Poised somewhere between 80s funk and early stormtrooper techno, "The Medicine Song" reached #12 on the R&B chart.

Mills enjoyed her greatest success with the MCA label. A bass-heavy, midtempo, MOR cover of **Angela Winbush**'s "I Have Learned To Respect The Power Of Love" gave Mills her first R&B #1 in 1986, while the slower, more saccharine "I Feel Good All Over" was just as successful the following year. She followed-up with two simpler, but over-produced, midtempo R&B #1 ballads: "(You're Puttin') A Rush On Me" and "Something In The Way (You Make Me Feel)". Her fifth #1

came with a song that used to wow 'em on Broadway, 1989's "Home".

After Mills made a brief return to her roots by appearing in a touring performance of *The Wiz* in 1990, her hit-making prowess began to desert her. She went back to her roots again on the gospel album *Personal Inspirations* in 1995 and returned to the dancefloor on 1999's "Latin Lover", produced by **Masters at Work**. Mills is still touring and recording, and 2004's *Born For This!* proved that her voice is still in remarkable form, although the album's production left much to be desired.

The Ultimate Collection
1999, Hip-O

As Stephanie Mills' records are strewn across different labels, this chronological 15-track CD is the only collection to compile material from her entire career. Hard-core disco and ballad fans might feel a little hard done by and there are some regrettable omissions, but *The Ultimate Collection* provides a fine overview of Mills' protean talents as a vocalist.

Garnet Mimms

Born on November 16, 1933 in Ashton, Virginia, but raised in Philadelphia, **Garnet Mimms** ranks among the finest of the early soul singers. Although he only achieved one hit commensurate with his talents, with hindsight it's easy to see that his vocal style was the blueprint for deep soul.

As a teenager, Mimms sang in Philadelphia gospel ensembles The Norfolk Four and The Evening Stars (with Howard Tate and **Little Joe Cook**). After a stint in the military, he founded a doo-wop group called **The Gainors** with Tate, **Sam Bell**, Willie Combo and John Jefferson and they scored local hits with "The Secret" and "You Must Be An Angel" on Cameo-Parkway in 1958. Further singles on Mercury and Talley-Ho failed to sell, and they broke up in 1961.

Mimms then formed **The Enchanters** with Bell, **Zola Parnell** and **Charles Boyer**. The first record that Garnet Mimms & The Enchanters cut with **Bert Berns** and **Jerry Ragovoy** at United Artists, 1963's "Cry Baby", counts as one of the greatest in the soul canon. Its lush uptown orchestration, Southern-fried guitar lines, dramatic arrangements and gospel phrasing fused to create the template followed by nearly all subsequent deep-soul ballads.

A magnificent version of Jerry Butler's "For Your Precious Love" followed later that year. "Tell Me Baby" in 1964 was more uptempo, but the group's hand-clapping interaction was delightful and Mimms was still powerful even at this higher speed. Other 1964 recordings included "One Girl", The Drifters-esque "A Quiet Place" and the splendid "Look Away". Mimms' 1965 cover of "A Little Bit Of Soap" wasn't as good as **The Jarmels**' original, but it became a Northern soul favourite nevertheless.

Mimms' final recordings for United Artists were among his best. The 1966 album *I'll Take Good Care Of You* included two stone-cold classics: the incredibly deep title track and the uptempo, Motown-ish "Prove It To Me", which had a great female chorus. Mimms moved to Verve with Ragavoy in 1968, but none of his four singles for the label had the impact of those by his former comrade Howard Tate. Mimms also recorded a couple of singles for Lloyd Price's GSF label in the early 70s, including the funky "Stop And Check Yourself" with **Joe Quartermain**'s band.

Mimms re-emerged in 1977 and released "What It Is" under the name of **Garnet Mimms & The Truckin' Company**. The record was a nice little Randy Muller disco production with Brass Construction in the background and it reached #44 on the UK pop charts. The surprisingly good 1978 album *Garnett Mimms Has It All* included "It's You", an aching deep-soul ballad that was quite different from his disco material of the era. However, shortly after the album's release, Mimms rediscovered Christianity and retired permanently from the music biz.

The Best Of Garnet Mimms: Cry Baby
1993, EMI

This superb 25-track compilation includes nearly everything Garnet Mimms recorded for United Artists between 1963 and 1966. Mimms created a lasting soul legacy at the label with the help of producer Jerry Ragovoy during those three years, and these are some of the most influential soul recordings ever made.

Mint Condition

Minneapolis's **Mint Condition** were one of the very, very few, if not the only, self-contained bands to make a significant impact on R&B during the 90s. Excelling at both post-New Jack Swing slow jams and post-Jam & Lewis funk, they were not afraid to show off their skills. Their one drawback was perhaps that they spread their chops too thin, throwing fusion, Latin music and even steel pans into their brand of R&B.

Mint Condition was formed in 1986 at St. Paul Central High School in Minnesota by guitarist **Homer O'Dell**, drummer/vocalist **Stokley Williams**, keyboardist **Lawrence Waddell** and saxophonist **Jeffrey Allen**. Along with bassist **Ricky Kinchen** and keyboardist **Keri Lewis**, they signed to Jam & Lewis's Perspective label in 1989. Their breakthrough was their second single, 1991's "Breakin' My Heart (Pretty Brown Eyes)", an old-fashioned romantic ballad in an age of he-man humpers which had just enough New Jack flourishes not to sound completely out of place on urban radio. It was a top-ten hit on both the pop and R&B charts. The following year's "Forever In Your Eyes" was cheesier and more MOR and had a couple of cringe-worthy sax solos.

The group's second album, 1993's *From The Mint Factory*, was both more consistent and more in tune with the times, with "Nobody Does it Betta" rocking **Teddy Riley**-style beats and "U Send Me Swingin'" sounding like **Take 6**. *Definition Of A Band* went gold in 1996 on the strength of the fidelity ballad "What Kind Of Man Would I Be" and the love-on-the-rebound seduction of "You Don't Have To Hurt No More".

Keri Lewis married Toni Braxton and left the group after they recorded *Life's Aquarium* in 1999. The album was tighter but less interesting than their previous albums because of its focus on loverman ballads. After a six-year hiatus, Mint Condition returned with a new album, *Livin' The Luxury Brown*, in 2005 on their own Cagedbird label. More indulgent than *Life's Aquarium*, it reinforced the group's standing as a collective unit free from the influence of the Svengalis who run R&B these days.

The Collection 1991–1998
1998, Perspective

Even though their albums are what makes Mint Condition unique, their overreaching eclecticism can be wearing at times. This 15-track compilation collects the hits and the highlights from their first three albums, making for a perfect introduction to a band that dared to put romance back into R&B.

The Moments

Against all the odds **The Moments** were one of the most consistent hit-making groups in the history of R&B. With a couple of exceptions, they recorded fairly formulaic sweet doo-wop-influenced soul during the funk and disco era for a label that didn't have the budget to lavish heavy orchestrations and sweetening on their records. Nevertheless, The Moments and **Ray, Goodman & Brown**, as they later became known, had a string of R&B hits between the late 60s and the late 80s.

Mark Greene, **Richie Horsley** and **John Morgan**, all from Washington, DC, signed to Joe and **Sylvia Robinson**'s All Platinum organization as The Moments in 1968. Their first single, the pleading ballad "Not On The Outside", reached #13 on the R&B chart that year. However, Greene and Horsley were fired by the label owners after a couple of gigs at the Apollo Theatre went badly. They were replaced by **Billy Brown**, who had previously been in The Broadways, and **Al Goodman**. The new line-up reached the R&B Top 10 the next year with the doo-woppy "I Do", but Morgan, the last original member of the group, was then replaced by Robinson's brother-in-law **John Moore**.

With Moore the group recorded "I'm So Lost" and "Lovely Way She Loves" in 1969, and their mega-hit, "Love On A Two-Way Street", in 1970. With its cavernous echo surrounding a chanking guitar and gentle bass undertow, the production on "Love On A Two-Way Street" highlighted Brown's wimpy falsetto, somehow suggesting that there was a full uptown orchestra behind him. It stayed at the top of the R&B chart for five weeks and reached #3 on the pop chart. However, just after the single was recorded, Moore left the group and was replaced by **Harry Ray**.

Ray sang lead on the group's next hit, "If I Didn't Care", while Brown took the lead on "All I Have". A string of faceless romantic ballads followed, before the release of the deliciously sleazy "Sexy Mama" in 1973, which set an early rhythm box against a string section to create a groove that presaged disco. The next year's "Sho Nuff Boogie", a duet with **Sylvia Robinson**, also featured drum-machine experimentation. The Moments linked up with labelmates The Whatnauts to record the early disco favourite "Girls" in 1974, which hit #3 on the UK pop chart.

"Look At Me (I'm In Love)", a typical Moments' ballad with an unusually lush string arrangement, reached the top of the R&B chart. As hard as they tried with out-and-out funk tracks, such as "Come In Girl" from 1976's *Moments With You* album, the group found it difficult to break a sweat. The disco years proved lean for The Moments, although they did manage to enter the UK Top 10 with "Dolly My Love" and "Jack In The Box". Times were also tough for All Platinum, and the group and the label parted company at the end of 1977.

As All Platinum owned The Moments' name, when the group signed to Polydor in 1979 it was as **Ray, Goodman & Brown**. The trio hit immediately with "Special Lady", a modern doo-wop record with a great hook. However, aside from "Another Day" – a favourite hip-hop sample thanks to its bouncy bass groove and spacey keyboard riff – the rest of their Polydor records were utterly nondescript doo-wop. Ray left the group in 1982 to pursue a solo career. His place was taken first by **Kevin "Ray" Owens** and then **Wade Elliott**, who stayed with the group until their final chart hit "Where Did You Get That Body, Baby?" in 1988.

Ray died of a stroke on October 1, 1992, but the group remained active on the oldies circuit throughout the 90s. In 2003 a line-up of Goodman, Brown, Owens and Larry "Ice" Winfree released two new albums, *Intimate Moments* and *A Moment With Friends* (a covers album), and they also performed backing vocals on Alicia Keys' "You Don't Know My Name" the following year.

The Best Of The Moments: Love On A Two-Way Street
1996, Rhino

This 18-track greatest hits package understandably focuses on The Moments' hit ballads, which are what they're best known for. Despite failing to include the disco track "Girls", which was a big hit everywhere but the US, it's the best available summation of their recording career from 1968 to 1982.

Monica

Along with her sometime partner **Brandy**, **Monica** set the stage and created the pattern for the supernova teenage hip-hop R&B diva, notching up a staggering six platinum singles in four years. Of course, while supernovas burn bright, they also burn out pretty darn quick.

Born **Monica Arnold** in Atlanta on October 24, 1980, she was discovered by producer **Dallas Austin**, who immediately signed her to his Rowdy Records label. Monica exploded onto the scene in 1995 with her debut "Don't Take It Personal (Just One of Dem Days)", which sampled **LL Cool J**'s "Back Seat (Of My Jeep). A whiny "I need my space" song, "Don't Take It Personal" reached #1 on the R&B chart and #2 pop. Monica's 1995 debut album *Miss Thang*, which was co-produced by Austin, spawned three more top-ten hits: "Before You Walk Out Of My Life", "Like This And Like That" and "Why I Love You So Much".

Yet another top-ten single, "For You I Will" from the *Space Jam* movie soundtrack, cemented her crossover appeal in 1997. However, it was her appearance on one of the biggest singles ever that truly established her as an R&B superstar. "The Boy Is Mine", a duet with Brandy, went double platinum in 1998 and spent thirteen weeks at #1, despite being a histrionic pile of rubbish in which Brandy and Monica sounded like a female version of Jodeci. Monica's solo 1998 single "The First Night" was far better – due in no small part to the ace sample of Diana Ross's "Love Hangover" – but Monica herself was also richer and more soulful. It was another blockbuster, spending five weeks at the top of the pop chart. The truly diabolical "Angel Of Mine" – a hideously sappy Hallmark card of a ballad – gave her another #1 that year, this time for four weeks.

As quickly as Monica arrived on the scene from nowhere, she went right back there just as fast. Nothing was heard from her for four years while she dealt with the suicide of her boyfriend and other personal problems. However, she returned to the limelight in 2003 with *After The Storm*, which was a surprisingly decent album, largely due to the presence of Missy Elliott on three tracks: "Set It Off", "So Gone" and "Knock Knock". There were no blockbusters on the album, however, reinforcing the old lesson that you gotta get it while the gettin's good.

(o) **After The Storm**
2003, J-Records

It may not be the multi-platinum success that her previous records were, but this is certainly Monica's most listenable album. The adenoidal, adolescent whine has become more womanly; the production is sharper; the lyrics are generally smarter and less crass; plus it has Missy Elliott.

Dorothy Moore

With a couple of huge singles, **Dorothy Moore** helped to redefine Southern soul in the mid-70s. Born in 1946 in Jackson, Mississippi, Moore first came to local prominence by winning a talent show at the city's Alamo Theatre and was eventually hired by local producer **Bob McRee** as a back-up singer. While at Jackson State University, Moore was in a group called **The Poppies** with Fern Kinney and Patsy McEwen. McRee got them signed to Epic, where they had a small pop hit with the Billy Sherrill-produced "Lullaby Of Love" in 1966. With a new line-up of Moore, Pet McClune and Rosemary Taylor, The Poppies recorded two more singles that became Northern soul favourites, "He's Ready" and "There's A Pain In My Heart".

The Poppies broke up after they were dropped by Epic in 1967. Moore then recorded a one-off single for the Josie label as **Dorothy & The Hesitations** – "Don't Set Me Up For The Kill" – and another for MGM as **Dottie Cambridge** – the uptempo, gogo-dancing "He's About A Mover". Recording for Buddah as **Chee Chee & Peppy** with **Keith Bolling**, Moore recorded a couple more Northern soul favourites in 1971, "My Love Will Never Fade Away" and "Never Never Never".

In 1971 Moore signed to Malaco, who licensed her first few singles to Avco and GSF. She hit the R&B chart with "Cry Like A Baby" and a version of Eddie Floyd's "We Can Love", recorded as a duet with King Floyd. Her breakout record was a stunning 1975 version of **Bob Montgomery**'s country song "Misty Blue". Moore was great, but what truly made the record special were the dry fills from Muscle Shoals guitarist **Jimmy Johnson** in the background. The song's traditionalism struck a chord with record buyers during the first year of the disco boom and it went to #3 on the pop chart.

Moore tried a similar trick in 1976 with a version of **Willie Nelson**'s "Funny How Time Slips Away", but the strings swamped the record. Better were the funky flip side, "Ain't That A Mother's Luck", and the follow-up, "For Old Time's Sake", which was recorded in Muscle Shoals. Unfortunately, Moore started to record some dreadful pop songs in 1977, including "I Believe You", which was, inexplicably, her second-biggest hit, and the tear-jerker "With Pen In Hand".

After leaving Malaco in 1980, Moore continued to record sporadically throughout the early 80s. Her recordings included a cover of Michael Murphey's "What's Forever For", the dance track "Just Another Broken Heart" and the traditionalist "We Just Came Apart At The Dreams". She then recorded two albums for the resurrected Volt label – 1988's *Time Out For Me* and 1989's *Winner* – before re-signing with Malaco in 1990.

The 1990 single "If You'll Give Me Your Heart" saw Moore return to her trademark country-tinged ballads, while she also made the lower reaches of the R&B chart with "All Night Blue". Her most remarkable recording during her second stint with Malaco was

"Please Don't Let Our Good Thing End", a beyond-the-grave duet with Z.Z. Hill from the 1994 tribute album *Z. Zelebration*.

Moore started her own independent record label in 2002, Farish Street Records, on which she has released several albums over the last few years, including a Christmas album and 2005's *I'm Doing Alright*.

Greatest Hits
2001, Varese Sarabande

This 14-track collection includes thirteen of Dorothy Moore's R&B chart hits plus a neat version of George Jones's classic "He Thinks I Still Care". Unfortunately, too many of the chart hits included here are the dreary pop songs that dragged her career down in the late 70s, but this compilation does show what a fine vocalist she is.

Jackie Moore

Southern soul vocalist **Jackie Moore** could sing it both sweet and tough, both downhome and uptown. While this malleability made her one of the very few Southern female singers who could make the transition to disco, it also meant that she was never able to fully develop her own style and personality, leaving her at the mercy of changing fads and her producers' whims.

Born in 1946 in Jacksonville, Florida, Moore moved to Philadelphia in the late 60s and hooked up with DJ/label impresario **Jimmy Bishop**. She recorded two singles for the Shout label in 1968, but her first record to make any noise was 1969's "Loser Again" on Wand, a slightly overwrought ballad adorned with wah-wah guitar.

Moving back to Florida in 1970, Moore started working with her cousin, producer **Dave Crawford**. That year's "Precious, Precious" – a classic Southern soul record with infectious horn charts and countrified guitar runs – sold a million copies despite only reaching #12 on the R&B chart and merely creeping into the pop Top 30. The funkier, more uptempo "Sometimes It's Got To Rain (In Your Love Life)" was recorded with **The Dixie Flyers** in 1971, while the disco hit, "Sweet Charlie Babe", followed in 1973 at the Sigma Studios in Philadelphia.

Moore's biggest R&B hit, reaching #6 on the chart, was 1975's "Make Me Feel Like A Woman", which was recorded at Criteria Studios in Miami with **Brad Shapiro**. While

wholeheartedly embracing disco on records such as "Disco Body (Shake It To The East, Shake It To The West)", she also continued to record traditional Southern soul tracks such as "Personally", produced by Paul Kelly. The soaring "This Time Baby", produced by key Philly session man **Bobby Eli** in 1979, was her finest disco record.

Moore made it into the lower reaches of the R&B chart again in the 80s, with "Love Won't Let Me Wait", with both Barry White and **Blue Lovett** from The Manhattans, in 1980 and the break-up ballad "Holding Back" in 1983. These days, aside from cutting the odd dance remake of her old hits, she can mostly be found performing on the disco revival circuit.

Precious, Precious: The Best Of Jackie Moore
1994, Ichiban

Compiling most of the material Moore recorded for Atlantic between 1970 and 1973, this 14-track CD includes some fine Southern soul. Although it contains her two biggest pop hits, the title track and "Sweet Charlie Babe", it doesn't include her big R&B hit, "Make Me Feel Like A Woman", nor any of her prime disco records, giving a somewhat incomplete portrait of this versatile vocalist.

Melba Moore

Like her contemporary Stephanie Mills, **Melba Moore** – a fine singer blessed with a four-octave range – has never been able fully to reconcile her Broadway roots with the demands of R&B. While she enjoyed some big R&B hits in the age of the power ballad, she has never crossed over to the pop chart. Unlike most African-American singers of her generation, however, Moore has had far more success in Europe where audiences have been more tolerant of her showbiz excesses.

She was born **Melba Hill** in New York on October 29, 1945 as the daughter of **Bonnie Davis** (a jazz singer who had an R&B #1 in 1943 with "Don't Stop Now" with the Bunny Banks Trio) and big-band leader **Teddy Hill**. After a short stint as a music teacher, she sang jingles and background vocals in the mid-60s. Then, in 1968, she replaced **Diane Keaton** as Sheila in the Broadway musical *Hair*, becoming the first African-American actress ever to replace a white actress in a leading role. Around this time, Moore recorded two singles for Musicor, "Don't Cry, Sing Along With The Music" and "The Magic Touch". Both eventually became favourites on the UK's Northern soul scene, especially "The Magic Touch", a jumpy, busy arrangement on which Moore sounded stunted, which remained unreleased until it was discovered in the vaults in 1986.

In 1970 Moore joined the cast of the musical *Purlie* and won a Tony Award as Best Supporting Actress in a Musical. Later that year she signed to Mercury and released the album *I Got Love*, arranged by **Thom Bell** and **Charlie Calello** and largely comprised of her Broadway numbers. After her two subsequent albums went nowhere, Moore was dropped by Mercury.

Signing to Buddah, Moore recorded "This Is It" in 1976, an effervescent disco confection produced by Van McCoy. A small hit in the US, it reached the Top 10 in the UK. With her blend of showbiz and jazziness, Moore was perfectly placed to be a big disco star, but she only had small club hits with two disco tracks, a cover of **The Bee-Gees'** "You Stepped Into My Life" – seek out the superb extended mix by DJ John Luongo – and the boogie classic, "Take My Love". Another stellar boogie track, "Love's Comin' At Ya", became a top-five R&B hit in 1982; it stalled outside the Top 100 in the US, but reached #15 in the UK charts. The follow-up, "Mind Up Tonight", was a British #22 that same year.

Moore didn't really break through in the US until she released a series of duets that proved her facility with the kind of MOR ballad that took over urban radio in the 80s:

"(Can't Take Half) All Of You" with **Lillo Thomas**; "Love The One I'm With (A Lot Of Love)" and "I'm In Love" with **Kashif**; and "It's Been So Long" with **Dennis Collin**. Her biggest hit, and her first R&B #1, was "A Little Bit More". A 1986 duet with Freddie Jackson, "A Little Bit More" was a syrupy ballad with production distressingly reminiscent of a Mr. Mister track. Moore didn't need any help from a male singing partner on 1987's mellow "Falling", which also became an R&B #1. During this time Moore had also continued to appear on Broadway in productions such as *Timbuktu* and *Inacent Black*.

After a prolonged hiatus following a difficult divorce and financial difficulties in 1990 that put a sudden end to her string of hits, Moore returned with a new album, *Happy Together*, in 1996. She also reappeared on Broadway that year in *Les Miserables* and, in 1998, toured the US with an autobiographical one-woman show, called *Sweet Songs Of The Soul*. Moore is still appearing on the Broadway stage and featured in the 2003 movie *The Fighting Temptations* alongside **Cuba Gooding, Jr.** and **Beyoncé Knowles**. She also continues to record new material from time to time, turning to gospel for the 2004 album, *Nobody But Jesus*.

This Is It: The Best Of Melba Moore
1995, Razor & Tie

This 16-track collection covers both incarnations of Melba Moore: the sprightly dance queen and the over-emotive balladeer. There are no real surprises, but it's nice to see a few album tracks sitting alongside all the big R&B hits from the 80s. This is the best, and most comprehensive, overview available.

The Neville Brothers

Soul music has had more than its fair share of illustrious families – The **Isleys**, the **Jacksons**, the **Houston/Warwicks** – but it wouldn't be too much of a stretch to say that its most talented clan was **The Neville Brothers**. Art (born December 17, 1937), Aaron (born January 24, 1941), Charles (born December 28, 1938) and Cyril (born January 10, 1948) epitomized what is arguably popular music's greatest tradition – the creole swing of New Orleans.

Keyboardist/vocalist **Art Neville** was the first member of the family to find fame. As one of **The Hawketts**, he cut the entrancing second-line groover "Mardi Gras Mambo" for the Chess label in 1954. The record remains one of the Crescent City's best-

loved Carnival classics. Art also recorded a couple of sides for Specialty in 1958, including the great "Cha-Dooky-Doo", one of the first records to feature a distorted guitar sound. When Art joined the navy in late 1958, his brothers **Aaron** (vocals) and **Charles** (saxophone) joined The Hawketts in his place.

Aaron's gorgeous vocal quaver made its first solo appearance on "Over You" in 1960; never has murdering one's baby sounded quite so seductive. Late-night ballads were clearly Aaron's strong point, and the only thing that kept "Reality" from being a huge hit the following year was its ridiculously out-of-place chorus. Returning from the navy in 1962, Art also achieved solo success with the gorgeous ballad "All These Things". The next year, Aaron was at his yearning, delicate best on the rock'n'roll-styled ballad "Wrong Number (I Am Sorry, Goodbye)". Charles, meanwhile, spent the best part of the 60s as a member of the house band at New Orleans' legendary Dew Drop Inn, where he backed anyone who was anyone in R&B and soul.

Recorded in 1965 but not released until late the following year, Aaron's "Tell It Like It Is" was his breakthrough record. With a killer hook and Aaron's incredible falsetto, it stayed at the top of the R&B chart for five weeks, and eventually became a pop #2. Aaron sounded out of place on the soft-soul track "She Took Me For A Ride" the next year, but sounded great on 1968's "You Can Give But You Can't Take", as did the Stax-inspired band accompanying him.

In 1966 Art founded **Art Neville and The Neville Sounds** with Aaron, Cyril, **George**

Porter, Leo Nocentelli and Ziggaboo Modeliste. Without Aaron and Cyril, that line-up eventually became one of New Orleans' greatest funk bands, The Meters. Art had a local solo hit in 1967 with a version of "Bo Diddley", souped up with an astounding funk beat by drummer Modeliste. The Meters backed Cyril on his solo debut, the ridiculously funky "Tell Me What's On Your Mind", and Aaron on the loping, funk record "Hercules".

While Art and The Meters were going from strength to strength, the rest of the Neville brothers were not having the same kind of success. During this period Aaron's solo career was mostly a series of dead ends and he had to work as a longshoreman on the banks of the Mississippi to make ends meet. Charles, meanwhile, moved to New York and played sax at a number of jazz gigs. However, when he returned to New Orleans he was arrested for possession of marijuana and served three years at the infamous Angola Prison Farm.

Their fortunes changed in 1976 when Aaron, Charles and Cyril joined forces with The Meters to create the 1976 funk masterpiece *The Wild Tchoupitoulas*, recording traditional songs with the eponymous Mardi Gras Indian tribe led by the Nevilles' uncle George Landry. After The Meters broke up in 1976, the four Neville brothers toured with The Wild Tchoupitoulas and then came together as The Neville Brothers for a self-titled album released on Capitol in 1978. Sadly, however, it was a wretched disco-by-numbers job produced by Jack Nitzsche. The Nevilles' next album, *Fiyo On The Bayou*, recorded in 1981 with producer Joel Dorn, was a critical, if not a commercial, success, showcasing the brothers as the preservers of New Orleans tradition.

Neville-ization, a live album recorded in 1984 at the legendary Big Easy nightspot Tipitana's, was the brothers' best record until they released their breakthrough *Yellow Moon* in 1989. Produced by Daniel Lanois, *Yellow Moon* elevated The Neville Brothers above both nostalgia and genericism, and even gave them a modest hit with the tribute to Rosa Parks, "Sister Rosa". Later that year, Aaron sang two duets with Linda Ronstadt, the #2 smash "Don't Know Much" and the #11 hit "All My Life", and he had a top-ten

PLAYLIST
The Neville Brothers

1 OVER YOU Aaron Neville from **Treacherous: A History Of The Neville Brothers**
Only the Louvin Brothers have made murder ballads more beautiful than this.

2 TELL IT LIKE IT IS Aaron Neville from **Treacherous: A History Of The Neville Brothers**
Aaron Neville's falsetto at its most gorgeous and shimmering.

3 HERCULES Aaron Neville from **Treacherous: A History Of The Neville Brothers**
Creeping, paranoid funk classic.

4 ALL THESE THINGS Art Neville from **Treacherous: A History Of The Neville Brothers**
A great ballad in the tradition of his brother Aaron.

5 BO DIDDLEY Art Neville from **Treacherous: A History Of The Neville Brothers**
Monster funk remake of the archetypal rock'n'roll beat.

6 FIRE ON THE BAYOU from **Treacherous: A History Of The Neville Brothers**
Perhaps not as funky as The Meters' version, but a party-hearty New Orleans anthem nonetheless.

7 MEET DE BOYS ON THE BATTLE FRONT from **Treacherous: A History Of The Neville Brothers**
The brothers meet up with their uncle's Mardi Gras Indian group for a percussive pow-wow.

8 SISTER ROSA from **Treacherous: A History Of The Neville Brothers**
Leaving aside the watery 80s keyboard sound and lame rap, this is a moving tribute to Rosa Parks.

hit in 1991 with the Ronstadt-produced "Everybody Plays The Fool".

In 1990 Ronstadt joined The Neville Brothers for their biggest hit, *Brother's Keeper*, but the album saw them slipping back into run-of-the-mill lite funk. They continued to follow the path of bland commercialism on albums such as 1992's *Family Groove*, 1994's *Live On Planet Earth*, 1996's *Mitakuye Oyasin Oyasin*, 1999's *Valence Street*, and by recording with Jimmy Buffett, Wyclef Jean, Kenny G., Trisha Yearwood and David Sanborn.

The group returned in 2004 with *Walkin' In The Shadow Of Life*, a more lively record that featured contributions from a second generation of Nevilles: Aaron's son **Ivan** on keyboards and Art's son **Ian** on guitar. However, it's in a live setting that the Nevilles truly excel – that's where their reputation was built – and their records just don't do their live performances justice. You owe it to yourself to see the first family of New Orleans R&B when they're next performing in your neighbourhood.

Treacherous: A History Of The Neville Brothers
1986, Rhino

The Nevilles have been at the forefront of the New Orleans R&B scene – and thus just about all of popular music – since the beginning. This decent 2-CD collection, together with its counterpart *Treacherous Too: A History Of The Neville Brothers, Vol. 2* (1991, Rhino), fully documents the breadth and range of the brothers' achievements.

New Birth / The Nite-Liters

The history of the fine mid-70s vocal group **New Birth** and the wicked instrumental funk band **The Nite-Liters** is maddeningly convoluted at best. The Nite-Liters are said to have been founded in 1963 in Louisville, Kentucky by industry veterans **Harvey Fuqua** and **Tony Churchill**, even though by then Fuqua was in Detroit working with Motown and Tri-Phi. During the late 60s, The Nite-Liters did session work at Motown and played live with vocal groups known as The New Birth, The Mint Juleps and The New Sound. Eventually, those groups merged into a single seventeen-person collective that included vocalists **Leslie** and **Melvin Wilson**, former Marvelette **Anne Bogan**, **Londee Loren**, Bobby Downs and Alan Frye; saxophonists Tony Churchill and Austin Lander; guitarists Carl McDaniel and Charlie Hearndon; keyboardist James Baker; trumpeter Robert Jackson; bassist Leroy Taylor and drummer Robin Russell.

Fuqua left Motown in 1970 to start his own production company in Louisville and he got the collective signed to RCA. The Nite-Liters, who were basically the instrumentalists, were the first to record. Their debut album, 1970's *The Nite–Liters*, contained great dancefloor cuts like "Down And Dirty", but they didn't find real success until *Morning, Noon And Nite-Liters* in 1971. Thanks to its streamlined arrangement, creamy guitar licks and kitschy horn charts, "K-Jee", their first top-forty hit, helped to pioneer the disco sound. The funkier "Tanga Boo Gonk" was almost as popular.

The New Birth had their own hit in 1971, an improbable funked-up cover of **Perry Como**'s "It's Impossible" featuring the vocals of Londee Loren. Recording as **Love, Peace & Happiness**, the Wilson brothers and Ann Bogan also charted in 1972 with a cover of Gladys Knight & The Pips' "I Don't Want To Do Wrong", before rejoining the rest of the ensemble for The New Birth's "Unh Song" later that year. Meanwhile, The Nite-Liters struck again with the super-funky "Afro Strut", which was essentially a scratchy clipped guitar riff with horns that swooped down into the bass groove.

From 1973's *Birth Day* album onwards, the collective concentrated on recording together as The New Birth. On their R&B Top 5 cover of Bobby Womack's "I Can Understand It", Leslie Wilson sounded very much like Womack himself, albeit with a couple of James Brown interjections. They also enjoyed success with **Elvis Presley**'s "Until It's Time For You To Go". However, the *Birth Day* album was most notable for the trippy psych-funk breakbeat classic "Got To Get A Knutt" and "Buck & The Preacher", the theme to the blaxploitation movie of the same name that had originally appeared on The Nite-Liters' 1972 album *Different Strokes*.

New Birth left both RCA and Harvey Fuqua in 1975. Signing with Buddah, they released *Blind Baby* that year, which included their one R&B #1, a cover of Jerry Butler's "Dream Merchant". Next, with Buddah in financial trouble, the group moved to Warner and recorded a dreadful version of "The Long And Winding Road". By now they were moving further and further into generic disco, although both the underground disco classic "Deeper" and the streamlined Meters' groove "Ain't That Something" managed to rise above the purely formulaic in 1977. Despite the success of "I Love You" in 1979, the group broke up soon after its release.

New Birth re-formed in 1994 with the Wilson brothers and new members **Barbara**

Wilson and Paulette Williams. They have toured sporadically ever since and recorded two new albums, *God's Children* in 1998 and *Lifetime* in 2005.

○ **The Very Best Of The New Birth: Where Soul Meets Funk**
1995, RCA

An excellent 16-track compilation of the RCA tenure of the whole New Birth collective: New Birth, The Nite-Liters and Love, Peace & Happiness. You'll probably wish there were more Nite-Liters tracks on this fine single-disc album, but it nevertheless proves New Birth, Inc. to be a much underrated funk-soul outfit.

New Edition

From Jackson 5 rip-offs to New Jack Swing pioneers to reality-show casualties, **New Edition** epitomized the R&B of the last quarter-century. The group was formed in 1981 in Boston's notorious Roxbury area by **Bobby Brown** (born February 5, 1969), **Ralph Tresvant** (born May 16, 1968), **Ricky Bell** (born September 18, 1967) and **Michael Bivins** (born August 10, 1968). Brook Payne helped out with choreography and his nephew, **Ronnie DeVoe** (born November 17, 1967), soon joined the group.

After the teenage group finished second in a talent contest at Boston's Strand Theatre, producer **Maurice Starr** got New Edition signed to the Streetwise label. Produced by Starr and his brother **Michael Jonzun** (from the Jonzun Crew), New Edition's 1983 debut "Candy Girl" was little more than a bubblegum update of the Jackson 5, but it reached #1 on the US R&B chart and #1 on the UK pop chart. Two more hits from their album *Candy Girl*, "Is This The End" and "Popcorn Love", followed that same year. The group then severed all ties with their manager Starr and signed with MCA.

Recorded with producers such as Ray Parker, Jr. in 1984, New Edition's self-titled second album was a smash. The first single from the album, "Cool It Now", became their first #1 on the American pop chart. While barely straying from the model of "Candy Girl", "Cool It Now" was a bit more modern and thoroughly infectious. More importantly, though, it was also one of the first R&B records to feature a rap interlude. Bobby Brown sang the lead on the group's

third R&B #1, "Mr Telephone Man", later that year because, although lead singer Ralph Tresvant had a whispy falsetto, he couldn't hit the song's high notes.

New Edition continued to have R&B hits in the mid-80s with records such as "Count Me Out" and "A Little Bit Of Love Is All It Takes". The success of the abysmal "Earth Angel" in 1986 prompted the group to cut an entire album of classic covers. Produced by former Jackson 5 producer **Freddie Perren**, *Under The Blue Moon* has to be one of the most shockingly awful records ever made. That same year, Brown left the group to pursue a solo career.

He got off to a terrible start with the **Larry Blackmon**-produced *King Of Stage* album in 1987, although its first single, "Girlfriend", was an R&B #1. However, with 1988's *Don't Be Cruel* Brown made one of the definitive documents of New Jack Swing. His vocals had picked up some attitude and assertiveness, while the beats, from **LA Reid**, Babyface and **Teddy Riley**, were sharp and angular, but had just enough melody not to turn off his old fans. On the strength of singles such as "My Prerogative" and the title track, the album sold six million copies.

Brown was replaced in New Edition by **Johnny Gill** (born on May 22, 1966), who had previously scored some middling R&B hits with Stacy Lattisaw. Working with Jam & Lewis on 1988's *Heart Break*, New Edition moved into much the same territory as Brown. While most of the album was in the harder New Jack Swing vein, its biggest hit was the Stylistics-inspired "Can You Stand The Rain", which made it to the top of the charts. New Edition broke up soon after it was released.

Johnny Gill had huge R&B chart success the following year with a duet with Stacy Lattisaw, "Where Do We Go From Here", and subsequently with "Rub You The Right Way", "My, My, My" and "Wrap My Body Tight". Ralph Tresvant also began his own solo career and had an R&B #1 in 1990 with the oversung "Sensitivity", produced by Jam & Lewis, who also acted as co-producers on his debut album, 1990's *Ralph Tresvant*.

Meanwhile, the remaining members of New Edition, Bell, Bivins and DeVoe, formed a new group called **Bell Biv DeVoe**. They mixed locker-room lust, nightclub misogyny and sweet, barely post-pubescent harmonies on the most slamming of New Jack Swing classics, 1990's "Poison" – you can't help but want to do the running man

to those heebie-jeebie, scratchy drums and punchy horn stabs. The equally successful "BBD (I Thought It Was Me)" from the 1990 album *Poison* was produced by Hank and

New Jack Swing

Although most of the world wasn't paying attention, the evolution of New Jack Swing– essentially the combination of soul singing and hip-hop-influenced beats – was inevitable in New York in the mid-80s. Traditional soul singing had become a moribund morass of bland upward mobility and schlocky Hollywood-style epics, while hip-hop was ruling the streets and the clubs but not the radio. Then producer **Teddy Riley** came onto the scene to bridge the gap.

New Edition's 1984 single "Cool It Now" may have been the first R&B record to feature a rap interlude, but it took Teddy Riley to make the merger anything more than a gimmick. Riley's first stab at the soul subgenre that would soon be called New Jack Swing was probably **Heavy D. & The Boyz**' "Mr Big Stuff" in 1986, a pop-rap remake of Jean Knight's soul-funk classic. However, "Mr Big Stuff" didn't feature much singing and a better landmark would be Keith Sweat's 1987 release "I Want Her".

Riley's synth stabs on "I Want Her" were light years away from the churchy keyboards of traditional soul, while Sweat's whiny melisma brought the street back to R&B in a way that hadn't been heard since the doo-wop revival of the early 60s. Sweat's predatory sexuality wasn't cloaked in the helium-high sweetness or sappy metaphors of doo-wop – no one had been this sexually suggestive since Donna Summer. Riley followed the "I Want Her" blueprint on records

for his own group, Guy, and then reproduced the formula again and again for countless others during the late 80s.

It didn't take long for other producers to get in on the game. Jam & Lewis, whose sharp keyboard lines were an obvious influence on Riley, had their own New Jack smashes with **Johnny Gill**'s "Rub You The Right Way" and **Ralph Tresvant**'s "Sensitivity". **Bell Biv DeVoe** recorded the swingbeat track "Poison" that same year, and **LA Reid** & Babyface jumped into the fray with Johnny Gill's "My, My, My" and Pebbles' "Giving You The Benefit", using tricks they had picked up working with Riley on Bobby Brown's *Don't Be Cruel*.

By 1991, however, the New Jack Swing sound was over and a new brand of hip-hop soul was taking over with **R. Kelly**'s "She's Got That Vibe", records by **TLC** and **SWV** and, perhaps most crucially, Mary J. Blige.

Various Artists: New Jack Swing Mastercuts Volume 1
1992, Beechwood/Mastercuts

The 12 tracks included here – both hits and relative obscurities – effectively sum up the New Jack Swing era. Unfortunately, this album doesn't feature the Teddy Riley-produced milestone, Keith Sweat's "I Want Her", but it does have such landmarks as Bell Biv DeVoe's "Poison", Johnny Gill's "Rub You The Right Way" and Wreck-N-Effect's "New Jack Swing".

PLAYLIST

1 MR BIG STUFF Heavy D & The Boyz from Living Large
The opening salvo in Teddy Riley's hip-hop soul revolution.

2 I WANT HER Keith Sweat from Make It Last Forever
Even more than the garish synth stabs and hip-hop beats, it was Sweat's street attitude that made this track the harbinger of New Jack Swing.

3 GROOVE ME Guy from Guy
The record that permanently changed the face of R&B.

4 MY PREROGATIVE Bobby Brown from Don't Be Cruel
No longer the shy boy with a quivering voice from his New Edition days, Brown now sings R&B like an assertive rapper.

5 JUST GOT PAID Johnny Kemp from Secrets Of Flying
Perhaps closer to House than hip-hop, this is a New Jack classic thanks to Kemp's unorthodox delivery.

6 NEW JACK SWING Wreck-N-Effect from New Jack Swing Mastercuts Volume 1
"Rump Shaker" was the bigger hit, but the rips of Das EFX and Kriss Kross make this track more stylistically apposite.

7 RUB YOU THE RIGHT WAY Johnny Gill from New Jack Swing Mastercuts Volume 1
Gill does his best Luther Vandross over the angular, skittering drums that are definitive New Jack Swing.

8 GIVING YOU THE BENEFIT Pebbles from Always
Consummate R&B craftsmanship even if LA and Babyface were interlopers on the scene.

Keith Shocklee and Eric Sadler, the team behind **Public Enemy**.

Apart from Tresvant and BBD hitching a ride with Luther Vandross and Janet Jackson on 1992's "The Best Things In Life Are Free", none of the former members of New Edition enjoyed significant success during the early 90s. However, in 1996 all six members reunited for *Home Again*, which was a brief sensation, going to #1 on the album chart. *Home Again*'s lead single, "Hit Me Off", also made it to #3 on the pop chart. The subsequent tour was a mess of ego conflicts, however, and the group broke up and returned to their solo projects as soon as the tour was over.

New Edition came back again in 2004, but this time minus Brown, and signed to **P. Diddy**'s Bad Boy label. That same year they released *One Love*, a mixed-up record on which, on the one hand, they sang relatively

mature ballads befitting men their age, and, on the other, they pretended they were 19 years old again and could still hump around and get the girls excited. Brown, of course, was too busy with his run-ins with the law and the filming of his car-crash of a reality TV show, *Being Bobby Brown*, with his wife, R&B diva Whitney Houston.

Hits
2004, Geffen

Although it lacks the material they recorded with Maurice Starr in 1983 for their debut *Candy Girl*, this 17-track collection holds all the New Edition that anyone who wasn't 13 years old in 1985 could want.

New Edition Solo Hits
1996, MCA

Bobby Brown, Ralph Tresvant and Bell Biv DeVoe – there's no sign of Johnny Gill – get four tracks each on this 12-track CD of their biggest solo hits. Its not an ideal compilation, perhaps, but it's not bad if you'd rather not wade through the extra baggage of their individual albums.

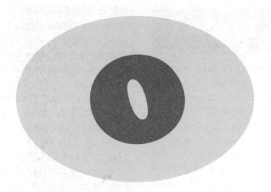

Billy Ocean

Billy Ocean is far and away the most successful British R&B singer in the United States, and probably the only one who was more successful in the US than in Britain. Indeed, he was one of the most successful pop artists of the 80s. Born **Leslie Sebastian Charles** in Fyzbad, Trinidad on January 21, 1950, Ocean moved to London when he was 7 years old. He later worked as a tailor on Savile Row and then on the assembly line at Ford Motors in Dagenham, while also moonlighting as a session singer. In 1974 he released his debut "On The Run" under the alias of **Scorched Earth**, but the following year he changed his name to Billy Ocean, in honour of the Frank Sinatra movie *Ocean's 11*, and signed to the GTO label.

In 1976, despite being a clumsy, leaden, utterly typical Euro-soul production, Billy Ocean's GTO debut, "Love Really Hurts Without You", reached #2 in the UK and #22 in the US. He enjoyed continued pop success in the UK with the similar records "LOD (Love On Delivery)", "Stop Me (If You've Heard It All Before)" and "Red Light Spells Danger". However, once the hits started to dry up, he moved to the US and started writing songs for other artists, including **LaToya Jackson**.

Signing to Epic in 1981, Ocean had a top-ten R&B hit with the breezy dance number "Night (Feel Like Getting Down)", and followed-up with the minor dancefloor hit, "Calypso Funkin'". His biggest success of all came in 1984 with the release of the *Suddenly* album on Jive. The album included "Caribbean Queen (No More Love On The Run)", which, with its unforgettable hook and definitive 80s groove, became a worldwide smash, reaching #1 in the US and the Top 10 in the UK. The jaunty "Loverboy" and the ballad "Suddenly" followed it into the American Top 10 that same year.

Although Ocean had at first seemed like a breath of fresh air, he quickly descended into ridiculousness. "When The Going Gets Tough, The Tough Get Going", the theme song to the 1985 film *The Jewel In The Nile*, was just silly, but it went to #2 in the US and was Ocean's only British #1. His second album with the Jive label, 1986's *Love Zone*, featured "There'll Be Sad Songs (To Make You Cry)", his second US #1, and "Love Zone", his third R&B #1. The **Mutt Lange**-produced *Tear Down These Walls* followed in 1988; its lead single, "Get Outta My Dreams, Get Into My Car", was as absurd as its title, but became his third US #1 single.

As the 80s ticked away, Billy Ocean's glossiness became as outdated as his wet-look Jheri curl and the hits soon stopped coming. Not even collaborations with **The Fresh Prince** – 1990's "I Sleep Much Better (In Someone Else's Bed)" – and R. Kelly – 1993's "Everything's So Different Without You" – could help.

The Ultimate Collection
2004, BMG/Jive

Billy Ocean's unique selling proposition – his West Indies' lilt – may have been barely discernible among all the synth washes and syn-drums on his records, but it gave him enough personality to make him the king of 80s corporate soul. If one single album sums up the middle-of-the-road R&B of the decade, then this 18-track hits compilation is it.

The Ohio Players

While **The Ohio Players** may be best known for their wink-wink-nudge-nudge party funk and their sexually explicit 70s album covers, their history dates back to the dawn of soul. In Dayton, Ohio, in 1959, guitarist **Robert Ward** formed **The Ohio Untouchables** with vocalist/saxophonist **Clarence Satchell**, trumpeter **Ralph "Pee Wee" Middlebrook** and bassist **Marshall Jones**. Ward was related to **Robert West**, the founder of Detroit's LuPine label, and the Untouchables backed The Falcons on "I Found A Love" in 1962.

The Ohio Untouchables' early releases on Lupine included "She's My Heart's Desire", the gorgeous, hypnotic early soul masterpiece "Love Is Amazing" and "I'm Tired", which all featured vocals by **Benny McCain**. After Ward – and his shimmering guitar – went solo in 1964, he was replaced by **Leroy "Sugarfoot" Bonner**. The group then changed their name to The Ohio Players and signed to Compass. Their 1967 and 1968 singles for the label, "Trespassin'" and "It's A Cryin' Shame", sounded vaguely like Parliament's records with their blend of soul and psychedelia.

The Players signed to Capitol in 1968 and released *Observations In Time*, an awkward blend of Southern soul and jazz, while their 1970 single for the Tangerine label, "A Thing Called Love", went nowhere. Eventually, the group's 1971 single "Pain", released on the local Top Hat label, was picked up by Westbound and became a minor R&B hit. With a line-up of Satchell, Middlebrook, Jones and Bonner, plus keyboardist **Walter "Junie" Morrison**, trumpeter **Bruce Napier**, trombonist **Marvin Pierce** and drummer **Greg Webster**, The Ohio Players followed up on that success later that year with the funky black rock album *Pain* on Westbound. The album had a notorious S&M cover design and included the outrageously funky track "Players Ballin'".

Their next Westbound album, 1972's *Pleasure*, with its similar sleeve art, gave the band their big breakthrough hit – the seemingly throw-away novelty tune, "Funky Worm". Morrison sang on the record like a demented granny, and the worm was embodied by a high-pitched synth squeal that went on to launch a thousand G-Funk records. Bumping like crazy, "Funky Worm" suggested that the group were moving away from their psych-soul sound towards more straight-up funk. That was confirmed by the title track of their 1973 album *Ecstasy*, which was another huge R&B hit and also saw **James "Diamond" Williams** replacing Webster as drummer.

When The Ohio Players moved to the Mercury label in 1974, Morrison, who was seen as the brains behind the group, stayed behind at Westbound. He released a couple of solo albums, 1975's *When We Do* and 1976's *Freeze*, before joining the **P-Funk** circus. *When We Do* included the track "Tight Rope", which featured Morrison's best Sly Stone impression on top of a potentially great groove that had one too many dead spaces. "Not As Good As You Should", from his *Freeze* album, was a spacy groove that sounded like Deep Purple as produced by **George Clinton**.

Meanwhile, **Billy Beck** replaced Morrison in The Ohio Players and, with his smooth synth sound, the group dominated the R&B charts for the next few years. The slightly bluesy and jazzy "Jive Turkey" did reasonably well in 1974, but it was the follow-up, "Skin Tight", that set the template for the group's dominance. Sugarfoot drawled like a hillbilly in heat about some fox's hot pants, over a thumping bassline and Beck's slick keyboards. "Fire" then followed this same formula exactly to become the group's first #1 pop hit.

The Players had three more hits in 1975. "Sweet Sticky Thing", a high-pitched, ethereal ballad that was just as lubricious as all their records and still bumped like crazy, went to #1 on the R&B chart; the yowsah "Love Rollercoaster" became their second pop #1; and "Fopp", which sounded like **Grand Funk Railroad** meeting **Earth Wind & Fire** – not necessarily a pretty combination – was another top-ten R&B hit.

After cutting a final R&B chart-topper in 1976, the jazzier but still nasty "Who'd She Coo?", the group started to lapse creatively. Perhaps they were spending too much time producing other groups such as **Faze-O** and **Kitty & The Haywoods**. The Players left Mercury for Arista in 1979, but their first release for the new label, the uncomfortable disco number "Everybody Up", showed that things hadn't really changed. The Players' fortunes continued to decline and, after releasing a couple of terrible albums, the group fizzled out.

The Ohio Players returned in 1988 with *Back* on Track Records, a synth-heavy album that held a couple of modest R&B hits, "Sweat" and "Let's Play (From Now On)". Both Satchell and Middlebrook died in the mid-90s, but an Ohio Players line-up that includes Sugarfoot, Williams and guitarist **Chet Willis** remains a popular draw on the funk scene today.

Funk On Fire: The Mercury Anthology
1995, Mercury

This 2-disc, 28-track compilation of The Ohio Players' peak years with Mercury may not get things quite right – almost half of it is unnecessary, yet it still manages to omit key tracks such as "Smoke" and "What The Hell" – but it is a smoking collection of prime 70s funk music nonetheless.

Orgasm: Best Of The Westbound Years
1998, Westbound

Before moving to Mercury in 1974 and scoring their biggest hits, The Ohio Players cut several fine albums for the Westbound label. A little more jam-oriented and a little more "out" than their later stuff, the best of that material from 1972 to 1974 is collected on this 15-track compilation, which is well worth checking out.

The O'Jays

Contrasting gruff, assertive gospel leads with gossamer harmonies, **The O'Jays'** dialectic between the rough and smooth perfectly articulated the tensions at the heart of the vision of producer-songwriters and Philadelphia International head honchos **Kenny Gamble** and **Leon Huff**. The O'Jays became the duo's greatest vehicle and one of the most important acts of the 70s.

Before joining forces with Gamble and Huff, The O'Jays were a group of journeymen who had formed a five-member vocal group in Canton, Ohio in 1958. When **Eddie Levert**, **Walter Williams**, **William Powell**, **Bobby Massey** and **Bill Isles** first teamed up they called themselves **The Triumphs**. After cutting a single on the Wayco label that went nowhere, they signed to King as **The Ascots** and released "Story Of My Heart" and "Lonely Rain" in 1960.

Renaming themselves after Cleveland disc jockey **Eddie O'Jay**, the group signed to **H.B. Barnum**'s Little Star label and moved to LA in 1961. After the doo-wop-flavoured "Crack Up Laughing" became a minor hit in 1963, they moved to Imperial and achieved their first chart hit with the Drifters-styled "Lonely Drifter", complete with the sound of waves crashing and seagulls swooping overhead. The next year's "Oh, How You Hurt Me" featured Eddie Levert's soaring tenor vocals, but their first substantial hit was 1965's "Lipstick Traces (On A Cigarette)". It wasn't a patch on **Benny Spellman**'s original, but the swooping chorus on The O'Jays' version was great.

Bill Isles left the group soon afterwards, and the remaining quartet reached #12 on the R&B chart with "Stand In For Love" in 1966. Subsequent releases such as "I'll Never Forget You", the easy-swinging "I Dig Your Act" and the uptempo stomper "Working On Your Case" all went on to become firm favourites on the UK's Northern soul scene.

Signing to Kenny Gamble's Neptune label in 1969, The O'Jays hit #15 on the R&B chart with "One Night Affair", a string-heavy arrangement recorded at a heart-attack-inducing pace that helped set the foundation for disco. They followed up successfully in 1970 with both "Deeper (In Love With You)" and "Looky Looky (Look At Me Girl)", before Bobby Massey left to become a producer. In 1972 the remaining O'Jays trio became the first signings to the Philadelphia International label, and finally they were journeymen no more.

The O'Jays' masterpiece, *Back Stabbers*, was released in their first year with the label. Its title track had the greatest riff on the "smiling faces" trope of 70s soul. Recorded when the full scale of **Nixon**'s Watergate treachery was beginning to emerge, when Gamble & Huff still believed that people needed to sing "We Shall Overcome" and when liberal Senator Daniel Moynihan was blaming the cycle of poverty on African-American men, "Back Stabbers"' refrain of "Smilin' faces sometimes tell lies (back stabbers)" resonated with a significance that went far beyond the tale of a man whose friends want to steal his woman. The atmosphere of spooks, dirty tricks and double-crossing was emphasized by the eerie piano, screeching strings and off-kilter percussion.

Elsewhere on the album, "Who Am I" was a brutally introspective track on which Eddie Levert chastised himself for believing that men shouldn't cry and for not listening to her enough. He was also plagued by "Shiftless, Shady, Jealous Kind Of People" on the track of the same name, but in amongst all the trouble and strife, there were also the stolen moments of bliss of "Listen To The Clock On The Wall". The final track, "Love Train", brought a little levity to the album and became The O'Jays' only pop #1. You'd almost expect the lyrics to be from some wispy flower child like **Scott McKenzie**, but The O'Jays gave it some old-time religion and turned "Love Train" into secular gospel of the highest order.

The follow-up album, 1973's *Ship Ahoy*, was almost as good as *Back Stabbers*, but the love songs had a little less bite – although "Now That We Found Love" became a standard and a hit for both **Third World** and **Heavy D**. "For The Love Of Money", on the other hand, was perhaps the toughest record The O'Jays ever recorded and it was one of the few tracks on which they were outshone by the groove. The album also included the stunning "Don't Call Me Brother", a shockingly direct castigation of fair-weather black nationalists.

With the release of *Survival* in 1975, disco had caught up with the Philly label and the group's music was less surprising and more formulaic. The album included message cuts such as "Rich Get Richer" and the R&B #1 "Give The People What They Want", but they lacked the simmering ferocity of old. That same year's *Family Reunion* album marked a further retreat, but it had two absolute dancefloor corkers in "I Love Music" and "Livin' For The Weekend".

By the time they got to *Message In Our Music* in 1976, The O'Jays were merely telling you that their songs were political. Despite, or perhaps because of, this, they were as successful as ever. "Message In Our Music", "Darlin', Darlin' Baby (Sweet, Tender, Love)" and the retro "Use Ta Be My Girl" all went #1 on the R&B chart. Sadly, just before the release of this final hit in 1977, Powell died of cancer. He was replaced by **Sammy Strain**, who used to sing with Little Anthony & The Imperials.

As disco went supernova in 1978 and 1979, The O'Jays went in the opposite direction. However, they failed to keep up with

PLAYLIST
The O'Jays

1 ONE NIGHT AFFAIR from **The O'Jays In Philadelphia**
Lush but fast-paced stormer that is an ancestral echo of disco.

2 BACK STABBERS from **Back Stabbers**
Perhaps the greatest intro in the history of popular music, and things only got better from here.

3 WHEN THE WORLD'S AT PEACE from **Back Stabbers**
Angry, bitter, dystopic yearning for brotherhood.

4 LOVE TRAIN from **The Essential O'Jays**
After spending too long staring at the brink, The O'Jays come up for air.

5 NOW THAT WE FOUND LOVE from **The Essential O'Jays**
A gauzy daydream of a love song.

6 FOR THE LOVE OF MONEY from **The Essential O'Jays**
Perhaps the best bassline ever.

7 DON'T CALL ME BROTHER from **Ship Ahoy**
The diametric opposite of Curtis Mayfield's brotherhood bromides.

8 GIVE THE PEOPLE WHAT THEY WANT from **The Essential O'Jays**
"For The Love Of Money" redux.

9 I LOVE MUSIC from **The Essential O'Jays**
Disco classic that is the foundation of House music.

10 USE TA BE MY GIRL from **The Essential O'Jays**
Disco-era streetcorner nostalgia.

the changing R&B climate and were largely seen as a nostalgia act in the early 80s. They also broke the United Nations' ban on playing in South Africa, although they refused to perform for segregated audiences. When Levert's sons gained fame in the mid-80s with their group **LeVert**, The O'Jays were given some renewed momentum. Their 1987 comeback record, "Lovin' You" – written by Gamble & Huff in the 70s, but never before recorded – became their first R&B #1 in nearly a decade. The go-go-styled "Have You Had Your Love Today" featured a rap from **Jaz** and also reached #1 in 1989. The O'Jays continued to have R&B hits with "Serious Hold On Me", "Don't Let Me Down" and a cover of **Bob Dylan**'s "Emotionally Yours".

Nathaniel Best replaced Sammy Strain in 1993, and was replaced in turn by **Eric Grant** in 1997 for the modest hits "What's Stopping You" and "Baby You Know". In 2001 the group recorded a new album, *For The Love...*, for MCA and in 2004 they signed to **Matthew Knowles**' Sanctuary Urban Records to release *Imagination*, a better-than-average album that had little impact on the charts, but included a few great tracks. The O'Jays continue to be an enormously popular live act decades after their first big hit.

Back Stabbers
1972, Philadelphia International

The O'Jays' breakthrough album for Philly International was, undoubtedly, their greatest – and also the album that put Gamble & Huff on the map. From the opening track, "When The World's At Peace", with its Civil Rights references and almost mocking James Brown horn riff, to the fine secular gospel of "Love Train", these ten tracks are some of the toughest, lushest soul music ever recorded.

Ship Ahoy
1973, Philadelphia International

This may not have stand-out tracks like "Back Stabbers" and "Love Train", but it is a consistent and high-quality album and the lengthier tracks give you a real sense of what the Philadelphia International sound was all about. Filled with message and social commentary, this is highlighted by their hit, "For The Love Of Money".

Love You to Tears
1997, Volcano

With expectations not high for a late-90s comeback, this O'Jays CD came as a real surprise. Leader Eddie Levert, who had a hand in writing most of the material, turns in a fine performance, and the updated production, making no attempt to replicate sounds of the past, works remarkably well. A fine, soulful release.

Alexander O'Neal

Born in Natchez, Mississippi on November 15, 1953, **Alexander O'Neal** must be the only artist in this book to have sung a **Def Leppard** song on stage, as he did regularly when fronting a black rock band called **Alexander in Minneapolis** during the mid-80s.

O'Neal moved to Minneapolis when he was 20 and worked as a petrol station attendant while playing local clubs with various groups. In 1978, he joined the group **Flyte Tyme**, which included **Jam & Lewis**, **Jesse Johnson**, **Monte Moir** and **Cynthia Johnson**, and soon became **Prince**'s backing band. However, O'Neal argued with Prince in 1980 and was replaced as lead singer by **Morris Day**. The band then shortened their name to **The Time**.

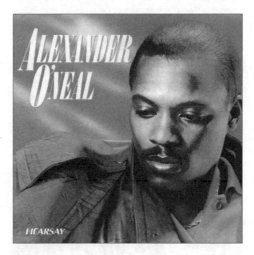

O'Neal recorded a couple of singles for the small Chicago label Erect before reuniting with Jimmy Jam, Terry Lewis and Monte Moir to record his debut album, *Alexander O'Neal*, in 1984. The album did OK, with tracks such as "Innocent" and "If You Were Here Tonight" enabling O'Neal to display his smooth but powerful voice that was a cross between **Luther Vandross** and **Colonel Abrams**. O'Neal's real breakthrough came in 1985 with "Saturday Love", a duet with **Cherrelle**. The duo reunited two years later for another MOR smash, "Never Knew Love Like This".

O'Neal's 1987 *Hearsay* album – and especially its big hit, "Fake" (his only R&B #1), with its drums, chirpy synth peals and lyrical obsession with first names – was essentially the masculine counterpart of **Janet Jackson**'s *Control*. The similar "Criticize", which featured a less angular, more House-like production, reached #4 in the UK, where O'Neal became a sizeable star, but wasn't as well received in the US. "The Lovers", a strange Frankenstein combination of **The Human League**'s "Human" and **Duran Duran**'s "Notorious", gave O'Neal another UK hit, but was virtually ignored at home.

O'Neal disappeared into drug and alcohol rehab for a couple of years in the late 80s, although a "Hitmix" of his records went into the UK's Top 20 in 1989. He returned in 1991 with the gospelish "All True Man", a top-five R&B hit, while his *All True Man* album reached the Top 10 in the UK. The hyperventilating sexuality of the New Jack Swingers in the early 90s made O'Neal's **Teddy Pendergrass**-style assertiveness and husky machismo passé, but he continued to have modest hits in the UK with 1993's "Love Makes No Sense" and 1996's "Let's Get Together". His *Saga Of A Married Man* was released only in Europe in 2002, as was his 2005 album, *Live At The Hammersmith Apollo London*.

⊙ Greatest Hits
2004, EMI

This fine 15-track compilation includes all Alexander O'Neal's hits, including the two duets with Cherrelle. Despite having the ideal voice for the 80s, O'Neal never achieved the commercial success he deserved, but this collection helps to preserve that voice for posterity.

One Way / The Soul Partners

During the late 70s and 80s, the many groups with which Detroit vocalist **Al Hudson** was involved – **The Soul Partners**, The Partners and **One Way** – became consistent mid-level hit-makers on the R&B charts, without ever really acquiring much of a profile of their own. This anonymity enabled them to float along with whatever the prevailing groove of the day might be without ever facing accusations of selling out.

Having recorded the ballad "Love Is" as a solo artist for Atco in 1976, Hudson formed The Soul Partners with four musicians from the Detroit club circuit: bassist/falsetto vocalist **Kevin McCord**, guitarist **Cortez Harris**, pianist **Jack Hall** and drummer **Theodore Dudley, Jr.** That year, the group recorded two more singles for Atco, "When You're Gone" and "Almost Ain't Never Enough", before moving to ABC and enjoying their first R&B hit with "I Got A Notion (You've Got The Motion)".

The Soul Partners' 1977 debut album, *Especially For You*, featured a couple of decent club tracks, most notably "Disco Lover", and a truly shocking cover of "Feelings". However, their shining moment came with "Spread Love" in 1978. The record was a glitterball mini-masterpiece with stellar string arrangement, whining keyboards and an upful bassline. Featuring new vocalist **Alicia Myers**, "You Can Do It" – released under the name of Al Hudson & The Partners – was a slinky, keyboard-heavy post-disco groover that was almost as good as "Spread Love".

In 1980 the group changed its name to One Way and made some personnel changes – **Gregory Green** replaced Dudley on drums, keyboardist **Jonathan Meadows** replaced pianist Hall, and **Dave Roberson** joined on guitar. One Way had modest club hits with "Music" and "Do Your Thang" in 1980, before Alicia Myers left the group to go solo. Her "I Want to Thank You" – produced by Hudson and McCord – with its breathy vocals and singsong melody, became an end-of-the-night club favourite in 1981, and eventually reached the R&B Top 40 a year later. While her "Don't Stop What You're Doin'" is now a rare groove boogie classic, Myers' biggest hit was 1984's "You Get The Best from Me (Say, Say, Say)".

Although Myers was replaced in One Way by **Candyce Edwards**, the group missed her distinctive vocals at first and they abandoned the dancefloor in the hope of scoring with quiet storm tracks. After their spare synth groove "Push" became a big R&B hit in 1981, however, One Way ditched the pretty stuff in favour of slamming but poppy funk tracks such as "Pull Fancy Dancer". They had certainly been listening to "More Bounce To The Ounce" and other **Zapp & Roger Troutman** records when they released their big hits "Cutie Pie" and the Vocoder jam "Mr. Groove" in the early 80s.

Working with **Eumir Deodato**, One Way had two more big hits in 1986 with the faceless uptempo cuts "Don't Think About It" and "You Better Quit". However, *New Beginnings* was an overly optimistic title for their 1989 album – they broke up soon after its release. Hudson reconvened One Way for the *Carnival* album in 1996, but most of their work these days is on the oldies circuit.

◉ **The Best Of One Way: Featuring Al Hudson & Alicia Myers**
1996, MCA

While it may not include "Music" or "Spread Love", this 14-track CD does feature Alicia Myers' solo records, "I Want To Thank You" and "You Get The Best From Me", and it is the best available One Way compilation. Amid all the uptempo tracks, 1984's "Lady You Are" proves they could slow it down with aplomb when they needed to.

Johnny Otis

Even if his greatest talent has been his ability to survive, **Johnny Otis** has long been a singular presence on the R&B scene as a talent scout, entrepreneur and musical weatherman. His records were seldom all that original, but they always had a certain *joie de vivre*. However, his main contribution was as a discoverer and nurturer of talent. Without Otis, it's possible that the world would be bereft of Etta James, Esther Phillips, Hank Ballard, Little Willie John, The Robins, Jackie Wilson and **Big Mama Thornton**.

Born **John Veliotes** to Greek parents on December 28, 1921, in Vallejo, California, Otis moved with his parents to a predominantly black neighbourhood of Oakland when he was a young boy. He grew up with black friends and neighbours and was effectively considered an honorary black from a young age. Otis was also particularly fond of jazz as a child and was a big fan of Count Basie's drummer **Philly Jo Jones**. Although Otis was Greek-American, by the time he was playing drums with **The Count Otis Matthews Houserockers** as a teenager, most people thought he was black. He moved to LA in 1943 and became a session musician, playing most notably on Illinois Jacquet's "Flying Home" and Johnny Moore's **Three Blazers**' "Driftin' Blues".

In 1945 Otis formed his own jump blues band, with future jazz stars **Hampton Hawes**, **Curtis Counce**, **Art Farmer** and **Buddy Collette**, as well as organist Bill Doggett. Their first record was "Drop Another Nickel In The Jukebox" for Excelsior, but their first hit was "Harlem Nocturne" in 1946. Together with jazz and R&B singer and bandleader **Bardu Ali**, Otis

Johnny Otis: "They told me it was a saxophone in the shop"

opened a club called The Barrelhouse on Central Avenue in the Watts area of LA in 1948. The club swiftly became one of the main R&B venues on the West Coast.

Using some of the vocalists they discovered at The Barrelhouse, **The Johnny Otis Orchestra** became a hit machine on the Savoy label in 1950. The group had a total of ten R&B hits that year, including three #1s – "Double Crossing Blues", "Mistrustin' Blues and "Cupid Boogie" – and the bluesy end-of-the-night lover's ballad "Cry Baby". "Double Crossing Blues", which had the bluesy and astringent Little Esther on lead vocals and The Robins in the background, spent nine weeks at the top of the R&B chart. It was replaced at #1 by "Mistrustin' Blues", an oil-and-vinegar duet between Esther and **Mel Walker**.

When **Little Esther** went solo in 1951, she was replaced by **Linda Hopkins**, who debuted on "Doggin' Blues". Hopkins sang lead on the daft "Mambo Boogie" and the fine "Gee Baby", which both charted in 1951, as did "Call Operator 210" the following year. After the hits dried up, Otis became a producer and arranger for **Don Robey**'s Peacock and Duke labels, most famously working on Big Mama Thornton's "Hound Dog" and Johnny Ace's "Pledging My Love". Otis also discovered Etta James, and he co-wrote – and played on – her rollicking 1955 debut "The Wallflower". Amid all that, Otis hosted radio and TV shows in LA that served as crucibles for the burgeoning rock'n'roll scene, and he started his own record label, Dig.

In 1957 Otis signed to Capitol Records, where he and his group recorded as **The Johnny Otis Show**. During this time, Otis also hosted his own TV variety show of the same name in LA. Otis and his band had a UK #2 on Capitol in 1957 with "Ma (He's Making Eyes At Me)", thanks to **Marie Adams**' bluesy vocals. The next year Otis enjoyed his only top-ten hit in the US pop chart with his fabulous version of the archetypal Bo Diddley beat, "Willie & The Hand Jive" – Otis oozed hipness as he rasped the surreal lyrics. However, the rapidly changing rock'n'roll climate soon left Otis out in the cold. After recording a couple of dud singles for Capitol and King in the late 50s and early 60s, he concentrated on his chicken ranch.

In due course, the emergence of his son Shuggie Otis as a guitarist prompted Johnny

PLAYLIST
Johnny Otis

1 **DOUBLE CROSSING BLUES** from
The Godfather Of Rhythm & Blues
Lovely, classy blues with the astringent Little Esther on vocals.

2 **CRY BABY** from
The Original Johnny Otis Show
Smoky blues ballad sung by the smooth Mel Walker.

3 **ALL NITE LONG** from
The Original Johnny Otis Show
Swinging merger of Louis Jordan and early rock'n'roll.

4 **WILLIE & THE HAND JIVE** from
The Greatest Johnny Otis Show
Shave and a haircut – two bits.

5 **MA (HE'S MAKING EYES AT ME)** from
The Greatest Johnny Otis Show
Showaddywaddy ripped this record off for their entire career, except they didn't have Marie Adams.

6 **COUNTRY GIRL** from **Watts Funky**
Lowdown and funky track with a fine guitar workout from teenager Shuggie Otis.

7 **SIGNIFYIN' MONKEY** from **Watts Funky**
The old trickster folk tale the way you probably would have heard it on the streets.

8 **WATTS BREAKAWAY** from **Watts Funky**
A tip of the hat to Sly & The Family Stone.

Otis to return to music. Credited to The Johnny Otis Show, the 1968 album *Cold Shot* featured 15-year-old Shuggie on guitar and updated Otis's straightforward R&B with a hint of funk, rock and soul. Besides the hit single "Country Girl", *Cold Shot* included "The Signifyin' Monkey, Pt. 1", a ribald telling of an old folk tale. That track's ribaldry and profanity were extended even further on 1969's *Snatch & The Poontangs* – essentially the Johnny Otis Show in dirtier clothes.

In 1971 Johnny Otis signed to Epic and released *Cuttin' Up*, which featured the churning "Watts Breakaway". He then set up the Hawk Sound and Lujon labels, and released the breakbeat classic "The Humpty Dump" by **The Vibrettes**. Becoming an ordained minister in 1974, Otis founded his own church, the Landmark Community

Church. He also recorded some so-so disco records in the mid-70s, but by the time he recorded *The New Johnny Otis Show* in 1982 he had settled into an enjoyable retro groove. Johnny Otis finally slowed down in the 80s, contenting himself with running a produce market, writing a couple of books and hosting a regular radio show on KPFA in California, which continues to this day.

The Original Johnny Otis Show
1994, Savoy

Irritatingly, this 27-track compilation doesn't include the #1 hit "Double Crossing Blues", sung by Little Esther and The Robins. However, it is still the finest anthology of Johnny Otis's early material for the Savoy label and it commemorates his remarkable chart run in 1950.

The Greatest Johnny Otis Show
1998, Ace

This 26-track collection features the best of Otis's delightful rock'n'roll records from the mid- to late 50s. As well as his own wonderful "Willie & The Hand Jive" and "Crazy Country Hop", the album also features records from other performers in The Johnny Otis Show, including Marie Adams, Mel Williams, Marci Lee and Jeannie Sterling.

Watts Funky
2001, BGP

Johnny Otis's son Shuggie plays a big role on this 20-track collection of funk recordings from the late 60s and early 70s. As well as Johnny Otis's "Country Girl" and "The Signifyin' Monkey", *Watts Funky* also includes crucial cuts by The Vibrettes, Preston Love and Debbie Lyndsey plus Shuggie Otis's original version of "Strawberry Letter 23".

Shuggie Otis

B orn Johnny Otis, Jr. on November 30, 1953 in Los Angeles, **Shuggie Otis** had R&B in his blood – he was the son of the legendary Johnny Otis. However, it was the blues that first brought Shuggie to prominence. At 15 years old, he played lead guitar on his father's 1968 comeback hit "Country Girl" and was immediately hailed as a guitar prodigy.

The following year Shuggie Otis contributed guitar to **Frank Zappa**'s "Peaches En Regalia" and released his own album debut, *Al Kooper Introduces Shuggie Otis*, which showed off his fiery, **Albert King**-influenced guitar style on tracks such as "12:15 Slow Goonbash Blues" and "Shuggie's Old Time (Dee-Di-Lee-Di-Leet-Deet/Slide Boogie)". His second album, 1970's *Here Comes Shuggie Otis*, was produced by his father and showed the beginnings of the style that would make Shuggie a cult hero. There were still traditional blues tracks to be sure, but "Oxford Gray" and "Jennie Lee" were strange amalgams of baroque R&B, psychedelic pop, Chicago blues and Sly & The Family Stone.

It was on 1971's *Freedom Flight* that Shuggie Otis's vision came together. Recorded with luminaries Wilton Felder, **George Duke**, Preston Love and Clydie King, and travelling a similar path to **Jimi Hendrix**, Otis seamlessly blended psychedelia, blues, soul and funk on *Freedom Flight* in a way that would later influence both Prince and **George Clinton**. "Me And My Woman" was a trippy, funky blues number with a super-fat bassline, while "Ice Cold Daydream" and "Strawberry Letter 23" (later a huge hit for The Brothers Johnson) both exemplified the cosmic, pan-sexual psych-funk groove that has been the goal of the black rock movement since the death of Hendrix.

Otis made 1974's *Inspiration Information* on his own, and although there were similarities – particularly the extensive use of the rhythm box – with Sly Stone's masterpiece *There's A Riot Goin' On*, Otis's album was not a black hole of bleakness. There were some stoned funk tracks, such as "Sparkle City", but "Happy House" and "Island Letter" were more upbeat and less blunted, and even a bit tropical. The title track was more akin to Sly Stone circa *Fresh*, while "XL-30" was a dubby experimental groove inspired by electric **Miles Davis** that was thirty years ahead of its time.

Unfortunately, *Inspiration Information* took so long to record that Otis was dropped by his label. At around the same time, he also declined an offer to audition for **The Rolling Stones**, who were looking to replace Mick Taylor. Otis played on Billy Preston's *It's My Pleasure* in 1975, before almost disappearing from the scene. Otis has since reappeared from time to time, playing with his father and his own son, bassist Lucky Otis. In 2001 *Inspiration Information* was reissued to rapturous acclaim.

Inspiration Information
1974, Luaka Bop

Perhaps not the out-and-out masterpiece that revisionist critics hailed it when it was re-released, *Inspiration Information* is, nevertheless, a strikingly original vision of soul, funk and psychedelia. As a bonus, the 2001 Luaka Bop reissue includes "Strawberry Letter 23", "Ice Cold Daydream" and "Freedom Flight" from Otis's equally fine *Freedom Flight* album.

Ray Parker Jr. / Raydio

Epitomizing the corporate soul of the 80s, Ray Parker Jr. sounded like a black **Huey Lewis** some of the time and like **Hall & Oates** for the rest. Born in Detroit on May 1, 1954, Parker started out as a session guitarist for Holland-Dozier-Holland's labels, and he appeared on Stevie Wonder's *Innervisions* and *Talking Book* albums. Moving to California in 1974, Parker worked with Leon Haywood, Gene Page and Ronnie McNeir, and co-wrote Rufus & Chaka Khan's "You Got The Love".

In 1977 Parker formed the group **Raydio** with **Arnell** and **Darren Carmichael**, **Jerry Knight**, **Larry Tolbert** and **Charles Fearing**. That year Knight sang lead on their first top-five hit for Arista, "Jack And Jill", a smooth and somewhat novel spin on the classic cheating song format. Raydio's brand of pop-funk adorned the Top 10 again in 1979, with Parker's most Hall & Oates-like moment, "You Can't Change That".

As **Ray Parker Jr. & Raydio**, the group had their first R&B #1 with "A Woman Needs Love (Just Like You Do)" in 1981. This was the first record on which Parker sang lead unaccompanied, and even though his vocals were forced and stilted, its success hastened his impending solo career. After Raydio broke up in 1982 and Parker moved on to a solo career, vocalist Knight also went on to further success. He teamed up with **Ollie Brown** to sing the theme songs to the 1984 movies *Breakin'* and *Breakin' 2: Electric Boogaloo* as **Ollie & Jerry**.

Meanwhile, Parker hit immediately with "The Other Woman", a perfect marriage of skinny-tie rock and pop-R&B that created the foundations for the rest of his career. Despite being another cheating song, "The Other Woman" somehow sounded tailor-made for the date montage of a teen flick. It also sounded a lot like the blueprint for **Huey Lewis & The News'** 1983 album *Sports*. Ironically, when Parker had his only pop #1 with the inescapable "Ghostbusters" – from the 1984 Dan Ackroyd movie of the same name – he was sued by Huey Lewis for its similarity to his "I Want A New Drug".

Despite the crossover success of "Ghostbusters", Parker's biggest hits were already behind him, although he did manage to have a modest follow-up hit with "Jamie" later that year. In the mid-80s Parker went on to have sizeable R&B hits with "I Don't Think That Man Should Sleep Alone" and "Over You", a duet with Natalie Cole, but he fared better when he concentrated on writing and producing other acts, including New Edition and Diana Ross.

Greatest Hits
1993, Arista

Who you gonna call if you need some middle-of-the-road R&B to keep the oldies happy at your daughter's Bat Mitzvah? – Ray Parker Jr. This compilation of Parker's biggest solo and Raydio material is basically fourteen tracks of bubblegum pop, with a hint of soul and funk thrown in. Sadly this is all so faceless and ignorable that it almost matches Brian Eno's notion of ambient music.

Parliament-Funkadelic

No one traversed the mind–booty divide more audaciously than **George Clinton** with his **Parliafunkadelicment Thang**. With an unhealthy interest in scatology – perhaps due to the fact that he was born in an outhouse in North Carolina in 1941 – Clinton attempted to solve Western philosophy's mind–body problem by merging the alternative universes he found in effluence, coitus, black radio, conspiracy theory, comic books, nursery rhymes and advertising slogans with the close-harmony singing, transcendence and physicality of the gospel tradition. With his equation of headspace and dancefloor, Clinton exposed the idea that black music was only capable of expressing the urges of the body as the racist fallacy that it was.

While Clinton was the conceptual ringleader of the P-Funk circus and had the ability to arrange individual instrumental voices into a whole, the Mothership would never have descended without the musicians he attracted. Clinton's **Funkateers** saw the funk everywhere they looked; no one except Isaac Hayes did more for the wah-wah pedal than **Eddie Hazel**, or more for the MiniMoog than **Bernie Worrell**. Worrell's willingness to explore the outer limits of technology and timbre ranked him as one of the most important keyboard players American music had

produced since be-bop. **Bootsy Collins** was, without a doubt, the most rhythmically gifted and inventive bassist since Jimmy Blanton; and the other James Brown refugees, the **Horny Horns** – saxophonist **Maceo Parker** and trombonist **Fred Wesley** – did as much for funk as either of their bosses.

With other key members such as vocalists Mudbone Cooper, Glen Goins, Lynn Mabry, Dawn Silva, Fuzzy Haskins and Grady Thomas, drummers Tiki Fulwood, Jerome Brailey and Tyrone Lampkin, bassist Boogie Mosson and guitarists Michael Hampton, **Catfish Collins**, Garry Shider, Dewayne McKnight and Junie Morrison, the P-Funk Mob skewed Sly Stone's integrationist vision into an assertion of the black roots of rock, funk and soul. Combined with Clinton's sci-fi trickster persona and his confidence games with racial stereotypes, the P-Funk legacy is the most complete, detailed and unique sound world ever committed to vinyl.

While future Dr. Funkenstein began his musical life as the leader of a straightforward doo-wop band called **The Parliaments** in New Jersey in 1956, the P-Funk experience only started to take shape when Clinton took the group to Detroit in the 60s in the hope of signing to Motown. **Berry Gordy** passed on the group, but signed Clinton as a producer and songwriter. However, Clinton spent most of his time moonlighting for local Motown rivals Revilot, Solid Hit and Groovesville where he produced and co wrote Northern soul gems for Darrell Banks, J.J. Barnes and **The Debonaires**.

The Parliaments' 1967 Revilot single, "(I Wanna) Testify", came from nowhere and reached the American Top 20. Predating Sly Stone's "Whole New Thing" and **Norman Whitfield**'s more experimental productions for The Temptations and The Undisputed Truth, "Testify" was the prescient, guitar-led blueprint for soul's hippy crossover success. Soon afterwards, Clinton would start dropping acid, grooving to the MC5 and digging John Sinclair's sexual liberation = political freedom spiel. With the addition of the hard funk bottom from Sly Stone, James Brown and **Jimi Hendrix**'s freak-outs, the strands of Clinton's twisted vision coalesced.

The suit and tie-wearing, doo-wopping Parliaments became the Afro-wearing, diaper-clad **Parliament**, while the fuzz-guitar-infested backing band became **Funkadelic**. Parliament released the first P-Funk album, *Osmium*, on Invictus in 1970. Named after the heaviest metal on the periodic table long before the term "heavy metal" was coined, *Osmium* set the vocalizing skills of Clinton, Haskins, Thomas, **Calvin Simon** and **Raymond Davis** against a backdrop of acid-drenched psych-outs, bagpipes and harpsichords. God only knows what label bosses Holland-Dozier-Holland must have thought.

Strangely, though, it was Funkadelic's first album that really toyed with the conventions of soul vocal group recordings. *Funkadelic* (1970) sounded like The Temptations and **Grand Funk Railroad** emerging together from the rubble left by Detroit's race riot. The blurred, murky sound of "I'll Bet You" and "Music For My Mother" and the aggressive distortion of "I Got A Thing, You Got A Thing, Everybody Got A Thing" – which they sing like they don't really believe – seemed to sum up the frustration of urban African-Americans after the back-handed double-dealings of the government. To Clinton, alternative realities offered the only hope of escaping both the physical ghetto and the ghettos of the mind.

Clinton invented his most potent catch phrase on the title track of Funkadelic's other 1970 album, *Free Your Mind...And Your Ass Will Follow*. By inverting the hippy belief that physical liberation led to intellectual freedom, Clinton showed that the supposed "natural" physicality of black people was simply a product of Norman Mailer's repressed imagination. Jimi Hendrix fully entered Clinton's synthesis via guitarist Eddie Hazel on the stinging riff of "I Wanna Know If It's Good To You" and the dangling hammer-ons at the beginning of "Funky Dollar Bill".

Although Clinton has denied it numerous times, rumour has it that 1971's *Maggot Brain* was so named because he had found his brother Robert's festering corpse after he overdosed on drugs. Whether it was that, or Vietnam, or the grim realities of life in Detroit, *Maggot Brain* was as bleak as Sly Stone's *There's A Riot Goin' On*, as washed-out as **The Rolling Stones**' *Exile On Main Street*, as aggressive as **Black Sabbath**'s *Paranoid* – and as brilliant as any of them. The bitingly sarcastic approach of "Back In Our Minds", which predated The O'Jays' "Back Stabbers" and "Don't Call Me

Brother" in its attack of false brotherhood sentiments, would be taken up and writ large on Funkadelic's next album.

Where Sly, the Stones and Sabbath all lightened their moods after trawling the depths with their masterpieces, Funkadelic sustained the mood with the unbearably bitter *America Eats Its Young* in 1972. Cloaked in a savage parody of the funky dollar bill that showed a be-fanged Statue of Liberty snacking on babies, the album featured sniping satires of their vocal-group contemporaries. It also saw the band borrowing **Gamble & Huff**'s Philly International sound with Worrell's keyboard riff and Clinton's string arrangement on "A Joyful Process". Clinton's childhood friend **Garry Shider** also became part of the group with the release of *America Eats Its Young*.

The 1973 *Cosmic Slop* album saw Clinton channel his lysergic visions and ghetto rage through his vocal-group experience more explicitly than before. While still featuring bizarre anti-war fantasies like "March To The Witch's Castle", the album was dominated by tracks like "You Can't Miss What You Can't Measure" – with its Motown-style basso profondo interjections – and the title track, which featured a lead vocal from Shider that wouldn't have been out of place on a **Swan Silvertones** record. Clinton's extremism may have been tempered, but it's hard to imagine how startling the title track must have sounded when it was released.

Clinton's other tales of sex and desire – "No Compute", "Nappy Dugout" and "Trash

The wild and glittering Parliament

A Go-Go" – were equally bold and outlandish. This new-found obsession with sexual politics was echoed by the somewhat scandalous first cartoon sleeve designed by **Pedro Bell**. Bell went on to provide the visual analogue of Clinton's increasingly sophisticated sound world on the rest of Funkadelic's albums, and on Clinton's solo records, until 1986's *R&B Skeleton In The Closet*.

Two other recruits proved even more crucial to the development of P-Funk. After a meeting with Bootsy and Catfish Collins, Clinton decided to reinstate the Parliament/ Funkadelic distinction. Parliament's first album for the Casablanca label, 1974's *Up For The Down Stroke*, updated their old material like "(I Wanna) Testify" and "The Goose That Laid The Golden Egg". It also contained "Up For The Down Stroke", the Collins brothers' first contribution to the Parliafunkadelicment Thang, which provided the groove-based direction the band would pursue in future. Meanwhile, the 1974 Funkadelic album, *Standing On The Verge Of Getting It On*, followed a more rock-orientated route, with tracks like "Red Hot Mama" and the title cut.

While Funkadelic continued to focus on Clinton's concern with trashy soft-core vignettes on *Let's Take It To The Stage* (1975)

and *Tales Of Kidd Funkadelic* (1976), Clinton saved his most original scenarios for the Parliament albums. The title track on 1975's *Chocolate City* may be the most multilayered, surreal and sophisticated piece of music that Clinton ever made. "Chocolate City" turned white stereotypes of insatiable black hypersexuality into a black power fantasy that would keep George Wallace and Enoch Powell awake at night, imagining the African-American electorate multiplying like rabbits. Referencing James Brown's "Night Train" and Martha & The Vandellas' "Dancing In The Street", Clinton turned the name-checking of predominantly black cities into the reading of election results that spelled the end of the white power structure. Unfortunately, they couldn't keep up that inventive pace for the rest of the album.

Parliament's 1975 album *Mothership Connection* was unrelenting in its musical and conceptual genius, and became the first of a series of "funk operas". Coming out of the same jam sessions that produced the basic tracks for Funkadelic's *Let's Take It To The Stage* and Bootsy Collins's *Stretchin' Out In Bootsy's Rubber Band*, *Mothership Connection* gave P-Funk their commercial breakthrough when "Give Up The Funk (Tear The Roof Off The Sucker)" reached the US Top 15. The DJ from the previous *Chocolate City* album was resurrected on *Mothership Connection* in the persona of Star Child, who "returned to claim the Pyramids" in the Mothership. Gospel's deliverance was no longer brought forth by the white cherubs of European imagination, but by chitlin'-eating, Afro-clad brothers from another planet.

The depth of Clinton's sci-fi fantasy was matched by the creation of a unique sound world. Bootsy's custom-made Space Bass and **Bigfoot Brailey**'s drums laid down an unfeasibly aqueous, molten bottom over which **Michael Hampton** and **Garry Shider** vamped in tiny gestures and with rocket-science precision. Bernie Worrell's trademark hi-pitched synth squiggles really started taking shape on *Mothership Connection*, as he sculpted the contours of Clinton's outer-space in sound.

Unlike label owners Berry Gordy and Juggy Murray, Clinton eschewed the tenets of self-sufficient black capitalism in favour of an attempt to take the record industry for all it was worth. Between 1976 and 1979, the various P-Funk projects (Parliament, Funkadelic, Brides of Funkenstein, Bootsy, Parlet, The Horny Horns, Fuzzy Haskins, Eddie Hazel and Bernie Worrell) released 23 albums for five labels – and that doesn't include the Quazar and Mutiny projects by refugees from the Mothership. While all of the side project albums had enough inspired lunacy to recommend them, the best were Bootsy Collins's first two records.

Taking on the persona of Casper the bass-playing ghost, Bootsy became a bespectacled caped crusader for funk. He was at once the superhero of childhood fantasies and the kinky love man that Clinton could never be within Parliament-Funkadelic's constraints of collective improvisation. While the grooves of "Psychoticbumpschool" and the title track from 1977's *Stretchin' Out*, and the title cut and "The Pinocchio Theory" from 1977's *Ahh... The Name Is Bootsy, Baby!* were as monolithic as anything created by the core bands, it was the utterly bizarre ballads that set Bootsy apart. *Ahh...*'s "Munchies For Your Love" was a ten-minute psycho-sexual odyssey complete with a bass solo, while *Stretchin' Out*'s "I'd Rather Be With You" and "Vanish In Our Sleep" were as scary as anything Clinton had come up with earlier in the decade.

Parliament's 1977 album *Funkentelechy Vs. The Placebo Syndrome* refined Clinton's slyly facetious futurism. It followed the success of the mammoth P-Funk Earth Tour, which spent a then unheard of $275,000 budget on descending Motherships, space pimp outfits and toy bop guns. Star Child, the hero of *Mothership Connection*, returned for this tale of cloning and mind control as "the protector of the pleasure principle" who

PLAYLIST
Parliament

1 (I WANNA) TESTIFY The Parliaments from **I Wanna Testify: A Historic Compilation Of Vintage Soul**
One of the very first blends of guitar psychedelia and vocal group harmonizing.

2 MAGGOT BRAIN Funkadelic from **Maggot Brain**
Ten minutes of devastatingly emotive guitar, this is the result of Clinton directing Eddie Hazel to play like his "mother had just died".

3 UP FOR THE DOWN STROKE Parliament from **Up For The Down Stroke**
Preposterously funky monolithic groove.

4 COSMIC SLOP Funkadelic from **Cosmic Slop**
A remarkable tale of a mother turning tricks to feed her kids.

5 CHOCOLATE CITY Parliament from **Chocolate City**
Combines the hipster jive of black radio personalities with a parody of election-night roll call.

6 GIVE UP THE FUNK (TEAR THE ROOF OFF THE SUCKER) Parliament from **Mothership Connection**
One of Clinton's most outlandish sci-fi fantasies.

7 VANISH IN OUR SLEEP Bootsy's Rubber Band from **Stretchin' Out In Bootsy's Rubber Band**
An acid-soaked conflation of Eros and Thanatos.

8 FLASH LIGHT Parliament from **Funkentelechy Vs. The Placebo Syndrome**
Their greatest groove and one of the first records to appreciate the synth as a rhythm machine.

9 ONE NATION UNDER A GROOVE Funkadelic from **One Nation Under A Groove**
Clinton's most unabashedly anthemic record.

10 ATOMIC DOG George Clinton from **Computer Games**
The synth stomp that launched a thousand G-Funk rap records.

invaded the "zone of zero funkativity" in order to make Sir Nose D'Voidoffunk dance and defeat the "Placebo Syndrome" with his "Bop Gun". While Clinton's comic-book scenarios obscured his messages behind the cartoon music and juvenile humour, it was hard to ignore the Civil Rights references: "Turn me loose, we shall overcome".

The "Bop Gun" was Clinton's metaphor for the life-affirming power of dancing in the face of the pleasure-denying, sexless Puritans who still ran America 200 years after they founded it. With the album's closing track, "Flash Light" – which spent three weeks at the top of the R&B chart on the strength of its bassline – he found a song that made his metaphor real. "Flash Light" was a landmark not only for its implausibly kinetic groove, but also for its ground-breaking use of technology. By taking advantage of the Moog's capacity for stacking notes to create a gargantuan bass sound, Worrell's synth bassline remains perhaps the most important musical moment of the past 25 years as it anticipated the use of synths as rhythm machines.

The Funk Mob's next single – "One Nation Under A Groove" – doubled that success, expressing a sentiment that was strangely out of touch with both the recessionary times and Clinton's previous work. Kicking off with a Temptations reference, the track proceeded to take licks and catch phrases from Funkadelic's contemporaries in an inclusive and celebratory fashion that was miles from the scornful piss-takes of old. The anthemic vibe of the title track was repeated on nearly every track of 1978's *One Nation Under A Groove*. An even more improbable moment came when the impeccably cool former (Detroit) Spinners' vocalist **Philippe Wynne** defrosted himself by boarding the Mothership to sing on the remarkable synth riff of "(Not Just) Knee Deep" on 1979's *Uncle Jam Wants You*.

While Parliament was expanding the funk opera's horizons with 1978's underwater sextravaganza *Motor Booty Affair*, Funkadelic was exploring the darkest corners of Clinton's ego. Starting with the groupie wet dreams of *Let's Take It To The Stage* in 1975 and culminating with his fantasy of freak multitudes coming under his sway on *Uncle Jam Wants You* in 1979, Clinton seemed obsessed with the idea that

he was a superstar. Combined with the band's impossible-to-maintain workload, legal wrangles and bizarre record company decisions, his delusions of grandeur tore the P-Funk Thang apart. Bigfoot Brailey and Glen Goins jumped ship to make albums as **Quazar** and **Mutiny**; Fuzzy Haskins tried to wrest control of the Funkadelic name away from Clinton; Bootsy's **Rubber Band** lost a lawsuit over its name initiated by a country group called the Rubber Band; and Warner Bros refused to sanction Pedro Bell's phallic rocket cover art for 1981's *Electric Spanking Of War Babies*, and allegedly pressed only 80,000 copies, although the previous two Funkadelic albums had sold over a million.

After the lacklustre single entendres of Parliament's *Gloryhallastoopid* (1979) and *Trombipulation* (1980), and with the P-Funk nomenclature in legal turmoil, Clinton released a "solo" project on Capitol in 1982. With help from Bootsy, Shider, Junie and Worrell, the Parliafunkadelicment Thang's swansong as a unified entity became the phenomenon's most enduring record. Although it never made the pop chart, the second single from 1982's *Computer Games*, "Atomic Dog", was an R&B #1 for a month, while its rhythm loop – a classic P-Funk hand clap appended to a backwards drum machine – and its "Why must I feel like that?/Why must I chase the cat?/Nothin' but the dog in me" refrain have remained in the language of pop music ever since. With Clinton reprising his proto-rap vocals, the video game samples, the synth licks and mechanical rhythm loops, *Computer Games* directly linked P-Funk with the new breed of funkateers like Prince, The Gap Band, Yarbrough & Peoples, **John Robie** and a generation of hip-hop and electro artists.

Clinton enjoyed intermittent success after *Computer Games*, but his momentum was lost to the bands that brought the P-Funk blueprint into the 80s. Despite making great groove records like the P-Funk All Stars' 1983 *Urban Dancefloor Guerillas* album and 1984's *You Shouldn't-Nuf Bit Fish*, Clinton's name was dirt in the music industry. Legal catastrophes seemed to follow him around, and he was reduced to recording with outcasts. Some were inspired, like his duet with Vanessa Williams on 1986's *R&B Skeletons In The Closet*; and some were not, like the duets with **Thomas Dolby** on 1985's *Some Of My Best Friends Are Jokes.*

Meanwhile, Bootsy Collins had to sign over his earnings to Warner Bros after losing the suit over the rights to the Rubber Band name. He didn't make another record under his own name from 1982 to 1988; however, during that time he fell in with the group participating in **Bill Laswell**'s astringent funk experiments and appeared on Sly & Robbie's *Rhythm Killers* album in 1987.

While George Clinton has been championed by Prince, and many P-Funk albums have been recorded with Bill Laswell, the bump and spirit – if not the sci-fi flights of fancy – of P-Funk's music have been kept alive by West Coast hip-hoppers. P-Funk was huge in Southern California, and ever since Roger Clayton's **Uncle Jam's Army** started making electro records in 1985, P-Funk's presence has always been felt in West Coast hip-hop. Almost none of the records made under **Dr. Dre**'s G-Funk umbrella can match the original P-Funk for wit, intelligence or groove, but they still stand as a testament to Clinton's enduring legacy that "All that is good is nasty".

Funkadelic – Maggot Brain
1971, Westbound

As soul and funk were turning their backs on crossover success and looking inwards, Funkadelic had their eyes firmly on "white" rock and, on *Maggot Brain*, they produced music more attuned to the realities of black life than any of their contemporaries. From the opening title track with its devastatingly emotive primal screaming guitar to the final track, "Wars Of Armageddon", which took John Lennon's tape loops into the ghetto, *Maggot Brain* expressed George Clinton's vision to its fullest.

Parliament – Funkentelechy Vs. The Placebo Syndrome
1997, Casablanca

Funkentelechy Vs. The Placebo Syndrome was the most outlandish and fully realized of his sci-fi fantasies. Lurking underneath all the cartoonish synth squiggles and comic-book personas of what is perhaps his greatest funk opera is a vivid, eye-popping politically charged fantasy about race, religion and cultural politics.

George Clinton – Computer Games
1982, Capitol

While gracefully passing the torch to a new generation of funkateers, *Computer Games* contains plenty of the classic elements that made everyone groove on the P-Funk thang in the first place: serious funk spanks like "Get Dressed", Clinton's most deranged love-song throwaway "Pot Sharing Tots", and the prototype Funkadelic guitar sound being updated by throwing in bits of Wendy Carlos's Moog effects.

Billy Paul

Although he was perhaps the least typical of the singers who had hits under the auspices of **Gamble & Huff** at Philadelphia International – indeed, he had just the one smash – **Billy Paul** laid the groundwork for Lou Rawls' major crossover success in the mid-70s. With his jazzy ballad style and deeply soulful voice, he was a fine smooth-soul vocalist who deserves a greater appreciation of his talent.

Billy Paul was born **Paul Williams** in Philadelphia on December 1, 1934. During the mid-40s he performed on The Kiddie Show on the radio with his childhood friends **Bill Cosby** and **Lola Falana**. His recording debut came in 1955 with "Why Am I" on the Jubilee label, and he later joined an early doo-wop version of Harold Melvin & The Blue Notes and one of the many **Flamingos** line-ups. By the mid-60s Paul had established himself as one of Philadelphia's finest jazz vocalists, and he recorded the scat-heavy *Feelin' Good At The Cadillac Club* for the Gamble label in 1967.

By the time he released *Ebony Woman* in 1969 Paul had moved away from jazz standards towards a more pop-savvy and message-oriented style, although you might not know it from his jaunty cover of "Mrs Robinson". In 1971 he signed to Philadelphia International and recorded *Going East*. Except for the scything strings, the album sounded nothing like Philly soul, but it was among the most novel of the Afrocentric jazz-soul albums of the period. Paul strangely resembled a mellow **Nina Simone** on the album's jazzy, spiritual "East".

Paul's next album, 1972's *360 Degrees Of Billy Paul*, provided the perfect setting for his style and included his biggest hit, "Me And Mrs Jones". *The* cheating ballad of the 70s and a #1 on the R&B and pop charts, "Me And Mrs Jones" was lush, sleazy and emotionally compelling at the same time, and Paul's improvisations weren't merely ornamentation. "Am I Black Enough For You?" was one of the few pro-black anthems that didn't resort to facile cheerleading or air-headed positivity and actually dared to ask questions, while Paul's version of **Elton**

Go-Go

If hip-hop hadn't been invented in New York and if it was played by live bands instead of DJs, it probably would have been go-go, a music phenomenon unique to Washington DC that combined funk, congas and a touch of hip-hop. Just like hip-hop, go-go focused on Latin-flavoured percussion breaks and vocals that were little more than exhortations to the crowd to get down and jam.

Go-go's genesis came in 1974 when **Chuck Brown & The Soul Searchers** released *Salt Of The Earth*. The album featured "Blow Your Whistle", a track that combined the rhythm of Grover Washington Jr.'s "Mr Magic" with percussion breaks inspired by Chuck Brown's tenure in a group called **Los Latinos**. This combination of a slow funk groove with congas and cowbells became go-go music. In 1979 Brown recorded the track that would become go-go's calling card, "Bustin' Loose", and the genre soon became the dominant sound in Washington DC.

Trouble Funk, a group that had originally formed in the 60s as the Trouble Band, soon supplanted the Soul Searchers as the biggest go-go band. Their first go-go single was "E Flat Boogie", but their breakthrough came when they signed to Sugarhill Records in 1982 and released "Drop The Bomb", which was quite simply one of the funkiest records ever, combining **Parliament**-style rhythms and keyboards with cowbells. The follow-up, "Pump Me Up", had percussion that

was like the Mau-Maus marching up the Potomac.

Other major groups from the early days of go-go were **E.U.** (Experience Unlimited), **Rare Essence**, Redds & The Boys, Mass Extension, Junk Yard Band and Hot Cold Sweat. There was a brief vogue for go-go in the UK in the mid-80s, and E.U. had a moderate hit with "Da Butt" in 1989 thanks to its appearance on the soundtrack to Spike Lee's *School Daze*. However, despite connverting almost anyone who hears it being played live, go-go music has never really made it outside of Washington DC.

Trouble Funk: Live
1996, American/Infinite Zero

A reissue of what is quite possibly one of the greatest live albums ever made, this 4-track double album is just one long jam. But unlike the soporific extended jams of, say, the Grateful Dead, this album is pure intensity from the get-go.

Various Artists: Meet Me At The Go-Go
2003, Sanctuary

Although this is perhaps not the very best mainstream compilation of go-go – seek out *Go-Go Crankin'* (1985, 4th & Broadway) – it's certainly the most readily available, and it still has plenty going for it. It features such classics as Trouble Funk's "E Flat Boogie" and "Let's Get Small", Chuck Brown & The Soul Searchers' "We Need Some Money" and Hot Cold Sweat's "Meet Me At The Go-Go", as well as obscurities like Arkade Funk's awesome "Tilt" and Ski Bone's "Take It To The Top".

John's "Your Song" eventually became a Top 40 hit in the UK.

The even more overtly political *War Of The Gods* album from 1973 included Paul's second-biggest hit, "Thanks For Saving My Life", which reached the R&B Top 10. While he had some success in subsequent years with uptempo tracks such as "Be Truthful To Me", Paul was at his best as a ballad singer. "Billy's Back Home" was similar to "Me And Mrs Jones", while the follow-up "Let's Make A Baby" was an ode to childhood and procreation.

By the mid-70s message tracks were no longer in vogue and Paul had only modest success with 1976's "People Power" and his cover of **Paul McCartney**'s "Let 'Em In", which featured snippets of speeches by both **Malcolm X** and **Martin Luther King Jr**. After leaving Philadelphia International in 1981, Paul recorded *Lately* for Total Experience in 1985 and *Wide Open* for

Ichiban in 1988. Although he retired from recording at the end of the 80s, Paul continues to perform on the jazz circuit today.

Me And Mrs Jones: The Best Of Billy Paul
1999, Epic/Legacy

Despite giving short shrift to his more spiritual message tracks, this 14-cut compilation is a fine introduction to Billy Paul's underrated vocal style. Paul's vocal chops allowed Gamble & Huff to indulge in their jazz fantasies and, in turn, they created some of their lushest, gooiest productions for him. This is Philly soul at its most unctuous.

Freda Payne

With her cabaret vocal style, **Freda Payne** was meant to be the new Diana Ross for Holland-Dozier-Holland's Invictus imprint. It didn't quite work out that way, but at her best Payne was a good foil for HDH's real female solo star, the assertive Laura Lee.

Born in Detroit on September 19, 1945, Payne made her way around the talent show circuit as a teenager. When she graduated from high school she performed with the likes of **Pearl Bailey**, Quincy Jones and **Lionel Hampton**; **Duke Ellington** even offered a long-term contract, which she turned down for business reasons. She was also the understudy for **Leslie Uggams** in the Broadway production of *Hallelujah, Baby!* Her first recording was an English version of "Desafinado" for ABC-Paramount in 1962. After cutting the lite jazz album, *After The Lights Go Down Low And Much More!*, for the Impulse! label in 1963, Payne recorded as part of **Bob Crosby's Bobcats** for MGM.

In 1969 Payne's old high school friend **Eddie Holland** asked her to ditch the cabaret vibe and join his new Invictus label. She sounded somewhat lost in the powerhouse arrangement on her first Invictus release, "The Unhooked Generation", which included an extraordinary fuzz guitar line that later became the basis for **JVC Force**'s hip-hop classic "Strong Island". However, HDH got things right for her next record, "Band Of Gold", a singsong tale of matrimonial frustration that became her all-time bestseller.

Payne was at her best on similarly breezy uptempo numbers like "Deeper & Deeper", "Cherish What Is Dear To You (While It's Near To You)" and "You Brought The Joy". In 1971 the anti-war song "Bring The Boys Home" was Payne's biggest R&B hit, charting at #3. For the rest of her stint at Invictus, Payne shied away from both controversy and soul, as with her releases "Two Wrongs Don't Make A Right" and "For No Reason".

When Invictus closed up shop in 1974, Payne signed to ABC-Dunhill and released a series of records that were more in keeping with her original supper-club jazz style. She had modest dancefloor success in the late 70s with stiff disco records such as "Love Magnet", "I'll Do Anything For You" and "In Motion". Following a 1981 stint hosting her own TV talk show, *Today's Black Woman*, Payne turned to acting. Although she has subsequently released a few live albums and the retro cabaret album *Come See About Me*, Payne has been more visible on television and the silver screen of late, appearing in such movies as 2000's *Nutty Professor II: The Klumps*.

○ **Unhooked Generation: The Complete Invictus Recordings**
2001, Castle

Payne may not have been their finest vehicle, but you have to admire Holland-Dozier-Holland for trying to push the boundaries of soul in the early 70s. While they successfully tackled male impotence ("Band Of Gold") and anti-war sentiments ("Bring The Boys Back") with Payne, she was best at the more conventional love songs they penned specifically for her. On this mammoth 41-track collection, both the adventurous and the conventional are fully represented.

Peaches & Herb

Much like their patron Van McCoy, **Peaches & Herb** managed to have hits in both the soul and disco eras – and lived to tell the tale. The Peaches & Herb duo was born on a fateful day in 1965 when McCoy walked into a record store in Washington DC to promote a single by girl group **The Sweet Things**. The salesman, **Herb Feemster**, convinced McCoy to give him an audition, and he was signed to Columbia subsidiary Date as a vocalist a week later.

Feemster issued a couple of solo singles under the name **Herb Fame** in 1966 – most notably "You're Messing Up My Mind", an uptempo track that later gained some play on Northern soul dancefloors in the UK – but to little success. With Feemster's career going nowhere, McCoy decided to pair him with the lead singer of The Sweet Things, **Francine Hurd Barker**, who had the childhood nickname "Peaches". The duo first recorded "We're In This Thing Together" as Peaches & Herb in 1966, but it went nowhere. However, a DJ in St Louis started to play the flip, a cover of **Eddy Duchin**'s "Let's Fall In Love", and it eventually reached #21 on the pop chart.

Peaches & Herb were quickly dubbed the "Sweethearts of Soul", and McCoy created a series of lush sweet soul ballads for them. Their version of **The Five Keys**' "Close Your Eyes" was a top-ten pop hit in 1967, and they also enjoyed substantial success that year with versions of **Ed Townshend**'s "For Your Love" and **Mickey & Sylvia**'s "Love Is Strange". Barker was replaced at live dates by session singer **Marlene Mack** in 1968, but continued to sing on their recordings, such as "Ten Commandments Of Love", "(We'll

Be) United" and "When He Touches Me (Nothing Else Matters)", in 1968 and 1969.

Although Feemster quit the duo in 1970 to become a police officer in Washington, they did record a version of **Simon & Garfunkel's** "The Sound Of Silence" in 1971. Peaches & Herb then largely lay dormant until the sight of McCoy riding high in the charts with "The Hustle" prompted Feemster to re-enter the music biz in the mid-70s. McCoy hooked him up with a new Peaches, **Linda Green**, a former model and member of **The Rondells**, but no one really cared about their 1977 MCA release, "We're Still Together".

The following year Feemster and Green started working with **Freddie Perren's** production company and signed to Polydor. Their "Shake Your Groove Thing" went gold in 1978, riding a funky disco sound, but it was the silky ballad "Reunited" that was a true smash hit, spending a month at the top of both the pop and R&B charts in 1979. However, when they tied their fortunes to disco with records like "Roller Skatin' Mate" and "Funtime", Peaches & Herb's hits dried up pretty quick. "I Pledge My Love", a carbon copy of "Reunited", was a top-twenty pop hit in 1979, but it was to be their last. The duo finally called it quits when Feemster returned to law enforcement in 1986, although he did briefly reconvene the act with **Patrice Hawthorne** in 1992, but to little real success.

(o) **The Best Of Peaches & Herb: Love Is Strange**
1996, Epic/Legacy

This 16-track compilation holds essentially all you need of the original incarnation of Peaches & Herb – Francine Barker and Herb Feemster – from 1966 to 1969. It's largely treacly Tin Pan Alley stuff with a hint of sweet soul, but the overall innocence remains quite charming.

(o) **20th Century Masters – The Millennium Collection: The Best Of Peaches & Herb**
2002, Universal

If you prefer Peaches & Herb's dancefloor tracks to their ballads, this 12-track compilation is the album for you. It is the best anthology of the disco-era version of the duo, which had Linda Green as Peaches, and it includes their big hit "Shake Your Groove Thing".

Pebbles

R eleasing a series of immaculately craft- ed dance-pop singles during the late 80s, **Pebbles** epitomized the strong, inde-

pendent female R&B persona that developed in the wake of Janet Jackson. However, a series of personal and business disasters then seemed to cut off her career at the legs.

Born **Perri Alette McKissack** on August 29, 1965 in Oakland, California, Pebbles was nicknamed by her godfather thanks to her childhood resemblance to a character in the cartoon *The Flintstones*. She studied opera and classical music before becoming a back-up singer and songwriter for Con Funk Shun and Sister Sledge. Signing to MCA as a solo artist in 1987, she released the compelling debut album, *Pebbles*, the following year. The album was largely self-produced, except for the two hit singles, "Girlfriend" and "Mercedes Boy". "Girlfriend", produced by **LA Reid** and Babyface, was a classic of the strut-pow-put-'em-out school of late-80s R&B. "Mercedes Boy", produced by The Gap Band's **Charlie Wilson**, was reminiscent of Janet Jackson's *Control* album, though its arrangement emphasized interlocking guitars rather than angular drum machine beats, which gave the track a spacier, less strident quality.

Pebbles married LA Reid in 1989, and LA and Babyface produced her second album, *Always*, in 1990. While the shine they gave Pebbles didn't hurt her chart placings any, it did, regrettably, smooth out the previous rough edges. Even so, "Giving You The Benefit" was consummate pop-R&B craftsmanship, while "Love Makes Things Happen" was in that wretched Babyface ballad style that ruled urban radio before hip-hop could no longer be ignored.

Pebbles then put together R&B/pop sensations TLC. She served as the girl group's manager until she divorced Reid in 1995 and sued his LaFace label for allegedly trying to wrest the group from her control. Amid all the chaos, Pebbles found the time to release her third album, *Straight From The Heart*, in 1995. It was a fine, more "mature" record with occasionally dazzling production from **Organized Noize** and P. Diddy. After that album, she quit the music biz entirely. Ditching the the name Pebbles, she is now known as Sister Perri and runs a Christian ministry for women in Atlanta, Georgia.

Freestyle

Like politics, pop music has always made for strange bedfellows. However, none of pop's miscegenated couplings were more bizarre than kids from the Bronx believing that Düsseldorf's showroom dummies **Kraftwerk** were the funkiest thing since James Brown. Borrowing heavily from Kraftwerk's "Trans-Europe Express" and "Numbers", **Afrika Bambaataa & The Soul Sonic Force**'s "Planet Rock" introduced the video game aesthetic that briefly dominated New York's dance music scene. With the increasing availability of fairly sophisticated technology, the Big Apple's early 80s clubscape was defined by the sound of harsh drum machines and piercing synthesizers on records like **C-Bank**'s "One More Shot", **Hashim**'s "Al-Naafiyish" and **Planet Patrol**'s "Play At Your Own Risk". Somewhere in this mechanical matrix, New York Latinos heard ancestral echoes of salsa piano lines and montuno rhythms. In the hands of producers like the Latin Rascals, Paul Robb, **Omar Santana** and **Andy "Panda" Tripoli**, the Pac-Man bleeps, synth stabs and Roland TR-808 clavés became an android descarga called Freestyle.

Of course, Freestyle was the kind of thing that could only happen in New York and, with the exception of Miami's large Hispanic community, it was largely ignored by the rest of the US. Make no mistake, though; Freestyle exerted an enormous influence on dance music producers and, with the exception of Latin Rock and the brief flourishes of East Side soul in LA, it was the first mainstream genre that Hispanic Americans could call their own. While Freestyle was often called "Latin hip-hop", the genre's insistence on melody and heartbreak vocals actually made it closer to Latin soul.

Freestyle's ground zero was **Shannon**'s 1983 single, "Let The Music Play". Although it didn't have the hi-hat sound that later characterized Freestyle percussion, the record's electro-wood-block-and-cow-bell percussion and kick drum/snare drum interaction provided the blueprint for Freestyle's street-smart tales of innocence and experience. "Please Don't Go" by 16-year-old **Nayobe** and producer Andy Panda further Latinized the formula established by "Let The Music Play", featuring keyboard patterns stolen from Patrice Rushen and **Eddie Palmieri** on top of synthesized timbale beats. Meanwhile, DJ **Jellybean Benitez** attempted to reclaim "The Mexican" for Latinos from both Ennio Morricone and prog rock group Babe Ruth.

Freestyle's biggest early star was **Lisa Lisa**, aka former Funhouse dancer Lisa Velez, who was discovered by production team **Full Force**. With a dubby synth effect stolen from John Robie's Emulator keyboard and a Roland woodblock pattern, **Lisa Lisa & Cult Jam**'s 1984 debut "I Wonder If I Take You Home" was an anthemic update of the eternal question first posed by The Shirelles – will you still love me tomorrow? It dented the Top 40 when it was re-released in 1985, but was a bigger hit in 2005 when it was sampled on "Don't Phunk With My Heart" by hip-hop crew **Black Eyed Peas**. Other early Freestyle stars included the proto-boy band **TKA** and "Latin Supremes" **The Cover Girls**.

Largely adenoidal teenagers, most of Freestyle's vocalists could barely hold a note without their voices cracking, let alone compete with the singers of the soul tradition. However, if, as its many guardians claim, soul music is about the direct expression of experience, then

Greatest Hits
2000, Hip-O

Although it lacks anything from her surprisingly decent third album, *Straight From The Heart*, this 14-track collection holds a satisfying wealth of Pebbles' bright, shiny dance-pop-with-attitude, including the hit singles "Girlfriend", "Mercedes Boy" and "Giving You The Benefit".

Ann Peebles

Although Memphis' **Hi Records** will be forever associated with Al Green, soulstress **Ann Peebles** created a body of work during the same period that was equally distinctive and almost as definitive as that of her more famous labelmate. While Green was redefining the soul man as a softly spoken gentleman torn between the spirit and the flesh, Peebles injected the long-suffering female soul persona with rage and rootsiness. Unlike the somewhat gimmicky feminism of Laura Lee, Peebles sang from a strong woman's perspective without abandoning the gospel-blues tradition. In doing so, she became perhaps the most compelling female soul singer in the post-Aretha Franklin era.

Born in East St. Louis on April 27, 1947, Peebles began singing in her church choir as a child. After performing on the local club circuit, she was given the chance to audition for **Willie Mitchell** at Hi Records while on a

Freestyle surely deserves a place in its pantheon. What could be more immediate than heartbroken adolescents exorcizing sexual confusion while dodging synth bullets and chopping edits that mirrored their changing voices? Freestyle transcended its largely crass teenybop foundations because of the producers and mixers. They not only created startling electronic music, but also made their knob-twiddling the musical representation of the young vocalists who were grasping for certainty while all around them was change and flux.

Various Artists: Freestyle's Greatest Beats: The Complete Collection Volume 1
1994, Tommy Boy/Timber

This collection contains most of the major recordings from Freestyle's golden age in the mid-80s. It is probably the single best collection available of this largely underappreciated genre and it includes important records by Lisa Lisa, TKA, The Cover Girls and Sa-Fire.

PLAYLIST

1 LET THE MUSIC PLAY Shannon from **Let The Music Play**
The sound of New York circa 1983.

2 ONE MORE SHOT C-Bank from **The Disco Years Volume 5**
This uses a snippet of the sound of breaking glass and all manner of weird synth striations and nasty scratches to give a grim edge to a tale of heartbreak and paranoia.

3 PLEASE DON'T GO Nayobe from **Freestyle's Greatest Beats: The Complete Collection Volume 1**
An electrified montuno beat that was one of the first true freestyle records.

4 I WONDER IF I TAKE YOU HOME Lisa Lisa & Cult Jam from **Freestyle's Greatest Beats: The Complete Collection Volume 1**
The Shirelles updated for Latino girls from el barrio.

5 RUNNING Information Society from **Freestyle's Greatest Beats: The Complete Collection Volume 1**
Depeche Mode doom and gloom plus Nuyorican drum programming equals Freestyle's strangest hit.

6 ONE WAY LOVE TKA from **Freestyle's Greatest Beats: The Complete Collection Volume 1**
The cavernous synth bass and the percussion stalactites make this irresistible.

7 SHOW ME Cover Girls from **Freestyle's Greatest Beats: The Complete Collection Volume 1**
Journalist Dave Tompkins calls the feeling created by productions like this "torque"; crank this high and when you peel yourself off the wall you'll see what he means.

8 SILENT MORNING Noel from **Freestyle's Greatest Beats: The Complete Collection Volume 1**
Another odd mix of dour European synth-pop and sparkling Latino pizzazz.

9 DREAM BOY/DREAM GIRL Cynthia/Johnny O from **Cynthia**
The biggest-selling Freestyle record ever, and one of the 90s' true teen anthems.

10 TOGETHER FOREVER Lisette Melendez from **Together Forever**
The android descarga updated for the early 90s.

trip to Memphis, and was signed to the label just before her 21st birthday. Her first single was 1969's "Walk Away". One of Mitchell's earliest productions, "Walk Away" was a classic Memphis blend of gospel feeling and country chords. While Peebles' phrasing was reminiscent of Aretha Franklin's, her voice was more direct, more ragged, more loveworn – not what you'd expect from a 22-year-old. Unfortunately, her debut album, *This Is Ann Peebles* – with its slightly awkward covers of tracks like Bettye Swann's "Make Me Yours" – didn't manage to live up to the power and promise of "Walk Away".

In 1970, however, her version of the blues evergreen, "Part Time Love", and the album of the same name, truly established Peebles as a great singer. The song had been a standard for male singers for years, but it sounded tailor-made for Peebles' tough, assertive wail and she attacked it with relish. The album had several other highlights, such as Peebles' self-penned "I'll Get Along" – a bluesy, testifying declaration of independence filled with downhome metaphors – and the devastating slow-burn, "I Still Love You".

Her 1972 cover of Bobby Bland's "I Pity The Fool" followed the same blueprint as "Part Time Love" to become another profound blast of break-up catharsis. "I Pity The Fool" was one of the two stand-out tracks on her *Straight From The Heart* album. The

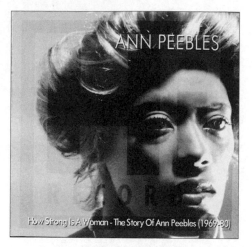

ANN PEEBLES

How Strong Is A Woman - The Story Of Ann Peebles (1969-80)

other was her definitive reading of "I Feel Like Breaking Up Somebody's Home". Once again, Peebles brought her forceful pipes and a feminine perspective to bear on a classic male cheating song, and the results rank alongside Aretha's reading of Otis Redding's "Respect".

Despite their perfect Southern soul credentials, Peebles' albums failed to sell, and it wasn't until 1973 that she achieved a commercial breakthrough with "I Can't Stand The Rain". The song's instantly memorable beginning might sound more like it emerged from a Parisian sound lab than from Willie Mitchell's joint in Memphis, but "I Can't Stand The Rain" remains a true classic of the Memphis sound. It had everything: Al Jackson's smouldering drums, a driving piano, those horn charts and, most of all, Peebles' ravaged vocals. The way she sang the first line has to be just about the most chilling moment in the history of popular music. Although it only reached #38, it was still Peebles' biggest pop hit and it was something of a miracle that a song so naked and raw could make the charts at all.

While "I Can't Stand The Rain" was Peebles' own property (she co-wrote it with husband Don Bryant), only fools and Paul Young would dare to match her version of "I'm Gonna Tear Your Playhouse Down". Although Willie Mitchell's by now formulaic production was perfectly suited for Al Green, it didn't always work with Peebles; this is definitely one instance where she outperformed her band and saved the record.

Peebles' mid- to late-70s recordings were a series of diminishing returns on which the

backing became increasingly faceless, but she remained a great singer capable of transcending tired musicians and weak material. Like Al Green, she focused exclusively on gospel music during the 80s, but she returned to secular material during the 90s and recorded a few fine albums that echoed classic Southern soul styles: *Call Me* (1990), *Full Time Love* (1992) and *Fill This World With Love* (1996).

Fill This World With Love
1996, Bullseye

With a body of work as strong as her early-70s Hi Records material behind her, it shouldn't be surprising that Ann Peebles came back with this deep-soul stunner in the 90s. Her vocal style is unchanged and the unassuming power of the downhome back-up gives her plenty of room to show off her often unacknowledged talent.

How Strong Is A Woman – The Story Of Ann Peebles (1969–80)
1998, Cream/Hi Records

An excellent 46-track, 2-CD compilation of Peebles' years with Willie Mitchell at Hi Records, this is probably the only Peebles material anyone needs to own. Her intensity, and her combination of bluesiness with Memphis groove, make her one of the definitive Southern soul singers.

Teddy Pendergrass

The bard of the boudoir, Philadelphia vocalist **Teddy Pendergrass** oozed machismo from every pore. He had a man-and-a-half growl like Wilson Pickett, but he was styled more like hot-buttered love men Isaac Hayes and Barry White, and during the height of his fame in the late-70s he frequently held "ladies only" concerts.

Pendergrass was born in Philadelphia on March 26, 1950. His mother was a nightclub singer and he spent much of his youth singing in church. As a teenager he joined a local group called **The Cadillacs** – not the ones who had a hit with "Speedo" – as the drummer. In 1969 the group became the backing band for Harold Melvin & The Blue Notes, and when that group's lead singer, **John Atkins**, left, Pendergrass took over his role. The Blue Notes then signed to **Gamble & Huff**'s Philadelphia International label and Pendergrass guided them to huge success throughout the first half of the 70s. However, tensions between Pendergrass and Melvin eventually caused the group to split in 1976.

Teddy Pendergrass stayed with Gamble & Huff and released his first solo album, *Teddy Pendergrass*, the following year. His debut set the style for which he became famous: rubbing his girl down with essential oils, and seducing her with his throaty baritone cushioned against Gamble & Huff's luxuriant strings and woodwinds. That said, the album's finest track, "You Can't Hide From Yourself", was an uptempo disco stormer with a pulsating bassline and piercing strings.

His second album, 1978's *Life Is A Song Worth Singing*, held another uptempo corker, the slightly more ridiculous "Get Up, Get Down, Get Funky, Get Loose", but its big hit was the classic he-man seduction song, "Close The Door", his first R&B #1. "Turn Off The Lights" followed in nearly identical style in 1979, although the "Teddy Bear" was slightly less husky. The next year's "Love TKO" boasted the same unctuous production, but this time Pendergrass was singing about failure and the record became a classic break-up ballad. "You're My Latest, My Greatest Inspiration", from his *It's Time For Love* album in 1981, was an even sappier version of the same formula.

Tragically, on March 18, 1982, Pendergrass crashed his Rolls Royce and suffered severe spinal cord injuries that left him paralyzed from the neck down. His voice was spared, however, and after two years of rehab he returned to singing in 1984 with "Hold Me", an icky duet with Whitney Houston. Although the hits didn't come so easily after the accident, Pendergrass scored his second R&B #1 in 1988 with "Joy", written and produced by Reggie and Vincent Calloway from Midnight Star. The follow-up, "2 AM", attempted to bring him back to his old sound, but its production values only made him sound thin. However, "2 AM" was still a #3 R&B hit.

In the early 90s the R&B #1 "It Should've Been You", and "Voodoo", written and produced by Gerald Levert, were far more successful attempts at returning Pendergrass to the love man throne. His final R&B chart hit was 1997's "Give It To Me", but he returned to live performance in May 2001. Since then, Pendergrass has also set up the Teddy Pendergrass Alliance, a charity for people suffering from spinal cord injuries.

 The Philly Years
1994, Philadelphia International

This double-disc, 32-track compilation is a near-perfect summation of Pendergrass's years at Philadelphia International – all that's missing is the great "You Can't Hide From Yourself". Otherwise, this has all the records that made the Teddy Bear one of the biggest soul icons in the 70s, and the model for nearly all the love men who followed in his wake.

The Persuaders

With their first few records, **The Persuaders** stood out as one of 70s soul's most remarkable vocal groups – not so much for their singing, which was, in truth, somewhat ragged, but for their subject matter and production, which was the diametric opposite of the sweet soul dominating the charts at the time.

Consisting of **James Barnes**, **Willie Holland**, **Charles Stodghill** and lead singer **Douglas "Smokey" Scott**, The Persuaders originally formed in New York in the mid-60s as **The Internationals**. In 1968 they were lured to the UK by a dodgy promoter who billed them as **The Showstoppers**, confident that no one would realize they weren't the group who recorded "Ain't Nothin' But A House Party". They were all furious, but they went ahead with the tour as they had no money and no way to get back home.

Having briefly split apart in their anger, they soon reformed as The Persuaders and hooked up with songwriter/producers **Richard and Robert Poindexter**. After the group cut a couple of singles, including 1970's "Give A Damn", that went nowhere on Bell, the Poindexters signed a deal with Atlantic. The Persuaders' first Atlantic release, the remarkable "Thin Line Between Love And Hate", spent two weeks at #1 on the R&B chart in 1971. With Scott's over-enunciated lead vocals and the old-fashioned melodrama of the arrangement, "Thin Line Between Love And Hate" was a pretty standard cautionary tale about adultery – until the last verse, where the put-upon wife exacts her revenge and sends the cheating bastard to the hospital.

The follow-up, "Love Gonna Pack Up (And Walk Out)", which also went into the Top 10 in 1971, was a lugubrious, reggae-inspired doom march that established The Persuaders as chroniclers of the dark side of love. The next year's "If This Is What You Call Love (I Don't Want No Part Of It)" was a less distinctive record, but was still full of misery and hurt.

With **John Tobias** and former Majestics' lead singer **Thomas Lee Hill** replacing Stodghill and Barnes, The Persuaders scored further R&B hits in 1972 with the more soothing "Peace In The Valley Of Love" and the run-of-the-mill "Bad, Bold And Beautiful Girl". The next year **Richard Gant** and **Willie Coleman** replaced Tobias and Holland, and the new line-up scored a big hit with the singsong "Some Guys Have All The Luck", which was later a smash for **Rod Stewart**. In 1974 "The Best Thing That Ever Happened To Me" made the R&B Top 30, but was drowned out by Gladys Knight & The Pips' version.

In 1977, with disco in full swing, The Persuaders enlisted the services of producer/arranger **Norman Harris** of Philadelphia International to add some glitterball polish to their *It's All About Love* album. The group suffered on the uptempo numbers, but had a modest hit with the pretty "I Need Love". However, these recordings proved to be the group's last sessions.

With the hits drying up, The Persuaders drifted apart, but varous line-ups continued to tour the revival circuit until Scott died in 1994. Tommy Hill re-formed the group with a new line-up in the mid-90s and they recorded a new album, *Stayed Away Too Long*, in 1997. Hill died in November 2002, but a current line-up of Richard Pindexter, **Alexander Brown**, **David Turner** and **Tony Riley** are still touring and they released *Made To Be Loved* in 2006.

⊙ **Thin Line Between Love & Hate: Golden Classics Edition**
1991, Collectables

Essentially their first album with the addition of "Peace In The Valley Of Love", this 12-track CD is the best available collection. While it doesn't have the dispensable, but popular, "Some Guys Have All The Luck", it offers all the tracks that made the group a unique presence on the vocal group scene in the early 70s.

Esther Phillips

Even if her astringent, nasal voice was obviously influenced by Dinah Washington, **Esther Phillips** will one day achieve her due recognition as a truly great female vocalist. Capable of injecting anything from pop standards to country weepies to disco baubles with fierce emotion, Phillips was such a towering singer that in 1973 Aretha Franklin gave her own Grammy for best performance by a female R&B singer to Phillips because she thought that she deserved it more.

Phillips was born **Esther Mae Jones** on December 23, 1935 in Galveston, Texas. Living in LA with her mother after her parents' divorce, she brought down the house as a 13-year-old at a 1949 talent show at Johnny Otis's Barrelhouse Club. Billed as **Little Esther**, she signed to Savoy and released a string of records with Johnny Otis's band that made her a superstar. "Double Crossing Blues" from 1950 was a standard lover's blues lament, but her piercing voice really connected with the lyrics, and it became an R&B #1 for nine weeks. She made the R&B Top 10 with Otis's band six more times over the next twelve months, including two more #1s: "Mistrustin' Blues" and "Cupid Boogie".

In 1951 Esther's mother was appointed as her legal guardian and she signed a disputed contract with **Syd Nathan**'s King/Federal labels. Her first record with Federal was the bizarre proto-rock'n'roll track "The Deacon Moves In", on which she shared the lead with **Charlie White** of The Dominoes and sounded reminiscent of Shirley & Lee. Although Little Esther stayed with Federal for three years, her only hit was the silly "Ring-a-Ding-Doo" in 1952, with her old sparring partner from Johnny Otis's band, **Mel Walker**. She signed with Decca at the end of 1953, but her jazzy records for the label, such as "Please Don't Send Me Home" and "Sit Back Down", were out of step with the burgeoning rock'n'roll sound.

For several years, while Esther was dogged by an addiction to heroin, her only record of any real significance was 1956's modest R&B hit "You Can Bet Your Life". She was largely forgotten by the early 60s and was performing at a Houston nightclub in 1962 when she was "rediscovered" by country-rock singer **Kenny Rogers**, and signed to his brother's Lenox label as **Esther Phillips**. According to legend, she took her name from a nearby Phillips petrol station. Thanks to Ray Charles' pioneering country recordings that year, her 1962 version of **Ray Price**'s "Release Me" came out of nowhere to reach #1 on the R&B chart and the pop Top 10. Phillips simply destroyed this country evergreen record with such piercing intensity that even the cornpone chorale sounded soulful.

The Lenox label went out of business the following year, but Phillips signed to Atlantic in 1964 and enjoyed success with **The Beatles**' "And I Love Him" and an answer record to Percy Sledge, "When A Woman Loves A Man". However, her best Atlantic record was probably 1965's "Hello Walls", with its overwrought choir and lush downtown soul arrangement. Phillips also had a minor R&B success with **Glen Campbell**'s "Too Late To Worry, Too Blue to Cry" for Roulette in 1969.

Signing to **Creed Taylor**'s Kudu label, Phillips released the stunning *From A Whisper To A Scream* album in 1972, which included fearsome renditions of Gil Scott-Heron's "Home Is Where The Hatred Is" and Marvin Gaye's "Baby, I'm For Real", as well as the belting ballad "That's All Right With Me". She scored another big hit in 1975 with a disco remake of **Dinah Washington**'s "What A Diff'rence A Day Makes", but failed to repeat the same trick with **Hal Kemp**'s "For All We Know" the next year.

Phillips signed to Mercury in 1977 and recorded four albums, but her only post-disco hit was 1983's "Turn Me Out", a final flirtation with the dancefloor. She suffered from serious health problems over the next year and, sadly, died from liver failure on August 7, 1984.

○ **Home Is Where The Hatred Is: The Kudu Years 1971–1977**
2004, Raven

Phillips may have made her name as a bluesy jazz and R&B singer in the early 50s, but she really shined during her stint at the Kudu label in the 70s. Phillips' pipes were still in remarkable shape at that time, and she brought incredible pathos and emotion to some remarkably challenging material.

Wilson Pickett

Journalist Dave Marsh has said that if **Wilson Pickett** "came along today, he'd be a rapper". It's hard to disagree with him – no one this side of Ice Cube has had more 'tude

than "the Wicked Pickett". While it's true that no matter how far away from the speakers you sit, Pickett always sounds like he's in your face – his voice so ravaged it's as if he's just downed more bottles of St. Ides than an entire cipher of Compton rappers – Pickett hits you with an emotional, gospel-derived force that no MC could hope to attain.

Born in Alabama in 1941, Pickett first came to prominence in Detroit as a member of The Falcons. During their career, the legendary group also featured Eddie Floyd, **Sir Mack Rice** and **Joe Stubbs** (who later found success as part of 100 Proof (Aged in Soul)). After the 1962 release of The Falcons' "I Found A Love", Pickett went solo and suffered the injustice of having Atlantic release a version of his "If You Need Me" by Solomon Burke, which effectively destroyed the chart potential of his record.

Nonetheless, Pickett was himself signed by Atlantic in 1964. He struggled at first with unsuitable material and was almost dropped from the label until he went to Memphis to record at the Stax studio. The first song that Pickett and guitarist **Steve Cropper** came up with was "In The Midnight Hour", which became Pickett's first hit in 1965. With a definitive Memphis horn line and drums inspired by producer **Jerry Wexler**'s attempt to do The Jerk, "In The Midnight Hour" was the perfect vehicle for Pickett's throat-shredding vocals. The follow-up "634-5789 (Soulsville, U.S.A.)" was a bit singsongy, but it proved Pickett could do more than just rupture his diaphragm and showcased his emotional range.

Pickett's next single, "Ninety-Nine And A Half Won't Do", was a definitive soul moment. Based on **Dorothy Love Coates**' 1956 gospel classic "99 1/2", it was a blasphemous transmogrification of religious ecstasy into the most salacious lust – dig the way he licks his chops on the line "Ain't no use in foolin' ourselves honey", as the song fades out. It made little impression on the charts, but the follow-up, a cover of **Chris Kenner**'s "Land Of 1,000 Dances" recorded at the Fame Studios in Muscle Shoals, Alabama, was an R&B chart-topper. Based largely on **Cannibal & The Headhunters**' garage-punk version, the record was a bundle of compressed energy, with the horns breaking up on impact and Roger Hawkins' pile-driving

Wilson Pickett and The MG's Steve Cropper having a laugh at Muscle Shoals Studios

drums pushing Pickett to rip his larynx asunder on the final "Ahh, help me"s. "Mustang Sally" returned Pickett to the wicked terrain that he had made his own in 1966 with "Ninety-Nine And A Half Won't Do", while his version of Dyke & The Blazers' "Funky Broadway" was another R&B #1, despite lacking the grit and grime of the original.

After 1967's surprisingly sweet "I'm In Love", Pickett floundered for a while, suffering from less than inspired arrangements and recording terrible covers like "Hey Jude", "Hey Joe", "Born To Be Wild" and "Sugar Sugar". An inspired move to Philadelphia International in 1970 and a brief partnership with **Gamble & Huff** led to two fabulous records, the cowbell and psych-guitar groover "Engine No. 9" and what could be the theme song of Philly soul, "Don't Let The Green Grass Fool You". After cutting a final R&B chart-topper at Miami's Criterion Studio, "Don't Knock My Love" in 1971, the Wicked One left Atlantic and slipped into complete irrelevance by covering such songs as **Captain & Tenille**'s "Love Will Keep Us Together".

Wilson Pickett made a welcome return in 1999, following a decade and a half of personal problems and run-ins with the law. He re-emerged onto the scene that year with the surprisingly decent *It's Harder Now*. The album found him in fine voice, and working with sympathetic arrangements. He continued to tour and perform regularly through the 90s and early 00s, before retiring in late 2004 due to ill health. Pickett died, aged 64, on January 19, 2006 following a heart attack near his home in Virginia.

Wilson Pickett In Philadelphia
1970, Atlantic

After his string of gritty Southern soul hits in the 60s, Atlantic sent the wicked Mr. Pickett to work with Gamble & Huff in 1970. The collaboration worked beyond expectations, with Gamble & Huff adding an element of sophistication and melody to Pickett's powerhouse style. Highlights include the hits "Engine No. 9" and "Don't Let The Green Grass Fool You".

A Man And A Half: The Best Of Wilson Pickett
1992, Rhino

If you only know The Commitments' versions of Wilson Pickett's songs, do yourself a favour and get this double-disc anthology pronto. An excellent collection of his career at Atlantic, this album includes everything from "I Found A Love" and "If You Need Me" to "Engine No. 9" and "Don't Knock My Love".

It's Harder Now
1999, Bullseye

Bullseye's formula for successful soul legends' comebacks is simple: put them together with a good back-up and let them do what they do best. This critically acclaimed CD is no exception. Clean and modern sounding, it bumps and grinds with Pickett's best material from the past, while highlights like "Outskirts Of Town" and the title track show that his command is undiminished.

PLAYLIST
Wilson Pickett

1 **I FOUND A LOVE** The Falcons from **I Found A Love**
Pickett was at his most powerful on this stunner.

2 **IN THE MIDNIGHT HOUR** from **A Man And A Half: The Best Of Wilson Pickett**
With the help of a classic horn line, this established Pickett as one of the titans of 60s soul.

3 **634-5789 (SOULSVILLE, U.S.A.)** from **A Man And A Half: The Best Of Wilson Pickett**
The love man is always on call.

4 **NINETY-NINE AND A HALF WON'T DO** from **A Man And A Half: The Best Of Wilson Pickett**
Sheer heresy, but a towering record nevertheless.

5 **LAND OF 1,000 DANCES** from **A Man And A Half: The Best Of Wilson Pickett**
The definitive version of this old chestnut.

6 **FUNKY BROADWAY** from **A Man And A Half: The Best Of Wilson Pickett**
It ain't as good as Dyke & The Blazers' version, but it still moves something.

7 **I'M IN LOVE** from **A Man And A Half: The Best Of Wilson Pickett**
The wicked one tries to get tender, but he still tears a hole in your speakers.

8 **ENGINE NO. 9** from **A Man And A Half: The Best Of Wilson Pickett**
Incredible, spacey funk.

9 **DON'T LET THE GREEN GRASS FOOL YOU** from **A Man And A Half: The Best Of Wilson Pickett**
Who woulda thunk it? Gamble & Huff tame the wicked one.

10 **DON'T KNOCK MY LOVE** from **A Man And A Half: The Best Of Wilson Pickett**
Pickett's last hit, but he still tears it up.

The Platters

The Platters were by far the most commercially successful of all the doo-wop era vocal groups. With their classy, pop-informed version of doo-wop, they became not only the undisputed champions of "make-out" music, but the first African-American rock'n'roll group to top the pop chart. A measure of just how much the R&B community have taken the group into their hearts is that close to a hundred versions of The Platters have toured the oldies circuit.

The Platters formed in 1952 in LA as **Tony Williams & The Platters**. With a line-up of Williams, **David Lynch**, **Herb Reed** and **Alex Hodge**, they released the generic "Give Thanks" on Federal in 1953. After several more lacklustre singles for Federal, including a version of "Beer Barrel Polka", they were brought under the wing of manager/songwriter **Buck Ram** in 1954. With **Paul Robi** replacing Hodge and the addition of new member **Zola Taylor**, who had sung with **Shirley Gunter & The Queens**, the group signed to Mercury.

At Mercury, Ram crafted some of the most enduring pop and rock'n'roll records. The first, 1955's "Only You (And You Alone)", had been rejected by Federal, but when it was released by Mercury, it spent seven weeks at the top of the R&B chart, thanks to Williams' soaring, hiccoughing tenor lead. The follow-up, "The Great Pretender", was even more significant. It topped the R&B chart, for eleven weeks and spent two weeks at #1 on the pop chart, making The Platters the first African-American rock'n'roll artists not to have their success spoiled by a wimpy white cover version.

After these first two records, The Platters slowly gravitated away from teenage themes towards more conventional pop material, as with their 1956 version of **Glenn Miller**'s "My Prayer", their second and biggest pop #1. Williams' high-flying, gospel-influenced falsetto made The Platters important forerunners of soul even though their late-50s material, such as "On My Word Of Honour", "My Dream", "Twilight Time", "Smoke Gets In Your Eyes" and "Harbor Lights", wasn't exactly grits and cornbread.

Tony Williams went solo in 1960, but his "Sleepless Nights" and "Come Along Now" went nowhere. He was replaced by former Metrotone vocalist **Charles "Sonny" Turner**, who sang lead on The Platters' final Mercury hit, "I'll Never Smile Again", in 1961. Taylor and Robi also left in 1962, to be replaced by **Sandra Dawn** and former Flamingo singer **Nate Nelson**.

After several godawful records and legal turmoil with Mercury, The Platters left the

Doo-Wop

Soul may have been born in the churches of the South, but an equally important birthplace was on the street corners of the Northern cities. Although they came after both, the doo-wop groups of the 50s attempted to take a middle ground between the classic style of early vocal groups like **The Ink Spots**, **The Ravens** and **The Orioles** and the harder, more gospel-informed records of **The Clovers** and **Clyde McPhatter**-era Drifters. Doo-wop is more often associated with rock'n'roll, but it is an important antecedent to soul, and groups like **The Dells** and **The Manhattans** tweaked the doo-wop format and had huge success on the soul scene.

The doo-wop sound probably grew most clearly from **The Ravens**' "Count Every Star" in 1950, with its soaring falsetto lead on top of a prominent bass pattern. However, the first record to truly articulate the wordless rapture that doo-wop aimed for was **The Crows**' "Gee". Lead singer Sonny Norton's youthful raggedness became an aural symbol of desire and ecstasy every bit as powerful as Ray Charles's once sanctified swoops and shouts. The up-tempo "Gee" included the immortal nonsense syllables "doo-do-do-doo doo-do-do-doo do-do-do-doo-do-doo". **The Penguins**' falsetto ballad "Earth Angel" was similarly all over the place, but it remains one of the all-time classics.

In addition to providing a forum for vocalists' flights of fancy, doo-wop helped create the integrationist aesthetic of soul music. The first integrated group to have success on the pop chart were **The Del-Vikings** from Pittsburgh, who had a mammoth hit in 1957 with the delightful "Come Go With Me". A year later, **Dion & The Belmonts** became the first all-white group to have a hit in the doo-wop style with "I Wonder Why".

Aside from doo-wop titans The Platters, the groups that made the biggest impact on soul were **The Moonglows** and **The Flamingos**. The Moonglows' signature record was "Sincerely", a gorgeous weave of intricate vocals and a wonderfully effective jazzy guitar riff. "Sincerely" replaced "Earth Angel" at #1 on the R&B chart, although an odious cover by The McGuire Sisters was the pop #1. The Moonglows excelled at ballads, and records like "Most Of All", "In My Diary", "We Go Together", "When I'm With You" and "Ten Commandments Of Love" proved that they were perhaps the best of the doo-wop groups. When they broke up in 1958, group founder **Harvey Fuqua** went on to have an illustrious career in R&B, working with the likes of Marvin Gaye, The Spinners and Sylvester.

The Flamingos, who formed in Chicago in the early 50s and signed to the Chance label, recorded the cult favourite "Golden Teardrops" in 1953. They also scored hits in 1955 with the uptempo "That's My Baby" and the ballad "I'll Be Home" on Checker, before a move to George Goldner's End label resulted in their biggest hit, "I Only Have Eyes For You". The group then reinvented itself in the mid-60s as a full-on soul group with "Boogaloo Party" and the funkier and darker "Buffalo Soldier".

Doo-wop suffered at the hands of the British Invasion in the 60s, but thanks to the likes of

---

label and signed to Musicor, where producer/songwriter **Luther Dixon** crafted an updated sound that gave them a new lease of life. The delightful, easy swingin' "I Love You 1000 Times" from 1966 somehow sounded both contemporary and like one of their early classics, while the more modern but no less charming "With This Ring" made the pop Top 20 in 1967. That same year, "Washed Ashore" followed in similar style, while "Sweet, Sweet Lovin'" betrayed more of a Motown influence.

Since Lynch and Reed left the group in 1969, a staggering number of Platters have continued to trade on the name on the nostalgia circuit. When The Platters were elected into the Rock'n'Roll Hall of Fame in 1990, sadly the only original member there to wit-

ness it was Tony Williams, and he later died of emphysema in August 1992.

Enchanted: The Best Of The Platters
1998, Rhino

This 20-track compilation is the only single-disc collection to include The Platters' biggest hits with both the Mercury and Musicor labels and with both Buck Ram and Luther Dixon. Tony Williams is clearly the star of the show, but the group's agreeable breezy soul period is also well represented.

The Pointer Sisters

Although they're now primarily remembered for 80s hits that brought a little

The Dells and The Manhattans, it never truly died. Instead it became a big part of the soul scene. The Falcons and The Impressions, among others, incorporated gospel fervour into their music in the late 50s, helping to keep the doo-wop style alive. In the 70s, as white folks were groovin' to Showaddywaddy and Sha Na Na, soul fans indulged in their own form of nostalgia, and records by The Manhattans and **Ray, Goodman & Brown** protected gentle ears from the disco craze with their retrograde street-corner crooning.

Various Artists: The Doo-Wop Box
1994, Rhino

A hundred tracks over 4 CDs may seem a little much, but this is the definitive collection of doo-wop and it deserves a spot in everyone's record collection. It's got everything from The Orioles, The Ravens, The Moonglows and The Flamingos to later post-doo-wop nonsense vocalizing like "I Do" by The Marvelows.

PLAYLIST

1 COUNT EVERY STAR The Ravens from **The Doo-Wop Box**
The doo-wop sound was born from the bass intro of this early vocal group classic.

2 IT'S TOO SOON TO KNOW The Orioles from **The Doo-Wop Box**
Too smooth for rock'n'roll, too gritty for classic pop, this is one of the early antecedents of soul.

3 GEE The Crows from **The Doo-Wop Box**
This utterly charming record is perhaps the first true doo-wop artefact.

4 GOODNITE SWEETHEART GOODNITE
The Spaniels from **The Doo-Wop Box**
Da-doo-doo-da-doo.

5 EARTH ANGEL The Penguins from **The Doo-Wop Box**
A record of rare beauty.

6 SINCERELY The Moonglows from **The Doo-Wop Box**
Perhaps the greatest vocal group record from the rock'n'roll era.

7 I ONLY HAVE EYES FOR YOU The Flamingos from **The Doo-Wop Box**
The ethereal vocals turn this pop chestnut into a classic.

8 COME GO WITH ME The Del-Vikings from **The Doo-Wop Box**
Truer words were never spoken: Dom-dom-dom-dom-dom-dom-be-doobie-dom-dom-dom-dom-dom-dom-be-doobie-dom-wah-wah-wah.

---

bit of Reagan-era "Neutron Dance" to R&B, **The Pointer Sisters** were key players in the liberation of the girl-group format. Along with their contemporaries LaBelle, they were quirky individualists whose expansive tastes and awesome vocal skills made the chiffon gowns of The Supremes a thing of the past.

Ruth, **Anita**, **Bonnie** and **June Pointer** grew up in Oakland, California, and learned to sing at the West Oakland Church of God, where their parents were both ministers. They began their secular careers as back-up singers for acts like Boz Scaggs, Taj Mahal, Cold Blood, Elvin Bishop and Tower of Power. When they weren't doing back-up work, the sisters donned thrift-store dresses and sang big band, blues and country numbers à la Lambert, Hendricks & Ross at nightclubs around the Bay Area. The group was originally signed to Atlantic, for whom they recorded an abortive 1972 session with **Wardell Quezergue**. The following year they released a self-titled debut album on Blue Thumb and had an R&B smash with Allen Toussaint's "Yes We Can Can", a seamless blend of New Orleans swing and West Coast funk. The sisters were at their most soulful – though it would have been hard not to be, with those drums and guitar licks.

That's A Plenty continued their funky blues-jazz nostalgia in 1974 with a dazzling range of covers like **Dizzy Gillespie**'s be-bop standard "Salt Peanuts", **Son House**'s intense delta blues "Grinning In Your Face", and "Steam Heat" from the Broadway musical *The Pajama Game*. The album also included

their first foray into country, the self-penned "Fairytale" which landed them a spot at the Grand Ol' Opry and a Grammy for Best Country Performance by a Duo or Group.

"How Long (Betcha Got A Chick On The Side)", from 1975's *Steppin'*, was their first and only R&B #1. The track started life as a straight country song before being combined with a hook from producer **David Rubinson** and an incredible guitar riff from **Wah-Wah Watson**. "Going Down Slowly", another slickly produced take on swamp funk, also made the R&B chart, while the rest of the album showed off the group's eclecticism with a fusion-y cover (featuring Herbie Hancock) of **Blind Willie McTell**'s "Chainey Do" and a medley tribute to **Duke Ellington**.

After a scene-stealing appearance in *Car Wash* in 1976, The Pointer Sisters released the disappointing *Having A Party* in 1977, an album troubled by clashes with the label and producers. Its one bright spot was the sleazy midtempo funk record "Don't It Drive You Crazy". Soon after the album's release, Bonnie decided to go solo and signed to Motown. She had a big R&B hit with "Free From My Freedom/Tie Me To A Tree (Handcuff Me)" in 1978, but her solo records were typically schlocky covers of Motown standards like "Heaven Must Have Sent You" and "I Can't Help Myself".

The remaining three sisters signed to **Richard Perry**'s Planet label in 1978. Perry produced that year's *Energy*, a more rock-oriented album that streamlined their sound and influences. Their cover of **Bruce Springsteen**'s "Fire" was a huge pop hit, and its electric sheen gave the group a new, radio-friendly sound. Two more gold records, "He's So Shy" and "Slow Hand", cemented their crossover success at the start of the 80s, and for the next few years they were more successful as a pop act than an R&B one.

Although it wasn't much of a hit at the time, only reaching #30 on the pop chart, 1982's "I'm So Excited" defined their new aesthetic and eventually became ubiquitous. Like Kool & The Gang's "Celebration", it was one of those sorta funky, sorta disco, high-energy pop records that seemed ready-made for a sports highlight montage or a deodorant advert. The 1984 album *Break Out* picked up where "I'm So Excited" left off, embracing the synthesizer wholesale and spawning four monster state-of-the-art singles: "Jump (For My Love)", "Automatic", "I Need You" and "Neutron Dance".

The group moved to RCA in 1985, but with the exception of that year's "Dare Me", the sparkle had worn off their records, and the rest of the world had caught up to Richard Perry's production values. Within three short years, instead of scoring blockbusters, their songs were appearing in duds like the 1988 movie *Action Jackson*. The Pointer Sisters' last chart hit came with the dull "Insanity" in 1990.

Since then, besides appearing on the nostalgia circuit, the sisters have recorded **Maya Angelou**'s poetry, as with 1994's "It Ain't A Man's World"; collaborated with country singer **Clint Black** on a cover of "Chain Of Fools"; and appeared in a Broadway revival of the **Fats Waller** musical *Ain't Misbehavin'* in 1995. They are still busy performing on the touring circuit and they released a live CD and DVD in 2004.

Fire: The Very Best Of The Pointer Sisters 1973–1986
1996, RCA

Two discs and 36 tracks is probably a tad excessive, but this is undoubtedly the most comprehensive Pointer Sisters retrospective. Even at such a length it misses a lot of key material, but it is the only collection to feature both their Blue Thumb and Planet releases.

Billy Preston

A musician of protean talents, these days **Billy Preston** is mostly remembered for his organ work on **The Beatles**' *White Album*,

Abbey Road and *Let It Be* albums, although in parts of Europe he is credited with having pioneered the Afro hairstyle. His real legacy, however, has to be as one of the funkiest organists to ever whomp a Wurlitzer or hammer a Hammond.

Born on September 9, 1946, in Houston, Texas, Billy Preston was a child prodigy. At age 10 he played alongside **Mahalia Jackson** at his mother's church, while at 12 he played the young W.C. Handy in the film *St. Louis Blues* (Nat "King" Cole played the older Handy). While playing keyboards for Sam Cooke and **Little Richard** on a European tour in 1962, Preston met not only The Beatles, but also an instrumental group called **Sound Incorporated**, who later introduced him to the producer of the television show *Shindig*. Preston became the show's resident keyboard player, and as a result was asked by Ray Charles to play on his *Crying Time* album in 1965.

After recording a couple of fine albums for Vee-Jay in 1965 – *Most Exciting Organ Ever* and *Hymns Speak From The Organ* – Preston signed to Capitol. There he released *The Wildest Organ In Town!* in 1966, a rollicking, mostly instrumental album featuring a hyperspeed Wurlitzer cover of Stevie Wonder's "Uptight" and "The Girl's Got It", an upbeat Chicago-style soul cut that became popular on the UK's Northern soul scene. 1967's *Club Meeting* followed in similar style; the noisy, funky Hammond and horn wig-outs of the glorious "Let The Music Play" paved the way for Sly Stone, with whom Preston later recorded a couple of demos.

Over the next few years Preston became a highly sought-after session musician. In addition to his work with The Beatles, he also played with **The Rolling Stones**, Aretha Franklin, Quincy Jones, Martha Reeves, **George Harrison** and **Ringo Starr**. Signing to The Beatles' Apple label, Preston achieved a UK #11 in 1969 with the sludgy psychedelic organ/guitar dirge "That's The Way God Planned It". His first US hit came when his version of George Harrison's "My Sweet Lord" made the R&B Top 30 in 1970.

Preston then signed to A&M in 1972 and had an R&B #1 with the preposterously funky "Outa-Space". Little more than a super-hot clavinet riff – it was the first time he'd ever played the instrument – "Outa-

Space" clearly spawned such records as The Commodores' "Machine Gun". The next year's "Will It Go Round In Circles", a blend of cheery organ, Little Stevie harmonica and lite gospel-isms, became his first pop #1. The follow-up, "Space Race", did for the Arp synthesizer what "Outa-Space" did for the clavinet; again it marked the first time Preston had played the instrument, and again it topped the R&B chart. It later served as the theme for *American Bandstand*.

Another easy-swinging funk track with a cryptic message, "Nothing From Nothing", topped the pop chart in 1974. It was to be Preston's last significant hit for some time, as disco obviated message tracks and everyone and his brother started tinkering with synthesizers and funny keyboard sounds. Still, this was about the time Preston wrote the huge-selling "You Are So Beautiful" for **Joe Cocker**, so the commercial dip didn't hurt too much.

Preston did, however, return to the pop charts in 1980 with "With You I'm Born Again", a duet with **Syreeta** recorded for the soundtrack to the Gabe Kaplan basketball flick *Fast Break*. The hideously saccharine ballad was a worldwide smash, reaching #4 on the US and #2 on the UK pop charts. Preston scored two more movies (he had previously written the theme tune to *Slaughter* and later *They Call Me Mr Tibbs* with Quincy Jones), *I'm Never Gonna Say Goodbye* in 1982 and *O'Hara's Wife* in 1983, without recapturing that success.

In recent years, Preston appeared in the film *Blues Brothers 2000*, performed at the tribute concert for George Harrison at London's Royal Albert Hall and played on Ray Charles's final album, 2004's *Genius Loves Company*. After touring extensively with **The Funk Brothers** and **Eric Clapton** in 2004, Preston started work on a tribute to The Beatles.

Ultimate Collection
2000, Hip-O

This 20-track retrospective has all Billy Preston's biggest hits (minus "That's The Way God Planned It" which most soul fans probably wouldn't want anyway), and is the best introduction to the music that made this most talented and funkiest of organists a household name.

The Wildest Organ In Town!/Club Meeting
2004, EMI

A real treat, this two-on-one reissue CD combines Preston's two Capitol albums from 1966 and 1967. These

rollicking albums hold the cream of his early instrumentals, including "Let The Music Play" and "Uptight"
– greasy and delightful in equal measure.

Prince

Prince was the pop star *par excellence* of
the 80s for two reasons. In an era of
faceless, corporate soul by the likes of Luther
Vandross and Freddie Jackson, Prince was
probably the only R&B artist able to synthe-
size his influences into an original vision.
Perhaps more importantly, aside from a
handful of hip-hop artists, Prince was the
only black performer to address the hope-
lessness and spiritual desolation of the
Reagan years. Like a century of African-
American musicians before him, this was
often channelled into bitter love songs and a
ribaldry so fierce that it would make Chaucer
or Petronius blush.

After running away from home at the age of
14, **Prince Rogers Nelson** – who was born in
Minneapolis, Minnesota on June 7, 1958 –
eventually ended up living in the basement of
his friend's mother's house. It was here that he
began writing songs, cutting himself off from
the outside world and jotting down his fantasies in his notebook. Around this time Prince
formed his first band, **Grand Central**, which
soon morphed into **Champagne**, a group that
included Terry Lewis and Morris Day. In
1976 he was the guitarist in a band called **94
East** with Colonel Abrams, Pepé Willie,
Wendell Thomas, Pierre Lewis and Dale
Alexander. After recording one single for
Polydor, they were quickly dropped.

The following year, somebody at Warner
Bros must have been in touch with the spirits when an 18-year-old nobody from
nowhere, along with his manager and attorney, managed to negotiate a deal that
allowed the artist to produce himself. Nearly
unprecedented in the history of the major
labels (particularly for a black artist), this
relative creative control given to Prince
allowed "His Royal Badness" to explore his
personal vision to the full.

The first fruit of that vision, 1978's *For
You*, was a Rick James-influenced disco-funk
hybrid. Things only really took off on the
first single, "Soft And Wet", which displayed
Prince's daring sexual imagery as well as his

extraordinary falsetto and gender-bending
experiments. His next album, 1979's *Prince*,
was more solid, and his rock-funk fusion
started to take hold (particularly on "Bambi",
with its post-Hendrix guitar). His breakthrough record was "I Wanna Be Your
Lover", a remarkable blend of The Jackson 5,
disco synths, new-wave dynamics and spacey
je ne sais quoi. The even more risqué "Sexy
Dancer" had a groove that was simultaneously ferocious and mellow. The album also
included "I Feel For You", which eventually
became a huge hit for Chaka Khan, whom,
strangely enough, Prince often resembled on
this record.

Prince's talent finally came to fruition on
his third album, 1980's *Dirty Mind*. Not
since James Brown's *Sex Machine* had an
album's title so matched its contents.
Produced, arranged, written and recorded
almost completely by Prince, and featuring
stories that could have come straight from
Penthouse magazine, *Dirty Mind* begat the
narcissism that plagues the contemporary
R&B scene. While subsequent singers followed his lead on subject matter, none has
been able to duplicate his skill as the best falsetto singer of the last thirty years. *Dirty
Mind* is Prince's most new-wave album: the
guitars were all trebly, the synth riffs simple
and direct, and some of the harmonies just
screamed skinny-tie band. The album may
have dated a bit because of this, but it does
contain "When You Were Mine", a pop song
that could have been as transcendent and
enduring as any of Prince's best-known
tracks were it not about a *ménage à trois*.

However, *Dirty Mind* was a commercial
failure. The following year's *Controversy* was
a more heavy-handed treatment of the same
themes with some explicit politics thrown in.
The title track slammed like crazy; "Do Me
Baby" was an old-fashioned slow jam where
Prince's voice was, well, soft and wet; "Jack U
Off" was Prince doing glam rock; and
"Ronnie, Talk To Russia" was just plain silly.
On the other hand, *1999* was a pop masterpiece. A double album from 1983 with three
killer singles – the title track, "Little Red
Corvette" and "Delirious" – it welded songs
about the apocalypse, race relations and dirty
sex to a bumping funk bottom and just
enough guitars to make Prince a mainstream
figure. While perhaps not as startlingly origi-

The Purple One in concert

Around The World In A Day came as a huge disappointment in 1985: it was all boring, dragging, crass cod-psychedelia, though at least "Raspberry Beret" had a hook. *Parade*, which followed the next year, represented a significant improvement. Yes, it could still be grotesquely self-indulgent, but "Kiss" remains a masterpiece of a pop single, and the lush "Mountains" and quirky "Girls And Boys" had just enough song to justify the mind-boggling production.

It was not until 1987, however, that Prince cut his greatest record yet. That year's *Sign O' The Times* was the best politically charged soul-funk-pop record since Marvin Gaye's *What's Going On* and Sly & The Family Stone's *There's A Riot Goin' On*. "U Got The Look" was what the James Brown guitar riff would sound like if the star of his band was **Eddie Van Halen** not **Bootsy Collins**. "It's Gonna Be A Beautiful Night" and "Housequake" were both P-Funk redux, while "If I Was Your Girlfriend" could have been an ode to Sylvester, the only falsetto vocalist who out-gender-fucks Prince.

Sign O' The Times didn't rely on history to make its point, however. As on *There's A Riot Goin' On*, the songs were often so muted that they felt half-finished, but unlike *Riot*, *Sign O' The Times* wasn't sapped of energy. Tracks like "If I Was Your Girlfriend", "The Cross" and "Sign O' The Times" were abstract, but Prince's vocal chops filled them out and pushed them over the top into the realm of pure pop. Then there were the grooves. "It's

nal as *Dirty Mind*, *1999* remains one of the all-time great pop albums.

While writing and producing for his protegées The Time, **Vanity 6**, **Appolonia 6** and **Sheila E.**, Prince managed to churn out the self-indulgent, semi-autobiographical movie *Purple Rain* in 1984. The film was a dud, but the soundtrack was a pop juggernaut that made Prince the biggest star of the decade after Jacko and **Madonna**. "When Doves Cry", an extraordinary marriage of guitar bombast and minimal plastic funk, became his first pop #1, while he welded gospel to megalomania on both the title track and "Let's Go Crazy".

Gonna Be A Beautiful Night", recorded live in Paris with **The Revolution**, absolutely smokes. "U Got The Look" was slamming, but it was also something far more than an intense funk track. The album's title track contextualized the record by mentioning AIDS (that "big disease with a little name") in the very first line.

With the Parents Music Resource Centre already on Prince's back for writing songs about masturbation and incest, he came up with the most dangerous record of his career. It may very well have featured the vacant dance-pop chanteuse **Sheena Easton** and a passage bordering on **Meatloaf**'s "Paradise By The Dashboard Light", but by combining seething funk with heavy metal guitar and lines like "Your body's heck-a-slammin'/If love is good, let's get to rammin'", "U Got The Look" was a melting pot of the moral guardians' two most hated forms of music that was all about quick, intense sex without thinking about the consequences. If Prince's obsession with freaky sex often sounded merely like a shock tactic, this was where it coalesced into something more than a fuckbook fantasy.

Inevitably, Prince has retreated ever since. The single "Alphabet St." aside, 1988's *Lovesexy* was pseudo-mystical cosmic religious claptrap wrapped in his usual ace production. Far better was *The Black Album* – a whomping bottom-end groove monster that was recorded at the same time as *Lovesexy*, but not officially released until 1994. His 1989 soundtrack to *Batman* was as crass as the movie itself, but "Batdance" was a neat throwaway merger of Minneapolis swing and Chicago house. *Music From Graffiti Bridge* in 1990 was a kind of revue album with way too much **Tevin Campbell**.

With his new band **New Power Generation**, 1991's *Diamonds And Pearls* at times slammed like *The Black Album* and at others was pointlessly baroque. "Cream" and "Gett Off" showed Prince could still marry vamp, hook and boundary breaking if he felt like it. The ♀ (aka *Love Symbol*) album in 1992 had great hip-hoppish jams like "Sexy MF" and "My Name Is Prince", but was ruined by the mystical mumbo-jumbo and "conceptual" voice-overs by Kirstie Alley.

The following year Prince legally changed his name to ♀ – the cryptic pan-gender glyph from the album of the same name – declaring that he was trying to free himself

PLAYLIST
Prince

1 I WANNA BE YOUR LOVER from **Prince**
A little bit Jackson-ish for comfort, but the King of Pop would never leave a pause that pregnant after "The only one who makes you come".

2 HEAD from **Dirty Mind**
If Tipper Gore had heard this instead of "Darling Nikki" all of America might be like the town in *Footloose*.

3 WHEN YOU WERE MINE from **Dirty Mind**
Hindsight is 20/20.

4 CONTROVERSY from **Controversy**
Perhaps Prince's greatest groove.

5 1999 from **1999**
Prince channels The Band's Garth Hudson on one of the great records about the apocalypse.

6 LITTLE RED CORVETTE from **1999**
The dick as car metaphor has never been this exciting.

7 WHEN DOVES CRY from **Purple Rain**
Pick up that guitar and talk to me.

8 KISS from **Parade**
Surely the only record ever to be inspired by Joan Collins.

9 IF I WAS YOUR GIRLFRIEND from **Sign O' The Times**
The master gender bender at work.

10 U GOT THE LOOK from **Sign O' The Times**
If you can make Sheena Easton this slamming, you deserve all the accolades in the world.

from his record company Warner Bros who used the name Prince as a marketing tool. ♀ or The Artist Formerly Known As Prince then declared that he was a slave to the recording industry and had a prolonged battle with Warner Bros until his contract ended in 1996. Throughout this period more seemed to be written about his image and "weirdness" than about his music.

Over the next decade every new release was hailed as a return to form by people desperate to believe that two or three decent tracks meant that the prodigal genius had returned. They were nearly always wrong, particularly with 2001's dreadful *Rainbow Children*, a concept album about his conversion to the

Jehovah's Witness faith. He was now simply making records for himself. It was also around this time that, free from record labels and publishing contracts, he finally dropped ♔ and returned to using the name Prince.

By 2004 Prince had grown tired of trying to dazzle himself and released the thoroughly enjoyable, if resolutely retro, *Musicology*. He followed with the slightly more contemporary, but still wildly uneven, *3121* in 2006. While the albums weren't exactly masterpieces, it was still good to have him back.

Dirty Mind
1980, Warner Bros

Still one of Prince's biggest aesthetic triumphs, *Dirty Mind* is an outstanding album. On top of sharp synth melodies and deep funk grooves that were among the best of the era, the lyrical details are a little less than radio friendly – no previous album had been so gleefully sexually explicit. The best, but filthiest, tracks on the album are the funky "Head" and the incestuous "Sister", but the album ends on a different note with the anti-war song "Partyup".

Sign O' The Times
1987, Paisley Park

Prince wrote, produced and recorded *Sign O' The Times* amost entirely on his own. Despite, or perhaps thanks to, this extreme solipsism, it's his greatest and most referential album. He was infatuated with the often politically explicit, psychedelic soul of the late 60s and early 70s, and unites these two facets like no artist since Marvin Gaye or Sly Stone, but he also manages to retain a sense of hope and faith amid the despair.

Professor Longhair

There are few musicians in the history of recorded sound who can truly be called unique. New Orleans' main musical treasure, **Roy Byrd** (aka **Professor Longhair** or Fess), is one such artist. Recording under such outrageous names as Professor Longhair And His Shuffling Hungarians or The Four Hairs Combo, Byrd approached **Jelly Roll Morton**'s piano shuffles, rhumba and calypso and **Champion Jack Dupree**'s barrelhouse boogie woogie with a rhythmic and vocal sensibility that can only be described as inebriated.

Despite having only one medium-sized national hit in the US (1950's "Bald Head"), Professor Longhair was – and is – a talisman of the New Orleans sound, a piano player whose influence extends in a direct line from **Fats Domino**, Huey "Piano" Smith, Allen

Toussaint to New Orleans' current king of keyboards, hip-hop producer **Mannie Fresh**.

Professor Longhair was born Henry Roeland Byrd on December 19, 1918 in Bogalusa, Louisiana. He moved to New Orleans as a child and made money by tap dancing for tips on Bourbon Street. By the time he was a teenager, he was sneaking into clubs to listen to piano players like Sullivan Rock, King Stormy Weather and Tuts Washington. Alongside his flourishing gambling career, Longhair began playing piano professionally in local clubs during his 20s, alongside Champion Jack Dupree and **Sonny Boy Williamson**. In 1948 he temporarily replaced Salvador Doucette in Dave Bartholomew's band at a gig at the Caldonia Inn – and the crowd went wild. Bartholomew was fired and Longhair hired, and he played at the club for the rest of the year.

The next year **Professor Longhair and His Shuffling Hungarians** recorded four sides for the Star Talent label: "Mardi Gras In New Orleans", "She Ain't Got No Hair", "Bye Bye Baby" and "Professor Longhair's Boogie". The sides were quickly recalled, however, because the sessions were non-union. Soon afterwards, Longhair recorded four sides for Mercury as **Roy Byrd And His Blue Jumpers**, including his only national hit, 1950's "Bald Head", a remake of "She Ain't Got No Hair" that introduced Longhair's wonderful combination of rhumba, calypso and straight-ahead R&B. "Hey Now Baby", recorded at the same sessions, introduced another classic piano figure that has since found its way into the repertoire of every piano player from the Crescent City.

Longhair re-recorded "Hey Now Baby" for Atlantic later that year, along with his anthem "Mardi Gras In New Orleans", complete with whistling and woodblock percussion. Still with Atlantic, he recorded the immortal "Tipitina" in 1953, which is one of the weirdest and most wonderful records in the R&B canon.

Sadly Professor Longhair suffered a mild stroke in the mid-50s, which affected his technique. However, he had recovered sufficiently by 1958 to record another version of "Mardi Gras In New Orleans" entitled "Go To The Mardi Gras". Although the booming New Orleans recording industry owed him a significant debt, Longhair was largely forgotten by the mid-60s. Aside from a couple of sides produced by **Wardell Quezergue** for the Rip label in 1962 and the very fine "Big Chief" for the Watch label in 1964, he stopped recording and performing, and soon disappeared altogether.

In 1971, at the age of 52, Professor Longhair made a remarkable comeback at that year's New Orleans Jazz & Heritage Festival. The organizers of the festival had found him packing goods and sweeping the floor at a local record store, and convinced him to get back behind the keyboard. As a result of his show-stopping performance at the festival, Longhair gained a lot of attention, toured Europe several times in the late 70s, got a record deal and recorded *Rock 'N' Roll Gumbo* (1975) and the excellent *Crawfish Fiesta* (1980). Unfortunately, *Crawfish Fiesta* was to be his last album; he died of a heart attack on January 30, 1980.

Fess: The Professor Longhair Anthology
1993, Rhino

Professor Longhair was the first musician to adapt the "second line" New Orleans rhythms, Afro-Caribbean roots and ritualistic boasts and dances of the Mardi Gras Indian tribes into R&B, thereby creating the signature New Orleans bounce. This 40-track compilation of the great pianist's legacy may have too much of his comeback work, but it's a fitting testament to one of the most influential musicians in American history.

James & Bobby Purify

J ames & Bobby Purify were solid if rarely stellar Southern soul performers who are often, somewhat unfairly, categorized as the poor man's Sam & Dave. The cousins from Pensacola, Florida, first joined forces in 1965 when **James Purify** (born May 12, 1944) was asked by **Robert Dickey** (born September 2, 1939) to replace both Magic Sam and Oscar Toney Jr. in **The Dothan Sextet**. Recognizing that their duets outshone the rest of the group, DJ/producer **Papa Don Schroeder** signed them up as a duo.

Recording in Muscle Shoals, James & Bobby Purify scored their biggest hit with their 1966 debut single, "I'm Your Puppet", written by **Dan Penn** and **Spooner Oldham**. Among the most creative Southern soul arrangements, the singsong lover's lullaby

reached the pop Top 10. The more uptempo "Wish You Didn't Have To Go", which followed in 1967, proved their flair for interpreting the simple songs upon which the Muscle Shoals sound depended.

Unfortunately, Schroeder then decided to move the duo to American Studios in Memphis, where they were saddled with poor cover material such as a flaccid version of "Shake A Tail Feather", which insultingly became a bigger hit than The Five Du-Tones' splendid original. Their cover of Sam & Dave's "I Take What I Want" merely served to show that they were second fiddle, but their "Let Love Come Between Us" was a far better record, reminiscent of Sam Cooke's "Havin' A Party" but with more singsongy horns. Their 1968 release "Do Unto Me", an awkward marriage of Southern grit and uptown polish, presaged their rapid slide into overproduction. That same year "I Can Remember" and "Help Yourself (To All Of My Love)" were treacly, airheaded stabs at commercial crossover that did better than they should have even if they didn't exactly light up the charts.

James Purify continued as a solo artist after Robert Dickey quit the duo in 1969, but two years later he invited former Tams' singer **Ben Moore** to assume the identity of Bobby Purify. The rejuvenated duo had a minor hit in the US with "Do Your Thing" in 1974, and reached #12 in the UK with a remake of "I'm Your Puppet" in 1976, but James Purify was soon beset by legal troubles and he quit music altogether in the late 70s.

Ben Moore reverted to his birth name in 1982 for the fine gospel album *He Believes In Me*, and used the Bobby Purify moniker on and off throughout the ensuing years. He lost his vision in 1998 and abandoned music until a conversation with Ray Charles inspired him to get back in the game. 2005's *Better To Have It*, credited to Bobby Purify, reunited Moore with Muscle Shoals stalwarts Dan Penn and Spooner Oldham, and marked a return to form in the vein of Solomon Burke's *Don't Give Up On Me*.

Shake A Tail Feather!: The Best Of James & Bobby Purify
2000, Sundazed

Weighing in at 28 tracks, this is far and away the best Purify collection on the market, even if it lacks country soul numbers like "Blame Me". The duo tried a maddening variety of styles besides their true forte, deep Southern soul, and they are all represented here.

Lou Rawls

S upper-club soul often gets a bad name, but if one practitioner can claim to have made it an art form, and made it signify at the same level as the more fiery gospel-derived soul, it is **Louis Allen Rawls**. That's probably because Rawls excelled at gospel singing before he donned a velvet tux and smoothed out his act. Blessed with a four-octave range, Rawls has a voice like a snifter of brandy: it can be rich and warm like Louis XIII, but if he needs it to, it can also be raspy and burn like cheap Applejack.

Rawls was born on December 1, 1935 on the Southside of Chicago, where he grew up with Sam Cooke. As adolescents, they both belonged to **The Teenage Kings of Harmony** gospel group, and in 1951 Rawls, then a member of The Holy Wonders, was chosen to replace Cooke in **The Highway QCs**. Rawls joined The Chosen Gospel Singers in 1953, but made a name for himself the following year by becoming a member of **The Pilgrim Travellers**. Touring with the group in 1958, Cooke and Rawls were involved in a serious car crash. Cooke sustained minor injuries, but Rawls lay in a coma for several days – at one stage he was even pronounced dead – and he didn't fully recover for another year. Around that time, Rawls ran away with young Candi Staton and the pair hoped to marry, but his disapproving mother sent Staton back home to finish school.

After recovering from his injuries, Rawls moved to LA and went secular, adding smooth jazz and urbane blues to his repertoire of melismatic swoops and testifying. As well as recording singles for small labels like Shar-Dee ("Love, Love, Love") and Candix ("In My Little Black Book" and "80 Ways"), in the early 60s he landed a small role on the television show *77 Sunset Strip*. Later he also appeared in *Fantasy Island* and was the singing voice of the cartoon cat Garfield. Rawls signed to Capitol in 1961, and sang back-up on Cooke's "Bring It On Home To Me" before releasing his own jazzy debut album, *Stormy Monday*, in 1962. He spent the next few years trying a variety of styles without ever quite establishing an identity.

Rawls had his first moderate hit with the dreamily funky "Three O'Clock In The Morning" in 1965, while the next year's *Live!* album revealed how at home he was in supper clubs. His superb showmanship was epitomized by his rap introductions, which brought an old church trick uptown. His true breakthrough came in 1966 with "Love Is A Hurtin' Thing". Loosening his bow tie, Rawls was at his most emotional as he bemoaned love. The arrangement was awesome – the interaction between the piano riff and chunky drum beat sublime – until the chipper horn lines ruined the whole thing.

Rawls hooked up with cult producer **David Axelrod** for "Dead End Street" in 1967. Despite his warm tone, you could feel Rawls howling down Michigan Avenue in the song's rap about the wind in Chicago and, when he started to sing, he was at his bluesiest and was, as usual, consummately professional. Rawls also recorded 1968's *Feelin' Good* with David Axelrod, which included an ultra-percussive version of "For What It's Worth" that found Rawls being distinctly "groovy". Rawls was in similarly silly form on 1969's crazy funky cover of "Season Of The Witch", but it was the A-side, a version of "Your Good Thing (Is About To End)", that proved what a great soul singer he could be.

Moving to MGM in 1971, Rawls had a hit with the extraordinary "Natural Man". Fusing **Nat "King" Cole** and **Gil Scott-Heron**, he created a protest song that wouldn't offend the clientele in the Vegas lounges where he regularly played, but was swinging and hard-hitting enough for the Southside streets he had grown up on. Unfortunately, none of his other MGM records hit with such force.

After brief stints recording with Bell and Arista, Rawls signed with Philadelphia International in 1976. It was a match made in heaven. That year's "You'll Never Find Another Love Like Mine" was just about perfect. Rawls was loungey and cabaret-ish on top of the gently galloping disco rhythm, but when the chorus hit he turned into one of the best ballad singers ever. The follow-up "Groovy People" was rather silly, but by the release of "Lady Love" the next year, Rawls' restrained crooning had become the new model for modern balladeers such as **Peabo Bryson** and **Freddie Jackson**.

A mainstream performer by the 80s, Rawls turned his status towards running the Lou Rawls Parade of Stars Telethons to benefit the United Negro College Fund. During the late 80s and early 90s, he recorded several albums for Blue Note in his old Joe Williams style; 1989's *At Last* was probably the best. Rawls then pursued film work, most notably in *Leaving Las Vegas*. Returning to gospel, he cut *I'm Blessed* in 2001 and *Oh Happy Day* in 2002. He released his final new album, *Rawls Sings Sinatra*, in 2003 before dying on January 6, 2006 in LA, after fighting a long battle with cancer.

(o) **Anthology**
2000, Capitol

This 33-track, double-disc collection covers Rawls' stint at Capitol Records from 1962 to 1970. Although it misses out important records like "Natural Man" and "You'll Never Find Another Love Like Mine" and it doesn't include any of his Philadelphia International tracks from the late 70s, it does offer the best overview of Rawls' protean talents.

(o) **All Things In Time / Unmistakably Lou**
2005, Edsel

After his long career at Capitol in the 60s, Rawls' mid-70s comeback was notable in that it produced his biggest hits

---

PLAYLIST
Lou Rawls

1 **TOBACCO ROAD** from **Anthology**
Lou Rawls as a jazzy, lounge hepcat.

2 **THREE O'CLOCK IN THE MORNING** from **Anthology**
Lazy funk so groovy that Billy Joel later covered it as part of The Hassles.

3 **LOVE IS A HURTIN' THING** from **Anthology**
Rawls at his most soulful, despite the arrangement's best attempts to drag him to Vegas.

4 **DEAD END STREET** from **Anthology**
One of the great rapprochements between the nightclub, blues, gospel and soul.

5 **SEASON OF THE WITCH** from **Anthology**
Can this be Rawls immersed in funk so deep?

6 **YOUR GOOD THING (IS ABOUT TO END)** from **Anthology**
The arrangement may be a bit busy, but Rawls absolutely kills it.

7 **NATURAL MAN** from **Natural Man**
A rather wonderful self-empowerment anthem that worked as well on the urban streets as it did in the supper club.

8 **YOU'LL NEVER FIND ANOTHER LOVE LIKE MINE** from **All Things In Time**
Rawls dons his velvet smoking jacket and comes on to his ex like Hugh Hefner.

9 **GROOVY PEOPLE** from **All Things In Time**
MOR disco for big ol' country boys.

10 **FROM NOW ON** from **All Things In Time**
Rousing disco pop with Rawls at his richest.

---

and best-known work. This single-disc reissue pairs his first two albums for Philadelphia International, 1976's *All Things In Time* and 1977's *Unmistakably Lou*. These albums were landmark collaborations between the elegant synergistic sweetness of Rawls' crooning style and Gamble & Huff's slick production.

Otis Redding

His finest records seem so timeless, so full of hard-earned authority that it's hard to believe that **Otis Redding** was only 26 when he died in 1967. The very embodiment of the "soul man", Redding was all grits, grunt and gospel fire. Being an archetype

Otis Redding: all grits, grunt and gospel fire on stage

didn't make him a caricature, however. Through sheer overwhelming presence, Redding tapped into the recesses of emotion that most men find so hard to express. Far from grotesque melodrama, as some have charged, his stylistic excess was the sound of someone so sensitive that his feelings only came out in floods.

Born in Dawson, Georgia, in 1941, the son of a father too sick with tuberculosis to work, Redding grew up dirt poor in nearby Macon. His formative influences, the shriek of **Little Richard** and the grace of Sam Cooke, represented the twin poles of soul style, and indeed he dropped out of high school to front Little Richard's former band, **The Upsetters**. Redding's first significant recording, "Shout Bamalama", cut in 1960 with Macon group **The Pinetoppers**, was pure Little Richard, but by the time he first entered the Stax studio in 1963, he had fused Richard and Cooke into an equal mix. "These Arms Of Mine" was an impromptu recording made after Redding had impressed Stax head **Jim Stewart** and after most of the musicians had finished for the day. With guitarist **Steve Cropper** sitting in for keyboardist Booker T. Jones, the arrangement was as basic as anything you might hear at a 10-year-old's piano recital, but it laid out the blueprint for country soul. The contrast between Redding's wrenching vocals and the stark background established a formula that was to be copied for the rest of the decade.

That same year, "Pain In My Heart" – a brazen steal from "Ruler Of My Heart" by Irma Thomas – gave Redding his first pop hit. Even better was 1965's "I've Been Loving You Too Long", written by Redding with Chicago soul man Jerry Butler. The song was tailor-made for Redding's style: only he could get away with those quavering notes and the pleading outro without turning it into an orgy of mawkishness. Of course, no one else is likely to enjoy the guitar interjections of Steve Cropper or the hung-over brass of the Memphis Horns.

Just as good, but never released as a single, was Redding's sublime reading of Eddie Thomas, Jerry Butler and Roy Lowe's smouldering ballad "Cigarettes And Coffee" from 1966. From the bleary horns to Booker T.'s ghost-town saloon keyboard and Al Jackson's exhausted beat, the arrangement evoked the song's quarter-to-three-in-the-morning atmosphere perfectly. The same year's "Try A Little Tenderness" was simply amazing. Bing Crosby had been singing this old piece of Tin Pan Alley frippery for thirty years, but in Redding's hands the track became a desperate plea.

Redding was equally adept at uptempo material. The essentially trivial "Fa-Fa-Fa-Fa-Fa (Sad Song)" might have been little more than a few lines about soul music attached to some nonsense syllables, but Redding sang it as though it contained the meaning of life. Meanwhile, "Tramp" had Redding playing a hayseed defending himself against the vicious taunts of cosmopolitan Carla Thomas to create the most irresistible of all the battle-of-the-sexes records. Amazingly, the only time Redding ever reached the pop Top 20 was with the last song he recorded before he died in a plane crash (along with four members of his band The Bar-Kays) on December 10, 1967 – the meditative, weary, semi-acoustic and eternal "(Sittin' On) The Dock Of The Bay".

The song was written in response to Redding's appearance at the Monterey International Pop Festival the preceding

PLAYLIST
Otis Redding

1 THESE ARMS OF MINE from **Dreams To Remember: The Otis Redding Anthology**
The archetype of the Southern soul ballad.

2 PAIN IN MY HEART from **Dreams To Remember: The Otis Redding Anthology**
This may be a rip-off of Irma Thomas's "Ruler Of My Heart", but it's every bit as good.

3 MR PITIFUL from **Dreams To Remember: The Otis Redding Anthology**
Few artists can be this self-reflexive and get away with it.

4 I'VE BEEN LOVING YOU TOO LONG from **Dreams To Remember: The Otis Redding Anthology**
A note to all aspiring love men: this song is forever off limits because Redding owns it.

5 CIGARETTES AND COFFEE from **Dreams To Remember: The Otis Redding Anthology**
Ragged, haggard late-night ballad that is one of Redding's finest performances.

6 TRY A LITTLE TENDERNESS from **Dreams To Remember: The Otis Redding Anthology**
Otis Redding lends weight and authority to a Bing Crosby standard.

7 FA-FA-FA-FA-FA (SAD SONG) from **Dreams To Remember: The Otis Redding Anthology**
Redding reveals the hermeneutics of soul music.

8 HARD TO HANDLE from **Dreams To Remember: The Otis Redding Anthology**
Put the Black Crowes' muddy, grooveless blasphemy out of your mind.

9 TRAMP from **Dreams To Remember: The Otis Redding Anthology**
An almighty funk classic riding one of the greatest drum beats ever.

10 (SITTIN' ON) THE DOCK OF THE BAY from **Dreams To Remember: The Otis Redding Anthology**
Perhaps not Redding's finest performance, but certainly the best hook he ever worked with.

summer. The quintessential soul love man had met the white "love crowd" (as he called them) on his own terms and won them over. That performance at Monterey and "(Sittin' On') The Dock Of The Bay" marked what could have been a potential musical and cultural revolution that was cut short by Redding's tragic premature death.

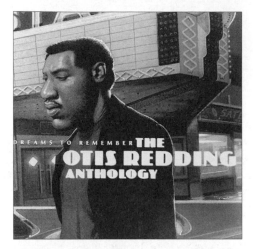

Dreams To Remember: The Otis Redding Anthology
1998, Atlantic

This magnificent double-disc, 50-track collection holds all of Otis Redding's hits and best-known songs, plus several revelatory album and previously unreleased tracks. It also features all five of the unforgettable tracks he performed live at the Monterey Festival in 1967.

In Person At The Whisky A Go Go
1968, Atco

If you've got *Dreams To Remember*, you've already got the best of his classic Stax material. However, this album, recorded live in LA in 1966, features vintage Redding in a club setting with his regular touring band. The set is so hot, you can almost feel the sweat as Redding pours his heart out. A second album of material recorded at the same live shows was released in 1993, *Good To Me: Live At The Whisky A Go Go*, and it's also well worth a look.

Della Reese

Long before she became a prime-time fixture on the TV drama *Touched By An Angel*, **Della Reese** was a cabaret singer of rare force and personality, due in no small part to her church background.

Born **Delloreese Patricia Early Taliafero** in Detroit on July 6, 1931, she began singing in church at age 6. Seven years later, she started a five-year stint singing back-up for **Mahalia Jackson**. In 1949 she enrolled at Wayne State University, where she majored in psychology and joined the influential gospel group **The Meditation Singers** with Laura Lee. Among their biggest fans were Diana Ross and Martha Reeves.

Shortening her name to Della Reese, she landed a gig with **Erskine Hawkins**'s jazz orchestra in 1953. Two years later her first single for the Jubilee label, "In The Still Of The Night", allegedly sold 500,000 copies. A further two years after that "And That Reminds Me" reached #12 on the pop charts, and positioned Reese somewhere between **Dinah Washington** and **Eartha Kitt**.

Signing with RCA in 1959, Reese worked with hacks like **Hugo & Luigi** and **Neal Hefti**, and scored a massive hit with "Don't You Know", a stiff, starchy old-fashioned pop record that topped the R&B chart and went #2 on the pop chart. Reese became more and more over the top at RCA, developing into a bawdy, schticky showstopper. However, when she was allowed to sing bluesier numbers such as "Someday (You'll Want Me To Want You)" in 1960 and "Call Me" in 1964, she nonetheless shone.

In 1964 Reese recorded a couple of Northern soul classics: the direct "If I Didn't Care" and "A Clock That's Got No Hands", which was a bizarre combination of the *Hawaii Five-O* theme, Tin Pan Alley and uptight 50s rock'n'roll. After a three-year stint at ABC-Paramount, releasing awful material such as "It Was A Very Good Year" and "Sunny", she signed to Avco and worked on more soul-oriented records like 1969's nice version of "Compared To What" and the uptempo Northern favourite "If It Feels Good Do It".

Reese was given her own television show, *The Della Reese Show*, in 1969. While it didn't last long, her band, including the great drummer **Earl Palmer**, may well have been the best ever assembled for such a venture. Television gradually pulled Reese away from music and she has since starred in *Chico & The Man*, *It Takes Two*, *The Royal Family* and, most famously, *Touched By An Angel*, as well as the 1989 Eddie Murphy film *Harlem Nights*. Reese has returned to music a few times over the last twenty years, releasing gospel material such as 1998's Grammy-nominated live album *My Soul Feels Better Right Now*.

Voice Of An Angel
1996, RCA

Unfortunately, there's no decent collection of Reese's more soulful material, so this 20-track overview of her RCA years will have to do. Despite the lack of material truly identifiable as "soul" on this album, it does show that Reese has a helluva voice, and when she lets rip on songs like "Call Me" it's a joy.

René & Angela

In the tradition of Ashford & Simpson, Womack & Womack, and even Peaches & Herb, René & Angela were the most consistent duet act of the 80s. Their tenor and soprano voices played off each other perfectly as they sang about the ups and downs of love, and about foibles and triumphs.

When they met in 1977, René Moore and Angela Winbush were both aspiring songwriters and backing singers. Winbush had previously sang back-up for Stevie Wonder, L.T.D. and Jean Carne; Moore had worked with Kim Weston. As songwriters, the two had crafted records for Millie Jackson, Janet Jackson and Lenny Williams. After hearing a demo tape of "Do You Really Love Me", Capitol Records vice-president Cecil Hale signed them to his label and released the record, which became their first minor hit, in 1980.

The duo's third single, 1981's "I Love You More" – a cult club classic that sounded like Chic but with a synth replacing Bernard Edwards – was a perfect example of the strange ghostly dancefloor style that ruled New York in the early 80s. Though they continued to have modest R&B hits with records like "Imaginary Playmates" and "My First Love", however, real success eluded René & Angela at Capitol.

Signing to Mercury in 1985, the duo started working with René's brother, Bobby Watson from Rufus. The resultant album, *Street Called Desire*, became a minor R&B sensation. The first single, "Save Your Love (For #1)", featured a rap from Kurtis Blow and topped the R&B charts, as did the plush ballad "Your Smile". However, the record's best track, was the amazing ghostly synth-funk track "I'll Be Good".

The duo split acrimoniously in 1987, after Angela Winbush wrote "Smooth Sailin' Tonight" for The Isley Brothers and Moore claimed she'd stolen the lyrics from him. Moore recorded two singles, "All Or Nothing" and "Never Say Goodbye To Love", which reached the R&B Top 20 in 1988, while Winbush enjoyed significant solo success. She had a solo R&B #1 with the ballad "Angel" in 1987, released the albums *Sharp* (1987) and *It's The Real Thing* (1989)

and continued to work with the Isleys. She wrote and produced most of Ronald Isley's 1989 solo album *Spend The Night*, and the pair eventually married in 1993.

A Street Called Desire And More
1997, Polygram

This 14-track reissue of 1985's *Street Called Desire* offers the entire original album plus some soundtrack throwaways and, more importantly, five 12" remixes, including the popular ballad "Your Smile" and a fabulous mix of "I'll Be Good".

The Best Of René And Angela: Come My Way
1996, Capitol

Capitol Records' René & Angela hits package is worth getting for its one absolutely crucial track, the fabulous "I Love You More". The rest – tracks like "Imaginary Playmates", "Bangin' The Boogie" and "Secret Rendezvous" – is good to middling 80s soul.

The Rivingtons

The clown princes of vocal group harmony, The Rivingtons (Al Frazier, Carl White, Sonny Harris and Turner Wilson Jr.) are known, if at all, as the progenitors of The Trashmen's towering surf-punk classic, "Surfin' Bird". While The Rivingtons' best-known songs are indeed nonsense records of the highest calibre, the truth is that the group was a classy combo capable of performing any material with panache.

Al Frazier sang baritone with a number of West Coast groups in the 40s and 50s, including The Mello-Moods, The Emanons and The Lamplighters. He then formed The Tenderfoots with White, Harris and Matthew Nelson. They recorded a few sides for Federal before backing Paul Anka as The Jacks. In 1956 they signed to the Jamie label as The Sharps and backed Thurston Harris and Duane Eddy. Turner Wilson then replaced Nelson and the group became The Crenshaws, providing backing vocals for Roy Milton and producer Kim Fowley.

Fooling around in the studio in the early 60s, Wilson came up with the preposterous sound, "papa-oom-mow-mow". The rest of the group, now going under the name The Rivingtons, loved the sound and designed a song around it. Eventually released in 1962 on Liberty, "Papa-Oom-Mow-Mow" reached #48 on the pop charts on the strength of the

California Soul

The lyrics of The Fifth Dimension's 1968 record "California Soul" may intimate that California soul is "a sound you hear that lingers in your ear … it's all in the air, it's everywhere", but the reality is that West Coast soul never had much of an identity, unlike its brethren in the South and Midwest or on the East Coast. The Left Coast's biggest soul stars were either transplants like Ray Charles or Sam Cooke, or unique artists like Sly Stone, who didn't drag anyone else along on their coat-tails.

Los Angeles was a significant force on the R&B and jump blues scenes. The city's pre-eminence extended to doo-wop, with groups like The Penguins releasing one of the classics of the genre, 1954's "Earth Angel". LA played host to a variety of excellent vocal groups, most notably The Robins, The Rivingtons and The Olympics. A latter incarnation of The Robins included H.B. Barnum, a singer and producer who crafted hits for Irma Thomas and The O'Jays and recorded two Northern soul favourites, "It Hurts Too Much To Cry" and "Call On Me".

Barnum was prone to over-orchestration in his productions and this easy-listening vibe characterized California's most successful and recognizable brand of soul. With records like The Incredibles' "I'll Make It Easy (If You'll Come On Home)", Leon Haywood's "It's Got To Be Mellow", The Fifth Dimension's numerous hits, Al Wilson's "The Snake" and "Show and Tell", and Sonny Charles & The Checkmates' "Black Pearl", LA was one of the centres of the sweet soul sound. This conventional attitude was later perfected by Lou Rawls and Bill Withers, and modified by Barry White. Dick Griffey's Solar label gave the city's soul artists another identity in the late 70s and early 80s, in the form of a string of bubbly, lite funk records by Shalamar, The Whispers, Lakeside, Carrie Lucas, Dynasty and Midnight Star.

The Bay Area had a much funkier sound than Southern California. The Galaxy label specialized in raw downhome records by bluesman Little Johnny Taylor ("Part Time Love"), Rodger Collins ("She's Looking Good"), The Debonaires ("I Want To Talk About It (World)"), Merl Saunders ("I Pity The Fool") and Lenny Williams. Williams recorded a few singles for Galaxy – most notably The Temptations' rip "I Love Her Too" and a cover of Creedence Clearwater Revival's "Feelin' Blue" – before becoming the lead singer of funk outfit Tower of Power, with their blend of funk feel and jazz chops. Going solo again in 1975, Williams had a big club hit with "You Got Me Running".

Various Artists: The Best Of Solar
1995, Castle

This is a neat and tidy 16-track overview of the neat and tidy dance-pop that made LA's Solar the label of choice for Bar Mitzvahs around the world in the early 80s.

PLAYLIST

1 PAPA OOM MOW MOW The Rivingtons from **The Golden Age Of American Rock'n'Roll Vol. 6**
The clown princes of soul answer life's imponderable mysteries.

2 IT HURTS TOO MUCH TO CRY H.B. Barnum from **Rare Collectable And Soulful**
One of the greatest drum-roll intros in the history of soul.

3 MERCY, MERCY, MERCY Larry Williams and Johnny "Guitar" Watson from **Best Of The OKeh Years**
A soft-soul classic that helped define the sound of Golden State soul.

4 GIMME LITTLE SIGN Brenton Wood from **Brenton Wood's 18 Best**
Delightful singsong pop-soul record.

5 SHE'S LOOKING GOOD Rodger Collins from **Get Your Lie Straight**
Searing, primal Oakland funk.

6 THANK YOU (FALETTINME BE MICE ELF AGIN) Sly & The Family Stone from **Anthology**
The meanest, angriest, most ornery record in soul's history, but also one of the best.

7 HARLEM Bill Withers from **The Best Of Bill Withers: Lean On Me**
An intense slow burn expressing the dark side of Withers' button-down persona.

8 I'M GONNA LOVE YOU JUST A LITTLE MORE BABY Barry White from **All-Time Greatest Hits**
The first, and best, of White's boudoir epics.

9 FANTASTIC VOYAGE Lakeside from **The Best Of Solar**
Utterly infectious bubblegum funk.

10 CALIFORNIA SOUL Marlena Shaw from **California Soul**
A bit more orchestral than the Left Coast norm, but still as pretty as the sun setting over the Pacific Coast Highway.

record's sheer *joie de vivre* and electricity. After releasing the purely ridiculous "Kickapoo Joy Juice" the next year, the group followed with "Mama-Oom-Mow-Mow" and "The Bird's The Word", which were essentially the same record as "Papa-Oom-Mow-Mow", but were still equally delightful.

The Rivingtons recorded several more sides throughout the 60s – most of which were rather wonderful – and bounced from one label to another, but they were never again able to recapture the commercial magic of "Papa-Oom-Mow-Mow".

The Liberty Years
1991, EMI

This collection of just about everything The Rivingtons recorded for Liberty in the early 60s shows that they were one of the most underrated of all the vocal groups. While they made their name with some of the most transcendent nonsense records ever made, they were also capable of making familiar rock'n'roll songs like "Long Tall Sally" all their own.

Smokey Robinson & The Miracles

S mokey Robinson was famously described as "America's greatest living poet" by no less an authority than **Bob Dylan**. Robinson wasn't necessarily one of popular music's premier songwriters because of his words, however. His lyrics were often rather trite, but his command of meter, rhyme and turn of phrase elevated his songs above the realm of pop schmaltz and into the rarified air of, well, poetry. While no one had done as much for vernacular language since Gutenberg, Robinson's biggest artistic triumph might have been his image. He wasn't a great singer, but his wounded, fragile, doo-wop-influenced high tenor admitted a vulnerability that few, if any, black male singers before him had dared to reveal, and his vision of love rather than lust paved the way for such non-traditional male personas as Al Green, The Stylistics and The Delfonics.

William "Smokey" Robinson was born in Detroit on February 19, 1940. He formed a group called **The Matadors** at Detroit Northern High School in 1955 with **Ron White, Warren "Pete" Moore, Bobby**

Rogers and **Emerson Rogers**. The following year Emerson Rogers was drafted into the army, so they enlisted his sister **Claudette** and changed their name to **The Miracles**. The group auditioned for, but failed to impress, Jackie Wilson's manager Nat Tarnapol, but there they met **Berry Gordy, Jr.** who was taken both with their voices and with Robinson's catalogue of 100 songs.

The group's first release, 1958's "Got A Job" – an answer song to **The Silhouettes'** "Get A Job" – reached the R&B charts, but it wasn't until 1960's "Shop Around" that they established themselves – and Motown (it was the label's first million-seller) – as a permanent fixture on the pop charts. Two years later "I'll Try Something New" surrounded Robinson in echo and strings, marking it as the first Motown record to aim for the pop charts with unrestrained ambition.

It was 1965's "Ooo Baby Baby" that truly embodied Robinson's art. The rhythm of his lyrics blended with his impossibly high, lachrymose vocals, set in an arrangement that was to be imitated hundreds of times, to create a record more moving than the lyrics would convey (check out **Linda Ronstadt**'s version for proof). Robinson's masterpiece, however, was probably "The Tracks Of My Tears". Again, lines like "My smile is my make-up I wear since my break-up with you" came to life inside an arrangement that welded classic crooning and street-corner harmony to a quintessential Motown beat, courtesy of studio band **The Funk Brothers**.

Of course, Robinson also wrote great dance music. The early-60s hits "I Gotta Dance To Keep From Crying", "Mickey's Monkey", "Come On Do The Jerk" and "Going To A Go-Go" were all proof of his multifaceted talent. Like all great craftsmen, he was never content to leave them as mere dance-craze trifles, and all of them featured moments of pure Smokey poetry. Catapulted by a trademark **James Jamerson** bassline and perfect percussion, 1967's "I Second That Emotion" blended both a dance imperative and heartbreak like few others. With lyrics like "Maybe you want to give me kisses sweet/But only for one night with no repeat", the record sounded more like a Shirelles song than something by a male soul singer.

Despite Robinson's talents and the quality of their records, The Miracles didn't have a pop #1 until 1970. That year's "The Tears Of A Clown" started off life as a **Stevie Wonder** instrumental, which Wonder gave to Robinson to write lyrics. Revisiting a theme he had previously conceived in 1964 for **Carolyn Crawford**'s "My Smile Is Just A Frown (Turned Upside Down)", Robinson wrote "The Tears Of A Clown" for inclusion on The Miracles' *Make It Happen* album in 1967. Released as a single in the UK three years later, it soon reached #1, so Motown released the track in the US and it quickly followed suit.

Robinson left The Miracles in January 1972, and was replaced by **Billy Griffin**. Although the group were never as successful again, they did achieve one more pop #1, with 1975's ridiculous "Love Machine". The single's vocals couldn't have sounded more different from Robinson's fragility. But as a solo artist Robinson also changed and he used his voice for very different ends. No longer the vulnerable nice guy of old, Robinson turned himself into a love man. The extraordinary 1974 release "Virgin Man" marked the transition between personas, while with his 1975 solo album, *A Quiet Storm*, Robinson single-handedly created the "quiet storm" subgenre of late-night, adult-oriented ballads that emphasized whispered vocals and ornate orchestrations, proving once again that he was one of popular music's singular talents.

On the fine 1979 ballad "Cruisin'", Robinson's fey falsetto almost dissolved into the lush guitar whirlpool, but he just man-

aged to keep his head above water. His huge 1981 hit "Being With You", on the other hand, may be the wimpiest love song ever recorded. Robinson's best record during this period – **Larry Levan**'s remix of Robinson's minor R&B hit, "And I Don't Love You" – barely featured him at all. One of the most famous voices in the history of popular music was merely mournfully intoning the title phrase a couple of times from behind a fog of echo and distended guitar.

Robinson continued to have R&B hits throughout the 80s, including the dreamy neo-doo-wop collaboration with **Rick James**, "Ebony Eyes", as well as the mainstream MOR crossover bids "Just To See Her", "One Heartbeat" and "Everything You Touch". After releasing the fairly awful *Double Good Everything* in 1991, Robinson was quiet for most of the 90s. However, he returned in 1999 with *Intimate*, yet another ignorable MOR ballad album. Although Robinson's voice was still in good shape, the relentlessly clean contemporary production styles tended to wash it away, and on his most recent album, the 2004 gospel disc *Food For The Spirit*, he was simply background noise.

Going To A Go-Go
1965, Tamla

This album has the cream of the crop of mid-60s Smokey Robinson & The Miracles. The album tracks are as great as the many hits included and, across the range of ballads and uptempo dance numbers, Smokey's impassioned vocals plead for redemptive love. Look out for the 2001 CD reissue that pairs this with the follow-up, 1967's *Away We A Go-Go*.

Anthology
1995, Motown

Motown has been woefully inconsistent with the stewardship of its catalogue in the digital age. This, however, is one CD collection that they got right. Two discs and 45 tracks of the music that made Motown what it is. The label certainly had more commercially successful acts, but none as important or as original as Smokey Robinson & The Miracles.

Smokey Robinson: The Ultimate Collection
1997, Motown

Smokey Robinson's solo career has been plagued with uneven albums filled out with mediocre material, but here is a case where a compilation of highlights really works. His best solo album, 1975's *A Quiet Storm*, is well represented, alongside the one or two great tracks from his subsequent outings. A concise, well-conceived and very listenable set.

PLAYLIST
Smokey Robinson

1 **SHOP AROUND** from **Anthology**
As hard-driving as Smokey ever got.

2 **YOU'VE REALLY GOT A HOLD ON ME** from **Anthology**
From its opening line, "I don't like you, but I love you", this truly established Robinson as the poet laureate of the lovelorn.

3 **OOO BABY BABY** from **Anthology**
Possibly Robinson's finest vocal performance.

4 **COME ON DO THE JERK** from **Anthology**
Undeniable finger-popping dance craze disc.

5 **THE TRACKS OF MY TEARS** from **Anthology**
Robinson's greatest achievement as a singer, songwriter and producer.

6 **GOING TO A GO-GO** from **Anthology**
Blaring, gaudy record with an utterly unstoppable momentum.

7 **I SECOND THAT EMOTION** from **Anthology**
This fine portrait of male vulnerability has yet to be topped.

8 **THE TEARS OF A CLOWN** from **Anthology**
The calliope and foghorn baritone sax may be the strangest instrumentation used on a Motown record, but the hook is undeniable.

9 **CRUISIN'** **Smokey Robinson** from **Cruisin'**
The most beautiful record of Robinson's frankly dull solo career.

10 **AND I DON'T LOVE YOU (REMIX)** **Smokey Robinson**
A remarkable dubby remix by the great Larry Levan turns Robinson into a ghost on his own record.

Rose Royce

One day everyone will understand the power of the hand clap; until then, we have **Rose Royce**. As the main late-70s vehicle for producer extraordinaire **Norman Whitfield**, Rose Royce were blessed with some of the best productions of the era, and Whitfield was never one to skimp on details like hand claps or cowbells.

The nucleus of the group came together in LA in 1970, when guitarist **Kenji Brown** (sporting one of the greatest Afros of all time), trumpeter/vocalist **Kenny "Captain Brown" Copeland**, keyboardist **Victor Nix**, trumpeter **Freddie Dunn**, saxophonist **Michael Moore** (no, not that one), bassist **Lequient "Duke" Jobe**, percussionist **Terral Santiel** and drummer **Henry Garner** formed a band called **Total Concept**. In 1973, touring Europe as Edwin Starr's backing band, they met Whitfield, who subsequently used them on projects for The Temptations, The Undisputed Truth and **Yvonne Fair**.

In 1975 Whitfield installed former Jewels' singer **Gwen Dickey** as the main vocalist, briefly changing her name to **Rose Norwalt**, and changed the group's name to Rose Royce. Around the same time, Whitfield was brought in as the producer of the soundtrack to Michael Schultz's 1976 movie *Car Wash*. He insisted that Rose Royce featured prominently on the soundtrack, and their three main contributions were all solid hits. Whitfield may have written the lyrics to "Car Wash" on a fast-food wrapper, but his production was anything but haphazard, and it included the greatest hand claps ever recorded. "Car Wash" became the group's only #1 hit. The ballad "I Wanna Get Next To You" featured Copeland on lead vocals and reached #10 on the pop chart, while Dickey's tour-de-force performance on the huge showstopper of a ballad "I'm Going Down" was later copied by Mary J. Blige.

The group's 1977 ablum *In Full Bloom* featured the killer cowbell-laden disco-funk cut "Do Your Dance" and the jazzy ballad "Ooh Boy". It also included "Wishing On A Star", a spare ballad that did nothing in the States, but was a #3 pop hit in the UK. The lively "It Makes You Feel Like Dancin'" was another UK hit, reaching #16. Dickey's finest vocal performance of all came on 1978's *Rose Royce III: Strikes Again!*, in the shape of "Love Don't Live Here Anymore", which was another massive UK hit.

Dickey suddenly left the group in 1980 and was replaced by **Ricci Benson**, while **Walter McKinney** took Brown's place as guitarist. The group's finest post-Dickey moment was "Pop Your Fingers", an electric roller-skating jam that somehow only reached #60 on the R&B chart. Benson was a less appealing vocalist than Dickey, but she gave some decent ballad performances on "Golden Touch", "Best Love" and "Still In Love".

Rose Royce split with Whitfield in 1984. Working with Philly mainstay **Bobby Eli** at the UK label Streetwave, they achieved a UK hit with "Magic Touch". They also had success on the American R&B chart in 1986 with "Doesn't Have To Be This Way" and "Lonely Road". The latter featured a sax solo from **Grover Washington, Jr.**

Gwen Dickey started performing again in 1984, and moved to London where she has become a star on the UK soul scene. Meanwhile, Rose Royce are still touring regularly and performing at private events around the world. Various revival movements in Britain have ensured that "Car Wash" is never too far from the UK Top 40 – it made it into the Top 20 in 1998 and into the Top 5 in 2004, when it was covered by Missy Elliott and **Christina Aguilera** for the movie *Shark Tale*.

⊙ **The Very Best Of Rose Royce**
2001, Rhino

This comprehensive 16-track collection is exactly what it says it is, and it has just about all the Rose Royce tracks anyone could want. Vinyl fans should seek out *Greatest Hits* (1980, Whitfield) which has one side of dance hits and one side of ballads – the way soul compilations were meant to be organized.

Diana Ross

You may love her or hate her, but you can't deny her star power. Like her over-the-top stylization, **Diana Ross** is bigger than life and an unquenchable force when she performs. Although her solo records were nowhere near as good as the ones she made with The Supremes when she started performing as a solo artist, her producers often found sounds that suited her far better than the Motown stomp of old.

Ross was born in Detroit, Michigan on March 26, 1944. As lead vocalist of Motown vocal group The Supremes, Ross had led the decade's most successful black act for the whole of the 60s, but she left the group to go solo in 1969. Her early solo career was tightly controlled by Motown boss **Berry Gordy** who gave her material by songwriting team Ashford & Simpson. Her first releases were covers of their tracks, like the wretched singsong "Reach Out And Touch (Somebody's Hand)" and a decent version of "Ain't No Mountain High Enough".

Ross's soundtrack to 1972's *Lady Sings The Blues* – the **Billie Holiday** biopic in which Ross also starred and for which she earned an Oscar nomination for best actress – was surprisingly acceptable. Since she knew she couldn't compete with Holiday's emotionalism, Ross remade Holiday's songs as easy-listening trinkets, an effective conceit. In 1973 Gordy roped in **Michael Masser** to write songs for Ross. Masser was responsible for her huge mid-70s hits, including "Touch Me In The Morning" and "Theme From Mahogany (Do You Know Where You're Going To)". Later in 1973 Ross also released a rather mediocre duet album with Marvin Gaye, *Diana & Marvin*. The album was notable only for "Don't Knock My Love", on which Ross managed

PLAYLIST
Diana Ross

1 AIN'T NO MOUNTAIN HIGH ENOUGH from **The Motown Anthology**
This isn't a patch on the original, but the showbiz excess has its pleasures.

2 TOUCH ME IN THE MORNING from **The Motown Anthology**
What Ross does best: gauzy easy listening suddenly exploding into razzle-dazzle.

3 SURRENDER from **The Motown Anthology**
This would have been better as a big, blowsy disco showstopper, but the arrangement plays to her strengths.

4 THEME FROM MAHOGANY (DO YOU KNOW WHERE YOU'RE GOING TO) from **The Motown Anthology**
Ross does her best Karen Carpenter impression.

5 LOVE HANGOVER from **The Motown Anthology**
Ross never sounded better than on this disco sleaze classic.

6 EASE ON DOWN THE ROAD from **The Wiz**
Not as good as Consumer Rapport's cult disco favourite, but it still makes you want to snap your suspender straps as you skip to work.

7 I'M COMING OUT from **Diana**
Chic save Ross from generic disco oblivion with backing as brittle and angular as her vocals.

8 UPSIDE DOWN from **Diana**
Anthemic, yet unsettling, this is another great production courtesy of Chic's Rodgers and Edwards.

331

Diana Ross with a twinkle in her eye

not to sound uptight for a whole two minutes.

The advent of disco should have been the best thing that ever happened to Ross, and initially it was. She was great on 1976's "Love Hangover": her forced breathiness sounded perfect next to the penthouse soul backing at the start, while as the temperature heated up, her soft-focus cooing provided the ideal counterpoint. However, the dancefloor hits quickly dried up, and not even "Ease On Down The Road", a perky, peppy duet with Michael Jackson from the disastrous film *The Wiz*, did significant business. Ross's disco years were summed up by "The Boss", a generic disco record on which Ross sounded even more like Michael Jackson.

Bernard Edwards and **Nile Rodgers** of Chic came to Ross's rescue in 1980. Their sharp lines and jagged grooves were a perfect foil for Ross's stiltedness, and their extensive involvement on that year's *Diana* helped make the album perhaps the best of her solo career. The album's defining moment was "Upside Down", with its weird, stunted, ghostly piano. In 1981 Ross teamed up with Lionel Richie for the rather hideous "Endless Love", which was an enormous hit and stayed at #1 for nine weeks.

Ross left Motown for RCA soon after that hit duet and immediately recorded a pointless remake of "Why Do Fools Fall In Love". As the 80s wore on, Ross gradually found it ever harder to make inroads into the charts. Even a move back to Motown in 1989 couldn't change her chart fortunes. By the early 90s she gradually turned away from pop music towards standards on albums like

Stolen Moments and *Take Me Higher*. Over the past few years she has also recorded a number of Christmas and children's albums, and in 2005 she released the shockingly awful "When You Tell Me That You Love Me" with British boy band **Westlife**.

In 2000 Ross reunited with The Supremes, although current members **Scherrie Payne** and **Lynda Laurence** had not actually been in the group when Ross was, in the 60s. Still, it was closure of some sort or another.

⊚ Diana
1980, Motown

Produced by Chic's Nile Rodgers and Bernard Edwards in an effort to update her sound, this great collaboration sent Ross back to the top of the charts. The great funk/disco sound of Chic that was so popular in the late 70s permeates this album, which is highlighted by the two monster hits, "Upside Down" and "I'm Coming Out".

⊚ The Motown Anthology
2001, Motown

Two discs and 38 tracks is more than enough solo Diana Ross for anyone, but this is by far the best collection of her solo work. *Diana* (1980, Motown) gets short shrift, with only "Upside Down" and "I'm Coming Out" appearing (where's "My Old Piano"?). Otherwise, this has everything you could ask for, including juicy rarities.

Rotary Connection

" I hate to criticize, but these groups that insist on playing louder than 85 decibels are not really keeping their image," producer/arranger **Charles Stepney** told *Downbeat* magazine in 1970. "I mean, they protest water and air pollution as a disease of our times, but go right ahead and commit ear pollution. That's as dangerous as cigarettes, as far as I'm concerned. It's a known fact that sounds above 85 decibels are dangerous to the ear. These rock-acid groups average over 100 decibels, and this erodes the highest layers of your audio perception." That pronouncement might hardly sound typical of a prophet of psychedelic soul, but producer/arranger Charles Stepney was as much a pioneer as Sly Stone or **Norman Whitfield**. He was just a bit quieter.

Stepney had joined the Chess Records fold as a member of Richard Evans's **Soulful Strings**, but in 1967 **Marshall Chess** asked him to come up with a psychedelic concept for the new Cadet Concept subsidiary label. Various session musicians – including guitarists Pete Cosey and Phil Upchurch, percussionist Henry Gibson and bassists Louis Satterfield and Mitch Aliotta – were drafted in. They were then teamed up with singers **Sidney Barnes** and **Minnie Riperton** – the latter had been with Chess since 1963 as part of The Gems and as a solo artist – and given the name **Rotary Connection**.

Released in March 1968, the *Rotary Connection* album was divided into two sides, "Trip I" and "Trip I Continued". Stepney set out to journey to the centre of his listeners' minds, not via overloaded dynamics and over-amped distortion but through over-the-top orchestration, hints of atonality and bizarre vocal and instrumental arrangements. "Memory Band" was a typical track, featuring an electric sitar; a slightly out-of-tune children's choir trying to sing along with Riperton's phenomenal multi-octave range; spaghetti western vibrato; and what sounds like a theremin in the background. Elsewhere on the album, the group turned "Like A Rolling Stone" into something approaching an "Up With People" rally led by the Edwin Hawkins Singers.

The same year's *Aladdin*, which was schmaltzier and a bit less psychedelic, featured Riperton more prominently and was less appealing as a result, while *Peace* was a good, but hardly essential, Christmas album. The fourth Rotary Connection album, 1969's *Songs*, featured nothing but cover versions – and, surprisingly, it just might be their best. Their totally unrecognizable rendition of "Respect" was certainly the most original version of that old chestnut: in place of the melody were chilly strings, an icy piano line that chimed like a death knell, a duet between Riperton and Barnes on top of a chorale of fallen angels, and Pete Cosey doing his thing. **Cream**'s "Sunshine Of Your Love" was transformed into a gospel symphony, like something producers **Hugo & Luigi** might have crafted for the blaxploitation era, while the vocal arrangement of **Hendrix**'s "The Burning Of The Midnight Lamp" might just be the most opulent thing ever recorded.

By 1970, when they released *Dinner Music* (or "Dog's Dinner Music", as it might more properly have been called), Rotary Connection were falling apart. The previous year Riperton had recorded the solo album

Come Into My Garden (released in 1971), on which Stepney perfected his chamber-soul sound. The final Rotary Connection album, 1971's *Hey Love*, featured a new vocal line-up of Riperton, **Dave Scott, Kitty Haywood** and **Shirley Wahls**. With the exception of the extraordinary track "I Am The Black Gold Of The Sun", Stepney's arrangements on the album seemed uninspired.

While Stepney went on to work with Earth Wind & Fire and The Dells, Riperton turned to Stevie Wonder, who wrote several songs – and played the drums – for her decent 1974 album *Perfect Angel*. The album found Riperton at her most sensuous and least mannered, and it included the monster hit "Lovin' You". Her solo follow-ups *Adventures In Paradise* (1975), *Stay In Love* (1977) and *Minnie* (1979) failed to repeat that success, however, and Riperton was doomed to remain a cult favourite. She died of breast cancer at just 31 years of age on July 12, 1979.

Songs / Hey Love
1998, BGP/Ace

Rotary Connection's *Songs* (1969) and *Hey Love* (1971) reissued together on one disc make the best introduction to the group's music. Although *Hey Love* is largely forgettable – except for the wonderful "I Am The Black Gold Of The Sun" – *Songs*, with its daring cover versions, is an often stunning album, thanks to Charles Stepney's startling arrangements.

Minnie Riperton: Perfect Angel
1974, Epic

Riperton sang vocals on Stevie Wonder's *Fulfillingness* album, and he returned the favour by co-producing and writing some songs for this mid-70s soul delight. Highlighted by her signature tune, "Loving You", this is Riperton's best album and the one that everyone remembers from her too short career. Her sparkling vocals shine throughout.

Barbara Roy

Barbara Roy (née Gaskins) was one of dance music's greatest vocalists and her fiery gospel vocals have graced countless club anthems, from the dawn of Northern soul through the early days of disco to the house explosion of the early 90s.

She was born in Kingston, North Carolina and later moved to New York where she formed the duo **Barbara & Brenda** with her niece **Brenda Gaskins**. Their first record was "Let's Get Together", but it was their second, 1964's "That's When You've Got Soul", released on the Heidi label, that got them noticed (albeit several years later when the Northern soul DJs picked up on it). After recording two more singles for Heidi, the duo started working with producer **Luther Dixon**, who signed them to the Musicor subsidiary label Dynamo. In 1968 Barbara & Brenda recorded the Northern soul classic, "Don't Wait Up For Me Mama", but Brenda got married shortly afterwards and decided to stop singing professionally. Barbara remained in the business and became a session player for Dynamo, most notably playing guitar on Inez Foxx's "You Shouldn't Have Set My Soul On Fire" in 1970.

In 1973, taking her father's first name as her surname, Barbara Roy formed **Ecstasy, Passion & Pain** with drummer **Althea "Cookie" Smith**, guitarist **Jimmy Clark**, keyboardist **Ronnie Foster**, bassist **Jimmy Williams** and percussionist **Carl Jordan**. Working with producer **Bobby Martin**, the group signed to Roulette and recorded a series of records that became hallmarks of the early disco sound. After their first single, "I Wouldn't Give You Up", became a moderate R&B hit, **Billy Gardner** replaced Foster and **Alan Tizer** replaced Jordan. However, aside from Barbara Roy, the line-up was rather immaterial because MFSB, the great Philadelphia International house band, played on almost all of their records and backing vocals were handled by **The Sweethearts of Sigma Sound**.

The group's biggest hit was 1974's "Good Things Don't Last Forever" – although it was simply pro forma Philly soul – but it was that same year's "Ask Me", written by Roy, that really endeared the group to the dancefloor. On top of a trademark pulsating Philly soul beat, Roy defined the disco diva with her mix of fierceness and desperation. The joyous "One Beautiful Day" was a bit more gospel-styled, but the follow-up "Touch And Go" was one of the truly great disco singles. Roy exorcized her pain as fiercely as anyone who has ever taken up a mic on top of a serious, serious disco beat and keyboards that gave life to a thousand house records.

After the 1977 releases of "Passion" and "Dance The Night Away", two fairly formulaic disco tracks, Ecstacy, Passion & Pain split. Roy then founded her own label, Roy B. Records, which had some disco success with **Soccer**'s "Dancin' Game" and "Give Me Your Love" in 1980. Briefly reuniting the next year, Ecstasy, Passion & Pain had a cult dance club hit with "I Want You". Roy continued to release solo dance club records like "With All My Love" and the modest R&B hit, "Gotta See You Tonight", in the mid-80s. In 1989 she also featured on producer **Paul Simpson**'s *One* album alongside fellow dance music all-stars Loleatta Holloway, Toney Lee, Fonda Rae, Will Downing and **Rochelle Fleming** as a group called **Togetherness**.

Although little has been heard from Barbara Roy since, her vocals from the great 70s dance track "Touch And Go" were sampled in 1989 on **Fidelfatti**'s Italo-house classic, "Just Wanna Touch Me". A different sample from the same record was also used as an anchor on **JX**'s huge European hit "Son Of A Gun" in 1994.

○ **Good Things: The Roulette Recordings 1973–77**
1999, Westside

This 28-track, double-disc collection literally has all the Ecstasy, Passion & Pain anyone could want – it has everything the group ever recorded, including demos and unreleased tracks. An essential purchase for anyone interested in the formative years of the disco sound.

Ruby & The Romantics

Perhaps the classiest of all the early precursors to the soft-soul vocal groups, **Ruby & The Romantics** managed to make the starchy stateliness of the early soul style signify and float with the élan of the more modern vocal style that came to prominence in the mid-60s.

The Romantics (**Leroy Fann, George Lee, Ronald Moseley** and **Ed Roberts**) began life in Akron, Ohio as a male vocal group called The Supremes. They recorded a couple of sides that went nowhere in the late 50s, before being joined by female vocalist **Ruby Nash Curtis** in 1961, and changing their name to Ruby & The Romantics. Ruby had a voice that somehow managed to be both sensual and prissy at the same time – a qual-

ity that made them the perfect transition group. True to form, their debut single, "Our Day Will Come", was a wonderful merger of classic pop style with new soul emotion and lusty grace. Thanks to the way Ruby sang the hook, the single topped both the pop and R&B charts in 1963.

The follow-ups "My Summer Love" and "Young Wings Can Fly (Higher Than You Know)" were less distinctive and more straightforwardly pop in style and conception. However, "Hey There Lonely Boy" was another lovely soft-soul shuffle. The song didn't achieve the success it deserved until **Eddie Holman** remade it in 1969 as "Hey There Lonely Girl" and took it to the top of the charts.

In 1964 "Our Everlasting Love" was more traditional, while "Baby Come Home" was a classic of soulful longing. "When You're Young And In Love" only reached #48 on the pop chart, but The Marvelettes' remake was more successful. The 1965 release "Your Baby Doesn't Love You Anymore" may have been Ruby & The Romantics' finest rapprochement between easy-listening orchestration and downtown soul, but it went nowhere commercially and the group split.

In 1966 Ruby organized a new bunch of Romantics – **Bill Evans, Ronald Jackson, Robert Lewis, Vincent McLeod** and **Richard Pryor** (no, not that one). The new line-up fully embraced easy listening on tracks such as "We Can Make It" and "I Know", but Ruby didn't sound as effortless as she once did and the hits quickly dried up. Ruby & The Romantics became an all-girl group on ABC in 1967, with **Denise Lewis** and **Cheryl Thomas** accompanying Ruby. Unfortunately, this realignment failed to change the group's fortunes and they fizzled out by the end of the decade.

○ **Our Day Will Come: The Very Best Of Ruby & The Romantics**
2003, RPM

This 2-disc, 42-track compilation has just about everything Ruby & The Romantics ever recorded. That may be more than most people need, but it includes crucial material like "Your Baby Doesn't Love You Anymore" and "Much Better Off Than I've Ever Been" that isn't on the single-disc *The Very Best Of Ruby & The Romantics* (1995, Taragon).

Jimmy Ruffin

Born on May 7, 1939 in Collinsville, Mississippi, **Jimmy Ruffin** was a decent singer who was always overshadowed by his younger brother **David Ruffin** of The Temptations. A far less distinctive vocalist than his brother, Jimmy Ruffin was doomed to make do with singsong pop bromides, while his brother's group were given masterpiece after masterpiece to record.

Jimmy Ruffin originally signed to the short-lived Motown subsidiary Miracle in 1961. He recorded the fine, Jackie Wilson-styled "Don't Feel Sorry For Me" for the label, but it went nowhere. He then became a member of **The Four Hollidays**, with whom he recorded two forgettable singles on the Markie label.

Ruffin returned to the Motown fold in 1964 with "Since I've Lost You". He proved his vocal talents the next year on the under-rated "How Can I Say I'm Sorry", but the song itself was cumbersome and it had a terrible chorus. Ruffin's biggest hit finally came with the rather sickly "What Becomes Of The Broken Hearted" in 1966. Several more records quickly followed in this same maudlin pop-soul vein – "I've Passed This Way Before", "Gonna Give Her All The Love I've Got" and "Don't You Miss Me a Little Bit Baby" – briefly establishing Ruffin as something of a mid-level star.

However, the hits quickly dried up again, even though sides like 1968's "Everybody Needs Love" were far better than his more successful records. Ruffin's 1969 *Ruff 'N Ready* album is worth seeking out for his surprisingly successful version of **? & The Mysterians'** "96 Tears". He then hit the UK's Top 10 with "Farewell Is A Lonely Sound", before teaming up with his brother in 1970 to release a version of **Ben E. King's** "Stand By Me", which also became his Motown swansong.

Ruffin re-emerged in 1974 with the fantastic "Tell Me What You Want" on the Chess label. He may have been ripping off Al Green, but the warm bass groove was enough to compensate for all of his sins as a vocalist. He reappeared on the scene in 1980, this time teaming up with Barry Gibb of **The Bee-Gees** for "Hold On To My Love". The record was a huge pop-disco hit on which Ruffin strangely sounded like Cat Stevens on occasion. His final appearance on the R&B charts came in 1982 with "Turn To Me", a duet with Maxine Nightingale.

⊙ 20th Century Masters: The Millennium Collection: The Best Of Jimmy Ruffin
2001, Universal

It doesn't have "Tell Me What You Want" or any of his obscure Motown sides, but this 11-track compilation does have all of Ruffin's Motown hits from "What Becomes Of The Broken Hearted" to "Stand By Me". It won't necessarily convince you of his greatness, but if you can't get enough singsongy Motown, this just might be for you.

Patrice Rushen

Just as they had done with funk a couple of years earlier, jazz fusioneers jumped right in line when disco took over the mainstream and they streamlined their grooves to be in touch with the temper of the times. Keyboardist **Patrice Rushen** was no exception. Her bouncy brand of easy rhythm and glossy synth sheen made her one of the most successful jazz and R&B crossover artists of the 80s.

Born into a musical family in LA on September 30, 1954, Rushen was a childhood piano prodigy, and she enrolled in a special musical education programme at the University of Southern California at age 3. After a performance at the Monterey Jazz Festival in 1972, Rushen signed with jazz label Prestige and released three albums – 1974's *Prelusion*, 1975's *Before The Dawn* and 1976's *Shout It Out*. Mostly fusion non-sense, typified by 1974's sort of funky track "Haw-Right Now", the albums barely sold. Rushen then turned to session work with the likes of **Lalo Schifrin**, The Blackbyrds, Ramsey Lewis and **Donald Byrd**.

Rushen had debuted her singing voice on "What's The Story" from *Before The Dawn*, and she was signed by Elektra in 1978 in the hope that she could cross over to the R&B market. The strategy started to pay dividends with the gently propulsive "Hang It Up" from her first Elektra album that year, *Patrice*. Already likeable but lightweight, her music was rendered even lighter by the success of the trite ballad "Haven't You Heard" in the R&B Top 10. That spawned successive overripe ballads in a typically awkward modern soul style, such as "This All I Know" from 1980's *Posh*.

Rushen's best album, 1982's *Straight From The Heart*, held plenty of formulaic pap to be sure, but it also offered fine grooves like "Number One" and "Remind Me", which didn't get too trapped by the gurgling whirl-pool of jazz-funk. *Straight From The Heart* also featured her biggest hit, "Forget Me Nots" – the bouncy bassline, well-placed hand claps, high-pitched keyboard hook and soft upbeat groove equalled dancefloor bliss.

From then on, however, Rushen's records were increasingly tainted by the synth glare of the 80s. She began to take on a variety of other projects, and over the past two decades she has composed scores for countless films and television programmes. In 1991 she was part of the soft jazz supergroup **The Meeting** with **Ernie Watts**, **Ndugu Chancler** and **Alphonso Johnson** and the musical director for Janet Jackson's tour. Her well-received album *Signature* returned Rushen to a jazz setting in 1997, while in 2000 she was part of the **Sisters Being Positively Real** project with **Sheree Brown**.

⊙ **Haven't You Heard: The Best Of Patrice Rushen**
1996, Rhino

This fine 14-track compilation includes nearly all her R&B hits, most of which were recorded for Elektra in the late 70s. The mainstream fusion sound can get a bit smarmy after a while, but when Rushen grooves and lets her slight but pleasant voice loose on uptempo material, you won't mind the bourgeois pretensions.

Sam & Dave

For four years and ten singles, the greatest duo in the history of pop music languished on fairly obscure Miami soul labels. Gospel-trained **Sam Moore** (born in Miami on October 12, 1935) and **Dave Prater** (born in Georgia on May 9, 1937) set out to be a pair of Sam Cookes, and as a result just sounded like everybody else. They were also saddled with lame material, and none of their early singles on Alston and Marlin achieved any success.

The turning point came in 1965, when they were signed by Atlantic. The label didn't really know what to do with them, and packed them off to the Stax studios in Memphis. Over the next few years, working primarily with the songwriting/production team of Isaac Hayes and **David Porter**, Sam & Dave crossed over to the mainstream with some of the hardest and deepest soul records ever created.

Sam & Dave's first record at Stax, released in March 1965, was David Porter's solo composition, "Goodnight Baby". With Prater singing lead, "Goodnight Baby" wasn't typical of the duo's output, but the gospel testifying at the end introduced what was to become their signature. Their second Stax effort, "I Take What I Want", written by both Porter and Hayes, featured Moore's straining lead. Like that other great rasper, James Brown, Moore wanted to be smooth and slick, but Hayes and Porter encouraged him to sing above his natural register, rendering his vocals that much more intense and anxious.

By the release of 1966's "You Don't Know Like I Know", the formula was just about perfected. Based on the gospel standard, "You Don't Know What The Lord Has Done For Me", the track showcased Sam & Dave alternating preaching ad-libs on top of a popping arrangement that steadily built towards the ultimate crash. If that only barely kept from boiling over, the next single, "Hold On I'm Comin'", was such a cauldron of energy that you could practically feel the sweat pouring from the speakers. One of the funkiest records ever, "Hold On" featured a mean chicken-scratch riff from guitarist **Steve Cropper**, while drummer **Al Jackson** Jr. served up his version of June Gardner's bad-ass "Get Out Of My Life Woman" beat. On top of the instrumental ferment, Sam & Dave traded lines like they were running from the flames.

Topping the R&B chart and reaching #21 in the pop charts, "Hold On, I'm Comin'"

was followed by "You Got Me Hummin'", with its slow-burn riff, classic Memphis horns and a whole lot of "unnngghh". The next year's "Soul Man" was the most bragging song this side of "Bo Diddley", with similarly elemental, searing guitar. Despite warning the world of Hayes's penchant for the clavinet, 1968's "I Thank You" found Sam & Dave singing hosannas about being baptized in love.

Although they were responsible for some of the most sexually predatory records ever made, Sam & Dave were just as effective on slower ballads. The finest secular preachers in the business, they got both river deep and mountain high on one of the truly great soul ballads, "When Something Is Wrong With My Baby", in 1967. That summer, they were also allowed to indulge their Sam Cooke fantasies by recording "Soothe Me". While they retained his sense of phrasing, Sam & Dave were no longer slavish imitators. Instead, they had become two of soul music's greatest and most individual stylists.

However, when Stax split with Atlantic in 1968, Sam & Dave were forced to work with producers and musicians who didn't understand them so well. Their own relationship also grew increasingly difficult, and the duo split after the release of 1969's fine "Soul Sister, Brown Sugar". They briefly reunited in 1974 and recorded the album *Back At 'Cha!* on United Artists, but the magic was gone. Sam Moore went on to have a small hit with a version of "Soul Man", which he recorded in 1987 with **Lou Reed**, but suffice to say it was neither man's finest work. Dave Prater died the following year in a car crash, but Sam Moore continues to perform, most recently singing "In The Midnight Hour" as a tribute to Wilson Pickett at the 2006 Grammy Awards.

○ **Soul Men**
1967, Stax

Though Stax tended to round out their artists' albums with filler of lesser quality, Sam & Dave's album tracks never falter here. Beside the only hit, "Soul Man", you get a fine mix of ballads and dance tracks with the duo's trademark harmonies on display throughout. Check out "Broke Down Piece Of Man" and "May I Baby".

○ **The Very Best Of Sam & Dave**
1995, Rhino

A concise, 16-track compilation that includes all of Sam & Dave's biggest hits for Stax/Atlantic, recorded with backing from Steve Cropper and Al Jackson of Booker T.

PLAYLIST
Sam & Dave

1 I TAKE WHAT I WANT from **The Very Best Of Sam & Dave**
A stomping tale of sexual urgency.

2 YOU DON'T KNOW LIKE I KNOW from **The Very Best Of Sam & Dave**
The band is even more intense than Sam & Dave on a Southern version of the Motown beat.

3 HOLD ON I'M COMIN' from **The Very Best Of Sam & Dave**
A brimstone-and-fire sermon of lust.

4 YOU GOT ME HUMMIN' from **The Very Best Of Sam & Dave**
Sam & Dave at their most sensual and least braggadocious.

5 SOUL MAN from **The Very Best Of Sam & Dave**
One of the truly great guitar licks and boasts that would make Bo Diddley blush.

6 I THANK YOU from **The Very Best Of Sam & Dave**
Plenty of old-fashioned soul clapping.

7 WRAP IT UP from **The Very Best Of Sam & Dave**
The flip side of "I Thank You" is a smoking girl-watching classic.

8 WHEN SOMETHING IS WRONG WITH MY BABY from **The Very Best Of Sam & Dave**
They weren't just about the fire down below – they could slow it down and be as tender as anyone.

9 SOOTHE ME from **The Very Best Of Sam & Dave**
Magnificent, churchy cover in which Sam & Dave channel Sam Cooke as effectively as anyone.

10 SOUL SISTER, BROWN SUGAR from **The Very Best Of Sam & Dave**
The killer intro of this track was pilfered by rappers MOP for the mighty "Ante Up".

& The MG's. If you want to dig deeper, *Sweat 'n' Soul: The Anthology (1965–71)* has just about everything worthwhile soul's greatest duo ever recorded.

Freddie Scott

Like Chuck Jackson, **Freddie Scott** brought a bit of grit into the rather frilly concoctions of New York soul. Although he was a New Englander, Scott could belt like a

Southern preacher, grounding the Brill Building's overwrought songs with his deep baritone vocal.

Born in Providence, Rhode Island on April 24, 1933, Freddie Scott sang in church as a young child. After a fateful experience at the Apollo Theatre's Amateur Night turned him towards songwriting, he worked as a staff writer for Screen Gems/Columbia during the early 60s, writing songs for **Paul Anka**, **Tommy Hunt** and Gene Chandler.

Scott also worked as a demo singer for New York's legendary Brill Building, where he recorded the demo of **Gerry Goffin** and **Carole King**'s "Hey Girl" in 1962. His miles-deep voice made the ballad the soul equivalent of **Bing Crosby**. Chuck Jackson declined the song, so Scott's demo recording was sweetened with strings, tympani and backing from **The Sweet Inspiration** and released, reaching the US Top 10 in 1963. As a result, Scott found himself saddled with inane arrangements and terrible material like "Where Have All The Flowers Gone?" for the next few years.

He was eventually rescued by **Bert Berns'** Shout Records label in 1966. Their first record together, "Are You Lonely For Me?", was a stone-cold classic. Although it was recorded in New York and had the hallmarks of later New York soul, it chugged like a Jacksonville-bound locomotive, while Scott's grit and passion were simply sensational. His version of **Solomon Burke**'s "Cry To Me" was a killer deep-soul ballad, while "(You) Got What I Need" was such a jammy jam that **Biz Markie** swiped it hook, line and sinker in 1989.

Scott's final R&B chart entry came in 1970 when he turned in a fine reading of **Bob Dylan**'s "I Shall Be Released". He basically disappeared from the limelight after that, but continued to appear on the oldies circuit. In 2001 he released an awkward comeback album, *Brand New Man*, which featured guest appearances from assorted luminaries, including Isaac Hayes, Graham Parker and Peter Wolf.

Cry To Me: The Best Of Freddie Scott
1998, Sony/Legacy

This 20-track compilation features the cream of the material this very fine singer recorded with Bert Berns for Shout Records from 1966 to 1970, which means it has pretty much everything except "Hey Girl".

Gil Scott-Heron

The career development of **Gil Scott-Heron** (born in Chicago on April 1, 1949) has taken him from radical, avant-garde poet to jazz-funk singer-songwriter with a conscience. That transformation began in 1970, when he recorded a reading of his volume of poetry, *Small Talk At 125th And Lenox*, to a **Last Poets**-style background of congas and bells for jazz producer **Bob Thiele**'s Flying Dutchman label. Released in 1972, *Small Talk At 125th And Lenox* documented the uncompromising world view of the Black Arts Movement with songs such as "Whitey On The Moon", a very funny attack on American economic priorities, and a skeletal early version of his most famous song, "The Revolution Will Not Be Televised". The latter was re-recorded and released on *Pieces Of A Man* in 1971 with a hard funk bassline that enhanced the moody menace of the lyrics.

As he added more instrumentation, Scott-Heron began to sing his poem-songs, allowing a more empathetic conception of politics to enter into his music. The first fully formed and successful work by the more musical Gil Scott-Heron was 1974's "The Bottle", a tough and danceable anti-alcohol song that featured **Brian Jackson**'s flute. The partnership between Scott-Heron and Jackson began when they were both students at Lincoln College in Pennsylvania and continued until the *1980* album. Another key factor in Scott-Heron's artistic (if not commercial) success was his underrated bassist **Robert Gordon** ("The Secretary of Entertainment") who was equally comfortable with virtuosic solos and fluid grooves.

Following the dancefloor success of "The Bottle" and a switch to the Arista label, "Johannesburg" (from the 1975 album *From South Africa To South Carolina*) proved that disco could celebrate something other than hedonism – in this instance the anti-apartheid struggle – and still move bodies. The mid-70s saw Scott-Heron become the most eloquent, if least famous, of music's anti-nuclear campaigners with the songs "South Carolina (Barnwell)", "We Almost Lost Detroit" and "Shut 'Um Down". Just as his music was starting to slip into a soft-jazz formula, Scott-Heron returned to a harsh, deep funk sound on his substantial black radio hit, "Angel Dust". Along with "Third World Revolution", the track anchored his strong 1978 album *Secrets*, with its spacey but direct groove-based attack on the latest scourge to wreck America's inner cities.

Scott-Heron furthered his brooding minimalism on the excellent albums *Reflections* (1981) and *Moving Target* (1982). "B Movie" from the *Reflections* album was perhaps the most bitter and explicitly political song ever to be a hit on radio. With its smart setting (a second-rate western) and savage characterizations of Reagan and his cronies, "B Movie" perfectly captured the Left's mood at the time. Despite his misgivings, Scott-Heron's collaboration with **Bill Laswell**, "Re-Ron", made explicit the underlying political slant of the mechanistic, urban funk of the 80s.

In spite of almost constant touring and probably because of his drug and alcohol problems, Scott-Heron didn't release any new material between 1984's "Re-Ron" and 1993's *Spirits*, a lacklustre album that suffered from weak material and the departure of bassist Robert Gordon. However, he came back with a vengeance in 1998. Linking up with TVT Records, Scott-Heron set up his own label, Rumal-Gia and re-released eleven of his albums from the 70s, bulked up with previously unreleased live tracks that featured his often hilarious rap-sermon-lectures on "bluesology".

The Best Of Gil Scott-Heron
1984, Arista

A nearly faultless greatest hits package, this collection surveys Gil Scott-Heron's singles from 1970's "The Revolution Will Not Be Televised" to 1984's "Re-Ron" in revelatory chronological order. You may not always agree with his politics, but the pleasure in Scott-Heron's music is not his message but the way he delivers it.

Shalamar

Belonging to the long and noble tradition of the manufactured pop group, **Shalamar** released a series of lightweight but infectious pop-disco-funk singles in the late 70s and early 80s that have stood the test of time far better than their initial chart placings would have suggested.

The first Shalamar recording was 1977's "Uptown Festival", a fairly horrific medley of

Motown hits ("Going To A Go-Go", "It's The Same Old Song", "I Can't Help Myself", "Stop! In The Name Of Love", etc) over a pile-driver kick drum that would have given even the most devoted disco habitué a migraine. The record was made by a bunch of studio musicians assembled by **Dick Griffey**, the booking agent for the television show *Soul Train*, and **Simon Soussan**, a legendary record collector and a notorious presence on Britain's Northern soul scene. When the song reached the R&B Top 10, they decided to put together a real Shalamar. They retained the original vocalist, **Gary Mumford**, and recruited two of the regular *Soul Train* dancers, **Jody Watley** (Jackie Wilson's goddaughter) and **Jeffrey Daniels**. This line-up recorded a similarly awful version of "Ooh Baby Baby" that same year.

Things really improved when the group moved to Griffey's Solar label and were released from Soussan's Motown fixation. Mumford was replaced by **Gerald Brown** and the group released "Take That To The Bank" in 1978. Despite its truly awful extended metaphor, the track was built on a rock-solid groove that made you forget how thin the vocals were. Brown left the group soon after the song's release and was replaced by **Howard Hewett**. The new line-up had an immediate hit with "The Second Time Around", a bright bubbly teen-pop record produced by **Leon Sylvers**.

"Right In The Socket", which followed in 1980, had a fabulous groove, but Watley trying to sing like a soul mama wasn't exactly convincing. Over the next few years Shalamar had hits with "Make That Move", the adenoidal, thin and fairly wretched "I Can Make You Feel Good" and "A Night To Remember". The group's air-headed feel-good dance music was much better received in Europe than it was in the US and Shalamar had big UK hits in 1982 and 1983 with "There It Is", "Friends", "Dead Giveaway" and "Over And Over", which were all largely ignored at home.

Watley and Daniels left the group at the end of 1983 and were replaced by **Micki Free** and former Miss Teen Georgia **Delisa Davis**. This version of the group contributed songs to the movie soundtracks *DC Cab* (1983), *Footloose* (1984) and *Beverly Hills Cop* (1985), before Hewett left for a solo career in

1985. He was replaced by **Sydney Justin**, a former member of the Los Angeles Rams' football team. The group had a couple more minor hits, but finally called it quits in 1990.

Howard Hewett had some solo success in the late 80s in a self-consciously pretty post-Luther Vandross crooning style with tracks like "I'm For Real", "Stay", "Show Me" and "Strange Relationship". However, the real solo star was Jody Watley. Her "Looking For A New Love", produced **Andre Cymone** and **David Z**, owed more than a little to Janet Jackson's *Control*, but Watley's cool, composed delivery fitted the production and mood perfectly and the "Hasta la vista baby" hook swiped from the movie *Terminator* didn't hurt either.

Watley's self-titled 1987 debut album was a huge hit. It spawned two more Top 10 singles, "Don't You Want Me" and "Some Kind Of Love", and won her a Grammy for Best New Artist. *Larger Than Life* followed in a similar style and with similar success in 1989; "Friends", "Everything" and "Real Love" all went into the Top 10. Watley's hits quickly dried up, however, and her last significant hit came in 1996 when she appeared alongside Hewett and Daniels on Babyface's remake of Shalamar's "This Is For The Lover In You". In 2003 she released *Midnight Lounge*, an album in a late-night club vibe with production from **Dave Warrin** and **King Britt**.

Jody Watley
1987, MCA

This album is a straight Janet Jackson rip, but if all band-wagon jumping was as good as this the world would be a better place. Having given no indication of her singing ability while with Shalamar, Watley is surprisingly good here, snarling and cooing in all the right places.

Shalamar: The Greatest Hits
1999, Capitol/Right Stuff

Here are seventeen tracks of inoffensive dance-pop records that are so harmless even your grandmother will love them. All of Shalamar's hits are present and correct – even the shockingly schlocky "Uptown Festival" – making this the collection to go for.

Dee Dee Sharp

Either damned with faint praise or unfairly dismissed as "the mashed potato queen", **Dee Dee Sharp** was far more than just dance-craze royalty. Sharp was a versatile vocalist with a strength and personality that was rare in the producer-moulded puppets of her age.

Dee Dee Sharp was born **Dione LaRue** in Philadelphia on September 9, 1945. She got her start as a teenager singing back-up on sessions by **Bobby Rydell**, Fabian, Freddie Cannon and **Frankie Avalon** for the teen-pop machine Cameo-Parkway. She also worked with Lloyd Price and Jackie Wilson before recording "Slow Twistin'" as a duet with **Chubby Checker** in 1962. Her first solo single was "Mashed Potato Time", a note-for-note rip-off of The Marvelettes' "Please Mr. Postman" that became a #2 pop hit in 1962. Being in Philadelphia, Sharp appeared on Dick Clark's *American Bandstand* TV show several times and became one of the first African-American female pop idols. She cut several dance-craze discs – "Gravy (For My Mashed Potatoes)", "Ride!", "Do The Bird" and "Wild!" – in quick succession in the early 60s, and all but the last reached the pop Top 10.

In 1965 "I Really Love You", a song written by her future husband, producer extraordinaire **Kenny Gamble**, set Sharp free from the teen shackles and proved her to be an excellent soul singer. However, the flip, "Standing In The Need Of Love", illustrated the problems with shifting styles – Sharp was fine, but the male chorus and the production were simpy terrible. Gamble also wrote the follow-up, "There Ain't Nothin' I Wouldn't Do For You", a record that later became a favourite on the Northern soul scene.

Sharp left Cameo-Parkway soon afterwards and moved to the Atco label. There she released a few singles in a deeper soul style, including 1968's "A Woman Will Do Wrong", a classic reading of a Southern soul ballad written by **Paul Kelly** and **Clarence Reid** that saw Sharp at her most emotional and preacherly. She also recorded a duet with Ben E. King, "We Got A Thing Goin' On", but they were both forcing it.

After several years of musical inaction, during which time she worked for her husband's new management company and record label, Sharp had a minor R&B hit on his Philadelphia International label with a novel reading of 10CC's "I'm Not In Love" in 1976. The single was featured on her 1976 album,

Happy 'Bout The Whole Thing, which also included the disco-happy title track and a fine reading of The Five Stairsteps' "Ooh Child". Recording as Dee Dee Sharp Gamble, she also had a minor R&B hit with the kiss-off record "I Love You Anyway" and a major club hit with "Breaking And Entering" in 1981. That was also the year that she and Kenny Gamble divorced. Although her chart career has taken a downturn since, she still performs regularly on the supper club oldies circuit.

All The Golden Hits
2004, Marginal

Dee Dee Sharp has been poorly served by the reissue market and this is the only available greatest hits package. It is a straight reissue of two Cameo-Parkway packages from the 60s, so it includes none of her later soul recordings and it gives short shrift to her talents as a vocalist. Despite these minor failings, however, this album remains a wonderful collection of teen-pop/dance-craze recordings.

The Shirelles

O ne of the standard articles of rock'n'roll faith is that no good music was made between **Buddy Holly**'s death and the arrival of **The Beatles**. The reason for this bit of dogma is clear: this was the era of the girl group and, as all serious music fans know, teenage girls are responsible for the worst music in creation. Of course, this is absolutely preposterous – the same kind of sexist (not to mention racist) nonsense that holds that jazz wasn't radical until Charlie Parker came along. The fact that girl groups, particularly **The Shirelles**, provided much of the material for the British Invasion always goes unmentioned: The Beatles, **Manfred Mann** and **The Merseybeats** all covered their songs. Two articles of faith that you *can* believe in, however, are that The Shirelles were among the first of the girl groups – after **The Chantels** they were the first to have any real success – and that they were the best.

Originally called The Poquellos, The Shirelles (**Shirley Owens, Beverly Lee, Doris Kenner** and **Addie "Micki" Harris**) were "discovered" by their schoolmate **Mary Jane Greenberg** at a school dance in Passaic, New Jersey. Greenberg's mother, Florence, owned a small record label and in 1959 she formed the Scepter label as an outlet for girls. At the time, the majority of the vocal groups were

male, but the virginal playground chanting of 1958's "I Met Him On A Sunday (Ronde-Ronde)" and the panting melodrama of 1960's "Tonight's The Night" would soon change all that.

The group's breakthrough was 1960's "Will You Love Me Tomorrow". Working with producer **Luther Dixon**, a former R&B singer who had written and produced songs for **Perry Como**, The Shirelles crafted probably the most enduring record about female sexuality ever made. Of course, **Gerry Goffin** and **Carole King**'s lyrics and melody made the task quite easy, but the zing-went-the-strings-of-my-heart production and surging beat borrowed from The Drifters, not to mention Shirley Owens's heartbreakingly naive vocals, really made the record. The flip side, "Boys", later covered by The Beatles, was all simmering lust and its arrangement came to signify the swinging 60s.

Perhaps even better than "Will You Love Me Tomorrow" was The Shirelles' rendition of The "5" Royales' "Dedicated To The One I Love". Released in 1959, the girls' version eventually climbed to #3 in the pop charts in 1961. With its plaintive lead vocal and thrilling doo-wop swoops, "Dedicated" took the puppy love romantic ideals of doo-wop away from the pretty-boy singers and put them in the mouths of the teenage girls who actually bought the records. It was a female doo-wop record taken from the pages of a teenage girl's diary rather than a street corner.

The Shirelles weren't all sweetness and light, however. "Mama Said" had a chorus with more schoolgirl sass than just about any other girl group record, while "Big John" teamed them with a rollicking blues rhythm more typically associated with strip joints and macho bad boys like **Wynonie Harris**. With its outrageous organ solo, "cheat, cheat" chorus and Owens' brilliant vocals, "Baby It's You" said just about everything you need to know about why girls fall in love with bad boys. Produced by the popularizer of the dance craze The Hustle, Van McCoy, 1962's "Stop The Music" was the best catfight this side of Crystal and Alexis trading blows on *Dynasty*, while "Foolish Little Girl" dished up the painful truth without pulling any punches.

The Shirelles hit #1 for the second time with "Soldier Boy" in 1962, but after the release of "Foolish Little Girl", which went to #4, the hits started to dry up. Their mid-60s records "Tonight You're Gonna Fall In Love With Me", "Sha-La-La" (which was covered by Manfred Mann), "Thank You Baby" and "Last Minute Miracle" reached the lower rungs of the R&B chart, but failed to make any impact on the popular consciousness.

The British Invasion is famously credited with stalling The Shirelles' career, but everything from legal disagreements with their label and the girls' marriages to the success of the unofficial "fifth Shirelle" Dionne Warwick, which meant they had to take a back seat, contributed to their downfall in the late 60s and 70s. Changing Shirelles line-ups continued to release a few new singles on a variety of labels during the 70s and they remained active on the oldies circuit until Harris died in 1982.

The Very Best Of The Shirelles
1994, Rhino

This excellent collection slights The Shirelles' later, non-hit records which aren't bad at all, but all their major hits are included. Their slightly adenoidal teenage voices might not have the gravitas of some of the great soul singers, but the longing, fervour and intensity of the best soul music are present and correct.

Shirley & Lee

If there is one group that best represents the sheer effervescence of old-school R&B it is the "Sweethearts of the Blues", **Shirley & Lee**. **Shirley Goodman** (born on June 19, 1936 in New Orleans) and **Leonard Lee** (born June 29, 1936 in New Orleans) recorded a demo tape, together with several other kids from their neighbourhood, at **Cosimo Matassa**'s studio in New Orleans. The demo was heard by **Eddie Messner** of the Aladdin label, who loved Goodman's singular nasal, shrill voice. He signed Lee and Goodman, who had both sung lead on the tape, as a duo and had them re-record the song, "I'm Gone", with a band that included the cream of the Crescent City's musicians (**Dave Bartholomew, Earl Palmer** and **Lee Allen**). The single was a #2 R&B hit in 1952.

Unfortunately, instead of playing up Lee's superb singing, Goodman's unique presence or the mighty swing of the studio band, Messner chose to market the duo as an ongoing teen soap opera on records like "Shirley Come Back To Me", "Shirley's Back", "The Proposal", "Lee Goofed" and "Confessin'". When the saga's commercial appeal ended in 1955, Messner allowed Shirley & Lee to be an R&B group again and they grabbed the chance with the wonderful "Feel So Good", which also reached #2 on the R&B chart.

The next year "Let The Good Times Roll" did one better on the R&B chart and became their first pop smash, reaching #20. One of the truly great R&B records, "Let The Good Times Roll" had it all: rollicking New Orleans rhythms and horns, Goodman at her most coquettish and Lee at his bluesy best, although they were both rarely in tune and alternated between flat and sharp seemingly randomly. The follow-up, "I Feel Good", was more typical rock'n'roll, but only slightly less delightful, while "The Flirt" was a more adult rendering of the music of their early days, but Shirley & Lee were more sly and the band cooked. Changing tastes in R&B quickly rendered the duo old hat, but they continued recording endearing trinkets – such as a version of "Bewildered" that sounded like **Eartha Kitt** on helium singing with **Lloyd Price** at Thano's Wurlitzer Lounge – until 1963.

Goodman moved to LA in the late 60s and, joining a large contingent of expats from New Orleans on the studio scene, she recorded with **Sonny & Cher**, Dr. John and **The Rolling Stones** (she appeared on *Exile On Main Street*). Shirley & Lee reunited as a duo for

Girl Groups

The "girl group sound" was the first genre of popular music that was, definitively, producer's music. As such, it had an ambiguous relationship with soul and R&B, even though all contemporary R&B is producer's music *par excellence*. Girl group music was just as utopian and impossibly passionate as the very best classic soul music – just maybe a little more innocent and a lot more chaste.

The girl group sound had its roots in doo-wop and, more specifically, in a record made by the first all-female vocal group to have a hit on the R&B charts, 1954's "Oop Shoop" by **Shirley Gunter & The Queens**. However, it was doo-wop impresario **George Goldner** that really created that quintessential, polished, girl group sound. Records such as 1957's "Maybe", which he produced for **The Chantels** – one of the very first girl groups – were archetypal girl group singles filled with virginal frustration and longing, and they became some of the genre's most definitive records. **The Bobbettes** had released "Mr Lee" slightly before The Chantels gave us "Maybe", but the earlier song's subject – the group's fifth-grade teacher – was not typical girl group stuff.

The greatest girl group of them all, The Shirelles, standardized the format and sound of female vocal groups in the early 60s and, with the help of Brill Building writers such as **Carole King** and **Gerry Goffin**, they brought a touch of pop craftsmanship to the genre's classic ragged vulnerability. In their wake came a deluge of similar groups: Kathy Young & The Innocents, **Rosie & The Originals**, The Paris Sisters, **The Marvelettes**, **The Sensations**, The Cookies, **The**

Exciters, **The Dixie Cup**s, etc. The true poet of the girl group sound was, of course, **Phil Spector**. As one of the most prominent producers working with girl groups in the 60s, Spector crafted hits for **The Crystals** and **The Ronettes** and, most memorably, for the phenomenal **Darlene Love**.

While Phil Spector codified the girl group sound as the surge and purge momentum of teenage heartbreak and desire, others were producing more atypical girl group records. Songs such as the amazingly ghostly "Sally Go 'Round The Roses" by **The Jaynetts**, the more mature "Mixed Up Shook Up Girl" by **Patty & The Emblems** and the Philly swing of "The 81" by **Candy & The Kisses** showed that the format was capable of more than just tingle and swoon.

Even though the girl group formula was later extended and tweaked by the likes of **The Supremes, Martha & The Vandellas, The Emotions** and **The Three Degrees**, the girl group sound, like doo-wop, was all but killed off by the British Invasion. Yet, ironically, many of the groups that brought about their demise, **The Beatles** included, borrowed extensively from the girl group catalogue.

Various Artists: The Best Of The Girl Groups Vol. 1
1990, Rhino

This album could have done without Cher and Skeeter Davis, but otherwise this 18-track compilation is a superb introduction to the sound that kept rock'n'roll alive while Elvis was in the army. The girl groups were a crucial force in the development of soul music.

PLAYLIST

1 MAYBE The Chantels from **Best Of The Chantels**
There's still a strong whiff of doo-wop here, but this is nevertheless where the girl group sound began.

2 WILL YOU STILL LOVE ME TOMORROW
The Shirelles from **The Very Best of The Shirelles**
Not only the best lyric about teenage sexuality, but also a sterling example of downtown studio craft.

3 SALLY GO ROUND THE ROSES The Jaynetts
from **The Best Of The Girl Groups Vol. 1**
An eerie, ghostly record that is the antithesis of the popular image of the girl group sound.

4 BE MY BABY The Ronettes from
The Best Of The Ronettes
One of the greatest drum intros ever and an utterly infectious chorus make this pop perfection.

5 HE'S SO FINE The Chiffons from
The Best Of The Chiffons

George Harrison was right: this record is so great, it's worth lifting hook, line and sinker.

6 HE'S A REBEL The Crystals from
The Best of The Crystals
Phil Spector's Wrecking Crew at their most potent.

7 TELL HIM The Exciters from
The Best Of The Girl Groups Vol. 2
As dramatic a record as any in the girl group canon.

8 CHAPEL OF LOVE Dixie Cups from
The Best Of The Girl Groups Vol. 1
No Wall of Sound hoodoo here; just a little finger snapping, a leftover jazz horn and an infernal singsong melody.

9 LOVE IS LIKE AN ITCHING IN MY HEART
The Supremes from **The Ultimate Collection**
The heart-attack drum beat makes this the quintessential girl group record.

some oldies shows in the early 70s, but Shirley Goodman then made a startling comeback in 1974 when her old rival **Sylvia Robinson** (formerly of the duo **Mickey & Sylvia**) asked her if she was interested in recording a song she had written. Goodman's cracked-glass voice was perfect on top of the discofied Bo Diddley beat of "Shame, Shame, Shame"– a song that was originally intended for **Donnie Elbert** – and she had her second R&B #1. Goodman continued working with Robinson on the follow-ups "Cry, Cry, Cry" and "I Like To Dance", but couldn't repeat the success of "Shame, Shame, Shame" and soon fell into obscurity. Leonard Lee died aged just 40 on October 23, 1976, while Goodman passed away more recently, on July 5, 2005.

Let The Good Times Roll
2000, Ace

Largely because of the singularity of Shirley Goodman's childlike voice and the novelty aspect of much of their material – most of which was self-penned – Shirley & Lee often don't get the respect they deserve. This 30-track collection of some of the most delightful R&B records ever made is their redemption.

Bunny Sigler

Bunny Sigler, or as he was known in the early days of his career, "Mr. Emotions", was a fine singer in the Marvin Gaye tradition, but his real contribution to the soul world was as Philadelphia's most valuable utility player. Sigler could play a variety of instruments – guitar, piano, bass and trombone – and was perhaps the city's most consistent songwriter after **Gamble & Huff**.

He was born **Walter Sigler** in Philadelphia on March 27, 1941, but nicknamed "Bunny" as a child because he had one prominent buck tooth. He started singing in church as a child and, by the time he was 12 years old, he was singing with his brothers **James** and **Benny** in a doo-wop called **The Opals**. In 1959 Sigler left the group and released the solo single "Promise Me" on the ABC subsidiary label HiLo. A cover of **Junior Parker**'s "Come On Home" followed on the minuscule Craig label in 1961, and Sigler then spent the next few years performing on the Philadelphia/South Jersey club circuit.

In the mid-60s Leon Huff caught Sigler's act and introduced him to producers **John** Madara and **Dave White**, who got him signed to Cameo-Parkway. Sigler recorded "Girl Don't Make Me Wait" with Madara and White for the label in 1966, as well as several uptempo dance records for Decca – "Comparatively Speaking", "For Cryin' Out Loud" and "Let Them Talk" – that later became in-demand tunes on the UK's Northern soul scene. However, Sigler's only hit during this period was a remake of Shirley & Lee's "Let The Good Times Roll", which he recorded in a contemporary uptempo fashion. Another Northern soul favourite, the record – from his 1967 debut album of the same name – was Sigler's biggest hit, reaching #22 on the pop chart.

When Cameo-Parkway folded, Sigler moved to Kenny Gamble's Neptune label. His 1969 release "Great Big Liar" was one of Gamble & Huff's first responses to **Norman Whitfield**'s psychedelic soul productions; Sigler was intense and Gamble & Huff's production was dense and thick, rather than creamy. Sigler's next record was a duet with **Cindy Scott**, "Sure Didn't Take Long (For The News To Get Around)", that was a step backwards in terms of its old-fashioned Motown production, even though both Sigler and Scott were great. Around this time Sigler also started to write and produce material with pianist **Ugene Dozier**. The first act they worked with together was **Talk of the Town**, a group that included **Gene McFadden** and **John Whitehead**.

When Gamble & Huff started their Philadelphia International label, Sigler worked with songwriter **Phil Hurtt** on "Sunshine", "Who Am I", "You Got Your Hooks In Me" and the awesome "Don't Call Me Brother" for The O'Jays; "International Playboy" for Wilson Pickett; "The Mirror Don't Lie" for Joe Simon; "I Could Dance All Night" for Archie Bell & The Drells; and "Sweet Charlie Babe" for Jackie Moore. Sigler also found time to record for the label, and had minor hits with the gorgeous Smokey Robinson-like ballad "Regina" and a funky remake of **Bobby Lewis**'s "Tossin' And Turnin'". His rather overripe reading of "That's How Long I'll Be Loving You" failed to chart in 1973, but his gospel remake of The O'Jays' "LoveTrain" was a substantial R&B hit the following year.

Sigler excelled during the disco era and crafted numerous hits for the group **Instant**

Funk, who had backed him up on "Love Train" as **The TNJs**. Sigler's own biggest hit during this period was 1977's "Let Me Party With You (Party, Party, Party)", a funky disco track not entirely unlike Marvin Gaye's "Got To Give It Up". His duet with **Loleatta Holloway**, "Only You", also packed dance-floors, but his best disco record was probably the pulsating "By The Way You Dance (I Knew It Was You)", which has since been sampled numerous times.

Bunny Sigler has largely concentrated on songwriting and back-up singing since the death of disco, but he did record a couple of singles as **Mr. B** for the Sugar Hill label during the formative days of hip-hop. He returned with his falsetto vocal still intact on *Let Me Love You Tonight* for the British soul label Grapevine in 2003.

⊙ **The Best Of Bunny Sigler: Sweeter Than The Berry**
1996, Epic/Legacy

Licensing restrictions and catalogue nightmares have meant that there has never been a decent retrospective of Sigler's underrated career. This 14-track collection covers his recordings for Philadelphia International, but has none of his Northern soul groovers or disco booty shakers. However, what's left is some very fine, if often overproduced, Philly soul in the trademark 70s style.

Silk

Not to be confused with the 70s vocal group from Philadelphia with the same name, this **Silk** is a five-member vocal group that was discovered by Keith Sweat at a bar-becue in Atlanta, Georgia in 1991. Sweat took the group under his wing and signed them to his Keia label, but not before firing one member of the group and hiring **Gary "Lil' G" Jenkins** from Nashville to be the group's lead singer.

With **Jimmy Gates**, **Timothy Cameron**, **Jonathan Rasboro** and **Gary "Big G" Glenn** following his lead, Jenkins sang Silk's huge hit, "Freak Me", in 1992, in that nasal whine cum melisma that became the sound of early-90s R&B in the wake of Boyz II Men. "Freak Me" was treaclier and perhaps even more explicit than R. Kelly or Jodeci's records and it stayed at the top of the R&B chart for two months and the pop chart for two weeks. Their debut album, 1992's *Lose*

Control, also included the adenoidal R&B top-ten hits, "Girl U For Me" and the title track, which at least had a decent **En Vogue**-style groove going for it.

After a disagreement with Sweat over the direction of the group, Silk left the Keia label for Elektra. On 1995's *Silk* they aimed for a more mature, less sexually suggestive sound with predictably lacklustre commercial appeal – the singing was still as forced as ever. Only "Hooked On You", a by-the-numbers mid-90s R&B jam with a high-pitched synth squeal, was a significant hit, reaching #12 on the R&B chart. Their third album, 1999's *Tonight*, was more of the same, although the group returned to the boudoir – and the upper reaches of the R&B chart – with "Meeting In My Bedroom" and "If You (Lovin' Me)".

Amazingly, by the release of *Love Session* in 2001, Silk's fan base still hadn't totally sickened of their smarmy come-ons and gra-tuitous vocal flourishes. Hopefully, they were turned off by the group's atrocious version of **Rick James** and **Smokey Robinson**'s "Ebony Eyes", however. *Silktime* from 2003 was released on indie label Liquid 8, an indi-cation that time had finally caught up with these saggy Lotharios.

⊙ **The Best Of Silk**
2004, Elektra

The group's singing was over the top at the best of times, so imagine how intolerable the album filler was. This 16-track compilation that hits all the highlights, but includes none of that filler, is surely all the Silk anyone needs.

Joe Simon

During his heyday, **Joe Simon** had one of the most original voices in soul. His bizarre baritone – as wide and deep as Jerry Butler's and, at the same time, constricted and tight – made him an incredibly effective interpreter of tormented country soul songs.

Simon was born on September 2, 1943 in Simmesport, Louisiana. At age 15 he moved with his family to Oakland, California and formed the vocal groups **The Silver Stars** and then **The Golden Tones** (not to be confused with the doo-wop group The Goldentones). The Golden Tones signed with the Hush label in 1959 and recorded "Doreetha" and the eerie doo-wop ballad "Ocean Of Tears", before Simon left for a solo career. Remaining at

Hush, he recorded tracks such as the uptempo "Troubles" and the mournful "I Keep Remembering" in the early 60s. He then recorded the gospel-influenced "Only A Dream" with **Eugene Blacknell**'s band for Irral in 1963, before signing to Vee Jay.

At the new label, Simon immediately had a moderate hit with the lilting "My Adorable One", a song that eventually became something of a country soul standard. However, it was 1965's "Let's Do It Over" – produced by **Rick Hall** in Muscle Shoals – that became his first big hit, thanks to his velvety vocals. Simon also started working with legendary Nashville DJ **John Richbourg** (aka John R), and, when Vee Jay folded soon after the release of "Let's Do It Over", he signed to John R's Sound Stage 7 label and recorded with a band of slumming country musicians. At Sound Stage 7, Simon had hits with "Teenager's Prayer", "My Special Prayer" and the uptempo "Put Your Trust In Me (Depend On Me)". However, it was 1967's "Nine Pound Steel" – a Southern soul classic on which Simon sounded quite like Solomon Burke – and 1968's "(You Keep Me) Hangin' On" that cemented Simon's reputation as a country soul singer of rare talent.

Simon was at his most countrified on a version of an old **Waylon Jennings** hit written by **Harlan Howard**, "The Chokin' Kind", which featured a wonderful bassline. While another Howard song, "Baby, Don't Be Looking In My Mind", along with "San Francisco Is A Lonely Town", showed Simon's propensity for moody ballads. Two more country soul hits, "Farther On Down The Road" and "Yours Love", followed in 1970, as did the country-flavoured "Your Time To Cry", produced by John R.

In 1970 Simon moved to the Spring label, and was soon shipped off to Philadelphia where he worked with the great production and songwriting team of **Gamble & Huff** to record the remarkable "Drowning In The Sea Of Love". The transition between **Norman Whitfield**'s psychedelic soul and the rise of the Philadelphia International sound was perhaps showcased by this record: it began with a Whitfield-style paranoid, overloaded soundworld, which was then replaced by an arrangement that was just as overloaded with rich creamy smooth licks. The juxtaposition of Simon's claxon of a

voice with the slinky Philly soul arrangement was strangely affective and paid dividends on later records, such as "The Power Of Love" and "Theme From Cleopatra Jones", which had an air of excess and melodrama that suited Simon perfectly.

Simon's biggest hit came while he was working with producer **Raeford Gerald**, who had previously crafted tracks for Millie Jackson and had a hit as **Act One** with "Tom The Peeper". The resulting track, 1975's "Get Down, Get Down (On The Floor)", was a disco smash and Simon's only entry into the pop Top 10. While he had follow-up hits with "Music In My Bones" and "I Need You, You Need Me", "Get Down" effectively stymied Simon's career by forcing him to put aside his interpretive abilities and try dance-floor material on every subsequent record.

Bizarrely, Simon signed to the Nashville-based Posse label in 1981. Working with country hack **Porter Wagoner**, he released the funky *You Came My Way* and had a couple of modest R&B hits with "Glad You Came My Way" and "Are We Breaking Up". He then recorded several sides in the old-fashioned country soul style, including a version of **Lee Greenwood**'s "It Turns Me Inside Out" in 1985, before dropping out of secular music altogether to became a minister at the Cathedral of Joy Church in Illinois.

Music In My Bones: The Best Of Joe Simon
1997, Rhino

This 20-track compilation chronologically covers every aspect of Simon's career from his stint at Sound Stage 7 to his Spring recordings. It is divided in half, with "Drowning In The Sea Of Love" the dividing line between the country soul of his early career and the lusher arrangements that characterized his 70s material, and it is an excellent introduction to one of the most original soul vocalists.

Sister Sledge

Atlantic Records were so grateful to Chic main men **Bernard Edwards** and **Nile Rodgers** for the colossal financial success of 1978's *Le Freak* that they offered them the choice of producing anyone on the label's roster. They could have chosen Aretha Franklin, The Spinners, Donny Hathaway, Roberta Flack... even **Crosby, Stills & Nash**, but, like the iconoclasts they were, they picked a group that had barely had a hint of a hit during their five years at the label. Chic wanted to work with a group that still lacked a fixed identity, and they chose run-of-the-mill girl group **Sister Sledge**.

Kathie, Joni, Debra and **Kim Sledge**, the granddaughters of opera singer Viola Williams, had started recording as Sisters Sledge as teenagers in 1971. Based in Philadelphia, they released some material on the Money Back label, and worked as back-up singers for **Gamble & Huff**'s Philadelphia International operation. After signing to Atlantic as Sister Sledge in 1973, they had some minor success with the proto-disco record "Love Don't Go Through No Changes On Me" and "Mama Never Told Me", which reached the British Top 20 in 1975. By and large, however, they toiled in the background for half a decade until Chic rescued them from obscurity. Recognizing that lead singer Kathie was, in traditional soul terms at least, one of the most skilled vocalists in disco, Rodgers and Edwards subtly changed the standard Chic formula. Instead of crafting the kind of strangely cryptic, ambivalent songs they wrote for Chic's female singers, Rodgers and Edwards gave Sister Sledge undeniably anthemic songs that downplayed Chic's disembodiment in favour of full-blooded disco-gospel release.

The first single from Sister Sledge's 1979 album *We Are Family* was "He's The Greatest Dancer". Led by an amazing, popping, guitar figure from Rodgers, the single became the group's first major hit, reaching the pop Top 10

and #1 on the R&B chart. It featured some of the Chic musicians' finest playing: Rodger's guitar, Edwards' fluid, if undermixed, bassline, **Tony Thompson**'s hard-hitting drums, **Raymond Jones**' best Fender Rhodes lines and some impeccable stuff from **Concert Master Gene Orloff**'s **Chic Strings**. As well as boasting one of the great disco breakdowns, the song also highlighted Rodgers and Edwards' songwriting prowess. Lines like "Arrogance, but not conceit/As a man he's complete" and the immortal rhyme, "Halston, Gucci, Fiorucci", showcased their gift for absurdist, plain-speech lyrics.

The album's best writing, however, was to be found on "Lost In Music". The song was never released as a single, but it struck a universal chord. Where Chic might have emphasized the "Caught in a trap/No turning back" part of the lyric with haunted vocals and deep spaces in the groove, Sister Sledge embodied the "I feel so alive/I quit my nine to five" refrain with Kathie's swoops and curlicues and Rodgers' surging, uplifting chicken-scratch riffing.

The album's title track was even bigger. Based on a riff stolen from Children of God (a group Rodgers admired when he was a hippy), "We Are Family" might have been a gospelesque get-happy tune about the joys of sisterhood, but it quickly became an all-purpose anthem used by everyone from feminists and gay rights activists to the Pittsburgh Pirates baseball team.

Sister Sledge's next album, 1980's *Love Somebody Today*, was also produced by the Chic Organization. However, Edwards and Rodgers were overextending themselves at that time and, despite containing one great single, "Got To Love Somebody", the album failed to recapture the same magic as *We Are Family*. **Narada Michael Walden** gave Sister Sledge a fine post-disco makeover on *All American Girls* the next year, while 1982's *The Sisters* included a minor hit cover of Mary Wells's "My Guy". However, as singers with more sass and less gospel flavour began to take over R&B, the Sledges fell out of favour with American audiences.

The fairly awful "Frankie" gave the group one last out-of-the-blue #1 hit in the UK in 1985. Kathy Sledge tried her hand at a solo career, releasing *Heart* in 1992 and fronting several pop-house productions in the early 90s, before reuniting with her sisters for the surprisingly strong *African Eyes* in 1997. Sister Sledge have since remained active on the concert circuit, releasing several live albums in recent years.

We Are Family
1979, Cotillion

Produced by Nile Rodgers and Bernard Edwards, who also co-wrote a number of the songs, this is as much a Chic album – and masterpiece – as it is the best original album by Sister Sledge. A collaboration made in heaven, the men of Chic brought out the best in the four sisters and gave them their signature tune.

The Best Of Sister Sledge (1973–1985)
1992, Rhino

Although it lacks all of the stunning ballads from *We Are Family*, this is a decent 18-track compilation that chronologically traces the career of one of soul's most underrated singing groups. It holds just about everything that a non-obsessive could possibly want and is a good introduction to their lesser-known pre-Chic, pre-disco hits.

Slave

At their best, the Dayton, Ohio-based funk troupe **Slave** pushed the Parliament-Funkadelic sound to its extreme thanks to their guitarist **Mark "Drac" Hicks**, who played in a Black Sabbath heavy metal cover band before joining Slave. However, at their worst, Slave made funk that was as weak as water.

Slave was formed in 1975 by trumpeter **Steve Washington**, the nephew of Ohio Players' Ralph "Pee Wee" Middlebrook. The group was originally called **Black Satin Soul** and included Hicks and drummer **Tim Dozier** before bassist Mark Adams, horn players Floyd Miller and **Tom Lockett**, guitarist Danny Webster and keyboardist Carter Bradley joined. Working with New Jersey radio DJ **Jeff Dixon**, the renamed Slave had their first R&B #1 with their very first record, the gimmicky but thumping "Slide", for the Cotillion label in 1977. The group's self-titled debut album, released that same year, had more monstrous grooves in the form of "Screw Your Wig On Tight", "Party Harty" and "Son Of Slide", while the follow-up *The Hardness Of The World* jammed almost as hard with tracks like "The Party Song" and the synth-heavy "Baby Sinister".

In 1978 **Rodger Parker** replaced Tim Dozier as drummer and new vocalists **Steve Arrington** and **Starleana Young** came on board, which smoothed out the group's sound. This more streamlined brand of funk engendered a big hit with "Just A Touch Of Love", in which Steve Arrington was at his least offensive on top of the best groove the band ever came up with.

Soon afterwards, however, the group's founder Steve Washington left to form the new group **Aurra** with Young, Lockett and vocalist **Curtis Jones**. Aurra had a cult disco hit in 1980 with "When I Come Home", which was mixed by the great **Larry Levan**, but their biggest hit was the following year's sublime post-disco R&B record "Make Up Your Mind". After a few more minor dancefloor hits in a similar style, Aurra fizzled out, but Jones and Young reorganized in 1987 as **Déja** and had a big R&B hit with "You And Me Tonight".

Slave, meanwhile, continued to have hits with a more straight-ahead brand of 80s funk. "Watching You" was one of the definitive 80s R&B tracks: the funk was shackled to the keyboards rather than vice-versa, and Arrington perfected that forced vocal sound that would become the bane of R&B. "Snap Shot" began a bit like one of the **Clash**'s funk excursions before metamorphosing into a weird matrix of slap bass, gurgling guitar, wild synth washes, scything strings and Arrington singing like Michael Jackson having an orgasm. Other tracks, such as 1981's "Party Lites", were more straightforward disco records, only three years too late.

In 1982 Steve Arrington left Slave for a solo career. His debut, *Steve Arrington's Hall Of Fame*, released on Atlantic in 1983, was another definitive 80s R&B platter. It included both party-rockers (the eternal "Weak At The Knees" and the bass-heavy "Nobody Can Be You") and smooth bedroom ballads ("Beddy-Biey"). By the mid-80s, Arrington's plodding inflectionless vocals became too much to bear, although he continued to have a few more hits with the awful "Feel So Real" and "Dancin' In The Key Of Life".

Following Arrington's departure, Slave had became increasingly uninspired. After the release of their single "Shake It Up" in 1983, subsequent records, such as "Ooohh" and "Juicy-O", failed to shake anyone up. The group plodded on until 1996's *Masters Of The Funk*, an album of new recordings of their biggest hits.

⊙ **Stellar Fungk: The Best Of Slave Featuring Steve Arrington**
1994, Rhino

This 15-track compilation gives short shrift to Mark Hicks' guitar antics, but it does nail all of the group's highlights. As a bonus, it includes five of Steve Arrington's solo tracks, which, for better or worse, helped shape the course of R&B during the 80s.

Percy Sledge

Few soul singers have become so completely identified with a single song as **Percy Sledge**. His very first recording, 1966's "When A Man Loves A Woman", became the first Southern soul record to hit #1 in the US pop charts and remains perhaps the most-played slow dance tune of all time.

You've probably heard it a thousand times, but if you actually listen to it carefully you may well realize that it's not quite what it seems. While couples embrace tightly and shuffle slowly across dancefloors wherever "When A Man Loves A Woman" is played, the lyrics, written by **Cameron Lewis** and **Andrew Wright**, don't exactly encourage you to cuddle up to your baby.

A mixture of a cautionary tale about being played for a fool and a plea to a woman not to take advantage of the singer, "When A Man Loves A Woman" is a forlorn ballad in the classic Southern soul tradition. While the funereal organ and the tick-tocking cymbal seem to suggest that the singer and his "loving eyes that don't see" will repeat the same mistakes all over again, Sledge doesn't quite sing it that way. Resigned to the fact that he's doomed to love the wrong woman, but determined that his passion won't be taken for granted this time, Sledge turns the song into an affirmation of the power of love to transcend all reason.

It's this combination of passion and long-sufferance that makes Percy Sledge one of the finest Southern soul singers. An unholy conjugation of **Ernest Tubb** and Otis Redding, Sledge combined the boohoos of country with the pow of soul. Born in Leighton, Alabama, in 1941, Sledge was working as a nurse when he joined vocal group **The Esquires Combo** in the early 60s. After going solo a few years later, he started to record in nearby Sheffield under the auspices of local disc jockey **Quin Ivy**. He was backed by the same session men who were to make the name of Fame Studios in nearby Muscle Shoals: guitarist **Jimmy Johnson**, organist **Spooner Oldham**, bassist **Junior Lowe** and drummer **Roger Hawkins**. It's not just that all these guys – aside from Sledge – were white that made his music remarkable, it was the fact that they managed to fuse allegedly incompatible black and white musical styles while racial turmoil raged all around them.

The follow-up to "When A Man Loves A Woman", "Warm And Tender Love", was about as country as a soul singer could get without being **Conway Twitty**. By contrast, Sledge's third single of 1966, "It Tears Me Up", adhered to the standard Southern soul formula – clockwork percussion, dragging tempo, church organ, bleary horn interjections and twangy guitar punctuation. However, Sledge's performance was anything but standard. He portrayed an anguish so deep that it made you want to tear your hair out. His rendition of "Drown In My Own Tears" the following year never approached the bluesy exhaustion of Ray Charles's version; instead, Sledge sounded like he was writing a suicide note. That same year, the smouldering ballad "Out Of Left Field" found Sledge reprising the atmosphere of "When A Man Loves A Woman", but his second major hit didn't come until "Take Time To Know Her" in 1968, one of soul's great cautionary tales.

By the end of the 60s, Sledge's popularity had waned. Neither "My Special Prayer" nor "Any Day Now" did more than dent the R&B charts in 1969, and in 1973 the Atlantic promos department dreamed up the idea of having new signings Sister Sledge provide the backing vocals on his "Sunshine". The following year, Sledge signed to Capricorn and, in the face of the Southern rock explosion, cut one of the last soul albums recorded in Muscle Shoals, *I'll Be Your Everything*, in 1974. A mix of classic Southern soul and a sprinkling of country covers, the album yielded Sledge's last hit when the title track surprisingly climbed into the R&B Top 20.

Sledge continued to tour throughout the 70s and 80s, and proved particularly popular with white country audiences. In 1985 he recorded a country album, *Wanted Again*, which wasn't released until 1989 and featured slightly hokey versions of standards like George Jones's "She Thinks I Still Care" and Jim Reeves' "He'll Have To Go". In 1994 the well-received comeback album *Blue Night* found Sledge on more stable soul/blues terrain. He has maintained a busy touring schedule ever since and, in 2004, he belatedly followed-up once again with *Shining Through The Rain*, a similar take on contemporary country soul.

 It Tears Me Up: The Best Of Percy Sledge
1992, Rhino/Atlantic

Percy Sledge is rivalled only by Joe Tex as the definitive country soul singer, thanks to his histrionic style that has much in common with his cry-in-your-beer cousins from the other side of the tracks. Apart from perhaps "Love Me Tender", there are no overt country covers on this collection of his best Atlantic sides, but the empathy between the two genres shines through.

Blue Nights
1994, Pointblank/Virgin

This Grammy contender from the mid-90s is not to be missed. Despite having one of the most immediately recognizable voices of 60s soul, Percy Sledge had fallen into virtual obscurity prior to this release. With strong material, superb production and a diversity of styles, *Blue Nights* is a contemporary soul *tour de force*.

Sly & The Family Stone

The Beatles, the Rolling Stones, The Temptations and James Brown may have had more hits, but no one epitomized the late 60s and early 70s more than Sly & The Family Stone. While other bands paid lip service to such 60s ideals as racial integration, sexual equality and fighting the establishment, the erstwhile Sylvester Stewart and his clan put the rhetoric into practice with some of the most radical, perfectly crafted, galvanizing music ever. Of course, when the 60s were shown up as nothing but lies, damned lies, no one felt the effects, or raged against the dying of the light, as much as Sly Stone.

Born March 15, 1944 on the outskirts of Dallas, Texas, Sylvester Stewart first recorded as an 8-year-old with his brother and sisters as The Stewart Four on the record, "On The Battlefield For My Lord", put out by the Church of God in Christ. As part of The Stewart Brothers, he then recorded a couple of daft secular singles before becoming part of the Bay Area band scene while in high school. His group The Viscaynes released a few singles for various local labels and Sly started to DJ at a couple of local radio stations, most prominently KSOL and KDIA.

Sylvester Stewart became an in-house producer and songwriter at San Francisco's Autumn Records label in 1964. Originally crafting Bobby Freeman's dance-craze hit, "C'mon And Swim", Stewart then went on to produce chart hits for white rock bands like the Beau Brummels and The Mojo Men as well as his own less successful records like "Buttermilk" and "I Just Learned How To Swim". However, after attempting to rein in the chaos of psychedelic bands like The Warlocks (soon to become The Grateful

Sly Stone learning to deal with his tonsurophobia (look it up)

Dead) and forcing Great Society to do 200 takes of "Free Advice", Stewart got fed up with the Haight-Ashbury scene, changed his name to Sly Stone and created his own variant of psychedelia.

In order to create his fantasy world in which the libertarian axioms of Haight-Ashbury's privileged white bohemia were actually applied to the struggle for civil rights, Sly recruited trumpeter **Cynthia Robinson**, sax player **Jerry Martini**, pianist **Rosie Stone** (his sister), guitarist **Freddie Stone** (his brother), drummer **Greg Errico** and bassist **Larry Graham**. The group's creation was an undeniable combination of stadium rock propulsion, gratuitous effects, proto-funk grooves and gospel-style positivity applied to the real world that made politics sound fun and fun sound like politics. While black nationalists were preaching sep-

Soul-Rock

The lines between soul and rock'n'roll have always been blurred: is doo-wop proto-soul or proto-rock'n'roll? How do you categorize **Little Richard** and **Fats Domino**? What about **Elvis Presley** who has 34 Top 20 R&B hits? Or **The Beatles** and **The Rolling Stones** who both drew enormous inspiration from soul and covered many soul records? Then, of course, there's Parliament-Funkadelic who rocked harder and out-grooved just about everyone in both genres. Unfortunately, the boundaries between soul and rock have become delineated across racial, rather than stylistic, lines.

Unquestionably, the two greatest soul-rock artists were Sly & The Family Stone and Parliament-Funkadelic because they seamlessly fused the guitar-crunching imperatives of rock with grooves and the communitarian spirit of soul better than anyone else. However, the first soul-rock artists were **The Chambers Brothers** from rural Mississippi. When they moved to New York in the 60s, they recruited white drummer **Brian Keenan**, who pushed their music in a more rock-orientated direction. Their first records were in a gospel-folk style, but in 1966 with "All Strung Out Over You", which sounded like a British Invasion cover of a Motown tune, they started adding rock guitars to their gospel vocal chops. On 1967's *The Time Has Come* they ventured further into psychedelia with "Time Has Come Today" and rocked up their soul harmonies on "I Can't Stand It" and "Uptown".

While it often seemed that psychedelic soul was nothing more than a fuzz guitar on top of a standard vocal group arrangement, it wasn't all one-way traffic – rock took just as much influence from soul as it gave. Before joining Motown, **Rare Earth** was a gigging Detroit group in the mould of the great white R&B band, Mitch Ryder & The Detroit Wheels. In 1968 Rare Earth recorded an album for the Verve label under the direction of **Mike Theodore** and **Dennis Coffey**, who pushed them in a more psychedelic direction. When the group moved to Motown in 1970, they were put under the control of **Norman Whitfield**, who turned them into a sort of Pat Boone in reverse: they covered his "Get Ready", "(I Know) I'm Losing You", "Smiling Faces Sometimes", "Hum Along And Dance". Their lack of singing abilty allowed Whitfield to indulge his most psychedelic tendencies, particularly on their ludicrous 21-minute version of "Get Ready". However, drummer **Pete Rivera** was the star of the show. He enamoured the group to both the early disco scene (several DJs made their own edits of "(I Know) I'm Losing You" and "Happy Song") and to beat diggers.

While the British Invasion would have been impossible without African-American music, only a handful of British groups had any impact on Afro-America. The late 60s beat combo **Timebox** recorded a few stellar covers of soul records, but their most important disc was a string-filled 1968 version of The Four Season's "Beggin'", which became one of the first disco records. Organist **Brian Auger**'s records with **Julie Driscoll** and his band **Oblivion Express** have also been popular sources of hip-hop beats.

The disco boom saw many rock artists make disco records in the hopes of shifting product:

aratism, the diverse racial make-up of the Family Stone made crossover seem like a political utopia. Perhaps even more radical was the crucial role women played as instrumentalists, not just vocal wallpaper to round out the band's sound.

Both gorgeous cacophony ("I Want To Take You Higher" and "Sing A Simple Song") and perfectly crafted pop bliss ("Everyday People" and "Hot Fun In The Summertime"), the band's music gave life to the greatest protest songs ever written. The messages were so strong that the band became a totem for the Woodstock nation and they tore the joint up at Yasgur's farm. The band's arrangements, which perfectly mirrored the lyrics, emphasized the variety of individual voices, both instrumental and vocal. While nearly all of soul's vocal groups grew out of the tradition of gospel harmonizing which featured tight ensemble singing and a defined lead singer, on tracks like "Dance To The Music" and "M'Lady" the Family Stone emphasized each group member's unique voice in arrangements that felt as if they were off the cuff and free-form, even though they were obsessively produced down to the last detail.

By 1970, however, 60s idealism was dead and buried and its promises had been revealed as lies. Sly responded with a single far removed from the anthemic heights of old. One of the five greatest singles ever, "Thank You (Falettinme Be Mice Elf Agin)"

Rod Stewart, The Rolling Stones, Bryan Adams, Rick Wakeman, Kiss. However, when disco went back underground it merged with that other outlaw music, post-punk, to create a potent meeting of groove and grate whose effects are still being felt in music today. Most notable among these were records by **James White & The Blacks**, **Was (Not Was)**, Delta 5, Gang of Four, A Certain Ratio, ESG, Liquid Liquid, Konk and Pigbag.

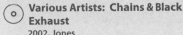

Various Artists: Chains & Black Exhaust
2002, Jones

Chains & Black Exhaust is a stunning compilation of black rock tracks from the early 70s put together by record collector extraordinaire Dante Carfagna. The rhythm tracks on just about all the records may be hotter and funkier than any rock jam this side of Atomic Rooster and The James Gang, but these are resolutely guitar records and often completely hallucinogenic ones at that: check out the wild and gratuitous feedback on The Young Senators' "Ringing Bells, Part 2" and Jade's ferocious "Paper Man".

PLAYLIST

1 TIME HAS COME TODAY The Chambers Brothers from **Time Has Come: The Best Of The Chambers Brothers**
Soul and psychedelic excess: two great tastes that taste great together.

2 DON'T CALL ME WHITEY, NIGGER Sly & The Family Stone from **Stand!**
Rock, soul, who cares?

3 SUPER STUPID Funkadelic from **Maggot Brain**
Still the greatest heavy metal record ever.

4 DEVIL WITH A BLUE DRESS ON/GOOD GOLLY MISS MOLLY Mitch Ryder & The Detroit Wheels from **Rev Up: The Best Of Mitch Ryder & The Detroit Wheels**
High-octane frat rock mash-up of Shorty Long and Little Richard.

5 HAPPY SONG Rare Earth from **Back To Earth**
Motown melody and percussion plus hairy mastodon stomp equals soul-rock perfection.

6 BEGGIN' Timebox from **Club Au Go-Go Volume Seven**
They may have evolved into prog-boogie nightmares, but Timebox's single stroke of genius is this Four Seasons cover that was a favourite in the early New York discos.

7 CYNTHY RUTH Black Merda from **Chains & Black Exhaust**
Punk-funk decades before the fact.

8 PAPER MAN Jade from **Chains & Black Exhaust**
One word: cowbell. A few more: what an amazin' riff.

9 CONTORT YOURSELF James White & The Blacks from **Mutant Disco**
Archetypal twitchy funk-punk guitar riff from the great Robert Quine.

10 WHEEL ME OUT Was (Not Was) from **Out Come The Freaks**
Cathartic yet eerie and uncomfortable, cryptically political, full of nuance and intrigue: everything great about the merging of post-punk and dance music in the early 80s.

was the group's most uncompromisingly funky record yet. Beginning with a vignette where Sly wrestled with "the devil", "Thank You (Falettinme Be Mice Elf Agin)" went on to vent Sly's anger at his betrayal: "Thank you for the party, but I could never stay", "Dying young is hard to take, but selling out is harder". He then mocked the catch phrases of his old hits and, with the sardonic title phrase, the message was clear.

By 1971 the group's new album was endlessly delayed, Sly wasn't showing up for concerts, he was wrestling with drug addiction, he was getting death threats and there were rumours that black nationalist leaders were trying to force him to make his music more radical. When *There's A Riot Goin' On*

finally emerged in November 1971, the joy, the gorgeous mosaic of voices and the "different strokes for different folks" tolerance had vanished. In their places were scorn, derision and dead spots so vast you felt like you'd just fallen off the end of the world. The deadest spot of all was the title track which clocked in at 0:00. While Marvin Gaye was making *What's Going On* as an article of faith in the power of pop music, Sly was highlighting his pessimism by sardonically pointing out that nothing was going on.

At times, listening to *There's A Riot Goin' On* is a bit like being stuck at a party with an incoherent drunk struggling not to pass out. When he wasn't gurgling and wailing like a hungry baby, Sly sang like he was talking to

PLAYLIST
Sly & The Family Stone

1 DANCE TO THE MUSIC from
Dance To The Music
Blends James Brown and The Who so seamlessly that you can't figure out where the rock stops and the soul begins.

2 M'LADY from **Life**
Churning funk almost identical to the above, but the groove is so ferocious you won't care.

3 I WANT TO TAKE YOU HIGHER from **Stand!**
Boom-lacka-lacka-lacka-boom.

4 EVERYDAY PEOPLE from **Stand!**
Sly took pop's great subject, "everybody is a star", and made it a political statement of empowerment, belonging and belief.

5 STAND from **Stand!**
Sly desperately tries to apply the solipsism of acid rock to the real world.

6 THANK YOU (FALETTINME BE MICE ELF AGIN) from **Greatest Hits**
Snarling funk vamp that is one of the group's greatest records.

7 FAMILY AFFAIR from **There's A Riot Goin' On**
Perhaps Sly Stone's best record about being trapped by fate.

8 QUE SERA SERA (WHATEVER WILL BE, WILL BE) from **Fresh**
Sly turns a sickly sweet Doris Day chestnut into a gospel hymn.

9 IF YOU WANT ME TO STAY from **Fresh**
As savage and brutal a kiss-off as Bob Dylan's "Positively Fourth Street".

10 LOOSE BOOTY from **Small Talk**
A record that pops with weird energy, but what do Shadrach, Meshach and Abednego have to do with loose booty?

his chest. However, for all that, Sly was the only one telling the truth, and those bits and pieces that you can make out from his mumble and the instrumental fog hit like a boot to the gut: "Out and down, ain't got a friend/ Don't know who turned you in", "Time they say is the answer/But I don't believe it", "Dying young is hard to take, but selling out is harder".

The music felt just as incomplete as the lyrics, but perhaps only in comparison to the glorious overload of the group's old records. With its early use of a primitive drum machine, slow – really slow – tempos, scratchy guitar, one-note organ drones, deconstructed James Brown horn riffs and almost schematic basslines, *There's A Riot Goin' On* was Sly & The Family Stone in dub, or maybe in photo-negative. It was as precisely detailed as "I Want to Take You Higher" or "Dance To The Music", only dragged through the ringer.

On 1973's *Fresh*, Sly may have retreated from such an uncompromising vision, but when you stare down the barrel of the gun and survive (sort of), there's nowhere else to go. Many members of the Family Stone had departed by the release of *Fresh*, and although the sound was lighter than *Riot*, it wasn't exactly the barrel full of monkeys of old. Sly may have been singing love songs again, but he also sang about "Babies Making Babies" and gave us a sardonic gospel version of Doris Day's "Que Sera Sera".

The follow-up album, 1974's *Small Talk*, was even more of a retreat. The vibe was summed up by the title of "Can't Strain My Brain". However, the album did include "Loose Booty", Sly's best post-golden age record. The diastrous *High On You* the following year was credited only to Sly, but reorganizing a new Family Stone for 1976's *Heard Ya Missed Me, Well I'm Back* didn't change matters any.

Back On The Right Track was a significant improvement in 1979, if only because tracks such as "Remember Who You Are" sounded like an outtake from *Fresh*. On the other hand, "The Same Thing (Makes You Laugh, Makes You Cry)" just dragged and sounded too much like **Peter Frampton**. That same year, Epic decided to release the shockingly awful *Ten Years Too Soon*, a collection of dreadfully dull disco remixes of the group's classic hits.

Sly spent 1981 hanging around the most talented of his progeny, **George Clinton**. He appeared on Funkadelic's *Electric Spanking Of War Babies* in 1981 and on the P-Funk All-Stars' *Urban Dancefloor Guerillas* in 1983. These sessions also produced much of the music for Sly's own 1983 album, *Ain't But The One Way*, an engaging but way too lightweight collection of period funk pieces.

Sly Stone's final hit was a surprise #2 on the R&B chart with **Jesse Johnson**, 1986's

"Crazay", but he then turned right around and recorded "Love And Affection" with The Motels' **Martha Davis** for the *Soul Man* soundtrack. In 1989 Stone was arrested on cocaine charges and, ever since, he has made only sporadic public appearances. One of the saddest endings to one of the most brilliant careers in popular music.

Stand!
1969, Epic

Stand! is the best early-era Sly & The Family Stone album: a no-holds-barred heavyweight. Here Sly Stone achieved his vision of hard party funk with a biting message. Anchored by the big hit, "Everyday People", the show-stopping "Want To Take You Higher" and the monster jam, "Sex Machine", the effervescent energy of this great band never lets up.

There's A Riot Goin' On
1971, Epic

There's A Riot Goin' On is one of the greatest albums of the 70s because it practised what it preached. The opening line, "Feels so good inside myself, don't wanna move", is its most joyous and one of the few moments when there are voices other than Sly's. The rest of *There's A Riot Goin' On*, cataloguing why Sly doesn't want to move, is set to sketchy, slo-mo grooves too frugged to try to fight their way through the narcotic haze. Rarely have sound and vision been unified to such an extent.

Anthology
1981, Epic

This 20-track collection highlights Sly's golden age, from 1968's "Dance To The Music" to 1973's *Fresh*. A mixture of rock and soul, pop and funk, whites and blacks, men and women, Sly & The Family Stone represented the words of the 60s dream made flesh. While the rock community paid lip service to tolerance and loving each other, the Family Stone were living it. The protest singers may have made their world a drag to live in, but the Family Stone made a joyful noise out of collectivity.

Huey "Piano" Smith

Like every other New Orleans keyboardist, Huey "Piano" Smith (born in New Orleans on January 26, 1934) was a Professor Longhair wannabe. Smith started out as a teenager playing for Guitar Slim and later Earl King. As a session pianist in the 50s, he played on the records of Lloyd Price and Little Richard, before becoming the main songwriter and arranger at New Orleans' Ace label in 1956. At the label, Smith began recording with a group called the Rhythm Aces, who later became **Smith & The Clowns**. Their main achievement was to incorporate Longhair's piano style and parade rhythms into rock'n'roll with a playfulness so infectious that no one seemed to be bothered that **Bobby Marchan**, The Clowns' lead singer, was a drag queen. If their musical legacy wasn't enough, the band's driver was none other than future *Dolemite* and *Avenging Disco Godfather* star **Rudy Ray Moore**.

Smith's first single with The Clowns at Ace was the wonderful double-sided "Everybody's Whalin'/Little Liza Jane", one of the most infectious R&B discs ever. However, he had his first hit in 1957 with the daft novelty record "Rockin' Pneumonia And The Boogie Woogie Flu". Far better was the double-sided "Don't You Just Know It/High Blood Pressure" the following year, which featured Smith's weird piano swing, the drunken horns of **Lee Allen** and **Red Tyler** and the breathtaking pace and feel of drummer **Charles "Hungry" Williams**. The record reached #9 on the pop chart and became Smith's biggest hit.

Smith & The Clowns backed **Frankie Ford** on the irresistible "Sea Cruise" and "Roberta" in 1959, before having their own modest hit with "Don't You Know Yokomo". However, the group started recording trash like the ridiculous "Tu-Ber-Cu-Lucas And The Sinus Blues" and the rote doo-wop single "Dearest Darling" later that year, and sounded very behind the times. They then recorded a few novelty singles for Imperial, before returning to Ace in 1962 and cutting the great dance craze disc, "Pop-Eye". The follow-up "At The Mardi Gras" was a further tribute to the sound of the Crescent City.

In the mid-60s Smith started working with a group called **The Pitter-Pats** and released "It Do Me Good", "Baby You Hurt Me", "I've Got Everything" and "Bury Me Dead" for the Instant label. Around the same time, he also recorded with **The Hueys** and a local hit with the humorous double sider "Coo Coo Over You/You Ain't No Hippie" in 1968. Towards the end of the decade, Smith released some funky New Orleans boogie sides under his own name, including "Two Way Pockaway", "You Got Too" and "The Whatcha Call 'Em". Unfortunately, these would be Smith's last recordings before he became a Jehovah's Witness and quit the music biz entirely.

⊙ **This Is Huey "Piano" Smith**
1998, Music Club

Ever since Rhino withdrew *Serious Clownin'* sometime in the 80s, there were no decent CD retrospectives of Smith's work with the Clowns. However, Music Club rectified the situation in the late 90s with this collection of eighteen of the most gloriously demented and wildly swinging R&B tunes ever committed to tape.

SOS Band

Although these days they are not treated with the respect they deserve, the **SOS Band** were one of the great post-disco R&B groups of the 80s. Working with producers **Sigidi Abdullah** and Jam & Lewis, the SOS Band helped define the sound of the Reagan era, but what is often forgotten is that in androgynous-sounding lead singer **Mary Davis** they had one of the few great voices to emerge during the decade.

The group was formed in Atlanta in 1977 by keyboardist **Jason Bryant**. Originally called Santa Monica, the group also included guitarist Bruno Speight, horn players Willie "Sonny" Killebrew and Billy Ellis, bassist John Simpson and drummer James Earl Jones III. They signed to Tabu Records in 1979, changed their name to SOS Band (although they said in song that it stood for "Sounds of Success", it was actually inspired by Morse code) and recorded their debut single, "Take Your Time (Do It Right)" with Abdallah. With a monstrous synth bassline that would later characterize their records and sublime high-neck guitar

playing, "Take Your Time (Do It Right)" was one of the best and most original rewrites of the Chic formula. The group continued to score R&B hits with Abdallah, although none was as significant or original as "Take Your Time (Do It Right)". These hits included the Kool-&-The-Gang-meets-Studio-54 "SOS (Dit Dit Dit Dash Dash Dash Dit Dit Dit)", from their self-titled debut album in 1980, and the dance track "Do It Now", from their second album, 1982's *Too (SOS 2)*.

With the addition of trumpeter/percussionist **Abdul Ra'oof** and new drummer Jerome Thomas, SOS Band worked with producers **Gene Dozier** and **Ricky Sylvers** on *SOS Band III* in 1982. However, it was a song written by the production team of Jimmy Jam and Terry Lewis that really marked the group as something special. Although "High Hopes" only reached #25 on the R&B chart, its shimmering sheen, synth bassline and slightly angular rhythm defined the sound of the next few years.

The group's 1983 album *On The Rise* was also produced by Jam & Lewis and featured the great "Just Be Good To Me". Despite the pretentious beginning, Mary Davis's vocals and the preposterously fat synth bassline saved the track from drowning in Jam & Lewis's egos and sent it to #2 on the R&B chart. "Tell Me If You Still Care" followed it into the R&B Top 10. The title track of 1984's *Just The Way You Like It* had another ridiculously fat synth bassline underpinning a disembodied ballad and cracked the R&B Top 10 again. "The Finest", a very effective combination of the Minneapolis sound and Loose Ends, reached #2 on the R&B chart, and the more typical "Borrowed Love" was almost as successful. However, these would be the SOS Band's last singles with Mary Davis, who left for a solo career and had modest R&B hits with "Steppin' Out" and "Don't Wear It Out".

With **Chandra Currelly** as lead singer and a new rhythm section of drummer Marcus Williams and bassist Kurt Mitchell, the group worked with producer **Curtis Williams** on 1989's *Diamonds In The Raw*. The new sound was a pop-friendly spin on New Jack Swing that spawned a Top 10 R&B hit with "I'm Still Missing Your Love". The SOS band then had a final R&B chart hit with "Sometimes I Wonder", before disbanding in 1991.

Mary Davis, Jason Bryant and Abdul Ra'oof reunited in 1995. Putting together a new SOS Band, they toured with the comedian Sinbad and appeared on the 1999 *United We Funk* compilation of re-formed old funk bands.

○ **Greatest Hits**
2004, Tabu

This excellent 15-track collection focuses mainly on the SOS Band's dance tracks, but it also include many examples of what they truly excelled at: strangely disembodied semi-ballads with pulsating synth lines that exploited Mary Davis's unique timbre. This is definitive 80s R&B that deserves a far better rep than it has.

Soul II Soul

It sometimes seems as though there are about one hundred people who listen to current R&B in Britain, a condition that tends to give the country's aspiring soul singers a perilous choice: stay trapped in a taste ghetto for the duration of your career or try to compete with the likes of **Jamiroquai** and produce crossover pap for middle-management types. With a combination of genius marketing, a good catch phrase, a couple of great tunes and innovative production, **Soul II Soul** actually managed to take their own agenda into the mainstream rather than being dictated by it.

Soul II Soul was the baby of **Beresford Romeo**, aka **Jazzie B**, a first-generation Briton born on January 26, 1963, the son of Antiguan parents. After graduating from high school, Jazzie and **Philip "Daddae" Harvey** started the Soul II Soul sound system which was modelled after the mobile DJ/dub crews of Jamaica. In 1985 they were hired by Bristol's **Wild Bunch** crew of DJs, producers and party throwers to bring their equipment for a London party. Jazzie and Harvey thought they were being hired as DJs and the misunderstanding escalated into a fight. However, in the way these things usually happen, the Wild Bunch's **Nellee Hooper** and Jazzie went to the pub, became friends, and Hooper joined Soul II Soul.

With a successful club night at Covent Garden's Africa Centre to their name, the group recorded a single, "Fairplay", which was picked up by Virgin subsidiary 10 Records and reached the lower end of the UK's Top 100 in 1988. Engineered by future U2 collaborator **Howie B**, produced and arranged by Jazzie and Hooper and sung by **Rose Windross**, "Fairplay" set out the Soul II Soul formula with tag-lines like "It's all about expression" leaping out from the jazzy keyboard washes. The follow-up single, "Feel Free", featured great Chic-style strings from the **Reggae Philharmonic Orchestra**. It was less focused and the sound never gelled, but it reached #63 in the UK charts nevertheless.

It was on their third single, "Keep On Movin'", that everything came together to produce a Top 5 UK hit and an American R&B #1. Riding the beat from **The Soul Searchers**' "Ashley's Roach Clip", "Keep On Movin'" was one of those singles that immediately announced themselves as something great, inevitable and undeniable. Hooper's production (particularly the strings and the ghostly piano parts) revealed that he had been extensively studying the Chic songbook, while **Caron Wheeler** (who had been promoted from singing back-up on "Feel Free") managed to make the British soul fan's obsession with jazzy oversinging into something more than bohemian irrelevance. In an R&B climate dominated by the likes of Atlantic Starr, **Bobby Brown** and Babyface, "Keep On Movin'" proved that you didn't have to be callow to have an R&B hit.

"Keep On Movin'" anchored their debut album, 1989's *Club Classics Vol. One* (which was released as *Keep On Movin'* in the US), but it wasn't the only standout track. The great "Back To Life" was also included in its original a cappella form, rather than the version issued as a single (their second R&B #1 in the US). Another album track, "Jazzie's Groove", featured what would become Soul II Soul's catch phrase: "A happy face, a thumpin' bass for a lovin' race". "Jazzie's Groove" epitomized the times with its horn stabs and cut-up James Brown beat. As the Soul II Soul collective expanded to include fashion emporiums selling T-shirts, "A happy face..." threatened to become little more than a Frankie Goes to Hollywood-style slogan. But with the explosion of dance music in Britain at the time and the increasing visibility of Britain's black community, the catch phrase became more than a cheap marketing scam and was emblematic of the optimism that accompanied the end of Thatcherism.

Unfortunately, that optimism quickly turned into overextension and in-fighting

British Soul

The first black soul artist to perform regularly in the UK was probably **Mel Turner**. An American who had sung with one of the many Five Crowns line-ups (before they became The Drifters), Turner moved to Britain in 1960 and performed in a style similar to that of Clyde McPhatter. A few years later African-American GIs stationed in the UK started to form soul bands – **Geno Washington & The Ram Jam Band**, Herbie Goins & The Nightimers – as did Caribbean immigrants like Jimmy James & The Vagabonds and Mac & Katie Kissoon.

These displaced singers collided with British musicians who played Motown and Stax like they were reading from a fake book and pop hacks who put "moon-June-spoon" and showbiz glitz into soul's gospel-derived vernacular. It was a strange, uncomfortable combination, perhaps best exemplified by **The Foundations** and their transatlantic hits "Baby, Now That I've Found You" and "Build Me Up Buttercup". Although the group's lead singer Clem Curtis was from Trinidad, he sounded like he was singing phonetic English. The music was similarly awkward, with the reggae-derived guitar chank sitting uneasily with Tom Jones-esque horn charts and cod-Motown rhythms.

Unwittingly, The Foundations had stumbled on the formula that, with minor alterations, came to define a peculiar strain of popular music known as "Europop". The apotheosis of the early Europop style was **Johnny Johnson & The Bandwagon**'s "(Blame It On The) Pony Express": all tortuous metaphors, singsong strings and a Motown beat that was more a dull thud than a strutting stomp. Ironically the group was entirely American and had only relocated to the UK after the British success of "Breakin' Down The Walls Of Heartache".

Of all the early British soul groups, none was more important than **The Equals**. A multiracial band from North London, The Equals were led by **Eddy Grant** from Guyana. Their first single, "Hold Me Closer", was released in 1966, but no one noticed it until the flip side, "Baby Come

Back", became a #1 hit in the Netherlands and Germany. "Baby Come Back" was the perfect Europop record: a singer with a seemingly tentative grasp of English, a bubblegum melody, one of the most metronomic beats imaginable, a trebly guitar and even a bit of ska thrown in at the end. However, The Equals' greatest record was undoubtedly "Black Skin Blue-Eyed Boys". With its relentless energy, driving, ultra-fast bassline, rock-solid drums, woodblock percussion and punchy, Santana-ish guitar style, "Black Skin Blue-Eyed Boys" was one of disco's earliest floor-fillers and first anthems.

Elton John's duet partner **Kiki Dee** was the first British act to be signed to Motown and released "The Day Will Come Between Sunday And Monday" in 1970. But perhaps the best British soul record (aside from Dusty Springfield's *Dusty In Memphis*, which doesn't count because it was recorded in the US) was **The Flirtations**' "Nothing But A Heartache". The Flirtations' lead singer sounded very much like Springfield and the arrangement was chunky and clunky in all the right ways.

In the early 70s the British soul scene fell into the hands of the hacks. Arranger/producer **Gerry Shury** reinforced the pop aspect of British soul in an effort to increase its commercial viability, arranging and producing British hits in a mock soul style for The Fantastics, The Pearls and **Sweet Dreams**. Sweet Dreams were a duo of reggae singer Tony Jackson and Polly Brown, a white singer who occasionally performed in blackface. Shury produced "Up In A Puff Of Smoke" for Brown, a record that got significant play in New York discos thanks to Brown's Diana Ross impersonation and a crunching kick drum/bass/synth bottom end.

In 1974 Gerry Shury hooked up with a producer called **Biddu**, who was working with unknown UK-based soul artists at Nova Studios in Marble Arch. Biddu had been born in 1944 in India, but moved to England in the late 60s where he started making records that imitated the Motown beat and became big on the UK's

for Soul II Soul. Caron Wheeler left the group, while Jazzie seemed more concerned with arranging **Sinead O'Connor**'s "Nothing Compares 2 U" and starting a record label, film production company and talent agency. *Vol. II: 1990, A New Decade* was a comparative dud, with only "Get A Life" and "A Dream's A Dream" approaching the heights of their fine debut album.

Two years later Soul II Soul released their third effort, *Vol. III: Just Right*, which, despite including a couple of OK singles in the shape of "Joy" and "Move Me No Mountain", showed that the life had gone from the band. Hooper had already left the group by this point to concentrate on **Massive Attack**, leaving Jazzie to fumble in the dark on his own. Their next two studio albums, 1995's *Vol. V: Believe* and 1997's *Time For Change*, were

Northern soul scene. Biddu was working with Jamaican soul singer **Carl Douglas** in 1974 on a song called "I Want To Give You My Everything". When they needed a flip side for the single, Douglas suggested one of his own numbers. In the remaining ten minutes of studio time, the song was arranged by Shury, sung by Douglas and recorded by Biddu. It was, of course, "Kung Fu Fighting", the record that kicked down the door and brought Eurodisco to the US.

The British undoubtedly committed numerous crimes in the name of disco, but **Hi-Tension**'s "Hi-Tension" (1978) and **The Real Thing**'s "Can You Feel The Force" (1979) brought some respectability back to British soul. The "woo woo woo" bit on "Can You Feel The Force" was one of the few great hooks that British soul bands have come up with – shame about the rest of the record, though.

In the 1980s **Linx**, David Grant and Peter "Sketch" Martin had transatlantic success with utterly generic bass grooves like "You're Lying"

and "Together We Can Shine". **Imagination** – singer Leee John, keyboardist Ashley Ingram and drummer Errol Kennedy – worked a similar territory and had hits with bright 80s dance pop tunes like "Just An Illusion". Other 80s acts, including Loose Ends and Soul II Soul, managed to improve the image of British soul, but nostalgic pastiche acts like The Pasadenas and pop-soul nonsense like Gabrielle's "Dreams" soon brought it right back down again.

Various Artists: British Hustle: The Sound Of British Jazz-Funk From 1974–1982
2003, Soul Jazz

Perhaps not the most representative of compilations, but in this instance that's no bad thing. The Brits excelled at jazz-funk perhaps because the pop sheen demanded by the UK market doesn't have to clash with grit. These thirteen tracks by groups like Hi-Tension, Central Line, The Real Thing, Olympic Runners and Atmosfear show that the US and UK don't have to be two countries separated by a common tongue.

 **PLAYLIST**

1 SON OF A PREACHER MAN **Dusty Springfield** from **Dusty In Memphis**
What all British soul should sound like – probably because it was recorded in America.

2 BLACK SKIN BLUE-EYED BOYS **The Equals** from **The Best Of The Equals**
Eddie Grant's finest moment and Britain's biggest contribution to disco.

3 NOTHING BUT A HEARTACHE **The Flirtations** from **One Kiss Can Lead To Another: Girl Group Sounds Lost And Found**
A rare record where the singer's limitations don't matter because she's swept along with the great arrangement.

4 HANGIN' ON A STRING (CONTEMPLATING) **Loose Ends** from **The Best Of Loose Ends**
A masterpiece of mid-80s production, and one of the few records of the era to wrench some emotion out of the stereo panning and the drum-machine woodblock sounds.

5 MAMA USED TO SAY **Junior** from **Ji**
Sure it begins like a U2 record, but then the synth bass smacks you in the gut and the growling, soaring chorus impels you to the dancefloor.

6 BABY, NOW THAT I'VE FOUND YOU **The Foundations** from **Now That I've Found You**
Singsong, pleading cod-soul that is the fundamental building block of all Europop.

7 BACK TO LIFE **Soul II Soul** from **Club Classics Vol. 1**
Here the hipper-than-thou Brit soul intelligentsia finally decides to communicate to the hoi polloi.

8 HI-TENSION **Hi-Tension** from **Hi-Tension**
The first single by this journeyman British jazz funk group did to the Chic guitar riff what Nile Rodgers did to the James Brown chicken scratch: magnified its intensity in order to reinterpret and refocus the funk.

even worse. Soul II Soul have since carried on largely as they were originally founded – as a sound system, party-throwing collective – and they host an R&B/reggae festival every spring in Antigua.

Club Classics Vol. One
1989, 10/Virgin

Soul II Soul's first album was the first, and only, time that modern British soul music has managed to make its fashion statement shtick signify. With tracks as great as "Keep

On Movin'" and "Back To Life", even distance and over-familiarity haven't worn this album thin. The 1999 tenth anniversary reissue of this album includes the single version of "Keep On Movin'" and several other remixes.

The Spaniels

One of the most important of the early vocal groups, **The Spaniels** were also one of the few to have any sort of success during the soul era. The whimpering voice of lead singer **Thornton James "Pookie" Hudson** became one of the building blocks of doo-wop and influenced later soul singers like **Aaron Neville**.

Hudson was originally the lead singer of a high-school group called The Four Bees in Gary, Indiana. All the other members of the group graduated a year before Hudson, so in 1952 he joined another high-school group that included **Opal Courtney**, **Gerald Gregory**, **Willie Jackson** and **Ernest Warren**. Calling themselves Pookie Hudson & The Hudsonaires, they were spotted by **Vivian Carter** and **Jimmy Bracken** who had just founded their Vee-Jay label. For their first record, 1953's "Baby, It's You", the group was renamed The Spaniels after Gregory's wife said that they sounded like a bunch of dogs. The interaction between Hudson's pleading and Gregory's mildly comic bassline made "Baby, It's You" one of the archetypal doo-wop records.

The next year's "Goodnite Sweetheart, Goodnite" was even better and would have been a huge hit for the group were it not for The McGuire Sisters' wretched cover version which reached the pop Top 10 and destroyed The Spaniels' thunder. Before their next chart hit, "You Painted Pictures", Courtney and Warren were both drafted, and they were replaced by **James Cochran**. Hudson also briefly left the group, but returned in 1956 for the great "You Gave Me Piece Of Mind", a commercial flop that is now treasured by doo-wop collectors.

The Spaniels had modest pop success in 1957 with "Everyone's Laughing", but missed out on potential superstardom that year when they declined Hank Ballard's immortal dance-craze tune "The Twist". A swinging version of "Stormy Weather" and the cha-cha record "I Know" soon followed, but The Spaniels already sounded a bit too archaic by this point and they broke up in 1961.

Going solo, Hudson recorded a fairly lame solo version of Huey "Piano" Smith's "John Brown" in 1962, before teaming up with **The Imperials** (minus **Little Anthony**) for "Jealous Heart". Hudson struggled somewhat with the new style, but the purity of his tone and the zinging strings rescued the record. In 1966 he recorded the Northern

soul classic "This Gets To Me", which was a dead ringer for "This Old Heart Of Mine", for the Jamie label.

Joining a new line-up of Spaniels in 1970, Hudson hit the R&B chart for the final time with the **Lloyd Price**-produced "Fairy Tales". With various line-ups that always included Hudson and often Gregory, the group recorded for a number of labels until 1975. They remain a popular draw on the oldies circuit, but unfortunately now without Gregory, who died on February 12, 1999.

Goodnite Sweetheart, Goodnite
1997, Charly

This excellent 30-track collection covers The Spaniels' stint with Vee-Jay from 1953 to 1960 and features some of the best vocal group/doo-wop recordings ever made. It includes all of their hits, as well as important album cuts like "Red Sails In The Sunset" and wonderful novelties like "Bounce".

Phil Spector

Pop music mythology has **Phil Spector** down as a tortured musical genius hiding behind his "Wall of Sound", working in megalomaniacal isolation to perfect his teen symphonies. The fact is, however, that Spector's masterpieces would be nothing without the songs of **Jeff Barry**, **Ellie Greenwich**, **Barry Mann** and **Cynthia Weill**, or the engineering of Jack Nitzsche and the drumming of Hal Blaine. Spector's records may have had a Wagnerian grandeur that pointed the way towards The Beatles and The Beach Boys, but his ultimate contribution to soul music was the voices he discovered, in particular **Darlene Love**, who was perhaps the only singer in history who could stand up to his monumental architecture.

Spector was born in The Bronx, New York on December 25, 1940 and moved to LA at age 12. In 1958 he formed a trio called **The Teddy Bears** with high-school classmates Annette Kleinbard (aka Carol Connors) and Marshall Lieb. They recorded two Spector originals, "Don't You Worry My Pretty Pet" and "To Know Him Is To Love Him", which were released together on the Dore label. The record eventually sold a million copies and spent three weeks at #1 on the pop chart thanks to what was originally the B-side, "To Know Him Is To Love Him". The Teddy

Bears' subsequent releases failed to sell and they broke up shortly afterwards, leaving Spector (who had never been very comfortable performing) to concentrate on writing and producing.

After producing **Ray Peterson**'s hit version of "Corinna, Corinna" in 1960, Spector helped produce Ben E. King's "Spanish Harlem", Curtis Lee's "Pretty Little Angel Eyes", **Gene Pitney**'s "Every Breath I Take" and The Paris Sisters' "I Love How You Love Me". He then teamed up with fellow producer **Lester Sill** to form their own Philles record label. Spector's Philles records are the ones he is most famous for. It was on these that he created his "wall of sound": three-minute mini-symphonies filled with a thousand ideas and nearly as many instruments that mapped out the last detail. While his records could often be overblown, when he got it right Spector created a magnificent melodrama perfectly suited to the emotional torment of the girl-group songs.

In the early 60s Spector recorded the so-so "There's No Other (Like My Baby)" and "Uptown" with **The Crystals** (La La Brooks, Barbara Alston, Dee Dee Kinnibrew, Mary Thomas and Priscilla Wright), before coming across Gene Pitney's song "He's A Rebel". Spector wanted The Crystals to record it, but they were still in high school and couldn't make the session. He hired **The Blossoms**, led by Darlene Love, to sing as The Crystals on the record, and Love's husky, breathless vocals sent "He's A Rebel" to #1 in 1962. The equally booming "He's Sure The Boy I Love" followed later that year, before the real Crystals returned for the equally wonderful "Da Doo Ron Ron" in 1963.

Darlene Love returned as the lead singer of **Bob B. Soxx & The Blue Jeans** on "Why Do Lovers Break Each Other's Hearts" and the lesser "Zip-A-Dee-Doo-Dah". Working with Spector, Love went on to have modest hits as a solo artist with "A Fine, Fine Boy", "Wait Til' My Bobby Gets Home" and "Today I Met The Boy I'm Gonna Marry". Shockingly, her 1963 Christmas record, "Christmas Baby (Please Come Home)", saw no chart action whatsoever. Despite her lack of significant chart success, Love deserves to be recognized as one of popular music's great singers.

Although Darlene Love's vocals were the best accompaniment to Spector's sound, he was also capable of making great music with not so great voices; his records with girl group **The Ronettes** being a prime example. The Ronettes were led by **Ronnie Bennett**, a singer of uncertain pitch and even less reliable interpretive skills. However, her quavering voice was the perfect foil for Spector's monuments and their early-60s hits "Be My Baby", "Baby, I Love You" and "Do I Love You" rank among pop music's classics. Spector soon became smitten with Bennett and the pair eventually married after he forced her to retire.

With the British Invasion signalling the beginning of the end for his girl-group sound in the mid-60s, Spector began to concentrate on **The Righteous Brothers**. He created often ridiculously overblown tracks for this white Southern California duo, like "Unchained Melody", "You've Lost That Lovin' Feelin'" and "Just Once In My Life", which were all huge hits. Spector also crafted the disastrous "River Deep, Mountain High" for Ike & Tina Turner in 1966. He considered the record his masterpiece, but it was roundly ignored in the US. After this spectacular failure, Spector rarely ventured out of his Hollywood mansion.

He made a brief comeback in the late 60s, producing his final soul record of any consequence, "Black Pearl", for **Sonny Charles & The Checkmates** in 1969. He was then drafted in to work on **The Beatles**' *Let It Be* album in 1970 and produced solo albums for John Lennon and George Harrison. Spector became even more reclusive from the late 70s onwards, only occasionally reappearing to produce albums for, among others, **Leonard Cohen** and punk rockers **The Ramones**. Spector most recently returned to the spotlight when he was arrested for allegedly murdering actress Lana Clarkson in 2003.

Various Artists: Back To Mono (1958–1969)
1991, ABKCO

This 4-disc, 73-track collection includes nearly all of Phil Spector's classic baroque pop productions from the early to mid-60s, when his sound dominated pop music. While Spector is clearly the star, the album also gives overdue praise to Darlene Love who toiled in the shadows for far too long. The fourth disc is the legendary 1963 album, *A Christmas Gift To You From Phil Spector*, which remains the only decent Christmas album in pop history.

Dusty Springfield wonders, "how am I gonna get down from here?"

Dusty Springfield

Dusty Springfield was born **Mary O'Brien** in London on April 16, 1939. She began her career in the late 50s as part of The Lana Sisters, a forgettable pop vocal group, but in 1960 she formed the folk-pop trio The Springfields with her brother **Dion** O'Brien and friend **Tim Field**. The group had big hits with "Bambino", "Silver Thread And Golden Needles" and "Say I Won't Be There", but broke up just before the dawn of the British Invasion.

Hearing girl-group records for the first time during a tour of America with the group in the early 60s inspired Springfield to go solo. She transformed herself into a gutsy vocalist and became, along with Dionne

Warwick, the new generation's best inter-
preter of the Brill Building's pop material.
While she sounded great on huge Phil
Spector-style productions like "I Only Want
To Be With You" and "Wishin' And
Hopin'", she sounded distinctly out of place
on "Can I Get A Witness", which wasn't
exactly Marvin Gaye or The Rolling Stones.

Even more impressive than her records
was her political commitment. Springfield
was one of the very few white singers in the
African-American idiom to acknowledge the
fact, and in 1964 she was thrown out of
South Africa for refusing to perform in front
of segregated audiences. Her music, however, was still showing signs of growing pains.
"Long After Tonight Is All Over" was the
kind of stuffy, string-laden, over-the-top
exorcism that British soul fans love, while
"You Don't Have To Say You Love Me" was
a wrenching ballad that showed she could
sing when given the right material.

Dusty Springfield came into her own as a
bona fide soul singer in the late 60s. On top
of production that was sort of a combination
between Motown and garage rock with its
stomping beat, swirling strings and tremolo
guitar runs, 1967's "What's It Gonna Be"
featured a really great performance from
Springfield that was full of smoky desperation. Equally superb was the similarly styled
"Don't Forget About Me". Her fine performance on "I'll Try Anything" was undone by
the wink-wink-nudge-nudge arrangement,
whic was also the case with the rather cheesy
"The Look Of Love".

Springfield never sounded as credible or
as powerful as she did on the fine 1968
album *Dusty In Memphis*. Recorded at **Chips
Moman**'s American Sound Studio in
Memphis, *Dusty In Memphis* was easily the
best album of her career and quite possibly
the greatest "blue-eyed soul" album ever.
The album's key players – **The 827 Thomas
Street Band** and backing vocalists **The Sweet
Inspirations** – must take a lot of the credit.
Although co-producer **Arif Mardin** gussied
up the Memphis sound with Concert Master
Gene Orloff's strings, the Al Jackson-
inspired drums, churchy keyboards, guitar
slurs and driving basslines ensured that
enough barbecue grease dripped from the
arrangements. The Sweet Inspirations,
meanwhile, took Springfield to church,

injecting a bit of sass into the proceedings. It
all rubbed off on Springfield and, unlike
many imports to Memphis, she didn't sound
out of place.

Her next album, 1970's *A Brand New Me*,
was recorded in Philadelphia with **Gamble &
Huff** who created "Silly, Silly Fool", which
was perhaps her most soulful performance
and one of the great ricocheting guitar

PLAYLIST
Dusty Springfield

1 I ONLY WANT TO BE WITH YOU from
The Very Best Of Dusty Springfield
Among the finest Phil Spector impressions ever
recorded.

2 WISHIN' AND HOPIN' from
The Very Best Of Dusty Springfield
Among the finest Dionne Warwick impressions
ever recorded.

3 YOU DON'T HAVE TO SAY YOU LOVE ME
from **The Very Best Of Dusty Springfield**
Completely and absurdly overblown, but all the
more effective for it.

4 WHAT'S IT GONNA BE from
The Very Best Of Dusty Springfield
Dusty at her best on top of a brilliant arrangement.

5 DON'T FORGET ABOUT ME from
The Very Best Of Dusty Springfield
Springfield excelled at the desperation blues –
this might be her best.

6 I'LL TRY ANYTHING from
The Very Best Of Dusty Springfield
Try to ignore the production and you'll hear Dusty
at her most emotional.

7 SON OF A PREACHER MAN from
The Very Best Of Dusty Springfield
Springfield rides the killer memphis groove for all
it's worth.

8 BREAKFAST IN BED from
The Very Best Of Dusty Springfield
She comes on like a cross between Al Green and
Bill Medley on this gauzy postcoital reverie.

9 WILLIE AND LAURA MAE JONES from
The Very Best Of Dusty Springfield
Springfield's fake countryisms are a bit annoying,
but the groove is pretty great.

10 SILLY, SILLY FOOL from
The Very Best Of Dusty Springfield
Springfield at her most soulful, with the bonus of
a wonderfully cheesy dangling wah-wah riff.

365

Blue-Eyed Soul

"Blue-eyed soul" may be the worst term ever applied to music by a critic. The history of soul is largely the history of integration; the history of white musicians, producers and arrangers interacting with black musicians, producers and arrangers. That white singers should be singled out seems stupid and antithetical to the aims of soul. Nevertheless, some first-rate white soul artists, who were labelled with this incongruous term during the mid-60s, thrived throughout the 60s and 70s and produced a wealth of classic soul records.

Perhaps the first of the many fine white soul singers was **Timi Yuro**. Growing up singing in her family's Italian restaurant in LA, Yuro sounded like a less restrained Dionne Warwick. She had two big pop/R&B hits in the early 60s with a version of Roy Hamilton's "Hurt" and the monumental "What's A Matter Baby (Is It Hurting You)". She continued recording throughout the 60s, with her obscure 1968 B-side "It'll Never Be Over For Me" proving a huge record on the Northern soul scene, before she put her career on hold to raise a family. Timi Yuro came back to record an album with **Willie Nelson** in the 80s before throat cancer sadly put an end to her singing career.

Also in LA, and at around the same time that Yuro started recording, **Bill Medley** and **Bobby Hatfield** recorded a few singles as The Paramours before changing their name to **The Righteous Brothers**. According to legend, the new name came from the reaction of African-American patrons at their gigs – "That's righteous, brothers." The duo borrowed substantially from Pasadena's Don & Dewey, including the modest hits "Koko Joe" and "Justine", before hooking up with Phil Spector for the towering "You've Lost That Lovin' Feelin'" and the flat-out irritating "Unchained Melody" in the mid-60s.

One of the most important sites of soul miscegenation was **Chips Moman**'s American Sound Studio in Memphis. Moman was a kid from rural Georgia who had formed an integrated band with Booker T. Jones in the late 50s. He had also helped **Jim Stewart** at Stax during the label's early days, before they fell out and Moman decided to set up his own studio in 1964. His American Sound Studio used a band mostly made up of ex-country players (guitarist Reggie Young, bassist Tommy Cogbill, drummer Gene Chrisman and keyboardists Bobby Emmons and Bobby Wood) to cut soul sides by the likes of James & Bobby Purify, Joe Tex, Roy Hamilton, **Oscar Toney Jr.** and Joe Simon. In 1968 Atlantic sent British singer Dusty Springfield down to Memphis to work at American, and the result was perhaps the best blue-eyed soul album ever recorded, *Dusty In Memphis*.

Before Motown found success with Norman Whitfield's recordings, which featured white guitarist **Dennis Coffey**, and Rare Earth's rock versions of Motown classics, its VIP subsidiary released one of the all-time blue-eyed soul classics in 1966, **R. Dean Taylor**'s "There's A Ghost In My House". With its fuzz guitar riff and a keyboard-heavy version of the archetypal Motown beat (reminiscent of Mitch Ryder), "There's A Ghost In My House" sounded more like garage rock than soul, but its easy pulsating beat made it a floor-filler at Northern soul events and, when it was re-released in 1974, it rose to #3 on the UK charts.

Other soul centres had their own avatars of the blue-eyed soul: Philadelphia International had **The Soul Survivors**, whose 1967 "Expressway To Your Heart" helped put songwriters Gamble & Huff on the map; Stax had **Johnny Daye** (né Johnny DiBucci), who recorded the superb "Stay Baby Stay" for the label in 1968 after his modest success working with Johnny Nash on Jomanda; Holland-Dozier-Holland crafted several hits for **The Flaming Ember**, including Westbound #9 and "I'm Not My Brother's Keeper"; Scepter had several countrified hits with **BJ Thomas**, but "Wendy" showed

intros. *Cameo*, recorded in LA in 1973, featured "Breakin' Up A Happy Home", one of her best vocals of the 70s and 80s which was almost ruined by the clumsy arrangement.

After a decade's worth of inactivity and utterly forgettable records, Springfield made a triumphant return in 1987 on a duet with **The Pet Shop Boys**, "What Have I Done To Deserve This?". Neil Tenant and Chris Lowe also produced several tracks for *Reputation* in 1990, her best album in nearly 20 years.

After releasing a couple more records in the 90s, Springfield died of breast cancer on March 2, 1999.

Dusty In Memphis
1968, Atlantic

Springfield's finest album has as its signature song "Son Of A Preacher Man", one of the most perfect matches between downhome values and mainstream pop sensibilities. The funky, Memphis soul stew is evident across the whole album; she shouts convincingly on "Don't Forget About Me" and has all the heartache of Lorraine Ellison on "I Can't Make It Alone".

Thomas's more soulful side and is another Northern soul favourite. Perhaps the best of these artists was **Eddie Hinton**, who worked at Muscle Shoals as a guitarist and songwriter. He recorded a couple of singles – "Leaving On A Jet Plane" and "Dreamer" in the 60s – before recording his own stellar album, *Very Extremely Dangerous* in 1977.

Contemporary R&B isn't as conducive to white singers as hip-hop is, but more traditionally styled white vocalists have continued to carry the blue-eyed soul mantle in recent years. **Lisa Stansfield** has been one of the most successful, having huge American R&B hits in the late 80s and early 90s with "All Around The World", "You Can't Deny It" and "All Woman". The only recent white singers to have any real success with music born from R&B have been boy bands, such as **The Backstreet Boys** and **N'Sync** – even **Britney Spears**'s team-up with R&B producers **The Neptunes** on the 2001 single "I'm A Slave 4 U" fell flat on its face.

⊙ **Various Artists: Soul Shots Volume 6: Blue-Eyed Soul**
1988, Rhino

Sadly, this record has never been released on CD, but it remains the best overview of this questionable genre. It includes records by The Soul Survivors, Bill Deal & The Rondells, Dean Parrish, Bob Kuban & The In-Men, Roy Head and Tony Joe White. Also worth checking out is Dusty Springfield's *Dusty In Memphis* (1968, Atlantic), which remains the greatest blue-eyed soul album ever recorded with a blend of funky Memphis soul.

▣ PLAYLIST

1 WHAT'S A MATTER BABY (IS IT HURTING YOU) **Timi Yuro** from **The Best Of Timi Yuro**
The gutsiest performance from the gutsiest of the blue-eyed soul singers.

2 YOU'VE LOST THAT LOVIN' FEELIN' **Righteous Brothers** from **Back To Mono**
Grandiosity is not one of pop's greater virtues, but the apocalyptic desolation conjured up here somehow evokes universality, not megalomania.

3 THERE'S A GHOST IN MY HOUSE **R. Dean Taylor** from **There's A Ghost In My House**
Garage rock with an unstoppable Motown beat.

4 THE CHEATER **Bob Kuban & The In-Men** from **Look Out For The Cheater**
Irresistible marriage of easy listening, Motown and the South Carolina boardwalk.

5 EXPRESSWAY TO YOUR HEART **The Soul Survivors** from **The Philly Sound**
Gamble & Huff at their rockiest and funkiest.

6 STAY BABY STAY **Johnny Daye** from **Complete Stax-Volt Singles Vol. 2**
A killer Southern soul side by perhaps the best of all the blue-eyed vocalists.

7 SON OF A PREACHER MAN **Dusty Springfield** from **Dusty In Memphis**
A classic marriage of mainstream pop and Memphis soul.

8 GET READY **Rare Earth** from **Get Ready**
Epic but thoroughly groovy psych-rock-soul.

9 WESTBOUND #9 **Flaming Ember** from **The Best Of Flaming Ember**
Holland Dozier Holland specialized in the buzzing fuzz guitar lick in the early 70s and this is the chirpiest and cheeriest of 'em all.

10 HARD LUCK GUY **Eddie Hinton** from **Hard Luck Guy**
A white guy doing the most precise Otis Redding interpretation ever says everything about the miscegenetic instinct at the heart of Southern soul.

The Staple Singers

The Staple Singers were one of the true treasures of American music. As perhaps the only soul group to span nearly the entirety of twentieth-century African-American music, from the Delta blues through classic gospel to Southern soul and funk and even a little reggae, The Staple Singers were tradition in flesh and blood.

The Staple Singers story dates back to 1915 when **Roebuck "Pops" Staples** was born in Winona, Mississippi. As a teenager, the aspiring guitarist knew the legendary Delta blues performer **Charley Patton**, whom he met playing at bars and parties throughout the Mississippi Delta. Staples was soon drawn to the church and began performing with **The Golden Trumpets**. In the mid- to late 30s, Staples moved to Chicago and, after teaching his three children **Cleotha**, **Pervis** and **Mavis** to sing, he formed The Staple Singers in 1951. Mavis, with her earthy contralto vocals, became the group's lead singer.

The Staple Singers released their first single, "They Are They", in 1952 on their own Royal label, before signing with United the following year. Their most significant recording at United was "This May Be The Last Time", a record that inspired **The Rolling Stones**' "The Last Time" and was covered by **The Grateful Dead**. Signing to Vee Jay, they had a hit with "Uncloudy Day" in 1955. With Pops' unique guitar sound that shimmered like heat on Texas blacktop and Mavis's powerful voice, "Uncloudy Day" was a stunning gospel record.

At Vee Jay, The Staple Singers continued to record gospel sides – "Swing Down Chariot", "Help Me Jesus", "I'm Leaving" and "So Soon" – that were utterly singular, yet sounded as primal and ancient as Mississippi mud. In 1960 Pops recorded a solo version of "Will The Circle Be Unbroken", which presaged the group's direction when they signed to the Riverside label later that year.

At Riverside the group started to blend gospel with the folk music of the Civil Rights Movement on *The 25th Day Of December* (1962), *Gamblin' Man* (1963) and *This Little Light* (1964). They then moved to Epic and some modest pop success in 1967 with "Why (Am I Treated So Bad)", produced by **Larry Williams**, and a version of "For What It's Worth".

Switching labels again, The Staple Singers signed to Stax and released *Soul Folk In Action* in 1968. The album included the Civil Rights song "Long Walk To DC", which had a slow momentum that really suited Mavis, and "The Ghetto", a churchy secular hymn that was made a bit mawkish by an Elvisy guitar figure and sickly strings. Their second Stax album, 1969's *We'll Get Over*, followed in similar style with tracks like "When Will We Be Paid?" and the **Al Kooper**-produced unsubtle secular gospel hymn "Brand New Day". The next year brought several changes, with Pervis leaving the group and being replaced by his sister **Yvonne** and **Al Bell** coming in as producer.

Bell immediately took The Staple Singers down to Muscle Shoals to get some funk in their folk. Their first record with Bell was a rousing version of "Heavy Makes You Happy (Sha-Na-Boom-Boom)", which got them into trouble with the gospel traditionalists. The group's music was already thoroughly secular by this point, so the reaction was a bit of a mystery. The traditionalists should have saved their rage for the follow-up, the fiery, gutsy "Respect Yourself", a #12 pop hit that truly established The Staple Singers as crossover artists. The utopian, but definitely earthly, "I'll Take You There" became the group's first pop #1 in 1972. The track's opening was stolen wholesale from the intro to **Harry J. All-Star**'s reggae hit, "The Liquidator", and it then wed the Muscle Shoals Rhythm Section with Pops' guitar and Mavis's voluptuous gospel vocals.

PLAYLIST
The Staple Singers

1 THIS MAY BE THE LAST TIME from **The Ultimate Staple Singers: A Family Affair**
Stark, solemn folk-gospel that became something of a rock standard.

2 UNCLOUDY DAY from **The Ultimate Staple Singers: A Family Affair**
One of the greatest religious recordings ever made.

3 WHY (AM I TREATED SO BAD) from **The Ultimate Staple Singers: A Family Affair**
The group's first foray into pop territory still features Mavis's gospel gravitas.

4 LONG WALK TO DC from **The Ultimate Staple Singers: A Family Affair**
Earthy, folky Civil Rights song that Mavis just kills.

5 RESPECT YOURSELF from **The Ultimate Staple Singers: A Family Affair**
Mavis's fearsome plea for self-respect.

6 I'LL TAKE YOU THERE from **The Ultimate Staple Singers: A Family Affair**
One of pop music's great utopian visions.

7 IF YOU'RE READY (COME GO WITH ME) from **The Ultimate Staple Singers: A Family Affair**
"I'll Take You There" part II.

8 SLIPPERY PEOPLE from **The Ultimate Staple Singers: A Family Affair**
Adds gospel authority to Talking Heads.

More hits followed with the funky "This World" and the clap-happy "Oh La De Da", and "If You're Ready (Come Go With Me)" was also equally successful, topping the R&B chart for two weeks. The Staple Singers' 1974 follow-up singles "Touch A Hand, Make A Friend" and "City In The Sky" were more mawkish and became the group's last recordings with Stax before the label folded.

Signing with Warner Bros in 1975, The Staple Singers scored their second pop #1 with a song written and produced by Curtis Mayfield for the Sidney Poitier and Bill Cosby movie *Let's Do it Again*. Recording as The Staples, the group didn't fare so well during the disco era and moved to the Private I label in 1980. There they had small hits in 1984 with a fabulous cover of Talking Heads' "Slippery People" and with "H-A-T-E (Don't Live Here Anymore)", but were unable to sustain the momentum and soon drifted out of sight again.

Mavis and Pops had both maintained relatively successful solo careers alongside their work with the rest of the family. Mavis had begun releasing material at Stax in 1969, but her solo career took a back seat to The Staple Singers until the 80s and 90s. In 1991 she hit the top of the R&B chart when she appeared on Bebe and Cece Winans' cover of "I'll Take You There" and she recorded a tribute album to Mahalia Jackson in 1996. Pops also began to concentrate more on solo material in the 90s, and he won a Grammy for his *Father, Father* album in 1995. Pops sadly passed away on December 19, 2000 from injuries sustained after a fall, but Mavis has gone from strength to strength, releasing the fine *Have A Little Faith* album in 2004.

○ **Be Altitude: Respect Yourself**
1972, Stax

Al Bell produced a string of great records for The Staple Singers in the early 70s, and this is the best. Here gospel meets the Stax house band with explosive results, as Bell slickly captures in the studio the great spirit of the group's live performances. This includes their best-known hit, "I'll Take You There", but everything here is a contender.

○ **The Ultimate Staple Singers: A Family Affair**
2004, Ace

Leave it to the fine folks at Ace to finally put together the collection that The Staple Singers' talent warrants. Two discs and 44 tracks is certainly no more than the group deserves – and certainly no more than you need. The more straightforwardly folky stuff may not appeal to soul fans, but this is, nevertheless, a fine testimony to one of America's true music treasures.

Edwin Starr

Edwin Starr was the gruffest, most assertive and swashbuckling vocalist ever to record at Motown. He was also the most over the top, meaning that he had a difficult time getting his records past Motown's Quality Control, who believed that they would never cross over. When Starr finally proved them wrong, he did so with characteristic bravado.

Starr was born Charles Edwin Hatcher on January 21, 1942 in Nashville, Tennessee and was raised in Cleveland, Ohio. As a teenager he joined a local doo-wop group called The Futuretones, who recorded "Roll On" in 1957. Starr left the group when he was drafted to serve in the military in Germany, and when he returned he fronted Bill Doggett's combo from 1963 to 1965. Signing to the Ric-Tic label in 1965, Starr had a hit with his first self-penned single, "Agent Double-O-Soul". This piece of James Bond schtick was silly, but Starr and the moonlighting Funk Brothers were anything but, and the record reached #21 on the pop chart.

Starr's less substantial hits for Ric-Tic – "Back Street", the soulful "Headline News" and "Stop Her On Sight (SOS)" (which sounded like Starr at his least demonstrative singing on top of a Supremes record) – later became big hits on the Northern soul circuit. If the label could have figured out a way to better incorporate Starr's rough-and-tumble vocals with the sweetness of the backing, he could have been a superstar.

When Ric-Tic was sold to Motown in 1967, Starr's contract was part of the deal. He struggled for a couple of years with weak material, such as "My Weakness Is You" (pro-forma Motown that made it big in the north of England because of its stomping beat), until the label relented to his demands that "Twenty-Five Miles" be released as a single. With the exception of the pulsating bassline, "Twenty-Five Miles" sounded nothing like a Motown record, but the funky drums, Starr's he-man performance, the horn charts like power chords and the wonderful countdown breakdown ensured that the single would reach the pop Top 10.

"Running Back And Forth", the B-side to 1970's "Time", tried to smooth out Starr's rough edges, but his biggest hit, released later that year, did nothing of the sort. Maybe the most stentorian record ever made, the anti-war protest song "War" found Starr shouting down even the fuzz guitars provided by producer **Norman Whitfield**. Starr tried to follow this #1 pop hit with "Stop The War Now", but he couldn't reproduce the magic. Less controversial footstompers like 1971's "Funky Music Sho Nuff Turns Me On" also failed to re-create his previous success.

In 1974 Starr worked on the soundtrack to the blaxploitation flick *Hell Up In Harlem*. Starr was perfectly suited to a blaxploitation score because the genre's instrumental tracks were usually as bombastic as his vocal style. Starr's ludicrously over-the-top score (created with producer-songwriters **Freddie Perren** and **Fonce Mizell**) didn't disappoint.

Starr signed with the Granite label the next year and had a small hit with "Abyssinia Jones", before moving to 20th Century and becoming one of the more bizarre disco hitmakers. Starr was terribly mannered on 1977's "I Just Wanna Do My Thing" and the beat and arrangement were plodding, but the cowbell rhythm at the beginning was almost worth the price of admission. Starr had big European hits in the late 70s with the proto-Hi-NRG "Contact" and "H.A.P.P.Y. Radio", which was perhaps the worst song he was saddled with during his career. However, this was a strangely effective disco move for this most assertive of soul vocalists.

In the mid-80s Starr moved to the UK where he was revered on the Northern soul scene. He recorded several sides for some of the old Northern soul boys who worshipped his records, including, bizarrely, **Stock, Aitken & Waterman**. He also performed regularly on the Northern soul revival circuit over the years and appeared on occasional Europop remakes of his old hits, such as Utah Saints' version of "Funky Music". He died of a heart attack in Nottingham, England on April 2, 2003.

The Very Best Of Edwin Starr
1998, Motown

This excellent 14-track collection includes the best of Starr's work for both Ric-Tic and Motown, making it the only Starr compilation to buy unless you're a disco freak. His rough, intense, more Memphis-like vocals sometimes threatened to tear at the fibre that held Motown together, but on the tracks included here the fire-and-ice marriage works perfectly.

Candi Staton

During her tenure at Muscle Shoals, Alabama, **Candi Staton** was one of the great female soul singers – her testifying, bordering-on-hoarse voice fitted the Southern grooves like a glove. Unfortunately, while she had some decent-sized hits there, greater fame didn't come until she left Alabama and recorded one of the most popular pop-disco hits, "Young Hearts Run Free".

Staton was born **Canzetta Maria Staton** in Hanceville, Alabama on March 13, 1943. She grew up in rural Alabama where all she had for company was the town's Baptist church and country radio. She joined the local gospel group The Four Echoes at the age of 8, but was then sent off to boarding school in Tennessee, where she joined The Jewel Gospel Trio. They recorded several sides for the Nashboro label during the 50s, including the excellent "Praying Time". While touring with The Jewel Gospel Trio, Staton attempted to elope with Lou Rawls, who was in **The Pilgrim Travellers** at the time, but his mother intervened and sent her home.

In 1960 Staton married an abusive man, who soon forbade her from singing. However, one night in 1967 she walked out on her husband and went to a club in Birmingham, Alabama. She sang "Do Right Woman – Do Right Man" and was hired on the spot by the club owner. Reigniting her career, Staton recorded the solo record, "Now You Got The Upper Hand", for the Unity label in 1967. The track was a Northern soul-style stomper with an overbearing chorus that drowned out Staton's very fine vocals. However, she soon caught the attention of Clarence Carter, who took her down to Muscle Shoals with him and later married her.

The first side Staton recorded at **Rick Hall's** Fame Studios in Muscle Shoals was 1969's "I'd Rather Be An Old Man's Sweetheart". She laid out the advantages of loving an older man over monstrous drums and a great Southern groove, and the record became an R&B top-ten hit. "I'm Just A Prisoner (Of Your Good Lovin')" followed in a similar style with another stunning performance by Staton. Although the arrangement of her rendition of "Stand By Your Man" was a bit stilted and the chorus was a mess, she sang the heck out of the verses and convincingly soulified **Tammy Wynette**. She wasn't all sass, however, as her killer reading of "That's How Strong My Love Is" proved.

In the early 70s Staton's lovely versions of "He Called Me Baby", "Mr And Mrs Untrue" and "Something's Burning" continued to show that she could be as graceful and emotional on slower country soul ballads as she was on the more fiery gospel-infused tracks. Staton moved to Warner Bros in 1974 (divorcing Carter the same year), but Rick Hall continued to produce fine Southern soul records, such as "As Long As He Takes Care Of Home", for her until the following year when she started recording in LA with producer **Dave Crawford**.

Recorded with a bunch of LA studio musicians (including Ray Parker, Jr. on guitar), Staton's "Young Hearts Run Free" was a huge disco hit in 1976, becoming her first R&B #1 in the US and a #2 pop hit in the UK. Staton sang more clearly on "Young Hearts Run Free" than she had on any of her Muscle Shoals records, a trend that she continued the next year on her versions of **The Bee-Gees'** "Nights On Broadway" and **The Doobie Brothers'** "Listen To The Music".

Staton revisited the Southern soul style that had made her name on "So Blue" in 1978, but returned to the dancefloor again the next year with "When You Wake Up Tomorrow". This cult disco record was co-written by **Patrick Adams** in the style he would later perfect with the short-lived disco group **Inner Life**. However, Staton's grit wasn't really suited to the discotheque, no matter what "Young Hearts" may have indicated. In 1982 she had a UK hit with a dance version of "Suspicious Minds" on the Sugarhill label before returning to gospel.

Most of Staton's gospel material was recorded for her own Beracah label, including the 1986 a cappella track "You Got The Love". An enterprising UK house producer calling himself **The Source** fused her track with **Jamie Principal**'s instrumental "Your Love" and one of the most popular bootleg mixes ever was born. The record became a huge hit in the UK in 1991, and allegedly sold 200,000 copies (remixes returned to the UK Top 10 again in 1997 and 2006). Staton

returned to secular music in 1999 with *Outside In*, an album of dance-pop aimed at the British market.

 Candi Staton
2004, Honest Jon's/Astralwerks

Candi Staton is the most successful female Southern soul singer, yet this is the first comprehensive collection of her great Muscle Shoals recordings. If you like Southern soul even a smidgen, you need this superb 26-track compilation in your collection. Quite simply, this is some of the best soul music ever recorded.

Billy Stewart

With a sparkling voice and a unique vocal technique somewhere between stuttering and scatting, **Billy Stewart** was one of the great soft-soul artists. His voice was seemingly tailor-made for the lush post-doo-wop arrangements of Chicago, but his jazzy vocal style wore thin and became too gimmicky – he had such a strong voice that he didn't need to rely on trickery.

Born in Washington DC on March 24, 1937, Stewart grew up singing with his family in The Stewart Gospel Singers. As a teenager he joined the doo-wop group The Rainbows with **Don Covay**, but his break came when he was discovered playing piano in a Washington bar by **Bo Diddley**. While touring with Diddley's band, Stewart recorded "Billy's Blues" in 1956 for the Chess label. The track featured a riff from Diddley that was later reused on **Mickey & Sylvia**'s "Love Is Strange". The next year Stewart recorded "Billy's Heartache" on OKeh with **The Marquees**, a group that included Marvin Gaye and that was also produced by Diddley.

In the early 60s Stewart started a songwriting/producing partnership with **Billy Davis** at Chess. The duo also wrote and produced several of Stewart's own records, including his first R&B hit, "Reap What You Sow", and "True Fine Lovin'". However, it was 1963's wonderfully gossamer "Strange Feeling" that first displayed Stewart's talent for soft-soul. After cutting several silly records, such as "A Fat Boy Can Cry", on which he made the most of the nonsense lyrics, Stewart recorded two of the all-time great soft-soul tracks, "I Do Love You" and "Sitting In The Park", on which he improvised like a resourceful saxophonist on top of classic Chicago piano-led productions.

Stewart's biggest pop hit, 1966's "Summertime", is one of the stranger records in the soul canon. His version of this Gershwin standard was full of showmanship and tricks that drove the crowds wild, while the big-band arrangement was Vegas in the extreme and the ending was one of the silliest things ever recorded, but somehow it worked. After a similar reconstruction of the old Doris Day hit "Secret Love" later that year, Stewart's records started to become less surprising and more formulaic, and the hits began to dry up. Tragically, before he had any chance of attempting a comeback, Stewart and three of his musicians were killed on January 17, 1970 when their car ran off the road and plunged into the Neuse River after a gig in North Carolina.

One More Time: The Chess Years
1990, Chess

Before he became a bit of a one-trick pony, Billy Stewart's jazzy voice on top of beautiful Chicago soul arrangements made him a superb soft-soul stylist. This 20-track compilation collects the best of his records, most of which were made before 1967 when a formulaic approach and health problems derailed his career.

The Stylistics

Simultaneously rather ridiculous and rather wonderful, **The Stylistics** took the

Philly Soul

Philadelphia has been a presence on the national soul scene since 1961. That was the year that vocal group **The Pentagons** recorded "Until Then", a tentative stab at a mix of dinner-club orchestral arrangement and storefront-church passion. This was perfected just two years later by Garnet Mimms when he recorded one of the most influential early soul records, "Cry Baby", in New York with fellow Philadelphian exile **Jerry Ragavoy**.

The song that really put Philadelphia soul on the map was Barbara Mason's "Yes I'm Ready", which became a #5 pop hit in the spring of 1965. The record was produced by the Dyno-Dynamic Productions team: **Luther Randolph**, organist **Johnny Styles**, lead singer of The Larks **Weldon McDougal III** and local radio DJ **Jimmy Bishop**. They used the Larks' backing band – guitarists **Norman Harris** and **Bobby Eli**, drummer **Earl Young** and bassist **Ronnie Baker** – as their house band, and a young songwriter called Kenny Gamble as backing singer. While not entirely stylistically apposite, the record established both the talent pool and the impossibly lush strings that worked with the rhythm rather than against it that would come to characterize the Philly soul sound.

Equally crucial, although not as popular, were a series of records by a vocal group called **The Volcanos**. Released a couple of months after Mason's "Yes I'm Ready", The Volcanos' "Storm Warning" was a significant advance on the blueprint thanks to the jazzy guitar that introduced the record and the vibraphone chimes throughout. This was where Philadelphia's jazz scene really made its mark on soul music. On "Storm Warning" vibist **Vince Montana** fleshed out the melody led by an undermixed piano – and the lead being played by a piano and vibraphone soon became a critical component in the Philly sound.

Eddie Holman's 1965 hit, "This Can't Be True", was the archetypal Philly soul record. Holman's helium falsetto vocals against a background of dangling guitar phrases laced with cavernous reverb, a dragging bassline that reached down to the centre of the earth and a slow shuffle drum beat that recalled doo-wop rhythms reinvented the sound of male vulnerability. This was the beginning of the sweet soul sound, perfected by **Thom Bell** with his work for The Delfonics, The Stylistics, The Spinners, **Ronny Dyson** and **New York City**. Soon after his initial success with The Delfonics, Bell's soft-soul sound became something of a cottage industry in Philadelphia. During the late 60s and early 70s numerous arrangers and producers tried their hand at it on records such as **The Ethics'** "Think About Tomorrow" and **The Ambassadors'** "I Really Love You".

Of course, Philadelphia's main contribution to soul was the work of **Kenny Gamble** and **Leon Huff** and their Philadelphia International label. As well as helping to define the sound of the 70s with their upwardly mobile, jazz-tinged signature sound, their studio band, **MFSB**, helped create disco thanks to the battery of drummer Earl Young and bassist Ronnie Baker, who discovered an eternal groove that still keeps feet dancing today.

artifice of pop love and spirituality to its most extreme, most beatified, most chaste realm. Based around the divine falsetto of lead singer **Russell Thompkins Jr.** and the impossibly sumptuous productions of **Thom Bell**, The Stylistics became one of the most successful vocal groups of the 70s.

The Stylistics formed in 1968 at Benjamin Franklin High School in Philadelphia when two vocal groups, The Monarchs and The Percussions, broke up. Thompkins, **James Smith** and **Airrion Love** from The Monarchs joined forces with **Herb Murrell** and **James Dunn** from The Percussions at the instigation of one of their teachers. The group performed on the local club circuit for about a year before being signed by the local Sebring label. The bland and teen-flavoured "You're A Big Girl Now" became a sizeable local hit in 1970 and outgrew Sebring's distribution capabilities. The group quickly signed to Avco Records and "You're A Big Girl Now" eventually rose to #7 on the R&B chart.

Working with producer-songwriter Thom Bell at Avco, The Stylistics had another top-ten R&B hit with "Stop, Look, Listen (To Your Heart)" before truly crossing over to the pop chart with the ultra-lush "You Are Everything". "Betcha By Golly Wow", their biggest hit, followed in 1972 and is quite possibly the wimpiest declaration of eternal love ever. No longer simply luxurious, this was where Bell's vision of heaven became nothing more than a penthouse suite.

Various Artists: Northern Soul: On The Philadelphia Beat Vol. 1
1995, Bear Family

Although the Northern soul focus gives a slightly skewed take on the early days of Philly soul (i.e. it contains mostly four-on-the-floor stompers), this is a fine collection of some of the City of Brotherly Love's more obscure gems, including The Volcanos' "Storm Warning", The Ethics' "Standing In The Darkness" and some early solo material by Kenny Gamble.

Various Artists: Philadelphia Roots
2001, Soul Jazz

Focusing on how Philadelphia helped spawn disco, this excellent compilation showcases some of the lesser-known records in Philly's vast treasure trove and shows why "disco" should not be considered a five-letter word. Also worth checking out is *The Sound Of Philadelphia* (2004, Soul Jazz).

▣ PLAYLIST

1 YES, I'M READY Barbara Mason from **Yes, I'm Ready**
With its gushing string cascades, this torrent of teen longing was a prototype for the genre.

2 LA-LA MEANS I LOVE YOU The Delfonics from **La-La Means I Love You**
Is this the most unctuous record ever made?

3 ONLY THE STRONG SURVIVE Jerry Butler from **The Iceman Cometh**
A richly upholstered classic given a deep, resonating sound by the creamy guitar and vibraphone.

4 DROWNING IN THE SEA OF LOVE Joe Simon from **Drowning In The Sea Of Love**
Simon's foghorn vocals are contrasted with the rolling waves of strings, horns and guitar.

5 BACK STABBERS The O'Jays from **Back Stabbers**
One of Gamble & Huff's, and Philly soul's, greatest achievements with its superb introduction, eerie piano and political resonance.

6 THE LOVE I LOST Harold Melvin & The Blue Notes from **Black & Blue**
Drummer Earl Young basically invents disco with his snare pattern and hi-hat work on this gem.

7 I'LL ALWAYS LOVE MY MAM The Intruders from **Save The Children**
An almost African-sounding guitar line makes this a sheer delight, even if the lead singer wanders off pitch like a drunk trying to walk a straight line.

8 LOVE IS THE MESSAGE MFSB from **Love Is The Message**
The fast section is the national anthem of disco.

9 DO IT ANY WAY YOU WANNA People's Choice from **Boogie Down USA**
Philly soul at its funkiest.

10 LIFE ON MARS Dexter Wansel from **Life On Mars**
The cosmic synths of keyboardist Wansel take Philly into outer space.

The more subdued "People Make The World Go Round" was far better, even if the message was quite sickly, while "I'm Stone In Love With You" and "Break Up To Make Up" were positively minimal in comparison. The next year's "Rockin' Roll Baby" was an attempt at an uptempo track, but it swung about as hard as **The Osmonds**. Nevertheless, it went to #3 on the R&B chart. "You Make Me Feel Brand New" featured Airrion Love singing lead, rather than Thompkins, and it became the group's biggest hit, reaching #2 on the pop chart. It was also the last record they made with Bell, who had crafted their nine consecutive top-ten R&B singles.

Beginning with "Let's Put It All Together" in 1974, The Stylistics began working with Van McCoy and **Hugo & Luigi**. They initially kept to the same formula as Bell, but as time wore on they went further and further into disco, a move that didn't particularly suit The Stylistics, with one exception, 1975's "Hey Girl, Come And Get It". With the group's commercial prospects diminishing at home, McCoy reworked the group's sound – by making it more loungy – for the European market. The ploy worked, and in 1975 and 1976 the records "Sing Baby Sing", "Can't Give You Anything (But My Love)", "Na Na Is The Saddest Word", "Funky Weekend", "Can't Help Falling In Love" and "16 Bars" all reached the UK Top 10, while only being middling R&B hits in the US. However, their hits dried up in Europe just as quickly, and James Dunn left the group.

In the late 70s The Stylistics moved to the Mercury label and worked with producer **Teddy Randazzo**. However, he was hopelessly out of his element during the disco era and their records flopped. A move to Philadelphia International, where they worked with **Dexter Wansel**, didn't help matters any, but 1980's "Hurry Up This Way Again" was their best record in years. The group teamed up with Bell again the following year, but the magic was gone and Philadelphia International was in trouble.

Reduced to a trio with the departure of James Smith, The Stylistics bizarrely signed to electro-dance label Streetwise in 1984. This, too, did little to change their fortunes and the group finally settled into a comfortable career on the nostalgia circuit.

The Stylistics
1971, Avco Embassy

Thom Bell's lush production and The Stylistics' glistening harmonies raised the bar on the competition with this Philly soul masterpiece, which established the group's winning formula. "You Are Everything" and "Betcha By Golly, Wow" you already know, but all the tracks shine – there's no dead wood here.

The Best Of The Stylistics
1990, Amherst

There are no decent Stylistics compilations on the market at the moment, so this one will have to do. It has only ten tracks, but a little Stylistics goes a long way and too much of their sweet fluff could give you tooth decay. Ten tracks is also enough to get almost the full range that could be squeezed out of their helium harmonies.

Donna Summer

Soul music is supposed to be all about *the voice* making the specific universal, turning pain into ecstasy and maybe even transcending the human condition altogether. With a couple of exceptions, though, soul is as much the sum of nearly interchangeable parts as any teenybop subgenre you care to name. Aside from maybe Motown, nowhere in the soul continuum is this more obvious than with **Donna Summer** (born Adrian Donna Gaines on December 31, 1948 in Boston). Disco is producer's music *par excellence*, and with Donna Summer disco found its ultimate blank canvas.

Disco's naysayers criticize disco singers for having more in common with Broadway vocalists than with soul's more "authentic" expressionists. With Summer they've got a point: her phrasing wasn't all that different from **Ethel Merman**, and even though she was supposed to have sung in church you sure couldn't find any evidence of it. In fact, Summer was an unknown singer from Boston who was in the Munich production of *Godspell* in 1974 when she met **Giorgio Moroder**. Moroder was a producer from the Tyrolian ski resort of Val Gardena until he happened across the Moog synthesizer at the dawn of the 70s. The Moog's distinctly space-age timbres inspired Moroder to write "Son Of My Father" which, in the hands of a group of slumming glam-rockers called **Chicory Tip**, became the first #1 record to feature a synthesizer. As glorious a piece of pop ephemera as "Son Of My Father" was, however, Moroder was still a journeyman.

With Summer and fellow producer **Pete Bellotte**, however, he defined the union of flesh and machine in dance music. Little more than Donna Summer simulating an orgasm or three over a background of blaxploitation cymbals, wah-wah guitars, a funky-butt clavinet riff and some synth chimes, 1975's "Love To Love You Baby" was extended into a 17-minute mini-symphony at the request of Casablanca Records chief **Neil Bogart** who wanted a soundtrack for his sexual exploits. Apparently Bogart wasn't alone in his taste for concupiscent soundtracks as the song reached #2 on the American pop chart.

Even more of a landmark was 1977's "I Feel Love", which had more fake-orgasm vocals from Summer set against an entirely synthesized background. Introducing both the syn-drum and the galloping Moog bassline that would come to categorize the strain of disco called Hi-NRG, "I Feel Love" was a masterpiece of mechano-eroticism. The epitome of the cocaine chill and metal gloss of the 70s, "I Feel Love" could only have better encapsulated the decade's obsession with the detachment of anonymous sex if the record was sheathed in latex. Where synth-based records by Jean-Jacques Perrey, **Kraftwerk**, Tangerine Dream and Tonto's Expanding Head Band had used Moogs to imagine the whooshing speed and gurgling weirdness of a possible future, Moroder considered what implications the machine would have on the human body.

As Summer became a bigger and bigger star, however, Moroder and Bellotte backed away from the world of artifice towards a more conventional pop soundworld that featured massed strings and guitar solos from the likes of studio hack **Jeff "Skunk" Baxter**. While her version of "MacArthur Park", her first #1 single, was as bad as any record Don Johnson or Bruce Willis ever made and more proof of disco's affinity for showbiz, "Last Dance", "Bad Girls" and "On The Radio" belong on anyone's dancefloor. Her duet with **Barbra Streisand**, "No More Tears (Enough Is Enough)", was camper than Nelson Eddy and Jeanette McDonald singing together in the shower.

Summer's greatest record was one she made with Quincy Jones. With Summer singing the first two verses in a mock Puerto Rican accent to an electro-reggae lilt, 1982's "State Of Independence" worked from camp theatricality and kitsch exotica to the soaring emotion of reciprocated love and the orchestral grandeur of synthesized strings and gospel chorus. Like "I Feel Love", "State Of Independence" was a synth masterpiece that revelled in artifice.

After one final smash, 1983's "She Works Hard For The Money", Summer gradually faded from the music scene. Hooking up with the production team of **Stock, Aitken & Waterman** in 1989, she had one final fling on the pop charts with "This Time I Know It's For Real". She reappeared once again in 1997, when she reunited with Moroder to record "Carry On", which won a Grammy for Best Dance Recording. Summer still pops up from time to time performing at disco reunion concerts and the like, and ably demonstrates that her pipes are still in remarkably good condition.

Endless Summer
1994, Casablanca/Polygram

Donna Summer may have had only two epochal recordings (most artists should be so lucky), but this 19-track greatest hits package shows why she was the undisputed queen of disco. Despite there being plenty of showbiz sclockiness in her music, she undoubtedly deserves a place in the soul pantheon.

The Supremes

If one Motown act epitomized the label as "the sound of young America", it was **The Supremes**. During the 60s only The Beatles were more successful, and Michael Jackson is the only black artist to achieve more pop

The Supremes: "Stop! In the name of love"

#1s. Like Jackson, however, The Supremes were more successful on the pop chart than they were on the R&B chart. Motown founder **Berry Gordy** wanted nothing more than to belong to the establishment, and The Supremes were his meal ticket. Astringent, angular, uptight, overly stylized lead singer Diana Ross wasn't that great a pop singer, much less a mediocre R&B singer. The reason that The Supremes belong in this book is what's going on behind the scenes and underneath the vocals.

The Supremes started life in the late 50s as a Detroit quartet called **The Primettes**, with a line-up of Diana Ross (born March 26, 1944), **Florence Ballard** (born June 30, 1943, died February 22, 1976), **Mary Wilson** (born March 4, 1944) and **Barbara Martin**. Even in the early days, they were more pop than R&B, covering chestnuts like "Moonlight In Vermont" and "Canadian Sunset". They recorded just one single for the Lupine label as The Primettes, 1960's "Tears Of Sorrow", before signing to Motown in 1961. Renamed

The Supremes, they released eight singles on Motown that went nowhere and Barbara Martin left after the release of the first. They were then teamed up with songwriting and producing team Holland-Dozier-Holland and enjoyed their first chart success with "When The Lovelight Starts Shining Through His Eyes" in 1963.

The Supremes remained the exclusive property of Holland-Dozier-Holland until 1968, when the producers left Motown to start their own label. HDH's Motown formula was simple, but incredibly effective. Ross's thin vocals were surrounded by insistent, simple guitar riffs that prefigured reggae, 21-horn salutes, bells and **James Jamerson**'s huge bass undertow. On early hits such as "Where Did Our Love Go", "Stop! In The Name Of Love" and "You Can't Hurry Love", Ross was given simple, singsong melodies that bristled with stripped-down momentum. Later, on records such as "You Keep Me Hangin' On" (what the Four Tops would have sounded like if Ross was their lead singer), "Love Is Like An Itching In My Heart" (The Supremes' best record and the birth of Hi-NRG) and "Love Child" (which had the upwardly mobile supper club backing of Ross and Gordy's dreams), the basic Supremes' formula was progressively expanded upon. While Ross's voice didn't crack with the emotional intensity the lyrics deserved, the music did – and that's what soul is all about.

After ten #1 singles between 1964 and 1967, the group began to break apart and their chart placings began to falter. Ballard left in 1967, to be replaced by former Bluebelle **Cindy Birdsong**, and the group, now officially known as **Diana Ross & The Supremes**, set about pursuing the supper-club dream shared by both Ross and Gordy. Their new MOR sound, as heard on 1968's "Love Child", continued to sell, but the tension and crackle of their old records were gone. Ross left the group to pursue a solo career at Motown after "Someday We'll Be Together" in 1969, and **Jean Terrell** came aboard. Even without Ross, The Supremes' profile remained high enough for the hits – "Stoned Love", "Nathan Jones" and "Floy Joy" – to keep on coming in the early 70s. However, when Birdsong was herself replaced by **Lynda Lawrence** in 1972, the writing was clearly on the wall. The Supremes name was retired in 1977, but Ross, **Scherrie Payne** (who had been in the mid-70s line-up that featured Mary Wilson and Cindy Birdsong for her second stint) and Lynda Lawrence reunited as The Supremes for a few performances in 2000. Ironically, none of them had ever actually been in The Supremes together.

⊙ Where Did Our Love Go?
1964, Motown

Holland-Dozier-Holland, who produced and wrote most of this, launched The Supremes to greatness. The girls were primarily a singles group, but this breakout release demonstrates that there was enough quality material left over to fill albums. The best way to get this now is on the 2000 reissue that pairs it with 1966's *I Hear A Symphony*.

⊙ The Ultimate Collection
1997, Motown

This 25-track compilation delivers "just the hits, ma'am", plus embarrassing renditions of "Funny Girl", "The Boy From Ipanema" and "Funny How Time Slips Away". No one but a Supremes obsessive really needs to own anything more than this.

Al B Sure!

With a laid-back, sexy voice that blended into the watery keys that dominated his records, former high-school star quarterback **Al B Sure!** was one of the biggest R&B stars of the late 80s and early 90s.

Born **Al Brown** in Boston, Massachusetts in 1969, Al B Sure! was raised in Mount Vernon, New York. When he wasn't playing football, he was writing songs with his cousin **Kyle West**. Through his friendship with DJ Eddie F, Sure sang backing vocals on Heavy D's "Money Earning Mount Vernon" in 1987. This introduced Sure to Andre Harrell, Heavy D's manager, who in turn introduced him to **Benny Medina**, one of the heads of black music at Warner Bros. That same year Sure won a songwriting competition with a song he had written as a 15-year-old and was signed to Warner Bros.

That song, "Nite And Day", became Sure's first single in 1988. One of the rare R&B tracks hip enough to be played on the younger, more cutting-edge urban radio stations as well as the more conservative ones and even the MOR stations, "Nite And Day" was a smash, reaching the top of the R&B chart and the pop Top 10. His debut album *In Effect Mode* went multi-platinum and also made it to the top of the charts.

The follow-up single "Off On Your Own (Girl)" was tougher and more angular, but Sure's voice (which sounded like **Philip Bailey** filtered through Michael Jackson and **El Debarge**) tempered the hip-hop elements, making it another R&B #1. When he cut more strutting tracks like "Rescue Me", Sure suffered – and the less said about his version of Roberta Flack's "Killing Me Softly" the better – but by the end of 1988 he had already established himself as a star.

After appearing on Quincy Jones's all-star quiet storm session, "The Secret Garden (Sweet Seduction Suite)", Sure had another R&B chart-topper with "Missunderstanding" in 1990. It was a harder New Jack Swing style track and Sure wasn't as sharp as he needed to be, but it was still another R&B #1. Later that year he also held his own on the rather sickly ballad "No Matter What You Do (Young 'N' Strong)" with Diana Ross.

Sure had his last R&B #1 with "Right Now" in 1992. Subsequent singles from his third album, *Sexy Versus*, failed to sell and Sure took a break from recording to work in an A&R position at Motown. He was involved in a serious car accident in 1996, but he has since recovered. He currently hosts his own "The Secret Garden" syndicated radio show and runs his own label, ABS Entertainment.

The Very Best Of Al B Sure!
2003, Rhino

This 16-track collection of the lighter side of New Jack Swing is all the Al B Sure! anyone needs – although no one really needs to hear his version of The Eagles' "Hotel California" either. Sure was at his best when his delicate falsetto could float off into the background and mesh with the production, but that's not to say that he didn't have personality as a singer – just that he preferred smooth talking over macking.

Swamp Dogg

A legend on the British "deep soul" scene, Jerry Williams, Jr. is one of the most original, unhinged and unheralded talents to ever cut a soul side. As a producer, Williams has been responsible for good to great records by C & The Shells, **The Exciters**, Charlie & Inez Foxx, Gary US Bonds, Irma

Thomas and, most famously, **Doris Duke** (see 2005's *I'm A Loser: The Swamp Dogg Sessions And More*). It's his records as **Swamp Dogg**, however, that ensure Williams a place in the soul pantheon. Alongside **Norman Whitfield**'s productions for The Temptations, Sly Stone and George Clinton's **Parliafunkadelicment Thang**, Swamp Dogg was responsible for expanding soul's parameters in the early 70s. In many ways, he was probably the most radical of them all.

Born in Portsmouth, Virginia on July 12, 1942, Williams was raised in a musical family that included stepfather guitarist **Nat Cross** and local drummer **Miss Vera**. His unique take on soul can perhaps be traced to his Catholic upbringing, which meant that he didn't have the usual gospel training or grounding in tradition of most soul singers. Williams recorded his first record, "HTD Blues", in 1956 as a 14-year-old, calling himself **Little Jerry**. He also received plenty of exposure in Virginia where he opened for whatever national acts were touring at the time. By the time he was 18, Williams had written a book of poetry, two plays and a novel, and produced a local TV show.

Little Jerry's "There Ain't Enough Love" was produced by **Dave "Baby" Cortez** in 1960, but the next year Williams took on the producer's role himself, on records by Tony Middleton, Jay Dee Bryant and a young Gino Vanelli, who later went on to disco fame. In the mid-60s Williams started recording for the Calla label and had his first hit, as Little Jerry Williams, with "Baby, You're My Everything". The follow-up, "If You Ask Me (Because I Love You)", recorded as Jerry Williams, did nothing at the time, but would eventually become one of the big records at the Wigan Casino.

After a decade as a journeyman producer and singer, Williams came up with the Swamp Dogg persona as a reaction to the standard packaging formulas of the record industry. As outrageous as **George Clinton**, as in your face as a punk **Little Richard** and as down and dirty as Dyke & The Blazers, Swamp Dogg was what **Otis Redding** might have sounded like if he had dropped acid with the "love crowd" after the Monterey International Pop Festival and stayed with them through the disillusionment of the Chicago Democratic Convention and the Kent State massacre.

Originally released on Canyon Records in 1970, Swamp Dogg's *Total Destruction To Your Mind* was housed in a cover that showed a guy sitting on the back of a truck with shorts and boots on and a metal pot on his head. The music inside was fairly typical Southern soul in the Stax/Muscle Shoals mould with a rougher edge and a bit more drive. Like the music, his voice was as raw as you could imagine; Robert Christgau has described it as "an Afro-American air-raid siren". The album's big hit was a blues ditty called "Mama's Baby, Daddy's Maybe" in which the singer's wife gives birth to a baby with blue eyes that's "a little brighter, a wee bit lighter than anybody in our families". It was in the classic cheating-song vein, but the details subtly subverted the form and gave the song a dimension no one else would have dared broach.

Total Destruction was a *cause célèbre* among hip soul fans and the press reaction helped get the Dogg signed to Elektra. His only album for the label was 1971's *Rat On*. Although *Rat On* couldn't recapture *Total Destruction*'s inspired lunacy, it did feature two songs as remarkable as anything on *Total Destruction*. "God Bless America, For What" brought a lawsuit from the Irving Berlin Foundation for using the name of Berlin's song in vain, while "Remember I Said Tomorrow" was the best indictment of political hypocrisy that **Bob Dylan** never wrote.

After being dropped by Elektra, Williams continued to produce other artists for his Mankind label, including Doris Duke, Z.Z. Hill and **Freddie North**. In 1973 he recorded an amazing version of John Prine's anti-war song "Sam Stone" and the twisted *Gag A Maggot*, which included a track called "I Couldn't Pay For What I Got Last Night" – a love song. He recorded several more singles for various different labels, including his own Stonedogg imprint with TK, before he made it into the R&B chart again in 1977 with "My Heart Can't Stop Dancing", a disco track recorded with a group called **Riders of the New Funk**.

I'm Not Selling Out, I'm Buying In was released on the Takoma label in 1981 and found Swamp Dogg ranting about abortion and El Salvador and collaborating with Esther Phillips. On his newly formed SDEG label, 1989's *I Asked For A Rope And They Threw Me A Rock* went back to more traditional soul, although the Dogg's trademark eccentricities were still very much intact. Ten years later, he returned once again with *Surfin' In Harlem*, which included a song with perhaps the best title ever, "I've Never Been To Africa (And It's Your Fault)" – it nearly lived up to the greatness of the title.

In the ensuing years, Williams has been concentrating on hip-hop projects, working with Flint, Michigan rappers **MC Breed** and **DFC**, and releasing holiday novelties like "She Left Me For Rudolph" with Xmas Balls, a group featuring Williams, Ned McElroy and Monty Lane Allen.

⊙ Total Destruction To Your Mind/Rat On
1991, Charly

Combining his two greatest albums (from 1970 and 1971) on a single disc, this is the best introduction to one of soul's most original and eccentric artists. Swamp Dogg was one of the few soul artists to dare to openly take on the establishment, and *Total Destruction*'s triumph is that the message comes across loud and clear without being cloying or crass. His version of Joe South's "Redneck" is probably the most daring song ever recorded by a black singer, while "I Was Born Blue" is one of the most moving.

Bettye Swann

Equally comfortable with the sweet teen-oriented soul of the mid-60s and the deep country soul material she recorded in the 70s, **Bettye Swann** is one of soul's more underrated vocalists. Her problem wasn't the usual one of being burdened with weak material, but that her style was often too busy for the music she sang.

She was born **Betty Jean Champion** in Shreveport, Louisiana on October 24, 1944, and grew up singing in church. Moving with her family to California in the late 50s, she sang in a female vocal group called The Fawns in high school. She signed to the Money label as a solo artist in 1964 and immediately had a top-thirty R&B hit with a version of **Carolyn Franklin**'s (Aretha Franklin's sister) "Don't Wait Too Long". Real success came with her fourth single, "Make Me Yours", in 1967. The record had one of the most meaningful guitar chanks in soul history. Swann was slightly breathless, but that just made the record that much more convincing.

Swann signed with Capitol in 1968, where she was produced by **Wayne Shuler**. On her first record there, "My Heart Is Closed For The Season", she developed a new, less girlish persona than she'd had in the past – she'd been wronged, but was rising above the fray. Shame about the busy production, though. Later that year, her version of **Hank Cochran**'s "Don't Touch Me" had a horn arrangement that was a bit Vegas. Swann's vocals didn't fit comfortably with all that showbiz, but the record became her second-biggest hit anyway.

Moving to Atlantic in 1971, Swann started working with **Rick Hall**, the owner of Fame Studios in Muscle Shoals, and his less baroque productions suited her far better. The light arrangement of 1971's "Victim Of A Foolish Heart", with its whining keyboard, positive cod-Motown beat and cheesy horns, was far more fitting than Shuler's busy, showbiz arrangements. She followed that with modest hits with killer versions of **Merle Haggard**'s "Today I Started Loving You Again" and **Tammy Wynette**'s "Till I Get it Right".

Swann moved away from country soul and towards the prevailing Philadelphia style with "The Boy Next Door" and "Kiss My Love Goodbye" in 1974. However, the following year she moved back to her favoured territory, country soul, with producer **Brad Shapiro** (no relation) on "All The Way In Or All the Way Out" and the very fine "Be

Strong Enough To Hold On". Unfortunately, the latter was her last record as she faded from the scene soon after its release.

Bettye Swann
2004, Honest Jon's/Astralwerks

Unfortunately, the compilation of Swann's Atlantic years, *Elegant Soul* (1981, Atlantic), was only released in Japan, but this collection of her Capitol recordings is the next best thing. The finest productions here are those that are the most restrained – such as the versions of Otis Redding's "These Arms Of Mine" and Patsy Cline's "Sweet Dreams" – but elsewhere the arrangements are often too busy and the sound too sweeping for Swann's voice. Fans of her earlier, sweeter recordings should opt for *The Money Recordings* (2001, Kent).

Keith Sweat

His nasal, pleading vocal style – based largely on Slave's **Steve Arrington** – may be an acquired taste, but the fact remains, however sadly, that **Keith Sweat** is one of the best singers in contemporary R&B, although he doesn't have that much competition.

Keith Sweat was born in New York on July 22, 1961, and he grew up in Harlem's Grant Housing Projects. While attending City College, he became the lead singer of a funk group called Jamilah, and, although he didn't stay with the group for long, it was through them that he met **Teddy Riley**, who was then a member of rival band Total Climax. A couple of years later, while working as a commodities broker, Sweat hooked up with Riley once again. Riley co-wrote and produced Sweat's debut "I Want Her", one of the most important singles of the last 25 years. With its garish synth stabs, hip-hop beats and street attitude, "I Want Her" marked the birth of New Jack Swing and became a huge hit on both the R&B and pop charts in 1987.

"Something Just Ain't Right" followed the next year and, although it sounded more like a Colonel Abrams record than his debut, it was another big R&B hit. "Make It Last Forever", a duet with **Jacci McGhee**, was a fairly standard "I'm gonna rub you down" ballad, while "Don't Stop Your Love" had production reminiscent of a slowed down **Nu Shooz** record. All of these tracks went into the Top 10 on the R&B chart and Sweat was now the new love man prototype.

The self-produced "Make You Sweat" became his second R&B #1 in 1990. It was more humping and pumping than his previous records, but had a slightly different style to his Teddy Riley-produced tracks. The follow-up ballad "I'll Give All My Love To You" was his second-biggest pop hit, reaching #7 on the pop chart, while the next year's "Why Me Baby?" basically created the formula for Jodeci.

After releasing the lacklustre *Keep On It* in 1994, Sweat returned to the top of the R&B chart with 1996's *Keith Sweat*, which included two platinum singles, "Twisted" and "Nobody". Sweat also went platinum with "My Body", a track he recorded as part of the all-star group **LSG** with **Gerald Levert** and **Johnny Gill**, which spent seven weeks at #1 on the R&B chart. In 1998 *Still In The Game* saw Sweat pointlessly celebrating a decade in the love man game with rappers like Too $hort and Erick Sermon, although "Come And Get With Me", a collaboration with **Snoop Dogg**, was a fine record, in a Montell Jordan kind of way. At the turn of the century, *Didn't See Me Coming* (2000) and *Rebirth* (2002) continued Sweat's remarkable run as one of R&B's top stallions.

Make It Last Forever
1987, Vintertainment/Elektra

For better or worse, this album has come to define the R&B of the last 20 years. Working with producer Teddy Riley, Sweat remade R&B with a hip-hop attitude – even on the ballads – and his whining tenor became *the* male R&B voice. Whether this album is your definition of soul or not is immaterial; it's now become everyone else's.

SWV

Sisters With Voices was one of the biggest R&B groups of the 90s. More street than En Vogue but less sassy than TLC, the all-female group SWV – **Cheryl "Coko" Gamble**, **Tamara "Taj" Johnson** and **Leanne "Lelee" Lyons** – hit the perfect middle ground for radio programmers.

The members of **SWV** were all New York City high-school friends who were originally in a group called Female Edition, named after New Edition. In 1990 they changed their name to SWV and briefly performed as a gospel group, before hooking up with producer **Brian Alexander Morgan**. Their debut

single, "Right Here", which was released on RCA in 1992, was a decent R&B hit. That same year, their debut album, *It's About Time*, became a smash thanks to the singles "I'm So Into You", "Weak" and "Always On My Mind", the latter being their most soulful track, not that that's saying much. Their pop #1 "Weak" was probably the apotheosis – or nadir, depending on your view – of the decade's overenunciated, adenoidal vocal style.

A **Teddy Riley** remix of "Right Here", which featured prominent samples of Michael Jackson's "Human Nature", spent seven weeks at the top of the R&B chart in 1993 and was only kept from the pop chart top spot by Mariah Carey's "Dreamlover". The following year SWV collaborated with hip-hop crew **The Wu-Tang Clan** on the R&B top-ten "Anything" from the *Above The Rim* soundtrack.

The girls' second album, 1996's *New Beginning*, had a richer sound than their debut, perhaps because Johnson and Lyons took a greater role, whereas Gamble had been the dominant voice on *It's About Time*. "You're The One" was another R&B #1, but subsequent singles "Use Your Heart" and "It's All About U" failed to keep up the momentum. In 1997 *Release Some Tension* found them going back to the streets with production from **P. Diddy** and an array of guest appearances from the likes of **Snoop Dogg**, Missy Elliott, Redman and E-40. The single "Someone" featured P. Diddy and several **Notorious BIG** samples and it went gold, while "Rain" was built on the foundation of Jaco Pastorius's "Portrait Of Tracy".

SWV broke up in 1998. Gamble released a solo album, *Hot Coko*, the following year and she had a modest hit with the single "Sunshine", produced by **Rodney Jerkins**. Rumours of a reunion surfaced in 2002 and again in 2005 and SWV have recently begun touring again, but at the time of writing, no new material has been released.

Best Of SWV
2001, RCA

If you need to hear the descent of R&B into the adenoids of oversexed, sentimental teenagers, then look no further than this 16-track collection. It includes all of SWV's R&B hits from the early 90s, but none of the unnecessary filler from their other albums.

The Sylvers

They were terribly derivative of The Jackson 5, but of all the family groups that followed in the wake of that pop phenomenon, Memphis's **The Sylvers** were surely the best. At the very least, they were better than **The DeFranco Family**.

The Sylvers began life as The Little Angels when opera singer **Shirley Sylvers** organized her children **Leon III, Charmaine, Olympia-Ann** and **James** into a singing group in the late 60s. The group served as the opening act for the likes of **Ray Charles** and **Johnny Mathis** before moving to LA in 1970. With the addition of younger siblings **Foster, Edmund** and **Ricky** in 1971, the group changed their name to The Sylvers and signed to the MGM subsidiary Pride. Their first two singles, "Fool's Paradise" and "Wish That I Could Talk to You", were produced by **Jerry Butler** and **Keg Johnson** and reached the R&B Top 20.

While largely a commercial failure, 1973's *The Sylvers II* has since become a cult favourite thanks to killer production from Johnson and **Jerry Peters**. "Stay Away From Me" had one of those great dramatic intros that made early 70s soul so appealing, while "We Can Make It If We Try" had monstrous chicken scratch guitars and a very chunky beat. That same year Foster released the solo single "Misdemeanor", which had similarly brilliant production and became an early disco classic and later a hip-hop favourite.

The Sylvers moved to the Capitol label in 1975, where they recorded three new albums and worked with former Jackson 5 producer **Freddie Perren**. He concocted a series of infectious teen disco records for the group in the mid-70s: "Boogie Fever", "Cotton Candy", "Hot Line" and "High School Dance".

Moving labels again in 1978, The Sylvers released *Forever Yours* on the Casablanca label. The album was produced by one of the older Sylver brothers, Leon III, who created the underrated disco-funk cut "Don't Stop, Get Off". The next year's *Disco Fever* was produced by **Giorgio Moroder** and was an undersung classic of the Eurodisco sound. The group then moved to the Solar label, before winding down their career in the mid-80s on Geffen.

Leon later became something of a star producer at Solar, working with **The Brothers Johnson**, Five Star and **Howard Hewett**. Meanwhile, his brother Foster went on to work with **Shalamar**, The Whispers, **Janet Jackson** and **Evelyn "Champagne" King** as an arranger-producer.

Boogie Fever: The Best Of The Sylvers
1995, Razor & Tie

Since it concentrates on their hits, this collection doesn't have nearly enough material from the fine *The Sylvers II*, but it is still 16 cuts of thoroughly enjoyable pop soul. It also includes Foster's superb solo release "Misdemeanor" and Edmund's less great "That Burning Love".

Sylvester

In a just world, **Sylvester** would have been as big as **Michael Jackson** or **Prince**. With his flamboyance, shimmer, sexual charisma and fierce high-energy beats, Sylvester was everything pop music is meant to be. Aside from **Chic** and the NYC **Peech Boys**, no one else of his time seemed to recognize that disco was both utopia and hell – the tension from which all truly great dance music is born. Most significantly, his use of his gospel-trained falsetto in the explicit service of gay desire and pleasure surely represents the most radical rewrite of pop's lingua franca ever attempted, while his success stands as a testament to the beauty and openness of the African-American musical tradition.

Born in 1947, **Sylvester James**, like most singers of his generation, learned his craft in church. By his teens, the music of **Bessie Smith** and **Billie Holiday** had supplanted gospel in his affections, and after moving to San Francisco in the late 60s he starred in a cabaret show called *Women Of The Blues*. In 1970 he joined the cross-dressing revue troupe The Cockettes and quickly became an underground star. When he kicked off his solo career as Sylvester & The Hot Band in 1973, he was covering Neil Young and James Taylor, and he continued down this rock path until he hooked up with former Moonglow **Harvey Fuqua** in 1977.

Sylvester then moved in a more soul-oriented direction. His first album with Fuqua, *Sylvester*, contained the solid disco floor-burner "Down, Down, Down", which may have been formulaic first-wave disco with its surging strings, galloping bassline, awkward horns and workmanlike arrangement, but had enough energy and pace to become a modest club hit in New York. However, it was another track off the album, a version of Ashford & Simpson's "Over And Over", that propelled Sylvester towards disco superstardom. Rather than the dancefloor heat for which he became known, "Over And Over" was an intense slowburn with stupendous backing vocals from **Izora Rhodes** and **Martha Wash**.

Following this somewhat limited success, 1978's *Step II* briefly carried Sylvester into the mainstream. The album's first single, "Dance (Disco Heat)" – a fairly mindless but enthralling disco track in which Rhodes and Wash (now known as Two Tons o' Fun) played a prominent role – reached the American Top 20 at the peak of disco fever. Although the follow-up, "You Make Me Feel (Mighty Real)", barely crept into the US Top 40, it is Sylvester's greatest record. With its synth licks, mechanized bassline and drum-machine beats, the song was the genesis of the disco sub-genre known as Hi-NRG. In other hands the genre was seldom more than an aural fantasy of a futuristic club populated entirely by cybernetic Tom of Finland studs, but the Hi-NRG created by Sylvester, Fuqua and synth player **Patrick Cowley** interrogated the African-American musical tradition and demanded to know what "realness" means for gay, black men who are forced to hide their true identities for most of their lives.

Cowley played a bigger role in Sylvester's music from then on, and eventually became his producer during the 80s. He penned 1979's "Stars (Everybody Is One)", a celebration of disco's fantasy world in which everyone could be who they wanted to be. Other tracks from that year, such as "Body Strong" and "I (Who Have Nothing)", shared that otherworldly quality, as the rigidly insistent mechanistic throbs of the synthesizers sought to upset the "natural" order of things. Sylvester's union of flesh, emotion and machine reinforced his status as the ultimate disco star.

Recording for Cowley's Megatone label in the early 80s, Sylvester specialized in

PLAYLIST
Sylvester

1 OVER AND OVER from
Star: The Best Of Sylvester
A guitar-and-bass slowburn that owes its intensity to the impassioned vocals by Sylvester and backing singers Izora Rhodes and Martha Wash.

2 DANCE (DISCO HEAT) from
Star: The Best Of Sylvester
Irresistible disco bounce-along.

3 YOU MAKE ME FEEL (MIGHTY REAL)
from **Star: The Best Of Sylvester**
An out-and-out disco masterpiece.

4 STARS (EVERYBODY IS ONE) from
Star: The Best Of Sylvester
A great exposition of pop's greatest subject.

5 I NEED SOMEBODY TO LOVE TONIGHT
from **Star: The Best Of Sylvester**
Eerie, slightly sleazy synth-reggae song of horny desperation.

6 I (WHO HAVE NOTHING) from
Star: The Best Of Sylvester
Over-the-top disco remake of Ben E. King.

7 DOWN DOWN DOWN from
Star: The Best Of Sylvester
Superfast disco gospel.

8 DO YOU WANNA FUNK from
Star: The Best Of Sylvester
One of the best examples of the clinical San Francisco sound of the early 80s.

Cowley's trademark San Francisco sound, performing relentlessly upbeat, ultra-mechanized, clinically clean uptempo disco songs. Whether wailing on top of Hi-NRG synths or delivering slow-burn ballads, Sylvester remained one of dance music's most distinctive vocalists until his AIDS-related death on December 16, 1988.

Star: The Best Of Sylvester
1989, Southbound/Ace

The best of Sylvester's work with Harvey Fuqua for the Fantasy label can be found on this 11-track compilation, which includes the disco hits "Over And Over" and "Down, Down, Down" and the great Hi-HRG tracks "You Make Me Feel (Mighty Real)" and "Stars (Everybody Is One)". Essential not only for disco fans, but for anyone interested in the breadth of soul's vision and inclusivity.

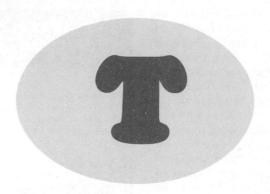

The Tams

Formed in the late 50s in Atlanta, **The Tams** have enjoyed a longevity out of all proportion to their chart success. Comprised of **Joseph** and **Charles Pope**, **Robert Lee Smith**, **Floyd Ashton** and **Horace Key**, the group started out as The Four Dots, but was renamed after their signature Scottish Tam O'Shanter caps.

The Tams' first hit came in 1962 with the shuffling "Untie Me", which they recorded at Fame Studios in Muscle Shoals. On the strength of its delightful interplay between the rough-voiced lead vocals of Joseph Pope and the bass of Smith, the flute-driven "What Kind Of Fool (Do You Think I Am)" reached the pop Top 10 the following year. Next came "Hey Girl Don't Bother Me", which featured a quasi-Latin beat reminiscent of Ben E. King's "Spanish Harlem" and a gently effervescent swing.

Although they couldn't maintain this steady chart success, The Tams quickly became favourites on the beach music scene in the Carolinas. They continued to record with songwriter/producers like **Ray Whiteley** and **Joe South** in the mid- to late 60s. That duo wrote The Tams' last American chart hit, the wonderful "Be Young, Be Foolish, Be Happy", in 1968.

Bizarrely, a 1971 reissue of "Hey Girl Don't Bother Me" reached #1 on the British pop charts, but the group remained largely invisible to everyone but their fanatical fans along the boardwalks from Wilmington to Charleston. In 1987 the film *Shag* inspired a mini beach music craze in the UK, and The Tams reached the Top 30 once again with "There Ain't Nothing Like Shaggin'", although probably because of the song's unintentional double entendre to British ears. To this day, The Tams still enjoy hits on the beach music circuit with recent records such as the bluesy "It Happens Every Time" and "Walkin' Dr. Bill".

The Best Of The Tams
1995, Ripete

This 14-track retrospective collects all of The Tams' ABC-Paramount singles from 1963 to 1969. They may have been Atlanta's biggest soul group during the 60s, but the easy swing and dated doo-wop feel of these tracks shows why their main audience was located a couple of hundred miles to the east.

Howard Tate

The geographical landmarks of country soul are as legendary as the music they produced: Memphis, Tennessee; Muscle Shoals, Alabama; Jackson, Mississippi. So how does Englewood Cliffs, New Jersey fit into that litany? **Rudy Van Gelder**'s studio in his living room in suburban New Jersey may be sacred ground in jazz circles, but it's hardly on the map for soul fans. Nonetheless, in the person of **Howard Tate**, this unlikely locale produced some of the greatest deep-soul sides ever recorded.

Until his recent re-emergence, Howard Tate was a bit of a mystery man. Even the European soul obsessives who have dug up every possible biographical detail about the most obscure artists have been stymied in their efforts to track down the elusive Tate. What is know is that Tate was born in

Beach Music

The American equivalent of the British Northern soul phenomenon, "beach music" had its roots in the forced integration of areas like Norfolk and Virginia Beach during the war effort in the mid-40s. Jump blues and R&B records started to appear on jukeboxes in white clubs in this seaside area, attracting fans from nearby frat houses and among the slightly bohemian lifeguard community.

R&B records quickly became the music of choice for clubs along the beach and for frat parties at nearby universities. The sound then spread down the coast to the Carolinas, where it fit perfectly with a 50s dance craze called "The Shag". In Myrtle Beach, South Carolina and Wilmington, North Carolina, teenagers gathered to dance the Shag to R&B records during summer vacations. The "shaggers" took any R&B record with a shuffling beat to their hearts, and obscure groups like The Tams, **The Embers**, The Showmen, **Bill Deal & The Rhondels** and **The Catalinas** became huge in the Carolinas.

In the 60s the music of choice was Motown, but like the Northern soul DJs, beach music scenesters preferred rarer, less obvious, records such as The Showmen's "39-21-46" (1963), **Fontella Bass & Bobby McLure**'s "You'll Miss Me (When I'm Gone)" (1965) and **The Monzas'** "Hey I Know" (1966). The growing influence of funk and disco in the late 60s and 70s threatened to destroy the scene, but **The Tymes'** "Ms Grace" (1974), The Catalinas' "Summertime's Calling Me" (1975) and The Embers' "I Love Beach Music" (1979) helped keep the shaggers happy.

Riding a wave of nostalgia, the beach music scene came back as strong as ever in the 80s. Blues harmonica player **Delbert McClinton**'s "Maybe Someday Baby" became one of the scene's biggest songs and reinvigorated a movement that had been based largely on old records. Beach music is still going strong today and its preservation society, the Society of Stranders, holds gatherings of up to 10,000 people every year.

◉ **Various Artists: Ocean Boulevard: The Ultimate Beach Box**
1999, Ripete

From Sticks McGhee's 1949 classic "Drinkin' Wine Spo-Dee-O-Dee" to current shag faves by The Band of Oz, this 4-disc set covers the entire beach music scene and serves as a wonderful alternative history of R&B.

Macon, Georgia in 1938 and whiled away his adolescence doo-wopping in Philadelphia with Garnet Mimms. In the early 60s, he was the lead singer in Bill Doggett's band. Other than that, his life before and after these "legendary sessions" is pretty sketchy. What remains most mysterious about Tate, however, is how a man who spent most of his life above the Mason-Dixon line acquired such an affinity for downhome sounds?

Recorded in April 1966, Tate's debut, "Ain't Nobody Home", was released by the Verve label and became his biggest hit, reaching #12 on the R&B chart and #63 pop. With a groove laid down by keyboardist **Richard Tee**, guitarist **Cornell Dupree**, bassist **Chuck Rainey** and drummer **Herb Lovell**, the production of "Ain't Nobody Home" by **Jerry Ragavoy** both borrowed from and influenced the music coming from Memphis and Muscle Shoals, and set the precedent for Atlantic's first recordings with Aretha Franklin. While the music was great, however, it was Tate's vocals that made the record. Sounding like a less overwrought Percy Sledge, Tate's simultaneously Northern and Southern phrasing was impeccable, and the economical use of his falsetto made it all the more effective.

The follow-up, "Look At Granny Run Run", a **Mort Shuman** throwaway turned into an enjoyable romp, did almost as well on the charts. Tate's third single, "Get It While You Can", was another Shuman/ Ragavoy collaboration and it sounded like it had come straight out of west Tennessee. The bleary horns and comping guitar screamed Memphis, while Tate outdid Solomon Burke in the secular-preacher-of-love stakes. Despite being an archetypal soul classic, it failed to make an impression on the charts until **Janis Joplin** got hold of it and turned it into a hippy travesty. More near-perfect church soul followed in the form of "I Learned It All The Hard Way", but it also failed to dent the charts.

Despite his affinity for sermonizing, Tate's best record was 1968's "Stop". An infectious groove created from the greatest non-Memphis piano line ever and a horn-arranging masterclass from **Garry Sherman**, "Stop" perfected the sound Ragavoy had constructed on "Ain't Nobody Home". Tate once again stole the show with his blues-rooted economy and restrained, but emotional, melisma.

After recording a couple of minor hits for Lloyd Price's Turntable label, Tate released *Howard Tate* on Atlantic in 1972. The album included covers of **Bob Dylan**'s "Girl From The North Country" and **The Band**'s "Jemima Surrender". A single for Epic followed in 1974, but Tate then vanished from view, apparently because he was forced underground by a dependency problem.

Tate eventually found religion and was working as a minister in New Jersey when a former member of **Harold Melvin & The Blue Notes** ran into him in a supermarket in 2003. Reunited with Jerry Ragavoy, Tate released *Rediscovered* that year, a decent if not great album that's compelling mostly because of the story behind it.

⊙ Get It While You Can: The Legendary Sessions
1995, Mercury

Tate's not the greatest soul singer ever, but he deserves more than just a cult following, and this 17-track collection of his Verve singles should give him that. Bluesier than most of his contemporaries, thanks largely to a childhood fascination with BB King, he consistently brings an extra emotional depth to his work.

Tavares

While most of the vocal groups of the 70s were clean-cut (aside from their Afros, of course), **Tavares** were perhaps the only group you could take home to your mother. The five Tavares brothers – **Antone** ("Chubby"), **Arthur** ("Pooch"), **Feliciano** ("Butch"), **Perry Lee** ("Tiny") and **Ralph** – specialized in a nice, safe brand of vocal harmony that certainly wasn't as zany as **Parliament**'s or **Skull Snaps**' nor as asexual as **The Stylistics**', just middle-of-the-road.

The Tavares brothers of Cape Verdean descent formed a vocal group called Chubby & The Turnpikes in 1964 in their home town of New Bedford, Massachusetts. They changed their name to Tavares in 1969 and signed to Capitol Records four years later. Their first single, "Check It Out", was a decent, although rather faceless, ballad in the prevailing soft-soul style. It made the R&B Top 5 in 1973 and was quickly followed into the Top 10 by the funkier, Temptations-styled "That's The Sound That Lonely Makes" and the Philly-styled "Too Late".

A 1974 cover of **Hall & Oates**' "She's Gone" became Tavares' first R&B #1, even though it wasn't as bright as the original. However, their first substantial crossover hit was the next year's pop-disco classic "It Only Takes A Minute", which borrowed liberally from The **Four Tops**' "Are You Man Enough". After their faithful and perky cover of Edgar Winter's "Free Ride", the group released the biggest hit of their career, 1976's "Heaven Must Be Missing An Angel", an easy-listening/disco crossover track of consummate professionalism. "Whodunnit", a silly track that used the *Dragnet* theme in its intro, became their third R&B #1, while "Don't Take Away The Music" was a big disco hit. Their less polished (which was its attraction) version of **The Bee Gees**' "More Than A Woman" was included on the *Saturday Night Fever* soundtrack.

With the exception of "Never Had A Love Like This Before", "Bad Times" and "Deeper In Love", which all made it into the R&B Top 10, the group's late-70s and early-80s records were middling hits at best. Tavares may now be firmly associated with disco, but the craze effectively put an end to their surprising chart run. However, records like "A Penny For Your Thoughts" – that had such sickly sweet singsong melodies that no urban radio programmer could, in good conscience, play them during the hip-hop era – also played their part in the group's decline.

Although the group's 1981 collaboration with **Kashif**, "Loveline", briefly made them sound modern again, they couldn't keep up the momentum and they disappeared from the charts entirely in the early 80s. Ralph and Tiny soon left the group, but the remaining three brothers are still touring and performing on the oldies circuit.

⊙ Capitol Gold: The Best Of Tavares
1996, Capitol

There's no fuss and no muss on this album, which is easily the best of the numerous Tavares compilations on the market. Here are their 15 biggest R&B hits plus "More Than A Woman". Unlike most of their contemporaries, Tavares made the transition to disco with ease, becoming one of the emblematic pop groups of the mid-70s.

Johnnie Taylor

Johnnie Taylor, "The soul philosopher", was one of soul's greatest and most versatile vocalists. Unlike most singers who find one style or groove and stick with it for their entire career, Taylor was able to fit his voice to the circumstance, moving from a Sam Cooke-influenced style to a harder, more Southern testifying style to disco sleazeball and back again during his career.

Taylor was born on May 5, 1938 in Crawfordsville, Arkansas, but moved to Chicago as a teenager. There he sang with gospel groups The Melody Makers, The Five Echoes and The Highway QCs. The QCs were essentially the understudies for The Soul Stirrers, and, when Sam Cooke left the group in 1957, Taylor was his replacement. Taylor sounded very much in Cooke's thrall during his tenure with the group, a situation that didn't change when he followed his mentor's lead, went secular and signed with the Sar label in 1961. Taylor's early records "Whole Lotta Woman" (his first secular recording) and "Baby, We've Got Love" (his first chart hit) were essentially carbon copies of the master.

When Taylor joined Stax in 1966, he had a bit more grit to his voice. The Cooke-derived urbane swoop was absent on bluesy, testifying tracks like "I Had A Dream", the Otis Redding-like "Changes", the ridiculously funky version of the Tennessee Ernie Ford standard "Sixteen Tons" and "Somebody's Sleeping In My Bed". Instead of the usual funereal ballads about cheating, Stax drummer Al Jackson cranked up the tempo, bassist Donald "Duck" Dunn came up with the best bassline of his illustrious career and Taylor howled like a hell hound on his 1968 breakthrough, "Who's Making Love", his first record with producer Don Davis.

With Davis's involvement, Taylor's "Take Care Of Your Homework", "Testify (I Wanna)", "Love Bones" and "Jody's Got Your Girl And Gone" (the genesis of the Jody cheating saga with a great, Detroit-style chorus in the background) all followed in a broadly similar style and were all big R&B hits. Taylor could still nail the country soul ballads, though, as his great versions of

"Separation Line" and "Steal Away" showed. Taylor returned to his Cooke-influenced intimacy in the early 70s on "I Believe In You (You Believe in Me)" and "We're Getting Careless With Our Love", while "Cheaper To Keep Her" was a reminder that he could still growl if he had to.

When Stax folded in 1975, Taylor moved to Columbia and had the biggest hit of his career with the reprehensible "Disco Lady". The platinum single which went to #1 on the R&B and pop charts was, unquestionably, his worst record so far. Unfortunately, he continued in this style throughout the latter half of the 70s with "Somebody's Gettin' It", "Love Is Better In The AM", "Your Love Is Rated X" and "Keep On Dancing".

Taylor recorded two albums and a song about Reaganomics for the smaller Beverly Glen label in the early 80s, before moving to Malaco in 1984. The label seemed to suit him; he released a number of albums with them over the next fifteen years and had modest chart success with bluesy ballads like "Lady, My Whole World Is You" and slightly sterile funk tracks like "Wall To Wall". In 1990 the country-ish rebound ballad "Still Crazy" made it into the R&B chart, thanks to a fine performance from Taylor, while 1996's "Good Love" was a surprisingly affective combination of old and new which saw Taylor riding the contemporary beats in his classic style and proved that you could teach an old jack new tricks. "Good Love" was his biggest hit in over a decade.

Unfortunately, that success inspired Malaco to release "Disco Lady 2000" in 1998, which didn't improve on the original. The song proved to be his final chart appearance, as he died of a heart attack at his home in Dallas, Texas on May 31, 2000.

Taylored In Silk
1973, Stax

Taylor's verstaile deep-soul testifying easily bridged classic 60s soul and the more contemporary 70s style. His early-70s studio albums for Stax are full of extraordinary bluesy soul, and *Taylored In Silk* – highlighted by the gritty "Highjackin' Love" and the aching "Getting Careless With Our Love" – is the best of them.

Chronicle: The 20 Greatest Hits
1977, Stax

This 20-track collection doesn't include many of Taylor's ballads, which is a shame because he shined at slower tempos. However, it does have plenty of him testifying at mid- to blistering tempos, which, thankfully, he also excelled at. As this focuses exclusively on his Stax material, the fine *The Roots Of Johnnie Taylor* (1999, Soul City) is also worth checking out for his Sar recordings.

Ted Taylor

B orn Austin Taylor on February 16, 1934 in Okmulgee, Oklahoma, **Ted Taylor** has to be considered one of the great lost treasures of soul music. He used his powerful, dramatic falsetto with great control and economy on numerous records that perfectly combined soul, blues and gospel sensibilities. Taylor was also a rare artist who seemed to get better with age.

Taylor moved to California with his family at a young age and sang with gospel groups like The Glory Bound Travellers, The Mighty Clouds Of Joy and The Santa Monica Soul Seekers (where he sang with a young Lou Rawls). In 1954 he joined **Aaron Collins**' vocal group **The Jacks** – Collins, Taylor, Will Jones, Willie Davis and Lloyd McCraw – as a tenor. When the group signed to Modern/ RPM in 1955, the label wanted to give them two identities – they were The Jacks for Modern and **The Cadets** for RPM.

The group's first release was a cover of Nappy Brown's "Don't Be Angry" as The Cadets in 1955, but their first hit came as The Jacks that same year, when "Why Don't You Write Me?" hit #3 on the R&B chart. It's also worth seeking out the rock'n'roll ballad "So Wrong", with its wonderful sax solo. The Cadets scored a big hit in 1956 with one of the all-time great rock'n'roll songs, "Stranded In The Jungle", a comedic paranoid lover's exotic travelogue that managed to combine Stagger Lee, **Harvey & The Moonglows**, Rudyard Kipling, Andre Williams and Kid Creole in a blast of sheer delight that you just don't get anymore.

Taylor left the group in 1957 to pursue a solo career and immediately had minor success with "Days Are Dark" on Ebb. His biggest early hit was "Be Ever Wonderful", released on the Duke label in 1959, a stratospheric falsetto ballad that must have given **Russell Thompkins** an idea or two. In 1962 Taylor worked with producer **Carl Davis** at OKeh where he re-recorded "Be Ever Wonderful" with full orchestration, making it even more heavenly. His fabulous early

soul album, 1963's *Be Ever Wonderful*, featured another ethereal ballad, "This Love Of Mine", a stunning version of "St. James Infirmary" and the stomping "You Give Me Nothing To Go On". This kind of uptempo jealous rage became Taylor's forte at OKeh on killer tracks such as "Somebody's Always Trying", "Stay Away From My Baby" and the incredible "(Love Is Like A) Ramblin' Rose", which was later covered by **The MC5**.

Signing to Atco in 1965, Taylor released the great Southern soul pleaders "Try Me Again" and "Feed The Flame". Moving to **Stan Lewis**'s Ronn label in 1968, he helped pioneer the new Southern blend of blues and soul on early-70s records like "Something Strange Is Goin' On In My House", "How's Your Love Life Baby", "Only The Lonely Know" and the remarkably titled "(I'm Just A Crumb) In Your Breadbox Of Love". His best record during this period was 1973's "Cry It Out Baby", an uplifting duet with **Little Johnny Taylor** (no relation).

In 1975 Taylor moved to Alarm, where he recorded some fine Southern soul sides such as "Gonna Hate Myself In The Morning", on which he was reminiscent of an older Al Green, and some less distinguished records like "Ghetto Disco". After recording the largely ignored *Keeping My Head Above Water* in 1978, Taylor started his own Solpugdits label. He continued to release the odd single and album until he died in a car crash on October 22, 1987.

Ted Taylor's Greatest Hits
1995, Collectables

No really good Taylor compilations are currently available, so this far-from-perfect 18-track overview of his OKeh years will have to do. Interested parties are advised to seek out his early original albums *Be Ever Wonderful* (1963), *Taylor Made* (1970), which was reissued on CD a few years ago, and *You Can Dig It* (1970).

The Temptations

F rom the almost naive sweetness of their early records with Smokey Robinson to the dark paranoia of their later records with **Norman Whitfield**, **The Temptations** were certainly Motown's – and probably all of popular music's – best and most versatile vocal group. Unlike The Supremes, with whom they're often paired, The Temptations

The Temptations: "You put your right leg in…"

were modelled on the classic harmony group foundation laid down by gospel groups like The Soul Stirrers and Swan Silvertones. With **David Ruffin**'s rough-hewn leads and **Eddie Kendricks'** floating falsetto, The Temptations had two of soul's finest and most recognizable vocalists.

The Temptations grew out of several Detroit vocal groups — The Distants, The Primes and The Voice Masters – and cut their first recordings, "Oh Mother" and "Check Yourself", for the Miracle label in 1961. The original line-up of Eddie Kendricks, **Otis Williams**, **Melvin Franklin**, **Paul Williams** and **Elbridge Bryant** then cut their first record for Motown, "Dream Come True", the next year, but it wasn't until David Ruffin replaced Bryant in 1964 that they had their first substantial hit. With an almost singsong arrangement and hokey lines like "The way you swept me off my feet, you could have been a broom/You smell so sweet, you could have been perfume", their first hit, "The Way You Do The Things You Do", was pure Smokey Robinson, but The Temptations became Robinson's best vehicle because only singers as talented as Ruffin and Kendricks could ride the jaunty melody and give it any sort of conviction. With its

sublime melody, perfect arrangement and instantly memorable bass and finger-snap breakdown, perhaps anyone could have sung "My Girl" and made it a hit, but Ruffin's swoops and the group's harmonies made it such an enduring pop shibboleth.

The group had several more hits with Robinson, including the "Since I Lost My Baby" and "Get Ready", before switching to producer Norman Whitfield in 1966 for "Ain't Too Proud To Beg". Whitfield is one of the greatest producers in the history of popular music, as his records with The Temptations testify. From the intro, which had Ruffin rasping over a sanctified, Holy Roller beat to the "chanking" guitar and Whitfield's prostrate lyrics, "Ain't Too Proud To Beg" was a whole new sound for the group that emphasized their gospel roots.

After the slight "Beauty Is Only Skin Deep", the group's next big hit was one of the calling cards of paranoid soul. "(I Know) I'm Losing You" began with an ominous guitar line that set the stage for the roiling horns and Ruffin's amazing portrayal of overwhelming jealousy. After the incredibly lush "You're My Everything" – with its whirlpooling strings, cod-Latin bongo patterns, classic Motown guitar part, ringing bells and the richest vocal arrangement of The Temptations' career – the paranoia of "(I Know) I'm Losing You" became both Whitfield and the group's signature sound.

With the success of records by Sly & The Family Stone, Whitfield knew that the days of the traditional Motown sound were numbered. In 1968 songwriters Holland-Dozier-Holland left Motown and distinctive co-lead singer David Ruffin left The Temptations, leaving both the label and group in upheaval, which gave Whitfield the freedom to re-craft the Motown sound. Ruffin's sandpaper vocals were replaced by Dennis Edwards' sackfuls of gravel and his steamroller power. Edwards gave the group a more stentorian quality, and Whitfield and his songwriting partner Barrett Strong wrote new, challenging material that matched this intensity.

Instead of the usual tales of heartache and puppy love, Whitfield and Strong wrote about drug addiction, runaways, war and Black Power on records for the Cloud Nine, Puzzle People and Psychedelic Shack albums. Of course, they also crafted music that was just as forceful. Whitfield brought in Detroit session guitarist Dennis Coffey and his wah-wah pedal, and created dark, noisy, funky music, dubbed "psychedelic soul", on tracks like the epochal "Cloud Nine", the towering "I Can't Get Next To You", "Runaway Child, Running Wild", "Psychedelic Shack", "Don't Let The Joneses Get You Down" and "Ball Of Confusion".

Eddie Kendricks and Paul Williams both left the group in 1971; Kendricks pursued a solo career, but Williams sadly died of a self-inflicted gunshot wound on August 17, 1973. After they were replaced by Richard Street and Damon Harris, Whitfield crafted the record that was perhaps his and the group's finest moment, "Papa Was A Rolling Stone". With a bassline that was more like a black hole than a groove, a frenetic wah-wah guitar part and just about the most dramatic arrangement imaginable, "Papa" was a searing interrogation of black masculine stereotypes.

The 1973 follow-ups "Masterpiece" and "Plastic Man" were more ungainly rewrites of "Papa Was A Rolling Stone", but the remarkable "Law Of The Land", which was never released as a single, proved that Whitfield was still at the top of his game. With a strict 4/4 drum beat that embodied the immutability of human nature described in the song, Whitfield made his apocalyptic funk even more dystopic on "Law Of The Land" and created the mechanized beat that was the birthplace of disco.

While The Temptations continued to have gold and platinum success, the solo careers of their former leads were shakier. David Ruffin started promisingly with the great "My Whole World Ended (The Moment You Left Me)" in 1969, but the hits dried up almost immediately afterwards. He had some modest success during the disco era, particularly with the Van McCoy-produced "Walk Away From Love" in 1975, but aside from a brief reunion with Kendricks in the mid-80s, his post-Temptations career was a struggle.

Eddie Kendricks' solo career started slowly with some middling hits, although his 1972 People...Hold On album was an underrated gem. "Date With The Rain" was one of the most gorgeous tracks of his career, but the most important track on the album was "Girl You Need A Change of Mind", one of the crucial building blocks of disco. Kendricks hit his commercial peak during the mid-70s with lesser, but still fun, records like "Keep On Truckin'", "Boogie Down", "Son Of Sagittarius" and "Shoeshine Boy", but the hits dried up by the end of the decade.

Meanwhile, The Temptations stopped working with Norman Whitfield in 1974. Their first post-Whitfield album was 1975's A Song For You, a strange mix of a more discofied version of Whitfield templates on "The Prophet" and "Happy People" and a harder funk sound on "Shakey Ground" and "Glasshouse", which featured guitar from Eddie Hazel and a bassline from Billy "Bass" Nelson, both Parliament-Funkadelic alumni. This album marked the end of The Temptations' stunning chart run as they struggled to find a way to stay current without sounding like mutton dressed as lamb. Harris left the group after A Song for You and was replaced by Glenn Leonard from The Unifics. Dennis Edwards briefly left the group from 1977 to 1979, during which time he was replaced by Louis Price.

The group signed to Atlantic in 1977, but the switch didn't help matters as they tried, unsuccessfully, to appeal to the disco crowd. Returning to Motown in 1980, The Temptations were reunited with Ruffin and

PLAYLIST
The Temptations

1 THE WAY YOU DO THE THINGS YOU DO
from **Anthology**
The rhymes are pretty appalling on paper, but become poetry when sung by voices as gorgeous as Kendricks' and Ruffin's.

2 MY GIRL from **Anthology**
Another Smokey Robinson Hallmark card, but Ruffin gives weight to the melody and the words.

3 GET READY from **Anthology**
It ain't exactly Sam & Dave, but, heck, it's still The Temptations.

4 AIN'T TOO PROUD TO BEG from **Anthology**
Norman Whitfield's first single with the group emphasizes their churchiness.

5 (I KNOW) I'M LOSING YOU from **Anthology**
The birth of the paranoid soul style that became The Temptations' *raison d'être*.

6 CLOUD NINE from **Anthology**
The buzzing guitar riff creates a sense of drama far greater than Motown's often prissy arrangements and ushered in the era of psychedelic soul.

7 I CAN'T GET NEXT TO YOU from **Anthology**
The street-corner pimp's lament.

8 JUST MY IMAGINATION (RUNNING AWAY WITH ME) from **Anthology**
This might not be psychedelic in style, but its vision of love as madness is just as lysergic.

9 PAPA WAS A ROLLING STONE from **Anthology**
Father Divine tries to scramble out of a black hole.

10 LAW OF THE LAND from **Masterpiece**
Perhaps the first disco record and, unquestionably, one of the best.

Ruffin, Kendricks and Franklin, but the group still managed to record new albums every so often. With Otis Williams the only original member in the current line-up, The Temptations are now essentially an oldies act, although they won a Grammy for their *Ear-Resistable* album in 2001.

The Temptin' Temptations
1965, Gordy

The Temptations' third album shows the original group in full stride, totally on top of their game. The hits are great, the album tracks are great, and Ruffin and Kendricks can do no wrong. If you want to be swept away by their smooth harmonies and classic Motown groove, this brilliantly remastered CD will take you there.

All Directions
1972, Gordy

With Ruffin and Kendricks gone, there were doubts about The Temptations' future, but All Directions – brilliantly produced by Norman Whitfield – proved that the group would not just survive, but thrive, in their aftermath. The full-length "Papa Was A Rolling Stone" is the standout track, joined by a selection of classic 70s soul harmonies.

Anthology
1995, Motown

As is irritatingly typical of Motown, The Temptations have been poorly served by the reissue market. This superb 2-CD, 46-track collection is no longer in print, but it remains their best. The 1-CD 1997 *Ultimate Collection* has too many omissions to make it worthwhile, while the 4-CD 1994 *Emperors Of Soul* is too comprehensive for most fans. It's worth making the effort to find this collection – the perfect overview of the greatest vocal group in history.

Joe Tex

Although they are often viewed as diametric opposites, soul and country music are really flip sides of the same coin, and the two genres have greatly influenced one another. With his hillbilly name and trademark ten-gallon Stetson hat, **Joe Tex** was perhaps the most conspicuous musician to blur this generic and racial boundary. Like many soul singers (Al Green, Ray Charles, Isaac Hayes, to name a few) Tex was a fan of **Hank Williams** and wanted to be a country singer. Despite the fact that many country artists were taught by black musicians, Tex was unable to cross the country's colour barrier, and he became a soul singer instead. Ironically, Tex's producer, **Buddy Killen**, was one of Nashville's biggest music publishers and Tex's songs were later covered by country stars **Johnny Cash** and **Barbara**

Kendricks and recorded "Standing On The Top", which became their first entry into the R&B Top 10 in six years. In 1983 **Ron Tyson** replaced Glenn Leonard and the group had another R&B hit with "Treat Her Like A Lady". Dennis Edwards left for a second time, but returned again in 1987.

Despite this personnel turmoil, the group continued to hit the R&B Top 10 in the latter half of the 80s with retro-flavoured ballads like "Lady Soul", "I Wonder Who She's Seeing Now" and "Special". The 90s were marred by the tragically premature deaths of

Psychedelic Soul

In 1964, a decade after Ray Charles first explicitly blended Saturday night and Sunday morning, soul music was starting to get really funky. It was becoming dirtier, greasier, rawer and more secular, paradoxically by imitating gospel's most hardcore aspects – its shouting, hand-clapping, speaking-in-tongues expressivity, its Holy Roller dementia, its relentless rhythms. In this climate the journeymen soul group The Isley Brothers sensed that soul's emphasis was shifting from the horns and keyboards to the guitar and bottom end, and set about recruiting a guitar player. Some guy called James Hendrix wowed the group so much that he earned a starring role on their next singles, the amazing "Testify" and the strutting, echo-filled "Move Over And Let Me Dance".

Jimi Hendrix immediately became the star of the group. While the others wore the crisp, matching gold lamé suits of the chitlin' circuit, Hendrix sported multicoloured sashes, ruffled shirts and a car chain as a belt. On the road, Hendrix regaled the Isleys with his dreams of guitars that would breathe fire and amps so loud that the audience would think Armageddon was coming. Soul was not only becoming funkier, it was also becoming infected by the lysergic emanations of the 60s.

At around the same time, another African-American visionary with mad style and ridiculous talent was beginning his own border crossings in San Francisco. By day Sylvester Stewart was producing white rock groups for the Autumn label. By night he was **Sly Stone**, jamming at R&B nightclubs in North Beach and DJing for radio station KSOL Super Soul. Stone tried to bring these two worlds together in early 1967 by forming Sly & The Family Stone, famed in the Bay Area for their wild outfits – brightly coloured polka-dot shirts, fringe vests, puffy sleeves and military jackets.

Sly's vision of integration began to be perfected on the group's first single, "Dance To The Music", released at the end of 1967. Although the record had all the logic of a good essay

– it said what it was going to do, did it, then told you that it did it – "Dance To The Music" was the first real salvo of psychedelic soul. The group blended James Brown and The Who so seamlessly that you couldn't figure out where the rock stopped and the soul began. Never before had the beloved community promised by Civil Rights and the hippy love-in been so gloriously or emphatically pronounced. Sly tried to apply the solipsism of acid rock to the real world and inspired a generation of soul musicians to imagine impossible worlds and to realize that segregation was just a state of mind.

That same year Parliament recorded "(I Wanna) Testify", another blueprint for soul's hippy crossover success. "Testify" was such an effective crossover record that the rest of the group ribbed **George Clinton** about how "white" his lead vocals sounded. The Parliaments had started out as a doo-wop group, but the changing nature of soul, the political/pharmacological climate in Detroit and a fateful encounter with **Vanilla Fudge**'s Marshall stacks at a gig in Connecticut turned the group into the Afro-wearing, diaper-clad Parliament and the fuzz-guitar-infested Funkadelic.

Other artists with their own takes on psychedelic soul included Rotary Connection, with their lushly orchestrated, trippy chamber soul; Swamp Dogg, who served up an acid-drenched anti-establishment and anti-racism message on top of a standard Southern soul gumbo; **Barbara & Ernie**, whose soul folky soul featured weirdly affecting autoharp and doomy piano lines; **Rasputin's Stash**, purveyors of lumbering keyboard-heavy soul that showed the link between Sly Stone and Deep Purple's Jon Lord; Eugene McDaniels, a folky merger of Bob Dylan and Miles Davis with politically charged lyrics; and Cymande, who blended Afro-Caribbean percussion with Santana-style guitar runs, spaced-out trance chants and flutes.

The chief popularizer of the mini-genre was producer **Norman Whitfield**, through his

Mandrell. Perhaps the biggest irony was that while Tex wanted nothing more than to play the *Grand Ole Opry*, his legacy is as one of the definitive Southern soul artists.

The major influence on the young Joe Tex, who was born **Joseph Arrington, Jr.**, was the black church. He utilized the homilies and hosannas of the black preacher to such an extent that he was the first soul singer to be nicknamed "The Rapper". In

truth, he felt that he wasn't a very good singer, so he would lay down a rap in an effort to reach people and get his message across. After almost a decade of trying, via such records as the bizarre Davy Crockett novelty, "Davy You Upset My Home", Tex's first hit was little more than a sermon about fidelity over a dragging beat, bleary horn charts and a wheezy organ. "Hold What You've Got" was Southern soul's first big work with **The Temptations**. From the moment Whitfield heard "Dance To The Music", he knew that the old singsong **Holland-Dozier-Holland** heartbreak melodies had had their day. In 1968 Whitfield called in Detroit guitarist **Dennis Coffey** to play on a session for The Temptations. Coffey had been experimenting with the wah-wah pedal in a traditional soul environment, and his flanged guitar sound had just the eerie but funky quality Whitfield was looking for. The result was "Cloud Nine", one of Motown's most monumental records. Coffey's buzzing guitar riff at the record's outset created a sense of drama never before seen on a Motown arrangement. While Coffey's dangling chicken-scratch riffs got all the attention, "Cloud Nine" was also the first Motown record to feature two drummers, and the complexity of the rhythms, particularly the double-time shuffles on the hi-hats, were just as revolutionary. Almost half the black music of the next decade came from this one record: **Isaac Hayes**, **The Jackson 5**, Marvin Gaye's *What's Goin' On?*, disco and, of course, every record that was dubbed "psychedelic soul".

○ **The Temptations: Psychedelic Soul**
2003, Motown/Universal

Norman Whitfield churned out single after single, album after album for The Temptations following the "Cloud Nine" blueprint, and the best of that material is collected here. Each little tweak of the formula seemed to open up chasms of paranoia, and records like "Runaway Child, Running Wild", "I Can't Get Next To You", "Message From A Black Man", "Ball Of Confusion" and "Papa Was A Rolling Stone" never seem like mere genre exercises.

PLAYLIST

1 MOVE OVER AND LET ME DANCE
The Isley Brothers from **It's Your Thing: The Story Of The Isley Brothers**
Hendrix plus the Isleys equals psych soul a few years early.

2 DANCE TO THE MUSIC Sly & The Family Stone from **Anthology**
A riotously joyous noise.

3 (I WANNA) TESTIFY The Parliaments from **I Wanna Testify: A Historic Compilation of Vintage Soul**
The first incarnation of George Clinton's lysergic Parliafunkadelicment Thang.

4 CLOUD NINE The Temptations from **Psychedelic Soul**
Thanks to guitarist Dennis Coffey's wah-wah licks, this is one of the most epochal records in Motown's history.

5 PAPA WAS A ROLLING STONE The Temptations from **Psychedelic Soul**
Sonically and thematically this masterpiece explores the black hole at the heart of soul music.

6 THANK YOU (FALETTINME BE MICE ELF AGIN)
Sly & The Family Stone from **Anthology**
The meanest, nastiest, gnarliest funk record ever.

7 THE BURNING OF THE MIDNIGHT LAMP
Rotary Connection from **Songs**
This Hendrix cover just might be the most opulent thing ever recorded.

8 SOMEBODY TO LOVE Barbara & Ernie from **Prelude To...**
A nearly unrecognizable cover of the old Jefferson Airplane warhorse thanks to a crawling tempo and a vibe not dissimilar to Dr. John in his night tripper phase.

9 JAGGER THE DAGGER Eugene McDaniels from **Headless Heroes Of The Apocalypse**
McDaniels takes a cheap shot at The Rolling Stones and provides A Tribe Called Quest with one of their most enduring beats.

10 BRA Cymande from **Cymande**
Great bass psychedelia from the underrated Steve Scipio.

crossover hit, reaching #5 in 1964. Although it was Southern soul's calling card, "Hold What You've Got" was atypical of the style and lacked the overt emotionalism of stars like Otis Redding and Sam & Dave. Tex hardly sang at all after the introduction, opting instead for the measured cadences of a minister preaching to his congregation. With the exception of the horn arrangement, the shuffling music sounds more like an early rock'n'roll ballad than the punchy rhythm of Southern soul.

With his solemn preachy style, Tex's next hits were, perhaps inevitably, more testaments to faithfulness. "I Want To (Do Everything For You)", an R&B #1, actually had Tex singing, but it still couldn't escape the rhythms of the church with the answering chorus and Tex's dramatic punctuations. His second R&B #1, "A Sweet Woman Like

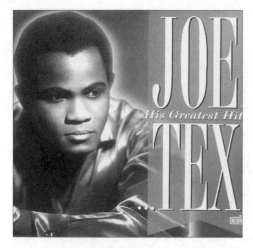

You", was another homiletic track that managed to bring in a touch of melody. More original, though, were his message tracks, including the amazing "The Love You Save (May Be Your Own)" and "Don't Make Your Children Pay (For Your Mistakes)". They're quite unlike anything else in the soul canon, thanks largely to Tex's ragged, rasping voice – he'd deliberately shout himself hoarse before recording sessions.

In time Tex's sermons stopped hitting the charts and he resorted to recording novelty songs. Even these, with Killen's production and Tex's unique style, tended to be pretty great. Moody, stretched out and deeply, deeply funky, "Papa Was Too" was Tex's entry into the "Tramp" saga started by **Lowell Fulson**. "Show Me" was countrified Motown dripping with barbecue grease, while "Skinny Legs And All" combined girl-watching, locker-room humour, Tex's preaching and patriarchy in one ridiculously catchy package. He returned to preaching in the late 60s with records like "Men Are Getting Scarce", "Buying A Book" and "Give The Baby Anything The Baby Wants". However, the biggest hit of Tex's career, came with another novelty number, 1971's preposterously funky "I Gotcha", which reached #2 on the pop charts.

After a two-year hiatus during which he converted to Islam and changed his name to Yusuf Hazziez, Tex returned with another novelty record, 1976's disco smash, "Ain't Gonna Bump No More (With No Big Fat Woman)". He continued in the same vein for the rest of his career, writing and recording songs about getting corns on his feet and

the like, but how can anyone resist records with titles like "You Might Be Diggin' The Garden (But Somebody's Picking Your Plums)" and "Finger Popped Myself Into the Poor House"?

Sadly, a year after he took part in 1981's short-lived Soul Clan reunion, alongside **Wilson Pickett, Solomon Burke, Don Covay** and **Ben E. King**, Joe Tex died of a heart attack aged just 49.

The Love You Save
1966, Dial/Atlantic

If you're looking for more than the hits, check out this album from Joe Tex's prime period. His album tracks are generally just a notch below the hits, but he recorded a lot of material in the same style. The 2001 CD reissue from Connoisseur Collection pairs this with *I've Got To Do A Little Bit Better*, another fine album from 1966.

His Greatest Hits
1996, Charly

This 2-CD collection spans almost the entire breadth of Joe Tex's recording career and makes a convincing argument for his being one of soul's unique talents. While it doesn't have his early novelty numbers, it does hold all his big hits, except, oddly, for "Give The Baby Anything The Baby Wants".

Irma Thomas

While producer extraordinaire **Allen Toussaint** is primarily known for his Carnival sound records with **Ernie K-Doe**, Lee Dorsey and The Meters, his most emotive, and perhaps most soulful, records were made with **Irma Thomas**. Like many of America's great songwriters and arrangers, Toussaint wrote songs specifically for each artist's individual voice, and in Thomas he found a singer who was perhaps the perfect transition figure between R&B and soul. Her voice had as much blues in it as gospel, she was more rhythmically dextrous than most female singers of the day, and she was just as effective doing a slow smoulder as she was on the more breathless, uptempo numbers. Thus, with Thomas, Toussaint crafted deep, dark records that were the antithesis of the Crescent City's party-hearty reputation.

Irma Thomas was born in February 1941 in Ponchatoula, Louisiana, but by the time she was 14 she was living in New Orleans and was pregnant with her first child. Four years later, she was married for the second time, had three kids and was working as a waitress at New Orleans' Pimloco Club, which was the residence of **Tommy Ridgley's** band. One night she persuaded him to let her sing with his band and blew him away. A week later she was recording her first record with Ridgley for **Joe Ruffino's** Ron label. The result, the bluesy "(You Can Have My Husband, But Please) Don't Mess With My Man", was a modest R&B hit, but she didn't really hit her stride until she started to record for Minit Records and Allen Toussaint the following year.

Thomas's first Minit release, the sublime "Cry On", was nearly perfect, although it went nowhere: a lachrymose organ and a drunken rhythm section set the backing for Thomas's defeated, but very sexy, vocals. On 1963's "It's Raining", Thomas again made Toussaint seem like a genius by giving depth to a fairly standard rock'n'roll ballad arrangement. A huge hit in her home town, "It's Raining" again failed to garner any national attention.

It wasn't all doom and gloom for Thomas, however. On "I Done Got Over It" she gave some restrained gospel oomph to one of Toussaint's trademark, comic Mardi Gras beats, while on "Hittin' On Nothing" she was as tough and sassy as any female singer around. Her best record with Minit, however, was "Ruler Of My Heart", which took the ancient New Orleans second-line rhythm on a journey through a cold night of the soul. One quarter devotional hymn, one quarter bayou hoodoo, one quarter lovelorn torture, one quarter bar-room blues, "Ruler Of My Heart" was such a devastating record that Otis Redding re-recorded it as "Pain In My Heart" and brought the song to its rightful place in the pop charts.

After Toussaint was drafted in late 1963, Minit rapidly foundered, so Thomas went out to LA and recorded for Imperial Records. Working with producer **H.B. Barnum**, she finally had a national hit in 1964 with the self-penned "Wish Someone Would Care". The dragging drums and funereal bells couldn't have been further from her New Orleans sound, but the atmosphere combined with her own ravaged vocals to create a devastating anthem of self-pity. Thomas's chart career then unjustly stalled, despite the fact that "Time Is On My Side", the B-side of her follow-up single, was copied note for

note by **The Rolling Stones** and became their first American hit.

After a string of fine but underperforming singles for Imperial, largely derivative of Motown and Dionne Warwick, but including the excellent end-of-the-night New Orleans blues "Nobody Wants To Hear Nobody's Troubles", Thomas left Imperial for Chess. There she had her final national hit with a version of Otis Redding's "Good To Me", recorded in Muscle Shoals.

Thomas moved to LA in 1969 and worked in a department store in between recording sides for companies like Canyon, Roker, Cotillion and Swamp Dogg's Fungus label. She then moved back to New Orleans where a resurgent pride in the city's vast musical heritage gave her career a new lease of life. She had a small disco hit with "Safe With Me" in 1979, and has since become a very fine repertoire singer on a series of albums for Rounder, the best of which are 1988's *The Way I Feel*, 1991's *Live! Simply The Best* and 1992's *True Believer*.

True Believer
1992, Rounder

If you've already got the 60s hits that made Thomas an R&B icon and the "Queen of New Orleans", it's worth checking out her more recent CDs. This is filled with soulful weepers and doesn't miss from beginning to end. Thomas can still bring it all to a performance, which is why she remains a perennial downhome favourite.

Sweet Soul Queen Of New Orleans: The Irma Thomas Collection
1996, Razor & Tie

This is the best available collection of Thomas's prime Minit and Imperial recordings, even though it gives short shrift to her uptempo records. Thomas is one of the finest blues singers, male or female, from a city with a long tradition of blues singing.

Rufus Thomas

Known as "the world's oldest teenager" and "the crown prince of dance", Rufus Thomas was one of the most endearing and enduring presences on the R&B scene for almost 60 years. A natural entertainer, he wore dozens of hats during the course of his career, acted as the mentor for virtually all of the Memphis soul scene and started more dance crazes than James Brown.

Thomas was born on March 26, 1917 in Cayce, Mississippi. He became a singer,

Rufus Thomas tries to start another new dance craze

dancer and comedian in the Rabbit Foot Minstrels in the early 30s, and in the 40s started dozens of variety shows in Memphis, including the famous Amateur Night at the Palace Theatre on Beale Street where **BB King**, Bobby "Blue" Bland and **Little Junior Parker** were all discovered. Thomas also began hosting his "Hoot And Holler" radio show in 1947 and stayed there until 1974.

Thomas's first record was 1950s' "I'll Be A Good Boy" on the Star Talent label, but he didn't have a hit until 1953 with the release of "Bear Cat" on Sun, a savagely funny retort to **Big Mama Thornton**'s "Hound Dog". In

1959, "'Cause I Love You", a duet with his daughter **Carla Thomas**, was licensed to the R&B giant Atlantic, starting the relationship between Atlantic and a budding Memphis label then known as Satellite, but soon to become Stax. Thomas started his first dance craze in 1963 with "The Dog", quickly following up with the even better "Walking The Dog", then "Can Your Monkey Do The Dog" and finally "Somebody Stole My Dog"– he was 46 when he recorded these novelties, but he was so damn funky that no one noticed.

Working at Stax with producer **Don Nix**, with whom he made most of his later records, Thomas started the "Sissy" craze with "Sophisticated Sissy" in 1967. He then cut the incredibly funky "The Memphis Train", on which guitarist **Steve Cropper** smoked throughout, before really hitting his stride with "Do The Funky Chicken", which featured a great rap interlude. Working with Nix, **The Bar-Kays** and his pianist son **Marvell Thomas**, Rufus Thomas released a series of crazy funky dance-craze discs in the early 70s: "Do The Push and Pull", his only R&B #1; "The Breakdown", with its bizarrely minimal wah-wah riff and a drum beat that has been sampled loads of times; "Do The Funky Penguin"; and the monstrous groove

of "Itch And Scratch", one of the great hip-hop breaks. This run of records cemented Thomas's reputation as the second-funkiest man alive.

Thomas continued to release similarly funky records in the mid- to late 70s with varying degrees of success. "The Funky Robot" was a bit rote and didn't do so well, but he soon returned to the charts with "The Funky Bird", "Boogie Ain't Nuttin' (But Gettin' Down)" and "Do The Double Bump", despite the problems his label was experiencing at that time. When Stax finally folded, he signed to AVI and had his final chart hit with "If There Were No Music" in 1976.

Dance Craze Discs

In pre-Beatles America just about the only records that mattered were the ones that, as they used to say on *American Bandstand*, "had a good beat that you could dance to." This simple maxim applied as much to early soul as it did to any other form of popular music. Just about all of soul's greatest legends made records that either capitalized on or started dance crazes: Sam Cooke's "Shake" and "Everybody Loves To Cha Cha Cha", Marvin Gaye's "Hitch Hike" and about half of James Brown's records. Whatever the self-appointed guardians of black music may claim about soaring emotion, true-to-life renderings of heartbreak and "soulfulness", back then even ballads were little more than excuses for couples to get close on the dancefloor.

Dance-craze discs came in all shapes and sizes. Arranged by omnipresent studio hack **Gene Page** and kicked off with a grandiose horn and tympani intro, Bob & Earl's 1963 "Harlem Shuffle" was that rarest of tracks: an orchestral dance record. Perhaps even denser was **Little Eva**'s "The Loco-Motion". Everything about "The Loco-Motion" seemed wrong – the lyrics were overwritten for a dance-craze novelty, the arrangement was plodding, Little Eva (song-writers' **Gerry Goffin** and **Carole King**'s babysit-ter) couldn't sing – but somehow it all worked fantastically and "The Loco-Motion" became an irresistible pop record.

Bert Berns is better known as the producer of records by The Drifters, **Van Morrison** and Solomon Burke, but his two contributions to the dance-craze oeuvre are unbeatable. The Isley Brothers' "Twist And Shout" was produced and written by Berns, while **Russell Byrd**'s "Hitch Hike" was a pairing of Berns's kitschy vocals on top of **King Curtis**'s band, producing a definitive document of 60s cool.

Before he changed the face of soul music in the late 60s and early 70s, Sly Stone was the in-house producer, arranger and A&R man for the San Francisco label Autumn Records. During his tenure there he wrote and produced Bobby Freeman's intense and swinging "C'mon And Swim". One of the most copied of all the dance-craze records was Cliff Nobles & Co.'s "The Horse", which was essentially a showpiece for the rhythmic skills of the musicians who later became Philadelphia International's house band, MFSB.

The undisputed king of the dance-craze disc was the great Rufus Thomas, but, more often than not, great dance-craze records were created by one-hit wonders who would never be heard from again. **The Capitols**' great "Cool Jerk" managed to work an honest-to-good-ness narrative into their hand-clapping barn-stormer, and, before writing Betty Wright's "Clean Up Woman", **Steve Alaimo** made one of the great blue-eyed soul hits, a wild cover of James Brown's "Mashed Potatoes". The super-syncopated "The Walk" by **Jimmy McCracklin** (who *was* heard from again) was the sound of a down-on-his-luck blues singer trying his damnedest to get a hit single, and succeeding.

⊙ **Various Artists: Land Of 1000 Dances**
1999, Ace

Land Of 1000 Dances is perhaps the only collection around that's not ashamed to admit the unrepentantly commercial, novelty origins of its records. If the only time you've ever done the limbo was at a children's party or if you're too young to remember any dance crazes earlier than the Hustle, the Electric Slide or the Macarena, this will be a complete eye-opener. It is a collection of gloriously simple tracks epitomizing pop's basic power – it will exorcize the ghosts of Van McCoy and Los Del Rio in no time.

In the 80s Thomas tried his hand at rapping on 1986's "Rappin' Rufus" and recorded the fine comic blues album *That Woman Is Poison* on Alligator in 1988. Around this time he also appeared in the films *Mystery Train* and *Great Balls Of Fire*. Thomas continued to perform throughout the 90s, singing at the Atlanta Olympics in 1996 and releasing a couple of blues albums, before undergoing open heart surgery in 1998. Sadly, "the world's oldest teenager" died of heart failure on December 15, 2001, aged 84.

Do The Funky Somethin': The Best Of Rufus Thomas
1996, Rhino

Although this 19-track retrospective criminally doesn't include the great "Itch And Scratch", it is the most complete look at Thomas's career. It includes "Bear Cat" as well as his early duets with his daughter Carla, the entire "Dog" saga and the later, funky dance-craze records.

The Three Degrees

The female vocal trio **The Three Degrees** were famously Prince Charles' favourite musical group in the 70s, performing at his 30th birthday. The royal seal of approval didn't really help this journeywoman group at home in America, where they were considered to be little more than also-rans with one brief shining moment. However, in Europe, where their stilted cabaret phrasing wasn't viewed with scorn and they enjoyed Chuck's patronage, they were huge.

The original Three Degrees line-up formed in Philadelphia in 1963 and recorded "Gee Baby (I'm Sorry)" for the Swan label. Their manager/producer **Richard Barrett** soon reorganized the group, however, and a new line-up of **Fayette Pickney**, **Janet Jones** and **Helen Scott** recorded versions of The Five Keys' "Close Your Eyes" and The Chantels' "Maybe" in the mid-60s.

Scott and Jones left the group soon after and were replaced by **Valerie Holiday** and **Sheila Ferguson**, who had previously recorded solo singles for Swan and Landa under Barrett's management. The new trio recorded material for ABC, Warner Bros and Metromedia, before releasing "What I See" on Kenny Gamble's Neptune label in 1970.

Their first big hit, "Maybe", which was released on Roulette, wedded their virginal tones to a psychedelic supper-club backing that made the most of their lack of grit.

The Three Degrees recorded a few more singles for Roulette, including "I Do Take You", their second top-ten R&B hit, before moving to **Gamble & Huff**'s Philadelphia International label in 1973. Their first single there, "Dirty Ol' Man", didn't do much in the charts, but it did introduce the phrase "age ain't nothing but a number" into the popular lexicon. The group also provided vocals on **MFSB**'s two most important records, "TSOP" and "Love Is The Message", before going platinum with the dreadfully saccharine "When Will I See You Again".

While they quickly disappeared from the upper reaches of the American charts in the mid-70s, The Three Degrees maintained their momentum in the UK with records such as "Take Good Care Of Yourself", "Long Lost Lover" and "Toast Of Love". With Helen Scott once again joining the group as a replacement for Fayette Pickney, the group signed to Ariola and concentrated on the European disco market.

They hooked up with **Giorgio Moroder** in 1978 for "Givin' Up Givin' In", an electronic disco track that just didn't work – largely because even they were too soulful and gritty for the backing. Nevertheless, the record's trashiness made it huge across Europe and it hit #12 in the UK. Moroder provided them with three fairly wretched entries into the British Top 10 in 1979: "Woman In Love", "My Simple Heart" and the proto-Hi-NRG track "The Runner".

The group continued to concentrate on the British market during the 80s, releasing a few UK-only albums during the Thatcher era. Their last record to hit the UK charts was "The Heaven I Need", produced by Stock, Aitken & Waterman, which was followed by an album on Ichiban in 1989. Although they disappeared from view in the early 90s, the Three Degrees can still be found touring all over the world.

Greatest Hits
2002, Goldies

Three CDs is way too much for a group that once opened for Englebert Humperdink. That said, this is the only collection that includes their recordings for Roulette, Philadelphia International and Ariola. If you want their earlier Swan recordings, some of which were big on the

UK's Northern soul scene, check out *Gee Baby I'm Sorry: The Best Of The Swan Years* (1997, Collectables).

The Time

The Time may have started off as little more than a side project for Prince, but they eventually grew into one of the tightest, most high-energy funk ensembles of the 80s. Although they had quite a few hit records, their métier was performing live concerts where they jammed every bit as hard as the master and may have even topped him in terms of sheer excitement.

The Time was originally conceived as a vehicle for singer **Morris Day**, who had been in the groups Grand Central and Champagne with Prince. Prince wrote, produced and played on most of the tracks on The Time's eponymous 1981 debut album under the pseudonym Jamie Starr. Day played drums and provided the vocals, while **Jesse Johnson** was the guitarist. The first single from the album, "Get It Up", reached the R&B Top 10 and found Prince at his most P-Funkish. "Cool", another top-ten R&B hit, followed with that characteristic early Minneapolis swing. When it was time to take the album on the road, keyboardists **Jimmy "Jam" Harris** and **Monte Moir**, bassist **Terry Lewis** and drummer **Jellybean Johnson** were recruited from two funk troupes, Flyte Tyme and Enterprise Band Of Pleasure.

In 1982 *What Time Is It?*, The Time's second album, featured the full group. It included the fierce funk track "Wild And Loose" and "777-9311", a sparse, angular track with a monstrous chorus surrounded by ricocheting synths. However, on "Gigolos Get Lonely Too", they proved that they could also nail the slow jam.

While the group were supporting Prince on his *1999* tour in 1983, Jam and Lewis decided to produce a record by the SOS Band, even though the schedules conflicted. They managed to make all the gigs *and* produce the record until they were snowed in at Atlanta airport and missed a concert. They were fired by Prince and replaced by dancer **Jerome Benton** and keyboardist **Paul Peterson**, but Jam & Lewis went on to become the most important production duo of the 80s.

The rest of The Time continued working on 1984's *Ice Cream Castle*, which became their best-selling album. The track "Jungle Love" became their best-known single thanks to its prominent appearance in the film *Purple Rain* and the fact that it is played at every single sporting event in the US. The group disbanded soon after the release of their third album.

Jesse Johnson went on to form Jesse Johnson's Revue, a largely featureless crew of Prince copycats that released three albums, *Jesse Johnson's Revue*, *Shockadelica* and *Every Shade Of Love*, in the 80s. His most notable tracks were "Free World" – a strange meeting between British synth-pop and 80s funk that wasn't entirely appealing, although the martial groove suited Johnson's stilted singing style better than most of his tracks – and "Crazay", which featured Sly Stone, although you couldn't really tell. Morris Day also released a few solo records after The Time broke up, most notably the 1988 R&B #1 "Fishnet", produced by Jam & Lewis.

The Time briefly reunited in 1990 to release the reunion album *Pandemonium*. Although the single "Jerk Out" went to #1 on the R&B chart and the album was fairly well received, no one's heart was in it and the group disbanded again soon afterwards.

What Time Is It?
1982, Warner Bros

A stone-cold classic party album that doesn't let up, except for the humorous ballad "Gigolos Get Lonely Too". "Wild And Loose", "777-9311" and "The Walk" are three of the best funk tracks of the decade and this album is just non-stop fun until Prince takes the keyboards away.

TLC

In their way, TLC were as revolutionary a girl group as **LaBelle**. Sure, they were sassy, independent women and all that bushwa, but at least in their early days they proved that women could be as dopey and cartoon stupid as the fellas. Inevitably, however, their spirited image spilled over into real life and the group became as famous for burning down houses and going bankrupt as they were for selling records.

TLC was formed in Atlanta in 1991 by **Tionne "T-Boz" Watkins**, **Lisa "Left Eye" Lopes** and **Rozanda "Chilli" Thomas** under

the wing of manager **Pebbles**. The group was signed to Pebbles' husband **LA Reid**'s LaFacc label in 1991. They worked with producers **Dallas Austin** and **Jermaine Dupri** on their debut, 1992's *Ooooooohh... On The TLC Tip*, a thoroughly energetic urban pop album. It spawned three hit singles, "Ain't 2 Proud 2 Beg", which had to be a hit with all those samples that needed to be cleared, the ballad "Baby-Baby-Baby" and "What About Your Friends", all of which made it into the R&B Top 2 and pop Top 10. The album also included "Hat 2 Da Back", which defended the flamboyant dress sense – Left Eye wore a condom over her left eye – that got them almost as much attention as their music.

Just before *CrazySexyCool* was released in 1994, Left Eye was arrested for burning down the house of her boyfriend, football player Andre Rison. She was in the news constantly, but the publicity certainly didn't hurt sales of this mellower, glossier album, or its two lead singles, "Creep" (an R&B #1 for nine weeks and pop #1 for four) and "Waterfalls" (a pop #1 for seven weeks). The album went on to sell 11 million copies.

Over the next two years the group filed for bankruptcy, split from Pebbles, announced that T-Boz had sickle cell anaemia, split from producer Austin, who had just had a child with Chilli, and had public fights with each other. However, when their third album, *Fanmail*, finally appeared in 1999 it reaffirmed their superstar status. "No Scrubs" spent a month at #1 on the pop chart and "Unpretty" three weeks, and *Fanmail* won a Grammy for best R&B album.

Left-Eye released "Block Party" solo in 2001, the best playground jam since Frankie Smith's "Double Dutch Bus". However, while on holiday in Honduras the following year she was inolved in a car accident and died from severe head trauma on April 25, 2002. The last tracks that the group had recorded together were released that same year as *3D*. The album was as slick and well produced as ever, but "Quickie" was a hyperactive, schizophrenic mess and there were a lot of mawkish tributes to Lopes which, understandable though they were, marred an otherwise fine album.

CrazySexyCool
1994, LaFace

At first pass, it's hard to know what all the fuss was about. The production was state of the art, but not jaw-dropping; the songs were fine, but hardly startling; and they couldn't sing terribly well. However, TLC mastered the art of getting mega sales: be just hip enough for the streets, just sexy enough for a teenage audience and ignorable enough that you can be played in the office all day.

Tony! Toni! Toné!

Not as self-consciously retro as artists such as **Erykah Badu** or **Angie Stone**, but still adhering to age-old soul and R&B values, **Tony! Toni! Toné!** were the acceptable face of neo-traditionalist soul.

Formed in Oakland, California by brothers **Raphael Saadiq** and **D'Wayne Wiggins** and their cousin **Timothy Christian Riley**, Tony! Toni! Toné! had an R&B #1 in 1988 with their first single, "Little Walter", a worldly rewrite of the old spiritual "Wade In The Water". Their debut abum, *Who?*, produced by **Denzil Foster** and **Thomas McElroy**, followed with a pleasant blend of old school soul and New Jack Swing and produced three more R&B top-ten hits: "Born Not To Know", "Baby Doll" and "For The Love Of You".

In 1990 the group released *The Revival*, an album that managed to blend hip-hop beats, contemporary balladry and good old-fashioned funk. "The Blues", a fine marriage of jeep beats, P-Funk and a blues guitar lick, was the first of the album's four R&B #1s. "Feels Good", New Jack Swing meets gospel, "It Never Rains (In Southern California)", not the same song that was a hit for Albert Hammond, and the sickly "Whatever You Want", followed "The Blues" to the top spot.

Sons Of Soul from 1993 was where the group's blend of old and new really gelled. Despite the sample claiming that there was "some New Jack Swing comin' at ya", "If I Had No Loot" was a breezy back-porch sing-along that made a country blues lick and a trigger beat sound like they were born to be together. "(Lay Your Head On My Pillow)" got closer to the classic Philly vocal group style than anyone else in the last 25 years, while "Gangsta Groove" managed not to waste its Meters sample and "My Ex-Girlfriend" merged a modified swing beat and distinctly modern lyrics with classic harmonies and a Sly Stone breakdown.

Their next album, 1996's *House Of Music*, was more of the same, with the group even more confident – they had to be if they were going to rip-off Al Green on the first track "Thinking Of You". "Let's Get Down" was slight but thoroughly enjoyable party funk, with a guest appearance from DJ Quik. However, soon after the album was released, the group broke up.

Wiggins recorded an overambitious solo album for Motown, *Eyes Never Lie*, in 2000, but it was Saadiq who went on to greater success. In 1999 he worked with Q-Tip on the very underrated "Get Involved", before forming Lucy Pearl with Ali Shaheed Muhammad and former En Vogue singer Dawn Robinson. The group's only album was 2000's lacklustre *Lucy Pearl*, which was self-consciously retro and bohemian in a way that Tony! Toni! Toné! never were. Dubbing his music "gospeldelic", Saadiq released his first solo album, *Instant Vintage*, in 2002. A strangely subdued album, it didn't have the hooks of the Tonys, but worked on a more textural level. *Ray Ray*, his half-baked blaxploitation concept album from 2004, was a bit forced, but again it sounded sweet when he really concentrated.

(o) **Hits**
1997, Mercury

Calling them the most accomplished R&B act of the 90s may be to damn them with faint praise, but that's exactly what Tony! Toni! Toné! were. Yet this was primarily because D'Angelo only recorded one album in the decade and Missy Elliott started too late. This 15-track collection includes all of the group's highlights and actually makes them look better than they were.

Allen Toussaint

As a producer, arranger, songwriter, session musician and performer, it would be hard to overestimate **Allen Toussaint**'s contributions to the music of New Orleans. Aside from his involvement in creating the signature sound of NOLA R&B, Toussaint has been involved with hits by Fats Domino, **Ernie K-Doe**, Jessie Hill, **Chris Kenner**, Benny Spellman, **The Showmen, Aaron Neville**, Eskew Reeder, Irma Thomas, Lee Dorsey, Betty Harris, The Meters, Dr. John, LaBelle, Chocolate Milk and **The Wild Tchoupitoulas**.

Toussaint was born on January 14, 1938 in New Orleans. By the time he was 13 he was playing piano in a group called The Flamingos (not the vocal group) with Snooks Eaglin. By 1958 Toussaint had became one of the mainstays in the Crescent City's studio scene, arranging **Lee Allen**'s "Walkin' With Mr Lee" and playing piano on **Fats Domino**'s "Young Schoolgirl". In 1958 he also recorded the instrumental album *The Wild Sound Of New Orleans* under the name Al Tousan. The album featured the novelty instrumental number "Java", which was rollicking good fun and later a hit for Al Hirt.

In 1960 Toussaint was hired as the A&R director of Minit Records. In reality, he produced and wrote most of the label's records, including many of the hits that made New Orleans synonymous with R&B. He stayed with Minit until he was drafted in 1963. While in the army, Toussaint wrote and recorded a little novelty number called "Whipped Cream", which was covered the following year by Herb Alpert & The Tijuana Brass and become one of the standards of easy listening.

Released from the army in 1965, Toussaint formed Sansu Enterprises with producer **Marshall Sehorn**. Toussaint was yet again involved with many more fabulous records, with help from house band The Meters. In 1971 he released *Toussaint* on Scepter, an album comprised mostly of tracks in a mellow, almost easy-listening vein, which disappointed fans of the New Orleans bounce that he had helped develop as a producer.

Signing to Warner Bros the following year, he released *Life, Love And Faith*, which featured The Meters on the sitar-fuelled "Goin'

Down" and on "Soul Sister", a somewhat patronizing but funky as hell praise song directed at liberated sisters with Afros. The Meters showed up again on *Southern Nights* in 1975. Toussaint's best album as a performer, *Southern Nights* was a quasi-psychedelic-funk gumbo concept album about Dixie that was a hair's breadth away from being a masterpiece. *Motion*, on the other hand, was a rather faceless album made with studio hacks in LA in 1978.

Toussaint continued to produce, write and play piano on a number of records after the release of *Motion*, but less prolifically. In 1996 he released his first studio album in years, *Connected*, on his own NYNO label. Thanks to a stellar supporting cast that included **Dave Bartholomew**, **Russell Batiste**, **Leo Nocentelli** and Chocolate Milk's Amadee Castanell, it was a surprisingly decent alum, even if the momentum of New Orleans had moved away from the more traditional R&B to the electrified gumbo of the city's hip-hop scene.

The Complete Warner Recordings
2003, Rhino Handmade

This superb 2-CD collection includes all three of his 70s albums for Warner Bros, as well as ten live recordings from 1975. It won't do anything to alter the fact that Toussaint's greatest contributions to music are as a producer, songwriter and arranger, but it makes the argument that much of his own material for Warner Bros would be considered masterpieces, if only he were a better singer.

Tower of Power

Coming from the San Francisco Bay Area, perhaps it was inevitable that **Tower of Power** would remake funk for hippies and musos. Horn-heavy, when the best funk troupes concentrated on the bottom end, and busy, when the best funk was simple and single-minded, Tower of Power's brand of funk was closer to a Las Vegas revue than a chicken shack at the end of town.

The original core of the group – saxophonist **Emilio Castillo**, drummer **Jack Castillo** and guitarist **Joe DeLopez** – came together as Black Orpheus in 1966. They soon added vocalist Rufus Miller, bassist Rocco Prestia, trumpeter Mic Gillette and saxophonists Stephen Kupka and Skip Mesquite to the line-up and changed their

name first to The Motowns and then to Tower of Power. In 1969 they landed a regular gig at the Fillmore and signed to Bill Graham's San Francisco label. Before recording their first single, 1970's "Sparkling In The Sand", DeLopez and Jack Castillo left the group and were replaced by Willie James Fulton and David Garibaldi.

Line-up problems plagued the group throughout their career. During the recording of their debut album, 1970's *East Bay Grease*, Gillette was replaced by Greg Adams and David Padron, while Miller was replaced by Rick Stevens. *East Bay Grease* laid down the format that they would follow for most of their career: meandering, blowhard funk jams that were just too damn busy.

Their 1972 follow-up, *Bump City*, featured a slicker, more commercial sound, which was most notable on their first charting single, the preachy message ballad "You're Still A Young Man". Mesquite and Stevens quit soon afterward, and were replaced by Lenny Pickett and **Lenny Williams**, who had previously recorded the solo singles "I Love Her Too" and "Feelin' Blue", which were both far funkier than anything Tower of Power ever released, for the Galaxy label.

With Lenny Williams as their new lead vocalist, the group released *Tower Of Power* in 1973. The album was their most commercially successful recording and the lead single, "So Very Hard To Go", broke the pop Top 20. The next year's *Back To Oakland* remains Tower of Power's funkiest album, if only because the ballads were kept to a minimum. However, after *Back To Oakland*, their records, with the exception of 1976's *Live And In Living Color*, were a faceless succession of bland discofied ballads and weak-as-water "jams".

Lenny Williams left the group in 1975. He went on to enjoy a successful solo career, the highlight of which was undoubtedly 1978's "You Got Me Running" – the high-speed walking bassline worked magic on disco dancefloors, but it was the incredible breakdown that really sent dancers into ecstasy. Meanwhile, with their chops and lack of restraint, Tower of Power became perhaps more successful as studio musicians, than as recording artists. They have backed everyone from Little Feat to Aaron Neville, Michael Bolton to Rod Stewart, and remain active in the studio and on the touring circuit.

At two discs and 35 tracks, this is certainly all the Tower of Power anyone needs. Although it includes too many ballads, this collection does largely separate the wheat from the chaff in their discography, highlighting their funkier side on tracks like "What Is Hip?", "Squib Cakes" and "You Got To Funkifize". The fact remains, however, that this is really funk for people who don't like funk.

The Trammps

The Trammps combined the vocal interplay of groups like The Coasters with gospel-like sermonizing and the driving beat of Philadelphia International's great session band MFSB. With their blend of roots and unabashed dancefloor appeal, The Trammps served as the bridge between the Philly soul sound and the discotheque. From their earliest hit, a cover of "Zing Went The Strings Of My Heart", which was originally popularized by Judy Garland, to their mid-70s heyday, The Trammps replaced the tension at the heart of Gamble & Huff's signature sound with a wholehearted embrace of disco. The group's drummer Earl Young was also the drummer for MFSB and The Salsoul Orchestra and pretty much invented the disco beat.

The Trammps grew out of the terribly underrated group The Volcanos, which was formed in 1964 by lead singer Gene Jones, keyboardist John Hart, bassist Stanley Wade, guitarist Harold Wade, vocalist Steve Kelly and drummer Earl Young. They signed to DJ Jimmy Bishop's Arctic label and recorded the ballad "Baby" in 1964. Their second single, "Storm Warning", was one of the building blocks of the Philly sound with its vibraphone chimes and piano-led arrangement. The following year, "Help Wanted!", written by aspiring songwriters Kenny Gamble and Leon Huff, was a more straightforward Motown-styled number, while "(It's Against) The Laws Of Love" was a fine marriage of Motown with the characteristic textural touches of Philadelphia. In 1966 they released their poppiest number, "You're Number One", which was presumably a last-ditch effort to make the charts – they were dropped from Arctic when the record failed to sell.

The Volcanos recorded two singles on the Harthon label, including the great dancer "It's Gotta Be A False Alarm", before Jones left the group in 1979. He later released a series of fine, collectable singles as Gene Faith, most notably the driving hard soul of "My Baby's Missing". After he left The Volcanos, the group first changed their name to The Moods and then to The Trammps. Originally consisting of Earl Young, Jimmy Ellis, Harold Wade, Stanley Wade and John Hart, The Trammps signed to Buddah in 1972 and released "Zing Went The Strings of My Heart", a nostalgic ballad with Young singing lead over a subtle driving beat that became popular in the early discos.

After releasing a silly version of "Sixty Minute Man" and the very fine "Pray All You Sinners", The Trammps confirmed their status as perhaps the best of the disco vocal groups with "Love Epidemic". The record owed more than a little to The O'Jays' "Love Train", but helped to create the blueprint for disco. The following year "Where Do We Go From Here" and "Trusting Heart" proved that The Trammps also excelled at midtempo traditional Philly soul.

Another midtempo number, the breezy and nostalgic "Hold Back The Night", became the group's biggest hit to date in 1975. However, The Trammps soon devoted themselves to disco and created perhaps the genre's greatest anthem to itself, "That's Where The Happy People Go", as well as their biggest hit, the irresistible "Disco Inferno". "The Night The Lights Went Out" was a wonderfully romantic reaction to the New York City blackout that summer, even if it glossed over all the turmoil. However, it was to be the group's last significant hit.

Their records were becoming more and more formulaic, perhaps because Earl Young was spreading himself too thin by this point, and titles like "Hard Rock And Disco" just wouldn't cut it anymore. In 1983, "Up On The Hill", an ode to a Philly make-out spot, was their last chart appearance, and they disbanded soon afterwards.

The Trammps have been unfairly tainted by their association with disco. Aside from making some of the best disco records ever, they also made some very solid soul records in a more traditional vein. Lead vocalist Jimmy Ellis could belt it out with the best of them, but he could also be surprisingly gentle. This fine 18-track collection makes a very convincing argument in their favour.

Ike & Tina Turner

Subtlety was an art lost on **Ike & Tina Turner**. Even before the jackhammer soul-rock records that made them household names in the early 70s, the Turners didn't exactly approach straight-ahead soul like wallflowers. Of course, it would have been impossible to do that with Tina's Molotov cocktail of a voice, but Ike, being a born huckster, liked big, bold colours and broad gestures too. Aside from their tempestuous relationship, Ike's hucksterism was their biggest problem. During the 60s and even into the 70s, he insisted on releasing dozens of haphazard records for a myriad of different labels, approaching the now standardized and somewhat legitimate music business as if he were still dealing with the pre-Civil Rights chitlin' circuit.

Ike Turner was born on November 5, 1931 in Clarksdale, Mississippi. By age 11, he was good enough on piano to have his own band that backed bluesmen like Sonny Boy Williamson II and Robert Nighthawk. Moving to Memphis in his late teens, he formed **Ike Turner & The Kings of Rhythm** and was a talent scout for Modern Records. With saxophonist **Jackie Brenston** singing lead, Turner's group went to **Sam Phillips'** studio – soon to be called Sun Studios – in 1951 and cut "Rocket 88". Credited to Jackie Brenston & His Delta Cats, "Rocket 88" was a pulsating jump blues record with a streamlined arrangement and it is regularly hailed as the "first rock'n'roll record". Around this time Turner also started playing guitar, backing Bobby "Blue" Bland, Little Junior Parker and Howlin' Wolf, and recording country as Icky Renrut.

Turner's band backed Billy Gayles on the smokin' "I'm Tore Up" in 1956, before moving to East St. Louis where they held court at the Club Manhattan. One night in 1956, a young woman named **Anna Mae Bullock** (born November 26, 1939 in Nutbush,

Tennessee) was dared by her sister to take the stage and sing with the band. She floored the crowd and Ike Turner, who added her to his show. He soon changed her name to Tina and, in 1958, married her.

In late 1959 Turner's group, now called The Ike & Tina Turner Revue, went into a studio to record "A Fool In Love". The band's male vocalist didn't show up, so Tina sang the lead. It was an inspired accident. Their backing singers **The Ikettes** may have been note-for-note copies of Ray Charles' **Raelettes**, but no one outside of a Holy Roller church sang like **Tina Turner** in 1960. "A Fool In Love" was a huge hit. Similarly styled, although somewhat less intense, records like "I Idolize You", "It's Gonna Work Out Fine", "Poor Fool" and "Tra La La La La" followed it into the R&B Top 10 over the next few years. Meanwhile, The Ikettes, **Delores Johnson**, **Jo Armstead** and **Eloise Hester** (with Tina singing back-up), had their own hit with the wonderful "I'm Blue (The Gong-Gong Song)", which showed how much you can do with a piano, drums, bass and some nonsense syllables.

In 1962 the Turners moved to California, where they cut sides for several labels that largely went nowhere: Kent, "I Can't Believe What You Say (For Seeing What You Do)"; Loma, "Tell Her I'm Not Home"; Sue, a dramatic version of "Stagger Lee & Billy", the uptempo bluesy stomp "Two Is A Couple" and the instrumental "The New Breed"; and Modern, "Good Bye, So Long". In 1966 they went into the studio with Phil Spector to record "River Deep, Mountain High", which was supposed to be Spector's retort to **The Beatles** and **Beach Boys** who had stolen his studio thunder. The record was a disaster of overload – at least an album's worth of sound in three minutes – and was virtually ignored in the US, although it became a #3 hit in the UK where it is hailed as a classic.

With Spector's delusions of grandeur and Tina's barrelhouse razmatazz, "River Deep, Mountain High" was preposterously over-ripe and overblown. While most of Ike & Tina's records had this tendency, on stage this was never a problem. Tina's scorched-earth vocals and her sleazy dynamism made for electric live performances, and the Ike & Tina Turner Revue – complete with nine musicians and the scantily clad Ikettes – became one of the hottest draws on both the

Tina Turner curls her lip at hubby Ike

chitlin and rock'n'roll circuits. The live setting was where the duo really made their reputation.

They had a small hit with "So Fine" in 1968 on the Innis label, before the very low-down and funky "Cussin', Cryin' And Carryin' On" on Pompeii hailed their future direction. "I Wanna Jump" was charcteristic of their new sound: Ike was absolutely ridiculous on fuzz guitar, but the arrangement, as was too often the case, had too much Vegas in it. "Bold Soul Sister" found Tina destroying her vocal chords over a supremely funky beat that has since become a hip-hop staple, while Ike's "Funky Mule" was a stone-cold breakbeat primer with a mastodon bassline. Ike & Tina were then chosen to be the opening act for **The Rolling Stones**' legendary 1969 tour, which brought them to the attention of a whole new audience. Thanks to this exposure, their version of The Beatles' "Come Together", although not nearly as audacious as their version of Creedence Clearwater Revival's "Proud Mary", was their first substantial hit in years.

Gaining some stability by signing with United Artists, Ike & Tina continued in this rock-funk vein in the early 70s with tracks such as "Doin' It", perhaps the dirtiest, funkiest track of their career, "Up In Heah", "Nutbush City Limits", Ike's "Garbage Man" – not his finest effort, but that clavinet line makes it worth putting up with his woeful **Melvin Van Peebles** imitation – and Tina's outrageous version of **Led Zeppelin**'s "Whole Lotta Love".

The Ike & Tina Revue kept rolling along until Tina had enough of Ike's physical and emotional abuse, which had been exacerbated by his addiction to cocaine since the late 60s. She divorced him in 1976 and, after several years of struggle, became the icon of survivordom when she returned to the top of the charts in 1984 with "What's Love Got To Do With It", "Better Be Good To Me" and "Private Dancer". Over the ensuing years, her recordings became more and more middle of the road and less and less relevant to a soul audience.

Despite the duo's evident talents, both Ike and Tina's legacies remain in question. Whatever Ike's significant contributions to the development of rock'n'roll, his reputation has been permanently tarnished as a wife beater and deadbeat. Tina, meanwhile, seems to be viewed these days as little more than a survivor who managed to escape from an abusive relationship with her legs and voice intact. Neither of them ever really made records commensurate with their obvious musical gifts, and at least one of them deserves better.

Tina Turner: Private Dancer
1984, Capitol

Tina Turner made a shocking comeback in 1984 and kick-started her solo career with this *tour de force*. Moving away from the soul belters of her early career to a more rock- and pop-oriented sound, she is both tender and defiant on this her best solo effort. Aside from her signature tune, "What's Love Got To Do With It", the album is filled with flourishes of sophisticated production and Tina maturely delivering her distinctive, gritty vocals.

Proud Mary: The Best Of Ike & Tina Turner
1991, EMI

There are about a thousand Ike & Tina Turner compilations on the market, but this does the best job of combining their first hit-making stint in the early 60s with the best material from their second in the late 60s/early 70s. A word of warning to baroque pop enthusiasts: the version of "River Deep, Mountain High" here is not the Phil Spector one, but the pared down version they recorded several years later.

Undisputed Truth

Super-producer **Norman Whitfield** formed **Undisputed Truth**, a male/female vocal group from Detroit, as a kind of sketch pad for his studio experimentation at Motown. He put together the initial line-up of **Joe Harris**, **Billie Rae Calvin** and **Brenda Joyce Evans** in 1970, shortly after he had ushered in the age of psychedelic soul with **The Temptations**.

The group's first single, 1971's "Save My Love For A Rainy Day", attracted little attention, but their second, "Smiling Faces Sometimes", from the same year, gave them their first – and only – US top-ten hit. With its massed chorales, swooping strings, gargantuan brass and woodwind sections, percussion that imitated both a ticking clock and a rattlesnake, and the "Can you dig it?" lyric that Isaac Hayes borrowed for "Shaft", "Smiling Faces" was the most fully realized orchestral soul production up to that point. While the arrangement mirrored those on Hayes's *Hot Buttered Soul*, the instrumental richness was denser, thicker and more claustrophobic, but also so sweet that it became almost cloying and fulsome, like false praise. When lead singer Joe Harris came in, he sang like a mourning **Levi Stubbs**, resigned to the fatalism of the lyrics and holding his power in reserve: "Smiling faces sometimes pretend to be your friend/Smiling faces show no traces of the evil that lurks within".

Similar gloom and portentousness pervaded "You Make Your Own Heaven And Hell Right Here On Earth", "What It Is" and the original version of "Papa Was A Rolling Stone". In 1973 Calvin and Evans left the group to be replaced by **Tyrone Berkeley**, **Tyrone Douglas**, **Virginia McDonald** and **Calvin Stevens**. Despite the personnel changes, their style remained the same and Whitfield crafted huge, swirling epics of wah-wah-infused paranoia on "Mama I Got A Brand New Thing (Don't Say No)" and "Law Of The Land".

The group had their biggest hit since "Smiling Faces" with 1974's "Help Yourself", which introduced synthesizers and a rhythm box into Whitfield's repertoire. More studio trickery was on display in 1975, on the P-Funk rip-off "UFOs" and the awkward soul-rocker "Higher Than High". When Whitfield left Motown later that year, he took Undisputed Truth with him to his own label, and Chaka Khan's sister **Taka Boom** joined the group when Douglas, Stevens and McDonald left. The group recorded one bona fide disco classic, "You + Me = Love", and two albums, *Method To The Madness* (1977) and *Smokin'* (1979), on the Whitfield label, before disbanding in the early 80s.

In 1991, however, Harris and Evans reunited with the former lead singer of Brainstorm, **Belita Woods**, to record a version of "Law Of The Land" for British producer and Hi-NRG impresario **Ian Levine's** Motor City project.

Best Of The Undisputed Truth
1991, Motown

While it may not have the glorious "You + Me = Love", this 12-track compilation holds essentially all of the group's significant Motown singles, including the only one that every soul fan needs, "Smiling Faces Sometimes".

Usher

Usher Raymond became the biggest male star in R&B in the 90s. Lithe and nimble on top of slick, ultra-produced dance tracks, he also croons sweetly enough on the ballads – crucially without oversinging as much as the majority of his peers – to make the girls go weak at the knees, although his willingness to show off his well-defined abs doesn't hurt either.

Born on October 14, 1978 in Chattanooga, Tennessee, Usher was discovered at the age of 14 by an executive for the LaFace label at a talent show in Atlanta, Georgia. When he later auditioned for label president **LA Reid**, he was signed on the spot. His first single, 1994's "Call Me A Mack", featured on the *Poetic Justice* soundtrack, sampled **Ice Cube** and was a teeny-bopperish attempt at being hard. His first album, *Usher*, released later that year, was executive produced by **P. Diddy**, but Usher was still a little bit green. However, the second single, "Think Of You", made it into the R&B Top 10 on the strength of a rap by **Biz Markie**.

When Usher graduated from high school, he recorded 1997's *My Way*, on which he co-wrote most of the tracks with producers **Jermaine Dupri** and Babyface. The ballad "You Make Me Wanna…" was little short of a sensation. It was an R&B #1 for 11 weeks, spending a staggering 71 weeks on the R&B chart in total, and was only kept out of the pop top spot by Elton John's "Candle In The Wind '97". In 1998 "Nice & Slow", became his first pop #1 and was an R&B #1 for two months, while the follow-up,"My Way", became the album's third platinum single.

After a couple of forgettable movie roles and a pointless and terrible live album, Usher returned with the dud *All About U* in 2000. That was followed in 2001 by *8701*, an album that was so slick it was bland and forgettable. However, 2004's *Confessions* was a real return to form. "Yeah!", produced by Lil' Jon, was the album's only dance track. It was a monster record that skidded and careened all over the place, bursting with manic energy – it was the year's best single. The rest of the album was extremely well produced, state-of-the-art love man.

Confessions
2004, Arista

Confessions was the best-selling album in the US in 2004 for two reasons: first, Usher's got charisma (unlike nearly everyone else on the R&B scene), and second, "Yeah!" was so great that it could even propel an overlong, over-produced album like this into the stratosphere. You could piece together all the obvious reference points on the album – Prince, The Chi-Lites, even R. Kelly – but it moves with such grace and élan that you don't really notice.

Luther Vandross

Luther Vandross was the best "pure" soul singer of the last 30 years. Eschewing the overwrought melisma that became the rage during his prime years, Vandross was easily the greatest male balladeer of his generation. The irony of this is that rather than taking inspiration from the usual male role models – Sam Cooke, **Eddie Kendricks**, Marvin Gaye – he learned to sing by aping female vocalists The Shirelles, Dionne Warwick and Diana Ross.

He was born in New York City on April 20, 1951. In the early 70s he worked as a jingle singer before becoming an in-demand session singer and vocal arranger, most famously singing backing vocals on **David Bowie**'s *Young Americans*. During the mid-70s Chic were effectively the backing band at his live gigs and he later sang on some of their records. He released a few solo singles for Cotillion in the mid-70s under the name Luther, including "It's Good For The Soul" and "Funky Music (Is A Part Of Me)".

In 1978 Vandross was a member of the session group Roundtree, with Chic's **Bernard Edwards**, that had a modest disco hit with "Get On Up (Get On Down)". Thanks to his work with Chic, Vandross was approached by producers **Mauro Malavasi** and **Jacques Fred Petrus** to work on their Chic rip-off project Change in 1980. He sang lead on "Searching", which sounded nothing like Chic, but more like an MOR radio hit from five years later, and "Glow Of Love", which was pure Chic.

Signing to Epic in 1981, he recorded his first solo album, *Never Too Much*. The title track was his first R&B #1 – and what a track. Self-produced (he had clearly learned a lot from Chic), "Never Too Much" was filled with cavernous spaces between the bass and guitar, the merest hints of strings and keyboards during the verses and gushes of sweetening during the chorus. The album also contained a fine version of Bacharach/David's "A House Is Not A Home", which heralded Vandross as the balladeer to bring back the slow jam.

In 1982 Vandross released "If This World Were Mine", a jazzy, overwrought duet with Cheryl Lynn, and "Bad Boy/Having A Party", a neat reinterpretation of Sam Cooke's "Having A Party". He then got the chance to work with his idol Dionne Warwick on the duet "How Many Times Can We Say Goodbye", before cutting another bold re-working, "Superstar/Until You Come Back To Me (That's What I'm Going To Do)", which was an unholy blend of The Carpenters and Aretha Franklin that somehow worked. He went uptempo again in 1985 on "'Til My Baby Comes Home", which had **Billy Preston** on organ giving a bit of grit to the usual unctuousness, and "It's Over Now", which was one of the decade's best break-up tracks thanks to his vocals, the slap bass and the post-Chic keyboard eeriness.

Beginning with 1986's "Give Me The Reason", from the *Ruthless People* sound-track, Vandross then became the voice of choice for the cheesy quiet storm/Hollywood date-montage ballad – which made him a superstar. He continued in this territory with records like "Any Love" – a thin, watery production that made you wish he was born twenty years earlier so he could sing on top of something with weight – "Here And Now" and "For You To Love". However, Vandross was at his best on funkier, more uptempo tracks like "I Really Didn't Mean It" and "The Best Things In Life Are Free", a duet with Janet Jackson, and on moodier ballads like "The Rush".

Vandross struggled during the 90s in the face of the commercial dominance of hip-hop and the oversexed, under-skilled young bucks who ran R&B. The one real exception was the dreadful 1994 remake of "Endless Love" with Mariah Carey that became only his second gold single (the first was "Here And Now"). He tried to be vaguely current on 2001's "Heaven Can Wait (Thunderpuss)" by singing on top of a fairly generic house beat, which had the effect of making him sound anonymous.

The autobiographical "Dance With My Father", from the album of the same name, was pure Hollywood schmaltz in 2003, but as usual Vandross sang it with consummate grace and won the Grammy for Song of the Year. In April of that year, however, just as the record was released, Vandross suffered a stroke that left him in a coma for two months. He never fully recovered and he died on July 1, 2005.

⊙ The Best Of Luther Vandross: The Best Of Love
1989, Epic

This 2-CD, 20-track collection has the edge over the more extensive *The Essential Luther Vandross* (2003, Epic/Legacy) because it includes the two Change tracks on which he sang lead, rather than all his schmaltzy ballads from the late 80s and early 90s. It's not only Vandross's comparatively melisma-less tone that set him apart from his peers, but his exquisite control – a concept totally lost on contemporary R&B singers.

Junior Walker & The All-Stars

Easily the funkiest and least typical of Motown's major signings, **Junior Walker** existed in his own greasy realm light years away from the deportment lessons forced on other Motown artists. Walker's squealing bluesy saxophone instrumentals sounded like they came from a sleazy stripjoint on the outskirts of town, not the urbane cocktail parties of **Berry Gordy**'s dreams.

Walker was born **Autry DeWalt** in Blytheville, Arkansas on June 14, 1931, although Motown lied about his age, presumably so the kids wouldn't know that it was an old geezer making them fingerpop. He grew up in South Bend, Indiana where he played in various jazz combos until the late 50s when he moved to Battle Creek, Michigan and formed **Jr. Walker & The All-Stars** with guitarist **Willie Woods**, organist **Victor Thomas** and drummer **James Graves**. They were discovered at the El Grotto Club in Battle Creek by Johnny Bristol and then signed to his friend **Harvey Fuqua**'s Harvey label. They recorded three singles for Harvey – "Twist Lackawanna", "Cleo's Mood" and "Good Rockin'" – in the early 60s, before the label was absorbed into Motown.

Their first single there for Motown, 1964's "Monkey Jump", went nowhere, but the follow-up became the group's biggest hit, reaching #1 on the R&B chart and #5 pop. "Shotgun" was the sort of grimy, dirty old-fashioned R&B Walker played at the El Grotto Club, but with Motown professionalism – the only All-Star to play on the record was Walker (who also sang); the rest of the group was made up of **The Funk Brothers**. The next year's "Shake And Fingerpop" was a thoroughly joyous record in which everything from the vocals to the sax and the organ stabs was guttural, slurred and low-down and another big chart hit.

The equally wonderful "(I'm A) Road Runner" followed the same blueprint, while "Any Way You Wannta", the B-side of the drab "Pucker Up Buttercup", was perhaps the funkiest record the band ever cut. Their 1969 album *Home Cookin'* featured tracks, such as "Baby Ain't You Shame", that sounded like James Brown from a few years earlier, but the group soon got slicker. "Hip City" sounded like a hotel lounge band letting their hair down, while "What Does It Take To Win Your Love" was positively mellow. Both "Gotta Hold On To This Feeling" and "Do You See My Love (For You Growing)" had warmer basslines and tempos that were more gently upbeat than full throttle.

By the release of "Walk In The Night" in 1972, the All-Stars sounded like they were imitating the soul music coming out of Philadelphia. Given the sound of that record, Walker's solo transition to disco should have been easy, but with the exceptions of "I'm So Glad", "Hot Shot" and an instrumental version of Rose Royce's "Wishin On A Star", he failed to chart at all in the mid- to late 70s. He famously appeared on Foreigner's "Urgent" in 1981, but imitators like **Grover Washington, Jr.** and **Kenny G.** began to steal his thunder. Although he continued to tour during the 80s and 90s, Walker soon disappeared from the charts, before sadly dying of cancer on November 23, 1995.

Shotgun
1965, Motown

The All-Stars were to Motown what The MG's were to Atlantic, and this sax-driven, largely instrumental debut catches them in their prime. The mid-60s Motown sound jams presented here are a dance-beat bonanza, with their funky title track joined by the equally devastating "Road Runner" and "Shake And Fingerpop".

The Ultimate Collection
1997, Motown

Twenty-five tracks is certainly all the Jr. Walker & The All-Stars non-fanatics need to own. However, this doesn't have their funkiest tracks like "Any Way You Wannta" or "Baby Ain't You Shame". On the other hand, it does have all of their early hits, which are so electric that you probably won't even notice.

War

Of all the bands to hail from LA, **War** probably came closest to embodying all the diverse images of the City of Angels – Hollywood glamour, endless beaches, palm-lined streets paved with gold, a gigantic smog-infested parking lot, a huge faceless suburb, Third World melting pot boiling over with racial strife. War was formed out of the ashes of a local group called **The Creators** when superstar defensive lineman for the LA Rams, Deacon Jones, was looking for a backing band as he tried to move into singing. A year later the group hooked up with former Animals lead singer **Eric Burdon**, whom they backed on two albums, producing the hits "Spill The Wine" and "They Can't Take Away Our Music".

In 1971 guitarist **Howard Scott**, bassist **B.B. Dickerson**, keyboardist **Lonnie Jordan**, drummer **Harold Brown**, percussionist **Papa Dee Allen**, horn player **Charles Miller** and Danish harmonica ace **Lee Oskar** got rid of Burdon and grabbed the spotlight for themselves. Their first album, 1971's *War*, was pretty faceless and didn't do much, but their second album that year, *All Day Music*, established the group as one of the most important funk troupes of the 70s. Picking up on one of the underappreciated currents of SoCal music, War concocted a potent blend of funk rhythms, rock force, harmony group vocal chops and Latin accents. Simultaneously joyful and frugged,

War sounded like a group of community activists brushing the smoke from the Watts riots out of their eyes. Unlike too many politically aware bands, however, War never forgot that pleasure has its own dialectic and their grooves spoke as emphatically as their lyrics.

The album's second track, "Get Down", may have been titled like an air-headed invitation to boogie, but its real intentions were clear by the second verse. The outrage of the lyrics ("Police and the justice laughing while they bust us") was matched by the seething menace of the percolating drum and bass groove. "Nappy Head" combined Santana-esque guitars, conga fills, *güiro* patterns, montuno piano and voices in the crowd yelling, "Viva La Raza", to create a Latino version of the soundtrack to Melvin Van Peebles' original blaxploitation flick, *Sweet Sweetback's Baadasss Song – ¡Sabroso!*. "Nappy Head" led into the album's masterpiece, "Slippin' Into Darkness", a dark, dubby track that stares over the edge of the abyss into the heart of the spiritual dissolution of America and deserves to be ranked alongside *There's A Riot Goin' On*, "Papa Was A Rolling Stone" and "Back Stabbers".

Half of their 1972 follow-up, *The World Is A Ghetto*, was just as good, including the percolating "Cisco Kid" and "City, Country, City", a 13-minute travelogue that mutated from mellow harmonica-led pastoral to humid, congested funk at the drop of a hat. The other half, unfortunately, meandered fairly aimlessly. *Deliver The Word* from 1973 was disappointingly similar, with too much progressive jazzy stuff. However, it did include the brilliant "Me And Baby Brother", a deceptively upbeat, celebratory number that told the tale of someone murdered by the cops ("Shot my baby brother/And they called it law and order").

Why Can't We Be Friends? from 1975 was perhaps the group's most mindlessly fun album, although it was hard to miss the message in the title track, and the mighty "Low Rider" was an anthem of Latino pride. *Why Can't We Be Friends?* was the group's last smash album, as disco started to take a bite out of funk sales in the late 70s. War tried to respond with "Galaxy" in 1977, a smoking disco-funk jam that was still unmistakably War, but perhaps that was the problem.

The group grew ever more faceless as time wore on. "Flying Machine", with its pronounced Latin flavour, was the only highlight to their 1978 *Youngblood* soundtrack. **Alice Tweed Smyth** joined on vocals in 1978 and Dickerson left the group, to be replaced by bassist **Luther Rabb**, horn player **Pat Rizzo** and percussionist **Ron Hammond**. Without Dickerson's characteristic basslines, War's records became nothing more than a series of anonymous slick disco jams that were virtually interchangeable with what was coming out of New York. Sadly, Charles Miller was murdered by an armed robber in 1980 and the group never recovered.

After releasing a series of commercially and artistically uninspired albums during the 80s, War became little more than a touring band. Sadly, Papa Dee Allen suffered a brain hemorrhage and died during a gig on August 30, 1988. In 1994 a War line-up of Jordan, Scott, Brown, Hammond, horn players Charley Green and Kerry Campbell, harmonica player Tetsuya Nakamura and percussionist Sal Rodriguez made a brief comeback with *Peace Sign*, which went nowhere and was to be their final studio album.

All Day Music
1971, Rhino

Producer Jerry Goldstein often edited tapes of War jamming in order to conjure "songs" from the instrumental morass. The slow and lazy ode to relaxation, "All Day Music", was born in this way. The rest of the album keeps the title cut's hazy groove, but is considerably less daydreamy – these tough, funky, political tracks take no prisoners with their grooves or their words.

Dionne Warwick

Certainly the only artist in this book with even the faintest connection to Marlene Dietrich, **Dionne Warwick** brought soul into the suburbs. Motown might have hooked kids with disposable incomes cruising in their cars, but Warwick's versions of Bacharach-David songs appealed to their leisure apparel-clad parents as well. With the sharp, piercing, intricate arrangements of **Burt Bacharach**, the almost-Cole Porter zing of **Hal David**'s wordplay and her own supper-club soft-gospel vocals, Warwick's early records marked the shift between R&B and

soul and laid the groundwork for soul's mainstream crossover.

Born in New Jersey on December 12, 1940, Marie Dionne Warwick formed a gospel trio, The Gospelaires, with her sister Dee Dee and her aunt Cissy Houston in the 50s. At the end of the decade Warwick began a career as a studio back-up singer. She was picked out of the crowd by Burt Bacharach, the former arranger for Marlene Dietrich's cabaret act, when she sang on The Drifters' "Mexican Divorce" in 1961. As the annointed voice for Bacharach-David productions, Warwick would score 22 hits in the American Top 40 over the following decade.

Warwick's first hit was 1962's "Don't Make Me Over". Not only a commercial success, it was an artistic triumph for the singer as she managed not to drown in the string undertow and, along with singers like Maxine Brown and Baby Washington, showed the way for female pop singers to escape the shackles of the girl group sound. Toning the melodrama down a bit, the follow-up, "Anyone Who Had A Heart", placed the strings a bit further back in the mix and showcased Warwick's voice which was a tower of strength even as she sang of vulnerability and heartbreak.

As close to pure pop as much of Warwick's best work was, her vocals never strayed too far from the gospel path. Possibly her best record, 1964's "Walk On By", was a masterpiece of churchy phrasing and subtle melisma that transcended that awful horn line which ensured that the song would forever be a staple of dentists' offices the world over. As The Beatles were conquering America,

New York Soul

As the centre of the American recording industry, New York has always had far too much activity for there ever to be a quantifiable New York sound. This is especially true of soul music. New York was the spiritual home of doo-wop thanks to **George Goldner** and **Bobby Robinson**, and the birthplace of the girl group sound thanks to **The Shirelles** and **The Chiffons**. However, in soul circles the Big Apple is most associated with a brief period in the late 50s and early 60s when the craftsmanship of the Brill Building songwriters, the artifice of producer-arrangers such as **Jerry Ragavoy**, **Luther Dixon**, **Burt Bacharach**, **Leiber & Stoller** and **Teddy Randazzo** and the gospel-trained voices of **Dionne Warwick**, **Chuck Jackson** and **Ben E. King** combined to create what became known as downtown soul.

The crucial downtown soul record was The Drifters' 1959 hit "There Goes My Baby". The pseudo-classical strings, the tympani and the group singing in a different key merged together to form an R&B sound of epic scope, a creation that could have only come from a plush Manhattan studio, not some greasy roadhouse down South.

After "There Goes My Baby" came a deluge of downtown soul records: Maxine Brown's "All In My Mind", The Shirelles' "Will You Still Love Me Tomorrow", Chuck Jackson's "I Don't Want To Cry", **The Exciters'** "Tell Him", Dionne Warwick's "Don't Make Me Over", Baby Washington's "That's How Heartaches Are Made", Freddie Scott's "Hey Girl" and Little Anthony & The Imperials' "Goin' Out Of My Head".

Aside from Atlantic – which was really too wide-ranging to be considered an exclusively New York soul label – the headquarters of the Big Apple sound was **Florence Greenberg**'s Scepter/Wand enterprise. Greenberg was a housewife who had no music business experience whatsoever when her daughter brought four classmates into her living room in 1957. Those four girls became The Shirelles – and the foundation of one of the most successful independent labels of the soul era. Scepter was also responsible for records by Chuck Jackson, Maxine Brown, Dionne Warwick, The Isley Brothers and many others.

While New York served as home base or produced records for dozens and dozens of soul singers with different styles – Brook Benton, J. J. Jackson, The Isley Brothers, Inez & Charlie Foxx, Lorraine Ellison, Doris Troy, The Manhattans, The Moments, **Donnie Elbert**, Jimmy Castor – it is with the Brill Building/downtown soul style that the city will forever be associated.

Various Artists: The Scepter Records Story
1992, Capricorn

This 2-CD, 65-track collection is a fabulous overview of Florence Greenberg's legendary New York-based Scepter label. It includes tracks by The Shirelles, Dionne Warwick, Chuck Jackson, Maxine Brown, BJ Thomas, Tommy Hunt, Roy Head, The Esquires, The Joe Jeffrey Group, The Isley Brothers and even The Kingsmen. More Scepter/Wand obscurities can be found on the excellent *Sweet Sound Of Success* (1995, Ace/Kent) and *New York Soul Serenade* (1997, Ace/Kent).

PLAYLIST

1 THERE GOES MY BABY The Drifters from Rockin' And Driftin': The Drifters Box
The first R&B record to feature strings, and therefore in many minds the very first soul record.

2 WILL YOU STILL LOVE ME TOMORROW The Shirelles from The Very Best Of The Shirelles
Female pop music's eternal question never posed better.

3 I DON'T WANT TO CRY Chuck Jackson from Any Day Now: The Very Best of Chuck Jackson 1961–1967
Jackson's throaty baritone juxtaposed against the chintzy strings is one of the hallmarks of downtown soul.

4 DON'T MAKE ME OVER Dionne Warwick from The Dionne Warwick Collection
How Warwick manages not to drown in the whirlpool of strings is one of the miracles of recorded sound.

5 HEY GIRL Freddie Scott from Birth Of Soul
Typical over-the-top New York sweetening and orchestration, but Scott still cuts through it all.

6 GOIN' OUT OF MY HEAD Little Anthony & The Imperials from 25 Greatest Hits
The lushest, most baroque downtown soul ever recorded

7 STAY WITH ME Lorraine Ellison from Stay With Me: The Best Of Lorraine Ellison
The most emotionally ravaged soul record.

8 THE NITTY GRITTY Shirley Ellis from The Complete Congress Recordings
The queen of playground soul at her best.

9 KISS AND SAY GOODBYE The Manhattans from Kiss And Say Goodbye: The Best Of The Manhattans
A break-up ballad so extravagant it made it to #1 during the disco era.

10 IT'S JUST BEGUN Jimmy Castor from The Everything Man: The Best of the Jimmy Castor Bunch
In which the "everything man" gives the drummer some.

413

Warwick continued to hit the charts with letter-perfect, controlled performances on songs like "Reach Out For Me" and "You'll Never Get To Heaven (If You Break My Heart)". Probably because she worked with the kings of middle-class respectability, Warwick hardly raised her voice after "Don't Make Me Over" and, like Nat "King" Cole, kept her pain beneath the surface. Where other soul mamas belted out their torment, Warwick took the classic pop road and masked her pain with extreme stylization.

No one since Cole himself was as good an interpreter of classic pop material as Warwick. Her soul mannerisms gave warmth to Bacharach's often acerbic arrangements and gravity to David's trifles like "Trains And Boats And Planes". Aside from her theme to *Valley Of The Dolls*, Warwick's biggest hit of the 60s was "I Say A Little Prayer", which epitomized her approach to Brill Building product. Although the gospelese call-and-response of "Walk On By" was replaced by bubble-machine "ba-ba-ba-bas" and "oo-oo-oos", Warwick modulated subtly between the church and the cabaret, and "I Say A Little Prayer" was a great co-mingling of chitlin-circuit grits and showbiz glitz.

Warwick's records with Bacharach-David were unprecedented, yet she didn't have a #1 single until after Bacharach and David broke up. Her 1974 hit with **The Spinners**, "Then Came You", was fine AM radio fodder, but it was hardly her best record. On records like "Track Of The Cat" she showed that her restrained vocals couldn't compete with the more rhythmically demanding arrangements of the disco/funk era. Unfortunately, her career sank to more bathetic lows in the 80s with "Heartbreaker" (with **Barry Gibb**), "I'll Never Love This Way Again" and "That's What Friends Are For" (with Gladys Knight, Elton John and Stevie Wonder) becoming some of the biggest hits of her career. Then, in the 90s there was the *Solid Gold* TV series and those adverts for the Psychic Friends Network…

Make Way For Dionne Warwick
1964, Scepter

Warwick's third album is a masterpiece of understated soul, brilliantly written and arranged by Burt Bacharach and Hal David. The control and reserve of her delivery are complemented by the lush precision of the studio back-up on these immaculately produced soul gems.

The Dionne Warwick Collection
1989, Rhino

This 24-track compilation represents the cream of Warwick's work in the 60s before she became an MOR hack. This isn't the soul music of fall-to-one's-knees intensity or gut-wrenching exorcism, but the restrained, subtle soulfulness of a perfectly in control singer deftly making pretentious pop trinkets signify despite themselves.

Baby Washington

Born Justine Washington on November 13, 1940 in Bamberg, South Carolina, **Jeanette "Baby" Washington** was one of the most underrated of the early soul vocalists. Sounding like a more powerful Dionne Warwick, Washington combined stately deportment with powerful bluesy wails on a series of fine records that helped define New York soul in the 60s.

She was discovered in a Harlem high school in 1956 by **Zell Sanders**, the owner of the J&S label. Sanders recruited her to be a member of **The Hearts**, a female doo-wop ensemble that had a hit with "Lonely Nights" in 1955. Washington sang on The Hearts' "Going Home To Stay" in 1956, before recording her first solo disc, "Everyday", the following year. She recorded four more singles with J&S before moving to **Donald Shaw**'s Neptune label (not to be confused with Kenny Gamble's later label of the same name) in 1958. Her first record for Neptune was "The Time", a classic of the tick-tocking rock'n'roll ballad genre and an early indicator that she would develop into a fine soul vocalist. "The Bells (On Our Wedding Day)" and "Nobody Cares (About Me)" followed in a similarly doom-laden style, and both reached the R&B Top 20.

Moving to **Juggy Murray**'s Sue label, Washington had a hit with "Handful Of Memories", a lovely early uptown soul production, before cutting her biggest hit, the lush "That's How Heartaches Are Made". In 1963 she sang in a slightly strained voice over the top of a classic uptown soul arrangement on "Hey Lonely One", but was at her most Warwick-like on "Leave Me Alone". The next year's "I Can't Wait Until I See My Baby's Face" had one of the most sympathetic arrangements she ever got – her gravitas worked perfectly with the ballroom jazz and dark-of-the-night guitar chank. Her delivery on that record also profoundly influenced British vocalist Dusty Springfield. After 1965's "Only Those In Love", Washington stopped recording for a couple of years.

Washington returned in 1968 on the Veep label with the album *With You In Mind*, hailed by many in the deep soul scene as a classic. On slow tracks like "I Got It Bad And That Ain't Good", her voice was so old-world that it sounded bizarre against the more modern arrangements, but more upt-empo tracks like "Think About the Good Times" were more successful. She had a minor hit on Cotillion with "I Don't Know" in 1969, before duetting with **Don Gardner** on the popular "Forever" in 1973.

After releasing several mediocre disco records in the late 70s, Washington's career petered out and she vanished from the scene. As a side note, she is not the same Jeanette Washington who sang with **James Brown** or as part of **George Clinton**'s girl group fantasy **Parlet** in the 80s.

> **I've Got A Feeling: The Best Of Baby Washington**
> 2005, EMI/Stateside

Capable of being both sweet and sultry and brazen and piercing, Baby Washington was one of the best of the early female soul singers. This superb 28-track compilation collects the best of the singles that she recorded for Sue between 1962 and 1967, as well as her more soulful Veep sides, and should go some way toward restoring the reputation of this unjustly forgotten vocalist.

Johnny "Guitar" Watson

Born in Houston, Texas on February 3, 1935, **Johnny "Guitar" Watson** wore more musical hats than just about anyone this side of Johnny Otis, with whom he briefly worked. As a teenager Watson garnered a formidable reputation as a piano player and frequently played alongside future blues legends **Albert Collins** and **Johnny Copeland**. When he was 15, he moved to LA to pursue music full-time and, after seeing a performance by Clarence "Gatemouth" Brown, decided to switch to guitar.

It was on piano, however, that he made his recording debut in 1952 on Chuck Higgins' "Motorhead Baby" and later "Highway 60".

As Young John Watson, he also recorded the outrageous guitar instrumental "Space Guitar" for Federal. It didn't sell at the time, but it was one of the most outlandish uses of primitive guitar effects and has since inspired many a surf guitar player. He then followed up with the far more sedate "Gettin' Drunk".

Inspired by the Joan Crawford film *Johnny Guitar*, he changed his name to Johnny "Guitar" Watson and signed to RPM/Modern in 1955. That same year the bluesy ballad "Those Lonely Nights" became his first hit, reaching the R&B Top 10. After releasing a few singles that failed to have an impact on the charts, Watson was dropped by Modern and, in 1958, signed to Keen, where he recorded the first version of his theme song, "Gangster Of Love".

Over the next few years Watson worked as a sideman with Don & Dewey, **Little Richard** and The Olympics. While working with producer and bandleader Johnny Otis, Watson briefly re-signed to King/Federal and had a big hit with "Cuttin' In" and a minor hit with a re-recorded, more soulful version of "Gangster Of Love". In 1964 Watson moved to the Chess label and recorded a loungy piano jazz album, *The Blues Soul Of Johnny "Guitar" Watson*.

Watson teamed up with New Orleans rock'n'roller **Larry Williams** in 1965. The two were equally flamboyant – Williams allegedly wore shoes with stacked plastic heels that had goldfish swimming in them – and made an enjoyable, if not truly great, pairing. They had a hit with the soft-soul classic "Mercy, Mercy, Mercy" in 1967, but most of their releases were high-energy up-tempo tracks like "A Quitter Never Wins" and "Two For The Price Of One". They were a bit mannered with all their asides and "yes y'alls", but both their falsettos were affecting when they let rip. On tracks like "Can't Find No Substitute For Love", which had a percolating bassline that was the precursor to **Ann Peebles**' "I Can't Stand The Rain", they were wonderfully charming, even if they didn't reach the depth of emotion that is the mark of the best soul. This was a problem on slower tracks like "I Could Love You", which sounded ridiculously mannered.

In the mid-70s Watson reinvented himself as a pimped-out funk bluesman. Signing to Fantasy in 1973, he recorded the underrated

Johnny "Guitar" Watson clearly lovin' his job

Listen album, which included the smoky slowburn blues ballad "You've Got A Hard Head" and the superfly pimp-silly "Loving You". He then had moderate hits with "Like I'm Not Your Man" and "I Don't Want To Be A Lone Ranger" – and played on **Frank Zappa**'s *One Size Fits All* in 1975 – before signing to the British DJM label.

At DJM he used funkier rhythms on "I Need It", "Superman Lover" and his biggest hit "A Real Mother for Ya" – by the way, *A Real Mother For Ya* might have the best album cover ever. In the late 70s and early 80s Watson continued to have modest R&B hits in the same formula, with yet another

"Gangster Of Love", "Love Jones", "The Planet Funk" and "Strike On Computers".

After a quiet ten years, Watson returned in 1994 with the not-half-bad, Grammy-nominated funk album *Bow Wow*, which he worked on with Tony! Toni! Toné!, and had modest hits with the title track and "Hook Me Up". However, while performing at the Yokohama Blues Café in Japan on May 17, 1996, he had a heart attack on stage and died.

The Very Best Of Johnny "Guitar" Watson
1999, Rhino

This excellent collection highlights Watson's early years as a jump blues piano player, fiery electric guitar player, blues balladeer and uptown soul singer. If you were being cruel you could say he was a jack of all trades and master of none, but these 18 tracks are uniformly delightful. Fans of his mid-70s funk rebirth are advised to pick up *The Very Best Of Johnny "Guitar" Watson: In Loving Memory* (1996, Collectables).

Mary Wells

During the label's early years, **Mary Wells** was, undoubtedly, Motown's biggest star. She was born on May 13, 1943 in Detroit and discovered at the age of 17 by Motown boss **Berry Gordy** when she was trying to get Jackie Wilson to record a song she had written. Instead of giving the song to Wilson, Gordy had Wells record "Bye Bye Baby" herself, and it became an R&B top-ten hit in 1960. "Bye Bye Baby" and its follow-up, "Don't Want To Take A Chance", were in that chugging post-rock'n'roll, not-quite-soul style of the time, and Wells' performance was accordingly full-throated.

With production and songwriting help from Smokey Robinson, Wells recorded three straight top-ten singles in 1962: "The One Who Really Loves You", "You Beat Me To The Punch" and "Two Lovers", all of which had Wells singing in a more demure, breathier style than her first few records. "Laughing Boy", "Your Old Stand By" and "You Lost The Sweetest Boy" continued her string of hits the next year, before she scored her only pop #1 with 1964's "My Guy".

After recording a duet with Marvin Gaye, "What's The Matter With You Baby", Wells left Motown and signed to 20th Century Fox after being promised acting roles at their studio. The film roles never materialized and Wells ended up recording overripe downtown records like "Never, Never Leave Me" and "He's A Lover". Wells' best record during her tenure at 20th Century was "Use Your Head", thanks to its easy swing and comparatively restrained arrangement, but she couldn't duplicate her Motown chart success at her new label. Signing to Atco in 1965, she released a few awkward records, including "Fancy Free" and "(Hey You) Set My Soul On Fire", on which Atlantic's studio pros desperately tried to merge downtown and Motown with fairly predictable results.

In the late 60s and early 70s, Wells started working with her husband **Cecil Womack**

and tried to change with the times. She signed with Reprise and recorded "I Found What I Wanted", on which she sounded a bit like Curtis Mayfield, and "If You Can't Love Her (Give Her Up)", but she just wasn't sassy enough to pull off straight-talking message songs. Although she recorded occasional one-offs like 1982's "Gigolo", recording dates and contracts were few and far between in the 80s, and Wells sadly died of throat cancer on July 26, 1992.

The Ultimate Collection
1998, Motown

This 25-track collection includes not only all of Mary Wells' major hits with Motown, but also "Dear Lover", her lone hit for Atco, and a couple of sides she recorded for 20th Century Fox. Although it doesn't include her fine, somewhat raunchy obscurity "Drop In The Bucket", this is the only Wells collection to own.

The Whispers

Before coming under the wing of impresario **Dick Griffey**, **The Whispers** were a journeymen vocal group who sang a series of cult post-doo-wop records in a sweet Temptations style. With Griffey, The Whispers tailored their style to pop-disco productions and became one of the very few vocal groups who were consistent hitmakers in the 60s, 70s, 80s and 90s.

The Whispers – identical twins **Walter** and **Wallace Scott**, **Gordy Harmon**, **Nicholas Caldwell** and **Marcus Hutson** – first got together at Jordan High School in LA in the early 60s. They signed to Lou Beddell's Dore label in 1964 and he named them after their soft singing style. At Dore, The Whispers released a number of records that weren't quite doo-wop or soul, but are now prized by collectors: "Take A Lesson From The Teacher", "I Was Born When You Kissed Me" and "Doctor Love".

In 1969 the group started recording for the Soul Clock label and had a regional hit with the neo-doo-wop record "Great Day", before breaking nationally with the smooth "The Time Will Come" and "Seems Like I Gotta Do Wrong". The following year they switched to the Janus label and had moderate success with a series of gentle ballads, including "There's A Love For Everyone", "Your Love Is So Doggone Good", "I Only

Boogie/Roller Skating Jams

What became known as "roller skating music" was a way for dance music producers to escape the gold lamé morass of mainstream disco. The main reason why it was more downtempo and less strictly 4/4 than classic disco was that you just can't skate to high-tempo music. Even so, it had little to do with the rubbish that accompanied the roller disco fad of 1978–79, such as Cher's "Hell On Wheels" and Citi's "Can You Do It On Skates?".

Instead, roller skating music developed in the early 80s from more R&B-flavoured disco, like **Patrick Adams**'s productions (Musique's "In The Bush" and "Keep On Jumpin'", Sine's "Just Let Me Do My Thing", Cloud One's "Disco Juice" and "Atmosphere Strutt" and Phreek's "Weekend"), **Brass Construction**'s funk hits and the Mizell Brothers' work on A Taste of Honey's "Boogie Oogie Oogie".

However, there was also a revisionist streak to this new music. At major New York roller rinks, including Manhattan's The Roxy and Brooklyn's Empire Rollerdrome, the DJs were playing records like **Shalamar**'s "Take That To The Bank" and "The Second Time Around", **The Whispers**' "And The Beat Goes On" and **Lakeside**'s "Fantastic Voyage" – all of which were released on LA's Solar label. Other favourites among the top roller rink DJs were **Rufus**'s "Do You Love What You Feel", **Rose Royce**'s "Pop Your Fingers" and **Vaughan Mason**'s "Bounce, Rock, Skate, Roll". While maintaining much of the groove of disco, all of these records marked a return of funk's "boom-slap", re-introducing a bouncy one-two feel to dance music after the 4/4 disco juggernaut.

Away from the roller rink, this funkier groove came to be known as "boogie" or "street music", distinguishing it not only from mainstream disco, but also from the heavily electronic dance music then popular in Europe and in gay communities in the US. Many of the early records in this style, such as the Fantastic Aleems' "Get Down Friday Night", Logg's "I Know You Will" and Convertion's "Let's Do It" – all featuring **Leroy Burgess** on vocals – as well as Central Line's "Walking Into Sunshine", were underground hits at New York's legendary Paradise Garage, where the disco flame was being kept alive. Pop trinkets like Indeep's "Last Night A DJ Saved My Life" had an across-the-board appeal.

Soon enough, though, records like Young & Company's "I Like What You're Doin' To Me", Goldie Alexander's "Show You My Love", Major Harris's "Gotta Make Up Your Mind", Kinky Foxx's "So Different" and Ceela's "I'm In Love" began to articulate a defiant R&B sensibility. Breaking away from the rainbow coalition that defined New York in the immediate post-disco era, they fed into R&B styles like the Minneapolis funk of **Jam & Lewis**, and the New Jack Swing of **Teddy Riley**, which severed any connection to disco or white music.

⊙ **Various Artists: The Perfect Beats Volumes 1–4**
1998, Tommy Boy

While no volume in this compilation set of New York's favourite early-80s dance music concentrates solely on roller skating music, they all provide a flavour of how skating hits like Shannon's "Let The Music Play" and the Aleems' "Release Yourself" fitted into the fabric of the time.

Meant To Wet My Feet" and "A Mother For My Children".

In 1973 **Leaveil Degree**, a former member of The Friends of Distinction, replaced Harmon after he injured his larynx in a car accident. The group then signed to Dick Griffey's Soul Train label and worked with disco producer **Norman Harris** on "One For The Money" and a remake of Bread's "Make It With You", which both broke the R&B Top 10 and became big disco hits. When Soul Train dissolved in 1978, Griffy brought the group over to his new label, Solar.

The Whispers' first record for Solar was the superb "(Let's Go) All The Way", a light and airy funk-disco track that soon became the signature sound of Solar. **Leon Sylvers**'

bubbly and vivacious "And the Beat Goes On" became the group's first R&B #1 in 1980. It set in motion a series of R&B hits in Solar's eminently enjoyable pop-disco style: "Imagination", a cult disco hit that was too messy to do anything off the dancefloor; "It's A Love Thing", with its definitive synth bassline, **Earth Wind & Fire**-style vocals, perfect keyboard interjections and one helluva hook (how did this not top the R&B chart?); the ballad "Lady"; "In The Raw"; "Emergency"; "Tonight"; and "Keep On Lovin' Me".

After 1984's funky "Contagious", The Whispers recorded "Some Kinda Lover", which was written by **Babyface**. Three years later, another Babyface song, "Rock Steady", became the group's biggest hit. Then, in 1990, they hit the R&B Top 10 three times with the ballads "Innocent", "My Heart Your Heart" and "Is It Good To You". Although no longer reaching the Top 10, The Whispers continued to hit the R&B charts with their smooth ballads into the latter half of the 90s. The group's last chart hit came in 1997 with a version of Babyface's "My, My, My", but they remain active on the oldies circuit today.

30th Anniversary Anthology
1994, Castle

This double-disc, 33-track collection includes most of The Whispers' hit singles from their days at Soul Clock, Janus, Soul Train and Solar, making this the best overview available. It's a model lesson in R&B longevity: be sweet enough to appeal to the ladies, but be bland enough never to outshine your producer.

Barry White

Granted, his records were a combination of Isaac Hayes and **Gene Page**, and Billy Stewart beat him to the punch as an overweight love man, but surely **Barry White** was one of the most singular presences in soul. Let's face it, it's not often that a 300-pound African-American becomes not only a sex symbol, but also one of the biggest cultural icons of his day.

White was born on September 12, 1944 in Galveston, Texas, but moved to LA with his family when he was 6 months old. At age 8 he was singing in the Greater Tabernacle Baptist

Barry White – the Walrus of Love

Church; by age 10 he was the choir's organist; and at age 12 he played piano on Jesse Belvin's R&B classic "Goodnight My Love". In high school he was in a vocal group called The Upfronts, who released several singles for the Lummtone label, including "Too Far To Turn Around", "Little Girl" and "I Stopped The Duke Of Earl". He then fronted **The Atlantics**, who released three singles for the Rampart, Linda and Faro labels in 1963. That same year, White arranged Bob & Earl's all-time great "Harlem Shuffle".

In 1966 White recorded a version of Elvis's "In The Ghetto" under the name of Gene West and then became a staff engineer and producer at Mustang-Bronco, where he produced records by the Bobby Fuller Four, Viola Wills and Felice Taylor. While with the label, White also released his first record under his own name, 1967's "All In The Run Of A Day". It was here that White met Gene Page, who gave him his taste for sweetening and unctuous arrangements.

While working on a session for Brendetta Davis, White met three backing singers – Diane Taylor and Linda and Glodean James – and proceeded to turn them into girl group **Love Unlimited**. He got the vocal trio signed to the Uni label and wrote and produced their "Walkin' In The Rain With The One I Love", a preposterous and cloying ballad that became a #6 R&B hit in 1972.

The next year White signed to 20th Century as a solo artist and released "I'm Gonna Love You Just A Little More Baby". The record was essentially a lubricious version of one of Isaac Hayes' ten-minute epics, but with steamier lyrics and more moaning. It was a huge hit. "I've Got So Much To Give", "Never, Never Gonna Give Ya Up" and "Honey Please, Can't Ya See" followed in swift succession and soon established White as a sensation.

While working on Love Unlimited's 1973 debut, *Under The Influence Of...*, White formed a mammoth 40-piece band called the **Love Unlimited Orchestra** (which included a 17-year-old **Kenny G.** on sax) to provide the backing. The orchestra's swirling, over-ripe instrumental "Love's Theme" was a big hit, and is often credited as being the first disco #1. Later, the group released two of White's funkiest tracks, "Strange Games And Things" from 1976's *My Sweet Summer*

PLAYLIST
Barry White

1 **I'M GONNA LOVE YOU JUST A LITTLE MORE BABY** from **All-Time Greatest Hits**
Even steamier and more ludicrous than Isaac Hayes.

2 **NEVER, NEVER GONNA GIVE YA UP** from **All-Time Greatest Hits**
White was at his best on more uptempo numbers, like this lithe groove.

3 **CAN'T GET ENOUGH OF YOUR LOVE, BABE** from **All-Time Greatest Hits**
The cowbell as metronome.

4 **YOU'RE THE FIRST, THE LAST, MY EVERYTHING** from **All-Time Greatest Hits**
Barry White at his most hedonistic – which is really saying something.

5 **THEME FROM TOGETHER BROTHERS** from **Together Brothers**
The Walrus of Love sheds some weight for this sleek groover.

6 **CAN'T SEEM TO FIND HIM** from **Together Brothers**
The funkiest track of White's career.

7 **PLAYING YOUR GAME, BABY** from **All-Time Greatest Hits**
White at his sleaziest and best.

8 **IT'S ECSTASY WHEN YOU LAY DOWN NEXT TO ME** from **All-Time Greatest Hits**
White at his least sleazy on top of swooping and scything strings.

Suite, with its simmering bassline, and 1977's "Theme From King Kong", with guitars that sounded almost African in the way they interlocked and never quite resolved.

On his own, White continued to have enormous success with records such as "Can't Get Enough Of Your Love, Babe" and "You're The First, The Last, My Everything", the latter of which featured White at his most overwrought, as the driving tempo forced him to over-emote and over-sing. However, if you think White is nothing but cheese, check out his 1974's *Together Brothers* – one of the stone-cold funkiest blaxploitation flick soundtracks, especially the main theme and the remarkable "Can't Seem To Find Him".

White's formula seemed to wear thin by 1976, but he returned to form the next year with the great "Playing Your Game, Baby" – this string arrangement was White's gift to the world, so baroquely symphonic, so sleazy – and the percolating "It's Ecstasy When You Lay Down Next To Me". White had a couple more hits with "Your Sweetness Is My Weakness" and a cover of Billy Joel's "Just The Way You Are", before signing to CBS where he was given his own custom label, Unlimited Gold.

The name of the label was a bit hopeful considering the disco backlash had already begun and White could only have got away with his signature schtick in the 70s. His next few albums were dismal failures and he stopped recording in 1983. However, not one to be kept down for long, he re-emerged in 1987 with "Sho' You Right", an uncharacteristically up-tempo track that was, remarkably for the time, still very lavish. In 1990 White made a guest appearance on Quincy Jones' ode to the quiet storm ballad, "Secret Garden (Sweet Seduction Suite)", and the following year he helped Big Daddy Kane get his mack on on "All Of Me".

This exposure to a new audience helped White's "Put Me In Your Mix" to become a #2 R&B hit later that year. He also teamed up with Isaac Hayes for the disappointing "Dark And Lovely (You Over There)", which featured on the *Put Me In Your Mix* album. In 1994 he once again hit the R&B top spot with "Practice What You Preach", a song written by Gerald Levert. White's musical career ended on a high when the title track to 1999's *Staying Power* gave him his first ever Grammy awards. Sadly, he was hospitalized due to kidney failure in 2002 and died on July 4, 2003.

All-Time Greatest Hits
1995, Mercury

Although this is White's best single-disc collection, it does have a few problems. First, although all of his major hits are included, they are the single edits, not the longer album versions. White was all about excess and delayed gratification, so why would you want edited versions that cut straight to the chase? Secondly, it neglects his often fabulous uptempo and funky dance tracks in favour of his ballads – although, if you want to cuddle up to the "Walrus of Love" for a night, this will serve you well.

Staying Power
1999, Private Music

White was never going to top the string of hits that are his late-70s legacy, but this, his final studio album, brought his signature style up to date. This contemporary recording is every bit as lush and sexy as the old days, and White raps and croons like no other, proving – as the title suggests – that he never lost his touch.

Andre Williams

Disguising his lack of singing talent with pure attitude, **Andre "Mr. Rhythm" Williams** has enjoyed one of the longest careers in R&B on the strength of a compelling persona that's like a more hip, more underworld **Huggy Bear**. Of course, his facility for crafting street-smart novelty discs hasn't hurt either.

Born in Bessemer, Alabama, in 1936, Williams was raised in Chicago, where he sang in his local church choir. In the early 50s, he moved to Detroit and joined a group called **The Five Dollars**, who recorded a couple of singles for the local Fortune label under assorted names. After "Bacon Fat", credited to Andre Williams & His New Group, but essentially a solo recording, created a stir in the Great Lakes in 1956, it was picked up by Epic and became a top-ten R&B hit the following year. The record epitomized Williams' style: his half-spoken, street-corner hepcat vocals over the top of primitive R&B backing recorded without reverb or EQ-ing. More wonderfully seedy records – "Jail Bait", "The Greasy Chicken", "Hey! Country Girl" and the fabulous "(Mmm… Andre Williams Is) Movin'" – soon followed in similar style but without the same success.

In 1961 Williams met **Berry Gordy** and spent the next few years flitting between Detroit and Chicago working for various labels as a freelance record producer/songwriter. At Motown he wrote Mary Wells'

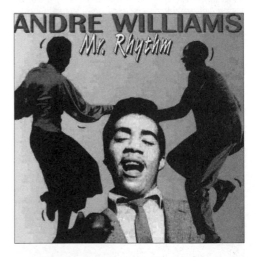

"Oh Little Boy (What Did You Do To Me)" – the flip side to "My Guy" – and produced some minor R&B hits for **The Contours**. In Chicago he co-wrote and produced the electric "Shake A Tail Feather" for The Five Du-Tones, as well as Mary Wells' post-Motown "Use Your Head" and **Alvin Cash & The Crawlers'** "Twine Time".

Williams returned to recording in 1966 with the single entendres of "Sweet Little Pussycat" and a swell instrumental called "Loose Juice". He then released a couple of pimptastic singles on the Checker label, "Cadillac Jack" and "It's Gonna Be Fine In '69", and he also produced the great "Funky Judge" for St. Louis group Bull & The Matadors. Williams then spent several years working with Ike & Tina Turner, The Chi-Lites and The Dramatics.

By the mid-70s he was struggling with drug addiction and, aside from recording the 1976 novelty record, "Streakin' Song", and appearing on Funkadelic's *Electric Spanking Of War Babies* in 1980, he wasn't heard from for many years. He finally re-emerged in 1996 with some retro greasy R&B records on Norton Records. While Williams had been previously championed by trash rockers **The Cramps**, his new albums – *Greasy* (1996), *Silky* (1997), *Red Dirt* (1999), *Is The Black Godfather* (2000), *Bait And Switch* (2001) and *Holland Shuffle* (2003) – and an appearance with the **Jon Spencer Blues Explosion** won him new fans among slumming punks and indie kids.

◉ Mr. Rhythm
1996, Eagle

Andre Williams recorded for so many different labels that the perfect compilation will probably never be issued. This anthology of his early sides, recorded mostly for Detroit's Fortune label, is a great place to start. *Mr. Rhythm Is Back* (1994, Revolvo) makes an ideal companion piece, collecting his late-60s recordings.

Deniece Williams

She may have grown up singing in the local Faith Temple Church of Christ in God, but **Deniece Williams'** rise to fame in the late 70s and early 80s had nothing to do with gospel intensity. Instead, her style was all about clarity – more akin to the pure pop singers of old than the brimstone and fire of her fellow choir members.

Williams was born **Deniece Chandler** on June 3, 1951 in Gary, Indiana. As a senior in high school, she recorded four singles for the Toddlin' Town label – "Love Is Tears", "Hey Baby", "I Don't Want To Cry" and "Come On Home To Me Baby" – and one for Lock, a cover of Barbara Mason's "Yes, I'm Ready". In 1971 her cousin introduced her to Stevie Wonder and she became a member of his backing troupe **Wonderlove**. She stayed with Wonder from 1972 to 1975, during which time she also recorded with Minnie Riperton and Roberta Flack.

Williams was also a songwriter, and The Emotions, Frankie Valli and **The Soul Train Gang** all recorded her compositions. In 1976 **Maurice White** of Earth Wind & Fire heard her singing on a demo of her own material and signed her as an artist to his Kalimba Productions company. Working with White and **Charles Stepney**, Williams released her debut, *This Is Niecy*, that same year. The lead single, "Free", was a serious bumper that was later sampled many times. It went to #2 on the R&B charts, but reached #1 in the UK. "That's What Friends Are For" also made it into the British Top 10 that year.

A duet with **Johnny Mathis**, "Too Much, Too Little, Too Late", was her first American #1, and inspired the duo to record an album of duets, 1978's *That's What Friends Are For*, which included a hit version of Marvin Gaye and **Tammi Terrell**'s "You're All I Need To Get By". Williams' own "I've Got The Next Dance" became a cult disco hit the following year. She then worked with producer **Thom Bell** on 1981's *My Melody* and 1982's *Niecy*, the latter of which included her second R&B chart-topper, a remake of The Royalettes' "It's Gonna Take A Miracle". Singing with Mathis again in 1984, she had a modest hit with "Love Won't Let Me Wait", but more importantly for pop culture junkies, they also got together to sing "Without Us", the theme to the sitcom *Family Ties*.

Working with **George Duke**, who had previously produced her R&B top-ten hit "Do What You Feel", Williams also recorded "Let's Hear It For The Boy" for the *Footloose* soundtrack that year. It was a definitive 80s production: rubbery synth bassline, tinkly and chirpy keyboard fills, deceptively complex rhythm programming and Williams' clean, slightly breathless vocals, with only a hint of gospel growl. The record's squeaky-clean perkiness defined the Reagan era and became her second American #1.

In the latter half of the 80s, Williams started to spend more time singing gospel, releasing her first gospel album, *So Glad I Know*, in 1986. The album contained two Grammy award-winning songs, "I Surrender All" and "They Say". Another gospel cut, "I Believe In You", won her a Grammy the following year. In 1988 she released her final secular album, *As Good As It Gets*, before concentrating exclusively on gospel music on albums such as *Special Love* (1989), *Lullabies To Dreamland* (1991), *Love Solves It All* (1996) and *This Is My Song* (1998).

The Best Of Deniece Williams: Gonna Take A Miracle
1996, Legacy

Although the sequencing can be irritating as it jumps around all over the place, this 16-track compilation is the best available Deniece Williams collection. She's a superb technical singer (a more powerful, more cosmic Dionne Warwick) and this is a singer's album – it focuses on tracks that highlight her strengths – and despite what many say, it's almost always the songs that make the singer.

Jackie Wilson

Even if **Jackie Wilson**, who was born in Detroit on June 9, 1934, did not make the very greatest of records, it's not hard to see why many soul aficionados consider him to be the finest singer of 'em all. Burdened with arrangements that trawled the depths of easy-listening territory, Wilson managed to excavate credible records from the most irredeemable schlock by virtue of his remarkable voice. Even at his very worst – check out 1960's "Night", which was shackled to an arrangement so archaic it would have sounded square to Lawrence Welk – Wilson always stamped his records with the authority of a consummate performer.

That peerless showmanship was the product of years spent at the altar of **Clyde McPhatter**. Not only was McPhatter one of the first secular singers to incorporate gospel phrasing, but he was also probably the first to incorporate its physicality into his act. McPhatter would shake, shimmy, glide, stride and drop to his knees while performing, and his enactment of ecstasy created one

of black showbiz's most enduring tropes. Wilson studied McPhatter so much that the moves became his own, and after being spotted at a Detroit talent show, he became the natural replacement for McPhatter when he left The Dominoes.

Wilson sang with The Dominoes for three years before going solo in 1957. Wilson met up with his cousin **Billy Davis**, who was writing (under the pseudonym Tyrone Carlo) with a failed record store owner called **Berry Gordy**, and they persuaded Wilson to record their song, "Reet Petite". Aside from starting the ball rolling for Gordy, "Reet Petite" also set the pattern that was to plague Wilson for most of his career. Gordy was a jazz fan who turned to writing pop only when his jazz record store closed down, and the lyrics and arrangement of "Reet Petite" were only as hip as a ten-year-old **Louis Jordan** record by almost the same name. Nonetheless, with his tongue rolls, stylized moans and sudden falsetto leaps, Wilson overcame it all to create a great record.

Gordy and Davis continued to write hits for Wilson over the next couple of years – "To Be Loved", "That's Why (I Love You So)", "I'll Be Satisfied" – the finest of which was 1958's "Lonely Teardrops". Despite that Swingle Singers chorus, "Lonely Teardrops" featured the best arrangement to grace a Wilson record until 1967. After Gordy moved on to start a little record company called Motown, Wilson continued to enjoy hits until 1963, such as 1960's "Doggin' Around". The song's accompaniment sounded like something from **Ray Charles'** C&W album from the next year, but Wilson's vocal was shattering, the sound of a man crying his guts out.

After 1963's "Baby Workout", on which Wilson triumphed over the overwrought backing to deliver a great performance, he didn't achieve another significant hit for three years. Then, finally working with a competent producer (**Carl Davis**), Wilson had material worthy of his talent on tracks like "I Don't Want To Lose You", "Whispers (Gettin' Louder)" and "I Get The Sweetest Feeling". Even on these records, Davis's Chicago soul style could be a bit sickly. However, on 1967's "(Your Love Keeps Lifting Me) Higher And Higher", with its rhythm section that actually drives, a female chorus that had heard of a blue note, and tasteful strings and horns that knew **The Bar-Kays** weren't a brand of margarine, Wilson sang like he'd found heaven.

Wilson's instincts got the worst of him again in 1968 when he worked with **Count Basie** on a series of re-recordings of soul classics, including "For Your Precious Love", "Uptight", "Chain Gang" and "Funky Broadway". He continued having minor R&B hits into the 70s with sappy records such as "(I Can Feel Those Vibrations) This Love Is Real", "Love Is Funny That Way" and "You Got Me Walking".

On September 25, 1975, Jackie Wilson collapsed on stage during a performance at the Latin Casino in Cherry Hill, New Jersey. He had suffered a severe stroke and fell into a coma. He remained in hospital for the rest of his life, finally giving up his fight for life on January 21, 1984.

⊚ Higher And Higher
1967, Brunswick

Carl Davis gave Wilson's career a jump start with this gem. Always a great, energetic performer, Wilson was more of a lounge act from an earlier generation when Davis's infusion of late 60s soul sent him back into the charts. A resurgent album and a breath of fresh air for a legend.

⊚ The Very Best Of Jackie Wilson
1987, Ace

"Mr. Excitement"'s story is among the saddest in soul, not just because of the tragic way this most dynamic singer's life ended, but because his enormous talent was so often drowned by producers who thought they knew better. This 24-track anthology, which has everything you could want and more, provides the best available testimony of Wilson's singular genius and how it was wasted.

Bill Withers

Working out of Los Angeles, **Bill Withers** was well-positioned to bring the singer-songwriter sensibility into soul music. The home of artists like Joni Mitchell, Crosby, Stills & Nash, James Taylor and Jackson Browne, LA's Laurel Canyon neighbourhood was the epicentre of the singer-songwriter movement that had a profound influence on pop music in the 70s. Using an understated, almost conversational, singing style and occasionally acoustic arrangements that were sparser than the norm for soul, Withers borrowed singer-songwriter conventions to deliver his childhood memories and lusty confessionals.

Born in Slab Fork, West Virginia on July 4, 1938, Bill Withers was a life-long stutterer who didn't try his hand at music until he was 29 years old. After a nine-year stint in the navy, Withers took on an array of odd jobs and, according to legend, started writing songs while working as a plumber installing toilets on aeroplanes. Following a move to LA, his compositions eventually caught the attention of Sussex Records boss **Clarence Avant**, who paired him with **Booker T. Jones** (of Booker T. & The MG's fame) for his debut, 1971's *Just As I Am*. The album was remarkable for its stripped-down approach to soul (it was similar to Willie Mitchell's productions with Al Green, perhaps because Al Jackson, Jr. was the drummer on both) and its striking songs, most notably "Ain't No Sunshine" and "Grandma's Hands". However, *Just As I Am*'s most influential track was "Harlem", one of the first disco hits, with its pulsating drum beat and surging but minimal string section.

Withers' second album, *Still Bill*, recorded in 1972 with members of the Watts 103rd Street Rhythm Band, was even better. "Lean On Me" was a perfect conjunction of message, vocals and beat, and Withers only #1 single. Beginning with a solemn keyboard pattern and hymnal humming, and moving to an uplifting hand-clapping rhythm underneath ensemble singing, "Lean On Me" was a classic example of a secular gospel arrangement. Unlike most soul singers who used gospel styles to describe the intensity of sex and love, Withers used the churchy atmosphere to deliver an ode to friendship that he said was inspired by his upbringing in a tight-knit rural community. Better still were the album's songs about love gone bad – "Use Me" and "Who Is He (And What Is He To You)", a mean and moody masterpiece of paranoia with a great string arrangement – that managed to work up searing levels of intensity with the merest of ingredients.

+*Justments* from 1974 was made with the same team as *Still Bill*, but it was less striking, partly because the arrangements were less surprising and partly because Withers was going through a divorce at the time. The next year's *Making Music* had the funky "Make Love To Your Mind", but little else, while 1976's *Naked And Warm* was a straight-up flop. *Menagerie* from 1977 featured "Lovely Day", on which Withers sounded as depressed as hell, but the bassline and the melody were as sunshiney as anything in the pop vernacular.

After a recording hiatus of several years, Withers worked with **Grover Washington Jr.** on "Just The Two of Us" and with Ralph McDonald on "In The Name Of Love". He also recorded one more album, the overproduced *Watching You, Watching Me*, in 1985, before going into semi-retirement and only performing the occasional live date.

○ **The Best Of Bill Withers: Lean On Me**
2000, Legacy

Not to be confused with *Lean On Me: The Best Of Bill Withers* (1994, Legacy), this is the collection to go for because it includes "Harlem", the most underrated yet important record in his catalogue. However, both collections lean too heavily towards his lacklustre later records. Another great option is the 2003 CD reissue combining his two best studio albums, *Just As I Am* and *Still Bill*.

Bobby Womack

Born in Cleveland, Ohio on March 4, 1944, **Bobby Womack** was one of soul's more mercurial talents. An excellent songwriter, fine guitar player and expressive singer with a forceful, throaty voice, he had all the tools to become one of soul's true greats, were it not for his penchant for overstatement, the disease of the longtime sideman.

With his brothers Cecil, Curtis, Friendly Jr. and Harry, Bobby formed the gospel troupe **The Womack Brothers** in the early 50s. The group opened for a lot of prominent gospel acts in Cleveland, most importantly **The Soul Stirrers**. That was how Bobby became friends with Sam Cooke, who signed the brothers to his own Sar label in 1960. They initially recorded gospel material, but when their records failed to sell, Cooke urged them to record pop. Their father, Friendly Sr., frowned on pop music and kicked them out of the house when he heard about their plans, but Cooke sent them money so they could go to the label's LA headquarters to record. Renamed **The Valentinos**, they recorded "Looking For A Love" in 1962, which started out in Sam Cooke style before Bobby started wailing and kicking gravel all over the Latinate track. They followed this R&B top-ten hit with "I'll Make It Alright" and "It's All Over Now", which was written by Bobby and later became a hit for **The Rolling Stones**. During this time, Bobby also became the guitarist in Cooke's live band.

A few months after Cooke's death in December 1964, Bobby married his widow **Barbara Campbell**, a move that was viewed with scorn in the R&B community. Bobby's first solo single, "I Found A True Love", released in 1965 on Checker, was a great secular gospel number that was completely ignored, as were the final Valentinos singles, "Do It Right" and "Sweeter Than The Day

Before". Womack then started working with **Chips Moman** at his American studios in Memphis. There he wrote songs for Wilson Pickett ("I'm In Love" and "I'm A Midnight Mover") and played guitar on sessions by Ray Charles, Solomon Burke, Joe Tex and Aretha Franklin.

Signing to Minit in 1967, Womack recorded "Baby, I Can't Stand It", one of his most affecting and least mannered performances, which was framed perfectly by Moman's spare production. That same year he cut "Broadway Walk", a "Funky Broadway" rip-off that was backed by the excellent "Somebody Special", on which he was at his most full-throated and testifying in a classic Southern soul vein. Womack's first solo hit was 1968's "What Is This", a rapprochement between funk and Motown on which he grunted like Syl Johnson. However, he then had bigger success with a series of schlocky pop covers – "Fly Me To The Moon", "California Dreamin'" and "I Left My Heart In San Francsico" – that indulged his worst instincts. His best record from this period was a version of "I'm A Midnight Mover", which was as mannered as most of his other records, but featured Stax-style backing that grounded him a bit.

Womack played guitar on Sly & The Family Stone's *There's A Riot Goin' On* at the start of the 70s, and the downbeat sparseness of that album rubbed off on him. In 1971 *Communication*, on which he had full artistic control, became Womack's most successful album to date. The tortured "That's The Way I Feel About Cha" was his breakthrough, going to #2 on the R&B chart, while the title track featured some gnarly guitar work that was somewhat undercut by his mean-spirited preaching. The next year's *Understanding* included the great early disco hit "I Can Understand It", as well as his first R&B #1, the bitter "Woman's Gotta Have It", and the scornful "Harry Hippie".

Womack recorded the fantastic theme song to the blaxploitation flick *Across 110th Street* in 1973, before scoring his second R&B #1 the next year with a re-recording of "Lookin' For A Love". He had further hits with the clavinet-led "You're Welcome, Stop On By", the half-hearted disco track "Check It Out" and the imitative Philly soul record "Daylight", and recorded the 1975 country album *BW Goes C&W* before moving to

Columbia Records. There he recorded a couple of albums that went nowhere, before putting his career on hold following a series of personal problems.

Returning in 1981 on the Beverly Glen label, Womack released *The Poet*, a critical cause célèbre that featured the fine ballad "If You Think You're Lonely Now". *The Poet II* from 1984 included another big R&B hit, "Love Has Finally Come At Last", which was a duet with Patti LaBelle. The next year Womack returned to country with "(No Matter How High I Get) I'll Still Be Looking Up To You" and had a top-five R&B hit with "I Wish He Didn't Trust Me So Much". He worked with Chips Moman again on 1986's *Womagic*, but failed to recapture the old magic. He slowed down considerably during the 90s, but still found time to record *Back To My Roots* in 1999, his first gospel album.

⊙ Understanding
1972, United Artists

Womack had been around for years before he finally recorded a string of albums in the early 70s that cemented his reputation – and this is the best. The original songs outshine the covers, and the laid-back funk of his Memphis back-up propels "Woman's Got To Have It" into the 70s soul canon.

⊙ Midnight Mover: The Bobby Womack Collection
1993, EMI

Although hardly complete (it has none of his pre-1967 material or anything from *The Poet*), this exhaustive 2-disc, 44-track compilation has just about all the Bobby Womack anyone could want. Stylistically it's all over the place, but it makes a convincing argument for Womack's versatility, if not his greatness.

Womack & Womack

Possibly the most talented family in soul history, the Womacks have been making rock-solid R&B in one form or another since the late 50s. The Womacks started out as a gospel-singing brother act before they changed their name to **The Valentinos** in the early 60s and signed to Sam Cooke's SAR label. After recording classics like "It's All Over Now" and "Lookin' For A Love", the group broke up and Bobby Womack went on to have an illustrious career as a solo performer, songwriter and sideman. His brother **Cecil**, meanwhile, became a producer and songwriter, working most notably with his first wife, Mary Wells, during the late 60s and early 70s.

After divorcing Wells, Cecil married Sam Cooke's daughter, **Linda**, and started the song-writing partnership responsible for the Teddy Pendergrass smash "Love T.K.O.". Together they formed **Womack & Womack** in the early 80s. Their first album, 1983's *Love Wars*, marked a rapprochement of age-old Southern soul verities with newfangled production values. Musically, it was reminiscent of an Al Green album, but with the Hi Rhythm Section replaced by Linn drums, Fender Rhodes and Ensoniq Mirages, and wrapped up in the kind of production sheen that was the hallmark of Philadelphia International during its last days under Dexter Wansel. *Love Wars* also recognized that there was a world of sound outside of Memphis, and Brazilian percussion master **Paulinho Da Costa** guested on a couple of tracks, while drummer **James Gadson** was surely listening to Guadeloupe's zouk kingpins Kassav' before coming up with his beat on "Baby, I'm Scared Of You". Best of all, unlike most 80s soul albums, there was only one garish, out-of-place guitar solo.

While their music didn't have the mytho-poeic force of great country soul, its smooth contours and easy lines channelled attention towards the words, which refined Southern soul's earthy metaphors for urban sophisticates. The resulting songs were among the finest duets since Marvin Gaye and **Tammi Terrell**. *Love Wars* was no cozy, lovey-dovey, private husband-and-wife thing. It was much closer to the brutal metaphors and bitter recriminations of Richard and Linda Thompson's *Shoot Out The Lights* than the domestic bliss of Paul and Linda McCartney.

Throughout their records Linda Womack was always hip to Cecil's sweet-talking. On "Catch And Don't Look Back", his "rap is kind of smooth, but [she] ain't gonna play [his] fool". On *Love Wars'* masterpiece, "Baby I'm Scared Of You", she warned against Houdinis and their tricks. Over a surging, lite-funk background that made the track a big American club hit, the two Womacks created the best wooing dialogue-cum-cautionary tale since **Mickey & Sylvia's** "Love Is Strange". Here, though, Linda didn't call lover boy, but left her suitor to pull rabbits out of his hat for someone else.

On *Radio M.U.S.I.C. Man*, which followed in 1985, the couple sounded like they were tired of fighting and had settled down in a less than blissful haze. The musicianship wasn't quite as interesting, the lyrics and the vocal performances didn't bite, and the two most notable songs were an unfinished Sam Cooke number ("Love's Calling") and a cover of **The Beatles'** "Here Comes The Sun". Their 1988 album, *Conscience*, was an improvement with its more pronounced Southern feel, even if the production values had a disconcertingly amateurish quality. The seemingly surefire hit "Teardrops" did nothing in the US, but reached the Top 3 in the UK.

At the start of the 90s, Cecil and Linda Womack travelled to Nigeria where they had a spiritual awakening and have since renamed themselves in honour of their African ancestors. Both 1991's *Family Spirit* and 1993's *Transformation To The House Of Zekkariyas* echoed this new spirituality – and suffered as a result.

Love Wars
1983, Elektra

Linda and Cecil Womack's debut album was also, undoubtedly, their best. These six tracks are a superb examination of the dynamics of a relationship, pitched somewhere between classic soul and earnest singer-songwriter confessional.

Stevie Wonder

Born on May 13, 1950 in Saginaw, Michigan, **Steveland Hardaway Judkins**

Stevie Wonder: musical visionary

(soon changed to Steveland Morris after his mother married) was a pop star by the time he was 13 years old. The harmonica (mostly) instrumental "Fingertips (Part 2)" might have seemed like a gimmick when it became a huge #1 hit in 1963, but the renamed **Stevie Wonder** never became a washed-up and bitter child star because he had a talent that extended well beyond flashy harp runs and youthful energy.

Wonder is one of the most eclectic geniuses in popular music, embracing everything from Tin Pan Alley pop to deep funk to reggae to salsa. He can record a saccharine ballad that reads like a Hallmark card one minute, and the next, write a searing indictment of America's racial politics. While everyone always notes that Wonder turned soul into a genre capable of album-length state-

ments, perhaps his most important innovation of the early 70s was that he collapsed the two oppositions of the male African-American vocal tradition – the fragile, feminized falsetto and the assertive, growling tenor – into each other, creating a persona that was as complex and multilayered as anyone in pop music, black or white.

Wonder was born prematurely, and he went blind while undergoing oxygen treatment. It quickly became apparent, however, that he was a musical prodigy. By the time he was 9, he had taught himself how to play the piano, drums and harmonica. In 1961 he was discovered by **The Miracles**' **Ronnie White**, who got him an audition with Motown's boss, **Berry Gordy**. He recorded two albums – *A Tribute To Uncle Ray*, a homage to his hero Ray Charles, and *The Jazz Soul Of Little Stevie* – before he made his breakthrough with "Fingertips".

After "Fingertips (Part 2)" and a few lesser hits, Wonder returned in 1965 with the self-penned "Uptight (Everything's Alright)", one of the most electric records in Motown's catalogue. His strange version of "Blowin' In The Wind" was an omen of the more political bent his career would later take, but more typical of his early records were "Hey Love" and "I Was Made To Love Her", which had an arrangement that created the blueprint for The Jackson 5, but with a more surging bassline.

While Wonder was capable of recording great pop songs, he was equally capable of creating mindless schmaltz such as "For Once In My Life" and "Shoo-Be-Doo-Be-Doo-Da-Day", which has a clavinet riff that presaged his drift away from the clutches of the studio system, as well as cheesy ballads like "My Cherie Amour" and "Yester-Me, Yester-You, Yesterday". "Signed, Sealed, Delivered, I'm Yours" (which was co-written with Syreeta Wright, whom he later married) was the kind of upbeat, joyful pop that he excelled at, while his singing on "Heaven Help Us All" elevated it from bathos.

In 1971 Wonder's contract with Motown was up for renewal and he demanded complete control over his projects. Like Marvin Gaye, who wanted similar terms, he eventually won, but not without a fight. You could argue that the contract problems Gaye and Wonder had with Motown weren't just about control, but also about a vision of the world. Motown had spent all of its history papering over the cracks of racial strife, creating a fantasy world where blacks and whites listened, danced, made out and broke up to the same music. When Gaye and Wonder demanded creative control of their records, they wanted to articulate a vision that was light years away from Berry Gordy's crossover Eden of deportment lessons, proper diction and smiling faces. In the face of race riots, Civil Rights legislation falling short of its promises and the innovations of Sly Stone, Wonder wanted to sing, "This place is cruel, nowhere could be much colder/If we don't change, the world will soon be over".

The first product of Wonder's new-found freedom was 1972's *Music Of My Mind*, written, produced and recorded almost entirely

PLAYLIST
Stevie Wonder

1 FINGERTIPS (PART 2) from **The Definitive Collection**
It's pretty rare – if not singular – that such a precocious talent also has such a sense of humour.

2 UPTIGHT (EVERYTHING'S ALRIGHT) from **The Definitive Collection**
Motown at its most frenzied.

3 I WAS MADE TO LOVE HER from **The Definitive Collection**
Stevie Wonder's finest love song.

4 SIGNED, SEALED, DELIVERED, I'M YOURS from **The Definitive Collection**
Just like Smokey Robinson, Wonder, at his best, can turn the utterly clichéd into perfect pop.

5 SUPERSTITION from **Talking Book**
Written for Jeff Beck, but only Wonder, and the ferocious synth riff, could have brought out all the lyric's nuances.

6 YOU ARE THE SUNSHINE OF MY LIFE from **Talking Book**
Sweet simplicity.

7 HIGHER GROUND from **Innervisions**
Perhaps his most complex song attached to one of his greatest grooves.

8 LIVING FOR THE CITY from **Innervisions**
The greatest hip-hop skit of all time.

9 DON'T YOU WORRY ABOUT A THING from **Innervisions**
Deep, pan-diasporic groove that is one of his finest purely musical achievements.

10 AS from **Songs In The Key Of Life**
Glorious secular gospel.

by himself. It was no masterpiece – it didn't have the songs to back up his mercurial wanderings across the boundaries of texture, timbre and taste. However, that same year's *Talking Book* undoubtedly was. On the album's highlight, "Superstition", he created a tough, buzzing Moog riff that seemed to mirror the chaos he was singing about, while on "Big Brother" he directly chastised the mysterious forces he was exorcizing on "Superstition". Although betrayed by it on "Maybe Your Baby", Wonder also held out hope for the redemptive power of love on "You Are The Sunshine Of My Life".

Wonder was still only 23 when he released 1973's *Innervisions*, his most fully realized, most political and best album. Recorded with synthesists **Robert Margouleff** and **Malcolm Cecil** (later to become Tonto's Expanding Head Band), *Innervisions* incorporated the resolutely unearthly sounds of the Moog into a sound world that explicitly engaged with the here and now. One of the album's obsessions was false religion, and even on the great "Higher Ground", a song about reaching heaven, the track faded out before the final lines according to the lyric sheet, "God is gonna show you higher ground/He's the only friend you have around". The equally great "Jesus Children Of America" had a similar riff and lyrics that chastised Holy Rollers, transcendental meditators and junkies who all tell lies when the truth is inside. Even the album's centrepiece, the very worldly "Living For The City", was constructed around a churchy organ line and conceived as a quasi-biblical parable. With such a tone, the "smiling faces" trope of 70s soul unsurprisingly reared its head on both "Don't You Worry About A Thing" and "He's Misstra Know-it-All".

Fulfillingness' First Finale (1974) was a step backward. Even though it included the savage "You Haven't Done Nothin'" and the boogying "Boogie On Reggae Woman", the songs were less accessible and more self-indulgent than those on Wonder's previous two albums. *Songs In The Key Of Life* (1976) was a sprawling, nearly two-hour-long double album (plus EP) that returned Wonder to the top of his game. The album was all over the place, but the songs themselves were tightly focused, going from gospel ("As") to caustic ("Village Ghetto Life") to devotional ("Another Star", "Have A Talk With God") to brassy ("Sir Duke").

After the utterly ignorable instrumental album *Journey Through The Secret Life Of Plants* (1979), Wonder released *Hotter Than July* in 1980. The excellent pop album didn't quite reach the heights of his 70s zenith, but it still featured great records like "Master Blaster (Jammin')" and "Happy Birthday", a track dedicated to **Martin Luther King** that at least showed that Wonder was still as committed as ever.

Over the next decade, Wonder's output declined in both quality and quantity.

"Ebony And Ivory", a racial harmony duet with **Paul McCartney**, was just dreadful, and it presaged Wonder's slip into cliché on mid-80s pop records like "That Girl", "I Just Called To Say I Love You" and "Part Time Lover". His 1987 album *Characters* was a slight return to form, featuring "Skeletons", a savage attack on Reagan, and "Get It", a mighty groove recorded with Michael Jackson. Wonder also recorded the soundtrack to Spike Lee's *Jungle Fever* in 1991 and tried to come to terms with hip-hop on his last studio album, 1995's *Conversation Peace*.

In 2005 Wonder released *A Time To Love*, his first studio album in a decade. Although it was hailed in some quarters as a masterpiece almost equal to his 70s work, it was really little more than a fine pop album with a couple of notable tracks ("So What The Fuss", "If Your Love Cannot Be Moved") and a lot of celebrity dead weight. What *A Time To Love* did show, however, was that the only facet of Wonder's brand of soul that translated to the contemporary R&B scene was not his expansive vision or heart, nor his political and spiritual commitment, but his unfortunate taste in vocal flourishes. Wonder deserves a better legacy than that.

Music Of My Mind
1972, Motown

His first album free from the constraints of Motown, this opened the door to Wonder's greatest and most productive period. Playing nearly every instrument himself and using synthesizers for the first time, he unleashed a set of songs that demanded attention. Incorporating soul and gospel, melody and funk, every track is a smash.

Innervisions
1973, Motown

Wonder's greatest album sought solace from the betrayals and lies of politics, drugs and false religion that plagued black America at that time. Unlike artists like Parliament-Funkadelic and Dexter Wansel who used the Moog to imagine a better world far away from earth, Wonder used the Moog to give instrumental voice to the back-stabbers, double-crossers and money men from whom he was trying to escape.

Songs In The Key Of Life
1976, Motown

This double album shows all the facets of Wonder's overwhelming, eclectic talent and includes many tracks that became the cornerstones of his career, with no filler. Joyous, bitter, contemplative, no single description can really do this masterpiece justice. An extraordinary album from an extraordinary artist.

Original Musiquarium I
1982, Motown

The definitive Stevie Wonder collection has yet to be released, so this double-disc album will have to do. Although his 70s albums were tightly structured, *Original Musiquarium I* cherry-picks his hits and high points from 1972 to 1980, and adds four new songs, including the trite "That Girl" and the jam with Dizzy Gillespie, "Do I Do".

Betty Wright

Betty Wright was one of soul's sassiest, most vibrant singers and one of its greatest chroniclers of cheating. Wright not only excelled at cautionary "the other woman" songs, but also – and perhaps more importantly – at songs about temptation and its consequences.

Wright was born in Miami, Florida on December 21, 1953 and she sang with her family's gospel group, The Echoes of Joy, from a young age. She was discovered at age 11 by Clarence Reid and Willie Clarke singing along to Billy Stewart's "Summertime" in a record store. She was signed to their Deep City label and had a small local hit with her 1966 debut, "Paralysed". The following year Clarke and Reid moved to Henry Stone's Alston label and took Wright with them. Her first release there, "Girls Can't Do What The Guys Do", was a strange record given Wright's assertive catalogue, and it sounded as though she was fighting with the chauvinistic lyrics.

In the early 70s Wright had modest hits on Alston with "Pure Love" and "I Love The Way You Love", before achieving a smash with "Clean Up Woman". The song was ostensibly a classic soul arrangement, but the interaction between the guitar and bass (and the lack of space between the two) made it sound strangely African. Her fiery "If You Love Me Like You Say You Love Me" was a crucial early disco record, while "Baby Sitter" was another cautionary tale in the vein of "Clean Up Woman".

The classic Caribbean-influenced Miami sound of the very funky "Let Me Be Your Lovemaker" followed, before "Secretary" made Wright soul's favourite teller of perfidious women tales in 1974. The excellent *Danger High Voltage* album, released that same year, included Allen Toussaint's New

Orleans-flavoured "Shoorah! Shoorah!", the gently levitating "Tonight's The Night" and the electric "Where Is The Love". However, 1976's *Explosion* suffered by being simple, unadorned Southern soul in the disco age.

"Sweet" from 1977's *This Time For Real* was jazzier than usual, but the mellow tempo suited Wright's not quite gravelly, not quite smooth, vocal style. Also from that album, "You Can't See For Lookin'" was a fine ballad, but again the plain production was no match for the disco blockbusters. Wright responded by contributing vocals to Peter Brown's disco smash "Dance With Me" and releasing 1978's *Betty Wright Live*, an excellent album that tried to distance her from canned dancefloor divas on a series of vibrant performances, including "Tonight Is The Night", "Where Is The Love" and "The Clean Up Woman Medley".

When Alston went bust in 1979, Wright signed with Epic for two lacklustre albums, the highlight of which was 1981's "What Are You Going To Do With It", produced by Stevie Wonder. A couple of slight dancefloor tracks followed in the mid-80s – "One Step Up, Two Steps Back" and "The Sun Don't Shine" – before she scored with a series of themed classic soul-styled singles for her own Ms B label: "Pain", "No Pain, No Gain", "After The Pain" and "From Pain To Joy". Wright continued to release albums throughout the 80s and 90s. She still performs frequently in the South and released a new studio album, *Fit For A King*, in 2001.

The Best Of Betty Wright
1992, Rhino

This 20-track collection is more substantial than Rhino's more recent *The Very Best Of Betty Wright* and displays Wright at her sassy best. Unfortunately, neither compilation includes her great "If You Love Me Like You Say You Love Me", but disco was never her forté, classic Southern soul was – and that's what this compilation has in spades.

O.V. Wright

Considered by many to be the greatest deep soul singer of 'em all, O.V. Wright may have crossed over from gospel, but he never truly left it behind. More than the records of any other soul singer, Wright's best releases were straight gospel records with different lyrics, and they had an intensity of feeling that could be matched only by some of James Carr's best sides.

Overton Vertis Wright was born on October 9, 1939 in Leno, Tennessee. He started singing gospel at an early age and joined the Memphis gospel group The Five Harmonaires as a teenager. He also spent time in The Spirit of Memphis Quartet and with The Highway QCs, but his most productive stint was with **The Sunset Travellers**. The Travellers recorded the great "On Jesus' Program" for Don Robey's Peacock label in 1964, before Wright recorded his solo debut, "That's How Strong My Love Is", written by his friend **Roosevelt Jamison**, for Goldwax. The record was as deep as night and utterly harrowing, filled with a sanctified intensity that not even Otis Redding could match when he recorded his own version a few months later.

Robey believed Wright was still under contract to him, so he persuaded Goldwax to transfer the contract over to his Back Beat label. Wright then had an R&B top-ten hit with the ballad "You're Gonna Make Me Cry", before cutting some of his best material with producer Willie Mitchell. "Eight Men, Four Women" was one of Wright's best deep-soul sides, despite the rather tortuous jury metaphor. The backing was as cold as a hanging judge's heart and Wright testified with everything he had. "Heartaches – Heartaches" was similarly intense, while "I Want Everyone To Know" was a shockingly under-regarded deep-soul ballad. Later records like 1970's "Love The Way You Love" – an awesome mix of Northern finger pop and Southern grease and grit – and "Ace Of Spade" had Wright letting rip on faster tempos without any loss of emotionalism.

After the wailing "A Nickel And A Nail" and the midtempo "I'd Rather Be (Blind, Cripple & Crazy)", Wright left Back Beat and joined Mitchell's Hi label. Instead of continuing in the same style, Mitchell tried to work some of his Al Green magic on Wright. Although Wright had modest hits in the mid-70s with "Into Something I Can't Shake Loose" and "Precious, Precious", he didn't fit this new soft approach. For instance on "Let's Straighten It Out", even though there was something compelling about hearing him struggle with the limitations of his own ravaged voice as well as the limitations of his lover, it wasn't easy listening. Wright's later records never matched the intensity of his early-70s material and, not long after their release, he sadly died of heart failure on November 16, 1980.

The Soul Of O.V. Wright
1992, MCA

This 18-track collection of his Back Beat recordings is the best available Wright album. It hits all the obvious high notes, but misses out on some crucial recordings. If you find yourself in a used record store in Tokyo, seek out *The Complete Recorded Works For ABC And Back Beat Label* (1991, P-Vine), which is no longer in print, but includes nearly all of his greatest recordings.

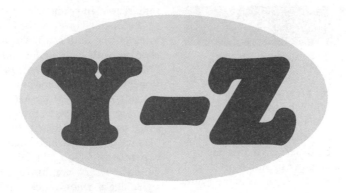

Yarbrough & Peoples

Although they are generally only associated with their masterpiece, "Don't Stop The Music", **Yarbrough & Peoples** were, in reality, the undisputed masters of the shimmering R&B sound of the 80s. No one else made that disconnect between the trebly guitar sound and walloping synth bass more of an art form than this Texas duo.

Calvin Yarbrough and **Alisa Peoples** first met when they were 6 and 4 years old respectively as pupils of the same piano teacher in Dallas, Texas and later sang together in the same church choir. In the mid-70s Yarbrough joined a Dallas group called Grand Theft, who released the cult funk-disco obscurity "Disco Dancing" on the Honey label in 1976. The Gap Band caught one of Grand Theft's gigs and offered Yarbrough a job as a backup singer on a tour with **Leon Russell**. Eventually, Yarbrough gave the group a demo tape that he had made with Peoples and they passed it on to their manager and producer, **Lonnie Simmons**, who quickly signed the duo.

Their first single was 1980's remarkable "Don't Stop The Music" – a minimal masterpiece featuring an oscillating bassline, sparse drum machine beat, repeating keyboard pattern and Peoples' forced vocals that gave the track an even eerier feel. Then the synth and cartoon voice breakdown came in. "Don't Stop The Music" spent five weeks at the top of the R&B chart and was one of the best records of the decade. It was followed the nest year by the far less singular "Third Degree", a misguided pop disco attempt.

In 1982 "Heartbeats" sounded alternately like the precursor to **Frankie Goes To Hollywood** and the blueprint for Robbie Robertson's late 80s comeback, while "Feels So Good" was a minimal rewrite of "Don't Stop The Music". The duo had their second R&B #1 in 1984 with "Don't Waste Your Time", which gave their signature sound a bit of **Sade** sheen and was another brilliant example of widescreen 80s R&B. That same year's "Be A Winner", on the other hand, was simply a clumsy, bungling attempt at blending electro, funk and pop.

Yarbrough and Peoples married in the mid-80s and their sound became sappier as a result. Peoples' singing also became slightly whinier on their last significant hits, "Guilty" and "I Wouldn't Lie", and on "Wrapped Around Your Finger", a 1986 ballad that owed more than a little to **Loose Ends**. In the late 80s, after Lonnie Simmons' Total Experience label collapsed, Yarbrough & Peoples left the music business and they haven't really been heard from since.

The Best Of Yarbrough & Peoples
1997, Mercury

This 14-track collection hits all the highlights and is undoubtedly all the Yarbrough & Peoples anyone needs to own. This is as breezy as R&B gets, but not in a light Grover Washington, Jr. kind of fashion – just simple, joyful grooves with sophisticated shading between light and dark and bottom end and top end.

Zapp

Zapp main man **Roger Troutman**'s unparalleled virtuosity with the talk box has unfortunately meant that he has been caricatured as merely the instrument's appendage rather than as one of soul's funkiest, grooviest cats, regardless of instrument, which is what he deserves. If there is one instrument that Troutman and Zapp should be associated with, however, it is the synth bass as they defined its role in funk.

Roger Troutman was born on November 29, 1951 in Hamilton, Ohio. He was the fourth of nine children in a musical family. By the time he was 11 years old, guitarist Roger and his younger brother **Lester** (drummer) played together in a band that was originally called "Lil" Roger and His Fabulous Vels and, later, The Essentials. In the early 70s, vocalist **Bobby Glover** and older brother **Larry Troutman** joined on percussion and they became **Roger & The Human Body**. Under that name, the group released the album *Introducing Roger* in 1975 on their own Troutman Bros label. The album mostly featured fairly generic funk cuts, but the track "Freedom" was marked by Roger's striking, rhythmic talk-boxing.

In 1977 another Troutman brother, **Terry** (aka "Zapp"), joined on synthesizers and keyboards and the group took his nickname as their own. Zapp the group signed with Warner Bros in 1979 and had a monster R&B hit with their first single, the incredible "More Bounce To The Ounce", in 1980. With the best synth bassline this side of Parliament's "Flash Light" and one of the all-time greatest hand-clap rhythms, "More Bounce" bumped like crazy – how it only reached #86 on the pop chart is a complete mystery. Produced by Roger Troutman and Bootsy Collins, the group's 1980 album, *Zapp*, also included the oft-sampled slow jam "Be Alright".

As well as leading Zapp, Roger Troutman also had a successful parallel solo career throughout the 80s and 90s. Under the name Roger and playing nearly all of the instruments himself, he released a solo album, *The Many Facets Of Roger*, in 1981 that was even more successful than Zapp's debut. Roger's

remarkable and somewhat ridiculous cover of "I Heard It Through The Grapevine" went to #1 on the R&B chart. The album was fleshed out with "So Ruff, So Tuff", a remake of "More Bounce To The Ounce", "Do It Roger", with its ferocious synth bassline, and the guitar wigout "Maxx Axe".

The group's 1982 album, *Zapp II*, featured their only R&B #1, the groovalicious "Dance Floor". It also included the R&B top-ten hit "Doo Wa Ditty (Blow That Thing)", which combined retro doo-wop, space-age harmonica, electro Latin percussion and a super-fat bassline. "I Can Make You Dance", from 1983's *Zapp III*, was more synth-heavy than their previous records, but it still reached the R&B Top 5, while the same album's "Heartbreaker" was more moody, but still retained that characteristic Zapp strut.

Roger again made the R&B Top 10 with the more electro-styled solo hit "In The Mix" in 1984, before achieving moderate hits with a cover of the classic soul record "Midnight Hour", featuring The Mighty Clouds of Joy, and the Prince-like "Girl, Cut It Out". Zapp, meanwhile, had a major R&B hit with one of the most original ballads in the soul/R&B idiom, 1985's "Computer Love".

Bizarrely, the biggest hit any of the Troutman family were ever involved with was Roger's "I Want To Be Your Man" in 1987. An R&B #1 and pop #3, "I Want To Be Your Man" was a slow jam that could have been Billy Ocean were it not for the occasional high-pitched talk-box squeals. In the latter half of the 80s Roger made a guest appearance on Scritti Politti's instantly forgettable "Boom! There She Was", and Zapp had a modest hit with a tired talk-box rendition of "Ooh Baby Baby".

In 1991 Roger got to grips with hip-hop on "(Everybody) Get Up", but Zapp already had plenty of standing in the hip-hop community thanks to groups like EPMD and Ice Cube sampling "More Bounce". Zapp's profile increased dramatically when **Dr Dre** sampled "Computer Love" on 2Pac's "I Get Around", indirectly leading to Roger's appearance in 1996 on 2Pac's "California Love", on which he made a star turn on the talk box. That same year Roger also appeared on H-Town's cover of "A Thin Line Between Love & Hate".

On April 25, 1999 Roger was found critically wounded outside a recording studio in Dayton, Ohio and later died in hospital. It soon shockingly transpired that he had been murdered by his brother Larry, who was found dead nearby, having apparently killed himself after first shooting Roger. A new Zapp line-up, led by Lester and Terry Troutman, started playing live dates again in 2001 to try to keep the memory of their brothers alive.

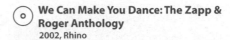

We Can Make You Dance: The Zapp & Roger Anthology
2002, Rhino

A superb 2-CD, 29-track collection that chronicles the work of Roger Troutman from the early 70s with Roger & The Human Body to the late 90s with H-Town. While it is justifiably heavy on the talk box, this album also shows how potent Zapp's synth grooves were and how they helped define the sound of the 80s and, by extension, the sound of West Coast hip-hop.

Index